WE SAW
SPAIN DIE

WE SAW SPAIN DIE

FOREIGN CORRESPONDENTS IN THE SPANISH CIVIL WAR

PAUL PRESTON

A Herman Graf Book
Skyhorse Publishing

Copyright © 2009 by Skyhorse Publishing, Inc.

All Rights Reserved. No part of this book may be reproduced in any manner without the express written consent of the publisher, except in the case of brief excerpts in critical reviews or articles. All inquiries should be addressed to Skyhorse Publishing, 555 Eighth Avenue, Suite 903, New York, NY 10018.

Skyhorse Publishing books may be purchased in bulk at special discounts for sales promotion, corporate gifts, fund-raising, or educational purposes. Special editions can also be created to specifications. For details, contact the Special Sales Department, Skyhorse Publishing, 555 Eighth Avenue, Suite 903, New York, NY 10018 or info@skyhorsepublishing.com.

www.skyhorsepublishing.com

10 9 8 7 6 5 4 3 2 1

Library of Congress Cataloging-in-Publication Data

Preston, Paul, 1946-
  We saw Spain die : foreign correspondents in the Spanish Civil War / Paul Preston.
     p. cm.
  Originally published: London : Constable, 2008.
  ISBN 978-1-60239-767-5
  1. Spain--History--Civil War, 1936–1939--Journalists. 2. Spain--History--Civil War, 1936–1939--Press coverage. 3. War correspondents--Spain--History--20th century. 4. Foreign correspondents--Spain--History--20th century. 5. War correspondents--Biography. 6. Foreign correspondents--Biography. 7. Journalism--Spain--History--20th century. 8. Journalism--History--20th century. I. Title.
  DP269.8.J68P74 2009
  070.4'49946081--dc22
                              2009010693

Printed and bound in the EU

CENTRAL ARKANSAS LIBRARY SYSTEM
LITTLE ROCK PUBLIC LIBRARY
100 ROCK STREET
LITTLE ROCK, ARKANSAS 72201

Contents

Acknowledgements   vii

List of Illustrations   x

Part One: Say that We Saw Spain Die   1

1   The Wound that Will Not Heal: Terror and Truth   3

2   The Capital of the World: The Correspondents and the Siege of Madrid   22

3   The Lost Generation Divided: Hemingway, Dos Passos and the Disappearance of José Robles   62

4   Love and Politics: The Correspondents in Valencia and Barcelona   93

5   The Rebel Zone: Intimidation in Salamanca and Burgos   134

Part Two: Beyond Journalism   171

6   Stalin's Eyes and Ears in Madrid? The Rise and Fall of Mikhail Koltsov   173

7   A Man of Influence: The Case of Louis Fischer   213

8   The Sentimental Adventurer: George Steer and the Quest for Lost Causes   263

9   Talking with Franco, Trouble with Hitler: Jay Allen   291

Part Three: After the War   339

10   The Humane Observer: Henry Buckley   341

11   A Lifetime's Struggle: Herbert Rutledge Southworth and the Undermining of the Franco Regime   351

12   Epilogue: Buried Treasure   364

Notes   368

Bibliography   414

Index   427

To the Memory of Herbert Rutledge Southworth (1908–99)

Acknowledgements

I would like to express my gratitude to all those who have helped to make this book possible. In particular, I must thank those who generously helped me locate the diaries, letters and other papers on which the book is principally based: the Very Reverend Dean Michael Allen and his daughter Sarah Wilson, for giving me access to the papers of Jay Allen; Patrick and Ramón Buckley, for lending me materials relating to their father Henry Buckley; Charlotte Kurzke, for granting permission for me to use the invaluable unpublished memoirs of her parents Jan Kurzke and Kate Mangan; Carmen Negrín, for providing access to the papers and photographs held in the Archivo Juan Negrín, Las Palmas de Gran Canaria; Paul Quintanilla, for giving me access to the papers of Luis Quintanilla; and David Wurtzel, for providing me with the diary and other papers of Lester Ziffren.

I am also very happy to record the help of numerous librarians who helped me locate particular papers. For the good-humoured tolerance with which they dealt with my complicated requests regarding the papers of Tom Wintringham and Kitty Bowler, I am indebted to the Staff of the Liddell Hart Centre for Military Archives, King's College London. Similarly, I am immensely grateful to Andrew Riley and Sandra Marsh of Churchill College Cambridge Archives Centre for their enthusiastic assistance in locating the correspondence between George Steer and Philip Noel-Baker. Gail Malmgreen has, for many years, been unfailingly helpful regarding requests and queries related to the ALBA Collection of the Tamiment Library, at New York University. Kelly Spring of the Sheridan Library, Johns Hopkins University, helped in the location of the Robles papers. Natalia Sciarini of the Beinecke Library, Yale University, went the extra mile in helping find particular items relating to Josephine Herbst. Above all, I want to thank Helene van Rossum of Princeton University Library for help and perceptive advice above and beyond the call of duty regarding the voluminous papers of Louis Fischer.

I am fortunate in the specific help I received regarding particular chapters. This is especially true of the chapter on Mikhail Koltsov, for which I must express my immense debt to Frank Schauff, whose unstinting help with Russian sources was indispensable. Robert Service, Denis Smyth, Ángel Viñas and Boris Volodarsky all contributed with sage advice and saved me from many errors. René Wolf and Gunther Schmigalle provided invaluable assistance on the German dimension of Koltsov's career. For the chapter on George Steer, I benefited from the generous help of Nick Rankin. I would also like to thank Christopher Holme of the *Glasgow Herald* for sending me material on his namesake who was with Steer in Guernica. For the chapter on José Robles, Will Watson generously shared his encyclopaedic knowledge of Hemingway in Spain, and José Nieto recounted his recollections of his conversations with John Dos Passos, Artur London and Luis Quintanilla. I was greatly stimulated by the enthusiastic response of Elinor Langer to my questions about Josephine Herbst. On the developments in the press office in Valencia, I benefited from the insights of Griffin Barry's daughter, Harriet Ward. I was also helped by David Fernbach in relation to the role of Tom Wintringham and Kitty Bowler. In Madrid, the indefatigable Mariano Sanz González was as helpful as ever. Regarding matters connected with the International Brigades, I turned to Richard Baxell and was never disappointed. I am also indebted to Larry Hannant of the University of Victoria and Professor David Lethbridge at Okanagan College, British Columbia for their help in unearthing material about Kajsa Rothman.

Surviving protagonists are unfortunately now few. I was thus especially glad to be able to benefit from the memories of three people who were in Spain: the late Sir Geoffrey Cox, whose chronicles from besieged Madrid remain important historical sources; Adelina Kondratieva, who was an interpreter with the Russian delegation; and Sam Lessor, who fought with the International Brigades and, after being wounded and invalided home, returned to Spain to work for the Republican propaganda services in Barcelona.

Four friends made a big difference. I ended up writing the book in the first place as a result of an invitation from Salvador Clotas to contribute to the catalogue of the splendid exhibition about foreign correspondents in Spain organized jointly by the Instituto Cervantes and the Fundación Pablo Iglesias. A trip to Lisbon to take part in the inauguration of the exhibition brought me into contact with its curator, Carlos García Santa Cecilia. To meet someone who shared my enthusiasm for the subject was an exhilarating experience and helped convince me that I was not engaged in a totally lunatic enterprise. Will Watson read several chapters with hawk-eyed precision. Lala Isla, as always, has been a fount of affectionate encouragement and I am immensely grateful for her close and sympathetic reading of all the chapters. The generous advice of Soledad Fox on sources and archives in the USA has been crucial. Without her unstinting encouragement and advice, this book would have been infinitely poorer.

It is with great pleasure that I also thank Andreas Campomar, my publisher and friend, for his faith in the project.

Finally, I want to thank the two people who have influenced this book the most. The first is my friend Herbert Southworth, who was a participant in much of what follows. Many years of conversations and correspondence with him taught me much about the Spanish Civil War in general and in particular about the correspondents with whom he had worked. The book is dedicated to him with deep gratitude for his friendship and his example. The other is my wife Gabrielle, who has always been my most lucid critic and reliable supporter. Her acute perceptions regarding the way in which unpalatable truths can be dismissed as bias have been an invaluable foundation for the book.

Illustrations

Every effort has been made to locate the rights holder to the pictures appearing in this book and to secure permission for usage from such persons. Any queries regarding the usage of such material should be addressed to the author c/o the publisher.

Henry Buckley and Louis Fischer in Barcelona, 1938. *Courtesy of the Buckley family.*

Jay Allen. *Courtesy of the Reverend Michael Allen.*

Lester Ziffren, Douglas Fairbanks and Juan Belmonte. *Courtesy of Didi Hunter.*

Sefton Delmer in Madrid. *Courtesy of Felix Sefton Delmer.*

Geoffrey Cox. *Courtesy of the late Sir Geoffrey Cox.*

Louis Delaprée. *Courtesy of the Instituto Cervantes.*

Arthur Koestler after his arrest in Málaga, February 1937. *Courtesy of El País*

Mikhail Koltsov and Buenaventura Durruti on the Aragón front at Bujaraloz, August 1936. *Courtesy of EFE.*

Ernest Hemingway, Communist General Enrique Líster, International Brigade Commander Hans Kahle and Vincent Sheean during the Battle of the Ebro. *Courtesy of the Buckley family.*

Mikhail Koltsov and Roman Karmen at the front outside Madrid, October 1936. *Courtesy of the Instituto Cervantes.*

Mikhail Koltsov and Maria Osten. *Courtesy of the Instituto Cervantes.*

Herbert Matthews and Ernest Hemingway in 'the Old Homestead'.

Illustrations

Herbert Matthews, Philip Jordan and Kajsa Rothman visit Alcalá de Henares. © *Vera Elkan Collection, Imperial War Museum* (HU 71630).

Josephine Herbst meets the villagers of Fuentidueña del Tajo, April 1937. *Courtesy of Elinor Langer.*

Liston Oak watches the front with Ernest Hemingway, Virginia Cowles and Kajsa Rothman, April 1937. Photographed by Joan Worthington.

Claud Cockburn, founder of the satirical news-sheet, *The Week* and Comintern agent Vittorio Vidali. © *Vera Elkan Collection, Imperial War Museum* (HU 71569).

Virginia Cowles of *Harpers' Bazaar,* autumn 1937. © *Angus McBean.*

Kajsa Rothman with a Swedish International Brigader. © *Arbetarrörelsens Arkiv och Bibliotek, Stockholm.*

George Lowther Steer with a group of French journalists, January 1937. *Courtesy of George Steer.*

Guernica after the German rehearsal for Blitzkrieg. *Courtesy of Museo de la Paz, Guernica.*

Jay Allen, Diana Sheean, Mrs Caspar Whitney, Juan Negrín, Muriel Draper and Louis Fischer discuss the display of Picasso's *Guernica* at the Paris Exhibition, summer 1937. *Courtesy of Carmen Negrín.*

Louis Fischer with the Soviet and Spanish Foreign Ministers, Maxim Litvinov and Julio Álvarez del Vayo at the League of Nations, Geneva, December 1936. *Courtesy of Carmen Negrín.*

Tom Wintringham, Commander of the British Battalion of the International Brigades, with Kitty Bowler. *Courtesy of Ben Wintringham.*

Safe-conduct issued to Kitty Bowler by the Catalan government. *Courtesy of Ben Wintringham.*

Kate Mangan and Jan Kurzke, in the hospital in Valencia. *Courtesy of Charlotte Kurzke.*

Kate Mangan's permission to attend a meeting of the Spanish parliament in Valencia on 30 September 1937. *Courtesy of Charlotte Kurzke.*

Luis Bolín. *Courtesy of the Instituto Cervantes.*

Clipping of *L'Intransigeant*'s report of the murder of its correspondent, Guy de Traversay. *Courtesy of the Instituto Cervantes.*

Harold Cardozo, Victor Console and Jean D'Hospital on the Madrid front, November 1936. *Courtesy of the Instituto Cervantes.*

John Dos Passos, Sydney Franklyn, Joris Ivens and Ernest Hemingway in the Hotel Florida, April 1937. © *Corbis.*

Kajsa Rothman fund-raising for the Republic in Stockholm. © *Arbetarrörelsens Arkiv och Bibliotek.*

Juan Negrín and Louis Fischer at a meeting of the League of Nations, September 1937. *Courtesy of Carmen Negrín.*

Gerda Grepp, Nordahl Grieg and Ludwig Renn. *Courtesy of Norges Kommunistiske Parti, Trondheim*

Ernest Hemingway, Henry Buckley and Herbert Matthews surveying the Ebro, November 1938. *Courtesy of the Buckley family.*

Ernest Hemingway rows Robert Capa, Herbert Matthews and Henry Buckley across the Ebro, November 1938.

Constancia de la Mora recovering after the war. Photographed by John Condax. *Courtesy of John and Laura Delano Condax.*

Jay Allen, captured by the Germans. *Courtesy of the Reverend Michael Allen.*

Arturo Barea and Ilsa Kulcsar together in their British exile. *Courtesy of Bruce and Margaret Weeden.*

Herbert Southworth in Sitges, April 1984. *Courtesy of Gabrielle Preston.*

PART ONE

SAY THAT WE SAW SPAIN DIE

1

The Wound that Will Not Heal:
Terror and Truth

'It was in Spain that men learned that one can be right and still be beaten, that force can vanquish spirit, that there are times when courage is not its own reward. It is this, without doubt, which explains why so many men throughout the world regard the Spanish drama as a personal tragedy.'

Albert Camus

When Spain's Second Republic was established on 14 April 1931, people thronged the streets of the country's cities and towns in an outburst of anticipatory joy. The new regime raised inordinate hopes among the most humble members of society and was seen as a threat by the most privileged, the landowners, industrialists and bankers, and their defenders in the armed forces and the Church. For the first time, control of the apparatus of the state had passed from the oligarchy to the moderate Left. This consisted of the reformist Socialists and a mixed bag of petty bourgeois Republicans. Together, they hoped, despite considerable disagreement over the finer details, to use state power to create a new Spain by curtailing the reactionary influence of the Church and the Army, by breaking up the great estates and by granting autonomy to the Basque Country and Catalonia. These hopes were soon blunted by the strength of the old order's defences.

Social and economic power – ownership of the land, the banks and industry, as well as of the principal newspapers and radio stations – remained unchanged. Those who held that power united with the Church and the Army to block any challenges to property, religion or national unity. Their repertoire of defence was rich and varied. Propaganda, through the Right's powerful press and radio networks and from the pulpit of every parish church, denounced the efforts at reform as the subversive work of Moscow. New right-wing political parties were founded and lavishly funded. Conspiracies were hatched to overthrow the new regime.

Rural and industrial lock-out became a regular response to legislation aimed at protecting worker interests.

So successfully was reform blocked that, by 1933, the disillusioned Socialists decided to leave their alliance with the liberal Republicans and go it alone. In a system heavily favouring coalitions, this handed power to the Right in the November 1933 elections. Employers and landowners now cut wages, sacked workers, evicted tenants and raised rents. Social legislation was dismantled and, one after another, the principal unions were weakened as strikes were provoked and crushed – notably a nation-wide stoppage by agricultural labourers in the summer of 1934. Tension was rising. The Left saw fascism in every action of the Right; the Right smelt revolution in every left-wing move.

On 6 October 1934, when the authoritarian Catholic party, the CEDA, entered the government, the Socialists called a revolutionary general strike. In most of Spain, it failed because of the swift declaration of martial law. In Barcelona, an independent state of Catalonia was short-lived. However, in the mining valleys of Asturias, there was a revolutionary movement organized jointly by the Socialist union, the Unión General de Trabajadores, the anarcho-syndicalist Confederación Nacional del Trabajo and, belatedly, the Communists. For nearly three weeks, a revolutionary commune heroically held out until finally the miners were reduced to submission by heavy artillery attacks and bombing raids co-ordinated by General Franco. The savage repression that followed was to be the fire in which was forged the Popular Front, essentially a re-creation of the Republican–Socialist coalition.

When elections were called for mid-February 1936, a well-financed right-wing campaign convinced the middle classes that Spain faced a life-or-death fight between good and evil, survival and destruction. The Popular Front campaign stressed the threat of fascism and demanded an amnesty for those imprisoned after October 1934. On 16 February, the Popular Front gained a narrow victory and thus shattered right-wing hopes of being able to impose legally an authoritarian, corporative state. Two years of aggressive rightist government had left the working masses, especially in the countryside, in a determined and vengeful mood. Having been blocked once in its reforming ambitions, the Left was now determined to proceed rapidly with meaningful agrarian reform. In response, right-wing leaders provoked social unrest, then used it in blood-curdling parliamentary speeches and articles, to present a military rising as the only alternative to catastrophe.

The central factor in the spring of 1936 was the weakness of the Popular Front government. The Socialist leader Francisco Largo Caballero had insisted that the liberal Republicans govern alone until the time came for them to make way for an all-Socialist government. He was mistakenly confident that, if reform provoked a fascist and/or military uprising, it would be defeated by the revolutionary action of the masses. So he used his power in the Socialist Party to prevent the formation of a strong government by his more realistic rival Indalecio Prieto. Mass hunger for reform saw a wave of land seizures in the south. Thoroughly alarmed, the Right prepared for war. A military conspiracy was headed by General Emilio Mola. The liberal Republicans of the Popular Front watched feebly as the terror squads of the growing fascist party, Falange Española, orchestrated a strategy of tension, its terrorism provoking left-wing reprisals and creating disorder to justify the imposition of an authoritarian regime. One such reprisal, the assassination on 13 July of the monarchist leader, José Calvo Sotelo, provided the signal for the conspirators.

The rising took place on the evening of 17 July in Spain's Moroccan colony and in the peninsula itself on the next morning. The plotters were confident that it would all be over in a few days. Had they faced only the Republican government, their predictions might have come true. The coup was successful in the Catholic small-holding areas which voted for the CEDA – the provincial capitals of rural León and Old Castile, cathedral market towns such as Avila, Burgos, Salamanca and Valladolid. However, in the left-wing strongholds of industrial Spain and the great estates of the deep south, the uprising was defeated by the spontaneous action of the working-class organizations. Yet, ominously, in major southern towns such as Cadiz, Cordoba, Granada and Seville, left-wing resistance was swiftly and savagely crushed.

Within days, the country was split into two war zones. The rebels controlled one-third of Spain in a northern block of Galicia, León, Old Castile, Aragón and part of Extremadura and an Andalusian triangle from Huelva to Seville to Cordoba. They had the great wheat-growing areas, but the main industrial centres remained in Republican hands. Vain efforts were made by the government to reach a compromise with the rebels. Then, to appease the Great Powers, a new cabinet of moderate Republicans was formed under the chemistry professor, José Giral. There was some reason to suppose that the Republic would be able to crush the rising. Giral's bourgeois Republican cabinet hoped to secure international assistance, and it controlled the nation's gold and currency reserves and virtually all of Spain's industrial capacity.

There would, however, be two big differences between the two sides that would eventually decide the conflict – the African Army and the help of the fascist powers. At first, the rebels' strongest card, the ferocious colonial army under Franco, was blockaded in Morocco by Republican warships. However, the fact that power in Spain's streets lay with the unions and their militia organizations – particularly as interpreted by the conservative newspapers of Europe and the United States – totally undermined the efforts of Giral's unrepresentative government to secure aid from the Western democracies. Republican requests for assistance met only hesitance from the Popular Front government in Paris. Inhibited by internal political divisions and sharing the British fear of revolution and of provoking a general war, the French premier Léon Blum soon drew back from early promises of aid. Franco, in contrast, was quickly able to persuade the local representatives of Nazi Germany and Fascist Italy that he was the man to back.

By the end of July, Junkers 52 and Savoia-Marchetti 81 transport aircraft were undertaking the first major military airlift in history. The bloodthirsty Foreign Legion and the so-called Native Regulars were carried across the Straits of Gibraltar to Seville. Fifteen thousand men crossed in ten days and a *coup d'état* going wrong became a long and bloody civil war. That crucial early aid was soon followed by a regular stream of high-technology assistance. In contrast to the state-of-the-art equipment arriving from Germany and Italy, complete with technicians, spare parts and the correct workshop manuals, the Republic, shunned by the democracies, had to make do with over-priced and obsolete equipment from private arms dealers.

While Mola attacked the Basque province of Guipúzcoa, cutting it off from the French border, Franco's Army of Africa advanced rapidly northwards to Madrid, leaving a horrific trail of slaughter in its wake, including the massacre at Badajoz where two thousand prisoners were shot. In part because of their iron control of the despatches of foreign correspondents, rebel atrocities made little impression on public opinion in the democracies. In contrast, revolutionary terror had a profound impact on foreign perceptions of the war, to a large extent because of the way in which it was treated by the conservative press. The subsequent sympathy of many foreign correspondents for the plight of the Republican population had therefore considerable obstacles to overcome before they could influence popular opinion in favour of the democratic cause.

One of the greatest was the fact that an inadvertent result of the coup was to leave the Republican government virtually without the structures of law and order. The consequent terrorism in the Republican zone, mainly directed against the supporters of right-wing parties and the clergy, predisposed foreign opinion in favour of the rebels. The disappearance of the police force and the judiciary had permitted revolutionary crowds to open the jails and release the common prisoners. Accordingly, for about four months, behind rhetoric of revolutionary justice, acts of violence of all kinds were perpetrated. Revenge was directed at the sections of society on whose behalf the military was acting. Thus, hatred of an oppressive social system found expression in the murder or humiliation of parish priests who justified it, Civil Guards and policemen who defended it, the wealthy who enjoyed it and the employers and landlords' agents who implemented it. In some cases, there was a revolutionary dimension – the burning of property records and land registries. But there were also criminal acts, murder, rape, theft and the settling of personal scores. Courts were replaced by revolutionary tribunals set up by political parties and trade unions.

About 55,000 civilians were killed in the Republican zone in the course of the war while more than three times that number were murdered in the rebel zone. Some, like the imprisoned army officers killed at Paracuellos del Jarama and Torrejón de Ardoz during the siege of Madrid, were victims of military decisions based on an assessment of their potential danger to the Republican cause. Some were executed as known fifth columnists. Others died in explosions of mass rage which occurred as news arrived of the savage purges being carried out in the Nationalist zone and especially of atrocities committed by Franco's Moors. Air-raids on Republican cities were another obvious trigger of popular fury. Whatever the reasons behind the violence, it seriously damaged the reputation of the Republic abroad and undermined its efforts to secure international support. Most notably, the near indiscriminate violence of anarchist elements in Barcelona in the first months of the war branded the Republic – whose authorities were desperately trying, with gradual success, to re-establish law and order – as a bloodstained regime of terror. In contrast, the atrocities in the Nationalist zone did nothing to diminish its standing in British and French government circles, let alone in Berlin or Rome.

In the first days after the military coup, the events in Catalonia saw newspapermen flocking from around the world. One of the first to arrive was the swashbuckling Sefton 'Tom' Delmer of the *Daily Express*. He had set off with his new wife Isabel for a holiday in Mallorca. The military coup in Spain took place while they were motoring through France. He managed to bluff their way through the frontier by flourishing his League of Nations press card. As they neared Barcelona, they were stopped by anarchists who either did not respect or could not read the card. However, the presence of a Siamese cat in a basket in the car convinced them that they were indeed dealing with holidaymakers. The couple were taken to the village of Mollet, just north of Barcelona. After just one night there, a night interrupted by the sounds of firing squads executing fascist sympathizers, they were obliged to return to France.[1]

From Perpignan, Delmer sent a report on their adventure which set the tone for much early reporting from the Republic zone. Under the headline ARMED REDS BAR WAY TO CITY OF TERROR, he relayed unsubstantiated gossip about thousands killed in Barcelona despite the fact that he had been prevented from visiting the city:

> The Red Terror wave that has broken out following the army's uprising has given the excuse for the settlement in the Barcelona district at least, of many private feuds. I heard of no fewer than three similar murders which had taken place during the last twenty-four hours in Mollet and the villages around.[2]

In the following days, reports from the Reuters correspondent were equally lurid. It was alleged that bodies were piled in the underground stations and that: 'The victorious Government civilian forces, composed of Anarchists, Communists and Socialists have burned and sacked practically every church and convent in Barcelona.' The Reuters report went on: 'The mob drunk with victory, afterwards paraded the streets of the city attired in the robes of ecclesiastical authorities.'[3]

Over the next few days the stories became ever gorier. The reign of terror was described under the sub-heading 'Priests Die Praying. The mob is uncontrollable and class hatred rules.' According to this account 'Priests are being dragged with a prayer on their lips from their monasteries to be shot – in the back – by firing squads. Some of them have had their heads and arms hacked off after death as a final vindictive act.' Delight in the bloodshed went hand in hand with an almost racist patronage of the simplicity of the perpetrators:

> like children with a new and dangerous toy which they scarcely understand. Alongside them on the firing line are city clerks who have let their beards grow and are heavy eyed with free liquor and days without sleep. The Robespierre of Barcelona sits on a pedestal fashioned like a throne on the balcony of a magnificent house in the Ramblas, the famous thoroughfare between the Plaza Cataluña and the port…On either side of the throne the leader's lieutenants sit on chairs with rifles over their knees and blood red silk scarves round head and waist. But for their menacing and unkempt appearance they would be like fancy-dress pirates. As armed men pass in the street below they salute the 'Committee' with a shout and shaking of the fist in the Communist salute.[4]

The Wound that Will Not Heal

The Canadian James M. Minifie left the Paris office of the *New York Herald Tribune* with the instructions of his bureau chief, Leland Stowe, ringing in his ears: 'Look under every stone and write what you find there.' Accordingly, he confined his reports to what he knew to be true. Like Delmer and many of his fellow newspapermen, on his arrival on the Catalan side of the Spanish–French frontier, Minifie was confronted by a gun-toting anarchist in blue overalls who gave him a safe-conduct which would be regarded as valid only by other members of the same faction:

> I found Catalan officials very gracious about giving interviews; they damned the Communists as little better than enemy agents, and blamed nightly murders and executions on them. I heard reports of mass graves, looted monasteries, raped nuns and the whole deck of cards; but I never found what I would accept as irrefutable evidence in support of these charges.

He did, however, find ample evidence of looting, whether of farms or urban luxury car showrooms. The anarchists had seized every Rolls Royce, Hispano-Suiza or Cadillac that they could lay their hands on, ostensibly to motorize their columns but often to destroy them in wild joy-rides. After a brief stay, the lack of decent cabling facilities obliged Minifie to return to Paris, prior to going to Madrid and capture by rebel forces three months later.[5]

As Minifie's example made clear, not all the visiting firemen were in search of a sensational scoop. Indeed, the journalists who knew Spain well wrote more sober accounts of what was happening. However, passing British journalists who visited His Majesty's Consul, Norman King, in search of orientation were treated to a gruesomely exaggerated account of what was happening. What he told them can be deduced from his consular despatches from Barcelona. He built a lurid picture in which 'anarchists, and the escaped criminals with other armed hooligans for a time spread terror throughout the town'.[6] Even when things had calmed down, he speculated almost gleefully that economic collapse 'will produce widespread distress, and possibly lead to a massacre', and predicted that 'a time is not far distant when a wave of xenophobia might set in'.[7] He confided in the British poet Stephen Spender that he wished Lluís Companys, the President of the Catalan Generalitat, had been shot after the rising of 1934.[8]

In stark contrast to King's alarmism about 'raw undisciplined youth armed to the teeth and mostly out of control' were the considered reflections of Lawrence Fernsworth. The distinguished, grey-haired Fernsworth, who was born in

Portland, Oregon in 1898, had lived in Barcelona for a decade and wrote for both *The Times* of London and the *New York Times*. He also wrote for a Jesuit weekly publication called *America*. A fervent Catholic, Fernsworth spoke both Spanish and Catalan. Reflecting on his first wartime experiences in Barcelona, he commented that 'our escorts and the Republican crowds in the towns, all armed to the teeth, were the most amiable and solicitous revolutionaries one might wish to meet' and that: 'The danger to foreigners in Barcelona seems small. Even the Communists and Anarchists have shown respect for foreigners.'[9] On 19 July, while the workers were fighting with the military rebels, Fernsworth noted groups of picnickers coming down the street with hampers hoping to get on a train for their customary Sunday trip out to the countryside. He also noted popular outrage that many military rebels and their civilian sympathizers had been permitted to establish machine-gun emplacements in numerous church towers before the coup. Fortified therein, these rebel supporters opened fire on the workers. The outrage fed the church burnings but, as Fernsworth also noted, the Catalan government made every effort to save those that it could, such as the cathedral. The Capuchin church in the Passeig de Gràcia was saved because the Franciscan friars were noted for their close relation to the poor. Of others, he wrote, 'I could hardly consider that these churches were being desecrated. In my eyes, they had already been desecrated by the anointed money-changers and were no longer holy temples of worship.' In describing the subsequent terror, in which those believed to be 'enemies of the people' were murdered, Fernsworth was careful to point out that the Catalan government, the Generalitat, was not responsible, and laboured incessantly to keep itself in business and to save property and lives. Of the efforts of the government to re-establish public order, Fernsworth wrote: 'Persons in official positions risked the anger of extremists, and consequently their lives, to save priests, nuns, bishops and certain other Spanish nationals by getting them aboard foreign ships or across the frontier.'[10]

Fernsworth felt a deep sympathy for the Republic, but had strict professional ethics. Not only did he not attempt to diminish what he knew about atrocities, but he actually took considerable risks to get stories out when he knew them to be true. In the early days of the war, he crossed clandestinely into France in order to send a report about the liquidation of the 'enemies of the people' in Barcelona:

> It was a dangerous story to bring out and I took care that my departure and return were unobserved and my passport had no telltale marks to show I had been in France. It was well that I did so, for the publication of the story caused a furore in Barcelona. It was an unpleasant task. I knew

> the facts would be harmful to the Republican cause for which, as an American, I felt a deep sympathy believing that in its essence the struggle was one for the rights of man. But it was the truth and had to be told. As a reporter I have never shirked at telling the truth regardless of whom it might please or displease.

He regularly used to board a Royal Navy cruiser in Barcelona harbour 'to visit the captain' and then be taken to Marseilles on a fast destroyer. Having sent his despatch, a day later he would step off the cruiser, having apparently just 'visited the captain'.[11]

The unnamed Barcelona correspondent of Lord Rothermere's *Daily Mail* had none of the Spanish experience of Fernsworth but nor, it would appear, did he have need for much prompting from Norman King. Five days before the military coup, an editorial had already claimed that 'The present year has seen Spain fall under the control of a Government bearing the sinister stamp of Bolshevism.' A few days later, another alleged that 'highly trained groups of revolutionaries were being sent to Spain, France and Belgium to direct operations on the spot'.[12] The rising itself was acclaimed as Spain's opportunity to be 'brought back to order or turned into a vassal of USSR' by the forces in Morocco and Spain gathered 'for a simultaneous effort of liberation' (printed in bold). The Socialist leader Francisco Largo Caballero, 'the Spanish Lenin', it was asserted, would try to 'force the pace to make Spain a vassal state of Soviet Russia'.[13]

When reports began to reach London from Barcelona, they were printed in the most sensationalist manner possible. Refugees were quoted to the effect that 'between 2,000–3,000 people' had been killed: 'The streets of Barcelona, they claim, are splattered with blood.' In contrast, Harold Cardozo with General Mola's forces at Soria approvingly quoted the general's declaration (printed in bold) that the purpose of the coup was 'to wrench out by the roots, for ever, all that represents the organisations and principles of Marxism'.[14] Some of the stories sent were not without their inadvertently comic elements. Under the headline, LONDONERS FORCED TO FIGHT FOR REDS. REFUGEES TELL OF SPANISH TERROR, ran a story of a man who had his car commandeered by 'some communists' and was forced to give them driving lessons for two hours.[15] The general line was that Republican Spain was in the hands of Moscow and that the crimes of the anarchists were committed at the behest of Soviet agents. An editorial declared: 'As Moscow is the stronghold of the Reds in the east, so Madrid has become their headquarters in the west.' In the same issue, under the headline MOB RULE PREVAILS IN BARCELONA TONIGHT, a report claimed that 'The flag of the sickle and hammer floats over many buildings. Homes of the Spanish nobility are being plundered and burned by Communists and anarchists.' Another asserted that 'Anxieties caused by the Communists' murderous reign of terror are spreading far beyond the frontiers of Spain.' To add spice to the red-baiting, there was added an element of misogyny. Under the headline THE WOMEN WHO BURN CHURCHES – SPAIN'S RED CARMENS, it was asserted that female volunteers in the militias were women who had 'thrown off religion, parental authority and all restraint'.[16]

The consequence was, as John Langdon-Davies of the *News Chronicle* wrote in September 1936, 'Today most English people have been convinced that the government supporters are not only "reds" but ghouls; that the reason why they have not defeated the fascists is that they spend their time raping nuns and watching them dance naked.'[17] Fernsworth, like Langdon-Davies, understood why things were happening as they were in Barcelona. It was not, as the *Daily Express* and the *Daily Mail* would have it, that it was to put a stop to the red terror that the military had risen, but rather that the coup had unleashed the red terror by removing the structures of law and order. As Fernsworth wrote later, 'the props were knocked out from under directing authority. Such local and provincial governments as existed in the large provincial capitals were like ships without rudder or motive power or sail, desperately battling ungovernable waves.'[18]

Langdon-Davies made every effort to present a more realistic view to a British audience. Since first visiting Catalonia in 1920, and living there during the years 1921–22 and 1927–29, Langdon-Davies had been an enthusiastic student and advocate of Catalan culture. His book, *Dancing Catalans*, published in 1929, reflected his admiration for the humanity and egalitarianism that he believed were the essence of social relations in rural Catalonia. The persecution of the Catalan language and popular culture under the dictatorship of General Miguel Primo de Rivera (1923–30) intensified Langdon-Davies' sympathies for Catalan nationalism. Unsurprisingly, the establishment of the democratic Second Republic on 14 April 1931 seemed to him to promise a freedom for the region that he loved.

On 6 August 1936, barely three weeks after the military coup, he arrived at Puigcerdà on the Spanish border on a second-hand motorcycle with his fifteen-year-old son, Robin. After leaving Robin with Catalan friends in Ripoll, he went on to Barcelona as a special correspondent of the liberal London daily, the *News Chronicle*. Between 11 August and 7 September, on an almost daily basis, he wrote articles in which he tried to put the disorder and church-burnings into their historical context. He believed that King's consular staff were contributing to an atmosphere of panic among British citizens in Barcelona: 'Many of these lost their heads completely, and one can sympathise with them, seeing that the British officials supposed to look after them completely lost theirs.' He claimed that Norman King 'became so childishly terrified that he refused to send a conservative newspaper-man a car to go to the local airport, saying that it was too dangerous, and that he would not risk the lives of his chauffeurs. This was in mid August when everyone else was settling down to normal existence.'[19] The man in question was almost certainly the correspondent of the *Daily Telegraph*, Cedric Salter.[20]

Thereafter, Langdon-Davies went to Valencia, Madrid and Toledo before returning to England on 19 September. He used the material gathered as the basis for lectures on behalf of the relief organization, Spanish Medical Aid, and for the book *Behind the Spanish Barricades* which he wrote in barely five weeks in the intervals between his lectures. During his brief time in Spain, Langdon-Davies was quickly convinced that the British policy of non-intervention was disastrous for both the Spanish Republic and for Britain. This brought him into direct conflict with the views being propounded by Norman King. In September 1936, he vainly visited the Foreign Office in London in an attempt to counteract the apocalyptic view emanating from right-wing sources about the Catalan President, Lluís Companys, and of the situation in Barcelona. Langdon-Davies mistakenly underestimated the scale of the killing in Barcelona, and this led to officials checking his figures with Norman King. The Consul gloated and he seized the opportunity to brand Langdon-Davies as a Communist, which he certainly was not.

Despite his sympathy with the Republic, Langdon-Davies did not try to pretend that revolutionary violence did not exist, but he made an effort to understand what lay behind it. In the case of the shooting of thirteen fascist sympathizers in Ripoll, the town where he left his son, he faced a grave moral dilemma:

> as I thought of those superb, simple-hearted working men and peasants
> in overalls, organising as best they could to keep the Moorish invasion
> from saving Christianity by killing Spanish Christians; as I thought of
> their gentleness, their zeal, their courtesy, and how in spite of it all they
> had been moved to get up and kill thirteen fairly harmless men, my heart
> hardened against those who had brought to Spain the most horrible
> atrocity of all, civil war.

The blame, he concluded, lay with 'those who let loose the supreme horror of civil war'.[21]

Langdon-Davies was one of the first to confront a problem that would bedevil the work of all those foreign correspondents who tried to write sympathetically about the uneven struggle of the Republic against fascist aggression and to awaken the governments of the democracies to the threat that faced them. As wild fantasies about Communist conspiracies and Muscovite skulduggery proliferated, he wrote:

> To the many readers who quite sincerely believe in the insincerities of our philo-fascist press I say, 'I beg of you to believe it possible that you have been misled. Read and imagine things in terms of human men and women; of simple folk, insulted and injured, whose hope of an end to the Dark Ages has been destroyed by rebellion subsidised from abroad. If you saw your family doomed to the conditions of the Spanish peasantry and workers, would you need Moscow gold to make you cling to the little you had and fight for a little more? Remember all that you have heard of the age-long tyrannies of Spain; do you realise that a victory for the Rebels means their re-imposition on the remnant left alive?.[22]

Within barely two months of the military coup, Langdon-Davies had put his finger on one of the greatest problems facing the most serious journalists and commentators. The early days of the terror, particularly in Barcelona, would colour subsequent perceptions and stand in the way of transmission of more profound truths about what was happening in Spain. Newspapermen in Spain would face the same problems as foreign correspondents in any war: local censorship and physical danger. However, in addition they faced the prejudices of editors who did not want to hear either about the plight of the Republican population or about the blind complacency of the Western decision-makers. Revolutionary violence fed the representation of a bloodstained Republic which made it possible to ignore the fact that the fascist powers were using Spain to alter the international balance of power against the democracies.

The British journalist Cedric Salter complained that to discuss the real issues in Spain was regarded in 'polite society' as 'not in quite the best of taste'. On one occasion, he sent to a London paper a powerful story about an old man caught trying to smuggle a few potatoes into Barcelona for his family. In the ensuing altercation, both a policeman and the old man were shot. The story was not printed and Salter was given the explanation that:

> Newspapers are mostly read at breakfast, and there is nothing better calculated to put a man off his second egg and rasher of bacon than reading a story forcing him to realize that not so very far away there are

people dying for a handful of potatoes. If one newspaper puts him off his breakfast he takes pains to buy another one. That we naturally wish to avoid.[23]

At the end of the conflict, the American newspaperman Frank Hanighen, who had briefly served as a correspondent in Spain, edited the reminiscences of several of his companions. He commented that:

> Almost every journalist assigned to Spain became a different man sometime or other after he crossed the Pyrenees…After he had been there a while, the queries of his editor in far-off New York or London seemed like trivial interruptions. For he had become a participant in, rather than an observer of, the horror, tragedy and adventure which constitutes war.[24]

The well-travelled American correspondent Louis Fischer similarly noted that:

> Many of the foreign correspondents who visited the Franco zone became Loyalists, but practically all of the numerous journalists and other visitors who went into Loyalist Spain became active friends of the cause. Even the foreign diplomats and military attachés scarcely disguised their admiration. Only a soulless idiot could have failed to understand and sympathize.[25]

Journalists of every political hue hastened to the Spanish Republic and were permitted to carry out their daily tasks. The only ones excluded were the representatives of the official media of Franco's allies: Hitler, Mussolini and Salazar. In contrast, the military rebels admitted to their zone only those journalists whom they believed to be sympathetic to their cause – those from Nazi Germany, Fascist Italy, Salazar's Portugal and the correspondents of the conservative press of the democracies. Of course, some of the latter were actually highly critical of the military atrocities that they saw, but were prevented by a fierce censorship from publishing them until they could write memoirs after leaving Spain.

Nearly one thousand newspaper correspondents went to Spain.[26] Along with the professional war correspondents, some hardened veterans of Abyssinia, others still to win their spurs, came some of the world's most prominent literary figures: Ernest Hemingway, John Dos Passos, Josephine Herbst and Martha Gellhorn from the United States; W. H. Auden, Stephen Spender and George Orwell from Britain; André Malraux and Antoine de Saint-Exupéry from France.

A few arrived as committed leftists, rather fewer as rightists, and plenty of those who spent brief periods in Spain were simply jobbing newspapermen.

However, as a result of what they saw, even some of those who arrived without commitment came to embrace the cause of the beleaguered Spanish Republic. Underlying their conversion was a deep admiration for the stoicism with which the Republican population resisted. Vernon Bartlett of the *News Chronicle* was impatient with the many political committees that had to be dealt with in the Republican zone. Nevertheless, he commented later 'My love of comfort and an easy life and my anger with the committees which did their best to rob me of them had taken away most of the enthusiasm for the Spanish Government with which I had left London. But when one saw the odds they had to face one's sympathy revived.'[27] In Madrid, Valencia and Barcelona, the correspondents saw the overcrowding caused by the endless flow of refugees fleeing from Franco's African columns and from the bombing of their homes. They saw the mangled corpses of innocent civilians bombed and shelled by Franco's Nazi and Fascist allies. And they saw the heroism of ordinary people hastening to take part in the struggle to defend their democratic Republic.

In trying to capture accurately what they saw, observation became indignation and sympathy became partisanship. As Louis Delaprée, the correspondent of *Paris-Soir*, wrote a mere eight days before his death in December 1936:

> What follows is not a set of prosecutor's charges. It is an actuary's process. I number the ruins, I count the dead, I weigh the blood spilt. All the images of martyred Madrid, which I will try to put before your eyes – and which most of the time defy description – I have seen them. I can be believed. I demand to be believed. I care nothing about propaganda literature or the sweetened reports of the Ministries. I do not follow any orders of parties or churches. And here you have my witness. You will draw your own conclusions.[28]

It was not just a question of correspondents describing what they witnessed. Many of them reflected on the implications for the rest of the world of events in Spain. What they saw and what they risked were perceived as portents of the future that faced the world if fascism was not stopped in Spain. Their experiences led them into a deep frustration and an impotent rage with the blind complacency of the policy-makers of Britain, France and America. They felt, in the words of Martha Gellhorn, that:

the Western democracies had two commanding obligations: they must save their honour by assisting a young, attacked fellow democracy, and they must save their skin, by fighting Hitler and Mussolini, at once, in Spain, instead of waiting until later, when the cost in human suffering would be unimaginably greater.[29]

Accordingly, they tried to convey what they saw as the injustice of the Republic having been left defenceless and forced into the arms of the Soviet Union because of the Western powers' short-sighted adoption of a policy of non-intervention.

Many journalists were driven by their indignation to write in favour of the loyalist cause, some, like Jay Allen and George Steer, to lobby in their own countries, and in a few cases even to take up arms for the Republic. Without going so far, many of the correspondents who experienced the horrors of the siege of Madrid and the inspiring popular spirit of resistance became convinced of the justice of the Republican cause. In some cases, such as Ernest Hemingway, Martha Gellhorn and Louis Fischer, they became resolute partisans, to the extent of activism yet not to the detriment of the accuracy or honesty of their reporting.[30] Indeed, some of the most committed correspondents produced some of the most accurate and lasting reportage of the war.

Like many others, Fischer found his emotions deeply engaged with the cause of the Republic. Comparing the impact of the Russian Revolution and the Spanish Civil War, he wrote:

> Bolshevism inspired vehement passions in its foreign adherents but little of the tenderness and intimacy which Loyalist Spain evoked. The pro-Loyalists loved the Spanish people and participated painfully in their ordeal by bullet, bomb and hunger. The Soviet system elicited intellectual approval, the Spanish struggle brought forth emotional identification. Loyalist Spain was always the weaker side, the loser, and its friends felt a constant, tense concern lest its strength end. Only those who lived with Spain through the thirty-three tragic months from July 1936 to March 1939 can fully understand the joy of victory and the more frequent pang of defeat which the ups and downs of the civil war brought to its millions of distant participants.[31]

Frank Hanighen believed that 'The Spanish war ushered in a new and by far the most dangerous phase in the history of newspaper reporting.'[32] He underlined the dangers faced by correspondents – at least five were killed during the war, numerous others wounded. On both sides, correspondents faced danger from snipers, the bombing and strafing of enemy aircraft. On both sides too, there were difficulties to be overcome with the censorship apparatus, although what could be irksome in the Republican zone was downright life-threatening in the rebel zone. More than thirty journalists were expelled from the Francoist zone, but only one by the Republicans. The rebels shot at least one, Guy de Traversay of *L'Intransigeant*, and arrested, interrogated and imprisoned about a dozen more for periods ranging from a few days to several months.[33]

There was physical risk from shelling and bombardment in both zones, although the rebel superiority in artillery and aircraft meant that it was greater for those posted in the Republic. Moreover, the close control exercised over correspondents in the rebel zone kept them away from danger at the front. Within the rebel zone, there were of course enthusiasts for Franco and fascism, and not just among the Nazi and Italian Fascist contingent. Nevertheless, the British, American and French Francoists were a minority. Many more of those who accompanied Franco's columns were repelled by the savagery they had witnessed with the rebel columns. Those in the rebel zone were kept under tight supervision and their published despatches were scoured to pick out any attempts to bypass the censorship. Transgressions were punished by harassment, and sometimes imprisonment and expulsion. Accordingly, they could not relate what they had seen in their daily despatches and did so only after the war, in their memoirs.

The correspondents in the Republican zone were given greater freedom of movement, although they too had to deal with a censorship machinery, albeit a much less crude and brutal one than its rebel equivalent. However, they faced another problem not encountered by their right-wing colleagues. Given that the bulk of the press in the democracies was in right-wing hands, pro-Republican correspondents found publicizing their views often more difficult than might have been expected. It was ironic that a high proportion of the world's best journalists and writers supported the Republic but often had difficulty in getting their material published as written.

In the United States, the debates over the issues of the Spanish war were especially embittered. The powerful Hearst press and several dailies such as the *Chicago Daily Tribune* were deeply hostile to the democratic Republic even before the military coup of 1936. Jay Allen, for instance, would be fired from the *Chicago Daily Tribune* because his articles provoked so much sympathy for the Republic. There were cases of the Catholic lobby using threats of boycott or the withdrawal of advertising to make smaller newspapers alter their stance on Spain. This had happened even before the outbreak of war. In late 1934, James M. Minifie went to report on the situation in the Basque Country for the *New York Herald Tribune*. Before leaving Paris, he was warned that 'the Power House' – the Roman Catholic hierarchy in St Patrick's Cathedral – was putting the heat on advertisers to insist that only 'reliable' news of Spain be printed: 'It worked by indirection, rarely telephoning the management, but making it clear to advertisers that they should not imperil their immortal souls or their pocket-books by dealing with supporters of leftists, pinkos, and radicals.'[34]

Such pressures intensified with the outbreak of war in Spain. Dr Edward Lodge Curran, President of the International Catholic Truth Society, boasted in December 1936 that his control of a large sum in advertising business permitted him to change the policy of a Brooklyn daily from pro-Loyalist to pro-rebel. Other more liberal newspapers were subjected to pressure to prevent the publication of pro-Loyalist news. Herbert L. Matthews, the meticulously honest *New York Times* correspondent, was constantly badgered with telegrams accusing him of sending propaganda. In 1938, the paper lost readers when the Roman Catholic Archdiocese of Brooklyn helped organize a campaign specifically aimed against Matthews and his reporting.[35] In Spain for the North American Newspaper Alliance, Hemingway also had cause for frequent complaint about his material being changed or simply not used.[36] He, Matthews and others believed that material deemed sympathetic to the Spanish Loyalists was edited or even omitted. In fact, both the cable desk and the night desk of the *New York Times* – effectively where it was decided what news would be printed – were manned by religious fanatics hostile to the Republican cause.[37]

The managing editor of the *New York Times* was the short, stick-toting Virginian, Edwin L. 'Jimmy' James. He wore brightly coloured suits, looked like a bookie and was nicknamed 'Dressy James' by Damon Runyon. A keen *bon viveur*, James was always keen to get off in the evening and so gave enormous freedom to the night managing editor, the deeply conservative Presbyterian, Raymond McCaw. In turn, McCaw gave considerable liberty to his deputy, Neil MacNeil, a fiercely partisan Catholic, and his assistant, the equally fanatical convert, Clarence Howell. These night editors controlled the group of desks in the newsroom known as the 'bullpen'. They decided what stories would get prominence and how they were edited.[38]

Matthews was convinced that these men treated his copy with 'suspicion, anger, and, at times, disbelief', tampered with his wording and buried entire stories because they were perceived to favour the Republican side. In contrast, they printed unashamedly partisan material from William P. Carney, his counterpart in the rebel zone, despite knowing that it was sometimes faked. McCaw issued orders that, whenever Matthews wrote about the 'Italian troops' who fought with the rebels, the phrase was to be replaced by 'insurgent troops'. Matthews had gone to Guadalajara after the Italian defeat there. He reported what Italian prisoners had told him and what he had seen of captured Italian weaponry and documents. McCaw's device made nonsense of his despatches. Moreover, McCaw cabled Matthews, accusing him of simply sending Republican propaganda handouts.[39]

Matthews, in fact, took enormous pride in his work and his personal ethic demanded that he never wrote a word that he did not fervently believe to be true. In Spain, he would endure the bitterness of seeing the side he supported lose. Over thirty years later, he concluded:

> All of us who lived the Spanish Civil War felt deeply emotional about it…I always felt the falseness and hypocrisy of those who claimed to be unbiased…those of us who championed the cause of the Republican government against the Franco Nationalists were right. It was, on balance, the cause of justice, morality, decency.[40]

Matthews was savagely denounced as 'a rabid Red partisan' by the leading Catholic propagandist Dr Joseph Thorning. Nevertheless, it did not diminish his passionate commitment to writing the truth as he saw it: 'the war also taught me that the truth will prevail in the long run. Journalism may seem to fail in its daily task of providing the material for history, but history will never fail so long as the newspaperman writes the truth.'[41]

Writing the truth meant, to quote Martha Gellhorn again, 'explaining that the Spanish Republic was neither a collection of blood-slathering Reds nor a cat's-paw of Russia'. She would have no truck with what she called 'all that objectivity shit', refusing to adopt a morally repugnant neutrality equidistant between two very different sides. Like Matthews and so many others, she felt that to write passionately and vividly about what they saw was no distortion of the truth. They came to believe that those who fought and those who died in defence of the Spanish Republic

> whatever their nationality and whether they were Communists, anarchists, Socialists, poets, plumbers, middle-class professional men, or the one Abyssinian prince, were brave and disinterested, as there were no rewards in Spain. They were fighting for us all, against the combined force of European fascism. They deserved our thanks and our respect and got neither.[42]

A few who became loyalist partisans went further than just writing the truth, indeed well beyond their journalistic duties. Hemingway gave an ambulance and dispensed advice to military commanders. Fischer helped both to organize the Republic's press services and to repatriate wounded International Brigaders. Jay Allen lobbied tirelessly for the Republic in America, then went into Vichy France to help Spanish refugees and imprisoned International Brigaders. In consequence, he suffered incarceration in a German prison. George Steer campaigned on behalf of the Basque government to get Britain to permit food supplies to get through to a blockaded Bilbao. The Russian, Mikhail Koltsov, wrote so enthusiastically about the revolutionary élan of the Spanish people that, in the atmosphere of the Soviet purges, he became an embarrassment and was executed.

It has been possible to reconstruct the experiences of some of the world's best newspapermen in Spain partly through their despatches, letters, diaries and memoirs. Moreover, many details of their activities and of their relations with the censorship apparatus have been revealed through the memoirs left by important figures in the Republican press bureaux in Madrid, Valencia and Barcelona: Arturo Barea, Kate Mangan and Constancia de la Mora. What was written by the foreign newspapermen was crucial at the time to the formation of public opinion in the democracies. Thereafter, the body of work produced by war correspondents during the Spanish conflict, endlessly mined by subsequent historians, was truly 'the first draft of history'. Herbert Matthews believed that 'a journalist who writes truthfully what he sees and knows on a given day is writing for posterity. The scepticism and criticisms that I met in some quarters during the Spanish conflict made me feel at times that I was working more for the historical record than for the daily reader.'[43]

2

The Capital of the World:
The Correspondents and the Siege of Madrid

On 21 September 1936, General Franco made a surprising decision that would affect the entire subsequent course of the Spanish Civil War. On that day, in their vertiginous advance from Seville to Madrid, his African columns had reached Maqueda in the province of Toledo from where the road north-east to the capital lay open. Madrid was at his mercy, yet Franco did not let his troops race onwards to an easy victory but decided instead to divert them south-east-wards to relieve the besieged Alcázar of Toledo. What seemed a major military blunder was actually a part of the orchestration of Franco's complex scheme to take control of the rebel forces, become Generalísimo and Caudillo. Ignoring warnings that he was throwing away an unrepeatable chance to sweep on to the Spanish capital before its defences were ready, Franco had decided that he would garner infinitely more prestige both among his fellow rebels and internationally if he liberated the besieged garrison. He thus chose to inflate his own political position by means of an emotional victory and a great propagandistic coup at the expense of the early defeat of the Republic. When his troops entered Toledo on 27 September, the accompanying war correspondents were prevented from witnessing the bloody massacre unleashed by the attacking legionaries and Moroccan *Regulares Indígenas*. They took no prisoners. Corpses littered the nar-row streets, down which trickled rivulets of blood. Webb Miller of the United Press told the US Ambassador that he had seen the beheaded corpses of militia-men. Four days later, Franco's fellow generals rewarded him by electing him Caudillo, head of the rebel armed forces and head of the rebel state.[1]

Although newspaper correspondents had been excluded, the gruesome story of what had happened got out soon enough. In any case, for two and a half months, refugees from the south had flooded north carrying horrendous tales of the slaughter unleashed by the African columns as they pillaged town after town. The massacre at Badajoz on 14 August had been intended as a warning to the citizens of Madrid of what would happen to them if they did not surrender. News of this latest horror in Toledo sent a shudder of terror through the city as, after a few days' rest, Franco's forces renewed their push on Madrid. In fact, the delay from 21 September until 6 October had inadvertently provided a breathing space which would eventually see Russian aircraft and tanks and the volunteers of the International Brigades arrive to help save Madrid. At the time, however, the population in the capital awaited the rebel assault with doom-laden trepidation. War correspondents from around the world, burning to be the first to announce the fall of the capital, constantly pestered the Republican authorities for passes to the front. One of the more persistent and intrepid was Hank Gorrell of Washington, DC.

Until 14 September, Gorrell had been working for the United Press in Rome but had fallen foul of the Fascist authorities. As a result of reporting a police round-up of a Communist resistance group, he had been summoned to Mussolini's Ministry of Information and 'invited' to leave Italy.[2] He was reassigned to Madrid, where he arrived one week later. On 3 October, with a Spanish colleague named Emilio Herrera, he had gone in a car provided by the Republican press office to the front just north of Toledo at the town of Olías del Teniente Castillo (previously Olías del Rey). They were stopped by Loyalist officers. Despite Hank carrying an American passport and a pass issued by the Ministry of War authorizing his visit to the front, they were arrested when he was heard speaking Italian. They were sent back to Madrid under motorcyclist escort, taken to a military headquarters located in the old royal palace and questioned. Having answered his interrogators satisfactorily, Gorrell was soon released, although Herrera was kept in custody. As Hank reported to the American Embassy,

> the officers who ordered me detained apologized profusely and told me that since I possessed the proper documents, I could proceed at any time thereafter to Cabanas and Olías. One officer recommended however that I request an additional pass for that particular war zone from the Colonel in command of the loyalist troops at Olías. I accepted the officer's apologies, telling them I was disposed to forget the incident.

On the following day, Hank Gorrell returned to the front at Olías and went to Loyalist headquarters to get the necessary pass. Before he could see the Colonel, he and his driver were detained by armed militiamen. The driver, Rafael Navarro, of Philippine origin, was also an American citizen. Under suspicion of being spies, they were held for four hours. They were then taken, on a bus full of more militia, to police headquarters in Madrid. There they were kept in considerable discomfort in a dirty cellar for several hours until the arrival of the chief of the Republican Foreign Ministry's press office, Luis Rubio Hidalgo, who quickly secured their release. When Gorrell reported on these two detentions, his principal complaint was that he had not been allowed to contact either his office or the American Embassy. Nevertheless, his captors had informed Rubio Hidalgo, who in turn alerted Lester Ziffren, the thirty-year-old head of the United Press bureau in Madrid. Ziffren had been in Madrid for over three years, knew his way around and was able to mobilize the aid of the Under-Secretary for War, General José Asensio Torrado. The consequence was not only the liberation of the prisoners and profuse official apologies but also an invitation to dinner at the Ministry of War.[3]

How different would be Hank Gorrell's experience three weeks later on another trip to the front. On 26 October, Hank set out from Madrid with a car and driver provided by the Republican press office. North of Aranjuez, he had been wandering behind the lines when advancing rebel troops opened fire on them. He was left behind when he ignored his driver's shouted invitation to jump for it and join him in dashing for Madrid. Hank took refuge in a ditch from an Italian whippet tank that was trying to run him down. When it toppled over, stunning the driver, Hank helped him out of the tank. He was rewarded for this when the rescued Italian officer intervened to prevent his execution by the Moors. However, the Moors did steal all his money, his gold watch and cuff links. He was taken to nearby Seseña where he was joined by two other correspondents, the Englishman Dennis Weaver of the *News Chronicle* and the Canadian James M. Minifie of the New York *Herald Tribune*, who had also ventured inadvertently beyond rebel lines and been captured.

The rebel authorities issued a statement to the effect that Gorrell, Weaver and Minifie were 'guests of the rebel command pending their departure for the border'. In fact, their situation was significantly more unpleasant than the press release implied. The driver and escort of Weaver and Minifie had been shot in front of them. They had been transported to Talavera, where the field commander of the African columns, General José Varela, had his headquarters. They were interrogated as spies and repeatedly told that they were about to be shot. Eventually, they were transferred to Salamanca for Franco himself to take the decision about what to do with them. There, they were harshly questioned by the notorious Luis Bolín, Rubio Hidalgo's counterpart in the rebel zone. The blustering Bolín threatened to have them hanged. After a further five unpleasant days in custody, and being obliged to send dispatches saying that they had been treated courteously, all three were expelled from Spain. Gorrell later returned to the Republican zone.[4] Not long after, Lester Ziffren narrowly escaped a similar fate: 'There was no indication where the respective lines lay. I missed being taken prisoner because a lone militiaman returning along a deserted road warned me that I was heading for Rebel territory.'[5]

Gorrell's three arrests showed that, in both zones, troops near the front were understandably jittery and indeed trigger-happy when confronted by prying civilians who might be spies. Nevertheless, the contrasting treatment received – apologies and dinner from the Republic's authorities, death threats and expulsion from the rebels – was representative of the attitudes of both sides towards journalists. To put it simply, the Republican press apparatus tended to facilitate rather than impede the work of correspondents. A section of the Ministerio de Estado (the Ministry of Foreign Affairs) had been set up within a few days of the military coup. The Madrid press office was housed in the thirteen-storey Telefónica building, the headquarters of the American International Telephone and Telegraph Company, situated on the central avenue known as the Gran Vía. It was from there that the journalists delivered their stories to the censors before they were allowed to telephone them to their papers. At night, camp beds were set up for those who were waiting to send out their stories. In a chaotic din of languages, ITT employees who acted as the first censors had to listen in to ensure that what was read out did not diverge from the censored text. If the newspapermen deviated from the approved wording, they were immediately cut off. By early November, as rebel forces approached, ready to occupy the city, the Telefónica, Madrid's tallest building, became a daily target for artillery fire and was regularly hit. Despite the shelling, the censors, the switchboard girls and the correspondents simply carried on.[6]

In the early days of the war, the censorship in Madrid was inefficient and sometimes heavy-handed. None of the early censors understood English and articles had to be submitted with a Spanish translation before approval for transmission was granted. There were no fixed guidelines and each censor exercised his authority as he thought best. One correspondent might see his dispatch passed for transmission while the same story worded differently by a colleague would be censored shortly after. Lester Ziffren described this situation in his diary on 23 August 1936:

> Rebel planes made their first raid on Madrid's environs and bombed the Getafe aerodrome. The government confirmed the news in its 10 p.m. broadcast. The censor would not permit transmission of cables carrying

the text of this broadcast. Apparently decided such news may be all right for the Spanish people but not for the press abroad. In view of this situation, I instructed my Paris office to pick up the official broadcasts because I could not send the texts out of Spain by cable.[7]

The position of the censorship was put on a more rational basis from the first week of September with the appointment as Foreign Minister in Largo Caballero's cabinet of Julio Álvarez del Vayo, himself a one-time journalist. Born in Madrid in 1891, the highly cosmopolitan Álvarez del Vayo had studied with Sydney and Beatrice Webb at the London School of Economics in 1912 and then in the following year at the University of Leipzig, where he became friends with Juan Negrín. He also came into contact with Rosa Luxembourg and Karl Liebknecht. He later wrote a biography of Rosa Luxembourg, *La senda roja* (Madrid: Espasa Calpe, 1934). In 1916, he met Lenin in Switzerland. He visited Russia several times and wrote two books about the Soviet experiment, *La nueva Rusia* (Madrid: Espasa Calpe, 1926), and *Rusia a los doce años* (Madrid: Espasa Calpe, 1929). On 18 September 1936, Álvarez del Vayo appointed his friend Luis Rubio Hidalgo, another experienced newspaperman, as Chief Censor at the Foreign Press and Propaganda Office of the Ministry.[8] Henceforth, it was much easier for correspondents to get their stories transmitted. Having known him for some years as a colleague, Lester Ziffren found Rubio Hidalgo to be helpful and co-operative. However, he was considered by others to be a suave scheming careerist. Rubio Hidalgo was, according to the highly experienced *Daily Express* correspondent, Sefton 'Tom' Delmer, 'an opportunist official who went out of his way to look as Machiavellian as he could with a thin streak of a black moustache on his upper lip, a superior cynical smile when he talked, and dark glasses hiding what were really timid eyes beneath the traditional mask of the international conspirator'.[9]

Ziffren felt that Rubio tried to make the censorship less irksome, and confined censorship to prohibiting references to troop movements, military plans or atrocities. Previously, the censorship had applied the same criteria to news for domestic use and the stories submitted by foreign correspondents: 'Defeats were never admitted in the Loyalist press which was engaged principally in publishing material intended to strengthen the public morale.' The hardened American journalist Louis Fischer was shocked by the fact that the Republican press did not tell all the truth:

The first question put to me when I arrived in Barcelona was, 'Have we lost Irún?' It has been lost weeks ago. The government has never announced it. Nor does the public know officially about the surrender of San Sebastián. The daily War Office reports are replete with victories; no repulse is recorded. It would be difficult to understand after collating all these broadcasts why the enemy is approaching Madrid. The Loyalists should, instead be approaching Madrid.[10]

Fischer put pressure on his friend Álvarez del Vayo to recognize that reporting of the truth would benefit the Republic. Rubio was authorized by Álvarez del Vayo to permit news of government defeats after he too had argued that it made more sense to admit a fact immediately rather than try to deny facts which would anyway be broadcast by the rebels. Consequently more accurate news had been published abroad about the true situation than was printed in Spain. Ziffren wrote warmly that Rubio Hidalgo's efforts to improve on the previously inefficient and clumsy censorship rendered it 'more tractable and workable'.[11] It is more than likely, however, that the changes noted by Ziffren were actually the work of others. It is certainly not difficult to find criticisms of Rubio Hidalgo from those who wanted to see the working conditions of correspondents made even easier, on the grounds that they would then be more likely to write in a manner that favoured the Republic.

As the rebel columns moving from the south came ever nearer to Madrid, the problems of the censorship machinery were merely part of the difficulties faced by the Republican government. As retreating militia units streamed back towards the capital, it would have been impossible to keep a blanket on news of what seemed like an impending defeat. Correspondents would drive south towards Toledo and in the small towns and villages to the south of the capital see, and indeed talk with, the demoralized Republican militiamen. The horror stories of the advancing columns of fierce foreign legionaries and Moorish mercenaries and the German and Italian aircraft which covered them could hardly be kept out of the press. Nevertheless, Rubio did his best. Louis Fischer was appalled when at dinner on 10 October, Madrid's longest-serving correspondent, Henry Buckley who reported for the *Daily Telegraph* and the *Observer*, told him that Rubio had commented blithely 'Wait six days. The tide will turn.' Fischer noted: 'The same story – they expect outside aid. They should also help themselves by organizing, introducing some discipline and generating a little energy.'[12] Rubio's optimism rang all the more false in the light of cases of correspondents being captured, imprisoned and mistreated by the rebels, as had happened with Dennis Weaver and Hank Gorrell. Indeed, behind the mask of optimism, the Republican government was so sure that Madrid would fall that arrangements would be made for its evacuation to Valencia. This would not happen until 6 November, when the city was to find itself entrusted to a rapidly improvised Defence Junta, a move that, for a time at least, would leave the machinery of press censorship in chaos.

In the weeks before the rebel forces had reached the outskirts of Madrid, some journalists stayed at the Hotel Florida, lower down the Gran Vía from the Telefónica. On the corner of the Plaza de Callao, the Florida was much nearer the front and would become a visible target. Before the siege, there had been some wild nights at the Florida. Frequented by prostitutes, the hotel housed young aviators, journalists and a bizarre mixture of arms dealers and spies. The pilots sported large knives and even larger revolvers. Once the prostitutes began to sidle in at siesta time after lunch, the noise and scandal would intensify until, in the early hours of the morning, there would be drunken rows and people running shouting into the corridors. The frenzied merry-making did not survive the worst of the siege. Once the rebel columns arrived and the hotel became a prominent artillery target, correspondents began to drift away from the Florida and then avoided it altogether.[13] During the worst days of the assault by Franco's forces throughout November 1936, many of the British and American newspapermen slept at their respective embassies. Some journalists lived in the Hotel Gran Vía, which was on the other side of the street opposite the Telefónica. Later, when the heat of the siege had cooled and the rebel attack blunted, correspondents started to use the Florida again and the revels recommenced.

In the Republican zone in general, but particularly in the besieged capital, the greatest hazards were bombing raids and material shortages. In the words of Lester Ziffren, 'For the first time in newspaper history, journalists felt the insecurity and chills which come to residents of a besieged city, ruthlessly torn to pieces day and night by relentless cannonading and bombing.'[14] Since coal from the Asturias mines could not reach Madrid, there was almost no heat or hot water in the hotels. The Madrileños took to eating dinner at 7.30 or 8 p.m., 'since bed was about the only warm place in any home, most residents were there by 9'. The young English journalist Kate Mangan wrote: 'The cold got into my bones. Nowhere was there any heating and, though I gave up washing and went to bed in most of my clothes, I was never warm and ached and shivered at night so that I could not sleep.' When her friend, the American reporter Kitty Bowler, visited Madrid in December 1936, it was so cold that her fingers stuck to the keys on her typewriter.[15]

Few restaurants were open for business and those that were had little to offer. Most foreign journalists ate in the grill in the basement of the Hotel Gran Vía. Run by the government, the restaurant was one of the few open in Madrid and its clientele was mainly policemen, soldiers, officials, journalists and prostitutes. Lester Ziffren recalled: 'We ate in our overcoats because there was no heat, and the meals consisted almost daily of beans, lentils, cauliflower, pickled sardines of unknown age, potatoes, cakes and fruit.'[16] As early as 28 September 1936, Louis Fischer, who had arrived to report for *The Nation* of New York, noted in his diary: 'I tried to eat in the Hotel Gran Vía this evening. They had practically nothing I wanted. Finally, the waiter said sourly: "Look at this menu. No meat, no chicken, no fish, no butter." That was true but much depends on the resourcefulness of the manager.'[17] Increasingly, correspondents were expected to forage for their own supplies. When he arrived in Madrid in November, having been expelled from the Nationalist zone in September, the *Daily Express* correspondent, Sefton Delmer, brought in food from France. 'Huge, burly, cosmopolitan, of Irish-Australian blood and born in Berlin', Delmer was a man of enormous self-confidence and ingenuity. In the midst of the siege, he took up residence, along with many others, in the British Embassy.[18]

Barely a week before the government and many journalists left Madrid, the new young correspondent of the *News Chronicle*, the Oxford-educated New Zealander Geoffrey Cox, arrived in Madrid. He was chosen because his paper did not want to risk losing a more celebrated reporter when the city fell. After discussing this immensely dangerous assignment with his wife, he decided that he had to go. The next day, 28 October, he flew to Paris, where he got the necessary authorization from the Spanish Embassy. While in the French capital, Cox also met one of the best-informed of all the correspondents who covered the Spanish war, Jay Allen of the *Chicago Daily Tribune*. Allen surprised him by predicting that Madrid would hold out. From Paris, Cox took the overnight train to Toulouse, where he took the next morning's Air France flight over the Pyrenees to Barcelona airport. There militiamen taught him the essential skill of drinking wine from the spout of a glass *porrón*. The next stage of the journey took him to Alicante. The long wait at the airfield there preyed on his nerves and he began to think to himself: 'It's quite extraordinary, what the hell am I doing here...a New Zealander in the worst bloody place? I'm sorry to say, had someone come along and said "Look, this isn't worth the bloody trouble. C'mon, you'd better board the helicopter and come back with me", I'd have been sorely tempted to do it, but as it was there was no escape thank God.' The sense of dread was livened only by the adrenalin flow on a flight to Madrid barely a few hundred feet above the hills. The only defence against possible attack by German or Italian aircraft came from a militiaman stationed by the open door with a light machine-gun.[19]

Despite the hair-rising circumstances of the flight, Cox arrived safely in Madrid on the evening of 29 October. He headed for the Hotel Gran Vía. At this stage of the battle for the capital, few correspondents went to the Hotel Florida. As Cox was checking in, a small, kindly, sandy-haired Englishman shook his hand and introduced himself as Jan Yindrich, one of the Madrid correspondents of the United Press. Yindrich took him over to the censorship office in the Telefónica and showed him the ropes. Cox quickly got to know that area to the south of Madrid into which Franco's troops were advancing. He was surprised by the freedom granted to correspondents: 'We were free to go where we would – or we dared.' Contrary to what happened in the rebel zone, there was no supervision by army officers obliging newspapermen to go only to approved areas. Once a correspondent was issued with a pass to visit the front and provided with a car and driver by the Ministry of War, he could go wherever he liked. What he wrote and tried to transmit was, however, subject to censorship. The consequence of such freedom of movement was that, like Gorrell and Weaver, correspondents ran the risk of mistakenly entering the other zone. This happened once to Cox when travelling with the Swedish correspondent, Barbro Alving, a stocky young blonde, who signed her articles 'Bang'. At a village south of the capital, they narrowly escaped capture by a convoy of Moorish troops.[20]

Cox always felt that his mentor in Madrid had been William Forrest, at the time working for the *Daily Express*, 'a small open-faced Glaswegian, with a quiet, wry manner'. Cox admired Forrest's ability to give colour to a story by the deft inclusion of a picturesque detail. He gave, as an example, the despatch that Willie began with the words: 'I took a two-penny tramride to the front this afternoon.' 'Tom' Delmer also admired Forrest, describing him as a 'shrewd little Scotsman, who had won everyone's respect for the cool-headedness with which, come air-raids, come bombs, come murders, come Franco's Moors, he could be counted on to get on the telephone every evening to dictate a graphic report on the ordeal of Madrid and its one and a half million citizens'. Forrest had previously been a sub-editor but had managed to persuade the editor of his newspaper that, as a member of the Communist Party, he would get access to places where other reporters would be excluded. This was the case, yet his reporting was notable for its objectivity. In any case, he would leave the Communist Party in 1939 in protest against the Soviet invasions of Poland and Finland.[21]

Despite the presence of some of the world's best newspapermen in Spain, many of whom later wrote memoirs, the most graphic record of the experience of correspondents during the siege of Madrid would come from the pen of a Spaniard, the Socialist Arturo Barea. In early September 1936, a few days after Largo

Caballero had formed his government, Barea had been offered a job at the press office through a Communist named Velilla who worked at the ministry. Barea was a quietly modest man, deeply thoughtful and entirely committed to the cause of the Spanish Republic. At the press office, he had to work with Rubio Hidalgo, whom he quickly came to see as a self-regarding opportunist. Barea worked at night in the Telefónica censoring press dispatches. Censorship may have been relaxed somewhat under Rubio, but Barea still found it to be too strict and aimed largely at the elimination of the slightest suggestion of anything other than a Republican victory. Although Franco's columns were coming inexorably nearer, newspaper reports were allowed only to talk of them being halted. Barea rightly regarded it as 'clumsy and futile'.[22] Indeed, the censorship was relatively easily circumvented by British, American and French journalists making creative use of slang. H. Edward Knoblaugh later boasted that 'By telling London that "the big shots were getting ready to take a run-out powder", I was able to scoop the other correspondents on the fact that the government was preparing to flee to Valencia.' One supercilious French journalist of the *Petit Parisien* tried so many tricks that, utterly exasperated, the normally mild-mannered Barea threatened to have him arrested.[23] Later on in the war, Herbert Matthews would evade the censorship by the even simpler device of having the Paris bureau of the *New York Times* telephone him at a time when the Spanish censor was having dinner. When Franco's forces split Republican Spain in two in mid-April 1938, the government tried to delay the news getting out. The censorship cut out sections of Vincent Sheean's report so, when he read it over the telephone to the Paris office of the *New York Herald Tribune*, he said 'censored' each time he reached a part that had been pencilled out. The story that appeared 'bristled with that ominous word in italics, and consequently looked fully as disastrous for the Republic as the events had actually been'.[24]

As the Francoist columns neared Madrid, its streets strewn with rubble and thronged with starving refugees, work in the Telefónica became more nightmarish. Bombing raids and artillery pounding were constant. When Barea appeared for work on the evening of 6 November, the crackle of rifle fire could be heard nearby. When he went to Rubio Hidalgo's office, papers were burning in the fireplace. With an urbanity bordering on satisfaction, Rubio told him that the government was leaving for Valencia. Declaring that the fall of the capital was inevitable, a white-faced Rubio gave Barea two months' wages and ordered him to close down the censorship apparatus, burn the remaining papers and save his own skin. Barea ignored Rubio's instructions and saved some important photographs of children killed in rebel bombing raids. He then worked as normal that night, preventing an American journalist from cabling that Madrid had already fallen.[25]

Certainly, virtually all of the foreign correspondents were entirely convinced that Madrid was about to fall. At a dinner at the beginning of November, nineteen of them had set up a sweepstake on the date that the rebels would enter the city. Eighteen of them chose dates within the following five weeks and only Jan Yindrich, just to be different, placed his bet on 'never'.[26] Rubio Hidalgo was only too happy to leave, offering William Forrest a seat in his escape car and telling him: 'if you come with me you will be the only British correspondent to get out of Madrid with the story. Have no fear of missing anything. The others will be caught here by the Fascists and will have no means of transportation or communications. But in any case, there will be no telephone calls to London and Paris after the government leaves tonight.' In fact, Forrest needed to get to Valencia because he wanted to return to England to campaign on behalf of the Republic. He was planning to resign from the *Daily Express*, so he accepted Rubio's offer. He was soon replaced in Madrid by Sefton Delmer. On arrival in Valencia, according to Delmer, 'Rubio, who had a talent for such things, quickly found himself a delightful old eighteenth-century *palacio*. And there, amid tapestries and brocades, he set himself up in a new and imposing Press and Public Relations Office.'[27] In fact, the tapestries were faded and the palace dilapidated. When, much later, in early December, Barea was summoned to Valencia, he found the palace to be as shabby as it was sumptuous, a veritable warren of small rooms overflowing with typewriters, rubber stamps and stacks of paper.[28]

Rubio also offered Geoffrey Cox a place in one of the cars leaving for Valencia, after ostentatiously showing him the flat automatic pistol that he carried in his elegant suit. Standing on the pavement outside the Hotel Gran Vía, the young New Zealander pondered his dilemma: 'I could validly argue that my work could now be better done from Valencia, that even if I witnessed the fall of the city Franco's censors would never allow me to send out the story, that I might find myself for several weeks in a Franco gaol. But I opted to stay. I did so less from a journalistic desire to cover the big story than from the feeling that history was about to be made, and I had the chance to witness it.' It was to be a momentous decision, since he found himself one of only three British journalists in the capital to cover Franco's attack. Out of his experiences would come some of the most important journalism on the siege of Madrid and one of the most enduring books on the Spanish Civil War. Later that afternoon, with the immensely knowledgeable Henry Buckley, an old hand who had been in Madrid since 1930, Cox walked down the Toledo road towards the rebel advance. They were surprised by the ferocity of the resistance that they witnessed and returned to the centre to sleep in the British Embassy, beginning to think the impossible, that maybe Madrid could hold out.[29]

On 7 November, with no censorship in Madrid, some correspondents, trying to get a scoop, had transmitted 'news' of the fall of the capital. In the case of those who were accompanying the rebel troops, the articles were especially imaginative. The most inventive was that of Hubert Renfro Knickerbocker, the chief foreign correspondent of the Hearst newspaper chain. 'Red' Knickerbocker, as he was known because of his flaming hair, was famous all over Europe. It was said that when he entered the lobby of a great hotel in Vienna, the manager greeted him with the words 'Mr Knickerbocker, welcome. Are things really so bad?' Now, he presented the apocryphal news of the 'fall of Madrid' with some verisimilitude, describing the triumphal march of the rebels into the city, roared on by cheering crowds and followed by a joyfully yapping little dog.[30] Somewhat more restrained was the equally famous English veteran, Harold Cardozo, who was accompanying the Francoist columns for the *Daily Mail*. His assistant, Frances Davis, recalled the great man writing a report on the fall of Madrid with blanks for the details to be filled in at a later date.[31] Cardozo himself later confessed:

> There flashed through the world the news that the Gran Vía and the great Telephone skyscraper were in the hands of Varela's troops who controlled the whole southern sector as far as the War Ministry. I must confess that I was confident of rapid victory and thought that the Nationalist advance had gone much farther than it really had. Later, when the disillusionment had somewhat faded, my colleague Paul Bewsher drew for our amusement a map of Madrid showing the points to which various over-sanguine correspondents had made the Nationalist troops advance. We were all to blame, though the lack of really reliable information and the feverish anxiety of the hour were valid excuses.[32]

Certainly, the news desks in Britain and America were taking it for granted that Madrid would fall. On the evening of 7 November, Henry Buckley telephoned a London Sunday newspaper and reported that the centre of Madrid was quiet and that Franco's troops were attacking the suburbs on the far side of the river Manzanares. The news editor at the other end of the line refused to believe him, because he had received so many other reports that the rebels were now inside Madrid. Buckley then received a call from a colleague in Paris who warned him that the Francoists were likely to shoot any journalists found in Madrid. A goodly number of correspondents had already left but, inspired by the sight of ordinary citizens going out to fight, Buckley and Cox had decided to stay on. As a result, Cox was able to secure the scoop of announcing to the world the arrival in Madrid of what he called 'the International Column of Anti-Fascists'.[33]

In the press office, Barea was outraged by 'reports breathing a malicious glee at the idea that Franco was, as they put it, inside the town'. He was appalled that the world was missing what he called 'the blaze of determination and fight' of the people of Madrid. His outrage was directed at Rubio Hidalgo: 'I had never been as completely convinced of the need for a war censorship as when I read those petty and deeply untrue reports and realized that the damage abroad had been done. It was a defeat inflicted by the man who had deserted.' Realizing that there had to be some censorship machinery, Barea ignored Rubio's orders and, believing that some control over the foreign press was required as long as Madrid held out, simply kept the service going.[34]

On the morning of 11 November, Barea was visited by the *Pravda* correspondent, Mikhail Koltsov, who was initially incandescent with rage that, after the flight of Rubio Hidalgo and before Barea had managed to set up alternative arrangements, some damaging despatches had got out. Koltov's intervention belied his status as merely the *Pravda* correspondent and reflected both his own energetic initiative and his semi-official position within the office of war commissars (the Comisariado General de Guerra). Once Koltsov had calmed down and heard Barea's story, he spirited him to the Ministry of War, where he secured permission from the newly appointed Junta de Defensa for the press office to carry on in Madrid under the auspices of the General War Commissariat. Barea himself was pleased to find himself under the authority of the Comisario General de Guerra, Julio Álvarez del Vayo, who in fact was already his boss in his capacity as Foreign Minister. Barea admired Álvarez del Vayo because he had been the first of the ministers to return to Madrid and get involved in the defence of the besieged city. Barea hoped vainly that, in the capital's besieged situation, the foreign press censorship would remain free of interference from the Foreign Ministry's bureaucracy, which remained in the Valencia rearguard. This hope was fostered by the written order that he received from the War Commissariat on 12 November:

> Having regard to the transfer to Valencia of the Ministry of Foreign
> Affairs and to the indispensable need for the Press Department of the
> aforesaid Ministry to continue functioning in Madrid, the General War
> Commissariat has decided that the aforementioned office of the Press

Department shall henceforward be dependent on the General War Commissariat, and furthermore that Arturo Barea Ogazón shall be in charge of the same, with the obligation to render a daily report of its activities to the General War Commissariat.[35]

Barea's optimism was short-lived. On the same evening, Rubio Hidalgo telephoned from Valencia to announce that he would return to Madrid to resolve the clash of authority. Barea informed the War Commissariat and was assured of their support. When Rubio Hidalgo arrived from Valencia, Barea received his old boss in his own office at his own desk. When he told him of the orders from the War Commissariat, Rubio went white, blinked but agreed to go to the ministry. There, he weathered the storm of 'crude, outspoken reprimands'. He then played his cards:

he was the Press Chief of the Foreign Ministry: the War Commissariat must be opposed to any wild and disorganized action, since it recognized the authority of the Government in which the Chief of the War Commissariat was a Minister. Rubio's legal position was unassailable. It was agreed that the Foreign Press and Censorship Office at Madrid would continue to depend on him in his capacity as Press Chief. It would be under the Madrid War Commissariat for current instructions, and through the Commissariat under the Junta de Defensa. The Foreign Ministry's Press Department would continue to cover the expenses of the Madrid office, the censored dispatches would continue to be sent to Rubio. He was suave and conciliatory. Back at the Foreign Ministry, he discussed the details of the service with me; the general rules for the censorship continued to be the same, while military security instructions would reach me from the Madrid authorities.

Despite this apparent agreement, Rubio Hidalgo would never forgive Barea's initiative, perceiving that his readiness to carry on under fire implied that he, like others who had gone to Valencia, was a deserter. As Barea put it: 'I knew that he hated me far more deeply than I hated him.'[36]

When Barea took over the censorship in a beleaguered Madrid, activities were briefly transferred to the historic ministry building in the Plaza de Santa Cruz near the Plaza Mayor. This meant that the correspondents had to make a hazardous journey through blacked-out streets from the Gran Vía where they lived or had their offices to the ministry for their copy to be censored and then back to the Telefónica building to telephone it out. The operation was transferred back to the Telefónica. Each night the censors, the telephonists and the journalists worked in appalling conditions, in candle-light, waiting for the whine of artillery shells or the drone of Franco's German and Italian bombers, until finally the shelling obliged a definitive move back to the ministry.[37]

Arturo Barea's deep commitment to the Republican cause would eventually see his health undermined by overwork, worry and the precariousness of his position with regard to Rubio Hidalgo. He had to juggle the competing instructions of the War Commissariat in Madrid and Rubio Hidalgo in Valencia. Catching a few hours of sleep on a camp bed in his office, Barea kept himself going on coffee, brandy and cigarettes. The toll that the work took on him can be discerned in the description left by Delmer of Barea as 'a cadaverous Spaniard with deep furrows of bitterness around his mouth, dug deeper by the shadows from his candle. He looked the very embodiment of Spanishness, tense and suspicious, clenched ready to take national umbrage.' Barea's job became easier only when he was joined, on a volunteer basis, by Ilsa Kulcsar, a thirty-four-year-old Austrian Socialist. She was short, plump and altogether unprepossessing: 'a round face with big eyes, blunt nose, wide forehead, a mass of dark hair that looked almost black, too-broad shoulders encased in a green or gray coat, or it may have been some other colour which the purple light made indefinite and ugly. She was over thirty and no beauty.'[38] Despite this unpromising start, as they talked night after night, he would soon fall in love with her. Theirs was to be one of several, and indeed one of the most enduring, love affairs that flowered in the midst of the war.

Born in Vienna in 1902, on the same day as, but five years after, Arturo Barea, Ilsa Kulcsar had studied economics and sociology. She joined the Communist Party before passing over to the Austrian Socialist Party in the mid-1920s. She had been involved in the Austrian resistance after the failed Vienna uprising of February 1934 and subsequently had fled with her husband to Czechoslovakia. She had come to Spain with credentials from some Czech and Norwegian left-wing papers, without a salary. Rubio Hidalgo, who appreciated her linguistic skills, had decreed that the press office would pay her services and she threw herself into its work with considerable enthusiasm. She not only helped out with her command of French, German, Magyar, English and other languages, but also persuaded Barea that the censorship should be more flexible. Her argument was that the conventional triumphalism imposed by the military mentality made the Republic's defeats and economic hardship inexplicable and its victories trivial. She easily convinced him that the truth about the government's difficulties could produce reporting that would eventually be to the benefit of the Republican cause.[39]

On their own initiative, Arturo and Ilsa relaxed the censorship and thereby established good relations with the correspondents. They helped them to get hotel rooms and petrol vouchers and often asked for their help in return. Risking the wrath of both Koltsov and Rubio Hidalgo, they allowed the correspondents to report the police raid on the abandoned German Embassy, which produced evidence of German collusion with the Francoist fifth column. They arranged interviews with members of the International Brigades, out of which came articles published by Louis Delaprée of *Paris-Soir*, Barbro Alving (Bang) of the *Dagens Nyheter* of Stockholm, Herbert Matthews of the *New York Times* and Louis Fischer for *The Nation*. All four wrote excellent and enthusiastic articles, but perhaps the most substantial was that by Louis Fischer. Having briefly served as quartermaster at International Brigade headquarters in Albacete, Fischer was a particularly privileged observer.[40]

Unfortunately for Delaprée, his newspaper increasingly considered his enthusiastic articles to be too pro-Republican, indeed 'communist', although he personally was not a Communist and was actually a lukewarm Catholic. Indeed, having been sent to Spain to cover the rebel zone, he had arrived in Burgos in the same aircraft as Sefton Delmer and Hubert Knickerbocker but had shortly after been expelled for visiting the front without an escort. Ironically, almost everyone that Delaprée met in Madrid considered that his newspaper was pro-fascist. Certainly as *Paris-Soir* showed ever more hunger for news about Edward VIII and the abdication crisis in England, his articles about Spain were rejected. Consequently, Delaprée decided to leave Spain. Geoffrey Cox described him, on the evening of 7 December 1936 in the Miami bar in Madrid, in a raincoat, red scarf and grey felt hat patiently explaining to a suspicious Madrileño that he was not a fascist and that he had actually been expelled from Burgos by the Francoists. Later that same night, Delaprée had sat on Arturo Barea's camp bed and told him that, when he got to Paris, he planned to protest about the pro-Franco activities of the French consulate. Unfortunately, on 8 December, the Air France plane on which he was flying to Toulouse was attacked by unknown aircraft near Guadalajara. Delaprée was hit in the hip and the back when the aircraft was machine-gunned from below. Delmer later claimed that Delaprée told him on his deathbed that the plane had been mistakenly fired on by Republican fighters. Although Delaprée was perplexed by this, Delmer was convinced that the attack had been ordered by the security services to prevent a pro-Franco diplomat taking a report on atrocities to Geneva, but he seems to have been alone in this view.

Although the pilot managed to crash-land in a remote field, it was three hours before help arrived. The nearest hospital lacked the equipment to deal with his wounds and it took another day before an ambulance from Madrid could get him to a better-equipped hospital. He died two days later after receiving the last sacraments and extreme unction. *Paris-Soir* reported his death with large headlines and numerous moving tributes. The French Government awarded him a posthumous Légion d'Honneur. He was buried in Paris with great ceremony. However, some days later the French Communist daily, *L'Humanité*, published the last message from Delaprée to his paper, which he had sent the day before he left Madrid. Because a carbon copy had remained in Barea's office in Madrid, it was possible for its contents to be made public. The duplicate, complete with the stamp of the Republican censorship, read:

> You have not published half my articles. That is your right. But I would
> have thought your friendship would have spared me useless work. For
> three weeks I have been getting up at 5 a.m. in order to give you the news
> for your first editions. You have made me work for the wastepaper basket.
> Thanks. I am taking a plane on Sunday unless I meet the fate of Guy de
> Traversay [a reporter for *L'Intransigeant*, a rival of *Paris-Soir*, who was
> killed by the rebels in Mallorca], which would be a good thing, wouldn't
> it, for thus you should have your martyr also. In the meantime, I am
> sending nothing more. It is not worth the trouble. The massacre of a
> hundred Spanish children is less interesting than a sigh from Mrs
> Simpson.

Geoffrey Cox wrote of Delaprée:

> It is easy to write good things of the dead, but Delaprée was a man of
> whom one would have written them willingly when he was alive.
> Without any exaggeration, he was one of the finest people I have met –
> intelligent, human, cheerful, courageous, good-looking. He was that
> rare type who is liked by both men and women. He was a journalist of
> the first rank, writing beautiful French prose. His descriptions of the air
> raids on Madrid might serve as classics of their type. Many fine men
> have gone to their deaths in the Spanish war. It is not the least of the
> tragedies of this struggle that Louis Delaprée should have been
> amongst them.[41]

Cox was right. Louis Delaprée's descriptions of the bombing of the capital count among the most moving writing produced during the war. Moreover, what he saw led him, like so many other correspondents, to a deep indignation with the blindness of the policy-makers of the democracies:

> I am only an accountant of the horror, a passive witness. However, let me make a comment, the strongest feeling that I have experienced today is not fear, or anger or even pity: IT IS SHAME. I feel ashamed of being a man when mankind shows itself capable of such massacres of the innocent. Oh old Europe, always busy with your petty games and great intrigues. God grant that all this blood should not choke you.[42]

The efforts of Arturo and Ilsa were a great success but did nothing to diminish the hostility of Rubio Hidalgo, who made sporadic efforts to remove them. First, Barea was summoned to Valencia in December 1936, where he realized how much resentment there was among those who had left the capital for those who had stayed. He learned that Rubio Hidalgo had expressed a desire to exile Barea to rot in the postal censorship in Valencia because he could not forgive his usurpation of his desk at the ministry. Ilsa also came to Valencia, where she was briefly arrested because her friendship with the Austrian Socialist leader Otto Bauer had led to her being denounced as a Trotskyist. When she was released, they finally admitted that their future lay together. Moreover, after an interview with Julio Álvarez del Vayo himself, Ilsa secured a reprieve for both of them. Rubio agreed to send them back to Madrid, with Arturo as head of the Foreign Press Censorship and Ilsa as his deputy.[43]

Barea's work in the censorship brought him into frequent contact with General Vladimir Gorev, the senior figure in Madrid of Russian military intelligence. As both military attaché and thus the principal Russian adviser to General José Miaja, the head of the Junta de Madrid, Gorev took a burning interest in the articles of the foreign correspondents. Every morning he would pore over the previous night's censored dispatches, sometimes disagreeing with Arturo Barea and Ilsa Kulcsar, sometimes explaining why certain military issues required censorship. He was fascinated by the way in which many correspondents had evolved from open animosity to the Republic to more objective reporting. He was inclined to attribute this to the greater freedom given to reporters by Arturo and Ilsa. His favourite articles were those by Herbert Matthews and Sefton Delmer. Ilsa believed that his liberal attitude may well have caused him problems with others in the Soviet delegation.[44]

Despite good relations both with Gorev and the majority of the foreign correspondents, the tensions between Valencia and Madrid continued. Finally, the combination of divorcing his wife in order to be with Ilsa and the strain of his work and the running struggle with Rubio took their toll. Barea was going through some kind of nervous breakdown and Ilsa was still dogged by accusations that she was a Trotskyist.

In April 1937, Arturo and Ilsa were visited in Madrid by the great American novelist, John Dos Passos, who helped them with their work one evening and later remembered 'a cadaverous Spaniard and a plump little pleasant-voiced Austrian woman'. Barea liked Dos Passos for the gentle and affectionate way he spoke about the plight of Spanish peasants. Dos Passos wrote sympathetically of the two censors:

> Only yesterday the Austrian woman came back to find that a shell fragment had set her room on fire and burned up all her shoes, and the censor had seen a woman made mincemeat of beside him when he stepped out to get a bite of lunch. It's not surprising that the censor is a nervous man; he looks underslept and underfed.[45]

Eventually, Barea was advised by Rubio's increasingly important assistant, and eventual successor, Constancia de la Mora, to take a holiday. He realized that part of the problem was that: 'she must have found it irksome that we in Madrid invariably acted as if we were independent of their – of her – authority. Tall, buxom, with full, dark eyes, the imperious bearing of a matriarch, a schoolgirl's simplicity of thought and the self-confidence of a grand-daughter of Antonio Maura, she grated on me, as I must have grated on her.' It was clear that he and Ilsa would not be permitted to return to their jobs in Madrid. Indeed, Constancia de la Mora had already selected Arturo's successor. He was replaced as Head of the Foreign Press and Censorship Department by Rosario del Olmo. Jay Allen remembered her as 'a darling, dedicated girl'. Described by Barea as a 'pale, inhibited girl', she had been secretary to the League of Anti-Fascist Intellectuals and had been recommended by María Teresa de León, the wife of Rafael Alberti and a friend of Constancia. In fact, Rosario would be a worthy successor to Barea, working in Madrid with bravery and dedication until the very last days of the siege in 1939. Barea himself was shunted into radio censorship and occasional broadcasting until eventually, his health broken, he and Ilsa would leave for England in 1938.[46]

In the meanwhile, the efficacy of the efforts of Arturo and Ilsa to facilitate the work of newspapermen was illustrated by the envious remarks of Sir Percival

Phillips, *Daily Telegraph* correspondent in the Nationalist zone. Irked by the aggressive rigidities of the Francoist censorship, Phillips reported what he had been told by colleagues who had experienced the Republican operation, where the press officer was usually a journalist himself and happy to welcome colleagues from London or New York: 'No need to wait three hours for an audience and then be told that you must come again tomorrow: you just blow in through the open door of the office, and help yourself to a drink or a cigar if the censor is busy. Sometimes he even asks you to lend him a hand or to give him some advice.' Phillips believed 'the humility and the camaraderie of those Red censors is so flattering and so touching that some Englishmen have actually dropped well-paid newspaper work in order to help them out'.[47] It is certainly the case that many journalists were moved by the camaraderie of the besieged population to work in favour of the Loyalist cause. Some reflected their sympathies in their writings, others by going back to lobby for the Republican cause in their own countries, and a small number of men by abandoning journalistic work altogether to join the International Brigades and take part in the fighting.

Louis Fischer, one of the most influential correspondents during the war, was a good example in that he did all three. His immensely well-informed and perspicacious articles for *The Nation* in New York and the *New Statesman and Nation* in London can still be read with profit by historians of the Spanish Civil War. He also served briefly in the International Brigades. Yet his importance was less because of what he published than because of what he did behind the scenes. Having been a correspondent in the Soviet Union for over a decade and a half, speaking fluent Russian, he had a remarkable range of high-level contacts in Moscow, especially in the Commissariat for Foreign Affairs. At the same time, he was considered in the United States to be one of the country's principal experts on Russia and its regime. Largely for that reason, he had access to the highest levels of government in Washington. He also enjoyed a number of important connections within the Spanish Government. In Moscow in the 1920s and later on a visit to Spain in 1934, Fischer had become friendly with the journalist Julio Álvarez del Vayo. On his 1934 trip, Fischer had also established friendships with the US Ambassador, Claude G. Bowers, himself a one-time newspaperman, and with other American correspondents, including Lester Ziffren and Jay Allen, through whom he met the then politically unknown Dr Juan Negrín.[48] Accordingly, he had a high degree of influence in all three countries.

When Fischer reached Spain in mid-September 1936, he had quickly renewed contact with Álvarez del Vayo, who barely two weeks earlier had been appointed Foreign Minister and two months later would be Comisario General de Guerra.

Álvarez del Vayo was trying, among a huge array of urgent tasks, to place the Republic's press and propaganda services on an efficient basis. In search of more professional assistance, he turned to Fischer, to Willi Münzenberg, the Comintern propaganda chief who specialized in anti-fascist activities, and to his deputy Otto Katz, the seductively mysterious Czech agent of the Comintern, widely regarded by friends and critics alike as a 'propagandist of genius'. Álvarez del Vayo had first met Münzenberg in Berlin in the early 1930s when he had been the Central European and Russian correspondent of *La Nación* of Buenos Aires. In late 1934, he had invited Willi Münzenberg and his wife Babette Gross to visit Spain and they had toured the south together.[49]

The multilingual Katz was remembered by Arthur Koestler as 'a smooth and slick operator[…]dark and handsome, with a somewhat seedy charm[…]He had the generosity of the adventurer, and he could be warm-hearted, spontaneous and helpful – as long as it did not conflict with his interests.' Claud Cockburn described him as 'a middle-sized man with a large, slightly cadaverous head in which the skull bones were unusually prominent. He had large melancholy eyes, a smile of singular sweetness and an air of mystery – a mystery into which he was prepared to induct you, you alone, because he loved and esteemed you so highly.' Otto claimed that he had once been married to Marlene Dietrich. Using the pseudonym 'André Simone', Katz became the unofficial organizer of the Spanish Republic's propaganda operation in Western Europe with financial support from both the Spanish Government and the Comintern. Katz was to be the guiding intelligence behind the Republic's Paris press agency, the Agence Espagne, which was finally set up at the beginning of 1937.[50]

Among those persuaded by Katz to campaign on behalf of the Republic was the Bavarian Catholic Prince Hubertus Friedrich of Loewenstein, a descendant of Queen Victoria. The Prince wrote a book on behalf of the Republic and accompanied Katz on a visit to Catholic bishops in the United States. Afterwards, the Prince said that he was 'still suffering from vertigo after seeing Otto Katz genuflect three times and kiss the ring of a reputedly progressive cardinal'.[51] In the main, Katz/Simone always remained in the shadows. Despite the importance of his role, there are few traces of his presence in the memoir literature of the time. Arturo Barea reported him holding a party for International Brigaders at the Hotel Gran Vía in early 1937. It may well have been on the same trip that Gustav Regler met him at the Hotel Florida in mid-April 1937.[52] In October 1937, Fischer stayed with the Republican Prime Minister Juan Negrín at his residence in Valencia and commented that Katz, 'who devoted his abilities to Loyalist propaganda abroad', was also there. Willi Münzenberg's widow, Babette Gross, said that he travelled between Paris, Barcelona and Valencia on behalf of the Agence Espagne throughout 1938.[53] Despite the scarcity of references to his role, there can be little doubt about the crucial, if shadowy, presence of Otto Katz within the efforts to present the Republican case to a world in which the bulk of the press was inclined to be hostile to a regime which was perceived as 'red', Communist and dangerous.

It was an irony that, for obvious economic reasons, a high proportion of newspapers were right-wing and thus supported the Spanish military rebels, yet a similarly high proportion of correspondents supported the Republic. Louis Fischer was far from alone in combining commitment to the Spanish Republic with honest journalism. Among the other correspondents who became converted to the Republican cause yet still produced accurate reporting, Martha Gellhorn, Jay Allen, Herbert Matthews and Geoffrey Cox are still quoted today for the vividness of their chronicles. Others who have since been forgotten, yet were greatly respected by their colleagues, include William Forrest and Lawrence Fernsworth. Forrest was a Communist Party member, yet anything but doctrinaire. Arthur Koestler was impressed by his dry humour, his generosity and the fact that 'he never used words like "dialectical", "concrete", or "mechanistic", whereas he used expressions like "decency", "fairness", "that wouldn't be right", and the like'.[54] A Scot, Forrest was not alone in his ethical commitment to the Republic. Decency and fairness mattered to all of these correspondents and that was why they identified with the cause of the democratic Republic.

This was particularly the case with the older hands who had been in Spain before the outbreak of war, such as Henry Buckley, Jay Allen and Lawrence Fernsworth, all of whom had witnessed, and sympathized with, the process whereby the newly established democratic regime had tried to modernize a deeply repressive society. According to Constancia de la Mora, Fernsworth 'knew Catalonia as few foreigners alive'. She was shocked by how little he earned: 'He began work at dawn, often driving hours to the front and back, then walking through dark streets to our Bureau to telephone his stories.' Like Buckley, Fernsworth was Roman Catholic. He was always well-groomed and exquisitely polite, always comporting himself with 'courtly gallantry'. Despite his exiguous earnings, he was an epicure and a wine connoisseur, yet his solidarity with the Spanish people was unquestionable and he wrote movingly of their plight during the Civil War.[55]

The commitment of the correspondents was immediately noted by the German novelist Gustav Regler when he arrived in Madrid in October 1936 as a volunteer for the International Brigades. Through a friendship first with Ilsa

Kulcsar and then Arturo Barea, Regler came into contact with several correspondents. At one point during the siege of Madrid, he met a group of newspapermen whom he found exhilarated by a visit from Julio Álvarez del Vayo: 'They loved the Spanish people, hoped for the victory of the Republic, and were all opposed to the official ambassadors of their own countries.'[56] This was a considerable overgeneralization, since the pro-Republican Americans knew that their sentiments were shared by their Ambassador Claude Bowers. There were also American correspondents who supported the rebels, such as Edward Knoblaugh, William Carney and Hubert Knickerbocker, but they tended to gravitate to the insurgent zone. Nevertheless, it was the case that a substantial number of correspondents became deeply committed to the Republic. Martha Gellhorn wrote in 1996: 'I believed in the cause of the Spanish Republic as I believed in nothing before or since.'[57] Regler was moved to note that, in the spring of 1937, she courageously went into no-man's land outside Madrid, helping the commander of the Garibaldi battalion of Italian volunteers, Randolfo Pacciardi, rolling bandages for the doctor who attended the wounded.[58]

Perhaps the best example of how the Republic could capture the emotions was the tall, gaunt and sad-eyed Herbert Lionel Matthews of the *New York Times*. The shy, bookish and melancholy New Yorker Matthews was thirty-six years old when he reached Spain in March 1937. There was little about his background to suggest that he would become an impassioned supporter of the Spanish Republic. He had volunteered for service in the First World War but reached France too late to take part in combat. On his return, he went to Columbia University, where he studied romance languages, ending up with a command of Italian, French and Spanish. After graduating, he had joined the *New York Times* as a secretary and stenographer for the business manager. Working nights so that he could continue studying, Matthews won a fellowship, which allowed him to spend 1925–26 in Europe. He studied Dante in Italy and acquired an admiration for the Fascist regime. On his return from France, he became a secretary in the news department of the *New York Times*. In 1929, he was offered the chance to take part in a five-month study tour of Japan, Korea, Manchuria and northern China funded by the Carnegie Endowment for International Peace and the Japanese Government. He returned as an admirer of Japanese economic dynamism and believing that the Japanese would be a progressive force within East Asia. From 1931 to 1935, Matthews worked in the Paris bureau of the *New York Times* until boredom drove him to grab the chance to cover the Italian invasion of Ethiopia in the autumn of 1935.[59]

Like many other Western correspondents in Ethiopia, Matthews praised 'the civilizing influence' and material progress brought by the Italians, commenting

'I never could withhold my admiration at seeing a difficult job superbly done'.[60] After Italian victory, in May 1936, Matthews returned to Paris, where his early articles on the French response to the Spanish Civil War were not notably sympathetic to the Republic.[61] Nevertheless, he became sufficiently fascinated by events in Spain that he asked for, and received, a posting there after Carney's abandonment of Republican Spain. Despite arriving with sympathies for the Italians, Matthews would write during the Spanish Civil War: 'No one who knows what is happening here and who has any pretense to intellectual honesty can forbear to take sides.' Shy and melancholy, he believed that the months passed in the besieged Spanish capital were the most glorious of his life. He wrote in 1938:

> Of all places to be in the world, Madrid is the most satisfactory. I thought
> so from the moment I arrived, and whenever I am away from it these days
> I cannot help longing to return. All of us feel the same way, so it is more
> than a personal impression. The drama, the thrills, the electrical
> optimism, the fighting spirit, the patient courage of these mad and
> wonderful people – these are things worth living for and seeing with one's
> own eyes.[62]

After the Second World War, he wrote: 'In those years we lived our best and what has come after and what there is to come can never carry us to those heights again. I, in my own field, have never done such work as I did in Spain, nor do I ever hope to equal it. We left our hearts there.' Like many correspondents, Matthews never lost his pride in supporting the Republic:

> I have already lived six years since the Spanish Civil War ended, and have
> seen much of greatness and glory and many beautiful things and places
> since then, and I may, with luck, live another twenty or thirty years, but
> I know, as surely as I know anything in this world, that nothing so
> wonderful will ever happen to me again as those two and a half years I
> spent in Spain. And it is not only I who say this, but everyone who lived
> through that period with the Spanish Republicans. Soldier or journalist,
> Spaniard or American or British or French or German or Italian, it did
> not matter. Spain was a melting pot in which the dross came out and pure
> gold remained. It made men ready to die gladly and proudly. It gave
> meaning to life; it gave courage and faith in humanity; it taught us what
> internationalism means, as no League of Nations or Dumbarton Oaks will
> ever do. There one learned that men could be brothers, that nations and

frontiers, religions and races were but outer trappings, and that nothing counted, nothing was worth fighting for, but the idea of liberty.[63]

Matthews was not alone in his visceral attachment to Madrid. Vincent 'Jimmy' Sheean wrote equally movingly:

> Madrid, the mushroom, the parasite, created by a monarch's whim, an aristocracy's extravagance and the heartless ostentation of the new rich had found its soul in the pride and courage of its workers. They had turned the brothel and show window of feudal Spain into this epic. Whatever the future might determine in the struggle against fascist barbarism, Madrid had already done so much more than its share that its name would lie forever across the mind of man, sometimes in reproach, sometimes in rebuke, sometimes as a reflex of the heroic tension that is still not lost from our race on earth. In this one place, if nowhere else, the dignity of the common man has stood firm against the world.[64]

Geoffrey Cox was also deeply affected by the social progress and the anti-fascist solidarity that he witnessed in the Republican zone:

> Facing a common danger gave all Madrid an unspoken, but very real, sense of common respect. *Compañero* – comrade – has an artificial ring in the comparative security of Britain. In Madrid, muttered by a sentry who saluted with clenched fist and gave the greeting, 'Salud', it was absolutely genuine. Here was an atmosphere in which realities like skill and strength, and, above all, courage, counted, and where dress and appearance and accent and schooling came in not at all. Individual pettiness, ambitions, jealousies, were to some extent merged in the common end and the common danger.

The defeat of Franco's assault on Madrid 'offered this extraordinary sense of hope, this sudden feeling…that not only was the threat of fascism removed, but all of a sudden there really seemed to be a sunny, a really marvellous exhilarating future open to Spain'.[65]

The hopes raised by the Republic, both in terms of its attempt to bring a better way of life to the dispossessed and as a beacon of anti-fascism, were shared by many others. The hardened veteran of the *News Chronicle*, Vernon Bartlett, wrote:

I have never had so keen a sense of the importance of freedom as I had in Spain. So keen that I have become terribly bitter against those who seek to limit it, and am no longer ashamed of my inability to be detached and clam. I have been glad enough to come out of Spain again and yet on each occasion I have found life elsewhere curiously flat, selfish and unimportant.[66]

Even the rather thick-skinned Sefton Delmer wrote, rather shamefacedly:

Despite all I had seen of the brutality and contempt for justice of the Reds, despite my own antipathy to Marxism as a demagogic fraud, despite all this and much more, I nevertheless found I was being swept along in the exhilaration of Madrid's refusal to abandon the fight. I found myself sharing the thrill of the reverses which the Reds were inflicting on the side I would certainly have chosen had I been a Spaniard and forced to decide between the ugly alternatives of Franco and Caballero.[67]

The sense that the cause of the Spanish Republic was worth supporting was linked to a close camaraderie among the correspondents. This was especially true of those who lived through the siege of Madrid, all of whom were converted into partisans of the Republic. The reasons were explained by Arthur Koestler, who suffered the bombing raids in the last week of October and the first days of November 1936. He wrote later:

Anyone who has lived through the hell of Madrid with his eyes, his nerves, his heart, his stomach – and then pretends to be objective, is a liar. If those who have at their command printing machines and printer's ink for the expression of their opinions, remain neutral and objective in the face of such bestiality, then Europe is lost. In that case let us all sit down and bury our heads in the sand and wait until the devil takes us. In that case it is time for Western civilization to say good night.[68]

Even those who arrived in the spring of 1937 felt the same. The British correspondents Sefton Delmer and Henry Buckley, who had been in Madrid since the earliest days of the siege, joined the Americans Herbert Matthews, Ernest Hemingway, Sidney Franklin, John Dos Passos, Martha Gellhorn and Virginia Cowles to watch battles at the front not from the Hotel Florida, but from a wrecked apartment building in the Paseo de Rosales overlooking the Casa de Campo. Hemingway referred to it as 'the old homestead', because it reminded him of his grandfather's house in Chicago. Dos Passos described it: 'The ground-glass door opens on air, at your feet, a well opens full of broken masonry and smashed furniture, then the empty avenue and beyond, across the Manzanares, a magnificent view of the enemy.'[69]

On 10 April 1937, Hemingway took the group there to observe a Loyalist offensive. Dos Passos was understandably apprehensive: 'The lines cross the valley below, but if you step out on the paseo you're in the full view of the enemy on the hills opposite, and the Moors are uncommonly good riflemen.' All was quiet because it was lunchtime. Nevertheless, the signs of activity in the apartment, the flashes of sunlight glinting off field glasses and Ivens' movie camera drew the attention of the rebels. In his later novelized account, *Century's Ebb*, Dos Passos recounted the scene, maliciously portraying the Hemingway character (George Elbert Warner) as a foolhardy idiot for walking along the Paseo de Rosales in full view of the rebel lines. When he was warned by a Republican corporal not to walk out in the open lest he draw enemy fire, he responded 'Who's chickenshit?' and strolled on. Once lunch was over, the rebels opened fire. Dos Passos wrote: 'as we were working our way back in the shelter of the smashed-up houses, all hell broke loose. I hate to think how many good guys lost their lives through that piece of bravado.' A similar incident is recounted by the British brigadier, Jason Gurney, who describes a visit to the front by Hemingway 'full of hearty and bogus *bonhomie*. He sat himself down behind the bullet-proof shield of a machine-gun and loosed off a whole belt of ammunition in the general direction of the enemy. This provoked a mortar bombardment for which he did not stay.'[70]

If correspondents faced dangers during the day, on their return to their hotel, they were confronted by lack of food. After leaving the British Embassy where, at the height of the siege of Madrid, Delmer had slept on the floor of the ballroom, he moved into the Florida, which he later described as 'the friendliest, funniest, and most adventure-laden Hotel' in which he had ever stayed. He had two rooms, a back room where he slept and a large front room, sunny but exposed to shell fire. This sitting room he used for reading, writing and 'roistering', the latter activity facilitated by the fact that he had installed electric burners and chafing dishes. He had also set up a bar in his bathroom, stocked with bottles that he had bought from anarchists who had looted the cellars of the royal palace. He was visited frequently by International Brigaders who helped him demolish his collection of rare and priceless vintages.[71]

As the war went on, journalists, like the rest of the Republican population, had to scrounge ever more desperately for food and cigarettes. Things would get gradually worse. When Martha Gellhorn arrived in Madrid on 27 March 1937, her first meal at the Gran Vía consisted of a minuscule portion of *garbanzos* (chickpeas) and strong-smelling *bacalao* (dried cod). The American novelist Josephine Herbst, who was there in April 1937, commented: 'Though food was on everyone's mind, I never heard anyone complain of the lack of it or because some of the dishes served at the restaurant on the Gran Vía stank to high heaven.' The altogether more celebrated American writer, John Dos Passos, there at the same time, also referred to 'the stink of the food at the Gran Vía'.[72] Virginia Cowles, an elegant and wealthy twenty-seven-year-old American, reached Madrid towards the end of March 1937. She was a friend of the Churchill family and had made her reputation writing travel pieces for *Harper's Bazaar* and the Hearst Sunday Syndicate. Having secured an interview with Mussolini in 1935, she managed to get a commission to cover the Spanish war. The dowdy Josephine Herbst enviously described her 'dressed in black, with heavy gold bracelets on her slender wrists and wearing tiny black shoes with incredibly high heels'.[73] Her room on the fifth floor of the Hotel Florida, overlooking the front and in the direct line of Franco's artillery, provoked a degree of nervousness. This was dissipated somewhat by the bustle of ordinary life which sprang forth every day in the square below like 'a huge movie set swarming with extras ready to play a part'. Virginia Cowles described the food at the Gran Vía as 'meagre and at times scarcely eatable', yet it was not so inedible as to deter hungry *Madrileños* from trying to force their way through the heavily guarded doors. When she arrived in Madrid, 'Tom' Delmer, with whom she struck up a friendship at the Florida, pointed out her error in failing to bring any food with her.[74]

As food got scarcer, Ernest Hemingway, who reached Madrid in March 1937, consolidated his popularity by dint of the inexhaustible store of bacon, eggs, coffee and marmalade, and drink, whisky and gin, that he kept in his room at the Florida. International Brigade volunteers were always welcome and would always find plenty of bottles and tinned food. His stocks were both replenished and distributed by his faithful crony, Sidney Franklin, the American bullfighter, described by John Dos Passos as 'a sallow slender blackhaired man with the skin so dark around the eyes he looked as if he had a couple of shiners'. Herbst referred to him as Hemingway's 'devoted friend and a sort of *"valet de chambre"*' largely because of his skills as a scrounger.[75] Such was the austerity of the Florida that a visit to the altogether better-provisioned Hotel Gaylord where the senior Russian advisers were housed was seen as a rare privilege. On 25 March 1937, Ilya Ehrenburg went there to visit the highly influential *Pravda* correspondent, Mikhail Koltsov. He went eagerly because 'you could get warm there and have a good meal'. On this occasion, in Koltsov's crowded room, Ehrenburg noticed a large ham and profusion of bottles, but forgot about both when he was introduced to Hemingway, a writer whose works he revered.

Ehrenburg gushingly tried to express his admiration to the already inebriated novelist, who was infinitely more interested in the large glass of whisky he held. Ehrenburg asked in French what he was doing in Madrid and Hemingway reluctantly explained in Spanish that he was there as the correspondent of the North American Newspaper Alliance. Ehrenburg then enquired if he had to telegraph just substantial articles or also news items (*nouvelles*). Hemingway was furious, having translated *nouvelles* into the Spanish *novelas* (novels). He jumped up and grabbed a bottle, with which he tried to hit Ehrenburg. Before serious bloodshed took place, he was restrained.[76] Hemingway clearly made a habit of creating scenes. In the winter of 1937, the beautiful American correspondent, Martha Gellhorn, had gone with Hemingway to another party in Mikhail Koltsov's room. She was distressed to be ushered away from the delicious food on offer when, once again, in characteristically boorish style, Hemingway had made a scene. Believing that the Communist commander Juan Modesto had made a pass at Martha, he had jealously challenged him to a duel of Russian roulette. After they circled each other menacingly, each with one end of a handkerchief between his teeth, they were unceremoniously separated and Hemingway, with a hungry Martha Gellhorn in tow, was required to leave.[77]

The Hotel Florida, like the Telefónica, was in the firing line of Nationalist artillery, but Hemingway assured his nightly guests that his room had a 'dead angle' and was therefore invulnerable. Tom Delmer's room, however, was eventually hit and his utensils destroyed. Given the impossibility of sleeping through artillery bombardments, every night became a fiesta either in the larger rooms or else in the patio around which the hotel was built. It was still frequented by prostitutes, nicknamed 'whores de combat' by Hemingway. To Gustav Regler, the German Communist writer, and commissar of the XII International Brigade, it was 'a noisy bordello'. Cedric Salter, who stayed at the Florida in the spring of 1937 while writing for the *Daily Telegraph*, complained of being unable to sleep because of

a dim roaring noise from below, not unlike that to be heard in the Lion House at the Zoo, shortly before feeding time. In desperation I rang and asked what caused this strange sound. That, I was told, was the Russian aviators having fun in the bar. Yes, to be sure, it always went on like that until dawn unless they drank more than usual, in which case they might fall asleep on the floors around 4 a.m.

Having managed, with the help of cotton wool in his ears, to fall asleep, Salter was awakened when a naked woman flung open his door and ran screaming into his bathroom, followed by a very large Russian dressed only in cotton underpants. Only with some difficulty could he persuade them to leave. Delmer agreed with Salter: 'it was not until three or four in the morning that the shrieking and brawling and flamenco singing died down'.[78] In contrast, more serious guests remembered principally the efforts of the staff to keep things as apparently normal as possible. Winston Churchill's cousin, Peter Spencer, otherwise known by his title as Viscount Churchill, was with the British medical aid unit and often stayed at the Florida. Kitty Bowler described him as 'the most distinguished living skeleton I have ever met'. His principal recollection from April 1937 was the fact that 'the chambermaid kept everything on her floor looking most elegant, although the end of the corridor was blasted, and from it you could see half across Madrid'.[79]

The bulk of those who stayed at the Florida tried hard to maintain a high level of objective and honest reporting. However, the standards aspired to by Matthews, Jay Allen, Henry Buckley, Lawrence Fernsworth and Geoffrey Cox and many others was not universal. It was certainly not achieved by the Oxford-educated Communist Claud Cockburn. He was the founder and editor of the satirical news-sheet, *The Week*, whose mimeographed sheets were highly influential in exposing the pro-fascist sympathies of the upper-class 'Cliveden Set' and the salon conspiracies that lay behind the farce of appeasement. Cockburn was on holiday in Salou near Tarragona when the Spanish Civil War began. The British Communist Party invited him to act as correspondent for its newspaper, the *Daily Worker*. He did so eventually, using the pseudonym 'Frank Pitcairn', but only after first going to Barcelona and then to Madrid. There he volunteered for the militia unit known as the Quinto Regimiento and fought in the sierra to the north. It was always the view of Koltsov and Otto Katz that good journalists could serve the cause better in front of their typewriters than in the trenches. Accordingly, like Arthur Koestler, he was persuaded to return to journalism. Having done so, as a result of a close friendship with both Mikhail Koltsov and Otto Katz, and a readiness to toe the party line, Cockburn received privileged information on a regular basis.[80]

What Cockburn published was not, however, always based on accurate information. On one notorious occasion, Katz and Cockburn worked together during the Republican push against Teruel. With urgently needed artillery held up on the French side of the border, Katz summoned Cockburn to Paris and announced; 'You are the first eyewitness of the revolt at Tetuán.' Cockburn, who had never set foot in Tetuán, sought elucidation. Katz explained that a delegation of French Communists and Socialists was about to try to persuade the premier, Léon Blum, to open the frontier. To get Blum into a receptive mood, Katz hoped to plant a newspaper story that would suggest that Franco was facing difficulties. Realizing that a story about some apocryphal Republican victory would have little influence, Katz decided to put out a story that would make it seem that Franco's power was crumbling in the very fount of its strength, Spanish Morocco. Together, they fabricated a military rebellion in Tetuán, using only the *Guide Bleu* and a couple of other travel guides to describe the streets and squares in which the mutiny had allegedly taken place. Complete with 'details' of places and participants, Cockburn remembered that it had 'emerged as one of the soundest, most factual pieces of war correspondence ever written'. When the delegation met Blum, all he could talk about was that morning's headlines about the 'revolt in Tetuán' and the frontier was reopened.[81]

Another journalist who could hardly be considered either objective or accurate was Hugh Slater, a handsome middle-class English Communist, who was a graduate of the Slade School of Art. In London, he used his real name, 'Humphrey', but, for Spain, had adopted the somewhat more proletarian 'Hugh'. Along with William Forrest, Slater had driven into Spain in an aged white Rolls Royce. His objective was to write for *Imprecor* (the International Press Correspondence), the Comintern's English-language newspaper. The Rolls Royce guzzled petrol and was 'dreadfully noticeable on the battlefield'. For some time, Forrest and Slater commuted from Madrid to Toledo each day to follow the siege of the Alcázar but Slater was dissatisfied with his journalistic work. Kate Mangan, who worked for a time as Slater's secretary in Madrid, noted: 'I had realised at length that Humphry [*sic*] was jealous of the soldiers. It sounds an odd thing to say but he envied them their heroism.'[82]

Wanting to do more than merely recite the party line in *Imprecor*, Slater joined the International Brigade and was appointed political commissar of the British battalion's anti-tank battery. His working-class comrades regarded him suspiciously as merely a middle-class ideologue, 'amiable and decorative' in the words of Fred Thomas, 'extremely arrogant' according to Tony McLean. A brigade report from May 1937 described him as 'generally unpopular due to sectarian activities etc. alleged. To some extent this may have been eliminated but manner is not one conducive to successful work with rank-and-file.' A later report commented that he 'was disliked by the majority of the men. They considered him a schemer.' Nevertheless, he was apparently a more than competent military tactician, and was named commander of the anti-tank battery on 30 July 1937. Three months later he was promoted to captain and on 8 April 1938, he was made chief of operations in the general staff of the XV Brigade. Official brigade reports described him as 'a leader almost of genius but too keen on his own comfort, which had a bad effect on his unit'. He was badly affected by a bout of typhoid and was repatriated in October 1938. After the Spanish Civil War, disillusioned with Stalinism, he became a novelist.[83]

The difficulties facing journalists who tried to maintain a commitment both to the Republican cause and to the ethics of their profession were illustrated by an incident on the Madrid front involving Louis Fischer. As the rebel Army of Africa approached the capital, Cockburn and Koltsov were joined by 'an American journalist' – Fischer – who had just published a brilliant and rather moving article about the demoralization of the Republican militia who were trying in vain to halt the advance of Franco's African columns. One of Fischer's recurrent themes was the imbalance between the rebels' well-armed, well-trained forces and the barely armed scratch militia of the Republic – 'untrained, inexperienced, undisciplined and badly officered. They melt away under fire.' He lamented that, on 25 September, two days before the city fell, he had witnessed frightened militiamen fleeing from German bombing raids on Toledo. Datelined 8 October, his article appeared two weeks later.[84] A couple of days after that, Fischer coincided with Cockburn and Koltsov south of Madrid.

When he saw Fischer get out of his car and walk towards them, a furious Koltsov spat on the ground in disgust and refused to shake hands with him. When Fischer asked what he had done wrong, Koltsov said that he had just received the text of the article from Moscow. Fischer remonstrated that he had merely reported the facts, saying: 'What's the good of pretending our militia here aren't demoralized and bewildered? Who's going to believe me if I tell the old story once again?' Koltsov responded sarcastically: 'Yes. Those are the facts. How extraordinarily observant and truthful you are.' The discussion grew more bitter. Koltsov said: 'You, with your reputation, you can really spread alarm and despondency. And that's what you've done. You've done more harm than thirty British MPs working for Franco. And you expect me to shake hands with you.' When Fischer persisted that the facts were the facts and that the readers had the right to know them, Koltsov replied: 'If you were a little more frank, you'd say that what you're really interested in is your damned reputation as a journalist. You're afraid that if you don't put out this stuff, and it comes through someone else, you'll be thought a bad reporter, can't see the facts under his nose. Probably in the pay of the Republicans. That's why you, as the French say, have lost an excellent opportunity to keep your mouth shut.' Cockburn himself agreed with Koltsov that the public did not necessarily have the right to read the truth. When his wife questioned this, he would respond angrily: 'Who gave them such a right? Perhaps when they have exerted themselves enough to alter the policy of their bloody government, and the Fascists are beaten in Spain, they will have such a right. This isn't an abstract question. It's a shooting war.'[85]

Despite his outburst against Fischer, Koltsov was not entirely comfortable with the need to tailor what he wrote to political necessity. This can be discerned in what another Soviet correspondent, Ilya Ehrenburg, wrote years later:

> The history of Soviet journalism knows no greater name, and his fame was well deserved. But having raised journalism to a high standard, having demonstrated to his readers that a report or an article could be a work of art, he did not believe it himself. More than once he said to me with wry irony: 'Other people write novels. But what will remain of me after I've gone? Newspaper articles are ephemeral stuff. Even an historian won't find them very useful, because we don't show in our articles what is going on in Spain, only what ought to be happening.'[86]

That it was possible to combine high professional standards with a passionate belief in the Spanish Republic was demonstrated by Matthews, Fischer, Buckley, Forrest, Cox, Fernsworth and many others, but perhaps most of all by Jay Allen. Like Buckley and Fernsworth, Allen had followed events in Spain for a long time, first working out of Paris in the 1920s and eventually going to live in Spain at the beginning of 1934. There he formed close friendships with many of the most prominent figures of the Socialist Party. A deep interest in the problems of rural Spain lay behind a warm appreciation of the Republic's attempts to introduce universal education and agrarian reform. Among many important articles written before and after the military coup of July 1936, Jay Allen filed what, along with Mario Neves' reports on the massacre of Badajoz and George Steer's report on the bombing of Guernica, were three of the most important, and frequently quoted, articles written during the war. These were an exclusive interview with Franco in Tetuán on 27 July 1936, his own account of the aftermath of the Nationalist capture of Badajoz and the last ever interview given by the about-to-be-executed founder of the Spanish fascist party, the Falange, José Antonio Primo de Rivera. The interview with Franco was remarkable for the rebel leader's declaration of his readiness to unleash mass slaughter in order to achieve his ends.[87] The immensely moving report from Badajoz led to Jay Allen being denigrated by right-wing broadcasters and journalists across the United States.[88]

A journalist who supplied defamatory material about Jay Allen, William P. Carney, was one of a small number of pro-rebel correspondents who worked for a time in the Republican zone. A thirty-eight-year-old Catholic from San Antonio, Texas, Carney had been covering Spanish Republican politics since 1931, on the basis of regular short trips from the *New York Times*'s Paris office.[89] Carney had spent the early months of the war as the *New York Times* correspondent in Madrid. After some friction with various Republican authorities, he was reassigned to Salamanca. In both zones, he frequently used his reports to benefit the Francoist cause and, in consequence, he was nicknamed 'General Bill' by other correspondents. As a correspondent of the rival *New York Herald Tribune*, James Minifie believed that Carney not only tilted articles in favour of the rebels, but also invented 'news' on the basis of 'eye-witness' reports. When these 'absentee eye-witness reports' appeared in the *New York Times*, Minifie would receive from his own paper queries about the episodes described. So blatant were they that he was able to respond adequately simply by cabling back the words 'Another Carney exclusive'. He remembered later the difficulties created for Herbert Matthews by Carney's practices. Matthews not only found his own credibility questioned but also, according to Minifie, 'was conscientious enough to check every wide-eyed Carney story that his paper had printed. He was then faced with the problem of straightening out the facts, without too obviously undercutting his colleague.'[90]

On leaving Madrid, Carney had gone to Paris, whence he sent a lengthy and virulently anti-Republican article to the *New York Times*, which was published on 7 December 1936. It appeared under the sub-heading 'All Semblance of Democratic Forms of Government in Spain Disappears – 25,000 Put to Death by Radicals – Priests, Nuns Slain'. Ignoring the fact that the conditions in a besieged capital demanded some form of censorship, he was outraged that he had been prevented from publishing pro-rebel articles, claiming falsely that: 'Any one engaged in reporting the course of events is in danger of being seized as a spy and perhaps shot summarily before he can prove his innocence.' Within the list of his hardships could be found the complaint that his apartment had been wrecked by a Francoist bombing raid, an incident which somehow intensified his resentment of the Republican authorities. Elsewhere in the article, he portrayed the deaths of civilians during the bombing of Madrid residential districts as the fault of the Republic by quoting the rebels to the effect that the government had made itself responsible for all the harm that may befall civilians by attempting to defend what they called an unfortified open city. Indeed, he was ready to express his annoyance because he had to walk through darkened streets during the black-out and because he had to wait his turn to phone out his stories.

There were many aspects of his article which, for obvious reasons, were not to the liking of the Republican authorities. Not least among them was the fact that they were simply untrue. He claimed for instance that the international volunteers who had come to help defend Madrid were mostly Russians and that 'for some time, Russia has been running the show in Spain in so far as the Madrid government's resistance to General Franco's insurgent movement is concerned'. He asserted that the Russian Ambassador, Marcel Rosenberg, had hand-picked the government of Largo Caballero and presided at cabinet meetings. He also complained that the staff of the censorship for the foreign press included a Russian and an Austrian Socialist, a reference to Ilsa Kulcsar. The latter was true, but he failed to take into account that it was not easy in the besieged city to find people capable of reading a wide range of Western and Eastern European languages. All of these claims were aimed at generating antipathy to the Republic in the United States. He also described in street-by-street detail how the rebels could take the capital. Such details would have been lost on the great majority of *New York Times* readers but might have been of some use to the rebels. Even more sensitive was his detailed account of the city's anti-aircraft defences:

> Machine guns and ridiculously ineffectual anti-aircraft guns firing one-pound shells are mounted on the tops of all the ministries and tall buildings in the centre of the city, such as the Fine Arts structure in Calle Alcalá, Madrid's main street, and the Palace of the Press in the Gran Vía. Batteries of six-inch guns have been placed in Callao Square, directly in front of the Palace of the Press, and in one corner of the Retiro, the vast public park; near the Prado Museum, the observatory and the Ministry of Public Works.

Graphically and accurately describing the appalling conditions of the starving capital, without light and heating, and often without shelter, Carney made it clear that its sufferings were the fault of the 'ferocious proletarian-directed determination to defend the city unto death'. The great popular mobilization in defence of the city was dismissed in contemptuous terms.[91]

Carney's article also included details of the activities of self-appointed extra-judicial squads, although by his own admission, his own encounters with them always ended with an apology by the authorities. Given the wealth of detail that it

provided about the persecution of priests, nuns and right-wingers, this unequiv-
ocally pro-Nationalist article was reprinted as a pamphlet by *Catholic Mind*, with
the sub-headings 'No democratic government in Spain', 'Russia's part in Spain's
civil war' and 'Murder and anti-religion in Spain'.[92] Once in the Nationalist zone,
Carney continued to write about Madrid in a hostile manner, describing it as a
'shabby, proletarian city', populated by hopeless and violent riff-raff.[93]

According to Constancia de la Mora, who was eventually to head the Republic's
censorship office, Carney had been given every facility to travel within the
Republican zone, 'although he was known to have fascist sympathies and fascist
friends'.[94] In his article, Carney had complained:

> the censorship established in Madrid, both for the Spanish press and for
> foreign correspondents, was on lines much more in keeping with Soviet
> ideas than with the customs of a democratic regime. All telephoned and
> telegraphed despatches had to be passed personally by a censor, and
> objections that the censors raised were constantly of such a nature as to
> exact strict adherence to government policy and the removal of all critical
> statements with regard to the situation in Madrid.

He seemed oblivious to the fact that such strictures were normal in wartime.
The fact that the only 'punishment' for journalists who transgressed the rules was
prohibition of the offending part of the despatch did not really sustain his claim
that these were Soviet-style restrictions. When he went to the Nationalist zone,
where transgressions of the censorship regularly provoked death threats, imprisonment and/or expulsion, he found the censorship arrangements to be admirable.
This was perhaps because his writings were so openly favourable to the rebels
that they never encountered difficulties with the censors.

Newspapermen would often try to cheat the censorship in both zones,
although the consequences were infinitely more severe in the rebel zone for those
caught doing so. The most frequently used trick, as noted by Edward Knoblaugh
and Virginia Cowles, was the use of incomprehensible slang. A different ruse was
attempted by Frederick Voigt, the Berlin correspondent of the Manchester
Guardian. He had arrived for a flying visit in Madrid at the end of April 1937 preceded by the apocryphal accolade that the Gestapo had put a price on his head.
Because he was also regarded as a confidant of the British Foreign Secretary,
Anthony Eden, Gustav Regler was deputed to give him an exhaustive tour of the
trenches outside Madrid. Jotting down her impressions of the trip, Josephine
Herbst found him to be unprepossessing: 'peculiar Voigt with his hair unwinding

around pinkish skull, small childish features but firm large chin and too heavy top of head grey wisps too long uncovering attempted covered baldness'. Voigt revealed his prejudices when he expressed his astonishment that the Republican Army was organized at all.[95] His anti-Republican views came out more explicitly in a conversation with Hemingway. On the morning after Voigt's arrival at the Hotel Florida, Hemingway asked him of his first impressions. No doubt influenced by what he read in Nazi Germany, Voigt replied: 'There is a terror here. There is evidence of it wherever you go. Thousands of bodies are being found.' When Hemingway asked where he had seen the bodies, Voigt replied that, although he had not actually been out yet, they were everywhere.

Already unimpressed by a man who tried to cover his baldness by carefully weaving long wisps of blond hair back and forth across his pate, Hemingway laboriously explained how the Republic had made huge efforts to impose order and that, apart from those executed for espionage, 'for months Madrid had been as safe and well policed from any terror as any capital in Europe'. This was something of an exaggeration but it was certainly true that massive strides had been made and that the streets were not littered with bodies as Voigt suggested. Not wanting to substantiate Voigt's obsession with terror, and because they were in Martha Gellhorn's room, Hemingway controlled his impulse to hit him. However, later on the same day, knowing that Ernest and Martha were about to return to the United States, Voigt gave her a sealed envelope and asked her to post it in France. He claimed that it contained a carbon copy of an already censored dispatch from the Teruel front which he wanted to make sure reached the *Guardian*. When Martha told Ernest, he insisted on taking it to Arturo Barea at the censorship office where the contents turned out to be an article denouncing the 'fact' that the bodies of thousands of the victims of the terror were lying around. Hemingway commented:

> It made liars out of every honest correspondent in Madrid. And this guy had written it without stirring from his hotel the first day he arrived. The only ugly thing was that the girl to whom he had entrusted it could, under the rules of war, have been shot as a spy if it had been found among her papers when she was leaving the country.[96]

Whatever 'the rules of war', there were very few cases of hostile journalists being imprisoned, let alone shot, by the Republic.

Although the Republican government had to exercise some control over dispatches sent to foreign newspapers, correspondents in the loyalist zone seemed to move around relatively unhindered. The Australian Noel Monks, a pious teetotal Catholic, was initially sympathetic to Franco but was deeply shocked by what he saw at Guernica, the dead, the dying and the refugees. He wrote later:

> Airplanes, bombs, bullets, fire. Within twenty-four hours Franco was going to brand these shocked homeless people as liars before the whole world. So-called British experts were going to come to Guernica months afterwards, when the smell of burnt human flesh had been replaced by petrol dumped here and there among the ruins, and deliver pompous judgements: 'Guernica was set on fire by the Reds.' My answer to them is unprintable. No government official had accompanied me to Guernica. I wandered among the ruins and survivors at will. I drove back to Bilbao and had to wake up the operator – it was two in the morning – to send my message. Censorship had been lifted. The man who sent my urgent dispatch couldn't read English. If the 'Reds' had destroyed Guernica, I for one could have blown the whole story for all they knew. And how I would have blown it had it been true![97]

Guernica was the subject of one of the most important articles produced during the Spanish Civil War. It was the work of George Lowther Steer, the special envoy of *The Times* with the Republican forces in Bilbao during the spring of 1937. He had been with Noel Monks in Bilbao on the night of 26 April when the news arrived that Guernica had been bombed. Together they drove to the burning town and spoke at length to the survivors. Steer's despatch, which appeared on 28 April in *The Times* and the *New York Times*, was factual and eschewed sensationalism. Without it, and those of Noel Monks, Christopher Holme of Reuters and Mathieu Corman of the Parisian *Ce Soir*, the truth might have been buried under the massive blanket of disinformation woven by the rebel press chief, Luis Bolín, and maintained by the Franco regime for a further thirty-five years. [98]

Despite all the efforts of Arturo Barea, Ilsa Kulcsar and later Constancia de la Mora and Rosario del Olmo to facilitate news-gathering within the Republican zone, the life of the correspondents was hard and often dangerous. In the last week of May 1938, dragging a suitcase containing tins of sardines, tuna, ham and butter, Vincent Sheean of the *New York Herald Tribune* came from Valencia to a now desperately hungry Madrid. In the Hotel Victoria in the Plaza del Ángel near the Puerta del Sol, he found that the standard fare was aged dried cod (*bacalao*) and lentils. The hotel was regularly shelled and fellow guests, such as Willy Forrest, urged him to take no notice of the machine-gun fire that could be heard from his room. It was just about tolerable for those, like Sheean, who were passing through as visiting firemen. Yet, Arturo Barea's successor as chief of the press office in Madrid, Rosario del Olmo, despite having been offered by Constancia de la Mora a job in the Barcelona bureau, had refused to leave the capital because it was her home. Sheean remembered Rosario as 'unobtrusive, severe and rectilinear as a schoolteacher with a crowd of refractory children, but possessed of such fixity of purpose that no difficulties could affect her inner sureness'. He heard later that she had fainted several times from under-nourishment. Geoffrey Brereton, who wrote for the *New Statesman and Nation*, paid tribute to the efforts of Rosario to ensure that journalists were fed, even if only on horsemeat, at the Hotel Victoria.[99] For those like Rosario del Olmo who stayed and went through the long siege of Madrid, the psychological effects were long-lasting. Barea's health never recovered and Lester Ziffren later recounted a common experience. According to Jay Allen, a close friend, after Webb Miller saw the carnage left after the massacre perpetrated when the rebels entered Toledo, he left Spain 'with a walking nervous break-down'.[100]

Ziffren wrote:

> During the war I had become accustomed to lack of food, the daily bombing and shelling, the absence of heating, the lack of hot water. The body adjusted itself to the increasingly bad conditions. But after I arrived in France a severe physical reaction set in. I saw persons living calmly, eating tranquilly and as much as they desired, free from the fear of bombs and bullets. When persons questioned me about Spain, I felt miserable and mournful. I began to suffer from nightmares. My dreams were of horrors. I used to wake several times a night in a cold sweat. If I could sleep four hours I was fortunate. For such are the after-effects of living through a veritable hell in a city which had survived days and nights such as no city in history has endured.[101]

Probably the last correspondent to leave Madrid was O'Dowd Gallagher of the *Daily Express*. Unshaven and scruffy, he was a hard-drinking half-Irish, half-South African, who had proved that a total disregard for personal appearance was no impediment to attracting streams of women. In this regard, Randolph Churchill once complained to Geoffrey Cox, 'Why should a grubby chap like that, without a bean, be able to get any woman he wants and I who have everything can't get a single one?'[102] It was freezing in Madrid; Gallagher and the remaining handful of correspondents huddled in their overcoats living on a diet of watery lentil or chickpea 'soup'. They lived the bewildering days following the anti-Negrín coup carried out on 4 March 1939 by Colonel Segismundo Casado in the naïve hope of a negotiated peace with Franco. The Casado action tapped into deep seams of war-weariness. Gallagher was aware that hunger and demoralization were rife in the central zone, where 'ordinary people had been worn down out by two and a half years of living below the bread line'. Nevertheless, he lived through the hair-raising experience of the fighting between Casado's men and the Communists. The President of the Madrid Defence Junta, the jovial General José Miaja, aligned himself with Casado. Gallagher enjoyed a glass of sherry with Miaja two days before the Francoists entered Madrid. He had stayed on in Madrid assuming that he would be writing about the last-ditch defence of the capital. In the event, he would write about the jubilant scenes of the city's right-wingers as the fifth column came out into the streets. On the morning that they arrived, he was awakened by the chants of '¡Franco! ¡Franco!' from the street below the apartment where he was staying. After rapidly pulling his clothes on, he set off through the crowds to the censor's office. It was nearly deserted. There was only one censor left, a woman, perhaps Rosario herself, who passed his first bulletins. By midday, she too had fled and he stamped his story with her official rubber stamps and faked her signature.[103] As Republican refugees streamed out of the capital towards the Mediterranean coast, he sent out a story about the scenes of jubilation beginning with the words 'Madrid, after a two and a half years' siege, surrendered today and tonight is completely under General Franco's control'.[104] Shortly afterwards, he was caught by Nationalist press officers, who told him that he was lucky not to be shot and expelled him from Spain.[105] It was a sad anticlimax to the collective efforts of the foreign journalists who had shared the vicissitudes of the besieged city.

3

The Lost Generation Divided:
Hemingway, Dos Passos and the
Disappearance of José Robles

'**M**orning: wake early suddenly, hearing two heavy thuds, shelling beginning, followed rapidly by crashes – house falling slam heavy as wall of water, voices in hall, doors opening, rising voices, more voices as shelling keeps up.' Josie Herbst was terrified, her hands shaking as she tried to find her clothes. She gave up, threw on a dressing gown and went out into the corridor where, in the darkness, other guests were milling. It was still dark and the revellers in the Hotel Florida had had little sleep when, at 6 a.m. on Thursday 22 April 1937, they were awakened by an artillery bombardment. Only a few hours earlier, their usual nightly carousing had been ended by a peevish complaint from Antoine de Saint-Exupéry, the correspondent of the Paris daily *L'Intransigeant*. According to Tom Delmer, 'All kinds of liaisons were revealed as people poured from their bedrooms to seek shelter in the basement, among them Ernest [Hemingway] and Martha [Gellhorn].' Martha was 'in pyjamas, uncombed, with a coat on' and putting on a brave face. Josie saw her with Virginia Cowles 'in semi-bravado laughter going to corner back room'.

Out from the rooms of correspondents and International Brigaders scuttled dozens of prostitutes, 'crying in high voices like birds' as Martha wrote in her diary. Awakened by the noise, John Dos Passos chose first to shave because 'a man feels safe shaving, sniffing the little customary odour of the usual shaving soap'. Emerging in a tartan bathrobe, he saw men and women 'in various stages of undress' dragging suitcases and mattresses into back rooms. One of the waiters from the restaurant came out of room after room with his arm around 'a different giggling or snivelling young woman. Great exhibitions of dishevelment and lingerie.' Rather miffed that no one noticed her, the dowdy Josie went back into her room and dressed, carefully starting with red socks. When she reappeared, Ernest Hemingway asked how she was. Finding her voice almost gone, she just said 'fine' in a funny voice, but thought to herself, 'but I didn't come here to die like a rat in a trap'. 'Shells seem to be tearing right into the room. Front of hotel seems ripping off. Expect any moment terrible scream, falling rocks and plaster.'

Despite the mayhem, the guests put on a show of serenity as the bombardment continued. Hemingway was 'very big and cheerful'. Dos Passos went back to bed for an hour, then appeared fully dressed, 'very composed and at ease'; Saint-Exupéry ('French gent emerges in blue pajamas') stood at the top of the stairs with a basket of grapefruits, bowed to each passing female, saying '*Voulez-vous une pamplemousse, Madame?*' Finally, a combination of Hemingway's bullfighting valet, Sidney Franklin, Claud Cockburn and Josie Herbst managed to get coffee going. The shelling went on relentlessly, the explosions outside sounding as if they were inside the hotel, 'actually were breaking in street outside, tearing up pavements, big 6 inch German shells'. Josie's scribbled and disorganized diary entry recorded the correspondents' attempts to construct some sort of normality in the midst of what seemed like their impending destruction:

> Frenchman with grapefruit reassembled in suit but with more grapefruits, continually pressed upon half-awake somewhat dazed behaving well crowd. Coburn, Klein, Frenchman, Dos, I have coffee Coburn's room, & makings 2 pieces toast made fringed brown on edges no bidders, crumbled bread on stand & coffee drunk gratefully, shelling bang bang Go to H's room. Gals gone. Gals (professionals) swarming in halls. As shelling subsides, what looks like 60 whores emerge from one room. More coffee made in Hem's room & then still another batch.[1]

As the shelling died down, one after another, Hemingway, Willie Forrest, Dos Passos, Josie Herbst and the other correspondents wandered out to see the damage in the Plaza de Callao. By now, the sun was blazing down and there were already workmen out repairing the pavement. Josie returned to the hotel to find it almost normal but gloomy after the glaring light outside and with a thick grey dust over all the furniture. After keeping their emotions in check during the terrifying morning ordeal, everyone was now touchy and on edge. Hemingway was talking to Cockburn but, noticing Josie, asked her why she was so grouchy. She replied that she was tired and didn't feel like playing the Girl Scout any more. This prompted Hemingway to invite her to his room for a drink. While they were standing around, there was a dramatic entry, recalled almost in passing when Josie wrote her diary that night: 'Dos comes in. Has found out Robles executed. Wants to investigate. Discuss with Hem danger of D. investigating. R. bad egg given fair trial – give away military secrets.'[2]

The two lines of this cryptic diary entry contain the bare bones of a story about which rivers of ink would flow over the next seventy years. It was a story that would involve John Dos Passos, Ernest Hemingway, Martha Gellhorn and Josephine Herbst, all stars of varying brightness in the American literary firmament. A story with many loose ends, it would come to be seen as the last straw, if not the key element, in the break-up of one of America's most celebrated literary friendships, that between Hemingway and Dos Passos. More recently, it has been taken up and wielded as 'proof' that the Spanish Republic, of which all four were staunch enthusiasts, had become simply an outpost of the most brutal Stalinism.[3] Yet, despite all this, at the heart of the story, there was a central character whose role remains an enigma: Robles, the man of whose death Dos Passos had just been informed.

José Robles Pazos was the translator into Spanish of the novels of John Dos Passos. The young American writer had met this tall dark nineteen-year-old Spaniard one Sunday morning in 1916 on a train from Madrid to Toledo and they visited the town's artistic treasures together. Dos Passos was entranced by Robles' cynical view on life and admired him as 'a man of vigorous, sceptical and inquiring mind'. They became close friends. Robles had later left Spain to escape the repressive environment of the Primo de Rivera dictatorship. He settled in America and taught Spanish literature at the Johns Hopkins University in Baltimore. In 1936, as he did every year, he had brought his family to spend the summer in Spain.[4] When the Civil War broke out, although Robles came from a reactionary monarchist family, he decided to remain and work for the Republic. Most commentators on the case follow John Dos Passos in stating that, because Robles knew Russian, he was drafted in as interpreter to General Vladimir Gorev, Soviet Military Attaché and GRU resident (local chief of the Soviet Military Intelligence), who arrived in Madrid at the end of August 1936. Robles was given the rank of lieutenant colonel and considerable responsibility within the Ministry of War.[5] Louis Fischer, who had high-level access both to the ministry and to Russians posted there, referred to Robles as Gorev's 'aide'. He believed that 'Gorev trusted him. Robles had a fine open face and pleasant face and looked the disinterested idealist.' He also recalled that, when the American military attaché Colonel Stephen O. Fuqua came to the ministry to get up-to-date information on the military situation, 'Gorev instructed Robles to talk to him'.[6]

That Robles should be given such a sensitive position as interpreter to the local head of Soviet Military Intelligence and such an exalted rank is extremely puzzling and surely significant. After all, the initial small group of high-ranking Russians had arrived with a team of twenty-five totally trusted interpreters and certainly had no need to recruit interpreters locally. Over the course of the war, over two hundred Russian interpreters were sent to Spain. They were, in general, neither sufficient in number nor, in some cases, sufficiently fluent in Spanish. However, Moscow intransigently insisted that only Soviet nationals or trusted foreign Communists trained in the USSR be allowed to work as interpreters in Spain, especially in the case of the top echelons of advisers. Since this meant the exclusion of virtually all Spaniards from the pool of potential interpreters, the employment of Robles as a GRU station chief's interpreter would have been, to say the very least, highly implausible. Gorev had as many interpreters as he needed, all of whom were GRU personnel. At first, there was Paulina Abramson and then Emma Wolf, who was a captain in the GRU.[7] Whatever Robles was doing with the Russians, it was almost certainly not interpreting.

According to his close friend, the novelist Francisco Ayala, Robles, at the time of his arrest, was actually working as a translator in the cipher department of the Russian Embassy.[8] If it makes little sense that the Russians would place someone who was allegedly just a pro-Republican academic from an American university in such an immensely senior and sensitive position as interpreter to the GRU station chief, it makes even less sense that such a person should be given access to Soviet code books. Why should Robles, a man who apparently had learned Russian in order to be able to read nineteenth-century novels in the original but had never lived in, or even visited, Russia, be offered either position? It might be the case, as Fischer suggests, that Robles was useful as a highly presentable individual who spoke excellent English.[9] However, leaving aside the fact that Gorev spoke English, Robles' possible usefulness as an English-speaker does not resolve the issue of his 'reliability' for the Russians. Even less does it resolve the even more mysterious question of his rank. Many totally trusted Communists who excelled on the battlefield had to wait many months for promotion. For Robles to be in such a situation suggested that he had more Communist credentials than has hitherto been assumed. What is much more likely is that Robles was a liaison officer between General Miaja, the Republican Minister of War, and Gorev (in his capacity as Soviet Military Attaché). This was the view of the American Military Attaché Colonel Stephen Fuqua, who described Robles as 'a very ardent socialist with strong communist leanings'.[10] This would, of course, have given him access to considerable sensitive material. Indeed, given that the international situation obliged the Republic to play down its reliance on Soviet aid, any knowledge of Russian activities was sensitive.

Another mystery regarding José Robles was his relationship with his younger brother. The thirty-seven-year-old Captain Ramón Robles Pazos was a conservative, indeed reactionary, army officer who had made his career in the brutal colonial Army of Africa. In 1936, he was on the staff of the Infantry Academy housed in the Alcázar of Toledo.[11] At the beginning of the war, he was in Madrid and he tried, on 21 July, to rejoin his comrades who had joined the rebellion and entrenched themselves in the Alcázar. He was arrested in Getafe in the south of the capital and taken to an improvised prison (*checa*) in the Paseo de Delicias in Madrid. After being detained for only a matter of hours, he was released and ordered to present himself at the Ministry of War. For him not to have been imprisoned or shot was highly unusual, unless his swift release was secured by the intervention of his brother José. If that were the case, it would suggest either that José already enjoyed extraordinary influence in the first days of the war or had somehow persuaded Ramón's captors that he could convert him to the Republican cause. Ramón then survived for three months in Madrid while still refusing to serve the Republic. This again suggests both the exercise of considerable influence by someone, presumably José.

A likely side-effect, however, would have been the accretion of some suspicion around José Robles for protecting an evident traitor. Ramón was arrested again on 16 October 1936 on charges of refusing to do military service for the Republic and was imprisoned in the Cárcel Modelo. He was there during the evacuation and subsequent massacre of right-wing prisoners on 7 November. The principal victims targeted in that operation were army officers who might want to join the rebels whose conquest of Madrid was assumed to be imminent. Yet Ramón was untouched. This curious history is explicable only in terms of the sort of influence that could be wielded by someone of power in the Ministry of War, someone such as José Robles. On 17 November, Ramón was transferred to the prison near the Ventas bullring where he remained until, on 26 January 1937, he was tried for *desafección al régimen* (hostility to the Republic). Having apparently withdrawn his refusal to serve in the Republican forces, he was released on *libertad provisional*.

The charmed existence of Ramón Robles inevitably raised suspicions that his brother José was in contact with the Francoist fifth column. The Russians viewed the parlous situation of the Republic with some paranoia, shocked by the levels of disorganization and also treachery within the higher levels of the army and the administration. Given the constant sabotage activities of the rebel fifth columnists within Madrid, it was an issue to which they and the Republic's own nascent security services were highly sensitive. Accordingly, even if the suspicions were misplaced, in protecting his brother, Robles was living dangerously. The slightest hint that he was playing a double game would have been sufficient for the NKVD to eliminate him and would certainly explain his arrest in December.[12] Dos Passos would later be told that Robles was killed by 'a special section'. This may well have been a unit known as the Brigada Especial, which had been created in Spain with the collaboration of the NKVD department known as 'Administration of Special Tasks'. One of its principal operatives was the twenty-three-year-old Lithuanian, the Spanish-speaking Iosif Romualdovich Grigulevich, who would later be involved in early attempts to murder Trotsky. Among the activities of the Brigada Especial was the rooting out of the fifth column.[13]

In fact, José had been in prison for a month when Ramón secured his own release by withdrawing his opposition to serving the Republic. However, far from joining the Popular Army as he had sworn he would do, on 28 January 1937 Ramón took refuge in the Chilean Embassy until, three weeks later, he managed to move to the French Embassy, where he remained until January 1938. Then, with the help of the French authorities, he managed to get evacuated to France. Ramón's desertion would not have helped José's case and would have intensified suspicion about the nature of the contacts between the brothers. At best, Ramón may have been motivated only by a desire eventually to get to the rebel zone. At worst, however, it is possible that he was provoked into going into hiding at the Chilean and French Embassies by fear that, under interrogation, José might reveal the real nature of those contacts. Certainly, there is nothing about Ramón's subsequent career to suggest that his discussions with José were focused on helping the Republic. From France, after some extremely complicated adventures, he reached the rebel zone in May 1938. After the standard investigation into his activities in the Republican zone, he was incorporated into the Nationalist forces as a major, a promotion back-dated to 10 December 1936. Because of his African service, he was given command of a unit of Moroccan mercenaries (*fuerzas regulares indígenas*). Further investigation into his role within the Republic produced favourable reports from fifth columnists of his complete commitment to the rebel cause (*manifiestan conocen al mismo, constándoles es persona de ideas completamente afectas al Movimiento Nacional*). He was promoted to lieutenant colonel and decorated several times. In 1942, he fought in Russia as a volunteer with the Blue Division, the force sent by Franco in support of Hitler. Thereafter, he enjoyed a highly distinguished military career, being promoted to brigadier general in

1952, to major general in 1957 and to the highest rank in the Spanish Army, lieutenant general, in 1961.[14]

That José Robles might indeed have had something to hide regarding his links with his brother might be inferred from two letters he wrote in the autumn of 1936. Sent to his friend and head of department at Johns Hopkins University, Professor Henry Carrington Lancaster, the letters suggest that his loyalty to the Republic was not all that Dos Passos and other later commentators have assumed. Both were written in French, which may not be of significance since Lancaster was a French specialist. On the other hand, it seems odd since Lancaster was American and Robles was totally fluent in English. Accordingly, it is just possible that by writing to Lancaster in French, Robles might have been sending him some previously agreed message. Both letters were sent from the Russian headquarters in the Hotel Palace.

In the first, undated but postmarked 20 October 1936, Robles made it quite clear that he wanted to leave, he wrote:

> The only thing that I'm lacking at present is a letter from you – on official notepaper – saying that you need me back as soon as possible. I don't need money, but it would be prudent to deposit my cheque in the National City Bank of N.Y. There is a branch here. I think that anything might happen. My wife is no longer here, and it is possible that, at a given moment, I will have to leave. That is why I would like to have a certain sum at my disposal. See you soon. I will have such things to tell you!!!

The second, also undated, and for which the envelope does not survive, expressed even more strongly Robles' desire to leave:

> I wish it were me arriving instead of this letter, but for the moment there is no way out. However, don't believe the exaggerations of fascist propaganda. We are fine here and things will be sorted out. I expect a resolution to my case in a few days. I will write to you soon, but probably not from Madrid. Thank you for your concern, but finances are not a problem. We don't need the cheque. Later on I'll tell you where to send it. Despite the situation, I am busying myself with the file-cards for M.L.N. [*Modern Language Notes*]. You'll get them.[15]

Without the date of the second letter, it is impossible to know if it was written before or after his arrest. The suggestion that his next letter would not come from

Madrid implies that the letter was written at the end of October or the beginning of November, just before the evacuation of the government to Valencia. In that case, the phrase 'a resolution to my case' would imply that Robles was awaiting permission to leave the Ministry of War and the service of the Russians. In the unlikely case that the letter post-dates his arrest, the phrase would refer to his arrest, implying that he did not consider himself to be in real danger and that he was merely the victim of a misunderstanding which he would be able to clear up. However, it is much more likely that it was before, given that it was addressed from the Hotel Palace and that he was still in a position to occupy himself with file-cards for a scholarly journal.

When the government moved to Valencia, Gorev remained throughout the siege of Madrid but Robles was among the staff evacuated. There, Robles soon became an assiduous member of the *tertulia* in the popular café known as the Ideal Room. One day in early December, he told the American Military Attaché, Colonel Stephen Fuqua, that 'he had to leave Madrid because he was being persecuted by someone who was ignorantly denouncing him'. This makes little sense and sounds like Robles preparing the ground in advance of a possible denunciation. Another habitué of the Ideal Room was the novelist Francisco Ayala. 'One day' (*cierto día*) – Ayala does not mention the date in his memoirs – Robles failed to appear after lunch as he normally did. That same evening, Robles' wife, the tiny brunette Márgara Fernández de Villegas, accompanied by her two children, was to be seen frantically going from café to café asking if anyone had seen her husband. Apparently, José had been detained the night before in his own apartment by a group of men in plain clothes. It appears that he accompanied them without fuss. At the Soviet Embassy, Márgara was told that no one knew anything. However, she soon discovered that he had been accused of treachery and taken to the Cárcel de Extranjeros on the banks of the river Turia. She was able to visit him there on two separate occasions and told their daughter to walk up and down the pavement outside so that he could see her. Robles himself told her not to worry, that there had been a misunderstanding and it would soon be cleared up.[16]

The visits must have taken place after 6 January 1937, for on that day, Robles' son Francisco 'Coco' wrote to Henry Lancaster, his father's friend and head of the Department of Romance Languages at Johns Hopkins University:

> Through misunderstanding and perhaps the personal feelings of people with whom he worked my father José Robles has suffered a rather disagreeable mishap. My father was working lately at the Ministry of War

and more recently in the Junta de Defensa of Madrid. Because of the designs of certain people he was obliged to come to Valencia where he worked with the Soviet Embassy. By orders from Madrid he was arrested there. Nobody, from the Minister of State and the Russian Embassy down, has been able to find out a concrete reason for his ridiculous arrest. He has been arrested nearly a month already.

This would place the arrest a couple of days either side of 9 December. Because the family was running out of money, Coco went on to ask for financial help from the university and that any moneys be sent in such a way as to avoid the need for José Robles' signature: 'He is incommunicated. We haven't been able to come in touch with him in any way.'[17]

Wild rumours flew around Valencia about the disappearance of Robles. Some said that he had been arrested on espionage charges and shot within the Soviet Embassy. Of all the reasons given for his subsequent death, the most widely believed was that, in a café conversation, he had carelessly let slip a piece of sensitive military information which he could have known only by dint of his privileged access to coded telegrams. This is what Ayala believed and Louis Fischer also heard the same rumours. In fact, Fischer's unique combination of access to both the Russian hierarchy in Spain and to the highest levels of the Spanish Government gives considerable credence to his comments on the case – written after he had broken all ties with Communism. He wrote:

> He was not shot by the government, and I do not know whether he was shot, but he vanished about that time without leaving a trace. People affirmed that he had been smuggled out of Spain against his will and taken by boat to Russia. Whispers said he had talked too much and revealed military secrets in Madrid cafés. If that could have been proved it might have warranted turning him over to the Spanish government for trial, but not 'taking him for a ride'.[18]

Louis Fischer was not in the habit of repeating rumours just for the sake of filling pages. He had strict journalistic ethics as well as high-level contacts. His contacts spoke to him uninhibitedly because they trusted him never to reveal more than they were comfortable with. Accordingly, this passage takes on considerable significance. His assertion that the Spanish Government was not involved carries some weight. He was a close friend of various ministers, including Julio Álvarez del Vayo, who at the time was both Foreign Minister and Chief

Commissar for War. If Fischer's elimination of the Republican Government as a suspect is accepted, the hint that Robles was killed by the Russians is doubly significant. Taken with the suspicion that, to get the position that he occupied, Robles had to have close connections with the Russian security services, it might well explain why, at this relatively early stage, they had no compunction in eliminating him. In other words, they regarded him as one of their own and not merely a Spanish employee. Enquiries about Robles directed by the present author to a hitherto helpful member of Gorev's staff, who was a GRU interpreter during the Civil War and knew about the case, were met with a brusque refusal to comment.

What would make the Robles case notorious was the interest taken in it by John Dos Passos. He arrived in Spain on 8 April 1937, on a trip that he later described as 'so typical of the blundering of well-intentioned American liberals trying to make themselves useful in the world'. Since the outbreak of the war, he had been working with 'various friends' to find ways of persuading the Roosevelt administration to lift the embargo which prevented the Spanish Republic buying arms. It having been decided that a documentary about the Civil War would help get public opinion behind the campaign, he was now en route to Madrid where he intended to link up with Ernest Hemingway and the Dutch director Joris Ivens to make the film *The Spanish Earth*. Dos Passos intended Pepe Robles to be his first port of call: 'I knew that with his knowledge and taste he would be the most useful man in Spain for the purposes of our documentary film.' On reaching Valencia, he headed for the press office in the Calle Campaneros. On a nearby street corner, Dos Passos was introduced by the American journalist Griffin Barry to Kate Mangan, who remembered him as 'yellow, small and bespectacled'.[19]

When he got to the press office, and began asking for Robles, Dos Passos recalled much later:'faces took on a strange embarrassment. Behind the embarrassment was fear. No one would tell me where he could be found. When at last I found his wife she told me. He had been arrested by some secret section or other and was being held for trial.' Márgara asked him to try to find out what had happened to her husband by using his influence as an internationally celebrated novelist who was identified with the Republic's cause. He began to make enquiries in an effort to discover what Robles had been accused of. If Robles had been arrested by Grigulevich's Brigada Especial or by some other section of the secret police, whether Russian or Spanish, none of the functionaries that he visited would have known anything. Nevertheless, Dos Passos regarded their ignorance as only feigned and thus as deeply sinister: 'again the run-around, the look of fear,

fear for their own lives, in the faces of republican officials'. Grasping around for a story with which to fob him off, 'the general impression that the higher-ups in Valencia tried to give was that if Robles were dead he had been kidnapped and shot by anarchist "uncontrollables"'.[20]

Not long after the arrest of Robles, at some point in January, his family had been evicted from their flat, which was unlikely to have been a coincidence. In an overcrowded Valencia, Robles had a decent apartment only because of his military rank and position in the Ministry of War. To pay the rent on the sleazy apartment to which they had to move, 'Coco' Robles had taken the job in the press office. Márgara told Dos Passos that the last time that she saw her husband was 'in the hands of a Communist group of secret police in Valencia' in late January 1937.[21] Thereafter, Robles was transferred from the prison on the banks of the Turia to Madrid where, presumably, he was executed. On 9 April, the day after Dos Passos reached Valencia, Coco was told that his father was dead. His informant was his immediate boss in the press and propaganda office, Liston Oak, the man responsible for the daily English-language news release. The gloomy, self-obsessed Oak was a member of the American Communist Party, but was developing sympathy for the anti-Stalinist POUM.[22] Those who worked in the press with 'Coco' were appalled by the news about his father. At the time, the most vocal in expressing her outrage was the outspoken American Milly Bennet. An English colleague, Kate Mangan, tried later in her memoirs to explain what had happened to Robles: 'he had been engaged in rather hush-hush work. What happened remained a mystery; it was inexplicable but it leaked out despite efforts to hush it up on the part of our communist friends.'[23]

Ironically, 'one of our communist friends' who not only did not hush the case up but was instrumental in giving it notoriety was that bundle of introspective misery and political contradictions, Liston Oak. His involvement in the Robles case and in the subsequent estrangement between Dos Passos and Hemingway was considerable. It derived in the first instance from his contact with Coco Robles and subsequently with Dos Passos. When Dos Passos went to the press office on 9 April and Coco Robles told him what Oak had said about the death of his father, they both chose to believe that this was merely a rumour. In fact, Coco, his sister and mother would go on believing for quite some time thereafter that José Robles was alive. On 20 April, Coco wrote to Henry Lancaster, saying: 'From my father there is no definite news. Some even say that he is free and at one of the Madrid fronts. I am not inclined to believe this. The whole affair continues to be surrounded with great mystery. We do not know what to think or expect next.' Then, in late April or early May, Maurice Coindreau heard from Márgara that 'for over a month she has not heard from her husband, that she thinks he is still in Madrid although she cannot understand why he doesn't communicate with her'. Coindreau was godfather to Robles' daughter Margarita (Miggie) and was also Dos Passos' French translator. As late as 17 July, Coco wrote to Professor Lancaster saying that there was still no news of his father.[24]

Meanwhile, on 9 April, Dos Passos was deeply affected by finding Márgara exhausted, her face drawn, living in a sordid and grimy apartment block, and by her desperate request that he try to find out what had happened to José. As a distinguished foreign visitor, Dos Passos was staying at the Hotel Colón, which had been renamed the Casa de Cultura and reserved for displaced and/or visiting intellectuals, artists and writers. Locally, it was known as the Casa de los Sabios (the house of the wise men), although Kate Mangan regarded it as 'a kind of zoo for intellectuals'.[25] When he was back in America, Dos Passos wrote about going back to his room and brooding on what Márgara had told him:

> It's quiet at night in the Casa de los Sabios. Lying in bed it's hard not to think of what one had heard during the day of the lives caught in a tangle, the prisoners huddled in stuffy rooms waiting to be questioned, the woman with her children barely able to pay for the cheap airless apartment while she waits for her husband. It's nothing they have told her, he was just taken away for questioning, certain little matters to be cleared up, wartime, no need for alarm. But the days have gone by, months, no news. The standing in line at the police station, the calling up of influential friends, the slow-growing terror tearing the woman to pieces.

He went on to imagine what had happened to his friend:

> And the man stepping out to be court-martialed by his own side. The conversational tone of the proceedings. A joke or a smile that lets the blood flow easy again, but the gradual freezing recognition of the hundred ways a man may be guilty, the remark you dropped in a café that somebody wrote down, the letter you wrote last year, the sentence you scribbled on a scratchpad, the fact that your cousin is in the ranks of the enemy, and the strange sound your own words make in your ears when they are quoted in the indictment. They shove a cigarette in your hand and you walk out into the courtyard to face six men you have never seen before. They take aim. They wait for the order. They fire.[26]

Those words were written months after. For now, Dos Passos was still uncertain of his friend's fate but he feared the worst. Playing on his celebrity, he had been to the Ministry of Foreign Affairs and asked to see the minister himself. His subsequent writings make it apparent that, although he had turned up without an appointment, he was mortified to be told that the minister could not see him until the following day. Julio Álvarez del Vayo, the Minister of Foreign Affairs and ultimate head of the press and propaganda machinery, was in fact an incredibly busy man. The government was in the throes of considerable internal upheaval. The Republic was fighting for its life, its forces exhausted after the battles of Jarama and Guadalajara, and facing a massive assault on the Basque Country. Del Vayo was the Commissar for War as well as Foreign Minister. In the latter capacity, he had to deal with the Republic's most difficult problem, the non-intervention policy of the British and French Governments that deprived it of the possibility of buying arms with which to defend itself. Inevitably, he did not just drop everything to see Dos Passos. Nevertheless, despite his myriad occupations, Álvarez del Vayo managed to make time to see him on the following day. Regarding Robles, he 'professed ignorance and chagrin'. This might have been expected and was almost certainly the truth. Nevertheless, he promised to try to find out what had happened.[27] Although Dos Passos would never forgive Álvarez del Vayo for what he considered to be his snub and his duplicity, there is no reason whatsoever why the Minister of Foreign Affairs would know anything about the fate of a functionary working in the Ministry of War with the representative of the Russian GRU.

Thereafter, Dos Passos went to Madrid to work on the film *Spanish Earth* and, if possible, pursue his investigations into the fate of Robles. To do that, he had two advantages: his celebrity as an internationally acclaimed novelist; and a prior acquaintance with the head of Republican counter-espionage (Comisario General de Investigación y Vigilancia), Pepe Quintanilla. He knew Pepe through his brother Luis, a famous Republican artist and one of his oldest and closest friends in Spain. Pepe and Luis were also good friends of Hemingway, who was going to be intensely displeased by Dos Passos' efforts to find out what had happened to Robles. There may have been some tension between them over the direction to be taken in *Spanish Earth*. Hemingway was more comfortable concentrating on the military achievements of the Republic, whereas Dos Passos was happier showing the suffering of ordinary people and the hopes raised by social revolution. Nevertheless, this was not a bone of contention. It is more likely that Dos Passos was becoming uncomfortable and suspicious about the growing influence of the Communists within the Republic as they endeavoured to impose order. In contrast, Hemingway regarded their activities as a crucial contribution to mounting an effective war effort.

When Dos Passos reached the Hotel Florida in Madrid, everything he did and said seemed to provoke Hemingway's scorn. He had failed to bring any food with him. There was also a certain friction deriving from the fact that Dos Passos and his wife Katy were close friends of Hemingway's wife Pauline. Dos Passos could not conceal his discomfort at the fact that Ernest was conducting a highly visible affair with Martha Gellhorn.[28] In his thinly fictionalized account, Dos Passos wrote of Martha: 'It becomes immediately clear that she doesn't like Jay [Dos Passos] any better than he likes her.'[29] Their mutual friend, Josephine Herbst, would be a privileged observer of the breakdown of the relationship between Hemingway and Dos Passos. She noted in her diary that Hemingway often made derogatory remarks about Dos Passos' wife Katy, irritated because she was such a good friend of Pauline. His annoyance was also reflected in complaints that Dos Passos had 'no guts' and 'no balls'.[30]

Trying to explain the friction between the two, Josie Herbst wrote later that Hemingway was determined to be '*the* war writer of his age' and that he 'seemed to be naively embracing on the simpler levels the current ideologies at the very moment when Dos Passos was urgently questioning them'. Perhaps too, as he posed ever more as the wise combat veteran, he resented the fact that Dos Passos knew how little combat he had actually seen. Or maybe he was just annoyed that Dos Passos did not share his visceral enjoyment of the war. Josie noted that there was 'a kind of splurging magnificence about Hemingway at the Florida, a crackling generosity whose underside was a kind of miserliness. He was stingy with his feelings to anyone who broke his code, even brutal, but it is only fair to say that Hemingway was never anything but faithful to the code he set up for himself.' However, it was not just that Dos Passos was anything but ostentatiously macho. Rather, the key issue was Hemingway's annoyance about his friend's insistent enquiries about Robles. Josie could feel the irritation growing between them: 'Hemingway was worried because Dos was conspicuously making inquiries and might get everybody into trouble if he persisted. "After all", he warned, "this is a war"', whereas Dos Passos refused to believe that his friend could be a traitor.[31]

In Dos Passos' fictional version, he gives a flavour of their disagreements over Robles. George Elbert Warner (the character based on Hemingway) asked the hero (Jay Pignatelli) why he was looking worried, saying: 'If it's your professor bloke's disappearance, think nothing of it…People disappear every day.' As soon as Sidney Franklin ('Cookie' in the novel) left the room, Warner screamed in Jay's ear: 'Don't put your mouth to this Echevarría [Robles] business…not even before

Cookie. Cookie's the rightest guy in the world, but he might get potted one night. The Fifth Column is everywhere. Just suppose your professor took a powder and joined the other side.' When Jay protested that Echevarria/Robles was of unimpeachable loyalty, Warner's girlfriend, Hilda Glendower (Martha Gellhorn), allegedly chipped in, 'like a blast of cold air', saying: 'Your enquiries have already caused us embarrassment.'[32]

Apart from *Century's Ebb*, the most commonly used source for the disagreements between Dos and Hemingway over Robles is the fragment of memoir by Josephine Herbst, 'The Starched Blue Sky of Spain', although her unpublished diary contains important additional information. Josie Herbst had arrived in Valencia about a week before Dos Passos. She had come to Spain not as a fully accredited correspondent of any newspaper. Rather, her biographer, Elinor Langer, considered that, as a lifelong leftist, Josie just wanted to be able to experience the revolutionary events there. According to Stephen Koch, she was a trusted Comintern operative and 'was sent to Spain to help monitor and control the American literary celebrities in Madrid'. To this end, he claimed, she had been invited by 'the Republic's propaganda office' to make radio broadcasts. It is highly unlikely that she had the sinister function attributed to her by Koch. Indeed, her personal notes reveal not the slightest interest in the political stances of anyone that she wrote about. However, she certainly made at least one broadcast 'from a cellar deep underground in Madrid'. It is true that she had set off for Spain rather precipitately, failing to get a newspaper assignment, and had secured only the vaguest expressions of interest from magazine editors who would be glad to consider articles from a 'human interest' or 'women's angle'. However, she seems to have written to Otto Katz, whom she had met briefly in Paris years before, to let him know about her trip and to ask his advice about getting into Spain. His wife, Ilsa, replied briefly, offering to help Josie should she encounter any difficulties.[33]

Thus, despite her lack of newspaper credentials, but because of her still current, albeit now forgotten, celebrity as a writer, she was supplied with a letter of introduction to Álvarez del Vayo from the Republican press agency in Paris, Otto Katz's Agence Espagne. If indeed he received her in Valencia, Álvarez del Vayo must quickly have passed her on to the press bureau. There, she was given anything but the privileged treatment that might have been expected if she was really an important Comintern agent on a mission personally backed by the Minister of Foreign Affairs. In fact, she was kept hanging around as befitted someone with no proper journalistic credentials. She complained: 'I had been assured at the press bureau that I would get to go places, but for days I was suspended, wondering. Where?'[34]

In the published memoir of her Spanish experience, she claims that it was told in strict confidence by someone in Valencia that Robles had been shot as a spy. She does not say who told her. Koch has claimed that the 'authority' in question was Julio Álvarez del Vayo, who had allegedly received Herbst for a lengthy conversation when she delivered her letter of introduction from the Agence Espagne, although there is no evidence for this. In fact, Josephine Herbst does not say that she was told by anyone in authority. However, in a letter to Bruce Bliven of the *New Republic,* she wrote: 'My informant was not an "American Communist sympathizer" but a Spaniard *and a responsible person* [added by hand] and I was told that he had worked in the Ministry of War and documents had been found in his possession proving or appearing to prove that he had direct connection with Franco's side.' This would rule out Liston Oak, whom she would have met when she visited the press office to arrange transport to Madrid. On the other hand, it would rule in Constancia de la Mora, whom she almost certainly saw as well. Her informant, whoever it was, told her that she must swear to keep the secret just as he had been sworn to secrecy by someone 'higher up'. This in itself eliminates Álvarez del Vayo, since the only person 'higher up' than the Foreign Minister was the prime minister, Francisco Largo Caballero, and it is inconceivable that that highly moral anti-Communist would be involved in covering up an apparent assassination by the Russians. The reason for all this secrecy was, she was told, that the authorities 'were beginning to be worried about Dos Passos's zeal, and fearing that he might turn against their cause if he discovered the truth, hoped to keep him from finding out anything about it while he was in Spain'. This makes it much more likely that her information originated in the press office. On the other hand, it does not explain why telling Josie increased the possibility of keeping the news from Dos Passos.[35]

Once in Madrid, she was given a safe-conduct by the military authorities, dated 3 April 1937.[36] Given that Dos Passos did not reach Valencia until 8 April, this would mean that she had enquired about Robles about a week before he arrived. It could be, as Elinor Langer suggests, that she was innocently asking for Robles simply because Dos Passos had given her his name as someone that she ought to meet. In her published account, her informant chose to unburden himself or herself to Josie about the authorities' concerns regarding Dos Passos and the Robles case only because, she was told, it was known that Dos Passos was an old friend of hers. If the informant was Constancia de la Mora, she could certainly have been told about this friendship by Liston Oak, a fellow American leftist and a mutual acquaintance of both Josie and Dos Passos. Yet for all that they were friends, in neither her published version nor in her unpublished diary did Josie record telling

Dos Passos anything about the case, although it is extremely unlikely that he had not confided in her his worries about Robles.

All subsequent accounts of the Robles case and its damaging impact on the Hemingway–Dos Passos friendship have taken their cue from Josephine Herbst's account published in 1960. That version goes as follows. For all that she was sworn to secrecy, Josie did choose to tell Hemingway. She says that he broached the subject first, after the particularly frightening artillery bombardment that shook the Hotel Florida at dawn on 22 April. Just after she had snapped at him, tired and tetchy, saying that she didn't feel like being a Girl Scout, he invited her to his room for a brandy, not so much to console her as to urge her to tell Dos Passos to stop stirring things up over the Robles case: 'It was going to throw suspicion on all of us and get us into trouble. This was a war.' He informed her that Pepe Quintanilla, the 'head of the Department of Justice', had already told Dos Passos that Robles was still alive and would get a fair trial. He went on to say that Quintanilla was 'a swell guy' and that she should get to know him. She was initially inhibited by her promise of secrecy, and less than impressed by his fears that Dos Passos' insistent enquiries were fomenting unease among the denizens of the Hotel Florida. However, in the face of Hemingway's brash confidence that all was well with Robles, she finally blurted out what she knew.

She portrays herself as outraged by what seemed to be Pepe Quintanilla's duplicity, although her memories of him were probably coloured by a later encounter with him: 'I could not believe Quintanilla so good a guy if he could let Dos Passos remain in anguished ignorance or if the evidence was so clear as not to admit contradiction. I felt that Dos should be told, not because he might bring danger down on us but because the man was dead.' Thus, she revealed that Robles had been shot as a spy – 'Quintanilla should have told Dos'. On hearing this, Hemingway apparently had no difficulty in accepting that Robles was a fascist spy. Josie insisted that Dos Passos be told but in a way that the information would not seem to be coming from her. She concocted a rather ramshackle and devious solution to safeguard her own promise of silence, although hardly the cruelly sinister one imagined by Stephen Koch in his book on the subject. She suggested that Ernest pass on the bad news but say only that he had been told by 'someone from Valencia who was passing through but whose name he must withhold'. Hemingway, who was happy to accept without question that Robles had been guilty of espionage, apparently agreed with 'too cheerful a readiness – I don't think he doubted for a minute that Robles was guilty if Quintanilla said so'. And there was an imminent opportunity to tell Dos Passos whatever it was they had planned, for all the correspondents were about to go to a lunch at the headquarters of the XV International Brigade that very afternoon.[37]

Now, it is certainly the case that, on the morning of 22 April, when he shaved so calmly and appeared so at ease, Dos Passos still entertained hope that Robles might not be dead. He had made enquiries at the United States Embassy and been told by a third party that Robles had been seen alive in a prison camp by the United States Military Attaché, Colonel Stephen Fuqua, on 26 March.[38] However, by mid-morning of 22 April, little hope remained. The encounter between Josie and Hemingway over a snifter of brandy did not take place quite as described in 'The Starched Blue Sky of Spain'. What Josie wrote in her diary at the time makes much more sense: 'Dos comes in. Has found out Robles executed. Wants to investigate. Discuss with Hem danger of D. investigating. R. bad egg given fair trial – give away military secrets.' Accordingly, there was no need for a devious plot to work out how to tell Dos Passos that Robles was dead. On the other hand, there was a need to explain to him why it had happened and perhaps thereby stop him stirring things up about it. It is reasonable to assume that Dos Passos had left the room when Josie and Hemingway started to discuss 'the danger of Dos investigating'. If Hemingway was right and Robles was 'a bad egg', had been given a fair trial and been found guilty of giving away military secrets, then that was what Dos Passos should be told. In her June 1939 letter to Bruce Bliven of the *New Republic*, Josephine Herbst wrote: 'It has always seemed to me and did then that it was a tragic mistake not to give Dos whatever evidence there was about the case and of the death.'[39] This suggests not that she had wanted him to be told that Robles was dead – after all, he already knew – but to be informed of the process that had led to his arrest and execution.

Later that day, a long lunch party took place at a castle that had once belonged to the Duque de Tovar, near El Escorial. The fiesta was being held to celebrate the incorporation of the XV International Brigade into the Republican Army. It was there that Dos Passos was to be told. But told what? He already knew that Robles was dead but not the circumstances. It is extremely likely that his informant that morning had been Pepe Quintanilla. As Comisario General de Investigación y Vigilancia, he was one of the very few people in a position to know what had happened and even to know about the existence of Grigulevich and the Brigada Especial. Moreover, as the brother of Dos Passos' intimate friend Luis Quintanilla, Pepe was the only person in the know prepared to talk to him. In 1939, Dos Passos referred to having been told regretfully by 'the then chief of the Republican counterespionage service' [Pepe Quintanilla] of Robles' death at the hands of 'a special section'. In his later novel, he invents a party where 'Juanito Posada' (Pepe

79

Quintanilla) told him: 'The man has been shot.' When 'Jay Pignatelli' (Dos) asked why, 'Juanito Posada' replied: 'Who knows? We are living in terrible times. To overcome them we have to be terrible ourselves.'[40] Although the time and place are different in the novel, there is no doubt that it was Pepe who revealed that Robles had been shot and that he did so on the morning of 22 April. The tone of what little is known of Pepe's explanation suggests a desire to let Dos Passos down as gently as possible. Years later, Luis Quintanilla told a friend in New York that Robles had been arrested because he was known to have handed sensitive information to the fifth column. To soften the blow, Pepe refrained from telling Dos Passos that his friend was a fascist spy. That is surely what Josie Herbst and Hemingway decided to tell him. If anything would make Dos Passos stop making awkward enquiries and embarrassing himself as well as them, surely that would.[41]

Whatever Hemingway told Dos Passos, he allegedly did so in the most abrupt and insensitive way. According to his biographer, Townsend Ludington, Dos Passos was distressed by 'Ernest's abrasive manner and secretiveness, which seemed to him a kind of treason'.[42] What happened that day at the fiesta for the XV Brigade has been widely seen as the culmination of the breakdown of the Hemingway–Dos Passos relationship. Certainly, Dos Passos wrote in his novel that: 'The fiesta out at the Fifteenth Brigade broke my heart.' Yet, in his contemporary factual account, 'The Fiesta at the Fifteenth Brigade', he made no mention of any unpleasantness with Hemingway. Nor, in her diary, does Josephine Herbst, who says only that he and Dos sat together at lunch. In her published version, she comments only on Dos' agitation at the fact that Hemingway would not reveal the identity of the 'someone from Valencia who was passing through'. Obviously he could not do so since the 'someone' was an invention of Josie. However, in her 1939 letter to Bruce Bliven, she wrote: 'It should be remembered that Dos hated war of all kinds and suffered in Madrid not only from the fate of his friend but from the attitude of certain people on the fringe of war who appeared to be taking it as a sport. A deep revulsion followed.'

According to Stephen Koch, what Josie and Hemingway planned to do at the International Brigade lunch was publicly to humiliate Dos Passos, expose him in public as the friend of a fascist spy: 'she had quietly and discreetly handed Hemingway the exact weapon she knew he was looking for. And then, just as quietly and discreetly, she had shown him how to use it.'[43] There is no evidence whatsoever to justify this assertion. Whatever Hemingway said to Dos Passos, he said quietly as they talked together. There is no mention of any of this malice in either of Josie's versions. And there is good reason to think that, if there was malice aforethought, she would have said so in her diary. For Josie Herbst was not without a nasty side, but it was focused not on the enemies of the Comintern but on women prettier than herself who got more attention than she did. While waiting for the car to go to lunch, she watched the glamorous Martha Gellhorn with loathing: 'Pushing whore like M gets pretty much around on what she's got. Don't mean in the head. The pants. Plays all. Take all. Never speaks of anyone not a name. Glib stupid tongue.' When they arrived at the fiesta, she switched her venom to María Teresa de León, the sensual blonde wife of the poet Rafael Alberti, who was the centre of all male attention: 'Marie T in coral earrings & brooch, scarf, stouter & lush.' Josie was irritated to see María Teresa, chirping trivialities like birdsong, surrounded by admiring men. The fact that less attention was paid to her than to the beautiful and the famous is by far the greatest preoccupation of Josie's account of the fiesta.[44]

Pepe Quintanilla's role in the Robles case was almost certainly confined to telling Dos Passos about the execution and giving him a sanitized version of how it had come about. However, he seems by association to have acquired an aura of guilt in the affair. This picture of Pepe Quintanilla as a monster who typified the Republican security services derives from the accounts by Josie Herbst and Virginia Cowles of a lunch with him and Hemingway on 28 April. Because of Josie's published account, and the fact that he is loosely portrayed as Antonio, the 'thin-lipped' security chief in Act II of Hemingway's *The Fifth Column*, Quintanilla has been enshrined in Carlos Baker's phrase as the 'thin-lipped executioner of Madrid'. A week after the fiesta for the XV Brigade, Hemingway, Virginia Cowles and Josephine Herbst were having lunch at the restaurant of the Hotel Gran Vía. Virginia noticed 'a fastidious-looking man dressed from head to toe in dove grey. He had the high forehead and long fingers of the intellectual and wore horn-rimmed spectacles which added to his thoughtful appearance.' Noticing her interest, Hemingway could not resist showing off his inside knowledge and his contacts, saying dramatically, 'That is the chief executioner of Madrid', and inviting Pepe to join them. He did so on the condition that they let him buy them another carafe of wine.

First Pepe regaled them with stories of the first days of the war when foolhardy *Madrileños* had stormed the Montaña barracks where the rebels had made their stronghold. As Quintanilla spoke, shells began to rain down and he coolly counted the explosions, pouring wine, one, talking, then two, three, four. By the time he got to ten, the air was thick with fear. As the wine flowed ever more freely, Pepe kept counting, flushed now and increasingly drunk. When Hemingway pressed Pepe to talk about the struggle against the fifth column, the atmosphere grew even thicker. Hemingway beamed and the women squirmed as he told them about an officer who soiled himself 'huddled in a corner' then 'had to be carried out and shot like a dog'. Nevertheless, when two soldiers and a girl walked, arm in arm, down the middle of the street in the direction from which the shells were coming, a frantic Quintanilla tried solicitously to stop them.

When Hemingway said he wanted to get back because he was worried about 'the blonde' (*la rubia*), Martha, Quintanilla wouldn't hear of it and insisted that they wait until the danger was over. He ordered brandy and began to flirt outrageously with Virginia, which did not endear him to Josie, who was sourly wondering how Miss Cowles managed to get down the rubble-strewn Gran Vía from the Florida to the restaurant on such high heels. Quintanilla said he would divorce his wife, marry Virginia and make his wife do the cooking. At the time, they all laughed but, in retrospect, Virginia Cowles remembered only what she took to be sadism in 'his bright marble-brown eyes'. When they left the restaurant, Hemingway said to her: 'Now remember, he's mine.' He thus gave the game away, revealing that he saw Pepe both as a prize with which to show off his own privileged status and also as a unique source and even as a character in a short story or a play. He later used the conversation about the deaths of rightists in his play *The Fifth Column*, rendering Pepe as 'Antonio'.[45]

This hair-raising lunch took place after a distressed Dos Passos had left Madrid. He spent some time in Fuentidueña del Tajo, a village where he wanted to film an irrigation project for the documentary *Spanish Earth*. Then he went back one more time to Valencia to tell Márgara Villegas what he had learned and to try in vain to get some answers from Julio Álvarez del Vayo. The minister still knew nothing, but at least he promised to try to secure a death certificate so that Márgara could collect José's life insurance.[46] The fact that he did not do so would rankle with Dos Passos in later years. However, in a letter to Claude Bowers at the time, he commented: 'As nothing has come from Del Vayo, I imagine he has forgotten about it, certainly he has enough on his shoulders not to remember small personal details.'[47] In fact, Del Vayo was replaced as Foreign Minister in mid-May 1937 and was unable to fulfil his promise. If Dos Passos did indeed inform Márgara Villegas of what he had been told, neither she nor her children chose to believe him. Letters written by Coco show that they continued to hope for more than two and a half months after Dos Passos' departure from Spain. At the end of April, Dos Passos left for France, stopping en route for a few days in Barcelona.

Someone else in the Catalan capital was Liston Oak, who had been trying to get away from his job in Valencia for some time, citing health problems. He had spent time in Madrid in April; he was investigating the possibility of opening a bureau there. He was photographed there with Hemingway and Virginia Cowles in mid-April. Given the camaraderie among the correspondents in the Hotel Florida, it is highly unlikely that he did not also see Dos Passos. Unnerved by the constant bombardments, he returned to Valencia. He stayed only long enough to collect his belongings and left for Barcelona, telling his boss, Constancia de la Mora, that it was merely for a short visit. It is not clear whether he planned to stay there, given a burgeoning sympathy with the POUM, or was already intending to return to the USA. At the Valencia press office, it took some weeks before they realized that he would not be coming back.[48]

In Barcelona, Dos Passos visited POUM headquarters and spoke with Juan Andrade and Andreu Nin.[49] According to his fictionalized account, in his hotel lobby, he also bumped into George Orwell:

> a gangling Englishman with his arm in a sling. He was wearing a threadbare uniform. A squashed overseas cap on the side of his head nestled in abundant wavy black hair. His long face with deep lines in the cheeks, was distinguished by a pair of exceptionally fine dark eyes. They had a farsighted look, like a seaman's eyes. [...] an extraordinary sense of relaxation came over him when he realized he was talking to an honest man. All these weeks since he'd landed in that horrid Casa de la Cultura in Valencia he hadn't dared talk frankly to anyone. At first he was afraid of saying something that would endanger his chances of smuggling Ramón [José Robles] out of the country and afterwards he was afraid some misinterpreted word of his might lessen Amparo's [Márgara] chances of getting out with the children.[50]

Although the notion of him smuggling José Robles and his family out of Spain was entirely invented, there is no reason to doubt that Dos Passos met Orwell. It is confirmed elsewhere, although it should be noted that, in the novel, he places the meeting during the May Days, when in fact he had already left Barcelona. Eighteen years later, in his factual account, Dos Passos wrote in similar terms of Orwell:

> His face had a sick drawn look. I suppose he was already suffering from the tuberculosis that later killed him. He seemed inexpressibly weary. We didn't talk very long but I can remember the sense of assuagement, of relief from strain I felt at last to be talking to an honest man. The officials I'd talked to in the past weeks had been gulls most of them, or self-deceivers, or else had been trying to pull the wool over my eyes.[51]

The drama surrounding the Robles case was now intensified one more time by Liston Oak. He visited Dos Passos one night in his Barcelona hotel claiming to be on the run from the security services after having been denounced as a Trotskyist. It is more than probable that Oak had become uncomfortable about the possible consequences of his lurch away from the American Communist Party and towards the anti-Stalinists of the POUM. This was surely related to his constant complaints about his health. However, this is some distance from Koch's assertion that 'Liston was also sick spiritually. There was a pestilence of fear and loathing in the depths of his soul.'[52] Liston Oak may have been 'sick with fear', but he was starkly dramatizing the circumstances of his leisurely separation from the Republican press service when he said that he had escaped by the skin of his teeth after discovering that he been reported to be politically unreliable. What actually happened is that he had gone to Barcelona, and made contact with Andreu Nin, the POUM leader. In late April, he had written an article mentioning his meeting with Nin and sympathizing with the POUM standpoint that the war could not be won if the revolution was crushed. The article was written before the events of May 1937 and the disappearance of Nin, but would be published in London only afterwards, in mid-May. George Orwell read it in hospital three weeks later and found it 'very good and well balanced'.[53] Having worked in the English-language section of the Republic's press office, Oak cannot have failed to realize that the publication of the article would be considered a subversive act, given the POUM's opposition to the government's policy of prioritizing the war effort over the revolution.

However, it is possible that, once in Barcelona, the already timorous Oak may have been startled into an outright funk by a chance meeting with a Russian agent whom he had known in New York as George Mink. His real name was Mink Djhordis and he was born in Lithuania. He was said to be closely related to Solomon Abramovich Lozovksy, the head of the Profintern, the Soviet international of trade unions. According to testimony given to the House Committee on Un-American Activities, he was a serving officer of Soviet military intelligence. Despite Mink being a taxi-driver in Philadelphia, and utterly ignorant of matters nautical, Lozovsky had used his influence to raise him to an important position in the Marine Workers' Industrial Union. He was arrested in Copenhagen in 1935 and jailed for eighteen months after police discovered espionage paraphernalia in his room. He was also linked to political assassinations in Germany and Spain. It has been suggested that he was one of the murderers of the Soviet defector, Ignace Reiss, in Switzerland.[54] Mink did not know of Oak's drift towards anti-Stalinist communism, invited him to have a drink and informed him that the Communists planned to move against the POUM and the anarchists in Barcelona within a couple of days. Oak, already jumpy, went into panic mode, assuming that he would be among those pursued.[55]

On the basis of Oak's panic-stricken pleas, Dos Passos sheltered him in his hotel room and then took him out of Spain as his 'private secretary'. In *Century's Ebb*, Dos Passos portrays Oak as 'Don Carp', suggesting both his endless whinge-ing and the fact that there was something fishy about him. In that version, he wrote: 'I thought that Carp was a down-the-line dyed-in-the-wool Party member, but it turned out the poor guy had associated with some splinter in Wisconsin.'[56] Back in Valencia, wrote Kate Mangan,

> it seeped through that Liston was consorting with the POUM a great deal in Barcelona. He left shortly before the May rising in that town, in haste, we heard, with the police on his track. It was much later that we heard from America that he had been conducting virulent written and spoken propaganda against the Spanish Republic and the war, and that he used his position 'employed in a responsible post by the Government' to lend authority to his statements.

This may be a reference to information received from Kitty Bowler who, on 22 June, wrote to Tom Wintringham that news of 'the Liston affair' had reached a left-wing friend in New York.[57]

The fact that Oak had written a pro-POUMist article, in the wartime circum-stances, would certainly have rendered unlikely his continued employment at the Valencia press office. It might even have attracted the attention of the secret police. However, Koch's suggestion that Oak feared that the NKVD would use its 'elite squad for foreign assassinations, the Bureau of Special Tasks' to hunt him relent-lessly to the ends of the earth is belied by the fact that, when he returned to the USA, Oak continued to publish numerous pro-anarchist and pro-POUM arti-cles fiercely critical of Communist policy. Oak's criticism of Stalin was even quoted, less than favourably, by Trotsky himself in an article entitled 'Stalinism and Bolshevism', written on 28 August 1937. Elsewhere, in an article entitled 'Their Morals and Ours', Trotsky wrote: 'Liston Oak until recently enjoyed such confidence from the Comintern that it entrusted him with conducting the English propaganda for Republican Spain. This did not, naturally, hinder him, once he had relinquished his post, from likewise relinquishing the Marxist alphabet.'[58] Most remarkably, for a man terrified of Russian hit-men in general and George Mink in particular, he wrote in one of his subsequent articles: 'I met George Mink,

American Communist, who boasted about his part in organizing the Spanish GPU and offered me a job – to put the finger on "untrustworthy" comrades entering Spain to fight against fascism, such as the members of the British Independent Labour Party (ILP) and the American Socialist Party.'[59]

Once over the Spanish frontier, Oak and Dos Passos continued on to the United States. While Dos Passos and his wife waited for the boat train in Paris, Hemingway came to the station to see them off. Their pleasure at this unexpected privilege was soon chilled when they saw that 'his face was a thundercloud'. Hemingway asked him what he planned to do about the Robles issue. Dos Passos replied: 'I'll tell the truth as I see it. Right now I've got to straighten out my ideas. You people are trying to believe it is one isolated instance. It isn't.' When Hemingway tried to point out the circumstances of the war, Dos Passos asked: 'What's the point of fighting a war for civil liberties, if you destroy civil liberties in the process?' A furious Hemingway growled: 'Civil liberties shit. Are you with us or are you against us?' When Dos Passos shrugged, Hemingway raised his fist as if to hit him and threatened: 'These people know how to turn you into a back number. I've seen them do it. What they did once they can do again.' Katy replied: 'Why, Ernest, I never heard anything so despicably opportunistic in my life.' If it was not quite the end of a great friendship, it was the beginning of the end.[60]

When Dos Passos finally reached New York, he met Maurice Coindreau and told him what he thought had happened to their friend. Coindreau wrote to Henry Lancaster, Robles' head of department at Johns Hopkins:

> The news he gave me are most distressing and <u>absolutely true</u> since he himself was in Valencia and Madrid and got his information on the spot. José Robles was shot sometime in the Winter. The last time that Márgara saw him was in January, in jail. (Therefore, no matter how much denial the government send, they just shamelessly lie). He told her that he was going to be transferred to Madrid. She never heard from him since. Dos Passos could not find out whether he was shot in Valencia or in Madrid, whether he was tried or simply executed.

Astonishingly, the letter ended with the request:

> will you be kind enough to mention to <u>no one</u> that the news were brought by Dos Passos. He has many connections with the Communist Party and he might get in trouble if they knew that he has revealed what the Spanish

government has done to an American professor who had never in his life taken any interest in politics neither on one side or the other.[61]

It looks as if Hemingway's contemptuous warning had had an effect.

In the spring and summer of 1937, Márgara was devastated and very ill. When she finally accepted that José was dead, she wrote to Esther Crooks, a friend from Baltimore: 'I feel so crushed and so sad that I am hardly alive. I have been left pathetically incomplete, incapable of doing anything'. To her grief was added worry over their financial situation and the need to get a death certificate in order to collect on José's life insurance. She wrote to Miss Crooks about her situation: 'so far, since the Government hasn't intervened, everything is still wrapped in mystery. No one can justify what happened and no one wants to admit a mistake. The internal situation is so complicated, so volatile and so complex that until this is all over, it's going to be difficult to get anything'.[62]

Strangely, despite the execution of José Robles, his family remained loyal to the Republic and stayed in Spain when it would have been relatively easy for them to return to the United States. In letters to Esther Crooks and Henry Lancaster, Márgara made it clear that she did not blame the Republic. To Miss Crooks, she wrote: 'It is still so incomprehensible for us that at times I think that I am going to awake from this nightmare. We still don't know anything concrete about what happened other than the fact of his death and that the government had nothing to do with it. Personal hatred or a fatal mistake appears to be the only explanation. And he had worked so hard and with such enthusiasm for the cause'. She wrote in similar terms to Henry Lancaster: 'Nothing makes sense to us. His loyalty to the Government was absolute. He gave everything and risked everything with such generosity in order to help what we consider such a just cause that the only explanation is a fatal error or an act of personal revenge'. Coco continued to work in the press office in Valencia and Miggie worked in a photographic laboratory of the Ministry of Propaganda. And once Márgara recovered her strength, she also began to work in the press office.[63]

Not long after Dos Passos left Spain, the press office received a visit from Elliott Paul, the American novelist who had just completed his book on the repression in Ibiza. Constancia de la Mora assigned Coco Robles to accompany him on a trip to Madrid. The middle-aged novelist and the boy became good friends on the journey. During one of their late-night discussions about literature, Elliott Paul mentioned Dos Passos and said: 'I don't know what has come over Dos Passos. I saw him in Paris and he won't even take an interest in Spain anymore – says he doesn't care. He is full of some story about a friend of his being shot as a spy, some college professor from Johns Hopkins.' With great sadness, but also notable firmness, Coco replied: 'I hope that will not make Mr Dos Passos lose his interest in the fight against fascism in Spain. The man he spoke of was my father.'[64]

Coco moved with the rest of the press office personnel when the capital was transferred from Valencia to Barcelona in November 1937. He had often tried to volunteer for the Republican army, lying about his age in order to do so. In 1938, he would eventually be successful. He joined a guerrilla unit, was captured on his first mission and spent many years in a Francoist prison. His sister Miggie joined the Communist Youth Movement, the Juventudes Unificadas Socialistas, and took part in morale-boosting visits to International Brigade units at the battle-front and a propaganda tour of the United States. After the government moved from Valencia to Barcelona, Márgara Villegas also continued to work in the press office with Coco and Constancia de la Mora. The Robles family became friendly not just with Constancia but also with Julio Álvarez del Vayo, despite Dos Passos' persistent belief that he had knowingly lied about the fate of José Robles. Márgara regularly used to take tea with Luisi, the Swiss wife of Álvarez del Vayo, and Maria Mikhailova Fiedelman, the estranged Russian wife of Juan Negrín.

It has been suggested by Ignacio Martínez de Pisón that Álvarez del Vayo's solicitude for the family was born of guilt. However, it is perfectly possible that he genuinely did not know what had happened to Robles, particularly if he had been arrested, imprisoned and executed by a Russian-run special section – all the more so if this was the unit led by Grigulevich. It is, of course, equally possible that he felt sympathy for the family precisely because he had been unable to do anything to prevent the murder of Robles, which does not mean necessarily that he was complicit therein. It has also been suggested that the actions of both Coco and Miggie were born of a desire somehow to show by their loyalty to the Republic that their father was innocent. It may be so, but other interpretations are possible. Márgara's letters to Esther Crooks and Henry Lancaster make it clear that the family was convinced that what had happened to José Robles had absolutely nothing to do with Constancia de la Mora or Julio Álvarez del Vayo. There is every possibility that they may even have feared that there had been good reasons for the action taken against Robles. In this regard, Constancia wrote: 'What John Dos Passos could not forgive, the man's wife and two children understood.' Kate Mangan, who worked with Coco, recalled him as 'crushed and wretched, so ashamed he never spoke of it'. Josie Herbst wrote in 1939: 'Several months after Robles had been shot I saw his son in Valencia on my way out of Spain. He was in Rubio's propaganda and censorship bureau and to my knowledge believed or said he believed in the proof of his father's guilt.' The family's collective commitment to the Republic remained undiminished, which would have been utterly inexplicable if they had harboured resentment against Álvarez del Vayo and other senior Republican politicians.[65]

Ironically, when the United States entered the Second World War after Pearl Harbor, Josie Herbst was given a job in Washington at the Office of the Coordinator of Information, a semi-independent intelligence and propaganda agency run by Colonel William J. Donovan. Her job was the preparation of radio scripts for propaganda broadcasts to Germany. However, she soon crossed the radar of the House Committee on un-American Activities, which was looking into the issue of the fitness of those serving the war effort. Many anti-fascists were being criticized for their support of the Spanish Republic and she was suddenly removed from her job on 21 May 1942. The circumstances remain mysterious. She was under investigation by the FBI, as were most people who, like her, had access to confidential information. A substantial report was compiled on the basis of a number of contradictory comments from various sources, including a particularly virulent one from Josie's friend, the novelist Katherine Anne Porter. In the event, it would appear that Porter's fabricated testimony was not the problem. Indeed, the final FBI report cleared Josephine Herbst of un-Americanism. It would appear that she had been sacked on the instructions of Bill Donovan because of her earlier sympathies for the Soviet Union and her support for the Spanish Republic. Her colleagues protested against the 'peremptory methods' and the undemocratic way in which she was refused the opportunity to defend herself.[66] Such things happened in a democracy in wartime, a fact forgotten by those outraged by the treatment of Liston Oak, whose betrayal of the Spanish Republic far outweighed anything done by Josie Herbst.

Dos Passos remained in touch with Márgara Villegas and tried to do what he could for the family, especially in relation to getting José Robles' life insurance paid out. He seems to have brooded on the issue and it was clearly one of the things that inclined him ever further to the right. He was initially cautious in what he wrote about the Robles case, as was to be expected in the light of his admonition to Maurice Coindreau to keep his name out of any public discussion of it. However, he did write an article entitled 'Farewell to Europe', in which he depicted the Communists in Spain crushing individual and local freedoms with a 'tremendously efficient and ruthless machine for power'. It was published in July 1937 in the magazine *Common Sense*. It provoked intensely critical responses from several of his friends. The next six months saw Dos Passos' anti-Communism become more explicit. In December 1937, he published another article in *Common Sense* entitled 'The Communist Party and the War Spirit: A Letter to a Friend Who is Probably a Party Member'. In it, he went beyond a generally fierce anti-Soviet line to make direct criticisms of the Spanish Republican Government. Speaking of the Communist Party's 'will to rule' and 'blind intolerance', he went on to claim that it had 'as it gained power, set itself to eliminating physically or otherwise all the men with possibilities of leadership who were not willing to put themselves under its orders'.[67]

Over the next year, perennially short of money, he decided to collect together some previously published plus some more recent pieces on Spain. The ensuing book, *Journey Between Wars*, included material in which both Robles and Márgara Villegas appeared anonymously as 'the man stepping out to be court-martialled by his own side' and 'the woman' waiting for her husband. It also provided an account of the fiesta at the XV Brigade in which he did not mention his conversation there with Hemingway but did describe the Soviet-trained General 'Walter', the Pole Karol Swierczewski – who would later be portrayed as Goltz in Hemingway's *For Whom the Bell Tolls*.[68] The most ferocious outrage was expressed by Hemingway who sent a cable from a transatlantic liner:

> When you decide to rat for money while better guys than you still fighting there's a war on you can always peddle it somewhere but in case you're incorporating your adventures in a book please check up and find Walter is a Pole not a Russian stop Meantime would appreciate small down payment on any your borrowings celebrate success trilogy regards hem.

The telegram was followed by a long letter, in which, after apologizing for the 'snotty' tone of the cable, he expressed his outrage at details in the book and in Dos Passos' articles which had effectively accused the Spanish Republican Government under Juan Negrín of being Russian puppets:

> The only trouble about this, Dos, is that Walter is a Pole. Just as Lucacz was a Hungarian, Petrov a Bulgarian, Hans a German, Copic a Yugo-Slav and so on. I'm sorry, Dos, but you didn't meet any Russian generals. The only reason I can see for your attacking, for money, the side that you were always supposed to be on is an unsuppressable desire to tell the truth. Then why not tell the truth? The thing is that you don't find out the truth in ten days or three weeks and this hasn't been a communist run war for a long time.[69]

Hardly surprisingly, it took a decade before Dos and Hemingway had a brief token reconciliation in Havana in September 1948. Meanwhile, they met in 1938 at the New York home of a mutual friend, the wealthy patron of the arts, Gerald Murphy. After a conversation with Hemingway on the balcony, Dos Passos came into the apartment and said to Murphy: 'You think for a long time you have a friend, and then you haven't.'[70] Dos Passos continued to blame Álvarez del Vayo for not helping him to discover Robles' fate. Nevertheless, he did not go explicitly public about the case until, in July 1939, he wrote a relatively measured account in the form of a letter to the *New Republic* in reply to a damning review of his novel *The Adventures of a Young Man* by the critic Malcolm Cowley. In it, Cowley had stated that Robles had been arrested as a fascist spy on the basis of damning evidence. Dos Passos' response showed that he still clung on to what Pepe Quintanilla had told him; he also wrote:

It is only too likely that Robles, like many others who were conscious of their own sincerity of purpose, laid himself open to a frame-up. For one thing, he had several interviews with his brother who was held prisoner in Madrid, to try to induce him to join the loyalist army. My impression is that the frame-up in his case was pushed to the point of execution because Russian secret agents felt that Robles knew too much about the relations between the Spanish war ministry and the Kremlin and was not, from their very special point of view, politically reliable. As always in such cases, personal enmities and social feuds probably contributed.

Dos Passos sent a copy to the editor of the anti-Stalinist *Partisan Review*, the radical critic Dwight Macdonald, accompanied by a letter in which he said: 'I rather underplayed the stupid way in which Del Vayo lied to me about the manner of Robles' death.'[71]

Over the years, Dos Passos' views hardened even more. By the mid-1950s, he had moved far to the right. In 1956, he published a selection of his articles with a commentary. When writing about the Robles affair, he presented the Russians as the brutal conquerors of the Spanish Republic. He described his enquiries into his friend's disappearance provoking 'the run around, the look of fear, fear for their own lives', which was surely an exaggeration. He wrote that he had kept silent on his return from Spain to the United States because: 'You didn't want to help the enemy, to add to the immense propaganda against the Spanish Republic fomented by so many different interests.'[72] In the atmosphere of the Cold War, he seems to have forgotten telling Maurice Coindreau to say nothing of his part in the Robles affair lest it damage his relationship with the Communist Party. By claiming that he had remained silent in order not to damage the Spanish Republic, he was not being honest. In his anxiety to protect his own reputation for integrity and discretion, he also seems to have forgotten his articles in the magazine *Common Sense* and in *Journeys Between Wars*. By the 1970s, the gloves were completely off. In his novel *Century's Ebb*, he vents his spleen against Hemingway, Martha Gellhorn, Sidney Franklin and Julio Álvarez del Vayo, who is portrayed as 'Juan Hernández del Río'.[73] In the meanwhile, however, when taking part in the 1964 presidential campaign of Senator Barry Goldwater, Dos Passos told one of his fellow campaign workers, who was a Spaniard with a particular interest in the Civil War, what he had been told at the time – perhaps at the fiesta at the XV Brigade. He said that Robles had actually been arrested with an envelope containing sensitive information about Russian aid to the Republic that he was about to give to the fifth column. This was, of course, never reflected in any of Dos Passos' public utterances. Significantly, in the early 1960s, Gustav Regler, long after he had turned against the Communist Party, told Josephine Herbst that Robles had been 'a bad egg'.[74]

4

Love and Politics: The Correspondents in Valencia and Barcelona

The first assault on Madrid in November 1936 had been beaten off. Subsequent rebel attempts to encircle the city, culminating in the battle of Jarama, had also been thwarted. After the Republican victory at Guadalajara in March 1937, rebel objectives changed. The capital was no longer the main target and Franco adopted a strategy of mopping up Republican territory by instalments, beginning in the north. Accordingly, by the early spring of 1937, the emphasis for correspondents tended to pass from Madrid to Valencia. Of course, there would always be correspondents and writers eager to visit the heroic city but, to get the requisite permits and passes, they had to apply at the press office of the new capital. The shift of the centre of gravity to Valencia was especially marked after the constitution of the government of Dr Juan Negrín on 16 May 1937. Barea was yesterday's man. Rubio Hidalgo resumed his old importance although he would soon be eclipsed by a figure of lasting significance, the tall and imposing Constancia de la Mora who, ironically, had once been married to the brother of Franco's press chief Luis Bolín.

Louis Fischer had met her in April 1936 at the home of Julio Álvarez del Vayo, the Socialist journalist whom he had known in Russia and had been for a time the Republican Ambassador in Mexico. Fischer was much taken by Constancia's Modigliani-style looks. By that time, she had divorced Bolín and married Ignacio Hidalgo de Cisneros, who had been Republican Military Attaché in Rome and, during the war, would be head of the air force. Fischer wrote later: 'She was a handsome dark Spanish woman, in revolt against her aristocratic, Catholic upbringing, who ran an antique and folk-art shop opposite the Cortes.' The shop, known as Arte Popular, actually belonged to Zenobia Camprubí, the wife of the poet Juan Ramón Jiménez. When the war broke out, Constancia had worked looking after refugee children. At the beginning of 1937, she had been persuaded by both Jay Allen and the poet Rafael Alberti to apply for a job in the Republic's foreign press office in Valencia, which was under the jurisdiction of the Ministry of Foreign Affairs. She asked Louis Fischer to speak on her behalf to Álvarez del Vayo, still Foreign Minister in the cabinet of Largo Caballero. A member of the Communist Party, married to Hidalgo de Cisneros, and with perfect English, French and German, Constancia was an ideal candidate.[1]

Once hired, like Barea before her, Constancia was unimpressed by the premises selected by Rubio Hidalgo: 'the offices themselves were up three flights of old wooden stairs, a suite of barn-like rooms with floors littered with papers, walls grim with peeling paint, old tables and chairs covered with torn posters, carbon paper, copies of Polish, Swiss, German, British and French newspapers'. She was even less impressed by Rubio himself, who

> lived like a mole in the middle of the Foreign Press Bureau. His office was practically pitch-dark. All the shades were drawn. The only daylight leaked in from cracks in the door. A shaded dim desk light made an eerie pool of green in the gloom. In the midst of this darkness sat Señor Rubio, partly bald, with a tiny moustache, pasty-coloured face, and dark glasses.[2]

At first, Rubio treated Constancia patronizingly and she was put to work in the censorship office. There she learned that newspapermen could say whatever they wanted as long as it was true and did not give away confidential military information. Accordingly, her job would be to filter out wild rumours, lies and coded military messages. It was in the press office that she met the glamorous would-be actress Gladys Green, who later married Burnett Bolloten, at the time a pro-Communist United Press correspondent and a daily visitor to the bureau. No one who worked with Rubio seemed to like him very much. Kate Mangan, who coincided with him in the press office, recalled:

> He never came to the office until the afternoon and stayed there until the small hours and had his supper and trays of black coffee taken into his private room. Rubio was pallid and bald and looked rather sinister as he had weak eyes and always wore dark glasses. The only light in his pitch-black office came from cracks in the door, his desk-light and that which was reflected off his shiny bald pate.

John Dos Passos described him as sitting 'owl-like in his big glasses'.[3]

As a result of Rubio Hidalgo's machinations, Barea was reduced to being a censor for the radio. By the summer of 1937, he noted that Constancia de la Mora 'had virtually assumed the control of the Censorship Department in Valencia and that she did not like Rubio; that she was an efficient organizer, very much a woman of the world who had joined the Left of her free choice, and that she had greatly improved the relationship between the Valencia office and the press'.[4] Although correspondents found the censorship infinitely less irksome than in the rebel zone, there were occasional disagreements. Vincent 'Jimmy' Sheean, of the *New York Herald Tribune*, thought it a mistake that the censorship never allowed journalists to mention the munitions factory at Sagunto. The censors' logic was incontrovertible but the frequent bombing of Sagunto made it obvious that the rebels already knew all about the factory. Despite the daily bombing raids, the town's munitions workers had chosen to remain at their jobs. The bombs had miraculously failed to hit the factory, while destroying the homes around it, but the workers knew that one direct hit on the explosives factory would blow the entire area to smithereens, yet they rejected chances to leave. Sheean thought that the censors had missed a great opportunity to publicize the workers' heroism.[5]

Joseph North, of the American *Daily Worker*, who arrived in Valencia in the second week of September 1937, found Rubio Hidalgo less than helpful. According to North, Rubio was 'a short, heavy man wearing smoked glasses, who had a sombre air and his welcome was tepid'. Apparently unaware of, or indifferent to, the fact that the *Daily Worker* was campaigning for Roosevelt to lift the arms embargo, Rubio put considerable difficulties in the way of North being able to send cables, which were certainly extremely expensive. Finally, he agreed to let him have the miserly amount of five hundred words per week. North was in despair until things changed after Rubio was eventually replaced by Constancia de la Mora, who gave him ample facilities for sending cables.[6]

Constancia's rise to domination of the press office was not without its difficulties. In October 1937, she had to overcome a serious crisis. One day, Louis Fischer bumped into her in the street in Valencia. Surprised to see the notorious workaholic away from her desk and looking upset, he asked her what had happened, to which she explained bitterly: 'I've been discharged...Prieto did it.' The reason was that Indalecio Prieto, as Minister of Defence, had issued a decree limiting the capacity of the Communists to proselytize within the armed forces. Although the decree was reported within Spain, Constancia had censored comments on it by foreign correspondents lest it damage the Communist Party. Kate Mangan refers obliquely to Constancia being 'under a temporary political cloud herself'. Prieto's reaction was understandable, since Constancia was effectively censoring her own government. He had telephoned José Giral, who had replaced

Álvarez del Vayo as Foreign Minister in May. The press office came under Giral's jurisdiction and he had dismissed her.

Shortly after meeting her, Fischer returned to the Presidencia, where he was staying along with Otto Katz. He said to Negrín over lunch: 'Prieto did a very foolish thing today.' When he explained, Negrín exclaimed: 'I would have put her in prison.' Fischer agreed that she had behaved unpardonably, but that she was irreplaceable in the press department: 'All the foreign visitors and journalists are pleased with her and there is nobody who would do nearly as well in her job.' Negrín shrugged his shoulders, said it was up to Prieto and recommended that Fischer go and see him. Fischer already had an appointment with him and at the end of their conversation raised the issue. Prieto replied that Constancia was essentially too high-handed: 'she is a Maura and like her famous grandfather Don Antonio Maura, Prime Minister of Spain, she is brusque and sometimes hysterical. She does things this way.' And he proceeded to imitate her dismissive manner, with wild gestures from side to side, saying 'bah, bah, bah'. In the end, Prieto said he was happy for Negrín to take the decision and Negrín said he would talk to Giral.

Fischer asked if it would help if there were a petition from all the foreign correspondents. Earlier in the day, 'a fair young United Press correspondent' (almost certainly Burnett Bolloten) had been collecting signatures, but Fischer had advised him to stop because in his Russian experience an official could be damaged by the support of foreign newspapermen. Once Negrín said that he thought a petition might help, Fischer himself signed and urged Bolloten to get other correspondents, including Ernest Hemingway and Herbert Matthews, to sign as well. A few days later Constancia was back at her office. However, since Bolloten had told her about Fischer's initial reluctance to sign the petition but not about his subsequent efforts on her behalf, she was furious and held him partly responsible for her dismissal. Although she said that she accepted his explanation that he had lobbied to have her reinstated, she never forgave him and refused ever to speak to him again.[7]

When the government moved from Valencia to Barcelona in November 1937, the foreign press bureau was forced to share premises with the Propaganda Department of the Ministry of Foreign Affairs. Luis Rubio Hidalgo was said to be piqued at what he perceived as a loss of independence and importance. However, he was chosen to go to Paris as titular head of the Spanish Republican News Agency, Agence Espagne. Constancia de la Mora, forgiven for her clash with Prieto, was made the director of the foreign press office.[8] These changes seem to have been made as a result of a report on the Republic's propaganda deficit prepared for Negrín by Louis Fischer.[9] The real brains behind the Agence Espagne was the Comintern's brilliant propagandist, Otto Katz. Kate Mangan met him on his occasional visits to Valencia, where he used his pseudonym of André Simon. She recalled later: 'No longer young, he was a very charming man, an artful propagandist amazingly good at ingratiating himself with the most diverse types and making use of them for propaganda purposes without their realising it.'[10] On her way back to England in the autumn of 1937, she met him in Paris with Louis Fischer and thought them both 'sweet'.[11]

Fischer's report, probably compiled after consultation with Katz, was crucial. As his own intensely felt yet perceptively analytical articles reveal, Fischer believed that the best thing a journalist could do for the Republic was to write as accurately as wartime conditions permitted. He had been introduced to Negrín by Jay Allen before the war. Now, he was drawn ever closer to the prime minister as he tried to implement his vision that the survival of the Republic required a change of policy from the democracies and that, in turn, depended on getting British, French and American public opinion to put pressure on their politicians to abandon non-intervention. Interestingly, Katz had been with Fischer in October 1937 when he accompanied Negrín on a visit to the International Brigade hospital at Benicasim. Fischer took Negrín around the hospital where, among the wounded, he introduced him to the English veteran Tom Wintringham, whom he already knew both from his time as quartermaster in the Brigades and through the young American correspondent Kitty Bowler.[12]

Not long after, on 9 November 1937, Fischer wrote to Negrín from Paris in terms that revealed just how close their collaboration had become:

> There is a general impression in Paris and London that *our* military situation is very bad and that Franco will soon win. [...] An effective method of counteracting this tendency is to give correct and optimistic statements regarding our military situation. Apart from the dry cold, official staff communiqués there is little that goes abroad about the republican military status. I propose the following: 1) A weekly survey of the military situation written by, say, Cruz Salido or some other good journalist. This is to be published in the Agence Espagne and simultaneously given to all foreign correspondents in Spain. [...] 2) From time to time, and preferably often, you or Prieto or Rojo should receive one or more foreign journalists and talk to them about *our* military situation and prospects. The world gets too little news out of Republican Spain. 3) The newspapers still complain that their correspondents cannot

go to the front. They cannot send their representatives to a country at war without a guarantee that these representatives can go to the scene of the fighting. For these and many other matters it is essential that you should have a department in your office for the foreign press. [...] It is also very necessary to take full advantage of Spanish radio facilities. These are not well exploited. You ought to have a radio director in your chancellery. Occasionally it is important to encourage correspondents and persons of prominence in political life to visit Spain. We thought, for instance, that in connection with the depression of favourable sentiment towards *us* a group of French and British journalists should go down for a special interview with you.[13]

Fischer was actually saying what the more perceptive staff on the ground in the main press offices in Madrid and Valencia, Ilsa Kulcsar and Constancia de la Mora, already knew. They had quickly reached the conclusion that the best way to counteract right-wing propaganda about the Republic was 'to give foreign correspondents every opportunity we could to see the truth, and then every facility possible for writing it and getting it sent abroad'. Like Ilsa before her, Constancia found that a policy of providing contacts with senior government officials and visits to the battle-fronts paid off, although there were occasional mishaps. One such was the case of William Carney, of the *New York Times*, who in 1936 revealed the details of Republican gun emplacements in Madrid to the benefit of his Francoist friends. Another case, infinitely less clear, related to the highly distinguished correspondent of the *Daily Express*, Sefton 'Tom' Delmer. Expelled by the Nationalists in September 1936 because his reporting was considered insufficiently favourable to their cause, Delmer then represented the *Daily Express* in the Republican zone. Although highly rated by his fellow newspapermen, who jokingly paid tribute to his ability to get a story by calling him 'Seldom Defter', the staff of the Valencia press office considered him to be hostile to the Republic.

In fact, Delmer was concerned only with the implications for British interests and told Virginia Cowles that 'the people over here are less dangerous to England'. She described him as being reasonably sympathetic to the Republic.[14] However, according to Constancia de la Mora, 'everyone in the Foreign Press Bureau disliked and distrusted Sefton Delmer'. She claimed that this was largely because he only pretended to be favourable to the Republic, although her view may have reflected her own snobbery:

He would always appear in my office in ancient ragged clothes, dirty shirts, mud-caked shoes, trousers stiff with grease. We considered his strange clothing an insult for we knew that in London he was something of a dandy. Madrid, Valencia and Barcelona were perfectly civilized cities – even if they were Spanish. Delmer always talked and behaved as though the Spanish people were some strange, benighted tribe of savages engaged in a rather silly, primitive type of bow-and-arrow contest.

Twenty years later, Delmer admitted that he had usually worn 'the dirtiest of shrunken and frayed grey flannels, a soup stained brown leather jacket over a khaki shirt'. He declared proudly in reply to Connie: 'I liked my get up. But it shocked the bourgeois prejudices of some of the Communists. They found it particularly shocking when I only wore a shirt and shorts.'[15]

However, the contemptuous and patronizing way in which Delmer generalized about Spaniards in his memoirs rather supported Connie's view. There he spoke of 'the amazing mixture of exaltation, fatalism and delight in sheer destruction that made up their attitude to life and to death'.[16] However, Geoffrey Cox, who had great admiration for Delmer's independent mind, thought it likely that what had infuriated Constancia was his apparently frivolous and mocking attitude.[17] However, a more substantial reason for her dislike of Delmer was related to his efforts to evade the censorship. Sam Russell, a young British Communist who had been invalided out of the International Brigades and returned to make English-language broadcasts from Barcelona, recalled a ferocious clash between the two. While the government was in Valencia, Delmer had written a series of articles which Constancia prevented him from transmitting. He had gone behind her back and had them sent to London via a British warship patrolling on the Spanish coast. He had then returned to England but later applied for a Spanish Republican visa in London, got it and returned to Spain. He went to the press office in Barcelona to see Connie to get the necessary passes. Sam was there as he came in and could hear through the flimsy partition her swearing at him. Apparently, her repertoire of English obscenity, learned while she was a convent girl in Ireland, was capable of peeling the wallpaper. She had no choice but to give Delmer the permits, but she never forgave him his earlier deceit.[18]

In the main, however, Connie was much more friendly and helpful to journalists than Rubio Hidalgo had ever been. He apparently had a phobia concerning journalists, keeping them at arm's length, making his dark office as unwelcoming as possible. Requests for passes or petrol vouchers for visits to the front would be left for days without response. Aware that Rubio's rudeness was leading to irritated correspondents making comments about inefficiency within the Republic, she suggested that the newspapermen be helped rather than hindered. Rubio was happy to be spared the chore of actually meeting the correspondents and left Constancia to deal with them. She set to enthusiastically, finding rooms for them in overcrowded Valencia, arranging transport and interviews: 'I knew, as all of us did – that the cause of the Republic depended on the world knowing the facts.' She secured for them passes and petrol for their cars so that they could get the facts for themselves.[19]

She was struck by the determination of correspondents such as Herbert Matthews to check facts for themselves and by their healthy suspicion of the official line:

> I came to admire terribly this passion for fact. I was irritated at first, I suppose, not to find myself believed. But I came to see that this, after all, was the way to get the facts into print, to have the men who sent them convinced of their accuracy because they themselves had got them. I have to smile when I hear stories of how we 'influenced' the foreign correspondents. And now, of course, as one looks back over their coverage, one sees that if they erred it was on the side of understatement.

Despite close friendships with Jay Allen, Henry Buckley, Burnett Bolloten and others, it was probably Herbert Matthews who most stimulated Constancia's fondness for the correspondents. Certainly, her affectionate description suggested as much:

> Tall, lean, and lanky, Matthews was one of the shyest, most diffident men in Spain. He used to come in every evening, always dressed in his gray flannels, after arduous and dangerous trips to the front, to telephone his story to Paris, whence it was cabled to New York. [...] For months he would not come near us except to telephone his stories – for fear, I suppose, that we might influence him somehow. He was so careful; he used to spend days tracking down some simple fact – how many churches in such and such a small town; what the Government's agricultural pro-gram was achieving in this or that region. Finally, when he discovered that we never tried to volunteer any information, even to the point of not offering him the latest press release unless he specifically requested it, he relaxed a little. Matthews had his own car and he used to drive to the front more often than almost any other reporter. We had to sell him the

gasoline from our own restricted stores, and he was always running out
of his monthly quota. Then he used to come to my desk, very shy, to beg
for more. And we always tried to find it for him: both because we liked
and respected him and because we did not want the *New York Times*
correspondent to lack gasoline to check the truth of our latest news
bulletin.[20]

She was referring to the fact that the press office in Valencia not only censored
the work of foreign correspondents, but made available to them a daily hand-out
on the progress of the war.

According to Louis Fischer, Constancia 'was a brilliant success. She knew languages and the psychology of foreigners, and the correspondents liked her.' Philip
Jordan of the *News Chronicle* wrote: 'no one was so kind as Constancia, or took
so much trouble to make life easy'.[21] Peter Spencer, Viscount Churchill (cousin to
Winston), spent nearly two years in Spain with the British group known as
Spanish Medical Aid. He later provided an account of the preconceptions of foreign journalists and of their reaction to Constancia de la Mora. They usually
arrived, he claimed in a considerable over-generalization, which perhaps contained an element of autobiography, already deeply frustrated by the deficiencies
of the transport available. In consequence, they were

in a state of fury and resentment, determined to stand no nonsense from
the peasants who were running things. What they did not know, because
the Press in most countries had failed to report it, was that some of the
finest brains in Spain were at the head of affairs on the Government side:
cultured, travelled people, many of them eminent in their various
professions.

Among them, he gave pride of place to

the head of the Foreign Press Bureau in the person of Constancia de la
Mora, the strikingly beautiful and brilliant wife of an ex-military attaché.
Constancia carried with her the unmistakable aura of the social and
diplomatic world of Paris, New York and London. She also had
considerable wit and was a linguist. Ushered into her presence the
foreigner was likely to become suddenly more conscious of his unshaven
chin than of his grievances.[22]

A similar tribute to the demands made on the diplomatic skills of the press office came from the memoirs of Kate Mangan, who wrote:

> There was often an awkward gap between the manners of our visitors and those of their hosts. Some of our visitors were exceedingly proletarian, crude and unpolished; the hosts were all urbane and civilised to Geneva League of Nations' standard. Many of the Spaniards and most of those in the Government must have seemed disappointingly moderate liberals to our guests.

Certainly not all correspondents were as polite and diffident as Herbert Matthews. Kate Mangan remembered having to cope with impatient demands for information from Lillian Hellman, the thirty-two-year-old American playwright, Hollywood scriptwriter and lover of Dashiell Hammett. Although not a Communist, the fellow-travelling Hellman was in Spain to participate in the making of the film *The Spanish Earth*, being made by the Dutch Communist Joris Ivens to a script by Ernest Hemingway and John Dos Passos, and also to write about the Abraham Lincoln battalion of the XV International Brigade. Although she helped to raise money for the Spanish Republic in the United States, during her stay in Valencia, Hellman 'made no allowance for the hasty and provisional nature of everything or the war'. Another prominent writer who left a less than favourable impression was Ilya Ehrenburg, whom Kate recalled as looking like 'an old grey rat'.[23]

The things that happened in and around the Valencia office were dramatically different from those that characterized the bureau in besieged Madrid. Hundreds of kilometres from the battle-front, Valencia lived little of the fear and none of the exhilaration of the capital. The straightforward life-or-death issues of the rebel shells whistling towards the Telefónica were unknown. The daily bombing raids did not come to Valencia until later and were never to be as intense as in Madrid or Barcelona. Philip Jordan arrived just after Christmas 1936. He wrote with some bitterness later that, when he arrived, 'I thought Valencia was a part of the war and I was excited by it', but 'how little, in fact, the embusqué of Valencia were doing for Madrid I did not learn until I had found it out for myself'.[24]

Stephen Spender visited the press office in the early summer of 1937 and remembered later: 'Valencia had a far more normal appearance than Madrid. Only on nights when there was a full moon like brilliant floodlighting exposing walls of bone-coloured palaces to the meticulous observing instruments of bombers, did it seem a city haunted by war.'[25] A similar comment was made in an

article by the American journalist Elizabeth O. Deeble – who signed her articles
E. O. Deeble because editors were reluctant to accept articles from a woman. This
became a joke with her friends, to whom she came to be known simply as 'Deeble'.
She wrote of the fact that, as of the end of 1936, no one had actually seen an
enemy bomber. On the other hand, the city was flooded with refugees:

> unhappy people whose poor homes no longer exist and who still carry
> their worldly goods upon their backs, are still pouring into Valencia at all
> hours. Were it not for the extraordinary efficiency with which they are fed,
> clothed, comforted and shipped out again to nearby towns and villages,
> they would indeed be a heavy problem, for this city of 400,000 inhabitants
> has received during the last month almost a million outsiders of one sort
> or another.[26]

The most pressing daily problems for foreign correspondents were the impossibility of finding a hotel room and the difficulty of getting transport for visits to
Madrid. Resolving these problems was one of the tasks undertaken by the office
of press and propaganda. The quality of daily life in Valencia, in terms of safety
and access to food, at times made it possible to forget that there was a war going
on. Philip Jordan managed to get a room at the rather grand Hotel Victoria, only
to discover that his fellow guests were vultures:

> armament men – most of them Germans – from every place you could
> think of, spies, harlots, more spies, job-hunters, propaganda men, sap-
> headed intellectuals who had never been properly appreciated in their
> own countries, drunken aviators, drummed out of other services: all riff-
> raff on the make in a town where gold was easy because the war was yet
> young.

Jordan expected, and was disappointed not to find, the heroic atmosphere of
besieged Madrid: 'Perpetual gala was not my idea of war, although it seemed to
be Valencia's.'[27] Vincent 'Jimmy' Sheean wrote as late as May 1938: 'Valencia was
a pleasant place. There was a good deal of food there in the spring, as all the crops
of vegetables and fruits had been excellent in the rich coastal plain of which it is
the capital. We had meat in Hotel Metropole twice a day, and one vegetable
(cauliflower or the like), with oranges to follow.' By that time, according to Sheean,
there were air-raids every day, but they were concentrated on the port district
and 'they did not come over the centre of the town at any time when I was there'.

He noted the lack of a wartime atmosphere and that you could buy most things in the shops.[28]

However, one issue that clouded the horizon for the press and propaganda office was the air of vigilance and the sense of intrigue that inevitably went with the need for a strategic control of information in the wartime capital. It is possible to get a vivid insight into much of what went on thanks to the surviving memoirs and letters left by various people who worked at or with the Valencia press bureau. Unique among these are the memoirs of Kate Mangan, who was employed there from early to mid-1937. Born in 1904 as Katherine Prideaux Foster, she was a beautiful model and artist, who had studied at the Slade School of Art in University College, London and also worked as a mannequin. She married the Irish-American left-wing writer Sherry Mangan in 1931. The marriage was not happy, partly because of financial constraints but also because he was jealous of her desire to write. After falling in love with Jan Kurzke, a German who had come to London on the run from the Nazis, she had divorced Sherry Mangan in 1935, although they remained friends. Jan Kurzke had volunteered to fight in the International Brigades and she had gone to Spain in October 1936 in the hope of being with him.[29] At first she had picked up casual jobs as an interpreter in Barcelona and then acted as secretary to an old friend from London, Hugh/Humphrey Slater, with whom she had studied at the Slade and with whom she had an affair in Spain.[30] Through Hugh Slater, she met Tom Wintringham, the senior British Communist who would soon be the commander of the British battalion in the International Brigades, although officially he had come to Spain as a correspondent of the CPGB's newspaper, the *Daily Worker*. Through both, she got to know a 'petite and vivacious American girl' called Katherine 'Kitty' Bowler ('Louise Mallory' in Kate Mangan's memoirs). Kate Mangan would eventually find herself sharing a hotel room with her and 'swept into the whirl of Louise's [Kitty's] life', which in turn would lead to her working in the Valencia press office.[31]

Kitty Bowler was an aspiring left-wing freelance journalist from a wealthy American family who had become Wintringham's lover not long after meeting him in Barcelona in September 1936. Her local newspaper in Plymouth, Massachusetts, described her as 'of less than medium height, slender, with large brown eyes and a short tousled bob, not unlike Amelia Earhart'.[32] A young woman of boundless energy, extremely pretty, with a mischievous look, she was ambitious but also deeply committed to the Popular Front cause. She had previously been in Moscow, where she had had a relationship with the famously pro-Stalinist *New York Times* correspondent there, the one-legged Liverpudlian Walter Duranty.[33] After a frantic period in August in Paris trying to get the necessary passes to get into Spain, she nervously crossed the border with recommendations from the American Communist Party and with a flimsy commission from the *People's Press* of New York, but with a fierce determination to make good. When she reached Barcelona along with a group of international volunteers, she met up with Duranty again and volunteered to work for the Generalitat's spontaneously assembled press and propaganda office. The Catalan Communist Party, the Partit Socialista Unificat de Catalunya, had arranged for her to have board and lodging at the Hotel Regina near the Plaça de Catalunya.[34] However, her hotel room was requisitioned to house a family of refugees. She wandered 'desolate and forlorn' to the Café Rambla, where she found a table around which sat a group of Englishmen wearing, shockingly for Catalan eyes, baggy shorts: 'Like the story book waif who peeks through the frosted pane at the happy family gathered round the fireside, I eyed the little group sitting at a corner table.' They looked at her coldly as, 'shy but desperate', she approached them. As she turned to leave, 'a soft-voiced bald man touched my arm. "You must join us".'[35]

It was Tom Wintringham. Balding, bespectacled and already married, Wintringham, while hardly handsome, had a romantic air. She was entranced by his fertile conversation, his gentle manner and humour, and they immediately became friends. Initially, Kitty was principally delighted to have found someone with the influence and contacts to help her gather information for her articles. However, they had quickly and passionately fallen in love. Shortly afterwards, Tom wrote an account of how their relationship had developed, an account that he later omitted from his memoir of the Spanish Civil War:

> She had been in Barcelona a few days when in the Rambla there appeared suddenly a moving forest of bare knees, some of which – for the English can appear incredibly tall – were almost on a level with her eyes. The first British medical unit, in shorts: and with it, vaguely attached to it, a bald-headed journalist whose name she knew from a book she had read in the States.

After a trip to a dark, lonely and frightened Madrid, she returned, feeling 'lost and small and afraid', but was cheered by his welcome:

> It went quickly then, though not very quickly: some meals together, coffee and cognac at the café Rambla where friendly waiters knew what was happening at least as soon as the pair of them did, and indicated with a nod or a lifted hand to the latecomer where to find the other. After that

there was the going home to her hotel, 'hell and gone' down the tramlines in the dark; she liked company on that lonely walk and he walked it with her three times before he kissed her goodnight.

Quite soon, just before going to the front for a few days, he had proposed to her 'curtly and nervously, without prejudice to any other interest either might have in other people a thousand or three thousand miles away'. While he was away, she had begun

> to think that she was in love with him (and he thought of little else). And a day before she expected he was back, to find her compact of tenderness, a warmth and reassurance of humanity. And someone in the room below had snored like a grass-cutter mowing, all night long. They heard it all night long, laughing a good deal at this but not because of this, they laughed because a loneliness and a strain was ended, with release and happiness.[36]

Kitty was not a member of the American Communist Party, but she belonged to the League Against War and Fascism. She threw herself into the work of prop- agating the Republican cause. She worked on a volunteer basis for the improvised propaganda department of the Catalan Generalitat. Aware that the relatively small amount of news about Catalonia that reached the United States was heavily weighted to give an impression of anarchist-inspired chaos and disorder, she per- suaded the recently created Catalan Commissariat for Propaganda to send photographs regularly to American left-wing organs such as *Fight*, the *New Masses* and the official Communist newspaper, the *Daily Worker*. Set up on 3 October 1936 under the direction of Jaume Miravitlles, a close friend of the President Lluís Companys, the Commissariat was the first state organism in the Republican zone to exercise some centralized control over the media. What she wrote to Joe North, when he was still in New York as the editor of the *Daily Worker*, informing him of this and asking for copies of the paper to be sent to the Generalitat, to herself and to the PSUC, is revealing of both of her efforts and her anxiety for recognition: 'A copy regularly to the CP headquarters here would be much appreciated. They were very pleased when we arranged for them to receive the English Worker regularly.' Rather coyly, she added: 'It would do me no harm if you mentioned the fact that I suggested that you send it.' She went on to explain that, 'I am working very closely here with Al Edwards and Tom Wintringham. They are both working very hard at other things so that I am doing most of the dirty work of getting out propaganda and also articles for the bourgeois press.'[37]

Thus, without the slightest doubt of her political reliability, Tom was delighted to let her act as a kind of secretary and messenger, something that would soon get both of them into serious trouble. Indeed, their relationship and her activities on his behalf would lead to her being one of the few correspondents ever arrested in, and then expelled from, the Republican zone. Kitty was soon writing on a regular basis, sending the articles to a friend in New York, the playwright Leslie Reade, in the hope that he could place them for her. When he could not find somewhere that would pay a fee, he was empowered to give them to left-wing papers such as *Fight*, the *New Masses* or the *Daily Worker*. She also wrote articles with Tom's help, publishing them under her own name in the British press and under his name in the British *Daily Worker*.[38] With his help, she got permission to tour the Aragón front in October and to visit the International Brigade hospital at Grañén in Huesca, where she worked briefly as a nurse. Equally, she was also writing her own lively and colourful articles for the Manchester *Guardian* and the *Daily Herald*, which drew on her own good relations with various left-wing groups in Catalonia – something that would later be held against her.[39] Indeed, it was an indication of how the relationship would be politically damaging to him that, shortly after he met Kitty, Tom was the object of a hostile report by two erstwhile friends, Sylvia Townsend Warner and Valentine Ackland. They wrote to CPGB headquarters: 'He is largely occupied with personal affairs and side issues of journalism.'[40]

This impression was confirmed in early November 1936. Kitty had gone to London in the hope of picking up some commissions for newspaper articles. She was successful in that the Manchester *Guardian* agreed for her to stand in for the more usual correspondent from Barcelona, her friend, Elizabeth Deeble. However, Tom had taken advantage of her journey to send various messages to London. These included one that involved her going to CPGB headquarters in King Street to try to persuade the Secretary General, Harry Pollitt, to raise more volunteers for Spain. Kitty was a less than prudent choice as an emissary given that, not only was Wintringham married to a respectably Marxist wife, Elizabeth, but he also had a lover in London with whom he had had a child. She, Millie, was another (married) party functionary who happened to have worked at King Street and to be a friend of Harry Pollitt. Matters were confused by the fact that, although they never married, Millie had changed her name to Wintringham by deed poll.

In this context, the arrival of the fragrant, uninhibited and voluble Kitty at the party offices in King Street could only have been shocking. Dr Kenneth Sinclair Loutit, who led the British Medical Unit, recalled later that: 'It was before drip-dry cottons but Kitty, though often dusty, always looked pretty good and smelt nice.' Kitty,

> who really wanted to do a job for Tom and who was at that time head over heels in love with her mystery man, rushed back to London and arrived at Victoria Station dirty and dusty. She went straight to Brown's Hotel, had a bath, put on her last approximately clean dress, walked around the block to Elizabeth Arden, had her hair done, bought herself a practical reversible autumn suit at Wetheralls, went back to Browns to pick up her brief case, was in a cab at CPGB H/Q King Street by 1100 hours. She bounced in as fresh as the dawn, looking as bright as a new dollar and bringing an unaccustomed waft of Elizabeth Arden fragrance through the dusty entrance.

Harry Pollitt was not there, but one of the other prudish comrades who saw her remarked later that she arrived 'smelling like a whorehouse and dressed like for the races'. Enthusing about what she had seen in Barcelona and the Aragón front, where she had mixed with anarchists and the POUM, she was immediately suspected of being 'a bourgeois tart' with Trotskyist tendencies. When she hectored a clearly uninterested Pollitt about the need for more volunteers, he responded sharply by accusing Wintringham of cowardice and suggested that she tell him to set an example by 'dying like Byron'.[41]

Wintringham's womanizing had already undermined his position within the CPGB. His sister Margaret wrote to Kitty pointing out that comrades in Spain had referred to 'Tom and his affairs rather as a joke' and were the occasion of sneers against him.[42] The highly influential British Communist Ralph Bates himself wrote to Pollitt in December 1936 to complain that:

> everyone here was very disappointed with Comrade Wintringham. He showed levity in taking a non-Party woman, in whom neither the PSUC nor the CPGB comrades have any confidence, to the Aragon front. We understand this person was entrusted with verbal messages to the Party in London. We are asked to send messages to Wintringham through this person rather than the Party headquarters here. The Party has punished members for far less serious examples of levity than this.[43]

Pollitt never relinquished his conviction that Kitty was a spy. When Wintringham asked him in 1937 why he thought that she was a spy, Pollitt replied:

'I can smell 'em' and recommended that Tom transfer his activities to 'these Spanish dames'.[44]

On her return from England in the second week of November, Kitty got a job broadcasting to the USA for the Catalan Communist Party's (PSUC) English-language service in Barcelona.[45] She also managed to become a member of the Socialist Union, the Unión General de Trabajadores, and made contact with the Socialist newspaper *Verdad*, which later became *Adelante*. As a result, she found it much easier to get information for her articles. She worked hard on behalf of Luis Rubio Hidalgo to get the Federated Press in New York to take news items from the Republican press service, even to the extent of trying to raise the money to pay for the exorbitantly expensive international cables. She wrote to Wintringham in December: 'have just heard of a hot story, have I been getting them lately, whoops, and I'm the darling of the censorship department'. Her connections with Tom Wintringham and Hugh Slater saw her get to Madrid in December 1936 in a car provided by the Socialist newspaper *Claridad*. She used the trip to get material for a story on how the International Brigades passed Christmas and New Year. It was so cold that her fingers stuck to her typewriter keys.[46]

After she returned to Valencia, there took place an incident on 21 January 1937 which provided the ammunition for those in the party who were outraged by Tom's relationship with Kitty. The Colt machine-guns used by the British battalion continually jammed and Tom asked Kitty to talk to two gunnery experts in Valencia about how to resolve the problem. Having got the information requested, she was unable to speak to Tom because the telephones were not functioning. Accordingly, the party authorities in Valencia suggested that she deliver it in person to the British battalion headquarters at Madrigueras, north of Albacete. She set off somewhat mischievously, knowing that journalists who were not Communist Party members were not welcome. Nevertheless, amused to have this vivacious and pretty girl in his office, Wilfred McCartney, the British commander, 'as a joke or as a compliment devised and signed a battalion order' naming her 'Colt machine-gun instructor' to the battalion and inviting her to stay for a few days. On the day after her departure, her room-mate Kate Mangan was being questioned by members of the security services as to her whereabouts. Her room was searched and private papers taken away. A mysterious individual (a German communist, Rudolf Selke) informed Kate that Kitty was about to be expelled from Spain.[47]

Unbeknownst to Kate, in the middle of her second night at Madrigueras, Kitty was awoken in the room of her pension by McCartney, who told her that two men had come to arrest her and take her to Albacete. He demanded that she return the paper with the battalion order. In her own later account, she referred to the two men who arrested her in Madrigueras as 'Tweedledee and Tweedledum':

> Two diminutive men, who looked exactly alike, in large overcoats and clumsy caps with visors and earflaps which buttoned back over the crown. The caps they removed occasionally but never the coats. One was Polish, the other Hungarian. Tweedledee spoke French and German and was friendly. Tweedledum also spoke some English and was convinced I was a dangerous siren.

At Albacete, she was interrogated by the Comintern's thuggish controller of the International Brigades, André Marty: 'Behind a roll-top desk sat an old man with a first class walrus moustache. He had pulled a coat on hastily over his pajamas. No wonder he was sleepy and irritable. He reminded me of a petty French bureaucrat.' Marty was more than irritable, he was a paranoid butcher. He threw all her Spanish papers back at her, including her UGT membership card.[48] According to Tom's later account to Victor Gollancz, this was because he 'considered the Spaniards a backward race unable to judge a foreigner politically'. Marty 'had the French belief that women travelling without their husbands (his own wife was with him) did so for no good purpose'. He charged her with going to Madrigueras without the necessary pass, entering a military establishment, being interested in the functioning of machine-guns and having visited Germany and Italy in 1933. All of this was incontrovertible proof for Marty that she was a Trotskyist spy. Despite the fact that she was an American and accredited as a correspondent of the Manchester *Guardian*, he was ready to have her shot right away.[49]

She was questioned in French for three days and nights by relays of interrogators. One was a German crony of Marty called Bill Neumann. When her luggage had been searched, Neumann had discovered, tucked in the pages of a book, a poem that Wintringham had written her. This he assumed to be a code and proof that she was a spy, a view shared by Marty. Neumann had visited Madrigueras, and tried to get the camp cook to inform on Wintringham. He had also spoken to Wintringham himself and told him that he should 'get rid of this young woman' – 'no way', wrote an outraged Tom, in one of his ongoing efforts to clear her name, 'to speak of a comrade who is sympathetic to the Party, who carries on our work as a journalist in the great liberal press'. When Kitty explained to one interrogator that she was in Madrigueras because of her relationship with Tom, he snapped that it was a lie and that she could not be in love with him because he had neither hair nor teeth. Her letters had been taken from him and scoured for incriminating material.[50] In fact, according to Sam Russell, the brigader working in the propaganda services of the Republic, Kitty's cheerful readiness to engage in conversation with everyone she met ensured that she was already being followed by the security services. A report, in Spanish, on the interrogation of Kitty and Neumann's questioning of Tom, was sent to Harry Pollitt. When it was translated for him by Russell, Pollitt burst out laughing and said 'the trouble with Tom is that he has gone through life with his cock standing straight in front of him'.[51]

While she was still in custody, Tom was aware of what was happening, was not allowed to see her but did manage to write to her. His anxiety about her fate was tempered by his party discipline:

> The length and seriousness of the enquiry seems to be due to the circulation of a description of a woman spy, this description resembling yourself. I expect you'll realise, when it's through, that this sort of job has to be done. But oh my dear, I hate to think of you under strain at this time. You impressed Marty as 'very, very strong, very clever, very intelligent'. Although this was said as a suspicious point against you – women journalists should be weak, stupid – I got a jump of pride from the words.[52]

Kitty was released, somewhat traumatized, although with Wintringham's help, she soon recovered her usual optimism.[53]

When she reached Valencia, she joked about her experience to Kate, grinning as she said:

> Hush, I've been in the jug. I had great fun at first and I saw Tom quite a lot which is something. All the Internationals wear uniforms now and they wear berets. The more important they are the bigger and more overhanging the beret and they wear them in the most individual ways. I was quizzed by André Marty, the Commander-in-Chief, and his is like a pagoda.

However, when she discovered that her room in Valencia had been searched and papers taken, she broke down and cried. Moreover, despite Tom's letters and reports to Albacete on her behalf, she continued to be subject to police surveillance, the investigation continued and she was sentenced to be expelled from Spain. Oddly, either because of bureaucratic inefficiency or because of her status as a foreign correspondent, the order was not implemented until July 1937.[54]

It was just as well that the order of expulsion did not reach Kitty. As a result of a shooting accident on 6 February 1937, McCartney was replaced as commander of the British battalion by Tom Wintringham. One week later, during the battle of Jarama, Tom was wounded in the leg. Kitty raced to Wintringham's bedside. She found him delirious with a raging fever. When no one in the International Brigades showed any interest, she went to the office of Largo Caballero and, with the help of two journalist friends, the American Griffin Barry and the English dilettante Basil Murray, browbeat his secretary into calling a specialist, Negrín's close friend, Dr Rafael Méndez, who diagnosed typhoid. Meanwhile, Tom's family had mounted pressure for the Spanish Medical Aid Committee to send out a nurse, the redoubtable Patience Darton, who, together with Kitty, certainly saved his life. With the help of Dr Méndez, Kitty managed to get Tom transferred to a private room in the Hospital Militar Pasionaria in Valencia, where Patience realized that he was also suffering from septicaemia, which she resolved with some improvised surgery. Kitty also managed to arrange for Tom to be seen by Dr Norman Bethune, the distinguished Canadian doctor whom she had interviewed about his experiences during the retreat from Málaga. Thereafter, she nursed him until he was fit to return to his unit. Their mutual friends considered that she had 'kept him here on earth by sheer force of will and work'.[55] At some point in April, Hemingway, accompanied by Martha Gellhorn, visited Tom in hospital. Since Kitty rarely left Tom's bedside, it may be supposed that she was present and was thus able to renew her acquaintanceship with Martha, her old classmate from Bryn Mawr, the New England women's college.[56]

In Valencia to be near the hospital, Kitty had strengthened her friendship with Kate Mangan, who had moved there in late 1936, although there was some slight tension between them over Tom's treatment. Griffin Barry and Basil Murray had tried to arrange with the British Embassy for Tom to be repatriated on a naval hospital ship. Kitty opposed this because she knew that, if Tom were conscious, he would refuse to go, but also because she knew that the very request to the British authorities would cause him problems with the Communist Party leadership. In a report that she wrote to Peter Kerrigan, Kitty wrote that, as a result of her opposition to the idea, 'Kate Mangan, member of the Spanish party, accused me of heartlessness, saying that if Comrade Wintringham was not put on the hospital ship he would surely die'. In the event, the British Embassy refused, but the incident caused such subsequent embarrassment for Tom that Kitty felt obliged to write the report.[57] Having suspended her journalistic work while she was caring for Tom, Kitty was just getting herself re-established as a correspondent when she went on 2 July to the Valencia authorities to get a pass to go to Madrid. When her records were checked, it was discovered that there was an order, dated January 1937, for her expulsion from Spain. Devastated to have to leave the Spanish cause to which she was so devoted, and still shocked, she wrote to Tom that 'it hasn't spoiled either my love for you nor Spain – only a deep hatred of the stupidities, cruelties and bureaucracy in life'.[58]

Kitty's frustration never degenerated into bitterness. Had she been of a mind to take some sort of revenge or merely profit from her experience, she would have had no trouble selling her story to a press hungry for anti-Communist stories in both Britain and the United States. As Tom later explained to the publisher Victor Gollancz:

> Journalists when arrested or expelled from some country usually find the story of their experiences worth printing. Kitty did not wish to give any publicity to her experiences, thinking anti-Fascism more important than any personal grievance. And until the outbreak of the present war we both ignored the political and personal slander which occasionally came our way, spread by the comrades; there was still some hope of a Popular Front in this country and these comrades were an essential factor in the movement towards that.

In retrospect, however, he concluded sadly that 'the decision made by Harry Pollitt and others to treat Kitty as a Fascist spy, to refuse any enquiry into her work in America or Spain, and to exclude me from the C.P. because I would not obey the order to leave the woman I was going to marry – these things had political roots as well as personal'. What he meant was that the sectarianism of the British Communist leadership prevented them from seeing the Popular Front as anything more than a short-term tactic, their inability 'to believe in the Popular Front as a real and human thing'.[59]

One important legacy of Kitty's time in Spain was her friendship with Kate Mangan. It had survived their disagreement over the hospital ship, not least because of all the help that she and Tom had given Kate in her efforts to get treatment for the wounded Jan Kurzke. Kitty had persuaded Norman Bethune to see Jan Kurzke, and was constantly visiting him in hospital, while Tom had sent him food and cigarettes and later helped in arranging for the brigade authorities to permit his return to England.[60] As result of the friendship between the two women, it is possible to reconstruct much of what happened in the Valencia press and propaganda office.

When Kate Mangan came to write her memoirs after the Spanish war, she portrayed Kitty Bowler as a typical New Yorker, endlessly and tryingly energetic, confident and intrusive, yet also thoughtful and willingly helpful. Eventually, she would come to find Kitty irritating. It was thanks to Kitty that Kate ended up in the press office and thus able to provide her unique insight into the people working there. Kitty had hoped vainly to get a job as a writer in the Valencia press office. The problem was largely that she was too occupied looking after Tom, although the suspicions still hanging over her may well have played their part. The job went to the much more experienced American journalist, Milly Bennett. Despite her own lack of success, Kitty suggested to Kate that she might be able to get a lesser position as a secretary and translator if she spoke to 'her friend' Liston Oak, who had been put in charge of the English-language press bulletin produced by the Valencia press office. A minor celebrity of the American left, Oak was a somewhat grey and depressive individual. In fact, according to Kate, 'Liston Oak, like most of the people Louise [Kitty] introduced me to, was not really a friend of hers'.[61] They may not have been friends – Oak seemed to have made few in Spain and was far too introspective to appeal to the ebullient Kitty – but she certainly knew Oak. In a letter in early November 1936, Tom had written to her: 'Would you please tell Oak I wanted to see him when he returns but that I couldn't, as you know.' Then, on 27 January 1937, Kitty wrote to Tom about the arrival at the Hotel Inglés in Valencia of 'a mob of new people all girating about Liston. A strange transplantation of English and American intellectual left, conversation, conversation, which seems so strangely out of place in this life.' It was not clear whether this latter comment was a reference to Liston Oak or to the mob of newcomers.[62] Prodded along by Kitty, and armed with an introduction from Hugh Slater, in late December 1936, Kate went to see, and was hired by, Liston Oak.

When she finally got to meet him in his gloomy hotel room, Kate found the 'rather pompous and habitually melancholy' Liston Oak to be decidedly unimpressive. She encountered 'a tall, distinguished-looking, middle-aged American with glasses and curling grey hair which he wore rather long at the back. He generally wore a large-size floppy beret.' Something about the spindly and hypochondriac Oak provoked Kate's suspicions: 'Liston was a chameleon kind of character. I always felt he was unreal and a faker though I did not know until afterwards what he was up to.' His politics tended to the libertarian. He expressed interest both in the FAI and the POUM, and held heated conversations with the

Austrian sociologist Franz Borkenau, who was passing through Valencia while doing research for his book *The Spanish Cockpit*. Nevertheless, Kate felt that 'even Liston's Trotskyism was unconvincing'.[63] By April of 1937, she would have some reason to alter that view: 'He was that most dangerous type of all – an ex-Communist. I do not know whether he had been expelled or had left the party. Apparently his old associates did not know, for he had come to Spain armed with what were, for a Leftist, unimpeachable letters of credit.'[64] According to the American writer Stephen Koch, Liston Oak was a Stalinist who, before coming to Spain, had been in Moscow, where he had been offered a job on an English-language newspaper for foreign visitors, the *Moscow Daily News*. However, before he took up the post, the Spanish Civil War had broken out and he got Louis Fischer to intercede on his behalf to get a job in Republican Spain. Despite his inability to speak Spanish, the 'unimpeachable letters of credit', recommendations from the American Communist Party and from Fischer, ensured that he was taken on. Kate's explanation of Oak's reason for being in Spain was rather less sinister: 'When I discovered that his second wife had left him I assumed that he had come to Spain to forget about it.' Nevertheless, Kate also commented on the fact that Oak carried a letter of introduction to someone referred to in her manuscript as 'Kellt, the former head of the foreign department'. It is difficult to identify 'Kellt'. Since Kellt did not speak English, Otto Katz, who did, may be eliminated as a candidate.[65]

At the press office, Kate also met Coco Robles, the sixteen-year-old son of John Dos Passos' friend, José Robles Pazos(see previous chapter). Having been educated in Baltimore, where his father was a professor at Johns Hopkins University, Coco spoke perfect American English as well as French, Spanish and some Russian. Kate remembered him as 'a lanky boy of sixteen with a dark skin, big white teeth and clear grey eyes with long lashes'. Constancia de la Mora regarded him as 'one of the most intelligent, able, and sweet-tempered boys I have known'.[66] Kate, Coco and Milly Bennett would scour the press and Republican news agency reports for stories that could be translated and issued to foreign journalists. They also translated speeches by Republican politicians such as Dolores Ibárruri and government ministers.[67] One of the things that struck Kate most forcibly was the extent to which the Republican authorities made every effort to facilitate the visits of foreign journalists, writers and politicians: 'the Spanish government is commendably and equally polite to all, real and fake, and we have all kinds from the film star Errol Flynn, who came here for publicity and staged a fake narrow escape for himself in Madrid, to the Dean of Canterbury, who had a real narrow escape in Durango'.[68]

One of the most colourful and fascinating characters to be employed by the Republican press office to help visiting writers and journalists was the striking

Swedish redhead Kajsa Hellin Rothman. According to Virginia Cowles, for whom she acted as interpreter, Kajsa 'had held jobs all over Europe ranging from governess to tourist guide and had finally ended up in Barcelona as a marathon dancer. On the twelfth day of the dance, war broke out and she went to the front as a nurse.' Born in Karlstad in 1903, she went to live in Paris when she was twenty and then worked as a nanny and a journalist. In 1925, she joined a dance troupe and toured all over Europe. In 1931, she gave it up after her manager absconded with her prize money leaving her high and dry in Cairo. She stayed in Romania for two years as a nanny before moving to Spain in 1934 where she helped set up a travel agency. During that time, she developed a passionate love of the country. Accordingly, on hearing of the military coup in July 1936, she became the first Swedish citizen to volunteer for the Republic, joining the Red Cross, as a nurse and being assigned to an anarchist militia unit, the Columna de Hierro.[69]

The war brought out in her a political commitment that soon became the driving force of her life. Believing that she could be more use in the besieged capital, she joined the Scottish Ambulance Unit that had arrived in Madrid in late September. The Unit was run by the puritanical and conservative Fernanda Jacobsen, who diverted food donated by Scottish workers for needy nursing mothers of the Spanish Republic, to right-wingers who had taken refuge in the British Embassy. Miss Jacobsen also permitted the Scottish Ambulance Unit to be used to smuggle rebel supporters out of Spain. In mid-December 1936, when the Unit returned to the UK on Christmas leave, by then much-depleted and with serious doubts as to its future, Kajsa left to seek other work. It was later alleged in a security report that she had actually been expelled for immorality. However, it seems more likely that she had protested about the use of the Unit to help Fifth Columnists and that Miss Jacobsen's accusations of 'loose morals' were a device to discredit Kajsa.[70]

By the end of December 1936, Kajsa had found work as secretary to the Canadian surgeon Dr Norman Bethune at the Hispano-Canadian Blood Transfusion Institute which he had established in Madrid. She made a great impact both in helping to improve the unit's organisational efficiency and in successfully publicising appeals for blood donors. She courageously delivered blood to the front during the battle of Jarama. T.C. Worsley, who drove Bethune's ambulance for a time, portrayed Kajsa in his memoir of that time as 'Gretchen': 'She was a big blonde Swede, more typically Aryan than any Nazi idealization. Where she had come from no one knew, but she could speak most languages, Swedish, French, German, Spanish, English.' He commented on her 'striking figure and warm nature' and her amazing range of contacts in Madrid.

Love and Politics

Kajsa had also become Bethune's lover and the jealousy aroused in a crucial member of his staff, Henning Sorenson, provoked a damaging conflict. The American sailor-turned journalist, Greg Moller, correspondent for the Copenhagen magazine *Politiken*, who knew both Bethune and Kajsa, wrote that her 'loveliness almost broke up the Canadian Blood Transfusion outfit'. Sorensen was the unit's liaison officer with the Spanish medical authorities and able to cause serious problems for Bethune. The situation was unsustainable. The Spanish doctors resented her steadfast defence of Bethune during his long fund-raising absences. Moreover, the confident manner of this tall redhead, exaggerated by her adoption of male attire, 'militia trousers and Sam Browne', made them rather uncomfortable. Nevertheless, Worsley recalled her as 'a person of great generosity, generous with her time, her help and her cheerfulness, quite unafraid and yet entirely unselfconscious in her whole attitude to the war. She never generalized about it, contenting herself with concentrating on the immediate problems whatever they might be.'

By the time that the Canadian blood transfusion team was absorbed into the Spanish medical services, on 2 March 1937, Kajsa had already left to join the Republican press office. She seems to have decided that it would be better for the unit and for Bethune if she broke with him and moved on. Despite this, she was inadvertently and peripherally involved in Bethune being forced out of Spain. His opposition to the absorption of his unit had already led to clashes with others in the unit and with the Republican authorities. At the beginning of April 1937, the anonymous report emanating from the Spanish security services absurdly accused Bethune of being a thief. It also insinuated, as a lever against him, that Kajsa might be a spy. Moreover, badly affected by the loss of Kajsa, he had begun to drink heavily and, on 5 April 1937, was persuaded to leave Spain.[71]

Kajsa herself remained deeply committed to the cause and made Swedish-language broadcasts for the Republican radio and also wrote articles for her home-town newspaper, the *Karlstad-tidningen*. That, plus her unique range of languages, made her an ideal recruit for the press office. Kate Mangan wrote of Kajsa:

> She was a handsome giantess with red-gold flowing hair. She was also correspondent for a Swedish paper and typing in Swedish involved putting in a lot of accents by hand. She had worked previously with Dr Bethune and had started in the war wearing trousers and riding a motorbike. With us, she wore flowing, Isidora Duncan garments. She was said to have worked for a travel agency before the war. She used to bawl into the telephone: 'Aquí, Kajsa, sabes, la sueca, alta, rubia!'

In the spring and summer of 1937, she worked in and around Madrid as guide and interpreter for Herbert Matthews, Philip Jordan, Willie Forrest, Josephine Herbst, and Virginia Cowles. At that time, as Virginia Cowles recalled, and as can be seen from the photograph with Hemingway and Liston Oak, when she was working on the Madrid front, she 'dressed in men's clothes and wore her hair in a Greta Garbo bob'.[72] According to Moller, Kajsa provided information which permitted him to expose in the Scandinavian press the extensive fifth-column organization run out of the Norwegian Legation by its German charge d'affaires, Felix Schlayer. This led to Schlayer's removal by the Norwegian government. In the autumn of 1937, Kajsa was recruited by the Svenska Spanienhjälpen (Swedish Relief for Spain) and worked tirelessly with refugee children. She opened an orphanage, to raise money for which she toured Sweden in 1938 and spoke to large audiences. She also wrote the text for a book of the children's drawings of the war (*Barnen ritar om kriget*). When the Republic was finally defeated, she fled to France with the rest of the press office where she helped organize the exodus to Mexico where she herself lived and worked as a tour guide until her death in 1969.[73]

An even more crucial member of the staff of the press office was the thirty-seven-year-old Californian 'Milly Bennett' (Mildred Jacqueline Bremler), 'Poppy' in Kate Mangan's memoirs. Like Kajsa, she greatly facilitated the work of the correspondents. Although, unlike her Swedish colleague, she was far from being a striking beauty, she had a thirst for life that ensured a steady supply of lovers. According to Kate, she was

> exceedingly popular with men and never without a romance of her own – probably because she was warm-hearted, such a genuine good sort, and also very amusing company. She was a first-rate newspaperwoman and quite well known as such and if it had not been for her Left sympathies, though she belonged to no political party, she would have been earning very good money. She had done so in the past. Only her left views and her love affairs, which made her rather a rolling stone, stood in her way. She had been everywhere, Honolulu, Shanghai and Moscow and never lacked a job as she was very competent.

After marrying an American, Mike Mitchell, in 1921, she worked as a reporter for the *Honolulu Star-Bulletin*. She divorced him in 1926 and went to cover the Chinese revolution of Chiang Kai-shek. She went to Moscow in 1931 and worked for an English-language newspaper for foreign visitors, the *Moscow Daily News*, as well as being a stringer for the *New York Times* and *Time* magazine. She became a good friend of the future commander of the Abraham Lincoln Battalion of the International Brigades, Robert Merriman, and his wife Marion, after they met her in Moscow in early 1935. Marion recalled: 'I could tell Milly was as "crazy" as I'd heard – an extrovert who knew no limits and whose curiosity demanded that she seek out virtually everything that came to mind.' In Moscow, Milly was working with the American journalist, Anna Louise Strong, who was briefly co-editor of the *Moscow Daily News*. After a brief visit to Madrid in mid-December 1936, Milly was given a job in the foreign press service in Valencia in the first week of January 1937.[74]

According to Marion Merriman: 'Milly Bennett was a wanderer who kept moving, from continent to continent, war to war, job to job, recording it all in whatever newspaper she could find to pay her at the moment.' Wherever she went, as Kate Mangan noted, she was extremely popular with men. Marion wrote:

> Milly was a homely woman, but she was blessed with an extraordinary figure. She didn't dress in a particularly sexy way, preferring the business skirts and blouses of the rather scruffy newspaper business. But her shapely figure turned the head of many a man with a roving eye. She was thirty-nine but looked years younger. Her face reflected her travels, her features craggy and rough-hewn. She was regarded as 'one of the boys' in the newspaper office and at the café bars where the journalists, crowd that included few women, gathered.

In 1931, she had married a Russian, Evgeni Konstantinov, but after he was arrested in 1934, she began to live with a ballet dancer. When Marion asked one of the other correspondents in Moscow the secret to Milly's attractiveness to men, he replied: '"Have you ever danced with her? No, of course you haven't", he added with a wink that suggested that Milly's charm lay not strictly in her ability to gather and write the news.'

James Minifie met Milly with an anarchist group south of Madrid. He described her as 'the homeliest woman I have ever seen; she had a muddy skin, poor teeth, unkempt black hair, and a bumpy figure'. Observing Minifie's dismay, an anarchist militiawoman told him: 'Don't underestimate Milly Bennett. She may not look like much, but she has a powerful attraction for men. She has charm.' Sefton Delmer had similar, if less affectionate memories of her. In a wildly exaggerated account, he wrote:

She was always clowning and mugging, and making a mock of herself and being a good fellow. Which was understandable. For Milly, with a mop of thick wiry hair, a sallow face, pebble lensed glasses perched on her thick stub of a nose, had one of those short, piano-legged, large torso bodies which are normally ignored by the courting males of our hemisphere.

Milly was, however, no pushover: 'She drank whiskey with the best of the correspondents, when they could get it, and vodka a good proportion of the rest of the time. Everybody liked Milly, and respected her. She was a pro.'

On the basis of her remarks to Robert Merriman in many heated conversations there could be little doubt that Milly Bennett was not a Communist. She was highly critical of the Soviet system and totally sceptical of the official line on its inexorable progress. When the Spanish Civil War broke out, she wanted to pursue a former lover, Wallace Burton, who had gone to join the International Brigades. With some difficulty, Milly managed to persuade her Russian employers to name her their correspondent in Spain. Burton was killed in action but Milly stayed on, writing occasional articles for the London *Times*, the Associated Press and United Press. She also worked in the press and propaganda office in Valencia, fell in love with a Swedish brigader called Hans Amlie and also helped gather material for Hemingway's *For Whom the Bell Tolls*.[75]

Although Milly was not a Communist, she fell foul of one of the more right-wing correspondents. Kate wrote of attending an event at which the President of the Republic, Manuel Azaña, made a speech:

> A very tall American journalist lifted me up so that I could see over all heads. Hank, the American, was a friend of Poppy and often used to take us out for a beer or invite us to cocktails at his flat. When he left Spain he wrote a pro-Franco book in which he said Poppy was a red agent sent straight from the Comintern and we laughed a lot about it but perhaps some people believed it.

The journalist in question was H. Edward Knoblaugh, the book *Correspondent in Spain*, and what he said highly damaging. Everything about Knoblaugh suggested a considerable political volatility and moral ambivalence. Other correspondents nicknamed him 'Doaks'.

In the first week of February 1937, Knoblaugh seemed to be relishing the likely capture of Málaga as a good story. The staff of the press office were reluctant to contemplate the consequences if the Andalusian port were to fall to the rebels and their Italian allies. One of their number, the louche Basil Murray, son of the Oxford classicist Gilbert Murray, went to find out for himself. Diminutive, perpetually disgruntled and often drunk, in Kate Mangan's opinion, he was 'a bit of a failure. He wore his hair long at the back, like Lloyd George, and was very sensitive. He had bright, dewy eyes like a stricken deer'. Murray was satirized by Evelyn Waugh (along with Peter Rodd, the husband of Nancy Mitford) as 'Basil Seal' in his novels *Black Mischief* (1932) and *Put Out More Flags* (1942). He had little stomach for war reporting. He returned from Málaga in a state of panic: 'It's too ghastly, that town is lost already. The bombardments are incessant and frightful. The morale of the people has broken under them. The cathedral is full of poor women with babies, camping, who have fled from the villages. You can't imagine the horror of it.' His colleagues shrugged him off as hysterical and his report went unpublished. When the Italians entered Málaga on 7 February, the flight of terrified refugees towards Almería witnessed one of the most tragic episodes of the war. Thousands of women, children and the elderly were bombarded from warships and strafed by Italian and German aircraft. The entire Republican zone was traumatized and the press office was not immune. Coco Robles wept uncontrollably and even Constancia de la Mora, who had tried to keep her emotions in check, cried in front of Kate Mangan.

Morale in the office had not been helped by the arrival of one of the last people to escape Málaga, the beautiful fresh-faced, brown-eyed young Norwegian journalist, Gerda Grepp, who later to have an affair with Louis Fischer. She had been sent to the town on her first assignment and become friends there with Arthur Koestler and local residents, ranging from anarchists to the English zoologist Sir Peter Chalmers-Mitchell. Now she arrived in a state of collapse and when news of the capture of the town came in 'she nearly went demented'. She had begged Koestler to leave with her but he had stayed on in the hope of reporting on the expected atrocities. Grepp was inconsolable, convinced that all the people she had met in Málaga would be murdered. She plunged into the darkest of Scandinavian depressions.[76]

Edward Knoblaugh was furious that he had not been immediately given a car to go and view the situation for himself. He later took his revenge on 'Poppy' and others in his book:

> A large bundle of material from the Ministry of Propaganda was delivered to my Valencia office twice each day. I rarely used any of this material without checking it carefully. Sometimes it was impossible to check. One of the articles I did use typifies the high degree of skill the propaganda

machine achieved within the space of a few short months. This was a story written by Milly Bennett, one of the talented young American writers on the government payroll, describing the evacuation of Malaga. My office had urgently requested coverage on the Malaga situation, but the government, denying there was any possibility of Malaga's falling, was not furnishing cars to correspondents to disprove its contention. The story, written by the Ministry of Propaganda employee, a gifted young woman fresh from seven years' training in Russia, was a 'ghosted interview' quoting Dr. Norman Bethune, Canadian head of a blood-transfusion unit working in Loyalist Spain, on the experiences she attributed to him among the refugees fleeing Malaga. Her well written 'interview' told of the 'inconceivable ferocity of the barbarian invaders', the 'innumerable scenes of horror created by the foreigners' and the 'terrible tragedy of these countless thousands forced to flee their homes'. It did not mention, of course, that the ones who did the 'forcing' were the Loyalists themselves. As happened later in Bilbao, many who did not want to leave were executed as 'counter-revolutionaries'. Even if it had mentioned this, I wouldn't have been able to send it. I had no doubt but that there *was* much suffering among the hungry Malaguenans struggling eastward along the highway toward Almeria. I had seen something of the hardships undergone by the refugees in other parts of Spain. I had no way of getting there to cover the story myself, so I used this prepared article, trimming out some of the more obvious propaganda with which the story was interlarded but letting it run pretty full.[77]

In fact, the text by Milly, to which Knoblaugh referred, was entirely accurate. After the war, she saw his book and wrote to him that she thought his insinuations about her being trained in Russia to be 'libellous, lowdown and mean'. In his remarkably insensitive reply, he had the audacity, or perhaps the obtuseness, to deny that it was meant to be 'a crack' at her or contained any 'nastiness': 'I think you are a fine newspaper woman and a swell pal, and certainly do not want you to feel that I went out of my way to take a slam at you.' To expect her not to be offended by his damaging statement that she had received 'seven years' training in Russia' and was thus a Soviet agent suggested either that he was very naïve or expected her to be.[78] He would display similar insensitivity in his dealings with Jay Allen.

The callous cynicism with which Knoblaugh viewed the plight of the refugees from Málaga contrasted with the attitude of Lawrence Fernsworth. He went with

Kate Mangan to cover the retreat and was deeply moved by the uncomplaining distress of the refugees he interviewed in Almería.[79] T. C. Worsley, who had been the driver of Bethune's ambulance during the retreat from Málaga, met Fernsworth shortly after his return to Valencia. He described him as grey-haired, wearing pince-nez and a 'Conservative democrat of the old school, who had become a staunch defender of the new Republic'. Fernsworth was anxious for Worsley to describe exactly what he had seen on the road from Málaga to Almeria. His reports, based on the interviews, had been published in *The Times* on 17 and 24 February, but had then been denied by the paper's correspondent with the rebels. The denial was shown to Fernsworth before printing and, when printed on 3 March, was accompanied by a statement from him that he had interviewed refugees on the road to Almería, in hospitals, in refugee camps and in barracks, and that it was 'beyond belief that they should all be engaged in a conspiracy to concoct the story'. In the hope of strengthening the point still further, Fernsworth now asked Worsley and Bethune to give him a signed statement of what they had seen. This they did, but nothing further was published by *The Times*.[80]

Not everyone in the office was as efficient as Milly Bennett. Yet, interestingly, in a letter to Kitty Bowler, Elizabeth Deeble wrote that Kitty would have been even better at the job in the press office than Milly. The scale of work expected from an employee of the press and propaganda can be deduced from Deeble's letter. As well as her own journalistic work for the Manchester *Guardian* and the *Washington Post*, she was working in Barcelona as Liston Oak's equivalent in the Catalan Comissariat de Propaganda with Jaume Miravitlles. As head of the English-language section there, she was

> editor (and write practically all of it) of English bulletin of propaganda
> under Miravitlles (laddie is well-named 'marvels' and does them), do
> most and supervise the rest of English translations for him, Companys,
> etc., translate into Spanish all letters that come in English, and translate
> the Spanish or Catalan replies back again into English, interpret for all
> English and American visitors, represent Agence Espagne here, help on
> religious bulletin, am trying to write a book on Spain in the few free
> seconds I have, keep track of all the English and most of the French press
> as well as the Spanish every day, and now and then march in a parade or
> have my photo taken for the good of the cause.

All this was recounted without complaint: 'Wish I could get along without sleep or without food, but find it impossible. As it is, I write some 5000 to 6000 words a day in various languages, some of it original, and find time to rush about doing other things as well.'[81]

In Valencia, Liston Oak certainly did not work on that scale. Indeed, he was regularly absent from his office and, when he was there, was notorious for his lack of diplomatic skills with visiting writers. For instance, he made a hash of relations with W. H. Auden, who had arrived in the belief that he could help the cause of the Republic by working in the press and propaganda office. Oak adopted a 'violently hostile attitude' out of sheer jealousy. Rubio commissioned Auden to translate a speech by Azaña, which he did with such elegance and imagination, according to Kate Mangan, as to improve upon the original. Eventually, Auden became exasperated with the politics and intrigue in Valencia and volunteered for the front as a stretcher-bearer.[82]

Liston Oak was involved peripherally in the scandal surrounding the death of José Robles Pazos and in the consequent fall-out. It was almost certainly Oak who was the first person to tell Coco Robles that he had heard that his father was dead. That was on 9 April, the day after John Dos Passos arrived in Valencia and visited the press office to get safe-conducts and make travel arrangements for his trip to Madrid. They must have known each other before, but the renewal of their acquaintance now would play some role in Dos Passos' drift into anti-Communism. Within three weeks, Oak would be in Barcelona pleading with Dos Passos to help him get out of Spain. The reason for his ostensible panic was that he had been increasingly indiscreet about his contacts with the POUM. Certainly, links with an organization regarded by the Russians as Trotskyist would do nothing to enhance his position as an employee of the Ministry of Foreign Affairs.

However, job security was probably not Liston Oak's main priority. According to Kate Mangan, Oak had already shown a desire to get out of Valencia: 'Liston was beginning to be a bit restless in his post, he was losing interest and discharging his duties more and more perfunctorily. He complained increasingly of his rheumatism. He said his health would not stand the damp climate in Valencia.' He went briefly to Madrid and talked vaguely of starting a bureau there. However, finding the besieged capital too dangerous, he came back to Valencia, but he soon left for Barcelona, claiming that it was merely for a visit. Constancia de la Mora pointed out that the climate there was even damper and cooler. However, Kate felt that Liston would be more at home in Catalonia, because of his sympathy with the POUM. He never formally resigned his post at the press office. Rubio Hidalgo thought highly of Oak and took it for granted that he would soon be back. The Valencia office continued to send him copies of their press releases and commissioned him to write articles on the Catalan economic situation. When he failed to respond to any of their communications and no articles materialized, 'at last we realized that he had deserted his post'. Milly Bennett commented: 'It's just like him to leave a job as soon as he has got it started. He has been a failure all his life.'[83]

The departure of Liston Oak hardly affected the functioning of the press office. The reorganization set off by Fischer's report on the Republic's propaganda deficit was still six months in the future. The late spring did, however, see one of the denizens of the office meet an unfortunate end. Since his marriage had broken up, Basil Murray had begun to drink. Having been persuaded not to join the International Brigades, he had devoted himself to a quest for romance, but every woman on whom he cast eyes turned him down. He became morose and, according to Delmer, 'what had once been charming eccentricity developed into a phobic moodiness and mad romantic exaltation'. Constancia de la Mora could not 'find much use for this disturbed and disturbing young man, who had come to Spain to play the part of Byron, and who could not be relied on to turn up at the office and play the part of a hack'. After losing his job at the press office, he joined the International News Service of William Randolph Hearst. He did not last long. He was amused by the fact that, in the square, there was a performing goat which balanced, with all four legs together, on top of a pole. His frequent mentions of the goat seemed a gratuitous frivolity to his employers and he was fired.

Unemployed, he drank more and his life became more aimless. Then he fell in love with a mysterious reporter. According to Delmer, she was called Mary Mulliner and appears in Kate Mangan's memoir as 'Geraldine O'Brien'. Kate recalled that she 'behaved so much like a spy that, in my opinion, it was impossible that she could have been one. If she was a spy I could not guess which side employed her'. Cockburn, who was working for the security service as some kind of counter-espionage agent devoted to vetting Anglo-Saxon visitors, had no doubts: 'had she had the words "I am a Nazi spy" printed on her hat, that could hardly have made her position clearer than it was'. Whatever else she was up to, the woman in question toyed with Basil, 'poor, dear, limp rag that he was', trying to make him jealous of other men. Then, suddenly she fled Valencia, heading, according to Cockburn, 'for Berlin, in the company of a high-ranking officer of the International Brigade, who proved also to be an agent of the enemy'. Basil inevitably became more gloomy than ever.

To distract Basil, Ed Knoblaugh took him drinking in the red light district of the port. At a street circus, Basil was entranced to see swinging on a trapeze 'a fine buxom she-ape with all the indications of her sex emphatically developed'. He offered to buy the ape and the reluctant owner was forced into selling by some watching militiamen. They, Basil, Knoblaugh and the ape then went off on a bar-crawl which ended at the Hotel Victoria. The Manager refused entry until, backed by the drunken militiamen, Basil successfully argued that this was intolerable dis-crimination: 'What about all the other apes in the hotel?' Knoblaugh told Delmer that the last he saw of Basil was 'when he turned on the water for his bath. "And now my poppet", he was saying as I closed the door, "you shall have a lovely warm bath with plenty of lovely lavender soap. Do you like soap, oh Queen of my heart?"' After a couple of days, there was no sign of Basil so Knoblaugh went back to the hotel. In the room, he found mayhem, the ape huddled in a nest of blankets and, a feverish Basil, both coughing helplessly. He had caught a virulent form of pneumonia from the ape. His enemies spread a rumour that it was a result of intimate relations with the ape; others that he had fallen into a drunken stupor and in an effort to rouse him, the bored ape had bitten him. Patience Darton arranged for him to be transferred to a British hospital ship. Basil recovered suf-ficiently to send proposals of marriage to several eligible girls in London, but died before reaching England.[84]

Distress over the fate of individuals was overshadowed by preoccupation with the progress of the war. The summer and the early autumn of 1937 saw some short-lived triumphs for the Republic, such as the initial successes at Brunete and Belchite, but also saw the disastrous loss of the north. Despite the gradual erosion of territory, morale remained high in Valencia. The move of the press office to Barcelona, along with the rest of the government, coincided with a reorganization of Republican resources, which seemed to bear fruit with the initial assault on Teruel in mid-December 1937 and its capture on 8 January 1938. In the first twelve days of the encounter, with Hemingway, Tom Delmer and Robert Capa, Herbert Matthews would drive each day from Valencia to the battle-front in bit-terly cold conditions. They drove nearly three thousand miles, and produced scoop after scoop, beating the other correspondents by anything up to four days. On 17 December 1937, Hemingway, Delmer and Matthews entered Teruel with the Republican attackers. They then drove back to Valencia. Matthews recalled later: 'after twenty hours on the go, I sat down at midnight, writing until four in the morning. It was the best story I got in the Spanish Civil War.'

Despite writing what he considered the best reporting of his life, Matthews found his piece brutally cut and buried on the inside pages of the *New York Times*, once again the victim of the pro-Catholic 'bull-pen'. They reprimanded him for the length of the piece. In contrast, the paper printed a vivid, but entirely faked, description by William Carney of the retaking of the city and the rescue of the besieged rebel garrison. Not for the first time, Carney, safely ensconced in

Zaragoza, had parroted, and then embellished, rebel press handouts that had over-confidently announced the recapture of the city. In contrast, Matthews had made the hazardous journey through snow and ice to Teruel and found it still in Republican hands. His vivid account utterly discredited what had been submitted by Carney. Nevertheless, the managing editor, Jimmy 'Dressy' James, issued Carney with no more than the most gentle reprimand.[85]

Hemingway was furious. When Matthews' book, *Two Wars and More to Come*, was due to come out some months later, he sent a telegram to the publishers:

> Herbert Matthews is the straightest the ablest and the bravest war correspondent writing today stop he has seen the truth where it was very dangerous to see and in this book he brings that rarest commodity to you stop in a world where faking now is far more successful than the truth he stands like a gaunt lighthouse of honesty stop and when the fakers are all dead they will read Matthews in the schools to find out what really happened stop I hope his office will keep some uncut copies of his dispatches in case he dies.[86]

The eventual rebel recapture of Teruel on 21 February opened the way to a massive rebel advance which reached the sea on 15 April and thus split the Republican zone in two. The end was in sight but Negrín was determined to fight on, refusing to believe that the democracies could go on being blind to the Axis threat. His optimism and commitment were shared by the majority of correspondents. Even when the situation grew ever more bleak for the Republic, there was no tightening of the censorship nor of working conditions for journalists beyond the hardships that they had to share with the rest of the population. In Barcelona, there was little food, no hot water for bathing, little by way of public transport and growing shortages of essential drugs.[87] Bombing raids on the Catalan capital were ever more intense and Franco's growing numerical superiority made visits to the front ever more dangerous.

In March 1938, Hemingway, another young correspondent, Jim Lardner, son of the novelist Ring Lardner, and Jimmy Sheean had all visited the press office situated in the broad avenue of the Diagonal in Barcelona. As with most other buildings in the city, the windows were criss-crossed with strips of gummed paper to prevent splintering from bomb blasts. Constancia de la Mora arranged hotel rooms for Sheean and Lardner. Feeling inadequate as a correspondent, Lardner would soon join the International Brigades and be killed at the battle of the Ebro.[88] Despite rebel advances through Aragón and the recent appalling bombing raids in Barcelona,

Sheean found Constancia de la Mora as cheerful and busy as ever. After the rebels broke through to the Mediterranean in mid-April, he was pleasantly surprised to note the deference with which the credentials issued by Connie's office were treated in both halves of the Republican zone. His work faced few restrictions:

> One time I went off to the front for three or four days by myself (rather against the advice of the local press attaché) and never had a moment's trouble. The boys who drove trucks of food or munitions were always ready to give me a lift; the military commanders were affable and informative; I could always find a place to sleep and a blanket to cover me.

In the ferocity of rebel attacks, 'the Republicans were inclined to assume that anybody who came up to the front was a friend. I never heard of a war in which a stray foreigner could roam about so freely, even with press credentials.' Far from being threatened, as was the fate of correspondents in the Nationalist zone, Sheean and others found themselves being invited to share the soldiers' meagre rations.[89]

In mid-1938, with the situation for the Republic worsening dramatically, Cedric Salter, who had worked for both the *Daily Telegraph* and the *News Chronicle* in Spain, was hoping to get a job representing the *Daily Mail*. Since Lord Rothermere's paper was notorious for its doggedly pro-fascist views, it seemed unlikely that it would want a correspondent in Spain or indeed that the Republican authorities would grant permission. However, Salter was persuaded by the Reuters correspondent, Bill Williams, to try his luck. The first part of the operation would be to persuade the Republican press office that to have relatively objective reporting in the hitherto ferociously Francoist *Daily Mail* would be to the infinite benefit of the Republic. The second part of the operation would be to persuade the editor of the *Daily Mail* that the inevitable fall of the Republic told from the inside would be a tremendous news story which, with no correspondent as things stood, they would be unable to report.

Accordingly, Salter went to see Constancia de la Mora, whom he described as 'the dictator of the Foreign Press Department'. Although he was suspicious of her commitment to the Communist Party, he was in awe of her:

> Few people and no other woman have ever impressed me with the same sense of latent mental power. She was in the middle thirties, rather masculine in manner and clothes, and had a nice taste in pretty secretaries. Everything that she did and said was quietly efficient, passionless, and far-seeing.

He argued the case that it might help the Republican cause to get a hearing in the *Daily Mail*. She granted her approval, albeit not without making it clear that she knew that he was motivated by the need for another job after being replaced as the *News Chronicle* correspondent by William Forrest: 'I always left Constancia feeling that she was at least three jumps ahead of me.' With her permission secured, Salter hastened to London and persuaded the *Daily Mail* to take him on as their first, last and only correspondent in Government Spain. He began his mission of reporting on the final days of the Republic at the beginning of June 1938.[90]

After Willie Forrest had returned to Spain in the spring of 1937, he impressed all who met him with his courage. According to Cedric Salter, Forrest never showed the slightest awareness of danger, 'strolling about happily with bullets whining uncomfortably close, and not bothering even to duck'. Apparently, the only sign that he recognized danger was that his Scottish accent intensified noticeably. During one of the most notorious artillery bombardments to affect the Hotel Florida, on 22 April 1937, Josephine Herbst described him as a sheep-faced man, 'behaving very well with grayish look'. However, it was his sensitive and realistic reporting that impressed every bit as much as his bravery. When Willie had been in Madrid during the worst days of the siege, Geoffrey Cox had recognized his uncanny ability to capture the intensity of the moment in his articles by the use of some concrete detail. Not all journalists were as impressed as Cox. Certainly not the interpreter assigned to Willie by the press office, the Swedish Kajsa Rothman. Not appreciating how he worked, she complained to Herbst that Willie 'always wants to know unimportant things'. Constancia de la Mora, however, shared Cox's appreciation of Forrest, regarding him as

> one of the best all-round correspondents covering the war. He had a fine Scotch sense of humour, which turned up at the most difficult moments. I never saw him flustered or worried. I never heard him complain. Bombardments never gave him the jitters, defeats never shook his faith in the Spanish people. He knew Spain intimately and used his knowledge to give his dispatches an informative and understanding tone few reporters achieved. He moved slowly around Valencia and Barcelona, apparently never in a hurry, never worried. Yet his dispatches were always on time and they always covered more facts than many reporters who stirred up lots of dust and trouble and got nothing for their pains.[91]

In acknowledging the bravery of some of the correspondents, an International Brigade veteran, Bernard Knox, commented that the one vital distinction between war reporter and soldier is that one can come and go when and where he chooses while the other must remain where he is ordered.[92] Nevertheless, several correspondents in the Republican zone increasingly found themselves in dangerous situations, chose to stay and frequently demonstrated a courage that went far beyond their immediate professional obligations. Cedric Salter remarked on the particular physical courage of Herbert Matthews, claiming that while in normal conditions he could often be short-tempered, under fire, he became 'one of the kindest, gentlest, and most considerate of men. If things were really bad he would go about doing little kindnesses and smiling amiably at anyone within sight. I formed the impression that only under circumstances of real danger was he really, deeply at peace with himself and his fellow men.'[93] There was no shortage of situations in which the correspondents' courage was put to the test.

Joseph North of the American *Daily Worker* recalled a revealing incident on May Day 1938. On the winding mountain roads around the Ebro, he, Matthews and Hemingway were in a car driving along behind a truck full of young soldiers singing Republican songs. Matthews was driving and

even he, somber and taciturn, seemed moved. Suddenly, as the truck rounded a sharp bend, the driver lost control and it somersaulted before our eyes, the scene of gaiety changed to horror as bodies lay bleeding on the ground. Matthews jammed the brakes on, we leaped out; I can never recall where Hemingway found a medicine kit, but he was on his knees bandaging the injured and solacing them. We worked away together, the blood of the dying on our hands. I noticed that Matthews strode among the bodies, bending down, not to help, but to interview the dying, jotting notes in a little notebook. After all, he was first and foremost, 'a *Times* man', and deadlines to even the most humane of *Times* men, were more urgent than death or life. To every man his loyalties. Hemingway started at the sight: 'You sonofabitch', he roared, 'get out or I'll kill you'. After this I felt a regard for him, a warmth, which has lasted to this day, for, I felt, thinking about it afterward, I had seen the real man; despite his tough-guy pose, here was a humanist, a partisan of humanity.[94]

Herbert Matthews, Jimmy Sheean, Robert Capa and Willie Forrest were among the last correspondents to leave Catalonia before the Francoists reached the French frontier. Sheean, Matthews, Buckley and Hemingway had been involved in a hair-raising crossing of the Ebro in a boat which was nearly smashed against some spikes. They were saved by Hemingway's brute strength and impetuousness.[95] They had then followed the retreating Republican army as it was bombed and strafed from Tarragona to Barcelona. In one of his most moving despatches, Matthews described the terrifying scene as streams of refugees were bombed near El Vendrell: 'We four correspondents and our chauffeur, as well as everyone else in the region, lived through the sort of hell that modern war brings to all and sundry.'[96] When the publisher of the *New York Times*, Arthur Hays Sulzberger, wrote to congratulate him on the article, Matthews replied: 'Thanks for the kind words about the Tarragona story, but I trust that you also noted that the desk preferred to front page Carney's story from faraway Burgos, meanwhile cutting my piece up.'[97]

Constancia de la Mora entered the press room in the Hotel Majestic on the night of 24 January 1939 and dramatically announced that, at noon the following day, the last cars would be leaving to evacuate the remaining correspondents. She solemnly took her leave, shaking hands with each of them. On the next day, William Forrest and O. D. Gallagher of the *Daily Express* loaded their luggage and set off. Cedric Salter, safe in the knowledge that the correspondent of the right-wing *Daily Mail* was unlikely to be molested by the Francoist occupiers, remained to be the last British correspondent in Barcelona. He quickly managed to ingratiate himself with the conquerors and sent out an eye-witness account of the fall of the city.[98] Gallagher, after crossing the French frontier, somehow managed to get to Madrid, where he was to be the last correspondent remaining when the Francoists took the capital.

As Barcelona fell, Negrín's government was installed in the fortress at Figueras in northern Girona. Herbert Matthews interviewed the prime minister, who declared his determination to fight on. Matthews was deeply impressed by the efforts being made by the Republicans to deal with the problems faced by the starving refugees who were sleeping in the streets of Figueras in the midst of regular rebel bombing raids.[99] After the last meeting of the Cortes on Spanish soil, Negrín remained in the fortress at Figueras until the last units of the Republican army had crossed the frontier on 9 February. Around the courtyard, the cabinet was installed in a room with the words 'council of ministers' roughly chalked on the wall next to the door. The town square, where the office of press and propaganda had been installed in a requisitioned house, was heaving with refugees. Luisi, Álvarez del Vayo's wife, was organizing food for the staff and the remaining journalists. The situation was chaotic, the office was noisy and dirty, with reporters coming then going around the clock on their way to the French border.

Anyone who had ever had anything remotely to do with the Foreign Ministry or had a relative who had once worked there headed for the flat where the press office had been installed. Correspondents and government officials squeezed in together, sharing what little food that could be obtained, sleeping on the floor. It was a symbol of the solidarity that had been established between many of the reporters and the Republic.

Sheean crossed the border in the bleakest mood imaginable and sent his last chronicle on the war from Perpignan. Like Herbert Matthews, like Henry Buckley, like Jay Allen, like Ernest Hemingway, like Martha Gellhorn, like Louis Fischer, like Willy Forrest, like so many foreign correspondents, Jimmy Sheean had become emotionally attached to the Spanish Republic. They had been inspired by the spirit with which the Republican population fought against overwhelming odds. They had shared some of their hardships and they left knowing that, since fascism had not been stopped in Spain, its aggression would now be felt by France, by Britain and eventually by the United States. Within five weeks Hitler had entered Prague and Neville Chamberlain declared that he was shocked and would no longer be able to take the Führer's word for anything. They had all of them – Fischer, Matthews, Allen, Sheean – argued passionately that the passivity of the democracies was paving the way to fascist victory. Now, it was with some bitterness that Sheean wrote:

> This strange, tardy awakening on the part of the Prime Minister was of no worth in the scales of history, and will do little to blind even his contemporaries to the true value of a man who has consistently put the interests of his own class and type above those of either his own nation or of humanity itself.[100]

Herbert Matthews, Willy Forrest and William Hickey of the *Daily Express* had crossed the border to send out stories but came back into Spain, although they too would have to leave shortly after. On the following day, Matthews wrote his last despatch. He had witnessed heart-rending scenes of the sick and the wounded crossing the frontier only to be thrown into rapidly organized and totally unhygienic concentration camps.[101] He looked back over his work in the previous two years' during which time he had written honestly while hoping for a Republican victory:

> The story that I told – of bravery, of tenacity, of discipline and high ideals – had been scoffed at by many. The dispatches describing the callousness

of the French and the cynicism of the British had been objected to and denied. I, too, was beaten and sick at heart and somewhat shell-shocked, as any person must be under the nerve strain of seven weeks of incessant danger, coming at the end of two years' campaigning. For a few years afterwards I suffered from a form of claustrophobia, brought on by being caught, as in a vise, in a refuge in Tarragona during one of the last bombings. So I was depressed, physically and mentally and morally. [...] But the lessons I had learned! They seemed worth a great deal. Even then, heartsick and discouraged as I was, something sang inside of me. I, like the Spaniards, had fought my war and lost, but I could not be persuaded that I had set too bad an example.[102]

5

The Rebel Zone: Intimidation in Salamanca and Burgos

Kate Mangan was struck by the extent to which her colleagues, in the Republican press office in Valencia, tried to facilitate the work of foreign journalists.[1] Such assistance was experienced in the rebel zone only by the correspondents from Fascist Italy, Nazi Germany and Portugal. This was a reflection not only of the prevailing military mentality, but also of the personnel chosen to oversee relations with the world's press. Anticipating his own future eminence, within a few days of arriving in Seville, Franco had set up a press and propaganda service. This Gabinete de Prensa was established on 9 August under the monarchist journalist, Juan Pujol Martínez, with practical responsibility for journalists being taken by Luis Antonio Bolín. Pujol was the choice of General Sanjurjo, having been involved in the preparation of his abortive military coup in August 1932; he had also been with him in Lisbon shortly before his death in an aircraft accident.[2] Pujol had worked for *ABC* before becoming editor of the right-wing *Informaciones*, where he accepted subsidies from the Third Reich in return for pro-Nazi and ferociously anti-Jewish articles, including one by Hitler himself entitled 'Why I am anti-Semitic'. He had opened its pages to leading Falangists and other Spanish fascist sympathizers. He was also a Cortes deputy for the Confederación Española de Derechas Autónomas for the Balearic Islands. His deputy was Joaquín Arrarás, a member of the ultra-rightist monarchist group, Acción Española, and close friend and first biographer of the Generalísimo himself. The Gabinete's name was changed on 24 August to Oficina de Prensa y Propaganda. Bolín, the one-time London correspondent for *ABC*, had attracted the attention of Franco because of his part in hiring the Dragon Rapide used to transport the rebel leader from the Canary Islands to Morocco. He would run the foreign press offices successively in Sevilla, Cáceres and Salamanca, and during the assaults on Málaga and Bilbao.[3] Ironically, his eventual counterpart in the Republican zone would be his sister-in-law, Constancia de la Mora.

When General José Millán Astray, the founder of the Spanish Foreign Legion, arrived in Seville, Franco quickly recruited him to propagate his cause throughout the Nationalist zone. He was installed at Franco's side along with his immediate staff in the Palacio de Yanduri in Seville.[4] Millán Astray devoted himself to the insistent proclamation of the future Caudillo's greatness. This adulation was sufficiently gratifying to Franco to persuade him, in the chill autumn of 1936, to replace the altogether less charismatic Pujol with his one-time mentor. Millán was placed in official charge of the expanded Oficina de Prensa y Propaganda in its improvised offices in the Instituto Anaya, an old palace which housed the Faculty of Sciences of the University of Salamanca.[5]

At first, a few correspondents were allowed to accompany the columns of the African Army, which advanced in early August from Seville towards Madrid. However, close control was quickly established since it was felt that the trail of slaughter was not something to be broadcast internationally. Accordingly, under the overall authority first of Pujol, and later of Millán Astray, responsibility for foreign correspondents was placed with Luis Bolín. Those who knew him as an Anglophile monarchist were taken aback to find him in Salamanca boasting the title Captain Bolín and living with other senior members of Franco's *cuartel general* in the Palacio de Monterrey, which had been loaned by the Duque de Alba. He could barely bring himself to talk to his old friends. Now, having been granted an honorary captaincy in the Foreign Legion as a reward for accompanying Franco on his journey, he had taken to dressing up as a legionnaire. Wearing breeches and high boots, against which he rapped a riding crop, he would strut menacingly through the press office glaring imperiously at the assembled journalists waiting for passes or other documentation. Although other Legion officers regarded him as a comic figure since he knew nothing of matters military, he exercised his spurious authority by making the correspondents line up as if they were soldiers at his orders. He strode menacingly among them with a fierce scowl.[6] During the Málaga campaign, Noel Monks of the *Daily Express* was shocked by Bolín's cruel streak: 'Whenever we saw a pathetic pile of freshly executed "Reds", their hands tied behind their backs – usually behind a farmhouse in every newly taken village – he would spit on them, saying "Vermin".'[7]

Sir Percival Phillips, correspondent of the *Daily Telegraph*, claimed that Bolín 'made himself hated like poison by the English and American correspondents'.[8] He was disliked and feared by the entire foreign press corps partly because he would not permit visits to the front other than under military escort, but much more as a result of his frequent threats to shoot newspapermen. The censorship never permitted any mention either of the atrocities committed by the

Nationalists or of the increasing numbers of Germans and Italians in their zone. Three days after the massacre of 14 August 1936, the cameraman René Brut of Pathé newsreels reached Badajoz and filmed piles of bodies. He was arrested in a Seville hotel on 5 September and imprisoned for several days, during which time he was threatened with death by Bolín. He escaped being shot only when Pathé sent a carefully doctored version of the film to Franco's headquarters.[9]

An account of the Badajoz massacre was published in the Paris edition of the *New York Herald Tribune* on the basis of a United Press agency report. The report used the name of Reynolds Packard, a UP journalist who had not in fact sent the story. When the original article was mentioned in the Manchester *Guardian* in January 1937, Bolín summoned Packard to Salamanca, where he threatened him. A terrified Packard cabled Webb Miller, the United Press' European Bureau chief in London, pleading with him to inform Bolín that he had not written the offending piece, which he did. A similar incident took place when Bolín made comparable demands of Jean d'Hospital, the representative of the Havas Agency in Nationalist Spain. Both the United Press and the Havas Agency pointed out that the cables in question had not come from Packard and d'Hospital, but they did not deny the veracity of the offending reports. Bolín then passed the replies on to the British enthusiast for the Francoist cause, Major Geoffrey McNeill-Moss, who used them to 'prove' that the reports of the Badajoz massacre had been fabricated.[10]

In the third week of August 1936, the correspondent of the French centre-right newspaper *L'Intransigeant*, Baron Guy de Traversay (sometimes rendered Traversée), was shot by the rebels in Mallorca. Traversay had travelled with the Republican expedition which had tried to recapture the island in mid-August. He carried credentials from the Catalan Generalitat signed by Jaume Miravitlles, who would later become the head of the Comissariat de Propaganda. When captured, Traversay had pointed out that he was a journalist. When the rebel officers saw the document signed by Miravitlles, they hesitated only briefly before shooting Traversay. The French Catholic writer, Georges Bernanos, was called upon to identify him and he was appalled to be confronted by the blackened and shiny cadaver of Traversay, which had been doused in petrol and burned on a beach along with the corpses of a number of Republican prisoners.[11]

On 25 September 1936, as the African columns moving on Madrid made their detour down from Maqueda towards Toledo, Webb Miller of the United Press was arrested at Torrijos. A telegram had been intercepted from his office requesting that he investigate rumours circulating about a plot to murder General Mola. The telegram had been read by the censors who misinterpreted the words 'RUMOURS PLOT ASSASSINATE GENERAL MOLA' as an instruction to Miller to carry out the murder himself. Apparently, shortly before Miller's arrival, a man claiming to be a newspaper correspondent had been executed in Burgos on suspicion of being involved in the plot. Without anything resembling an investigation, the rebel military authorities were about to shoot Miller when he had the good fortune to see the press officer attached to his group, the English-educated Captain Gonzalo Aguilera y Yeltes. After Miller had been left to sweat for some hours, told that he would soon be shot, Aguilera managed to sort out the misunderstanding.[12]

It was Bolín who ensured that no correspondents were permitted to enter Toledo during the two-day bloodbath that followed its occupation on 27 September 1936. The excuse given to correspondents who had previously been taken into battlefield situations was that it was 'too dangerous'. They knew only too well that it was to prevent them testifying to the atrocities taking place while, in the words of Yagüe, 'we make Toledo the whitest town in Spain'.[13] Accordingly, they had to make do with propaganda material given to them by Bolín. One such was the apocryphal story published in the *Daily Mail* by Harold Cardozo on 30 September 1936, in which it was claimed that Colonel Moscardó, the rebel commander of the Alcázar, was telephoned on 23 July by the Republican authorities and told that, if he did not surrender, his son would be shot. When Moscardó refused, it was alleged that his son was shot immediately. In fact, Luis Moscardó was killed, along with other prisoners, in reprisal for a Nationalist bombing attack on 23 August.[14]

Nevertheless, what they saw on entering the town two days later was still deeply disturbing. Webb Miller told Jay Allen that, after he saw what the rebels did to the wounded and to the nurses and the doctors in the hospital in Toledo, 'he came close to going off his rocker'. He began drinking more heavily than usual and, once in St Jean de Luz or Biarritz, telephoned the New York office saying that he absolutely had to write an account of it. The answer was that if he did so, the United Press would be thrown out of rebel Spain. Without a correspondent on the rebel side, the agency's best customers in Latin America, who were desperate for news of the Civil War, would be lost. Accordingly, Miller wrote nothing for the United Press about what he had seen and his 1937 memoirs are also relatively circumspect about it.[15]

On 26 October 1936, Denis Weaver of the *News Chronicle,* and the Canadian James M. Minifie of the *New York Herald Tribune,* set out from Madrid to tour the front in a car provided by the Republican press services, a chauffeur and an escort in the form of a white-haired retired seaman. Weaver had been in Madrid for only a week and had already had the hair-raising experience of lying in a ditch while his car was strafed by rebel aircraft. Now, driving from El Escorial to

Aranjuez, near Seseña, they were stopped by Moorish troops. The chauffeur and the seaman were shot immediately. The journalists were manhandled and threatened, and then were taken to General Varela's headquarters, where they found Henry T. Gorrell of the United Press, who had been captured in similar circumstances. After being interrogated as spies, they were detained, their concerns heightened by being repeatedly told that they were about to be shot, and seeing a lorry laden with terrified women and teenage prisoners being taken, presumably, for execution. Eventually, they were driven to Salamanca for Franco himself to decide their fate. Once there, they were individually interrogated by Luis Bolín, who threatened to have them hanged. Weaver learned later that on the same day that he had been captured, Bolín had refused a request by his paper, the *News Chronicle*, for permission to send a correspondent to the Francoist zone, and stated that 'if any representative of the *News Chronicle* were found in Franco territory it would be the worse for him'. After a further five days in custody, and being forced to send despatches saying that they had been treated courteously, Weaver, Minifie and Gorrell were expelled from Spain and into France.[16]

On reaching Hendaye, Weaver immediately wrote a disclaimer of the article that had secured his release. He described how, far from being given courteous treatment, he was repeatedly interrogated during his captivity. He pointed out that: 'My chauffeur was not killed by a stray bullet, but shot down in cold blood within a yard of me', adding that 'I was fired at, and from close range, repeatedly'. He went on to stress that:

> The report also failed to state that among the lethal weapons used to arrest two harmless journalists was a machine-gun in an Italian whippet tank, and that an Italian officer was among the many who raised venomous objections to my request to be taken to headquarters at once. [...] Even this morning in San Sebastian I was threatened with the cells if I persisted in asking to be allowed to telephone the British Consulate.[17]

Even before Weaver's arrest, because of the *News Chronicle*'s consistently pro-Republican stance, Franco's representative in London had already rejected outright its first application for permission to send an accredited correspondent to the insurgent zone. However, in late October 1936, the editor Gerald Barry had decided to take advantage of having a young reporter, the New Zealander, Geoffrey Cox, available in France to try again. Cox took the train to St Jean de Luz, the elegant border resort awash with diplomats and wealthy Franco supporters. At the Bar Basque, a nest of spies and arms dealers, he made contact with Franco's local agent, an Irishman. He agreed to pass on the newspaper's application but warned Cox: 'I doubt if they will let you in, and if they do, you had better watch your step. They detest the *News Chronicle*, and if you put one foot out of line, you could find yourself in gaol, if only as a hostage for better behaviour on the part of your paper.' While waiting for a favourable outcome, but mindful of the Irishman's dire warning, Cox made contact with the British Embassy in case he might later need help should he find himself thrown into a Francoist prison. The pompous and self-satisfied Ambassador, Sir Henry Chilton, a staunch admirer of Franco, had set up the embassy in a residence in St Jean de Luz, where he remained until his retirement in late 1937, rather than return to Republican Madrid. Chilton was not remotely sympathetic to Cox's potential situation, commenting irritably: 'I have never heard of anything like this in my diplomatic experience. You come here and tell me you are about to go into a foreign country and act in a way which may land you in gaol, and then expect us to get you out. If you obey the law – and I expect a British citizen to obey the laws of any country he enters – then you will come to no harm.' When Cox protested that the rebel generals were likely to be cavalier in their interpretation of the rule of law, Chilton dismissed him, saying: 'I know these generals. They will behave properly. If you don't, you can't expect us to help you.' In the event, it didn't matter since, three days later, Burgos bluntly refused the application. Ironically, as a result of Weaver's arrest, Cox would soon find himself in Madrid.[18]

With Madrid apparently about to fall, Gerald Barry had to get another correspondent to the besieged city to cover what was assumed to be Franco's final victorious attack. In the light of the hostility already demonstrated to the paper by Bolín and Franco, Barry believed that whoever his correspondent might be, he would face at best expulsion, and maybe imprisonment or at worst death. Accordingly, he was reluctant to send one of his stars such as Philip Jordan or Vernon Bartlett and so turned to someone he regarded as more expendable, the eager young Geoffrey Cox. On the afternoon of Tuesday 27 October 1936, the news editor put his head around the door of the reporters' room in London and said: 'I'm afraid you're for it Geoffrey. We've still no word of what has happened to Denis so you are to go to Madrid right away.'[19] Thus, as a result of the hostility of the Francoist authorities to foreign journalists, there was sent to Madrid a brilliant young correspondent whose writings would inspire immense sympathy for the cause of the Republic.

Later on the day of Weaver's arrest, two English businessmen from Madrid, out for a drive, also ran into Nationalists. They were arrested and later viciously interrogated by Bolín. One of them, Captain Christopher Lance, later celebrated as 'the Spanish Pimpernel' for his exploits in organizing the escape of Nationalists, remembered Bolín as 'sneering, sarcastic and contemptuous', 'quite the most unpleasant creature I've ever met'.[20] In late November 1936, Alex Small of the *Chicago Tribune* was arrested in Irún, where the military commander announced that he was to be shot for the crime of publishing an article in which he prophesied that Madrid would not fall. According to Arthur Koestler, the order to shoot Small emanated from Bolín personally. Small was saved only as a result of the fuss raised by another American colleague.[21]

In February 1937, the French right-wing newspaper, *Figaro*, which was fiercely pro-Franco, reported a similar case, that of Henri Malet-Dauban, the correspondent of the Havas Agency. Since his arrival five weeks earlier, Malet-Dauban had written articles that had been consistently in support of the rebel cause. He was a fluent Spanish-speaker who had once been secretary to Eduardo Aunós, of the extreme right-wing group Acción Española, a minister in the dictatorship of Primo de Rivera and to be so again under Franco. Nevertheless, Malet-Dauban had been arrested at his hotel in Ávila at the end of January. His room was searched and allegedly compromising documents were found, as a result of which he was accused of spying. He was imprisoned in solitary confinement and denied the right to communicate with anybody. The senior Havas correspondent, Jean D'Hospital, was prevented from communicating the news by the censorship and prevented from leaving rebel Spain. He managed to send messages to *Figaro* through both M. Perret of *Le Journal* and M. de Lagarde, the correspondent of the even more ferociously pro-rebel *Action Française*, who had been in Ávila and reported that they were seriously worried that Malet-Dauban was going to be shot, if he were not already dead. D'Hospital wrote to Franco asking what had happened and was told only that his colleague was suspected of espionage. Bolín made every effort to keep journalists from discussing the case of Malet-Dauban, but D'Hospital managed to get news out that a trial was imminent and that he feared that his colleague would be executed. In the event, Malet-Dauban was kept in prison for four months until, at the end of May 1937, the Basque Government managed to get him released as part of a prisoner exchange.[22]

One of the most dramatic examples of the mistreatment of correspondents by the rebels was the case of Arthur Koestler. He had worked sporadically for the Comintern propaganda wizard Willy Münzenberg between 1934 and 1936. When the military coup took place in Spain, Koestler approached Münzenberg for help in getting into Spain to join the International Brigades. When Münzenberg realized that Koestler carried a Hungarian passport and a press card for the conservative Budapest newspaper *Pester Lloyd*, he suggested that he use this 'semi-fascist' credential to get into the rebel zone and collect information on German and Italian intervention on behalf of Franco. Proof of Nazi and Fascist contravention of the non-intervention policy of the British and French Governments would be an important propaganda coup. In fact, the Hungarian press card had little validity, having been given to Koestler by a friendly editor, to facilitate his life as an exile in Paris. Even though Münzenberg, Otto Katz and Koestler assumed that no one in Franco's headquarters would bother to check, they did think that it was implausible that a small Hungarian newspaper would be able to afford a correspondent in Spain and so Katz arranged for him also to be accredited by the liberal London *News Chronicle*. En route to Seville, he stopped in Lisbon, where he discovered that his passport had expired. A visit to the Hungarian Consul, who was married to a fiercely right-wing Portuguese aristo-crat, led to introductions to the local circle of Franco supporters who took him to be a fellow rightist. As a result, he left Lisbon with two documents that would secure him entry into the lair of the bloodthirsty viceroy of Andalusia, General Gonzalo Queipo de Llano – a letter of introduction from Franco's unofficial ambassador in Lisbon, the leader of the Catholic CEDA party, José María Gil Robles, and a safe conduct signed by Franco's brother Nicolás, which described Koestler as a 'reliable friend of the National Revolution'.[23]

Koestler's trip was proving a success in terms of being able to gather informa-tion damaging to the rebels. In Lisbon, he had found ample proof of official Portuguese support for Franco. In Seville, he saw numerous German airmen whose Spanish air force overalls carried a small swastika in the middle of their pilot's wings. More dramatically, he managed to get an exclusive interview with Queipo de Llano, who happily repeated the same sort of virulent sexism that littered his daily radio broadcasts:

> For some ten minutes he described in a steady flood of words, which now and then became extremely racy, how the Marxists slit open the stomachs of pregnant women and speared the foetuses; how they had tied two eight-year-old girls on to their father's knees, violated them, poured petrol on them and set them on fire. This went on and on, unceasingly, one story following another – a perfect clinical demonstration in sexual psychopathology.[24]

However, on his second day in Seville, Koestler was recognized in a hotel lounge by a German journalist who knew that he was a Communist and denounced him to the airmen present. Shortly afterwards, a German officer demanded to see his papers. In an effort to bluff his way out of accusations that he was a spy, he demanded loudly that they telephone Luis Bolín. At that moment, into the hotel lobby swept Bolín himself, the 'tall, weak-faced, tough-acting officer of Scandinavian descent, who had already become famous for his rudeness to the foreign press'. When Koestler, still bluffing, demanded an apology from the German officer, a furious Bolín shouted brusquely that he was not interested in their silly quarrel. Koestler was able to use this to walk out of the hotel apparently 'in a huff'. He then left for Gibraltar as soon as he could. He learned later that a warrant for his arrest had been issued about an hour after his departure and that Bolín had been heard to swear that he would shoot Koestler 'like a mad dog if he ever got hold of him'.[25] Bolín's determination to exact punishment on Koestler can only have been intensified by the publication on 1 September of his powerful account of rebel Seville, ruled over by a deranged Queipo de Llano and thronged with Nazi officers.

Unfortunately for Koestler, five months later, Bolín did get hold of him. Indeed, Bolín would gain a kind of international fame by dint of his arrest and mistreatment of Arthur Koestler shortly after the Nationalist capture of Málaga in February 1937. In the intervening time, Koestler had been spending his time between London, Paris and Madrid working on pro-Republican propaganda with Münzenberg and Katz. In London and Paris, he worked for the Commission of Inquiry into Alleged Breaches of the Non-Intervention Agreement in Spain. Thought up by Willi Münzenberg, the commission was run by Otto Katz as a vehicle to campaign in favour of the Republic. By demonstrating the scale of Nazi and Fascist breaches of the non-intervention pact, it was hoped to demonstrate the absurdity of a British and French foreign policy that denied the Spanish Republic its rights in international law. In October 1936, Katz also arranged for him to receive an invitation from Julio Álvarez del Vayo to go to Madrid to search the papers of right-wing politicians who had fled, for material that would demonstrate that Nazi Germany had been involved in the preparation of the military coup. By the beginning of November, he felt that he had found as much material as he could and with the Franco forces apparently about to occupy the city, he was anxious to leave before Bolín arrived.

The suitcases of documents that he then took to Paris demonstrated a web of Nazi influence in the Spanish media, but provided no specific proof of involvement in the military coup. The material that he discovered was incorporated into the book produced by Otto Katz, with the title *The Nazi Conspiracy in Spain*. In Paris, Münzenberg persuaded Koestler to write a book on the origins of the Civil War, on the role of Hitler and Mussolini and the atrocities being committed by the rebels. Established in Otto Katz's own apartment, Koestler wrote fast. His book, complete with horrific photographs, was published in January 1937 as *L'Espagne ensanglantée* in French and as *Menschenopfer Unerhört* in German. An abridged version would eventually appear in English as the first part of *Spanish Testament*. In his autobiography, written when he had become fiercely anti-Communist, he disowned the book as too propagandistic, yet subsequent research has substantiated all of the atrocity stories recounted there.[26]

Having finished the book, Koestler was then commissioned by Otto Katz and the Republican news agency, Agence Espagne, to cover the war on the southern front. On 15 January 1937, armed with credentials from the *News Chronicle*, Koestler, accompanied by Willy Forrest, had gone to Valencia, where they had spent some time with Mikhail Koltsov. Nine days later, Koestler left Valencia en route to Málaga. When the beleagured city was occupied by rebel forces, he remained in the hope of getting a scoop by being able to witness and report on the expected massacre. He had become friendly with a retired English zoologist, Sir Peter Chalmers-Mitchell, whose villa on the outskirts of the city was next to that of Luis Bolín's uncle, Tomás, whose family he had sheltered. Despite that act of kindness to his uncle, Luis Bolín was determined to arrest Chalmers-Mitchell because on 22 October 1936, *The Times* had published a letter from him denouncing insurgent atrocities.

Rebel troops arrived at the house on 9 February accompanied by Bolín. He recognized Koestler and arrested him. So threatening was Bolín's manner that Koestler believed that he would be shot there and then. He was taken to a place where men were being executed by a gleeful mob of rebel soldiers. He was then held for four days in the prison at Málaga before being transferred to the central prison in Seville, where he was kept in solitary confinement for three months. He owed his life to the fact that the British authorities had intervened to save Sir Peter Chalmers-Mitchell, and this led Bolín to believe that Koestler also enjoyed powerful protection and that his execution would provoke an international incident. Nevertheless, in prison from 13 February to 14 May, Koestler's nights were punctuated by the sound of prisoners being taken out and shot. Although he was not officially informed of the fact, he had been sentenced to death for espionage. Confined on death row, he counted ninety-five executions before he worked out a technique of sleeping through the crucial hours. On Thursday 15 April 1937, the occupants of the cells on both sides of his were taken and shot after the warder had mistakenly tried to open his door. At one point, he was visited by a delegation of Falangists, who informed him that he would be sentenced to death but could get that sentence reduced to life imprisonment if he made a statement in favour of General Franco. After some hesitation, he had refused.

Meanwhile, Sir Peter Chalmers-Mitchell had managed to reach England, where he informed the *News Chronicle* of Koestler's plight. The news of his capture was printed by the paper on 15 February. A campaign for his release was set in motion by Koestler's wife Dorothy. With the assistance of Otto Katz, she managed to arrange a wave of newspaper articles, pleas to the Foreign Office to intervene and letters and telegrams of protest to Franco, some from Conservative MPs and clergymen. Winston Churchill wrote to the Foreign Office on Koestler's behalf. H. G. Wells sent a cable to Franco pleading for clemency. Katz even organized, fruitlessly as it happened, a trip by the English journalist Shiela Grant Duff to Málaga to intervene on Koestler's behalf. The British Consul advised her to forget about helping Koestler, pointing out that to raise questions about him would do him no good at all and bring considerable harm to her. Mikhail Koltsov commented to Gustav Regler: 'We know where he is. We've been shaking up the British Labour Party and the Foreign Office. The wires have been burning since yesterday. He's being looked after. We're the only people who can do that, you know – stir up the whole world on behalf of a single man. And the same time no one knows that we're at the back of it. That's something else only we can do.' Regarding the international campaign, both Koestler and Regler later reflected on the contradiction that similar campaigns were not mounted in favour of the old Bolsheviks being immolated in the purges in Moscow.[27] The Minister of Foreign Affairs in Negrín's new government, Professor José Giral, took a particular interest in the case and made it possible for Dr Marcel Junod of the International Red Cross finally to arrange an exchange of Koestler for the beautiful wife of the rebel air ace, Captain Carlos Haya. The lady in question was not in prison but merely under surveillance in the Hotel Inglés in Valencia.[28]

Six weeks after their triumph at Málaga, the rebels suffered the humiliating defeat of Guadalajara and made every attempt to keep news coverage to a minimum. Aware of what happened to journalists considered to be unfriendly, many correspondents tried to evade the censorship by ensuring that their papers did not use their by-line. After the news arrived of the Italian rout at Guadalajara, the Australian Noel Monks had driven to the French border and telephoned the story, insisting that his name be omitted. Unfortunately, the article appeared under his name. He was arrested in Seville, where Franco happened to be visiting, accompanied by Bolín. In his clipped Oxford English, a furious Bolín threatened Monks: 'You've put your foot in it now, Monks. Evading censorship is equivalent to spying and spies get short shrift in this country.' With Bolín ranting 'Shooting is too good for you journalists', Monks was taken before Franco himself. The paunchy rebel leader, 'the most unmilitary figure I have ever seen', glared at Monks with hard eyes and banged his fist on the table while repeating in Spanish that Monks was to be shot. When Bolín announced that he was to be taken before a firing squad, Monks protested: 'You can't shoot me. I'm British.' The remark provoked hoots of laughter from Franco when Bolín translated for him. In the event, Monks was expelled from Nationalist Spain for the sin of mentioning the presence of Italian and German forces and thereby refusing to be 'a party to Franco's hood-winking the world into believing that his revolt against the democratic Government of Spain was an all-Spanish affair, opposed to a gang of Moscow-led thugs'. The deeply Catholic Monks felt relief when he left: 'My six months in Franco Spain deeply shocked my religious sensibilities. And they were to receive further shocks when I went to Government Spain, but for totally different reasons.' As he commented sadly when he left Spain for the last time: 'one thing my assignment in Madrid taught me was that Republican Spain had the greatest cause of all – freedom. I suffered no religious restrictions in Madrid, and went to Mass as I willed.'[29]

During the latter stages of the march on Madrid of Franco's African columns, a press office had been set up at Talavera de la Reina shortly after its occupation on 3 September. The bureau was run by an aristocratic playboy, Pablo Merry del Val, who had been briefly the Paris correspondent of *El Debate* and was also a member of the Falange. He had been educated at Stonyhurst, the elite Jesuit school in north-west England, while his father had been Ambassador in London. Accordingly, he spoke fluent, aristocratic English. Peter Kemp, one of the few English volunteers for Franco, admired Merry del Val. He described him as still retaining

> the austere manner and appearance of a Sixth Form prefect confronted by a delinquent from the Lower Fourth; he became a very good friend of mine, and I am indebted to him for a great deal of kindness, but I always had the feeling that at any moment he might tell me to bend over and take six of the best.

Alan Dick, of the *Daily Telegraph*, met Merry del Val in Salamanca in the summer of 1937 and described him in similar but less benevolent terms:

> He was sleek and black, and very English in manner and speech. In fact, I was told that he was unpopular in some quarters because he spoke

broken Spanish. Not even Spain at war could crack the hard veneer of English public school and university. Outwardly he was the complete Spanish aristocrat. A stiff red Requeté beret – insignia of the Royalists of Navarre – sat like a pancake on his small oiled head. His lean face rarely abandoned its expression of tolerant hauteur. His voice was clipped and precise.

When he said 'I think we shall understand one another', Dick took it as a threat.[30]

Millán Astray remained in overall charge of the rebel press and propaganda machinery during the advance on Madrid. However, on 12 October 1936, he had brought the insurgent cause into considerable international disrepute by his behaviour during the celebrations of the anniversary of Christopher Columbus' discovery of America. He had clashed with the world-famous Rector of the University of Salamanca, the philosopher Miguel de Unamuno. His hysterical intervention had provoked from Unamuno words that went around the globe: 'You will win but you will not convince. You will win because you have more than enough brute force; but you will not convince because to convince means to persuade. And to persuade you need something which you lack: right and reason. It seems to me pointless to ask you to think about Spain'.[31] As far as Franco was concerned, Millán Astray had behaved as he should in his confrontation with Unamuno. Indeed, it was Franco himself who had recommended that Millán Astray take on, as his assistant, the deranged sycophant Ernesto Giménez Caballero, self-styled founder of Spanish surrealism, and author of a book admired by the Generalísimo, the extraordinary panegyric of fascist mysticism, *Genio de España*. Nevertheless, even Franco had to recognize that there was a need for a more tightly run operation than could be provided by Millán Astray and Giménez Caballero.[32]

Accordingly, on 24 January 1937, the Oficina de Prensa y Propaganda became the Delegación para Prensa y Propaganda, under the direction of Vicente Gay Forner, a virulently anti-Semitic professor of the University of Valladolid. Gay had contributed enthusiastically pro-Nazi, and virtually unreadable, articles to *Informaciones*, under the pseudonym Luis de Valencia. Vicente Gay had also received subsidies from Goebbels' Propaganda Ministry for his pro-Nazi writings, including the book *La revolución nacional-socialista*. He chose as his deputy Ramón Ruiz Alonso, the ex-CEDA deputy for Granada, who has been accused of responsibility for the murder of Federico García Lorca. Vicente Gay's lack of diplomatic skills and his ideological confusion soon earned him the hostility of most of the key groups in Salamanca. Ramón Serrano Suñer, Franco's brother-in-law and effectively his political factotum, replaced Gay in April 1937 with the military engineer Major Manuel Arias Paz, on the extraordinary grounds that he had built a radio transmitter in La Coruña. Arias Paz would be no more than a figurehead with the real task of organizing Nationalist propaganda assumed by the monarchist intellectual, Eugenio Vegas Latapié.[33]

The daily contact with journalists was left in the hands of Captain Gonzalo Aguilera y Yeltes, who was also a Stonyhurst product. For journalists already sympathetic to the rebels, the clipped Oxford English of these men gave an added credibility to their passing on of atrocity propaganda. Other journalists, especially Americans, tended to be much more sceptical, particularly of Aguilera. He was a deeply reactionary *latifundista* with lands in Salamanca and Cáceres, who told journalists that all Spain's problems were the result of the interference with the natural order constituted by the introduction of sewers.[34] He had retired from the army in protest at the requirement that officers swear an oath of loyalty to the Republic, taking advantage of the generous voluntary retirement terms of the decrees of 25 and 29 April 1931 promulgated by the newly installed Minister of War, Manuel Azaña.[35] On the outbreak of war, Aguilera had come out of retirement and volunteered for the nationalist forces. He had been informally attached to the general staff of General Mola, commander of the Army of the North. Because he spoke fluent English, French and German, he had been given the task of supervising the movements and the production of the foreign press correspondents – sometimes serving as a guide, others as a censor.[36] When Mola's Army of the North finally made contact with Franco's African columns in early September, Aguilera had moved south to take charge of the press accompanying the columns during the remainder of their march on Toledo and Madrid.[37]

Unlike most press officers, who felt responsible for the safety of the journalists assigned to them, Aguilera operated on the principle that, if risks had to be taken to get stories then, so long as they were favourable to the Nationalists, he would help the reporters take them. He regularly took his charges into the firing line and was 'bombed, machine-gunned and shelled' with them.[38] It was the most frequent complaint of the journalists in the Nationalist zone that they were expected to publish anodyne communiqués while being kept away from hard news. This was more often the case when the Nationalists were doing badly and especially so for journalists regarded as too 'independent'. Even favoured individuals were subjected to humiliating delays while waiting to be issued with passes for accompanied visits to the front.[39] Accordingly, Aguilera was extremely popular with the right-wing journalists who met him because he was prepared to take them dangerously near to the front and would use his influence with the censor to help them get their stories through.[40]

A journalist who had enormous personal regard for Aguilera was Sefton Delmer of the *Daily Express*. Delmer was most welcome in the Nationalist zone since he was reputed to be a personal friend of Hitler. Born and educated in Germany, he spoke the language fluently and had accompanied the Führer on Nazi election campaign tours. Indeed, he had famously joined Hitler when he inspected the smoking ruins of the Reichstag after the February 1933 fire. He made little secret of his admiration for the German leader.[41] On reaching Perpignan after leaving the anarchists of Mollet, his editor instructed him to head for Seville. He went to Toulouse, where he linked up with H. R. Knickerbocker, the internationally famous correspondent of the Hearst press, and Louis Delaprée of *Paris-Soir*, for the first leg of the flight which took them to Burgos. On arrival, Knickerbocker was especially outraged that his celebrity went unrecognized when they were all arrested and their aircraft commandeered. After an interview with General Mola, they were permitted to stay. Delmer discovered that Burgos shared with revolutionary Catalonia the inconvenience of nightly executions:

> Punctually at two o'clock every night I was awakened by volleys of shots. They were the shots fired by Mola's executions squads who night after night dragged their captives from the crowded prison to carry out the summary death sentences passed by the courts martial during the day. And day after day more prisoners – civilians, not soldiers taken in battle – were being brought in to take the places of those killed the night before.[42]

Delmer and the others were permitted to send reports to their papers only after they had pointed out that the more lenient conditions in the Republican zone favoured the enemy. Knickerbocker was deputed to take the reports of all three to Bordeaux for onward transmission. The many atrocities that Delmer witnessed were reported only years later in his memoirs. In his first article for the *Daily Express* from Burgos, he quoted the rebels' claims to be freeing Spain from the 'Red Marxist tyrants' and, understandably given the scale of censorship, failed to mention any rebel killings. Nevertheless, after six weeks, in September 1936, Aguilera expelled Delmer from Nationalist Spain on the grounds that one of his despatches published information likely to be of use to the enemy and also was 'calculated to make the Spanish armed forces look ridiculous'. The report in

THE OLD HANDS

above left) Henry Buckley (left, with Louis Fischer in Barcelona in 1938) had arrived in
pain in 1929 and was considered one of the two most knowledgeable of the newspapermen.
above right) Jay Allen (right) was the other one of the two best-informed correspondents. He
ad been coming to Spain since 1924 and had lived there since 1930.

.ester Ziffren (centre), head of the United Press Bureau in Madrid since 1933, with the actor
)ouglas Fairbanks (left) and his friend, the bullfighter Juan Belmonte.

FRESH BLOOD

(top left) The intrepid swashbuckler
Sefton Delmer in Madrid.
(top right) The young New Zealander
Geoffrey Cox became the chronicler of
the heroic defence of Madrid.
(bottom left) Louis Delaprée ('I
number the ruins, I count the dead'),
killed in December 1936, had recorded
the horrors of the bombing of Madrid.
(bottom right) Arthur Koestler after
his arrest in Málaga in February 1937.

WITH FRONTLINE COMMANDERS

Mikhail Koltsov of Pravda (right) with the legendary anarchist leader, Buenaventura Durruti, on the Aragón front at Bujaraloz, August 1936.

Ernest Hemingway chats with the Communist General Enrique Líster (second left) and International Brigade Commander Hans Kahle (first left) during the Battle of the Ebro, while Vincent Sheean looks away.

Koltsov (right) with the legendary Russian cameraman Roman Karmen at the front outside Madrid in October 1936.

Koltsov with his lover, the German journalist Maria Osten, who would be shot in Moscow in 1942.

WAR TOURISM?

Herbert Matthews and Hemingway in 'the Old Homestead' (a house on the Paseo de Rosales overlooking the Madrid front).

Herbert Matthews (left), Philip Jordan and their interpreter, Kajsa Rothman, visit the birthplace of Cervantes in Alcalá de Henares.

OBSERVING PEACE, OBSERVING WAR

Josephine Herbst, wearing beret, meets the villagers of Fuentidueña del Tajo, to the south-eas
of Madrid, where Joris Ivens' *The Spanish Earth* was being filmed (late April 1937).

Liston Oak (with beret) watches the front from the Paseo de Rosales in Madrid in 1937
with Hemingway (behind him, moustache-less), Virginia Cowles (with papers) and their
interpreter Kajsa Rothman (in leather jacket).

BEFORE AND AFTER THE BATTLE

(*top*) Claud Cockburn (right), founder of the satirical news-sheet, *The Week*, wrote under the pseudonym 'Frank Pitcairn' for the *Daily Worker*, before volunteering for the militia unit known as the Quinto Regimiento organized by the Comintern agent, Vittorio Vidali ('Carlos Contreras'), seen here on the left.

(*above left*) The glamorous American socialite, Virginia Cowles of *Harper's Bazaar*, in a studio portrait taken in London after her return from Spain in the autumn of 1937.

(*above right*) Kajsa Rothman with a Swedish International Brigader.

GUERNICA

George Lowther Steer, second from left with moustache, with a group of French journalists, visits the historic Casa de Juntas, the Basque parliament, in Guernica in January 1937.

Guernica after the German rehearsal for Blitzkrieg.

question had recounted an air-raid on Burgos by an aged Republican DC3. Delmer had described how, in the midst of it, a small British plane returning Knickerbocker from France had inadvertently arrived. It had been mistaken for an enemy aircraft, attracted the anti-aircraft fire of the Burgos batteries and still managed to land unscathed. The despatch, Aguilera told him over a drink, 'not only encourages the Reds to attack Burgos again. But it makes our ack-ack gunners look inefficient.'

Aguilera liked Delmer and so confided in him that he did not give a damn what the reporter said about the artillery since he was a cavalryman himself. He also told him that the real motive behind the incident was that German agents had requested that he be removed because they considered him, not without justification, to be an agent of British Intelligence.[43] Expelled by the Nationalists, Sefton Delmer then represented the *Daily Express* in the Republican zone. Other correspondents who knew him regarded him as fiercely independent and extremely clever but, in the Republican press office, he would be viewed with some suspicion. This was not entirely surprising given that in his memoirs he referred to Republicans throughout as 'Reds' and to Aguilera as 'dear Aggy'. Moreover, he and Aguilera were friends in London after the Spanish Civil War.[44]

The fiercely pro-Nationalist Harold Cardozo, of the *Daily Mail*, was considered something of a leader by other British and American correspondents – they called him 'the Major'.[45] Edmund Taylor thought Cardozo 'a courageous cool hand and a cheerful travelling companion, apart from politics'.[46] However, despite his enthusiasm for, and friendship with, Francoist officers, there was a noticeable tension between Bolín and Cardozo. Sir Percival Phillips thought that Bolín enjoyed bullying and humiliating correspondents in general but had a particular grudge against Cardozo. He claimed that, because the *Daily Mail* had refused to publish articles submitted by Bolín while he was in London, 'he's now treating the *Mail* men as if they were dirt beneath his feet'. Cardozo made little secret of his opinion that Bolín's articles had been rejected because they were 'damned rubbish'. Without mentioning Bolín by name, Cardozo complained that the Nationalist press censorship was rigidly applied even to those journalists, such as himself, who were 'heart and soul for the movement'. Frustrated by the bureaucratic obstacles imposed even on 'responsible war correspondents', he even commented enviously that in Madrid and Valencia, cables 'were transmitted with a fairly lenient censorship and with a minimum of delay'. Cardozo was not alone. The enthusiastically pro-Nazi Nigel Tangye, of the *Daily Mail*'s sister paper, the *Evening News*, despite a close personal relationship with Bolín, soon grew equally exasperated by the contemptuous treatment given to journalists. William F. Stirling, who briefly represented *The Times*, wrote to London to complain that Luis Bolín regularly hindered his work because he 'suffers from acute Anglophobia with *Times* complications'.[47]

Phillips similarly commented: 'on the other side, correspondents are treated much better. I have met dozens of fellows who are in Barcelona and Madrid, and they told me that, though there was hopeless confusion, they were always treated like brothers.'[48] The difference between the two zones in this regard was that, in Nationalist Spain, the military had no time for newspapermen. Phillips noticed that officers who were ready to be friendly with journalists were warned off by the press censors or by their own superiors: 'I never felt so isolated in any army. I cannot make contacts with anyone. There seems to be a deliberate policy to prevent the British and American correspondents from making any contacts.' When he was seen talking to an officer who spoke English, a member of the Press and Propaganda Office came and reprimanded the man, who never spoke to Phillips again. The result was an icy atmosphere: 'You go into a room full of officers, but the Press censor, who is with you, carefully forgets to introduce you to a single one of them, and a few whom you happen to know shake hands with you coldly, and then hastily turn their backs on you without a word.' He was told by one officer that 'all the generals begged the Generalísimo to exclude correspondents from the country till the war was over' and F. A. Rice, despite being the correspondent of the conservative *Morning Post*, was told by another that 'there are too many reporters here'.[49]

Randolph Churchill, who represented the *Daily Mail*, echoed Sir Percival's envy of the Republican press services. In March 1937, aware of the British Tory Arnold Lunn's close friendship with Bolín, he said to him: 'I wish you'd go back to Salamanca and tell those damned people at the Press Office that they're losing this war by their idiotic censorship. The Reds have got them beat so far as publicity is concerned. They let the Press go where they like, and consequently the Press send back great human stories from the front.' He was exaggerating, however, when he expostulated that 'in Salamanca they're more interested in killing stories than in killing Reds'. Sir Percival Phillips concluded with regard to Bolín's failings as a propagandist: 'I would describe him as a preventive rather than a propagandist: he has a positive genius for preventing news from getting out.'[50] It was illustrative of the military attitude to journalists that, while he was in charge of the Oficina de Prensa y Propaganda in Salamanca, each morning, General Millán Astray would summon with a whistle those journalists who were not at the front and form them up in lines to listen to his daily harangue. Bolín was clearly impressed by his example.[51]

The more junior press officers who were given the job of accompanying the correspondents were, according to Sir Percival Phillips:

> young grandees or diplomats, amiable weaklings for the most part, ruled by Bolín with a rod of iron. He telephones them at all hours of the day and night, scolding, ordering, but never advising, and, as a result of this drilling, they never express an opinion, even on the weather, lest some correspondent should cable that such-and-such a view is held 'in GHQ' or 'in well-informed circles' or 'by spokesmen of the Generalísimo'. As they also keep all officers away from us as carefully as if we had the plague, we are confined to the official Press reports and to the edifying but monotonous stories of Falangist valour which fill the Spanish newspapers every day.

The groups of correspondents were controlled by the press officers to the extent that they became 'like a bunch of schoolgirls under the guidance of a schoolmistress, or like a gang of Cook's tourists dragged around by a guide'.[52]

So tight was the censorship that the more critical journalists in the rebel zone would risk their lives to cheat the censors, as Noel Monks had done, by taking or sending despatches to France.[53] The young American journalist, Frances Davis, for instance, endeared herself to Harold Cardozo by offering to carry out his uncensored stories and those of Edmond Taylor, John Elliott and Bertrand de Jouvenal. She was in a position to do so because she had played on her ethereal good looks and apparent innocence to obtain the necessary safe-conducts. As a result, she managed to get a job with the *Daily Mail* as Cardozo's assistant. She actually took the copy out hidden in her girdle.[54] Edmond Taylor would send one story out to his paper while, as a cover, submitting other stories to Aguilera. However, he sometimes could not resist the temptation of leaving debatable material even in the submitted dummy copy. A notice was put up in the pressroom forbidding journalists to refer to the rebels as 'rebels' or 'insurgents', or to the Republicans as 'loyalists', 'governmentals' or 'Republicans'. The only permitted terms were 'Spanish national forces' or 'Nationalists' and 'Reds'.[55] One of the censors, a Barcelona millionaire named Captain Ignacio Rosales, whose racist views were similar to those of Aguilera, would react violently if he saw the word 'rebel' in a dispatch, shouting: '"Patriot" armies, "Nationalist" armies, "White" armies – any man who uses the term "rebel" will have his passes revoked and will leave the country!' Rosales made life unbearable for an American photographer, Tubby Cohen, because he was Jewish, refusing to issue him with passes and making remarks about his 'disgusting name'.[56]

Foreign newspapers were scoured for items considered hostile to the insurgents. Many British and American newspapers themselves censored mentions of Axis assistance, but any transgression of this rule by the correspondents was quickly punished. Karl Robson was expelled because his paper, the *Daily Express*, printed a leader which referred to the 'rebels', despite the fact that he was not the author.[57] While Aguilera was still running the censorship in Burgos, he ordered the detention on 11 September 1936 of F. A. Rice. His crime was to have sent two articles, one about Aguilera's English education, and another piece, sent from France and not therefore subjected to the rebel censorship, in which Rice had used the phrase 'insurgent frightfulness' in relation to the rebel attack on Irún on 1 September 1936. Aguilera regarded both articles as revealing 'a not wholly respectful attitude' either to himself or to his cause. After threatening Rice with the serious consequences awaiting journalists who referred to the rebels as 'insurgents', or to the Republicans as 'loyalists' or 'Government troops' instead of 'Reds', Aguilera told him to choose between leaving Spain or staying under strict vigilance, without permission to cross the frontier – which was the only way of filing a story outside the Francoist censorship. Rice chose to leave. His newspaper, the *Morning Post*, commented on his expulsion in an editorial: 'It proclaims *urbi et urbi* that any news emanating from Right sources belongs rather to the realm of propaganda than to that of fact.'[58]

It was generally recognized by those correspondents who served in the Nationalist zone that only the representatives of German, Italian and Portuguese newspapers could expect privileged treatment. In return, they produced the sort of stories that the rebels wanted to see, larded with praise for Nationalist heroism and with horrified accounts of 'red' atrocities. A good example was Curio Mortari, of *La Stampa* of Turin, the first foreign journalist to be given a safe-conduct by Franco's headquarters in Morocco. He later accompanied the rebel columns in their bloody progress from Seville to Badajoz. His admiring chronicles of their activities more than justified the rebels' faith in him.[59] The reports published in the Portuguese press were often highly revealing. It was admitted, for instance, that many refugees fleeing across the border from the massacre at Badajoz had been turned over by the local police to the Spanish army. More significant, perhaps, was what they revealed of the privileged position of Portuguese newspapermen. The correspondent of *Diario de la Manhã*, who covered the repressive activities of the brutal Columna Castejón, commented: 'I follow the operations by the side of the commander of the column'. In Seville, on 7 August, during one of his notorious broadcasts, the rebel leader there, General Gonzalo Queipo de Llano, after publicly welcoming a number of Portuguese journalists, introduced Félix Correia of the *Diario de Lisboa* over the radio, then actually turned the radio over to him. Correia was also invited to Franco's headquarters in the magnificent palace of the Marquesa de Yanduri and granted a long interview. Correia repaid his host in a long and sycophantic article by describing 'his radiant charm', presenting the diminutive general as a 'man of normal height' and comparing his patriotism to that of Hitler.[60]

On another occasion, Queipo invited Leopoldo Nunes of *O Seculo* to accompany him on a trip to Córdoba and spoke freely with him for the two hours of the car journey. The mutual sympathy thus established saw the sympathetic Nunes go even further than some of his colleagues. In late August 1936, Nunes drove from Ayamonte in Huelva to Riotinto, where Socialist miners were still holding out against the rebels. Claiming to have lost his way, he managed to conduct several interviews and he was allowed to leave unhindered. He then drove to Seville where he informed Queipo de Llano of the location, number and weaponry of the miners. On 27 August, *O Seculo* published an article by Nunes in praise of the military operation which had crushed the resistance of the miners. On the same evening, a delighted Queipo de Llano invited 'the distinguished Portuguese journalist' don Leopoldo Nunes to speak on his radio programme. Nunes declared that the Spanish Civil War was 'a struggle between a glorious army, supported by patriotic militias, and a herd of monsters who have nothing in common with human kind because they murder non-combatant men, women and children and then flee like cowardly vermin before the soldiers of the Nationalist army'.[61]

Franco's headquarters issued an order on 26 February 1937 to the armies of north and south: 'Except for Italian journalists with safe-conducts issued by these headquarters, only German and Spanish journalists who, as well as said document, also carry a special authorization to visit the sector under your command may do so. Those of other nationalities must be accompanied by a press officer with a safe-conduct as a credential as well as the previously mentioned requisites. No journalist will be allowed to remain in the sector without these requisites.'[62] The Italian and German correspondents themselves were apparently under instructions to avoid contact with journalists from Britain and America.[63] Ironically, the liberty given to the Italians by the censorship authorities could cause problems for correspondents. Indro Montanelli was with the Italian forces that entered Santander in August 1937. He sent an article to *Il Messagero* in which he wrote that the advance on the city had been '*una lunga passegiatta ed un solo nemico, il caldo*' (a leisurely parade with the heat the only enemy faced). What he had not realized was that the official line of the Italian commanders was that it had been a hard-fought and bloody battle which avenged the defeat of Guadalajara. Ready to distribute medals and promotions on the basis of this account, they furiously demanded the recall of Montanelli.[64]

There were a few exceptions to the harsh treatment meted out to correspondents from the democracies. These consisted mainly of several English extreme right-wing military men and Catholics. Arnold Lunn, a deeply reactionary old Harrovian, and a prominent Tory and Catholic, found a warm welcome from his old friend Luis Bolín, a fellow member of the right-wing *English Review* luncheon club in London. Lunn sympathized immediately with Bolín's difficulties running the censorship and was rewarded accordingly. He gushed that Bolín had 'a thankless task. He had to act as intermediary between the Military Command, whose job was to win the war, and the disgruntled journalists whose job was to report it. During my journey through Spain from Spain from Irún to Algeciras, I received every possible courtesy from Captain Bolín and his colleagues.' Lunn had complete sympathy with the fact that the Spanish military were determined to prevent journalists seeing anything that might embarrass their German and Italian allies. He wrote afterwards: 'The Germans, for instance, who are trying out their new anti-aircraft guns, are peculiarly sensitive to the propinquity of French journalists, some of whom may have been suspected, and one of whom has been arrested on a charge of spying on behalf of the French.'[65]

Another English journalist who received relatively favourable treatment was the aviation correspondent of the London *Evening News*, Nigel Tangye. On arrival, he had delighted Bolín because he carried enthusiastic recommendations from the Embassy of the Third Reich in London and other German contacts. In consequence, Tangye was accorded the rare privilege of being given a car and driver and allowed to travel with a camera without a military observer. However, firsthand contact with the situation did little to dent his astonishing ignorance. Moreover, although the falsities that he produced entirely favoured the rebels, that did not give him immunity from the same frustrating delays suffered by other correspondents. Regarding the Moorish mercenaries fighting on the rebel side, he claimed that 'the Sultan has sent the greater part of his magnificent army over to Spain, including his own personal bodyguard'. One of the reasons for this, he believed erroneously, was that Franco 'speaks Arabic fluently'. He described the Catholic Church as having no sympathy with either side until forced by the desecration of churches and the murder of priests to favour Franco. Most bizarrely of all, he claimed that the Trotskyist POUM had gained prominence because of Soviet aid.[66] However, Tangye's difficulties with the rebel censorship had nothing to do with his ignorance. They applied to all correspondents.

Accordingly, after the defeat at Guadalajara, the Italian military authorities began to cultivate the foreign press and take them to visit the Italian sectors of the Bilbao front. They also operated a special courier service to take their despatches from the front to St Jean de Luz. This allowed messages to reach London and New York between eight and twelve hours faster than those that had to pass through the Francoist censorship. Reynolds Packard of the United Press was given a severe dressing down by Major Manuel Lambarri y Yanguas, one of the rebel press officers at the office of the Oficina de Prensa in Vitoria. Threatening Packard with immediate expulsion if he visited the front with the Italians, he said: 'It's about time you fellows realize this is a Spanish war. We can't help it if we have to have some outside help. The other side has it, too. But we are determined that you are going to see this war through Spanish eyes.' However, the rebel censors faced enormous difficulties before they could prise the fiercely pro-Franco William P. Carney of the *New York Times* away from the Italian press officers, with whom he had established extremely close connections.[67]

In fact, among Bolín's subordinates, the portly Manuel de Lambarri y Yanguas was regarded as one of the more humane. He was a rather amiable incompetent who, in civilian life, had worked as a designer for the magazine *Vogue*, although, as a young man, he had attended the Toledo military academy with Franco. Lambarri had worked for *Vogue* in London and, according to the *Daily Telegraph* correspondent Alan Dick, 'still kept the soul of an artist beneath his khaki shirt'. Virginia Cowles remembered how he fluttered around like a demented Sunday School teacher trying to organize trips to the front which turned out 'like a mad tea-party from the pages of a bellicose *Alice in Wonderland*'. His English was less than fluent and, when the correspondents wanted to send a despatch that would meet censorship problems, they would take it to Lambarri. Rather than admit that he did not understand the dense cable-ese, he would cross out a couple of words at random and then approve it. Among his other endearing qualities was an ability to get his column of correspondents hopelessly lost.[68]

Lambarri was, however, an exception. John Whitaker, whom the rebels had good reason to regard as hostile to their cause, received altogether more sinister treatment at the hands of Aguilera. When, in the latter stages of the march on Madrid, Whitaker began to visit the front alone, Aguilera turned up at his lodgings with a Gestapo agent in the early hours of one morning and threatened to have him shot if he went near the front without a member of his staff: 'Next time you're unescorted at the front, and under fire, we'll shoot you. We'll say that you were a casualty to enemy action. You understand!'[69]

There were, of course, a small number of journalists whose enthusiasm for the Nationalist cause ensured that they had no problems with the censorship apparatus. One such was Cecil Gerahty of the *Daily Mail*. He had made no secret of his virulently anti-Republican views. Accordingly, he was delighted to be told that General Queipo de Llano 'would appreciate my giving a short talk on the wireless for the benefit of the fairly large number of English listeners, not only in Spain but in Gibraltar and Morocco'. After being primed with generous helpings of sherry, he made a speech which, he later claimed, provoked copious tears from the announcer. Among other adulatory remarks about what the rebels were doing, he proclaimed: 'Please remember that Spain is not struggling to provide interesting newspaper copy in a series of spectacular victories. A dreadful weed has been sown by aliens in her gardens, and these weeds have got to be eradicated.' Allegedly, Queipo de Llano was so moved, he had the speech translated and repeated it in his own broadcast on the following day. Either the amount of sherry consumed clouded Gerahty's memory or else the Nationalist media chose not to report the general's quotation of his words, for there was no mention of the speech in the Seville press.[70]

Gerahty was greatly outdone in his desire to please his hosts by F. Theo Rogers, an American Catholic born in Boston who had served in his country's wars against Spain in both Cuba and the Philippines, in the course of which he had developed a friendship with Colonel Theodore Roosevelt. Rogers became a journalist and eventually became editor of the *Philippines Free Press* and a relatively wealthy man. In the spring of 1936, he left the Philippines for a long vacation in Spain, where he had many friends among the aristocracy and the military. The fruit of his observations was *Spain: A Tragic Journey*, a fierce denunciation of the Republic and a hymn of praise for the rebels which sported an enthusiastic introduction by Theodore Roosevelt. In it, Rogers claimed that the election campaign for the Popular Front had been funded by Moscow and victory achieved by 'terroristic influences' and 'huge electoral frauds'. In fact, violence and electoral fraud had been exercised, but by the Right. Rogers also repeated the absurd story that there existed a Communist plot to impose a Soviet government in Spain. He portrayed the military rising as a reaction against the 'gangsterism' of the Republican Government.

With regard to the issue of foreign aid, Rogers quoted as 'absolutely true' the claim by his Spanish friends that 'there are entire regiments of Russians, officered by Russians, fighting for the Madrid government'. In contrast to his assertion about the Russians, he wrote that 'I have travelled through White Spain from end to end. I never saw an Italian soldier or officer. I saw probably 150 Germans at the most, all of them attached in a technical capacity to the foreign legions.' Elsewhere he praised Hitler's support of Franco on the grounds that the Führer 'is fearful of what Communism will do to our civilization'. Life in Republican Spain was described as a constant wave of terror, assassination, rape and theft. Of the mass shootings and the terror in the rebel zone, he was totally ignorant. Rogers asserted that, during his extensive travels in White Spain, 'I saw no trace of disorder, no sign of unorganized rabble'. His view of the Francoist repression was sanitized in the extreme. He knew of no violence, only of a few executions, 'but there was at least a trial, summary though it might be'. He gave a naïve account of what happened when the Francoists took a town: 'the word goes forth to the working men to return to their daily tasks. They may have heretofore sided with the Reds. Now they are to forget politics and war. It is their present and future that counts not their past.' He claimed even to have found 'workmen who approved of the executions ordered by the White forces'.

When Roger's book was published, a prominent Jesuit, Father Francis Talbot, wrote a preface in which he expressed his hope that *Spain: A Tragic Journey* would 'serve to disillusion every American who still backwardly believes in the myth of Spanish democracy as professed and practiced in the so-called Loyalist territories'. He went on to affirm that the book's conclusions indicted the Loyalists of 'abrogating fundamental rights, of violating every liberty, of producing a reign of terror and chaos. They affirm that Nationalist Spain fights for law, for order, for culture, for justice.'[71]

If not quite on a level with Rogers, William P. Carney of the *New York Times* was certainly an enthusiastic supporter of the rebels. In New York press circles, he was nicknamed 'General Franco's press agent on *The Times* payroll'.[72] To an extent he had paid his passage with his damning farewell article to the Republican zone which had been published as a pamphlet in the United States and helped influence Catholic opinion there in favour of Franco. Constancia de la Mora later claimed that, as a reward for revealing the exact details of the gun emplacements around Madrid, when Carney abandoned Madrid, the rebels rewarded him with 'a fine fascist uniform'. She also alleged that, after the Civil War, Carney signed a letter to Cardinal Gomá, the Primate of Spain, congratulating him on Franco's 'glorious victory'.[73] As a result, Carney tried to sue her for damages. His lawyer did not, as he could not have done, dispute the claim about the anti-aircraft guns, but argued rather feebly that Carney was 'not a fascist, never owned any uniform of a fascist, and certainly never wore one' and that the letter did not congratulate Gomá for glorious victory, but for the fact that Franco's victory had saved Spain for Catholicism.[74] On 18 May 1937, the American Ambassador Claude Bowers reported to the State Department that the Italian radio station in Salamanca was paying war correspondents up to ten thousand lire for propaganda speeches. William Carney had accepted and, in line with the conditions imposed, had ended his talk with the Francoist cry '¡Arriba España!'[75] Certainly, Carney was decorated after the Spanish Civil War by the United States Catholic fraternal Order of the Knights of Columbus. After the Second World War, he became a Cold War propagandist in the service of the US Government.[76]

It is certainly the case that, once in the Nationalist zone, Carney continued in a similar vein to that of the disputed Madrid article, manipulating the news in favour of the rebels and against the Republic. He began to quote the red atrocity stories from General Queipo de Llano's virulent propaganda broadcast as if they were factually accurate. On the day that Guernica was destroyed, he sent a triumphant telegram to the New York Times euphorically reporting the captures of Eibar and Durango and giving a wildly exaggerated account of Basque strength, including a claim that they had an abundance of modern artillery and an air force of one hundred aircraft when, in fact, their planes barely reached double figures.[77] After the bombing of Guernica, he was quick to join the ranks of the pro-Francoists who argued that the town had been dynamited by the Basques themselves. He visited Guernica and wrote that 'most of the destruction could have been the result of fires and dynamitings'. He also quoted approvingly the rebel slander of one of the prime witnesses, Father Alberto Onaindía, as 'an unfrocked young priest'.[78]

On 22 July 1937, he had interviewed the American pilot, Harold Dahl, captured after bailing out over Brunete. Although Dahl had been badly threatened, Carney quoted him as saying that he had been treated with 'kindness and consideration' and 'exquisite courtesy'. The bulk of the article was devoted to implying that the Republican air force was entirely Russian-controlled.[79] On other occasions too, he had invented details in his articles. In December 1937, when the Republicans were still defending the recently captured Teruel, the overconfident rebels issued a communiqué claiming that it had been reconquered. Carney both reprinted the communiqué and added colourful details of Franco's troops occupying the town. Herbert Matthews, disbelieving this, made a hazardous three-day trip from Barcelona to Teruel with Robert Capa, saw that the town was still in Republican hands and filed a story that implicitly reprimanded Carney. He wrote:

> the Rebels never reached the city, never made contact with the garrison
> and refugees in the cellars of Teruel, never captured any Government
> general staff officers and in short never really menaced the provincial
> capital which remains firmly in Government hands. It has been axiomatic

in this war that nothing can be learned with certainty unless one goes to the spot and sees with his own eyes.[80]

On reading Matthews' article, Jay Allen telegrammed Hemingway: 'TELL MATTHEWS HIS STUFF CREATED MAGNIFICENT IMPRESSION EVERYBODY. CARNEY VERY HOTWATER BECAUSE HIS THINKING NOW OBVIOUS.' In fact, the water in which Carney found himself remained barely lukewarm, receiving as he did only the mildest chiding from the *New York Times*' managing editor, Edwin James.[81]

In early April 1938, with some other reporters including Kim Philby, Carney visited the concentration camp at the Zaragoza military academy where captured International Brigaders were held. One of the Americans, Max Parker, said he would not talk to them if Carney was present because he believed him to be a Franco propagandist. Carney did not reveal his presence among the group of journalists and later published an account of the visit which bore no resemblance to the grim reality of the prisoners' conditions. He sympathetically quoted the head of Franco's juridical corps, Lieutenant Colonel Lorenzo Martínez Fuset, the man responsible for overseeing death sentences, to the effect that 'foreigners were treated exactly like Spanish prisoners'. Carney omitted to mention that this meant overcrowding, starvation, beatings, executions and disease for the international volunteers just as it did for Spanish Republicans. He claimed that the prisoners were delighted with their treatment, were astonished by how well they were fed and felt that their conditions in captivity were far better than they had been when fighting for the Republic. Parker revealed later that Carney had falsified interviews by using the prisoners' records made available to him by the Francoists. In the same article, Carney falsely reported that the North American Committee to Aid Spanish Democracy was recruiting volunteers, an assertion that damaged their subsequent fund-raising efforts. Later, he reported erroneously that the US Consul, Charles Bay, had claimed that the State Department would do nothing to defend American volunteers sentenced to death by the Francoists. He was obliged to print a retraction, but the intention to damage the recruiting efforts was obvious.[82]

Certainly Carney seemed very much at home in the rebel zone. Revealing of his ethics was the report that he produced after a visit on 9 July 1938 to the improvised Francoist concentration camp in the disused monastery of San Pedro de Cardeña six miles south-east of Burgos. Among the prisoners kept in the appallingly overcrowded conditions of the camp were a substantial number of International Brigaders. They were subject to regular beatings and torture. When the guards ordered the Americans to the assembly area to be interviewed by Carney, the prisoners quickly called the Irish brigader, Bob Doyle, having recently been savagely beaten, to substitute for one of them, and join another torture victim, Bob Steck. Carney interrogated the prisoners, demanding to know who had provided the funds to send them to Spain and how many of them were members of the Communist Party. The prisoners were convinced that Carney was looking for information to besmirch the brigaders back in the USA. The Americans' spokesmen, Lou Ornitz and Edgar Acken, himself a journalist, replied that all were anti-Fascists and they did not know how many Communists there were among them. They informed him about the atrocious living conditions and the beatings, but he was sceptical about their claims of brutality and refused to visit their quarters. So, they turned Doyle and Steck around and lifted their shirts to reveal the long red welts across their backs.

Carney was visibly shaken. Ornitz told Carney that if he was serious about helping the prisoners, he should tell the State Department about the appalling conditions. In fact, Carney informed the prison commander, Ornitz was beaten and had his rations reduced. Carney's dishonest report in the *New York Times* described the camp in idyllic terms, claiming that the prisoners had adequate space and good food and water. He stated that any mistreatment was provoked by the prisoners' rebellious attitudes. However, the publication of their names in the article ensured that they would not simply be executed by the Francoists.[83] Carney's article was lampooned in the prisoners' clandestine news-sheet the *San Pedro Jaily News*, with a cartoon by the British prisoner, Jimmy Moon, portraying the prisoners relaxing, reading and fishing in the river while the wounded were attended by a voluptuous nurse.[84]

When fourteen prisoners were exchanged on 8 October 1938, Carney was present as they crossed the international bridge at Hendaye to be received by David Amariglio, the representative of the Friends of the Abraham Lincoln Brigade. With funds passed to him by Louis Fischer from moneys made available by the Negrín government, Amariglio was there to arrange their passage home. According to Claude Bowers who was also there, Carney, 'whom they heartily dislike', was treated in a friendly manner. However, they reproached him for outright lies in his report from San Pedro:

> He blandly admitted it. Shamelessly he told us that he lied because 'it was the only way to get the story out' – another falsehood, since he could have sent it from France. His unqualified statement that we all admitted having been recruited by the Communist Party or the North American Committee was preposterous; the subject was never mentioned in the interview, and the facts were otherwise.

Carney's own account does not mention the questioning of his ethics, but it is at great pains to insist that Amariglio was a Communist and the FALB a Communist front organization.[85]

Carney was one of the American and British correspondents who had few problems with the rebel censorship apparatus. One who ran into serious problems was, astonishingly, the world-famous Hubert Knickerbocker. The incident was to cause Aguilera, and his superiors, considerable embarrassment. The red-haired Knickerbocker was a world-famous journalist who, through his articles in the Hearst press chain during the early months of the war, had done much for the Francoist cause, and yet he was arrested during the campaign against the Basque Country in April 1937.[86] When Knickerbocker had first wanted to join the African columns moving north from Seville, Juan Pujol, as head of the Gabinete de Prensa in Burgos, had written to Franco recommending him as an 'outstanding figure of North American journalism, who has done great work with his always accurate reports on our Movement'.[87]

However, when he tried to return in April 1936, he was refused permission. The American Ambassador, Claude Bowers, reported to Washington on the background to Knickerbocker's difficulties with the rebel authorities:

> General Franco is becoming more and more intolerant towards war correspondents with his armies. He turned them all away when the attack on Malaga began. The men he then turned away had been with him for months and had written the most pronounced pro-Franco articles. No war correspondent with him could have been more satisfactory to him than Knickerbocker who was convinced of his early and inevitable victory when I saw him frequently five months ago. He returned to America three months ago and has now been ordered back. I have seen him twice in Saint-Jean-de-Luz at my home. He was waiting for a permit to cross the border and to rejoin the army. He has just been informed that he 'cannot continue his journey to Spain'. I can only interpret this denial to mean that there must be something in the present situation that General Franco does not care to have blazoned to the world. I find Knickerbocker completely flabbergasted by the changed situation.[88]

Despite the prohibition on his proceeding into Spain, a week later the intrepid Knickerbocker sneaked over the frontier. He was caught and imprisoned in San Sebastián for thirty-six hours. His release was secured only after a considerable fuss was made by his friend and fellow newspaperman Randolph Churchill.

Knickerbocker was then expelled from Spain. Believing that his experience had been the consequence of a denunciation by Captain Aguilera, Knickerbocker took his revenge in a devastating fashion. He simply published, in the *Washington Times* on 10 May 1937, an account of what sort of society the military rebels planned to establish in Spain, which he based on Aguilera's anti-Semitic, misogynistic, anti-democratic opinions and, in particular, his claim that: 'We are going to shoot 50,000 in Madrid. And no matter where Azaña and Largo Caballero (the Premier) and all that crowd try to escape, we'll catch them and kill every last man, if it takes years of tracking them throughout the world.' Knickerbocker's article was quoted extensively in the US Congress by Jerry J. O'Connell of Montana on 11 May 1937. It may be presumed to have been a significant propaganda blow against the Francoists, coming as it did shortly after the bombing of Guernica.

Asking a hypothetical question about the kind of society that Franco would establish if he won the war, Knickerbocker answered using the words of Gonzalo Aguilera, rendered as a mythical Major Sánchez. Aguilera was quoted as saying:

> It is a race war, not merely a class war. You don't understand because you don't realize that there are two races in Spain – a slave race and a ruler race. Those reds, from President Azaña to the anarchists, are all slaves. It is our duty to put them back into their places – yes, put chains on them again, if you like. Modern sewer systems caused this war. Certainly – because unimpeded natural selection would have killed off most of the 'red' vermin. The example of Azaña is a typical case. He might have been carried off by infantile paralysis, but he was saved from it by these cursed sewers. We've got to do away with sewers.

Aguilera had apparently been melancholy for days when he had heard about the success of F. D. Roosevelt in the presidential election, commenting: 'What you can't grasp is that any stupid Democrats, so called, lend themselves blindly to the ends of "red" revolution. All you Democrats are just handmaidens of bolshevism. Hitler is the only one who knows a "red" when he sees one.' His most commonly used expression was 'take 'em out and shoot 'em!' He believed that trade unions should be abolished and membership of them made punishable by death. He advocated for industrial workers the paternal direction of the factory owners and for peasants a benevolent serfdom. His beliefs on the pernicious effects of education had also been expounded to Knickerbocker: 'We must destroy this spawn of "red" schools which the so-called republic installed to teach the slaves to revolt. It is sufficient for the masses to know just enough reading to understand orders.

We must restore the authority of the Church. Slaves need it to teach them to behave.' He had repeated to Knickerbocker views about women roughly similar to those to which he had treated Whitaker: 'It is damnable that women should vote. Nobody should vote – least of all women.' The Jews, he believed, were 'an international pest'. Liberty was 'a delusion employed by the "reds" to fool the so-called democrats. In our state, people are going to have the liberty to keep their mouths shut.'[89] It can have come as little surprise when one year later, the rebels again refused Knickerbocker permission to cover their drive to the Mediterranean.[90]

A correspondent who was ostensibly a rebel sympathizer was Harold A. R. Philby, nicknamed 'Kim' after the hero of Rudyard Kipling's tale about a spy. Like Knickerbocker, he would inflict damage on the rebels but in a very different way. He was welcomed with open arms in the Nationalist zone because he was the correspondent of *The Times* and, even more so, because of recommendations from the German Embassy in London. Ostensibly, he repaid this faith by producing pro-rebel articles that delighted his hosts, but he was actually a Russian spy. He had been recruited in London in the summer of 1934 by an NKVD talent scout, Edith Suschitzky, who was the wife of Dr Alex Tudor Hart (who would later serve in the International Brigade medical services in Spain) and a friend of Philby's Austrian wife, Litzi Friedman. Philby had then been paternalistically groomed by his 'control' or case officer, Arnold Deutsch, who was under the orders of the NKVD station chief in London, Alexander Orlov, a man who would later play a crucial role in the Spanish Civil War. Since Philby was known to have left-wing sympathies, in order to get him recruited into the Foreign Office or the security services, his past was buried by working for a small magazine called *Review of Reviews*, where he painstakingly built up an image of someone without political convictions, albeit vaguely liberal.[91]

From there, Philby was able to get a job with the *Anglo-Russian Trade Gazette*, a journal run by British financiers who had business interests in pre-revolutionary Russia and assumed by Moscow to be linked to British Intelligence. Since there was no chance of its backers getting their money back from the Russians, the *Gazette* was failing and the owners decided to turn it into an Anglo-German publication with backing from the Third Reich. Philby was installed as editor and also joined the Anglo-German Fellowship, an organization of pro-Nazi financiers, members of parliament and figures from high society – mocked by Churchill as the 'Heil Hitler Brigade'. This not only gave Kim credibility, but also allowed him to report to Moscow on the extent of British support for Hitler. Orlov, whose cover had been blown, left London and was replaced by the

Hungarian-born Theodore Mally. Because Philby had never adopted a fully pro-Nazi line, he was about to be sacked by the German Ministry of Propaganda when he was told by his Russian controllers that he was being sent to the rebel zone in Spain under the cover of being a freelance pro-Nazi journalist: 'I was told that my trip was very important to gather information but what was even more important was to gain a reputation and establish myself as journalist to obtain a more important job.' It was hoped that not only would he be able to gather information for the Russians about German and Italian military and political contributions to Franco's war effort, but also thereby to become attractive to British Intelligence as a potential informant.[92]

Philby's cover was that he would be a freelance, to which end, he had secured accreditation from the London *Evening Standard* and a German magazine called *Geopolitics*. Through the German Embassy, he was put in contact with Franco's diplomatic agent in Cavendish Square, the Duque de Alba, who provided him with letters of recommendation, one of which was to Pablo Merry del Val who, at the time, was in charge of the censorship at Talavera de la Reina. Philby later recalled:

> My immediate assignment was to get first-hand information on all
> aspects of the Fascist war effort. The arrangement was that I should
> transmit the bulk of my information by hand to Soviet contacts in France
> or, more occasionally, in England. But for urgent communications, I had
> been provided with a code and a number of cover-addresses outside
> Spain. Before I left England, instructions in the use of the code were
> committed to a tiny piece of a substance resembling rice-paper, which I
> habitually kept in the ticket-pocket of my trousers.

However, in fact, it was also intended that Philby might find a way to insinuate himself into Franco's headquarters. In order to facilitate an assassination attempt on the Caudillo, he was to report on anything to do with security routines, and personnel as well as any gaps therein. He left London on 3 February 1937 en route for Seville. At first he reported to his Russian contacts on the military situation, armaments deliveries, troop movements and the location of airfields. The information was then passed on to the Republicans.[93]

Although his cover held, in April 1937, he had nearly ended up in front of a firing squad in Córdoba, where he had gone after seeing a poster advertising a bullfight. He had been unable to resist the chance of combining a visit to the bullring with a trip to the front to the east of the city. Unfortunately, he had been misadvised about the need for a special pass to enter what was a restricted military area. He was arrested in the middle of the night by Civil Guards and taken to their headquarters. His luggage was minutely searched and he was questioned. He was worried that, when his clothing was searched, his secret codes would be found. When asked to turn out his pockets, he resourcefully spun his wallet across the table and, while his three interrogators scrambled after it, he managed to screw into a ball and swallow the code sheet.[94]

He returned to London in May 1937. After debriefing him, his controllers decided that he was completely unsuitable for 'a wet job' and recommended that he be relieved of the task of participating in any assassination plot against Franco. Instead, he was instructed to get hired as the correspondent of a major newspaper in order to get closer to British Intelligence. With help from his father, the immensely influential Arabist, Harold St John Bridger Philby, Kim got hired by *The Times* on 24 May to replace James Holburn, who had been covering the Basque campaign. He actually reached Spain in the last week of June 1937 after first revisiting the German Embassy. Once in Spain, he got considerable mileage out of his connection with Joaquim von Ribbentrop. Dazzled by such references, Bolín thought that Philby was 'a decent chap who inspired confidence in his reports because he was so objective', and, along with Merry del Val, considered him to be 'a gentleman'. On New Year's Eve 1937, during the battle of Teruel, he was a passenger in a car with three other correspondents eating lunch when it was hit by Republican artillery fire. The twenty-three-year-old Bradish Johnson of *Newsweek*, who had been in Spain for only three weeks, was killed instantly. Richard Sheepshanks, the star reporter of Reuters, was badly wounded, as was Edward J. Neil of the Associated Press. They were taken to hospital in Zaragoza, where they both died. The only one to survive was Philby, who suffered a minor head wound.[95] It was a tribute to his status as much to his minor head wound that, on 2 March 1938, he was decorated by Franco himself with the Red Cross of Military Merit. He recalled later: 'My wounding in Spain helped my work, both journalism and intelligence, no end – all sorts of doors opened for me.' After being honoured by the Caudillo, Philby reported on the rebel advances from Teruel to the sea and then on the battle of the Ebro. He was one of the first correspondents to enter Barcelona with the occupying forces – all of which he found deeply painful – 'the worst time of my life'.[96] Nevertheless, far more than the correspondents who tried to cheat the censorship by taking reports out to France, it may be supposed that he did the Francoist war effort some damage.

Had Philby's real purpose been discovered, the warmth of Bolín's welcome might well have embarrassed him. In fact, Bolín's time as head of the rebel press service soon came to an end. After the removal of Millán Astray, and the conversion in January 1937 of the Oficina de Prensa y Propaganda into the Delegación para Prensa y Propaganda, under Vicente Gay, Bolín had been left in charge of the press. He survived too the removal of Vicente Gay and his replacement by Manuel Arias Paz. However, Bolín's days overseeing the work of the correspondents were numbered after his bungled efforts to deny the bombing of Guernica.[97] The furore over the bombing had coincided with Arthur Koestler's release from prison with the attendant publicity about his arrest and Bolín's part in it.

Alarmed by the damage being done to the Nationalist cause, the Marqués del Moral, Frederick Ramón Bertodano y Wilson, the Anglo-Spanish co-ordinator of pro-Franco propaganda in London, hastened to Salamanca to warn Franco. Bertodano, like other Nationalist sympathizers, believed the story about Basque dynamiters, but was distressed by the damage being done to the Nationalists by reports about the bombing. He begged Franco to consent to an enquiry to allow the 'truth' to come out. Naturally, the Generalísimo refused and promised only to renew previous statements in other forms. However, the Marqués del Moral, together with another of Franco's British propagandists, Arthur Loveday, had a meeting with Manuel Arias Paz, shortly after his appointment as Delegado de Prensa y Propaganda, and convinced him that Bolín was provoking the hostility of otherwise favourable British correspondents. It seems likely that the pressure of all three led to Franco removing Bolín, who was replaced immediately after on 18 May by Pablo Merry del Val, who was promoted from head of press on the Madrid front to head of relations with the foreign press in Salamanca and Burgos. Thereafter, the treatment of correspondents was somewhat improved, even to the extent of Franco himself receiving a group of them on 15 July 1937 to tell them how much freer censorship was in his Spain than in the Republican zone. Bolín was appointed '*enviado especial de la Delegación en Inglaterra, Paises Escandinavos y Estados Unidos*', a post which involved him lobbying politicians and the media. In February 1938, he was named Jefe del Servicio Nacional de Turismo, which arranged sight-seeing tours of the rebel zone.[98]

The brutality with which the Nationalists went about 'managing' the news of Guernica was illustrated by the treatment received by the first reporter to arrive after the rebels had occupied the town. This was the Frenchman Georges Berniard, of *La Petite Gironde*, who had previously been with the rebel forces at San Sebastián, Oviedo and Toledo. Now, on 29 April, however, he had flown from Biarritz to Bilbao, received permits from the Basque Republican authorities and then driven to Guernica without realizing that it was now in rebel hands. He was immediately detained at gunpoint, accused of espionage. When an officer asked who Berniard and his guide were, their captors replied: 'They are communists who claim to be journalists.' He was saved by the intervention of an Italian correspondent, Sandro Sandri, who vouched for him and thus gave him the time in which to swallow some incriminating letters. He was then handed over to Captain Aguilera, who accepted that he was probably not a spy, but accused him of contravening a rebel decree condemning to death any foreign journalist who, having once covered the Francoist side, was found in the company of the Republican forces. Berniard was taken to Vitoria, where he was told that he was to be shot at dawn. His chauffeur was shot, as were two Basque journalists who had been with him that morning in Bilbao but, tired of waiting for him to get the necessary permits, had impatiently set off to Guernica on their own. After thirty-six hours under arrest, Berniard was told by Aguilera that he would be freed on condition that he wrote an article thanking Generals Franco, Mola and Solchaga for their clemency. This he duly did when he returned to France. The fact that Malet-Dauban was still in solitary confinement under sentence of death may well have influenced Berniard and indeed other journalists to go along with the rebel line. That seems to have been the case of Georges Botto, Malet-Dauban's replacement as Havas correspondent. Under Aguilera's guidance, he wrote a story that sustained the rebel line that Guernica had not been bombed but burned by the Basques themselves.[99]

The appointment of Merry del Val improved the day-to-day treatment of correspondents only as long as they did not ask awkward questions or try to send out embarrassing information. The German bombing of Guernica came into this category. Despite the removal of Bolín, the cover-up of Guernica would go on for many years and, in the short term, continued to involve all those in the press apparatus including Aguilera. This meant the close supervision of 'untrustworthy' journalists who tried to get near the ruins of the town and the expulsion of those who wrote unwelcome reports. It also extended to giving strong guidance to sympathetic journalists as to how their articles should be written.[100]

After the excitement of the Basque campaign, Aguilera was transferred from Mola's general staff to the Delegación del Estado para Prensa y Propaganda.[101] It made little difference to his readiness to be directly involved at the front. He took part in the subsequent assault on Santander, again accompanying the Navarrese Brigades. He actually entered the defeated city two hours before any other Nationalist forces, accompanied by the correspondent of *The Times*, Kim Philby. He drove through thousands of Republican militiamen, still armed but utterly paralysed and dejected by the rapidity of their defeat.[102] Shortly after, Virginia Cowles found herself in the recently captured city. Captain Aguilera offered to drive her to León, where she would be nearer Franco's headquarters as he continued with his attack on Asturias. He had a pale yellow Mercedes on the back seat of which he kept two large rifles and 'a chauffeur who drove so badly he was usually encouraged to sleep'. Wearing cavalry boots and spurs, a cap from which a blue tassel swung, he drove as if riding a racehorse. Since the roads were clogged by refugees and Italian troops, he would drive along cursing at other traffic. He occasionally complained: 'You never see any pretty girls. Any girl who hasn't got a face like a boot can get a ride in an Italian truck.' He gave little sign of being on his best behaviour for a foreign correspondent. If anything, the brutality of his speech was inflamed by the presence of Miss Cowles, an attractive woman who looked a little like Lauren Bacall. On stopping to ask the way and asking someone who turned out to be German, he said: 'Nice chaps, the Germans, but a bit too serious; they never seem to have any women around, but I suppose they didn't come for that. If they kill enough Reds, we can forgive them anything.'[103] 'Blast the Reds!' he said to Virginia Cowles, 'Why did they have to put ideas into people's heads? Everyone knows that people are fools and much better off told what to do than trying to run themselves. Hell is too good for the Reds. I'd like to impale every one and see them wriggling on poles like butterflies…' The Captain paused to see what impression his speech had made, but she said nothing, which seemed to anger him. 'There's only one thing I hate worse than a Red,' he blazed. 'What's that?' 'A sob-sister!'[104]

In the wake of the embarrassment over Guernica, ever stronger guidance was given to sympathetic journalists as to how their articles should be written. Virginia Cowles reached Nationalist Spain just before the entry of the Italians into Santander on 26 August 1937. She found the atmosphere in Salamanca reeking of paranoia. She wrote later:

> I found it dangerous to make contradictions. One woman, the wife of an official in the Foreign Office, asked me how I dared walk along the streets of Madrid. She had heard there was so much sniping from the windows that bodies were piled up by the curbs and left to rot in the gutters. When I denied this her tone became hostile, and I later learned she had denounced me as suspect. Another man asked if I had seen the Reds feeding prisoners to the animals in the Zoo. I told him the Zoo had been empty for months, and his manner froze. Still another, Pablo Merry del Val, the head of the Foreign Press, admired a gold bracelet I was wearing: 'I don't imagine you took that to Madrid with you,' he said, smiling. When I replied I had bought it in Madrid he was greatly affronted and from then on bowed coldly from a distance.[105]

On a trip to Asturias accompanied by Aguilera, she got on the wrong side of him, provoking his wrath by suggesting that the Republicans had blown up a bridge not out of wanton destructiveness but to hold up the Nationalists. He took his revenge by leaving her sitting alone in a car for several hours. In turn, she refused to greet a senior officer. Apoplectic with rage, he said: 'You have insulted the Nationalist cause. You will hear more of this later.' After a report from Aguilera, Merry del Val refused her the necessary permits for her to leave Spain. Other journalists told her that there was a warrant out for her arrest. She managed to get to Burgos with the help of the Duque de Montellano, whom she knew, and then on to San Sebastián thanks to another friend, the Conde Churruca. There, by a subterfuge, the First Secretary of the British Embassy, Geoffrey 'Tommy' Thompson, managed to spirit her across the border into France.[106] As Cowles' case revealed, the treatment meted out to correspondents by Bolín and Aguilera was a far cry from the efforts of Arturo Barea, Ilsa Kulcsar and Constancia de la Mora to facilitate the news-gathering of reporters in the Republican zone.

When the Francoists arrived in Barcelona, the foreign press was transported in a fleet of limousines. However, they were allowed to go nowhere unless accompanied by supervising officers. Cedric Salter, of the *Daily Mail*, had remained in the Catalan capital when the rest of the correspondents assigned to the Republic had been evacuated, confident that the right-wing and pro-fascist stance of his paper would protect him. Although he was treated contemptuously by the newly arrived conquerors, he was saved from major discomfort by a cable sent by the *Daily Mail* to Franco's headquarters in Burgos. He was called for interrogation by Manuel Lambarri, who had by now been promoted to Colonel. Lambarri was outraged to read in the newspaper's defence of its correspondent that he had reported the war 'absolutely objectively', something he regarded as deeply shocking. However, because Lambarri was under instructions to do nothing to displease the *Daily Mail*, Salter was to be sent to Burgos for a final decision on his fate. Once there, he was told by the urbane press chief, Pablo Merry del Val, that he could not work in Spain as a correspondent. There was, it seemed, a danger that he might repeat the sin of objectivity.[107]

PART TWO

BEYOND JOURNALISM

6

Stalin's Eyes and Ears in Madrid?
The Rise and Fall of Mikhail Koltsov

In the summer of 1938, Mikhail Koltsov, one of Russia's most successful writers and journalists, was elected to the Supreme Soviet of the Russian Socialist Federal Soviet Republic. It was a reward for a distinguished career which included an active, and indeed daring, role during the Spanish Civil War. His chronicles from Spain, published daily in *Pravda*, from 9 August 1936 to 6 November 1937, had been devoured avidly by the Russian public. During the spring and summer of 1938, his vivid diary of his Spanish exploits was serialized to enormous acclaim. He was at the apogee of his popularity. In the autumn of the same year, one evening at the Bolshoi, Stalin invited him to his box and told him how much he was enjoying the Spanish diary. The dictator then invited Koltsov to give a lecture to present the History of the Bolshevik Party, which he himself had edited. It was a notable token of official favour. Two days before the lecture, yet another honour came Koltsov's way – he was made a corresponding member of the Academy of Sciences. In the late afternoon of 12 December, a beaming Koltsov fulfilled his promise to Stalin and gave a warmly received lecture at the Writers' Union about Stalin's book. Late that night, shortly after he arrived at his *Pravda* office, agents of the NKVD (the People's Commissariat for Internal Security) arrived and took him away. After interrogation and torture over a period of nearly fourteen months, Koltsov was shot. To this day, the precise reasons for the fall from grace of such a celebrity remain a mystery.

Born in Kiev in 1898, the son of a Jewish artisan, Mikhail Efimovich Friedland Koltsov was to attain immense popularity in Soviet Russia. As a young man, he had left the Ukraine to study for a degree in medicine at the University of St Petersburg, but the outbreak of the Russian Revolution had seen him swept into politics. He took part in the Russian Civil War, producing political propaganda for the Red Army's Okna Yug ROSTA, an information bulletin on the southern front.

He joined the Communist Party in 1918 with a letter of recommendation signed by both Trotsky and the old Bolshevik Anatoly Lunacharsky, and participated in the repression of the sailors' revolt at Kronstadt in March 1921. Thereafter he became a prominent journalist. He was also an aviator who had taken part in long-distance flights, the most celebrated of which had opened up the route Moscow–Ankara–Teheran–Kabul. In 1931, he published the book *Khochu letat'* (I want to fly). He was an important pioneer in the nascent Soviet aircraft industry, participating in the fund-raising for construction of the gigantic aircraft 'Maxim Gorki'. He wrote colourfully realistic articles about his flying exploits, about his experiences as a taxi-driver and about his long journeys through Asia and Europe.[1] He believed that a journalist should see, feel and participate in everything he wrote about. From an early stage, his journalistic and literary work was larded with accounts of his own intrepid adventures. A tendency to self-publicity would accompany him throughout his career and may well have contributed to his ultimate fate.

Koltsov's political activities in the 1920s also contained the seeds of subsequent problems. He was a member of the left Opposition and the protégé of Lev Sosnovsky, an old Bolshevik, a close associate of Karl Radek and himself a gifted journalist. He joined the staff of *Pravda* in 1922 at the invitation of Lenin's sister, Maria Ulianova, one of the paper's senior editors. In 1923, to Stalin's annoyance, he had published a photo-montage 'A Day in the Life of Trotsky' in the magazine *Ogonyok*. After the deportation in 1927 of Leon Trotsky, Sosnovsky courageously bore the banner of his friend, an example not followed by Koltsov. When Sosnovsky was arrested in 1928, Koltsov quickly dissociated himself from his erstwhile mentor, which earned him a public slapping in the foyer of the Bolshoi Theatre from Sosnovsky's mistress, Olga.[2] Koltsov participated in Stalin's fiftieth-birthday celebrations in 1929 with a panegyric comparing him to Lenin.[3] Having reneged on his past, Koltsov quickly acquired considerable celebrity in the world of the Soviet press. He became editor of a host of journals – *Ogonyok* (1928–39), *Krokodil* (1934–38), *Chudak* (1928–30), *Za rubezhom* (1932–38), among others. He became acquainted with the top brass of the NKVD. Sofia Prokofieva, a colleague at *Ogonyok*, introduced him to her husband Georgi Prokofiev, deputy to the chief of the NKVD, Genrikh Grigorevich Yagoda. He also knew Yagoda's successor, the vicious Nikolai Yezhov, by dint of attending the literary salon run by his wife Yevgenia. He rose to be head of the powerful Soviet magazine and newspaper association, making him one of the most influential men in Soviet cultural policy of the 1930s. Moreover, as chairman of the foreign committee of the Soviet Writers' Union, he held a key function in propagating the policies of the Popular

Front.[4] Trotsky never forgave his conversion to Stalinism but Koltsov would never be free of the taint of Trotskyism.

Despite his growing pre-eminence in the literary world, Koltsov always retained a thirst for action. At the funeral of the great poet and playwright Vladimir Mayakovsky who had died on 14 April 1930, Koltsov volunteered to drive the hearse. It had been announced that Mayakovsky had committed suicide over a failed love affair. Certainly, he was demoralized and disillusioned by the drift of Soviet politics, but it was whispered by some that he had been murdered by the security services because of his increasingly individualistic writings. A huge crowd gathered to pay homage, walking behind the cortège as it drew away from the Writers' Union. However, Koltsov drove too fast, and lost the crowd. It is to be assumed that this was as a result of the impetuousness of the one-time taxi-driver rather than an official ploy to diminish the size of the popular homage to Mayakovsky and thus limit the negative publicity of his untimely death.[5]

A Moscow acquaintance, Paulina Abramson, then seventeen years old, met Koltsov in 1932 in the Soviet Embassy in Berlin and remembered him as 'of small stature, quite plump peering through thick-lensed spectacles'. The approbation with which he eyed her made it obvious that he was something of a womanizer.[6] Certainly, he was the very antithesis of a grey and dour apparatchik. An indication of Koltsov's boyish and irreverent style was given by the Hungarian Arthur Koestler. He recounted an episode in Paris in 1935 involving Koltsov, Maxim Litvinov, the Soviet Commissar for Foreign Affairs, and Aleksander Rado, a clandestine agent of Soviet Military Intelligence, the GRU. They were in Paris for some international diplomatic conference at which Litvinov was heading the Russian delegation and Rado attending under his cover as Paris representative of the Impress Bureau (Soviet Independent News Service). Koltsov arrived late for his meeting with Koestler: '"Forgive me," he said with his pale smile, "but I have a good excuse. I have been to a cinema." "At lunch-time?" I asked, surprised at such frivolity. "Yes, we were very naughty. We were playing truant. You will never guess who else." I didn't. The other two lunch-hour movie visitors had been Litvinov, incognito, and Alex Rado.' Interestingly, if Paulina Abramson remembered him as plump in 1932, by the time that they met in 1935, Koestler would describe him as 'a short, thin, insignificant-looking man, with a quiet manner and pale eyes'.[7] His weight loss could have been a reflection of the anxieties induced in an ex-member of the left opposition by the increasingly oppressive atmosphere in the Soviet Union.

That Koltsov was deeply uncomfortable about the turn of events in the USSR was immediately obvious to the German writer Gustav Regler, who visited him

at this time. Regler was horrified to find the Moscow bookshops full of outpour-
ings from exiles and from children which he likened to 'the stammerings of
terrified lackeys'. He protested to Koltsov about the stultifying atmosphere in
Russia, which was turning stormy petrels into parrots. An embarrassed Koltsov
told him of a recent decree, whereby destitute children had ceased to exist and
were to be put in camps, and laying down that children from the age of twelve
could be shot. Clearly appalled and ashamed, Koltsov said: 'Why don't you console yourself with the thought of the good that has been achieved? Or why don't
you simply tell yourself that I'm exaggerating, that even if the decree exists it isn't
being implemented, that no Russian would dream of shooting a child?' Distressed,
and pale, he stopped and said he had to leave.[8]

Although Koltsov enjoyed a high, not to say luxurious, standard of living in
Moscow, the chance to go to Spain must have come as an immense relief from
the ever more oppressive political atmosphere in Russia. En route, he met the son
of the Spanish Prime Minister José Giral in Paris on 6 August. It was an indication of Koltsov's perceived influence that the younger Giral asked him to inform
Moscow that the Republic needed 'trained officers, especially pilots, if a catastrophe is to be averted'.[9] Koltsov was the first Soviet newspaper correspondent to
reach Spain. On the evening of his arrival in Barcelona, he sent his first despatch
to *Pravda*.[10] Five years earlier, he had visited Spain, meeting the young
Communists Dolores Ibárruri in Bilbao and José Díaz in Seville and producing
a book entitled *Spanish Spring*.[11] Now back in Spain, Koltsov lost little time in
assuming a role as a political adviser to the Republican authorities. He carried
no credentials other than those of a *Pravda* editor and special correspondent,
but the importance of that was immediately recognized. Lieutenant Colonel
Felipe Díaz Sandino, Minister of Defence in the recently constituted Catalan
Government of Joan Casanovas, placed a car at his disposal. Within two days,
he had been received by the anarchist leader Juan García Oliver, by the leadership of the Catalan Communist Party, the Partit Socialista Unificat de Catalunya,
and by Casanovas himself. By the following day, he was at the front in Huesca
and happily giving advice to the local commander. He then expressed a desire to
meet the legendary anarchist leader, Buenaventura Durruti, who was on the
Aragón front at Bujaraloz. At first Durruti had no interest in talking to him
until he read in the letter of introduction from García Oliver the words 'Moscow'
and '*Pravda*'.

Despite enjoying such access to important politicians, like all correspondents,
Koltsov quickly ran into the difficulties of the censorship, the chronic shortage of
telephone lines and Spain's limited telegraph system.[12] He reached Madrid on

18 August and within twenty-four hours had spoken not just with leaders of the Communist Party but also with the prime minister, the Professor of Chemistry, Dr José Giral, and the Minister of War, Lieutenant Colonel Juan Hernández Saravia. Within a week, he had managed to interview the moderate Socialist Indalecio Prieto, who was effectively running the war effort from the shadows. It is a tribute both to Koltsov's journalistic ability and to his status that Prieto spoke to him with quite amazing frankness about his contempt for Largo Caballero. A day later, via the mediation of Julio Álvarez del Vayo, whom he knew from his days as a correspondent in Moscow, he was able to interview both President Manuel Azaña and Largo Caballero himself. In his unrestrained criticisms of the government of Dr Giral, Largo was as frank as Prieto had been.[13] Four days after becoming prime minister on 4 September 1937, Largo Caballero would receive Koltsov for another long conversation.[14]

There have been wild exaggerations about Koltsov's role in the Spanish Civil War. One German scholar claimed absurdly that he had arrived in Spain with the rank of general in the Soviet air force and with the job of establishing a Spanish equivalent of the NKVD.[15] It was bizarrely alleged that he spoke once or twice every day on the telephone with Stalin to give him news of the Spanish situation. This idea derived from Claud Cockburn, a Communist journalist who established a close friendship with Koltsov in Spain, and has subsequently gained wide currency despite its utter implausibility. Cockburn told the American author Peter Wyden that once, when he was speaking on the telephone to Stalin from Gaylord's Hotel, Koltsov allowed him to listen on an extension to the dictator's grunts. In an article, Cockburn exaggerated this hugely to the point of saying that Koltsov had 'a direct line from his room in the Palace Hotel, Madrid' to Stalin's desk in the Kremlin, and he talked, briefly or at length, with Stalin 'three or four times a week' and 'sometimes I could hear Stalin's voice asking questions from the other end'. Cockburn's wife Patricia elevated this further into something that happened once or twice every day.[16] The telephone connection from Madrid to Moscow, via Barcelona and Paris, was neither regularly functional nor sufficiently secure for any such conversations to be likely even had Stalin been sufficiently interested in daily bulletins from Spain. It is possible that, in exaggerating, Cockburn was simply building upon Koltsov's own boasts. However, as a letter to Stalin from Koltsov revealed, even the most senior Soviet emissaries were reluctant to send information even by telegraph, where it could be coded, let alone by telephone, which could be relatively easily tapped.[17]

It is inconceivable that Koltsov had a senior rank either in the Soviet air force or the NKVD. Nevertheless, it is certainly the case that although officially no more than the *Pravda* correspondent, Koltsov did play a role in Spain that went far beyond his journalistic responsibilities. Santiago Carrillo, who was Consejero de Orden Público in the Junta de Madrid, remembered him simply as having far greater influence than any other correspondent. During the siege of the capital, he seemed to be more important than the Ambassador Marcel Rosenberg. However, Carrillo categorically dismissed the idea of the daily telephone calls, recalling that regular reporting to the Kremlin took place from the embassy via coded radio transmissions. Usually, to get his *Pravda* despatches out during the siege of Madrid, Koltsov had to phone them to the Hotel Majestic in Barcelona, whence they were transmitted to Moscow. Direct telephone communication was a rarity, although it did take place occasionally.[18]

Beyond the more extreme exaggerations, many contemporary eye-witnesses noted Koltsov's importance. The well-informed Sovietologist, Louis Fischer, a man who came into frequent contact with Koltsov, described him as '*Pravda*'s correspondent in Spain and unofficially Stalin's eyes and ears in the country' – the first of several commentators to use the phrase.[19] Hemingway called Koltsov 'one of the three most important men in Spain', although that particular exaggeration was typical of his constant efforts to show that he was in the know and had access to everyone worth knowing.[20] The novelist Ilya Ehrenburg wrote:

> The Spaniards regarded him not only as a famous journalist but also as a political adviser. It would be difficult to visualize the first year of the Spanish war without Koltsov. Small, active courageous, so acute that his intelligence positively became a burden to him, he sized up a situation at a glance, saw all the weaknesses and never pampered himself with illusions.[21]

The NKVD agent (officer), Colonel Alexander Orlov (born Leiba Lazarevich Feldbin, he officially changed his name to Lev Lazarevich Nikolsky in 1920), claimed that Koltsov was sent to Spain 'by Stalin as his personal observer', which is not remarkable since it was very much what a *Pravda* editor would have been expected to be.[22] These views have been subsumed into the received wisdom on the Spanish Civil War. Hugh Thomas, for instance, presented Koltsov as 'probably Stalin's personal agent in Spain, with on occasion a direct line to the Kremlin'. The Russian historian Olga Novikova considered him as 'the liaison between Stalin and the Spanish authorities'.[23]

In his diary, Koltsov separated the journalistic tasks which he attributed to himself from the military-political ones, which he attributed to a Mexican by the name of 'Miguel Martínez' who had allegedly fought in the Mexican Revolution, yet, like Koltsov himself as a young man, had supposedly been involved in the First World War and the Russian Civil War. Moreover, Koltsov described 'Martínez' in terms that suggest that he was talking about himself: 'a Mexican Communist of below average height who, like me, had arrived yesterday'. Elsewhere we learn that he wears glasses.[24] The text is also littered with other clues that suggest that Koltsov and 'Martínez' were the same man. The author described Martínez's hair-raising flight from Paris to Barcelona in an aircraft piloted by Abel Guides. Suspecting that the pilot might have been planning to take him to the rebel zone, 'Miguel' contemplated shooting Guides and then piloting the plane himself – something that Koltsov was certainly capable of doing. On 8 June 1937 in Bilbao, Koltsov had a conversation with Guides about the incident from which it is quite clear that it was Koltsov himself who had considered shooting the pilot. He claimed that Miguel Martínez went every evening to the offices of the Communist newspaper, *Mundo Obrero*, and helped in the production of the following day's issue – precisely what Koltsov used to do. Elsewhere, during the retreat from Talavera, 'Miguel Martínez' saw a small pistol in the hands of the writer María Teresa de León; and later it is Koltsov who remembered seeing her with the pistol at the same place.[25] Koltsov's younger brother, the world-famous *Pravda* cartoonist, Boris Efimovich Friedland, known as Boris Efimov, his biographers, Skorokhodov and Rubashkin, and other scholars have all assumed that 'Miguel Martínez' was Koltsov himself. Enrique Líster, the commander of the Communist Quinto Regimiento, which was later to form the nucleus of the Popular Army, had frequent and regular contact with Koltsov, as the diary attests. He assured Ian Gibson that he had no doubt that Koltsov and 'Miguel Martínez' were the same person.[26]

There can be no doubt that many of the activities attributed to 'Miguel Martínez' were Koltsov's. It may well be, however, that the devotedly pro-Soviet Líster was endeavouring to conceal the true identity of 'Miguel Martínez' or at least of some component part thereof. In other words, it is possible that some of the activities attributed to 'Miguel Martínez' may not have been carried out by Koltsov. In his memoirs of the siege of Madrid, Vicente Rojo, the Republican Chief of Staff, writes of knowing 'Miguel Martínez' and of his work with the Quinto Regimiento. It is certainly the case that Koltsov knew Rojo and he wrote about him on more than one occasion.[27] However, the fact that Rojo did not identify 'Martínez' as Koltsov has provoked the suspicions of the Russian scholar Boris Volodarsky and of Spanish historian Ángel Viñas that there was a separate 'Miguel

Martínez' who had been in contact with Rojo. Based on the research of Boris Volodarsky in Russian security archives, they have reached the conclusion that at least some of the activities attributed to 'Miguel Martínez' were carried out not by Koltsov, but by a Soviet agent of Lithuanian origin. The man in question, Iosif Romualdovich Grigulevich, was a twenty-three-year-old member of the NKVD 'Administration of Special Tasks', a section specializing in assassination, terror and sabotage on foreign soil. He had learned Spanish in Argentina and reached Spain in September 1936. He would later head the first attempt on Trotsky's life in Mexico. Accordingly, the 'Miguel Martínez' portrayed by Koltsov may have been a composite portrait of various individuals – Koltsov himself, Grigulevich and possibly the Russian Military Attaché, General Vladimir Gorev. Station head of Soviet Military Intelligence (GRU) in Madrid, Gorev reported to Moscow that Koltsov 'carried out to the letter all the orders that I gave in relation to the defence of the city'.[28]

That Koltsov, as a *Pravda* editor, had a special status as an observer for Stalin is not in dispute. However, that does not explain the sheer scale of the active role played by Koltsov/'Miguel Martínez' in a wide range of political and military capacities. When the Republican militias retreated on 21 September 1936 from Maqueda, on the road from Talavera to Madrid, K/MM was to be found, pistol in hand, trying to stop the retreat – in this case, K/MM was probably Koltsov, since neither Gorev nor Grigulevich was likely to have been at the battle front. In the besieged capital, K/MM was a constant adviser to the Communist leadership and a close collaborator of Julio Álvarez del Vayo, who on 17 October had been named Commissar General of War, which effectively made him head of the Cuerpo de Comisarios. In terms of meetings with Del Vayo, 'Miguel Martínez' could at one point have been Koltsov and, at another, Gorev. Even before then, K/MM was being given copies of intercepted enemy radio traffic. Since the Republican army had no facilities to intercept enemy traffic, this task had to have been undertaken by three Soviet military specialists who arrived in October 1936. Accordingly, the person given the intercepts would most likely have been Gorev, as both Military Attaché and local head of Military Intelligence. On 28 October, K/MM could be found explaining to units of the Communist Quinto Regimiento how they should follow up tank attacks.[29] If this was Koltsov, he was merely passing on the advice of the real tank specialist, General Gorev, which leaves the suspicion that the person giving the explanations was Gorev himself.

One intervention by 'Miguel Martínez' of immense significance relates to the decision-making process about the evacuation and subsequent execution of imprisoned rightists from Madrid, one of the most controversial issues in the

Spanish Civil War. In the book, 'Miguel Martínez' insistently points out to the Communist leadership the dangers of letting the military personnel among the prisoners swell the ranks of the rebels. Worried about the 'eight thousand fascists who are locked in several prisons around Madrid' and who threaten to become a real problem as a dangerous 'fifth column', 'Miguel Martínez' went on several occasions both to Communist Party headquarters and also to the office of the War Commissariat to enquire what had been done and to suggest how an evacuation might be organized.[30] It is the view of Boris Volodarsky that, in describing the activities of 'Miguel Martínez' in relation to the evacuation of the right-wing political prisoners, Koltsov was actually recording those of Iosif Grigulevich. The eventual operation culminated in the murder of large numbers of the prisoners. The specific responsibility for the death of the prisoners remains unclear. The decision to evacuate involved many individuals and the eventual outcome developed gradually and cumulatively. Nevertheless, Grigulevich ran a special unit recruited from the Juventudes Socialistas Unificadas (JSU), and it appears that they played a key role on the night of 7 November and on the next day in the collection and transportation of prisoners.[31] Moreover, Grigulevich had become a close friend and collaborator of Santiago Carrillo who, as JSU leader and Consejero de Orden Público in the Madrid Defence Junta, has frequently been accused of responsibility in the affair.[32]

Koltsov's diary suggested that 'Miguel Martínez' was instrumental in the creation of the system of political commissars in order to raise morale among the troops. He claimed that 'Miguel Martínez' introduced the practice of the commissars sending regular political reports on their units to the military high command. Since this was standard Red Army practice at the time, it is possible either that Koltsov was merely passing on recommendations from his fellow Russian advisers such as Gorev, or that the 'Miguel Martínez' cited referred to Grigulevich or Gorev or some other 'adviser'. 'Miguel Martínez' was presented not only as having access to these reports but also, on occasion, writing them.[33] Exaggerating wildly on the basis of the diary, his first Soviet biographer claimed that, on 17 October 1936, Koltsov was officially named commissar of a brigade and helped to draft the instructions for the political commissars of the whole army.[34] While it is certainly true that the Spanish adoption of commissars was based on the model that emerged during the Russian Civil War, the name of Koltsov is not among those cited by Spanish sources as instrumental in developing the system in Spain. It is, however, possible that, through his close connection with the Communist Fifth Regiment, his advice was crucial.[35] He was on excellent terms with its commander, Enrique Líster, but then again, so was Iosif Grigulevich. *Milicia Popular*, the newspaper of the Fifth Regiment, serialized Koltsov's long article on the Red Army, 'El hombre del capote gris, el oficial y el jefe' (the man in the grey cape, the officer and the NCO).[36] It is impossible to be certain, but it is more likely that the 'Miguel Martínez' given such prominence in the development of the commissar system was someone other than Koltsov.

In his diary, Koltsov talks of Miguel's relationship with Álvarez del Vayo in such a way as to lend credence to his claims about his part in the commissar system. On 23 October 1936, he noted that, every day at six in the evening, Álvarez del Vayo, as Comisario General, held a meeting in the Ministry of War with the five vice-*comisarios*, two other commissars and 'Miguel Martínez'. If taken at face value, this would suggest that Koltsov was much more than a correspondent. It would, of course, be much more plausible if the participant in the meetings was Gorev, or Koltsov acting under Gorev's orders.[37]

Leaving aside the absurd suggestion of two French writers that Koltsov, who was openly in Spain as *Pravda* correspondent, was really 'a secret spokesman for Stalin', it is certainly the case that he had acquired considerable influence and authority in the Ministry of War.[38] This much has been attested by the Socialist Arturo Barea, at the time, working in the censorship department of the Foreign Ministry. In his memoirs, he vividly recounts an example of Koltsov's assertion of his own authority. Barea, on his own initiative, was desperately attempting to keep the press censorship going after the officials in charge had all fled to Valencia. Unaware of Barea's efforts, and infuriated by the fact that, before he had been able to set up some kind of new system, several foreign correspondents had managed to send out pessimistic reports, Koltsov burst into his office and imperiously demanded explanations. When Barea explained the situation and the fact that he was working on his own authority, Koltsov proclaimed: 'Your authority is the War Commissariat. Come along with us. Suzana will provide you with an order of the Secretariat.' 'Suzana', a woman who spoke Spanish with a French accent, had, rather like Barea himself, stayed on in Madrid, where she was a typist in the Ministry of War, and been made secretary to the Comisaría de Guerra. When they got to the ministry, Barea was amazed by the authority exercised by Koltsov: 'Groups of militia officers came and went, people burst in to shout that their consignment of arms had not arrived, and the man Koltsov intervened in most of the discussions on the authority of his vitality and arrogant will.'[39]

That Koltsov felt happier and more alive in Madrid than he had done in the bleak atmosphere of the purges is evident. He may have supported the purges publicly, but there is little doubt that he felt increasingly uncomfortable about them. He was overjoyed when the news came in that the Soviet Union had decided to send aeroplanes, tanks, artillery and other weaponry.[40] There can be no doubt of his astonishing capacity for work and his burning enthusiasm for the Spanish cause, although it is difficult not to suspect some authors of well-intentioned exaggeration. Gleb Skorokhodov, his first biographer, conflating Koltsov and 'Miguel Martínez', made the utterly absurd claim that, at the end of October, Koltsov was given the task of drawing up the the Ministry of War's orders for the defence of Madrid.[41] It is inconceivable that the strategists responsible, Generals Jan Berzin and Gorev, and the Republican Chief of Staff, Vicente Rojo, would have permitted such intrusion from an amateur. Skorokhodov's error is another indication not only that 'Miguel Martínez' was a composite figure, but also that an important component of that figure was Gorev.

According to the habitually unreliable Orlov, when the government left Madrid, only two members of the official Soviet group remained in the beleaguered capital: Koltsov and himself.[42] In fact, Gorev remained in the Ministry of Defence along with Koltsov's friend, the famous Soviet documentary-maker, Roman Karmen, and many other Russian officials. Nevertheless, Koltsov's courageous decision to stay was the prelude to his finest hour.

Gorev, who was unofficially advising General José Miaja, the president of the Madrid Junta de Defensa, spoke every day with Koltsov. Their meetings were evoked by Emma Wolf, Gorev's lover and interpreter. Gorev, she recalled, would listen closely to what Koltsov had to say, because he regarded him as the best-informed person around about what was going on both at the front and in the rearguard. The Russian historian of the KGB, Boris Volodarsky, has claimed that Gorev was actually afraid for his life and listened to Koltsov because he was the party's voice in Spain and could always report on him to Moscow. Gorev was equally attentive and respectful to Orlov, who reported on him anyway, in spite of Gorev's writing a flattering report to Moscow praising Orlov.[43]

Even leaving aside what seem to have been the activities of the other elements of 'Miguel Martínez', there can be no doubt that Koltsov was utterly devoted to the cause of the Republic. When things were going badly, he could not refrain from launching himself into action. Paulina Abramson reflected years later: 'At times it was quite shocking to see how he just got involved in issues and passed opinions that doubtless influenced the outcome. He did so because his education, his very nature and his knowledge of strategy would not let him just stand idly by when faced with the ubiquitous disorder'.[44] He could be tremendously acerbic and an unsympathetic Sefton Delmer recalled him as 'a dynamic raspwitted

Russian Jew', 'a small, stocky man, sharp-eyed and sneering, strutting around in martial-looking jackboots'.[45]

In the midst of the attack on Madrid, the first Soviet tanks went into action on 29 October 1936. They did well but, in the narrow streets of the villages, some got trapped and were vulnerable to the improvised incendiary devices such as Molotov cocktails thrown by Franco's troops. Three tanks were lost. When the Soviet tank commanders gathered that night in the Hotel Palace, the mood could not have been bleaker. Koltsov cheered them all up by pointing out that the attack had really been a great success. According to Orlov, he suggested that a telegram be sent to Stalin calling for all of the tank crews to be awarded the Order of Lenin and that the title of Hero of the Soviet Union be conferred upon the leader of the attack and the ten missing crew members. Orlov claimed improbably that a telegram signed by Koltsov, General Gorev and Orlov provoked a reply from the People's Commissar for Defence, Marshall Kliment Voroshilov, granting the request.[46]

It has been suggested that Koltsov even commanded a section of Russian tanks and played a significant part in the battles of Pozuelo and Aravaca (4–14 January 1937). This is certainly a wild exaggeration based on his adolescent enthusiasm for driving around the battlefield in an armoured car.[47] Certainly, despite an action-packed schedule, he sent a steady stream of long and vividly written articles back to Russia as well as having a journalistic presence in Spain. Roman Karmen was amazed at Koltsov's ability 'to write forty lines with astonishing speed, real wit and careful and thoughtful observation to give a perfectly finished portrait of the political situation'.[48]

However, it is impossible to say if Koltsov did any or all of these things on the basis of carrying some special authorization or accreditation from Stalin himself.[49] It is equally plausible that much of his astonishing prominence derived simply from the energy, self-confidence and impatience with Spanish disorganization, which saw him just steam into situations and give imperious advice. Perhaps he was allowed to take a prominent role precisely because it was believed that he had some sort of accreditation from Stalin. This was the view of Boris Efimov: 'Koltsov would not have been Koltsov if he had stayed within the confines of pure newspaper, journalistic work.' According to Boris Efimov: 'As far as I know no one especially delegated such work to Koltsov. He went to Spain only as a writer, as a *Pravda* correspondent.' However, like Vasily Grossman in the Second World War, Koltsov shared his opinions with those in charge because he believed that it was his duty as a Communist to do so. Moreover, given his enthusiastic and energetic personality, frustrated by the inadequacies of the Spanish defence of the Republic, Koltsov simply took it upon himself to give advice wherever any-one would listen to him. Already as a child, recalled Borís Efimov, his brother Mikhail had demonstrated a multi-faceted creativity: 'he was a restless child, he invented games, wrote plays'.[50]

A similar view can be derived from the memoirs of the cameraman Roman Karmen. 15 August 1936, the thirty-year-old Karmen had been instructed to go to Spain. He left Moscow on 19 August and, on the following day, was met in Paris by Ilya Ehrenburg and crossed the frontier at Hendaye.[51] After spending time in Irún and then Barcelona, he reached Madrid on 13 September: 'My meeting with Mikhail was a joy; he was waiting for us at the door of the Hotel Florida where we were also staying. From that moment on, we were virtually inseparable.' They went together to the siege of the Alcázar de Toledo. Later, from 7 to 17 October 1936, Karmen joined Koltsov on a tour of the northern fronts of the Basque Country and Asturias with Paulina Abramson as their interpreter. In the course of their visit, Koltsov spent time with local political and military leaders, includ-ing Juan Ambou, the young Communist who acted as defence chief in the Asturian Popular Front Committee, and José Antonio Aguirre, the Basque pres-ident.[52] Overriding the instructions of Marcel Rosenberg, both Koltsov and Karmen declined to join the evacuation to Valencia and stayed throughout the siege.[53] On 6 November, Karmen went to the Ministerio de Guerra, finding it deserted until he stumbled into a room containing the Communist leader, Antonio Mije, General Gorev and the chief of the Republican general staff, Vicente Rojo. From there he went to PCE headquarters, where he found Koltsov locked in conversation with Pedro Checa, who as Organization Secretary of the Central Committee was the acting head of the party.[54]

The memoirs of Karmen confirm Boris Efimov's view that Koltsov's official sta-tus was largely journalistic. He says that they were inseparable and that 'our friendship constituted a priceless education in militant journalism'. He often accompanied Koltsov as he moved around Madrid, visiting the defences, and claimed that he would read Koltsov's chronicles in *Pravda* a couple of days later, and was able to relive what they had seen, illuminated by what he called 'a divine spark, the wise, sharp and joyous spark of Koltsov's immense talent'. Karmen was entranced by the sheer energy and many facets of Koltsov: 'an acute chronicler of extraordinary events, a political being, an intrepid soldier', who also liked to live well and was always cheerful and jovial.[55] By the time that Hemingway arrived in the spring of 1937, Koltsov and Karmen had moved from the Hotel Florida, briefly to the Hotel Capitol on the other side of the Gran Vía, then to the Hotel Palace in the Carrera de San Jerónimo and then on to Gaylord's Hotel in Alfonso XII.[56]

Many of those who met Koltsov left descriptions. He was small, very Spanish-looking, had thick black hair and wore thick-lensed round spectacles. In a clearly autobiographical section of *For Whom the Bell Tolls*, Hemingway proclaimed him

> the most intelligent man he had ever met. Wearing black riding boots, grey breeches, and a grey tunic, with tiny hands and feet, puffily fragile of face and body, with a spitting way of talking through his bad teeth, he looked comic…but he had more brains and more inner dignity and outer insolence and humour than anybody he had ever known.[57]

Koltsov provided Hemingway with considerable amounts of material that was later incorporated into *For Whom the Bell Tolls*.[58] Orlov claimed that everything in Hemingway's portrayal of Koltsov in the form of the character of Karkov was exact.[59] Martha Gellhorn met Koltsov for the first time at a party in his warm and cosy room at the Hotel Gaylord. Writing at the end of her life, she remembered seeing 'a small thin man, with thick, well-cut, grey hair. He wore a dark, excellent suit. He had the kind of face that makes an immediate impression of brilliance, of wit, and the quiet manners of complete confidence. I thought he was forty or so, and more French than Russian.'[60]

As the comments of Ernest Hemingway, Martha Gellhorn, Emma Wolf, Roman Karmen, Paulina Abramson and others attest, Koltsov had a capacity to amuse, to impress and to generate affection and enthusiasm. The English Communist journalist, Claud Cockburn, became a close friend, as attracted as Karmen had been by Koltsov's wit and energy:

> I spent a great deal of my time in the company of Mikhail Koltsov, who then was Foreign Editor of *Pravda* and, more importantly still, was at that period – he disappeared later in Russia, presumed shot – the confidant and mouthpiece and direct agent of Stalin himself. He was a stocky little Jew from Odessa, I think – with a huge head and one of the most expressive faces of any man I ever met. What his face principally expressed was a kind of enthusiastically gleeful amusement – and a lively hope that you and everyone else would, however depressing the circumstances, do your best to make things more amusing still.

Cockburn described how easily Koltsov could provoke resentment and jealousy:

He had a savagely satirical tongue – and an attitude of entire ruthlessness towards people he thought either incompetent or even just pompous. People who did not know him well – particularly non-Russians – thought his conversation, his sharply pointed Jewish jokes, his derisive comments on all kinds of Sacred Cows, unbearably cynical. And others, who had known them both, said that he reminded them of Karl Radek (an ominous comparison). To myself it never seemed that anyone who had such a powerful enthusiasm for life – for the humour of life, for all manifestations of vigorous life from a tank battle to Elizabethan literature to a good circus – could possibly be described properly as 'cynical'. Realistic is perhaps the word – but that is not quite correct either, because it implies, or might imply, a dry practicality which was quite lacking from his nature. At any rate so far as his personal life and fate were concerned he unquestionably and positively enjoyed the sense of danger, and sometimes – by his political indiscretions, for instance, or his still more wildly indiscreet love affairs – deliberately created dangers which need not have existed.[61]

Cockburn was right that Koltsov's sharp wit was not to the liking of everyone. His interpreter, Paulina Abramson, wrote:

Many people who had the good fortune to know Koltsov were attracted by his temperament and by his ability to capture instantly the essence of any problem. I don't dare say that he was liked by everyone who knew him; indeed there were those who seriously disliked him. He was an intolerant person, to some extent, and just could not put up with limited or obtuse people.[62]

Ilya Ehrenburg commented: 'the friendship which he professed towards me was tainted by a touch of contempt'.[63]

Alongside his myriad literary and political activities, Koltsov also conducted intensely complicated personal relationships. His wife, the tall and angular journalist Elisabeta Ratmanova, arrived in Barcelona at the beginning of November 1936. She was there on behalf of the newspaper of the Komosomol (Communist youth) *Komsomolskaia Pravda*, although like all Russian personnel, she was also expected to provide reports for the NKVD about her compatriots.[64] The one conversation between the couple that is recorded in his diary is terse and cold. Lisa was understandably angry to have discovered that Koltsov had renewed his love affair with a voluptuous twenty-four-year-old German Communist writer, Maria Greßhöner. She was known by her pen-name Maria Osten, which she had taken because of her admiration for the Soviet Union. She was green-eyed with a sensual, almond-shaped face, and Koltsov had been in love with her ever since the composer Ernst Busch and the writer Ludwig Renn had introduced them in Berlin in 1932. He had subsequently arranged for her to work in Moscow for the German-language newspaper *Deutsche Zentral Zeitung*.

She lived with Koltsov and, in October 1934, they went to the Saarland on the German–French border, which was administered by the League of Nations. In January 1935 a plebiscite was to be held for the inhabitants to decide on union with France or Germany. Since the area's rich coal resources were being systematically plundered by the French as reparation for war damage, there was little chance of the people opting for union with France, all the more so given the efficacy of the Nazi propaganda in favour of union with the Third Reich. However, in the hope of damaging Hitler's prestige, the Comintern planned a campaign in favour of the area remaining under the League and that was why Koltsov and Maria Osten were there. In fact, the plebiscite of January 1935 saw a massive victory for the Nazis. It was in that context that they agreed to take back to the Soviet Union Hubert L'Hoste, the twelve-year-old son of a local Communist miner from the Saarland. The boy was a fanatical admirer of the Soviet system. Maria Osten and Koltsov wrote a hymn of praise to the Soviet Union as allegedly seen through the eyes of Hubert. Titled *Hubert im Wonderland* and with a preface by Georgi Dimitrov, it was a huge bestseller. Shortly after being posted to Spain, he arranged for Maria Osten to join him as the *Deutsche Zentral Zeitung* correspondent.[65]

It is difficult to know how much time Koltsov had to spend with Maria Osten in Spain, given his all-absorbing activities. According to Sefton Delmer's distorted recollection, Koltsov always turned up at the front or the ministries 'with one or more of his train of women. He would have with him either his wife, a neurotic-looking ex-ballerina, or Comrade "Bola", an enormous cheerful peasant who was his secretary assistant, or Maria Osten, a blond vivacious gamine of a young German Communist.'[66] There is certainly evidence that he went to the front with Maria Osten and little doubt that she was the love of his life.[67] Moreover, with or without female company, he seems to have been welcome at the front, not just because officers appreciated that he was prepared to risk his life along with their men, but also because of his ability to lift the spirits of those engaged in the battle. Ehrenburg wrote that he 'could hearten even those enthusiasts who easily fell into despair'. This was not the fruit of misplaced or frivolous optimism, but of grimly realistic ability to make the best of any situation. His philosophy could be summed up as 'grin and bear it', yet, however bleak the situation, 'an hour later he would be putting fresh heart into some Spanish politician by persuading him that victory was certain and so everything was alright'.[68]

The extent both of Koltsov's military knowledge and his ability to boost the morale of those around him was revealed by an incident during the battle of Jarama in the first week of February 1937. After a savage attack by Franco's Moorish troops, the crucial bridge near Arganda was lost. A demoralized Gustav Regler went to the Hotel Palace in Madrid hoping for some consolation from Koltsov. Before Regler could explain his depression, Koltsov said: 'I know all about it. The troops guarding the bridge were surprised. The Moors crept up on soft-soled sandals. You did not know that large numbers had been assembling on the plateau during the past few days. They knew every footpath, and they had had three days' rest.' Regler was struck by Koltsov's command of the details of the defeat. Polishing his glasses, Koltsov continued:

> The valley was asleep, you were asleep, the whole staff was asleep. You should have tested the telephone-lines – but you hadn't enough wire to carry out repairs. You should have sent a reconnaissance plane by daylight over the hill – but you hadn't a plane. You should have kept the hill under constant fire – but you only had one field gun, because the other's being overhauled. I know it all. I'm talking like a Pharisee. Why don't you shout at me? We should have sent you a tank-squadron – am I not right? Isn't that what you're thinking?

Replacing his glasses, he continued sadly and prophetically: 'Without glasses everything looks black to me. If they ever shoot me I shall have to ask them not to take my glasses off first.'[69]

To cheer Regler up, Koltsov took him to a farewell party for a Soviet engineer who had set up the searchlight installation for the International Brigade's anti-air-craft guns. He been recalled to Moscow and seemed cheerful, displaying the presents he was taking home for his family. Regler was astonished by the atmosphere at the party: 'Here there was none of the slavish terror of the Moscow intellectual. Under the hail of Fascist bullets they forgot the bullet in the back of the neck, the secret executions of the GPU. Their talk was relaxed, uncharged with double meanings, un-Asiatic.' The scene he described inadvertently explained why the advisers in Spain would be so unwelcome back in Moscow: 'in becoming partisans they were made whole again – they became new men! The stink of

Moscow was blown away by the winds of the Sierra and this heroic Spain.' On the next day, Koltsov visited the front and asked about the searchlights. When Regler said they were 'a legacy' from the engineer, Koltsov laughed sardonically and said: 'A legacy? That's the literal truth!' Alarmed, Regler asked if something had happened to him on his journey. 'On the journey? No,' replied Koltsov, 'but something will happen to him when he arrives. He'll be arrested when he reaches Odessa.' Regler was nauseated and puzzled about the previous night's party. Koltsov explained: 'The French give a man rum before they lead him out to the guillotine. In these days we give him champagne.' When Regler repeated that he felt unwell, Koltsov allegedly said: 'It's not easy for a European to get used to Asiatic customs.'[70]

Koltsov has been portrayed by the American writer Stephen Koch as a vicious and malevolent informer in Spain. He asserted without the slightest basis for doing so: 'It was Koltsov who concocted the disinformation used to destroy Andreu Nin; his articles in *Izvestiya* provided the Popular Front with the smears described by Orwell in *Homage to Catalonia*. [...] Koltsov regularly filed top-secret reports with the NKVD denouncing – thereby killing – "Trotskyite scum" in Spain.'[71] While this is certainly a wildly imaginative invention, Koltsov's links with the NKVD have also been remarked upon by Arkadi Vaksberg, a Russian expert on the purge trials.[72] All Soviet functionaries abroad were expected to report to the NKVD on what they saw. Koltsov, for instance, on 4 December 1937, reported on a Soviet Commissar named Kachelin, criticizing his 'demoralizing provocative reports at a meeting about the arrests in the Red Army'.[73] However, this does not mean that Koltsov, any more than the Soviet Ambassador Marcel Rosenberg or the General Consul in Barcelona, Vladimir Antonov-Ovseenko, were agents of the security services.

That Koltsov believed in the need for the Soviet security services is, on the other hand, indisputable. Three years before the outbreak of war in Spain, Koltsov had written a book about Soviet military life. In one of the chapters, he suggested that, given that the Soviet Revolution was always threatened by counter-revolutionaries, the terror exercised by the Cheka, the GPU and the NKVD were a necessary evil, 'the organ of defence and protection' of the working class. He wrote:

> 'Yet I don't know whether the work of the GPU is not the most important of them all. To do this work we need really honest, really unselfish, really reliable communist revolutionaries. We have them, and those whom the Party and the Soviet State have appointed to other posts must never

forget the services rendered by these men – ever watchful, ever alert, ever on the *qui vive*. Beyond our borders, in the general staffs of the mighty foreign powers, in the palaces of the industrial bosses, in the glittering cabarets and restaurants, strong and subtle plots are being fabricated; in front of huge fireproof safes, over heaps of gold, amidst the rustle of stocks and bonds, there is a barter going on for the heads of the Bolsheviks, for the lives of the workers and peasants, for their lives and factories. Over the champagne glasses, mercenaries and spies, assassins and frauds, provocateurs and gamblers are being given their instructions – to destroy the Soviet rule.[74]

It requires a substantial leap, however, to assume, as some commentators have done, that Koltsov was responsible for the horrific fate of Andreu Nin. Certainly, it is the case that in articles published in *Pravda* and *Izvestiya*, and reprinted in *L'Humanité* and other Communist newspapers in Europe, Koltsov denounced the POUM as 'a formation of Franco–Hitler–Mussolini agents who are organising treason in the front line and Trotskyist-terrorist assassinations in the rearguard'. His writings on the POUM, behind which he could see 'the criminal hand of Trotsky', were published in a pamphlet with the title 'Evidence of the Trotskyist Treachery'.[75] Trotsky's close collaborator in the Fourth International, the German Walter Held, wrote in early February 1937 that as part of his determination to annihilate the POUM, Stalin had sent to Spain: 'that journalistic scum Mikhail Koltsov, specialist in pogroms, who learned this honourable trade in the service of Petljura, the assassin of the Ukraine, in order to put in train a campaign of calumnies against the POUM'.[76] Although Koltsov was not in Spain from 2 April to 24 May 1937, he still wrote articles in *Pravda* reproducing the official Communist line that Andreu Nin had been rescued from custody by Nazi agents.[77] However, he was far from alone in this and his parroting of the party line on the POUM does not make him the assassin of Nin or the brains behind the assault on the POUM. In fact, the POUM appears fewer than ten times in Koltsov's diary. The longest entry, dated 21 January 1937, is ironic more than vicious in its description of the POUM leadership and virtually dismisses both the POUM and Trotskyism as insignificant.[78]

On 27 March 1937, Koltsov told Dolores Ibárruri that he had to go back to Moscow to report on the political and military situation in Spain but that he hoped to return soon. The need for him to report in person further undermines the idea that he spoke daily on the telephone with Stalin. He crossed the border from Spain into France on 2 April and remained in Moscow until the third week of May.[79] It is a sign of his importance that, on the evening of 15 April, for nearly two hours, he was grilled by Stalin himself, by Lazar Kaganovich, by the Soviet premier, Vyacheslav Molotov, by Marshal Voroshilov, and by Nikolai Yezhov, successor to the vicious Genrikh Grigorevich Yagoda as the head of the NKVD.[80] This was the narrow circle within which all major foreign-policy decisions were taken. With the Republic's Basque outpost about to fall, it was an especially bleak picture that Koltsov had to describe. To his surprise, Stalin seemed happy enough with what he heard. Nevertheless, with apparent despondency, he told Koltsov that he was distressed about the number of traitors being discovered in the USSR and that his only consolation was the performance of the Soviet mission in Spain.[81]

Later that evening, Koltsov recounted to his brother the bizarre ending to the meeting. Stalin began to clown around:

> He stood in front of me and, placing his arm across his chest, bowed and asked: 'What are you called in Spanish? Miguel?' I replied: 'Miguel, Comrade Stalin.' 'Very well, Don Miguel. We, noble Spaniards, thank you cordially for your most interesting report. We'll see you soon, Comrade Koltsov. Good luck, Don Miguel.' 'I am entirely at the service of the Soviet Union, Comrade Stalin.' I was just going to the door when he called me back again and a strange conversation ensued: 'Do you possess a revolver, Comrade Koltsov?' Completely thrown, I replied: 'Yes, Comrade Stalin.' 'You aren't thinking about committing suicide, are you?' Even more perplexed, I replied: 'Of course not. It has never occurred to me.' Stalin just said: 'Excellent. Excellent. Thank you again, Comrade Koltsov. We'll see you soon, Don Miguel.'

Koltsov then asked his brother: 'Do you know what I read with absolute certainty in Stalin's eyes?' 'What?' 'I read in them: He is just too smart.' On the following day, one of those present, probably Yezhov, told him: 'Remember, Mikhail, that you are appreciated, esteemed and trusted', but he couldn't get the idea of Stalin's mistrust out of his mind.[82]

That Koltsov had long since been worried about what was happening in Moscow was revealed by his remarks to Regler about the searchlight engineer. His anxiety level had been raised by the encounter with Stalin and would have been much greater had he known that, while he was still in Moscow, in mid-May 1937, according to the highly unreliable Orlov, a special courier who had previously worked in the Special Department of the NKVD arrived in Spain with the diplomatic pouch. One of Orlov's officers, who was a friend of the courier, reported that this man was telling 'strange stories', alleging that Koltsov had 'sold himself to the English and supplied Lord Beaverbrook with secret information about the Soviet Union'.[83] This is probably an invention, as was Orlov's claim that the NKVD chief, the cruel and malevolent Yezhov, nicknamed 'the blackberry' by Stalin, 'the poison dwarf' by others, was a close friend of Koltsov. Indeed, Orlov claimed that, on this trip to Moscow, Koltsov had taken with him a handsome, two-year-old Spanish orphan boy for Yezhov and his wife, Yevgenia Feigenberg, because they had recently lost their only child. It is certainly the case that Mikhail and Maria adopted an eighteen-month-old Spanish boy called José (Jusik) and took him to the Soviet Union, although it is unlikely that this was as a gift for Yezhov, since Maria was desperate for a child of her own.[84]

Koltsov certainly cultivated the sexually degenerate Yezhov. He had even described him in *Pravda* as 'a wonderful unyielding Bolshevik who, without getting up from his desk day and night is unravelling and cutting the threads of fascist conspiracy'.[85] Since both he and Boris Efimov were ex-members of the left opposition, they must have long since been dreading the late-night knock on the door. Koltsov may have felt safe as long as Yezhov remained head of the NKVD. On the other hand, his inveterate love of danger seems to have impelled him to have a brief affair with Yezhov's wife, the notoriously promiscuous Yevgenia Feigenberg.[86] It is a strange coincidence that Koltov's own downfall would coincide with the arrest and interrogation of her husband in December 1938, although the investigation that would damn Koltsov had already been ordered by the cuckolded security chief.

There was another meeting with Stalin on the afternoon of 14 May, at which Molotov was also present.[87] By 23 May, Koltsov was in France on his way back to Spain. From 24 May to 11 June, he spent a dangerous two weeks, first trying to get into the Basque Country and then reporting on the ever more desperate situation in Bilbao. Showing characteristic courage and daring, he flew back and forth from France to the Basque capital, where he interviewed the president, José Antonio Aguirre.[88] He then returned first to Barcelona and then to Valencia to help organize the international Anti-Fascist Writers' congress during the first two weeks of July. Although the principal purpose of the congress was to demonstrate that the bulk of the world's intellectuals supported the Republic, there was also a hidden agenda, which was to denounce the 'treachery' of André Gide's recently published critique of the USSR, *Retour de l'URSS*, which most of the delegates had not had a chance to read. The delegates were chauffeured in a fleet of limousines from Barcelona to Valencia and then on to Madrid, treated to banquet after banquet in a starving country. Stephen Spender, a British delegate, found something grotesque about 'this circus of intellectuals, treated like princes or ministers, carried for hundreds of miles through beautiful scenery and war-torn towns, to the sound of cheering voices, amid broken hearts, riding in Rolls Royces, banqueted, fêted, sung and danced to, photographed and drawn'. Jef Last, the Dutch novelist and poet, and a member of the International Brigades, attended the congress. Although a friend of Gide, he considered his book to be one-sided and inopportune, but he thought that the Russian obsession with attacking Trotskyism and Gide was utterly counter-productive.[89] Koltsov may well have agreed but, when the entire circus transferred to Madrid on 7 July, he made a speech praising the spirit of anti-fascism that brought the intellectuals together and denouncing Gide's *Retour de l'URSS* as a 'filthy slander'.

The version of Koltsov's speech published in the Spanish press on the following day includes a passage omitted in the diary. In it, in much the same spirit as had infused his 1933 essay on the GPU, he effectively described the terror in the Soviet Union as preventive:

> There are some people who are wondering why we, the Soviet writers, support the vigorous and pitiless measures of our government against traitors, spies and enemies of the people. These people ask how, despite being good Soviet patriots, as well as workers with peace-loving and defensive pens, can we leave all this to the immovable instruments of state and keep our distance from it; why we do not interfere and simply keep quiet about it, not drawing attention to it in the pages of our publications. No, colleagues and comrades, for us this is a matter of honour. The honour of the Soviet writer consists precisely in being at the forefront in the battle against treachery, against any attack on the liberty and independence of our people. We support our government and justify its actions not only because they are just but because [our government] will lead us to abundance and happiness. We support it because it is strong, its hand does not shake when punishing the enemy. Why are we fighting Franco now, when he has occupied the Spanish lands with the Foreign Legion, Moroccan infantry and German aircraft, and why was nothing done before when the same Franco was plotting his treachery? How many hundreds of thousands of lives would have been saved in Spain, how many bullets, shells and bombs would not have done their murderous work if a military tribunal and a firing squad had eliminated the

treacherous generals at a suitable moment? Our country is completely safeguarded against the adventures of big and small Francos. It is safeguarded because the Soviet security forces will stop the little Trotskyite Francos before they can start and the military tribunal, with support from the people, will punish them.[90]

Hemingway also quoted Koltsov/Karkov speaking with conviction of the need to shoot certain treacherous generals.[91] Ehrenburg, who was also a delegate, was surprised by the number of Soviet writers who referred to the liquidation in Russia of 'enemies of the people'. He asked several of them why and they refused to answer. When he commented on this to Koltsov, he grunted: 'Serves you right. You shouldn't ask.'[92]

It is difficult to avoid the conclusion that Koltsov was whistling in the dark, eulogizing the security services partly to underline his own reliability but also to make them seem less frightening to himself. Yet Koltsov was not alone in using the Spanish Civil War to justify the Soviet Terror. The German scholar Frank Schauff has identified a significant body of contemporary propaganda output justifying the Terror with reference to the Spanish Civil War, something he has called 'the Spanish parable of Terror'. Thus Koltsov, in this speech, was not doing anything exceptional but merely going along with the thrust of the mainstream Soviet press of those years. Koltsov and others wrote about Spain, but 'Spain' was read as meaning the Soviet Union. After all, if the moderate Spanish Republic and the incipient popular revolution were the victims of a major assault by the principal fascist powers, then it is inevitable that the Soviet Union, which is much richer and more tempting, is a target for fascist aggression. In order to face this attack and avoid the fate of the Spanish Republic, awareness of the hidden enemy within must be intensified.[93]

Shortly after his return to Spain, Koltsov had to witness the successive and deeply painful losses of the Basque Country, Santander and Asturias. He was also aware of the crippling cost to the Republic of the pyrrhic victories at Brunete and Belchite. Nevertheless, his optimism and enthusiasm for the Republic endured. His friend Claude Cockburn commented:

> As the Spanish War ground its way to its gruesome conclusion, and all
> over Europe people who had supported the Republic became truly
> cynical, despairing, without faith or enthusiasm for anything, I found
> myself looking forward more and more eagerly to conversations with
> Koltsov, journeys in his company, estimates from him of the course of

affairs. He was a man who could see the defeat for what it really was, could assume that half the big slogans were empty, and a lot of the big heroes stuffed, or charlatans, and yet not let that bother him at all, or sap his energy and enthusiasm.[94]

Nevertheless, it is difficult to imagine that Koltsov derived much satisfaction from following orders to write in praise of the NKVD's efforts to annihilate Trotskyism in Spain, since the affair had such echoes of what was happening to many of his friends at home. Viscount Chilston, the British Ambassador in Moscow, saw considerable significance in an article by Koltsov sent from Lérida and published in *Pravda* on 26 August. In it, Koltsov deplored the failure of the Spanish Republican authorities to take adequate steps against Trotskyists in Spain and repeated the story that Andreu Nin had escaped from prison with the help of a group of agents of the Gestapo. He went on to complain that the remainder of the Trotskyist leaders, though in prison, are treated too leniently and that the POUM newspaper, *Batalla*, although forbidden, continued to appear in an eight-page edition. The article claimed that Nin and the Spanish Trotskyists had been in cahoots with General Franco since 1935. Viscount Chilston went on:

> The foregoing considerations, the article continues, should serve as a lesson to those in Spain who are inclined to underestimate the Trotskist menace and dismiss it as a private quarrel of the Communist Party. The Trotskists are in fact the most dangerous detachment of Fascism. 'Woe', M. Koltsov concludes in a somewhat biblical strain, 'to those who do not see this danger or who do not wish to see it! Woe to those who make it possible for the Trotskist spies to continue their activities with impunity!' The present article, it will be seen, lays considerable stress on the menace which Trotskism constitutes to the Republican cause in Spain and criticises the Republican leaders in no measured terms for their failure to realise this and to take suitable action to avert the danger. Possibly this outburst merely forms part of the perennial anti-Trotskist drive which accounts for at least half the space in the Soviet press. It may be, on the other hand, that its purpose is to prepare the way in the case of a Republican debacle in Spain, which would then be attributed to the activities of Trotskists and to lack of vigilance on the part of the Republican leaders.[95]

Koltsov may have been painfully embarrassed to have to write such blatant untruths, an obligation imposed on every Soviet journalist at the time. Yet he had long since thrown in his lot with Stalin. With regard to Koltsov's contribution to the international propaganda offensive aimed at justifying the trial of the POUM and by implication that of Kameniev and Zinoviev, Leon Trotsky wrote: 'The entire press of the Communist International, fettered to Stalin by a golden chain, launched itself into an orgy of calumnies whose obscenity and baseness are without precedent. The role of leader of the orchestra has been assumed by such emissaries of Moscow as Mikhail Koltsov, Willi Münzenberg and other scum.'

What was going on around him in Spain and what was happening to friends in Moscow was preying ever more on his mind. When he was recalled, on 6 November 1937, Koltsov, aware of the worsening situation, persuaded Maria Osten not to join him. He arranged for her to be appointed as the *Deutsche Zentral Zeitung* correspondent in Paris.[96] On his return to Russia, he had short meetings with Stalin on 9 and 14 November. There cannot have been much time to discuss the Spanish situation in any detail since, nearly three weeks later, Koltsov wrote to request an interview with Stalin in order to review a lengthy list of issues relating to Republican Spain. There is no record of any such encounter in Stalin's desk diary, although this does not mean that they did not meet elsewhere or talk on the telephone.[97] Koltsov set himself the immediate task of converting his *Pravda* despatches into a book. A number of his reports and memories from Spain appeared in *Literaturnaya Gazeta*. The first part of his Diary of the Spanish Civil War appeared, to considerable critical acclaim, between April and September 1938 in the mass-circulation journal of the Soviet Writers' Association *Novyi Mir*, under the title 'Ispanskii dnevnik'.[98]

On 19 December 1937, Koltsov published an article in *Pravda* criticizing the informers who denounced their comrades. He recounted the story of a student who had been accused in a letter of duplicity, careerism and sycophancy. Without investigating the flimsy accusations, the party secretary of the Moscow institute where the boy was studying had simply accepted them and expelled him both from the party and the college as an enemy of the people. Koltsov roundly berated those who, to protect themselves, were ready to smear the innocent and claimed that the party, the government, the courts and public opinion would put a stop to such heartless liars who violated the rights of Soviet citizens. On 17 January 1938, he published a sequel in which he classified the mendacious informers as 'spear-chuckers' who would hurl their accusations randomly in order to strike down as many as possible and thus seem to be politically reliable and cover up their own dirty record; 'careerists' who informed on people in order to dominate their institutions and get promotion; and the 'cowardly and soulless bureaucrats' who would unquestioningly take action on the basis of groundless accusations. Soon, he wrote, the NKVD would put a stop to those guilty of such calumnies and slanders because they were contrary to the Soviet order. The articles had managed both to denounce widespread, and officially encouraged, practices, while suggesting that the regime was utterly opposed to them and would root them out. The motivations behind them were both personal and official. The articles clearly reflected an order from on high since, on 19 January 1938, a Central Committee decree was published on the errors of party organizations that expelled innocent members. At the same time, they allowed him to write about something that he found deeply disturbing.[99]

Vladimir Gorev's interpreter and lover Emma Wolf recounted a scene shortly after their return to Moscow, and before the disappearance of Gorev himself. They had been invited to a reception to celebrate the return from Spain of another of the 'advisers'. As they drank Soviet 'champagne' (sparkling wine from the Crimea), Koltsov asked her how she was finding her new job at Izvestiya. She told him that she was distraught to find that many of her old friends and colleagues had disappeared. Koltsov said nothing, just smiled sadly and shrugged his shoulders.[100] Clearly worried by the prevailing situation, Koltsov tried to present himself as a champion of Stalinist orthodoxy. On 11 March 1938, he wrote to his friend, the German Jewish novelist Lion Feuchtwanger, about the ongoing purge trials. He described how he had sat for a week in the courtroom, 'rendered speechless by the mountains of filth and crime'.[101] Despite his growing fears, certain issues brought forth the old courage. When Louis Fischer, who was in the process of breaking his ties with the Soviet Union, visited Moscow at the end of May 1938, none of his friends came to see him. They were too scared. Koltsov, however, took the risk of showing up at the home of the American. He was desperate for news from Spain. Fischer commented: 'Koltsov was very emotional about Spain. But when talking to strangers he wrapped himself in a smoke-screen which consisted of equal parts of brittle Pravda-editorial prose and literary spoofing. That made him seem pompous and cynical.'[102]

Through his newspaper articles, he also remained one of the most authoritative official voices, protecting himself by participating in the public denunciation of the accused in the Moscow purge trials. His attacks on Nikolai Bukharin were especially vehement.[103] There is reason to suppose that Koltsov's vehemence was defensive. One day, Lev Mekhlis, the editor of Pravda, had told Koltsov that a trusted colleague named Avgust was a spy. Mekhlis was close to Stalin and was often given advance notice of those under suspicion in order to prepare their public humiliation through the pages of the newspaper. Shocked, Koltsov replied that Avgust was a trusted Bolshevik who had been imprisoned under the Tsarist regime. Mekhlis replied that this counted for nothing because the Okhrana, the Tsarist secret service, recruited people just like Avgust. Yet, when Avgust himself came into the office, Mekhlis greeted him effusively. Koltsov told his brother that he had begun to fear that Mekhlis, who had previously been his protector, was harbouring some sort of suspicion. Koltsov now realized how little he could trust his boss.[104]

According to Boris Efimov, in the last weeks before his arrest, Koltsov

> worked furiously, almost obsessively, almost without respite, as if to escape his tortured thoughts. He believed deeply, honestly – and I am not afraid to say this – almost fanatically in Stalin's wisdom. My brother often told me in detail of his encounters with 'The Master' (*khozyain*), of his mannerisms in conversation, his remarks, turns of phrase and his jokes. He loved everything about Stalin.

However, another incident with Mekhlis in the late summer of 1938 intensified Koltsov's fears. He told Boris Efimov about a visit he had made to the new office of Mekhlis, shortly after he had been promoted to be head of the main political directorate of the armed forces. Mekhlis had shown him a thick green NKVD file containing the declarations of a recently arrested editor of *Izvestiya*, B. M. Tal. On it, in red pencil, was scribbled Stalin's order to both Mekhlis and Yezhov ordering them to arrest all those named in Tal's deposition.

Afterwards, nervously pacing up and down, Koltsov commented to Boris Efimov:

> I think and I think but I can't understand anything. What is going on? How did it turn out that we suddenly have so many enemies? These are people that we've known for years, that we lived with cheek-by-jowl for years! Army commanders, Civil War heroes, party veterans! And for some reason, no sooner have they disappeared behind bars than they immediately confess that they are enemies of the people, spies, agents of foreign intelligence services. What's going on? I think I'm going out of my mind. Surely, as a member of the editorial board of *Pravda*, a well-known journalist, a parliamentary deputy, I should be able to explain to others the meaning of what is going on, the reasons for so many

denunciations and arrests. But in fact I, like any terrified petty bourgeois, know nothing, understand nothing. I am bewildered, in the dark. Somebody perhaps, somewhere, maybe Yezhov, just gave vent to his [Stalin's] suspicions, hastily concocting all these conspiracies and betrayals? Or it was he [Stalin], himself, who constantly and eagerly encouraged Yezhov, mocking him for not being able to see the traitors and spies under his nose?[105]

At the end of September 1938, Koltsov was sent to Prague to report for *Pravda* on the Czech situation in the immediate wake of Munich, but before the arrival of German troops. What he saw as the last chance to stop Hitler deeply depressed him and was a bitter blow to his anti-fascist faith.[106] While there, he coincided with his friend Claud Cockburn, who was again reminded of the intensity with which Koltsov's anti-fascism burned. The episode in Prague provides another clue to Koltsov's fall from grace, since his enthusiasm for a possible Soviet intervention in favour of Czechoslovakia suggested that it was inevitable that he would have opposed the Molotov–Ribbentrop pact. Cockburn was moving between London, Paris, Geneva and Prague both as diplomatic correspondent and reporter of the *Daily Worker*, as well as reporting for his own satirical newssheet *The Week* and for a big new illustrated publication in Chicago called *Ken*. Then, in the autumn of 1938, Koltsov had appointed him London correspondent of *Pravda*, a position he held only briefly because Koltsov himself disappeared soon after.

Cockburn wrote:

I do not know to this day what Koltsov had done or was supposed to have done in Moscow. His fall – and one presumes execution – came at the height of his power there, and a lot of people when they heard of it could not believe it. They spread stories that he had been sent to China as a top-secret agent under another name. A lot of his friends went on believing that for years, as a kind of wishful thinking to soften their grief. Others were thrown into total disarray by the news, became despairing and totally cynical. For myself, though I missed him more than anyone I had known during that time, I cannot say I was surprised. And, oddly, I doubt if he was much surprised either. He had lived – and talked and joked – very dangerously, and he had absolutely no illusions so far as I know about the nature of the dangers. (Possibly his active taste for dangerous living had led him into some major conspiracy.) He would not, I thought, have been otherwise than satirically amused by some of the almost hysterically sentimental outcries which greeted his removal.[107]

Koltsov's earlier comment to Regler about keeping his glasses on in front of a firing squad had made it clear that he believed that eventual disgrace was highly likely. By the early autumn of 1938, he seems to have regarded it as inevitable. A meeting recalled by Cockburn suggested as much:

> Curiously enough, he once – a few weeks before his fall – entertained me at lunch with a kind of fantastic burlesque based on the imaginary future trial of himself for counter-revolutionary activities, taking in turn the part of a grimly furious Public Prosecutor and of himself in the role of a clown who has been caught out and still cannot resist making fatal jokes. This was in Prague at the height of the Munich crisis.

Cockburn, like Koltsov, was entirely aware of the desperate nature of the situation in Prague at the end of September and the beginning of October 1938:

> I spent a lot of time with Koltsov at the Russian Legation, for that was the place where, if anything decisive were to happen, it would happen. And I knew that Koltsov was at least as important a figure on the stage as the Russian Minister, and perhaps much more important because of his double position at *Pravda* and at the Kremlin.[108]

Cockburn forgot that Koltsov did not really hold a double position since *Pravda* was the organ of the Kremlin.

Koltsov seemed still to entertain hopes of Britain, France and the Soviet Union uniting on behalf of Czechoslovakia against Germany. The Czechoslovak army had been mobilized and was in fortified positions on the German frontier. Cockburn's account gave an improbably prominent role to Koltsov. He claimed that, in anticipation of Czech resistance against a Nazi invasion, an advance force of fighter planes and bombers had been secretly sent to Prague, and that the Soviet Ambassador and Koltsov were authorized to inform President Eduard Beneš that Russia was ready to send troops, artillery and aircraft when hostilities began. This is also a considerable exaggeration. For the USSR to aid Czechoslovakia, it would have required both the commitment of France and permission from Warsaw and Bucharest for Soviet troops to be transported through Poland and Romania to Czechoslovakia. Louis Fischer reported that Pierre Cot, the French Air Minister and Soviet sympathizer, told him that between May and September 1938, the USSR delivered three hundred aircraft to the Czechs. He also quotes Soviet documents to the effect that the Kremlin had put the Red air force on a war footing and was prepared to send 246 bombers and 302 fighters to Czechoslovakia.

Certainly, there were many rumours and reports flying around in the summer of 1938 about deliveries of Russian aircraft to Czechoslovakia and a Red air force delegation may well have flown to Prague to discuss possible collaboration. However, Stalin was unlikely to have made a commitment to the Czechs without knowing that he would be acting in concert with the French. In any case, Beneš, fearful that the Red Army would occupy Czechoslovakia, was resolved to fight only if the League of Nations, Britain and France were ready to fight. He was not prepared to resist Hitler's demands if that meant fighting a war with only the Soviet Union as an ally. With Koltsov and the embassy staff in despair, the Soviet air force delegation was despatched back eastwards. Then, just as they were airborne, it seemed as if Beneš had changed his mind and it appeared as if some agreement might be reached. Koltsov danced wildly, 'kissing people, throwing his big black beret repeatedly into the air'. His joy was short-lived. No agreement was reached between Stalin and Beneš and Koltsov was plunged into despair.[109]

Whether the lack of Soviet–Czech collaboration against the Germans was the fault of Stalin or Beneš, or even of the French and British, does not matter. Koltsov feared that it was the end for anti-fascism and that Stalin would now turn towards some kind of rapprochement with Hitler. Indeed, Stalin had never shared the uncompromising anti-fascism of Old Bolsheviks such as Bukharin and, indeed, Koltsov.[110] Koltsov's misery could be easily understood. The West had just effectively handed over to the Third Reich the substantial military resources of Czechoslovakia – more than fifteen hundred aircraft, over five hundred anti-aircraft guns, over two thousand artillery pieces, and large quantities of machine-guns, ammunition and vehicles. As Louis Fischer put it: 'Any planes, tanks, and other arms produced, any divisions trained and equipped by Britain and France between the end of September, 1938 (Munich), and September 1, 1939, when the war began, could not nearly match the power of Czechoslovakia's armed forces which the Anglo-French lost when Hitler dismembered that state.'[111]

It is far from clear that Koltsov had the 'position at the Kremlin' described by Cockburn or that he was the emissary responsible for negotiating with Beneš about possible Russian aid to Czechoslovakia. Whether Cockburn's view derived from his own tendency to exaggerate or from Koltsov's hyperbole is unclear. Martha Gellhorn got the same impression of Koltsov's crucial diplomatic importance when she met him in Prague. Having come from Barcelona to report on the Czech situation, she bumped into an utterly dejected Koltsov. She had found him, 'shrunken, all his brilliance gone', sitting on a wooden bench in a long, dark corridor of the Hradcany Palace: 'He took me to dinner in a small, bleak, workers' restaurant, not his sort of place. When the heavy bowls of soup were served, he began to talk. He had been waiting in that corridor in the Hradcany for four days.' Beneš would not receive him and had left him sitting in the public corridor. Gellhorn was distressed to see Koltsov so 'tired and hopeless. He foresaw everything exactly as it happened. We despaired further over thick, greasy food. Then we shook hands on a dark street corner and said goodbye.'[112]

Koltsov was equally despondent when he took his leave of Cockburn. They sat in a café, dissecting what had happened. The course of the conversation led them to the 'fantastic burlesque' mentioned by Cockburn. He had been anxious to get to a bank to exchange English pounds for Czech currency to pay his hotel bill and then catch a plane to London. Koltsov was reluctant to curtail the conversation. Pointing out that he had plenty of Koronas, he offered to change them into Sterling. As he took the pound notes from Cockburn, he commented: 'This, of course, may be the death of me.' When Cockburn asked what he meant, he went into a reverie, and proceeded to mount a one-man courtroom drama with himself playing three parts, himself as the accused, the judge and the public prosecutor. As the prosecutor, he was convincingly threatening: 'Do you deny, citizen Koltsov, that in Prague on the date in question you received British currency from the well-known British Intelligence Agent Cockburn? Do you deny that you insinuated that same agent into the Legation of the Soviet Union? Do you deny that you discussed with him the military disposition of the Soviet Union, including the operation of planes at the Prague military airfield?' After appointing Cockburn as the London correspondent of *Pravda*, he sadly took his leave, saying: 'the only thing to say is that in the little moment that remains to us between the crisis and the catastrophe, we may as well drink a glass of champagne'.[113] His gloomy sense that this was the end was intensified for another reason. He had hoped to be able to make a trip from Prague to Paris to see Maria Osten but, at the last minute, the Soviet Ambassador told him that he had received orders for his immediate return to Moscow. He must have known that the end of his hopes for a continuation of the anti-fascist struggle went hand in hand with his own destruction.[114]

Koltsov's evident sense of impending doom contrasted with his apparently burgeoning public prestige and acclaim. In the summer of 1938, he had been elected to the Supreme Soviet of the Russian Federation. According to his brother, despite his continuing faith in Stalin's wisdom, he was ever more concerned about the number of his friends being arrested. Although Koltsov still had occasional access to Stalin, he increasingly felt that something was wrong, especially when he was not invited to any high-level meetings when the head of the Spanish Republican air force, Ignacio Hidalgo de Cisneros, came to discuss supplies for the Republic. Ignacio was a friend of Koltsov and they had collaborated in Spain. It would have been logical for Koltsov, as an expert on Spain and aircraft, to be present at the discussions for more Soviet aid. On 9 December, Hidalgo de Cisneros had dinner with Koltsov. Koltsov was delighted to be told by him that the meeting with Stalin had gone well and that he had reacted positively to Spanish requests for aid. However, that Koltsov was still worried about Stalin's snub became clear when Boris Efimov arrived. On the previous day, the man whom Koltsov regarded as his protector, Nikolai Yezhov, was replaced by Lavrenti Beria as People's Commissar for Home Affairs. When Boris Efimov commented that this was good news and that the Terror of the Yezhovschina was over, Mikhail replied gloomily: 'Perhaps suspicion will now fall on those that Yezhov left untouched.'[115]

Koltsov's fears must have seemed groundless when, some weeks earlier, at an evening performance at the Bolshoi, Stalin had invited him to his box and had spoken warmly about the Spanish diary. This was the moment when he had been invited to give a lecture about the recently published History of the Bolshevik Party, which Stalin himself had meticulously edited and to which he had contributed a chapter. Koltsov had eagerly agreed, hoping that this signified a turn for the better. Certainly there were grounds for optimism, since two days before the lecture about Stalin's book, 'Compendium of the History of the Party', *Pravda* reported that Koltsov had been made a corresponding member of the Academy of Sciences, a very significant honour. In the late afternoon of 12 December, happy and smiling, he had made his last appearance in public. He fulfilled his promise to the dictator and addressed a full and appreciative house at the Writers' Union. Late in the evening, he went back to his office at *Pravda* to do some work. Shortly after his arrival, agents of the NKVD detained him. His apartment was searched and 'substantial writings' were removed by the sack-load and burnt.[116]

The real reasons for Koltsov's arrest have never been clarified. As late as 1964, Ilya Ehrenburg still could not work out why the intransigent and independent

Pasternak had survived while Koltsov, who 'honourably carried out every task assigned to him', had been liquidated.[117] There are many possibilities of which the most plausible is, in general terms, Koltsov's Spanish service. By late 1938, Stalin and his soon-to-be chief of state security, Lavrenti Beria, were collaborating on the show trials of a huge network of supposed spies. Stalin would soon enough be considering an improvement in relations with the Third Reich, but not yet. However, although Russian aid to the Spanish Republic had diminished some-what from late 1937 and throughout the summer of 1938, in the autumn Stalin had belatedly renewed his interest in Spain. Nevertheless, Koltsov, like many other army officers, pilots, diplomats, policemen and journalists who had served in the Spanish Civil War, was an object of suspicion, assumed somehow to have been infected by Trotskyist ideas while there.

A specific suggestion about Koltsov's 'offence' in relation to Spain came from Adelina Kondratieva, who, together with her sister Paulina, served as an inter-preter with the Soviet advisers in the Spanish Civil War, and was also an operative of the GRU. She believed that the immediate trigger for the arrest was a written denunciation emanating from André Marty, the French Communist who was head of the International Brigade's organization in Spain. Vaksberg also refers to Marty bypassing normal Comintern procedures and sending the denunciation directly to Stalin. Mediocre, envious, servile and cruel, Marty's qualities ensured his favoured position within the hierarchy of world Communism.[118] Marty's anti-Trotskyist paranoia and his suspicions of Koltsov's free-spirited energy and creativity were on a par with those of Stalin himself. Marty was noto-rious for his denunciations of suspected 'Trotskyists' in Spain. In addition to high-handed actions against International Brigaders, he also sent Stalin directly several devastating accusations against Soviet personnel. Hemingway recounts, with some verisimilitude, a scene in which Karkov (Koltsov) overturns a stupidly high-handed mistake by Marty. As he tells it, Koltsov threatens Marty, saying 'I am going to find out just how untouchable you are', and Marty watches him 'with no expression on his face except anger and dislike. There was nothing in his mind now but that Karkov/Koltsov had done something against him. Alright, Karkov, power and all, could watch out.' There is no proof that this incident took place. However, Josephine Herbst recalled that one of Hemingway's most useful contacts was an interpreter on Marty's staff who gave him information about the Frenchman's relations with the Russians.[119] Whether as a result of harbouring a grudge against Koltsov because of this incident or because of a more generalized resentment, Marty wrote a letter denouncing his unauthorized interference in military matters and his contacts with the POUM.

Although the latter accusations were absurd, they were received avidly in Moscow.[120]

According to General Dimitri Volkogonov, quoting an anonymous but 'prominent' NKVD source, prior to Marty's letter, someone else had already made a verbal denunciation of Koltsov's alleged contacts with foreign intelligence organizations, but Stalin had delayed taking action. However, it was the sight of written denunciations, possibly including the letter from Marty, that stirred the dictator to order Koltsov's arrest.[121] Nevertheless, Koltsov's fate has to be put in the general context of the imprisonment or execution of many of the most prominent men who had been advisers in Spain – General Vladimir Efimovich Gorev, who provided crucial advice during the defence of Madrid; Vladimir Antonov-Ovseenko, the consul in Barcelona; Marcel Rosenberg, the Ambassador in Madrid; General Emilio Kléber (Manfred Stern), briefly the commander of the International Brigades, to name just a few. All had participated in an inspiring revolutionary adventure within the anti-fascist struggle in Spain. The reasons were probably different in each case, although, where executions were concerned, Stalin did not need many reasons and their experience in the West sufficed to render them suspect. However, there is a more specific reason in Koltsov's case. His massively popular book recounted with passion the story of a country where revolutionary fervour and idealism still flourished, in direct contrast with the situation in the Soviet Union, where Stalin was crushing the life out of the revolution.[122] The Spanish situation had inspired Soviet youth with dreams that were the very antithesis of Stalin's policy and Koltsov was its chronicler. As Louis Fischer commented:

> The cause of Spain aroused intense enthusiasm throughout Russia. Many communists and non-communists hoped that the events in Spain might lend new life to the dying flame of the Russian revolution. Not Stalin. He had consented to sell the Spanish Republic arms. But not to make a revolution. He intended in the near future to snuff out the flame with Russian blood.[123]

However, Koltsov and others who went to Spain might have hoped that victory in Spain might bring about change back home.

Another contribution might well have been the fact that from late 1937, Koltsov had begun to be the object of slurs emanating from the Third Reich. A publication called *Bolshevism and the Jews* referred to him as 'Friedland-Kolzoff' and portrayed him as one of the most important Jews in Russian journalism.[124]

Given the scale of anti-Semitism within Stalin's immediate entourage, such attacks could not be simply dismissed as merely what was to be expected from the Nazis. Koltsov had the further disadvantage of being a friend of another prominent, albeit relatively untouchable, Jew, Maxim Litvinov. Now, in the wake of the Munich agreement, the policy of collective security, associated with Litvinov, had lost much of its attraction. Stalin would soon contemplate a possible link with the Third Reich. Seeing Munich as proof of the Western allies' readiness to encourage Hitler's eastward ambitions, Stalin was much less committed to the quest for alliances with the Western democracies.[125]

When Marty's denunciation arrived, Stalin would have been open to believing it, since he already harboured plenty of reasons for resentment against Koltsov. It would have confirmed the accusations made in the dossier from the NKVD, which he had received on 27 September 1938. It contained accusations that Koltsov maintained relationships with Trotskyists and counter-revolutionaries, and that he had criticized the Terror and the arrests related to it. The dossier, drawn up on the initiative of Yezhov, made much of Koltsov's friendship with Karl Radek and claimed that they had collaborated on a plot to kill Stalin. It claimed that there was something suspicious about Koltsov's close friendship with Maxim Gorki, whose biography he wrote, and whom he had visited regularly, once famously with André Malraux. His relationship with Maria Osten was portrayed as deeply sinister. In the report, Koltsov's lover was absurdly described as the daughter of 'a wealthy German Trotskyist landowner' and given the aristocratic title of Maria von Osten, when her real name was Maria Greßhöner and 'Maria Osten' her journalistic *nom de plume*. She was accused of Trotskyist agitation among German émigrés while living a life of luxury in Moscow before accompanying Koltsov to Spain and of going to France afterwards with a lover, Ernst Busch. In fact, she had taken refuge in Paris and the musician Busch was simply a friend.[126] It has been suggested that the malice of the accusations against Maria Osten derived from Lisa Ratmanova, Koltsov's jealous wife, who was friends with both Yezhov and Beria, and provided them with reports.[127] There was no shortage of accusations. Under interrogation, Beria's predecessor, the doomed Nikolai Yezhov, had denounced Koltsov along with several other literary figures, including Isaak Babel, who had slept with his wife, Yevgenia Feigenberg.[128]

Although he did not act immediately on the NKVD report, Stalin would have been receptive to its contents. The dictator's resentment towards Koltsov may have been masked by the invitation to lecture at the Writers' Union, but he harboured a number of specific grudges. He had found one in the diary of Mikhail

Prezent, a minor literary figure, the secretary of the journal *Soviet Construction*. In this diary, he had recorded the gossip of his many Trotskyist acquaintances. When he was arrested by the NKVD in 1935, its head, Genrikh Yagoda, handed the diary to Stalin. In it, the dictator read that Koltsov had ridiculed his habit of ruining books by opening their uncut pages with his greasy thumb. Certainly, Prezent's diary would also have reinforced Stalin's suspicions of Koltsov's Trotskyist past.[129] Stalin never forgot a slight, whether real or imagined.

Moreover, Stalin harboured a whole basket of grudges as a result of Koltsov's role in organizing, at the Salle Mutualité in Paris in June 1935, the World Congress of Writers for the Defence of Culture. In general terms, Stalin considered that Koltsov had concentrated too much on getting the participants to condemn Hitler instead of composing hymns of praise to Stalin. More specifically, he also believed that Koltsov had been the conduit for what he saw as an act of blackmail by the French delegates, who threatened to boycott the congress unless the USSR sent notable literary figures such as Isaak Babel or Boris Pasternak rather than party hacks. In fact, Koltsov had been trying to resolve the problems posed by the pitifully rigid performance of the hacks. Calls for more presentable Russian literary figures had come not just from the French, but also from Communist writers such as Gustav Regler. Having complied and sent Babel and Pasternak, Stalin then had to suffer the humiliation of seeing the French delegates and the Italian Gaetano Salvemini raise the case of Victor Serge, the French Trotskyist writer who had been in a Russian prison since 1933. Gide and Malraux as chairmen permitted the issue to be debated. The Russian delegates – including Koltsov, but excluding Pasternak – responded by denying that they knew anything of their fellow member of the Writers' Union, Victor Serge. Koltsov, described by Serge as 'a person in the innermost circle of Party confidence, a man as remarkable for his talent as for his pliant docility', insinuated that Serge was somehow implicated in the murder in December 1934 of Stalin's rival, the Leningrad party chief Sergei Kirov. Despite Koltsov's efforts, and as a result of the scandal generated at the congress, Serge had to be released. It was another offence for which Koltsov would not be forgiven. The same was true of his fraternization with French leftists who had later become critical of the USSR. These included André Malraux but, most damagingly, André Gide, whom Koltsov had invited to Russia and permitted to meet Soviet intellectuals without NKVD vigilance. Thereafter, Koltsov was held responsible for failing to prevent the publication of Gide's *Retour de l'URSS*.[130] He was also regarded as failing in his duty by not producing a convincing international response that would have totally discredited Gide, despite the fact that he was by then otherwise engaged in Spain.[131]

News of Koltsov's detention spread quickly. In intellectual circles, the notion that such a man, apparently a trusted patriotic hero and disseminator of the party line, could have fallen foul of the authorities generated first disbelief then panic. The demise of Yezhov had briefly raised hopes of an end to the purges, but Beria was soon to outdo both Yezhov and Yagoda in brutality. The British Embassy in Moscow reported: 'During the past fortnight, i.e. since Beria's formal accession to power there have been the usual arrests and rumours of arrests and there is no indication of any falling off in the "purge". After mentioning Koltsov's arrest and, presumably erroneously, that of Boris Efimovich, the despatch went on:

> We also learn on good authority that Nikolayev, who was head of the Special Section of the People's Commissariat for Internal Affairs under Yezhov, has been arrested as an enemy of the people, and it is even said that Yezhov's wife has been taken from the newspaper office where she worked. There seems to be little doubt that Yezhov is slipping fast. In spite of this, his portraits are still for sale in the shops and MacLean, on the occasion of his recent visit to the precincts of the Lubiyanka, was amused to notice in the room where he was received a life-sized portrait of the former 'master' and none of the new.[132]

Koltsov was astonished to discover that the semi-literate agent who took his first statement started to talk about his alleged involvement in an anti-Stalin conspiracy, along with all those major writers and poets not already in jail. The principal accusation was that he and Evgeni Gnedin, the press chief at the Commissariat of Foreign Affairs, were the ringleaders of an anti-Soviet plot involving intellectuals and diplomats. He had allegedly been recruited by the American, the French and the German Intelligence services. His extra-marital relationship with his German lover, Maria Osten, was regarded as proof. He was also accused of being an agent of Trotsky and of having collaborated with the POUM in Spain. Questioned by Beria's top interrogators Lev Shvartsman and Leonid Raikhman, Koltsov was tortured and finally signed statements admitting connections with a whole range of suspect individuals, some already executed, some under arrest and others still in high positions.

Gnedin survived to write memoirs in which he described being confronted with Koltsov in August 1939. The interrogators brought Koltsov into the room and Gnedin was shocked by how tired and worn he seemed. Nevertheless, Koltsov's eyes lit up when he saw his friend. It was a rare flash of the intelligence and humour which reminded Gnedin of the Koltsov of better times. He even managed a joke: 'Just look at you, Gnedin,' he grimaced, and paused before saying: 'Well, as bad as me, actually.' Gnedin found him a sick, broken man, weary from the months of arrest. Part of his disorientation came from the fact that his glasses had been taken from him and, as he had told Regler, without them 'everything looks black to me'. Thus, he was ready to admit anything of which he was accused. When he was asked to confess to conspiring with Gnedin and other journalists and diplomats against the Soviet state, he recited parrot-like a story that they had plotted at the apartment of Konstantin A. Umanskii, the Soviet Ambassador to the USA. Gnedin denied all knowledge of this.[133]

The interrogators had squeezed plenty out of Koltsov. He admitted that he had been friendly with Karl Radek. He had slept with Yezhov's wife, confessing to 'seducing' her. He had been recruited for French Intelligence by André Malraux. He had worked in Spain with the notorious NKVD defector, Aleksandr Orlov, somewhat ironic given that Orlov himself had been sent to Spain in September 1936 ostensibly as a political attaché with the exclusive task of combating Trotskyism, a task he had fulfilled with savage efficiency. Koltsov made the preposterous admission that he had links with the POUM. Shvartsman and Raikhman produced lists of those he was required to implicate, including the writers Babel, Pasternak, Ilya Ehrenburg and Aleksei Tolstoi, and diplomats including the Soviet Ambassadors Ivan Maisky in London, Konstantin Umanskii in Washington, right up to Maxim Litvinov, the Commissar for Foreign Affairs. He signed everything put in front of him.[134]

Within a few days of the arrest, Aleksandr Fadeiev, the influential Chairman of the Union of Writers, courageously sent a note to Stalin expressing doubts that Koltsov could have committed any kind of crime against the Soviet state, and requesting an audience to discuss the case. Barely a week before Koltsov's arrest, Fadeiev had published with Aleksei Tolstoi an article praising the Spanish diary as 'excellent, passionate, brave and poetic'.[135] Some months later, Stalin received Fadeiev and sent him into another room accompanied by Poskrëbyshev (Stalin's personal assistant), who gave him the two green folders with Koltsov's 'confessions'. After Fadeiev had read them, Stalin asked: 'So, now do you believe this?' to which an extremely uncomfortable Fadeiev answered: 'I have to.' Fadeiev later told members of the union, including Konstantin Simonov, that the declarations were terrifying, that Koltsov had 'admitted' to being a spy, a Trotskyist and a POUMista.[136] By August 1939, the NKVD had enough material to bring formal charges against Koltsov and Gnedin, of masterminding the anti-Soviet conspiracy of intellectuals and diplomats. Koltsov was tried under the infamous Article

58 of the Criminal Code, dealing with anti-Soviet, that is to say political, crimes, which served as the legal basis for the show trials.

When Koltsov was rehabilitated after Stalin's death, the official documentation revealed that he was tried for 'participation in an anti-Soviet conspiracy, espionage and carrying out anti-Soviet agitation'.[137] At his twenty-minute trial on 1 February 1940, Koltsov retracted his 'confessions' on the grounds that they had been extracted by means of horrific tortures.[138] He was found guilty and shot the same night or early the next morning. Ever since the assassination of Kirov on 1 December 1934, those sentenced to capital punishment usually had to be shot on the day that the decision was taken and no revision was possible. Nevertheless, Vasily Ulrikh, who presided at the trial, lied to Boris Efimov when he told him that Koltsov had been sentenced to 'ten years without right of correspondence' and thus was alive in a camp in the Urals. Ulrikh also blithely told Boris Efimov that 'for Koltsov to have been arrested, there had to have been proper authority for it'.[139] Koltsov was cremated and left in a common grave of unclaimed bodies at the Monastery of Donskoi in Moscow.[140] It is not known if his glasses had been returned to him before he faced the firing squad.

Some, but far from all, of those implicated by his 'confessions' were also shot. Gnedin served fifteen years in a concentration camp but survived to write the memoirs in which he described his 'confrontation' with Koltsov. Konstantin Umanskii, the Soviet Ambassador to the USA, died in an accident in Mexico and was buried with honours in Moscow. Koltsov's lover Maria Osten also met with a tragic fate. Against the advice of her friends in Paris, on hearing of Koltsov's arrest, she had immediately journeyed to Moscow in the hope of being able to help him.[141] When she arrived, with the now five-year-old Jusik, Hubert L'Hoste, fearful of being associated with 'an enemy of the people' after Koltsov's arrest, rejected her. When she asked, 'Do you really believe for a minute that nightmare about Mikhail?', he responded: 'Do you think everyone around you is mistaken? How can one individual be more intelligent and correct than everyone else?' Recently married and wanting the Koltsov apartment for himself and his new bride, he barred the door to Maria and Jusik, who had to go to a seedy hotel.

Convinced of Koltsov's innocence, Maria stayed on and took work as a translator at the Writers' Union. Few of their old friends had time for her, although Ignacio Hidalgo de Cisneros was one of those who did. When she appealed for help to the exiled leadership of the German Communist Party, Walter Ulbricht refused and recommended that she be investigated as someone who had benefited from the protection of Koltsov. Unaware of the KPD investigation, as late as the

211

summer of 1939, she was optimistic that Koltsov would soon be freed. However, on 14 October 1939, Ulbricht's machinations bore fruit when she was expelled from the Communist Party on the grounds of 'insufficient engagement with Party history and the theory of Marxism-Leninism'. In a vain attempt to find security, she took Soviet citizenship. On 22 June 1941, the day of the German invasion of the Soviet Union, she was arrested as a Nazi spy and her adopted son Jusik taken away. Her relationship with Koltsov was regarded as proof of guilt, just as Koltsov's guilt was taken as proven by his relationship with Osten. Despite the most horrendous tortures, she refused to 'confess' to being a Gestapo agent and was shot in the late summer of 1942. In 1947, Hubert L'Hoste was accused of anti-Soviet propaganda and sent to a concentration camp in Siberia. He was released after the death of Stalin and died in 1959.[142]

7

A Man of Influence:
The Case of Louis Fischer

On many mornings, while shaving and then while soaking in the bath, the Republican prime minister, Juan Negrín, would discuss the international situation in German with a journalist who sat on the toilet seat. Negrín was a man of enormous energy and even greater talent who had little time for the niceties of protocol. To maintain a war effort required an endless struggle with the twin problems of controlling the disparate component forces within Republican politics and of trying to reverse the British, French and American policies of non-intervention that deprived the Republic of the capacity to defend itself. Although immensely discreet, he would take advice where he thought it was useful and evidently one such place was in his bathroom. The man on the toilet seat also dispensed advice to senior Soviet leaders, albeit not at the same time. He was an inveterate traveller whose family lived in Moscow. In the same apartment building lived the notoriously prickly Soviet Foreign Minister Maxim Litvinov. Negrín's friend, who also spoke fluent Russian, had gained Litvinov's confidence to the extent that they would regularly sit in the evenings with children on their laps discussing burning issues of international relations. This German- and Russian-speaking newspaperman was actually an American and one with unusually direct access to the highest circles in Washington, where he had little difficulty in getting to talk to Cordell Hull or Eleanor Roosevelt. Tall, darkly saturnine with hooded eyes, Louis Fischer cut a striking figure among the correspondents in Spain.

The contacts enjoyed among Spanish, Russian and American leaders by Louis Fischer gave a remarkable authority to what he wrote. The bulk of Fischer's writing during the Spanish Civil War was first for the New York left-wing weekly *The Nation* and the *New Statesman and Nation* of London and then syndicated to more newspapers. Accordingly, his articles are much longer and more reflective than most journalistic despatches during the conflict. In consequence, they fully repay close reading even today. It has been suggested that Fischer constituted 'the

clearest case of complete commitment and almost total abandonment of objectivity' among the foreign correspondents.[1] There can be no doubt about his
commitment, although it was hardly greater than that of Herbert Matthews or
Jay Allen, or many other respected newspapermen. His vivid and well-informed
articles were clearly pro-Republican, but cannot be described as propaganda in
the negative sense.

Because of the range of activities that he undertook on behalf of the
Republican cause, the extraordinary energy that he devoted to that cause, and
the remarkable and highly unusual level of influence that he seemed to wield in
the highest levels of government in both Spain and the United States, Fischer was
unique. His influence was actually based on the fact that politicians trusted him
because he brought as much information as he took away. He was opinionated
and hard-faced, devoid of embarrassment, but trusted because, if he was asked to
keep something to himself, he did. Yet, the consequent level of understanding
with statesmen and diplomats has been given a sinister spin in some quarters.
The furiously anti-Communist cultural critic Stephen Koch portrays Fischer as
one of the many tools of Willi Münzenberg and Otto Katz, the men whom he
sees as the masterminds of what he calls 'the secret Soviet war of ideas against the
West'.[2] The most extreme, not to say deranged, version of this view of Fischer as
a Soviet agent emanated from the one-time Socialist civil governor of Albacete,
Justo Martínez Amutio, a fervent follower of Francisco Largo Caballero. Deeply
embittered by the Communist campaign to remove Largo, which interrupted his
own political career, Martínez Amutio wrote memoirs in which he vented his
spleen and wildly exaggerated his own importance and knowledge.

Of Fischer, Martínez Amutio wrote with a characteristic mix of ignorance,
invention and malice:

> He was thought to be a German writer fleeing from the Nazis, but other
> reports presented him as Austrian or Hungarian and also as Czech. The
> only thing proved for certain was that he acted as a Soviet agent, although
> he would say that he was not a Communist and that no one had sent him
> to Spain from Moscow. He got much support from Álvarez del Vayo, who
> claimed to be an old friend, but Luis Araquistain, who knew him during
> the period that he was the Republic's Ambassador in Berlin, warned us of
> what he really was, a covert Communist and the direct agent of Stalin.

Martínez Amutio claimed that the political orientation of the entire
Communist press and propaganda operation during the Spanish Civil War was

in the hands of Fischer. He went even further, making the ludicrous allegation that, together with Artur Stashevsky, the Soviet commercial attaché, and Palmiro Togliatti, the Comintern representative, Fischer cultivated Juan Negrín and, by dint of organizing banquets and orgies for him, turned him into a 'docile and adaptable' instrument of Kremlin policy. Martínez Amutio also claimed absurdly that Fischer was one of the Soviet agents who orchestrated the crisis of May 1937, a crisis whose long-term origins in the subsistence problems of Catalonia were beyond any form of orchestration.[3] Somewhat more restrained is the version of the historian Stanley G. Payne, who refers to Fischer as 'an important American correspondent who served as a sort of Soviet agent or source of information in the Republican zone'.[4]

The truth about Fischer's nationality and importance to Soviet policy was rather different. He was born on 29 February 1896 in the Jewish ghetto of Philadelphia, the son of Russian immigrants, although he was not to learn the language of his parents until a quarter of a century later. In 1917, he volunteered to serve in the British Army and served from 8 April 1918 to 14 June 1920 in the 38th Royal Fusiliers, principally as part of the Jewish Legion, spending fifteen months in Palestine. He saw no fighting against the Germans, since the war was over, although he did help defend Jewish settlers from Arab attack. In consequence, he had numerous conflicts with his British officers and was once confined to a brutal punishment camp in the desert for two weeks for going absent without leave. Despite this, the time in Palestine 'dimmed my Zionism, and Soviet Russia later extinguished it'. He claimed never to have felt deeply Jewish: 'Palestine and the Jews never stirred me as much as the Spanish Republicans in their struggle against Fascism.'[5]

On his return to the USA, he worked in a news agency in New York, where he met the Russian-born pianist Bertha 'Markoosha' Mark, with whom he fell in love, following her in 1921 to Berlin. He learned German and began contributing occasional articles to the *New York Evening Post*. In 1922, he and Markoosha moved to Moscow, where they married and remained for the next nine months. Although both travelled widely, they eventually settled back in Moscow in 1928, where they had two sons, George and Victor. Markoosha was seven years older than Louis and there was always an element of maternal tolerance in her attitude towards him, reflected in the fact that she referred to him in letters as 'Louinka my dear boy'. There was also a strong element of friendship and mutual support, although their correspondence makes it clear that their way of life – he constantly absent, she carrying the burden of care of the family – was his choice, not hers. Louis was not a monogamous man and on his endless travels he had

215

relationships with many women who, despite his egoism, found him irresistibly attractive.

One of them, Tatiana Lestchenko, a Russian singer and translator, had an affair with him in the early 1930s and bore him a son called Vanya. Her letters to him reveal an intelligent and independent woman who, as many others would be, was captivated by his sheer energy: 'And near you I always feel so warm and silently joyous – as if I were lying in the sunshine.' She wrote later to a friend: 'I feel that I am only grateful to LF for giving me the happiness of such a son. All my resentment to LF for his caddish, scoundrely behaviour toward me because I became pregnant – melts. I did love him. And the best of him I kept. I have.'[6] Whether it was politics or love, Louis Fischer would always be driven on by a voracious appetite and numerous women would suffer in consequence.

During his stint in Moscow, Fischer worked on a piece-rate basis for the Jewish Telegraphic Agency and, even more sporadically, for the *New York Evening Post*. He wrote later of how he divided his time between Moscow and the provinces, and lamented that, during his first period in Soviet Russia, 'I learned much less than I should have'. The reason was, paradoxically, because he spent so much time with his professional colleagues: 'We correspondents were one big, almost permanent poker party." When they weren't playing cards, his colleagues generally expressed anti-Soviet attitudes, which seemed to Fischer to be 'based less on knowledge than on prejudice'. In reaction to this, he developed deep sympathy for the Soviet experiment. At first, while working as a freelancer, he would not start a new article until he knew that the previous one had been published and that he would be paid for it. Because he needed 'the encouragement of publication', he wrote less but did much more research than the average correspondent. As he wrote later:

> I think my strongest instinct is curiosity. When aroused, I suffer if I do
> not know what I want to know, and Moscow aroused me powerfully.
> Under the bombardment of its kaleidoscopically changing events,
> there could be no intellectual laziness or complacency. I read a lot,
> travelled, and talked with those foreign correspondents who felt
> Moscow's excitement.[7]

In the summer of 1923, he returned to Germany and wrote five substantial articles on Soviet Russia. He then took them to New York, where he hoped to use them to get an assignment from the left-wing weekly magazine *The Nation*. He had first contributed to the magazine in 1920 with an article about Palestine.[8]

His Russian articles made a favourable impression on one of the magazine's principal editors, Freda Kirchwey, who decided to publish all five of them, and this led to him being appointed as *The Nation*'s special European correspondent. Returning to Europe, he wrote articles on Russia and Germany for both *The Nation* and other newspapers. Eventually, his articles would be syndicated to several papers including the *Baltimore Sun, Reynolds News* in London and others in Prague, Oslo, Stockholm, Paris, Brussels and Amsterdam. This would provide him with sufficient income to travel widely. On 3 June 1925, he published an article commenting on the fact that Hitler got six months for his part in the beer hall putsch whereas Communists who planned an insurrection got ten to fifteen years' hard labour. Hitler wrote a letter of complaint, pointing out that he had actually served thirteen months in jail. In fact, it was partly Fischer's observations of the rise of Nazism in Germany that intensified his sympathy for the Soviet Union: 'Each time I got disgusted with Russia I had only to return to central and western Europe. The disgust dwindled.' In the summer of 1927, along with a delegation of prominent American labour leaders and intellectuals, Fischer spent over six hours in Stalin's company. He noted that he had 'crafty eyes', a 'low forehead' and 'ugly, short black and gold teeth', but was impressed by his slow, methodical method of argument. Fischer left convinced that Stalin was 'unsentimental, steel-willed, unscrupulous, and irresistible'.[9]

The other motivation behind Fischer's sympathy for the Soviet Union was what he called its 'spectacle of creation and self-sacrifice'. Having witnessed on his many travels the degrading poverty of much of rural Russia, he was enthusiastic about the prospect of the revolution bringing better food, hygiene, education and medical care. He had been struck, as he travelled across the steppes by night train, by the hundreds of miles of unrelenting blackness: 'Now the electric bulb was invading the bleak black village; steel and iron were vanquishing Russia's wood civilization. I translated Five Year Plan statistics into human values.' In the grim years of the depression in America and Western Europe, the Soviet experiment seemed to Fischer, as to many other Western observers, to be a beacon of hope. At his Moscow apartment, he welcomed streams of American, British and European liberal enthusiasts who shared his views. Among them was the Spanish journalist Julio Álvarez del Vayo. He would contact him again in Spain in 1934 and yet again in 1936, by which time del Vayo would be Foreign Minister. Thus, Fischer came to know a huge array of influential intellectuals and politicians, most of them only too eager to believe the best of the Soviet system. He claimed acquaintance with George Bernard Shaw and Theodore Dreiser, with Sydney and Beatrice Webb and Harold Laski, with Jawaharwal Nehru and Rabindrath Tagore, with Lord Lothian and Lady Astor. He would never be shy about re-establishing contact with them in the future, particularly when he began to lobby on behalf of the Spanish Republic.[10]

These individuals – and their reactions to the Soviet Union – fascinated Fischer. After one tour with a group, he wrote to Freda Kirchwey:

> those tourists whom I bossed around the country for forty days taught me a great deal…though I showed them the good and the bad, and finally delivered a whole lecture on Soviet weaknesses, they all went away as Soviet patriots. Indeed, towards the end, I was trying to check their enthusiasm and make them more critical because I have often noticed excitement over the USSR evaporate at the first contact with a cold wind of shortcomings unless the excitement is tempered with understanding.[11]

One of his colleagues who, retrospectively at least, did not share Fischer's enthusiasms, no matter how tempered, was Malcolm Muggeridge, the correspondent of the Manchester *Guardian*. Years later, converted to Catholicism, he wrote with jaundiced hindsight of the same people whose presence had delighted Fischer. Their credulity provided only 'comic relief', their praise for the system 'as though a vegetarian society had come out with a passionate plea for cannibalism'. He mocked Fischer's readiness to give the Soviet experiment time to deal with centuries of backwardness: 'Fischer was a sallow, ponderous, inordinately earnest man, dear to Oumansky [Konstantin Oumansky was then head of the Press Department of the Commissariat for Foreign Affairs] as one who had never once through the years veered from virtuously following the Party Line.'[12]

It is certainly the case that Fischer, like most other correspondents, failed to report fully the great famine of 1932, although whether the Soviet censorship would have let them do so is a moot point. How much he knew is also a consideration, although he did occasionally refer to the famine as an unfortunate consequence of a necessary restructuring of Russian agriculture. Although he always looked at the Soviet experiment with hopeful expectancy, Fischer would, of course, eventually be disillusioned by the all-pervading sense of terror and insecurity. After the murder of Kirov, when the murderously repressive nature of Stalinism intensified with the judicial murder of the Old Bolsheviks in the Moscow trials, Fischer's faith began slowly to be undermined. At first, he made a distinction between the trials and the social progress. To Freda Kirchwey, he wrote at the beginning of 1934:

you can't shoot 103 whites thus giving the impression of a whiteguard plot and then exile Zinoviev etc. as the inspirers of the deed…I can't write on it yet because the matter is not clear in my mind…I am convinced this is a regrettable and serious interruption, but only an interruption in Russia's progress towards greater liberalism, but not much liberalism, nevertheless.

Just before leaving to cover the Spanish Civil War, he wrote in similar terms to his friend Max Lerner: 'I believe that even the Zinoviev etc trial will not stop the growth of democracy. That growth is the product of economic improvement and social peace – the existence of both these phenomena is not subject to the slightest doubt.'[13] His gradual, but unmistakable, change of heart would eventually earn him the hostility of the famous pro-Stalinist *New York Times* correspondent Walter Duranty, who would later refer to him as 'the rat who left the sinking ship that didn't sink'.[14]

During these years in Russia and Germany, Fischer perfected the technique that was to give him such influence, an influence that reached its apogee during the Spanish Civil War. In order to understand the Soviet situation, he travelled widely, but he also made a concerted effort to become personally acquainted with key politicians and then demonstrate to them that he was to be trusted:

> The Bolsheviks were pleased to see a serious approach to the life of their country. Moreover, politicians talk freely when they are certain they will not be quoted – some politicians, I should say – and I gave proof in Moscow that I would be discreet. What I was told in secret I kept secret. I went on the good journalistic principle that a statesman's information is his own until he releases it for publication. (Death also releases.) Besides, I am a good listener, and most men will talk about themselves or their work to a sympathetic listener.[15]

As he would later in Spain, he travelled in order to talk to ordinary people and to contrast their perceptions with what he had been told by the great and good. Through the success of his book *Oil Imperialism: The International Struggle for Petroleum* (1926), which was translated into French, German and Russian, he was commissioned to give lectures in the USA. In the course of research for his next book *The Soviets in World Affairs* (1930), he came to know the Commissar for Foreign Affairs Georgi Chicherin and his deputy and, from 1930, successor, Maxim Litvinov. He enjoyed a warm friendship and a rich correspondence with

Chicherin, helped no doubt by the fact that his wife, Markoosha, had once worked as secretary to the great man. At first, Litvinov was highly suspicious of journalists and difficult to interview. By dint of persistence, and because they had apartments in the same building, Fischer gradually won his confidence. With his young children next to him in the evenings, Litvinov would tell Fischer of his meetings with Briand, Chamberlain and Lloyd George. With Litvinov's help, he gained access to the exiled Trotskyist Kristian Rakovsky, who had been Soviet Ambassador in London and Paris before being exiled. Rakovsky uninhibitedly shared with Fischer both his memories and swathes of important documents. His two-volume work *The Soviets in World Affairs* (1930) was thus immensely well-informed. It was translated into French, German and Russian, but the Nazis came into power before the German edition could appear and Stalin refused permission for the Russian edition. Nevertheless, the book saw Fischer recognized in the United States as a leading expert on Russian politics and this eventually secured him ready access to successive Secretaries of State, Henry L. Stimson and Cordell Hull.[16]

Fischer was an immensely gregarious man. He prided himself on having regular bouts of laziness: 'In Moscow, Berlin, Paris, London and New York I loafed, played tennis, met journalists, family, relatives and friends and played poker with a passion. Once in Berlin I participated in a correspondents' all-night poker game in which I won one hundred and twenty-five dollars. It seemed like a million in those days.' He loved to talk shop with his fellow correspondents. In Moscow, he established friendships with many who would later share his support of the Spanish Republic, including John Gunther, Dorothy Thompson, Walter Duranty, Anna Louise Strong and James Vincent Sheean. In Berlin, he met Edgar A. Mowrer, Hubert R. Knickerbocker and the man who became his closest friend, Frederick Robert Kuh of the United Press. While Fischer concentrated on meeting people, his wife Markoosha supported herself and their two children. In fact, he seemed never to put much energy into his marriage or his children and had girlfriends in various parts of Europe. He started to make a decent living from 1929 and only then was able to accept 'partial financial responsibility for the family'. He remained jealous of his independence:

> I have never been a member of any political party or of a trade union or, after my youth, of any club. I am essentially a libertarian and resent shackles, even personal ones. I can impose discipline upon myself but I would fight its imposition on me by others. This applies especially to intellectual discipline. For me the question of joining the Communist

party never arose because I would not allow another person to tell me what to write or what to think.

He was often accused of being either a Communist or else in the pay of the Soviet regime, which he always categorically denied, stating: 'If I had been a Communist I should not have been ashamed or afraid to affirm it.'[17]

Fischer's eminence as a Sovietologist and as someone who moved back and forth to Russia led to British Intelligence taking an interest in him. Guy Liddell, the head of the security services, wrote that he 'has written several books very favourable to Soviet Russia, and who, if not actually a Communist, is a very deep shade of pink'.[18] They were equally interested in his friend Frederick Kuh, a pro-Communist journalist who used to be the correspondent of the *Daily Herald* in Vienna and was now the London representative of the United Press Association. In a letter to Kuh, somehow intercepted by the British security services, Fischer wrote from Moscow: 'I haven't seen anybody yet. I merely walk the streets to gather impressions.' He wrote in an oblique reference to Stalin:

> I heard that their big chief has frequent and more frequent fits of hysteria, has stamped his feet and raged even in interview with diplomats, and yells at the top of his voice and tears his hair when seeing his own people. He does not brook any opposition in even slight matters. The whole structure, however, is very strong. But the personal intrigues are endless, everybody being against everybody else.[19]

Fischer first visited Spain from late February to late March 1934. He travelled widely in the rural south. He interviewed numerous professors, journalists, parliamentary deputies and ex-ministers, including the ex-prime minister, Manuel Azaña.[20] He renewed his friendship with Luis Araquistain Quevedo, whom he had met in Berlin when he was Spanish Ambassador there. A close adviser to Largo Caballero, Araquistain was founder and editor of the Socialist theoretical journal *Leviatán*, to which he had invited Fischer to contribute. He did, in fact, write six major articles for the journal, five on the Soviet Union and one on Poland, between June 1934 and June 1936.[21] In Spain, Araquistain introduced Fischer into Socialist circles. Married to a Swiss woman called Trudy Graa, Araquistain brought Fischer back into contact with his brother-in-law, the journalist Julio Álvarez del Vayo, who was married to Trudy's sister Luisi. Álvarez del Vayo, whom Fischer had first met in Moscow, was also close to Largo Caballero and had been his Ambassador in Mexico. Fischer carried a letter of introduction from Frederick Kuh to Lester Ziffren, the chief of the United Press bureau in Madrid, who thus became his guide to the circle of foreign and Spanish correspondents. He also hit it off immediately with the US Ambassador, Claude G. Bowers, with whom he became firm friends, united with him in commitment to the Republican cause. He also established close friendships with the artist Luis Quintanilla, who drew his portrait; with the physiologist, Dr Juan Negrín, with whom he spoke German; and with the American journalist, Jay Allen. Fischer quickly set off for a tour of rural Spain and what he saw made him fall in love with the country. It also left him with the conviction that so much poverty would lead to bloodshed. Indeed, he was shocked by a lack of food that seemed more acute than in a poor Ukrainian village and by the fact that thousands of peasants lived in caves.[22]

Fischer wrote later of the beginnings of his friendship with Negrín. Together with Jay Allen, they had taken a taxi together to Colmenar Viejo, forty kilometres north of Madrid, and talked to the working men in the plaza and in their homes. Negrín was indignant about the all-pervading poverty and even talked about the need to distribute arms to the proletariat:

> We went into the cold stone house of a family which subsisted on bean soup and black coffee. The woman told us that her children had died of pneumonia. Negrín, who is a physician, said it was probably from undernourishment. A third child, seven months old, lay in a crib sick with hernia. The husband had not worked for months. They were in debt up to their ears, and saw no way out.

What particularly struck him was the dignity with which Spanish peasants bore their poverty, something he contrasted with the abject servility of their Russian and Ukrainian counterparts: 'The working men in blue cotton shirts, small, puny men, wore a proud look. Their eyes said, "I am a man", even though life was treating them like dogs.'[23]

At the end of September 1935, Fischer suggested to Freda Kirchwey of *The Nation* that she commission a series of articles about the growing crisis in international relations under the heading 'Arms over Europe'. 'I will need a lot of money,' he wrote. As a great admirer of the work of 'our favourite author', she replied: 'We are very eager to have you write for us and us alone.' After discussing it with the other editors, she replied: 'I am authorized to offer you the stupendous sum of $125 an article for a series of six to eight pieces.' This was indeed a fabulous offer, about three times their normal top rate. Fischer acknowledged the generosity of the offer, but commented that his expenses would be such as to ensure that 'my own income will be next to nothing. But I don't care. I wanted to do this and I am glad you enable me to do it.' In one of his letters to Freda Kirchwey, he revealed the seriousness with which he regarded his work: 'I keep repeating to myself what I always keep in mind when writing: Don't make predictions.' He was desperate to avoid writing things that might later be proved wrong: 'I think you will find me cautious in this series. I check every sentence with innumerable people, with my own background and with documents when they are available. You do not, I am sure, want sensations.'[24]

In the course of his visits in the last quarter of 1935 and early 1936, to London, Paris, Rome, Vienna, Prague, Berlin, Warsaw and Moscow, he consolidated his remarkable network of influential contacts among statesmen, ambassadors and journalists. He started at the League of Nations in Geneva. There, he renewed his acquaintanceship with a Soviet diplomat who was Russia's member of the League secretariat, Marcel Rosenberg: 'A hunchback with deep flaming eyes, he had made a big impression in Paris as Counsellor of the Soviet Embassy, and Paris salons angled for his visits.' Fischer had known him there and in Moscow where they had often argued about the deficiencies of the Soviet system. His readiness to argue robustly with Soviet leaders led to him establishing a friendship with the head of the Comintern, the Hungarian revolutionary, Bela Kun.[25]

'My head and files are full of material,' wrote Fischer to Freda Kirchwey, and, in consequence, he wrote more articles than was originally planned. Freda was delighted with the quality, although she lamented that he did not employ a more personal 'eye-witness' tone. Moreover, the process of getting them and actually publishing them was immensely revealing. Fischer was both a perfectionist and sported a massive ego. He wanted the articles published in their entirety and as they were received, but *The Nation* simply had insufficient space. Two other problems were that, while travelling, Fischer did not see what else the magazine was publishing on the same subject and that there were inevitable delays in his copy arriving. Inevitably, some of what he wrote overlapped with other things already printed or seemed dated by the time that it arrived. This necessitated editorial intervention on his copy, which in turn led to a sharp response from Louis:

> I feel very badly about the way you are using my series. I feel that you
> ruin this whole big piece of work by stretching it out so long. All the
> articles were connected in my mind and are connected in subject matter,
> and to print them over a period of four months just precludes a single,

homogeneous impression. [...] I cannot stand this way of destroying a piece of work to which I attached such importance and to which I gave so much energy and time and interest.

Valuing Fischer's work so highly, Freda's reply was conciliatory: 'you are right, but if we had used them consecutively we should have had to sacrifice other articles that seemed important. These editorial choices are often difficult, and I do not claim that they are always wisely made.' He finally apologized for being oversensitive, but continued to make comments about 'mutilations' to which she continually reassured him that 'we have been as gentle as circumstances seemed to permit'.[26]

In early April 1936, having completed the series, Fischer returned to Spain, where he got in touch with Julio Álvarez del Vayo. Through him, he secured interviews with the new prime minister, and future President of the Republic, Manuel Azaña, and with the Socialist leader Francisco Largo Caballero. Azaña remembered Fischer from his previous visit, saying: 'Ah, Fischer, that's the man who made fun of me. But not more fun that I make of myself. He's a wise journalist. I'd like to see him again.' Since he still did not speak Spanish, he took along an interpreter in the person of Constancia de la Mora, whom he described as 'a gorgeous maiden' in a letter to Freda Kirchwey. She replied: 'We all admire your capacity for finding señoritas wherever you go.'[27] He had met Constancia at the homes of both Araquistain and Álvarez del Vayo. It was to be the beginning of an important, if somewhat conflictive, friendship.

On 10 April, he set off on a short but hectic trip through Extremadura and Andalusia in the company of Jay Allen, who was collecting material for a book on the need for agrarian reform. What he saw accounted for the fact that, as he wrote later, 'the Spanish people had won my heart'. At one point, in the small town of Barcarrota in the province of Badajoz, they arrived just as a Socialist meeting was due to start. Since the advertised speaker, the local Socialist deputy Margarita Nelken, had not arrived, Fischer took over the meeting and got the local peasants to explain their situation. Throughout a trip of twelve hundred miles, he reached the unavoidable conclusion that the Spanish countryside was a time bomb and that the Right was pinning its hopes on the army to prevent agrarian reform.[28]

After a week in the south of Spain, he went on to Barcelona, whence he took a ship to Genoa. As he had written to Freda, 'I want to see Vesuvius spout and perhaps – I know I am sanguine – hear Mussolini do the same.' In the event, the interview with the Duce did not materialize. After a brief interlude in Paris with

Markoosha, he returned to Russia for the shared birthday, 4 May, of his two sons.[29] Accordingly, the outbreak of the Spanish Civil War found Fischer in Moscow but, regarding Spain as 'the front line against Fascism, I gladly left Russia to be close to the battle'.[30] After a holiday in Czechoslovakia, he journeyed to Paris, took a train to Toulouse and after a night in the station hotel, left at 6 a.m. on 16 September 1936 on the regular ten-passenger Air France flight to Barcelona.

Two days later, he wrote in his diary:

> I am full of impressions and information. If I am bombarded in this way much longer I shall forget things I would like to remember and record. The brain makes a little comment, a picture flashes before one's eyes in the street or on the aerodrome, one feels an emotion. [...] But this civil war situation is so rich, thrilling and interesting that I hate to lose any of it.

After some delay, he managed to get on a plane which, after failing to cross the mountains to Madrid, landed in Valencia. There, after further interruptions, it was decided to proceed by car, but appalling weather persuaded him to wait until he could get a train to the capital. To his amazement, no one would let him pay for his travel or his food. He went for a walk and was equally fascinated to hear discussions between anarchists, who wanted to collectivize everything, and Socialists and Communists, who argued that it was ridiculous to want to confiscate the property of small businessmen and artisans. When his train finally reached Madrid, after an incident-packed night, there were no taxis to be found at the station, so he and Victor Schiff of the London *Daily Herald* hired the only available vehicle – a double-decker bus – to take them to the Hotel Florida.[31]

In Madrid, Fischer quickly re-established contact with the Spaniards he had met on his previous visits. First among them was his closest friend, Luis Araquistain. By now editor of the left-Socialist daily, *Claridad*, Araquistain was in a curiously contradictory position. For most of his life, Araquistain had oscillated within a narrow political spectrum of liberalism, Fabianism and social democracy. However, from 1933 to 1937, he was the theoretician behind the adoption of revolutionary rhetoric by the Spanish Socialist leader, Francisco Largo Caballero. Araquistain's radicalism was the result of a frustrating spell as Undersecretary of Labour and Social Welfare under Largo Caballero and what he saw as Spanish Ambassador in Berlin in 1932 and 1933. Witnessing the rise of Nazism and its appalling consequences, he became an advocate of a united working-class revolutionary response to fascism. He came to despair of Socialist participation in bourgeois democracy as a determined and aggressive right wing blocked all attempts at reform. Through the pages of his journal *Leviatán*, Araquistain argued that the only choice lay between fascist or socialist dictatorship. It was at this time that he coined the phrase 'the Spanish Lenin' to describe Largo Caballero. He argued for the Bolshevization of the party and the adoption of Leninist tactics. At first, radicalization carried the PSOE nearer to the Communists, but Araquistain, like Largo Caballero, opposed the popular front policy because it meant further collaboration with bourgeois liberals. Ironically, popular frontism was to bring together the Communists and the right Socialists led by Largo Caballero's arch-rival Indalecio Prieto. This would eventually bring about a bitter confrontation between Araquistain and his brother-in-law, Julio Álvarez del Vayo, which would inevitably affect Araquistain's relationship with Fischer.

In September, Álvarez del Vayo had just been made Foreign Minister, apparently because Prieto had vetoed Araquistain, Largo Caballero's first choice. Uncomfortable about having his brother-in-law as his boss, Araquistain was about to go to Paris as Republican Ambassador. When Fischer met him, he did not hesitate to give Araquistain forthright advice on the military situation. In particular, he was amazed by the government's failure to break the resistance of the rebel troops besieged in the Alcázar of Toledo. He pointed out that the deadlock over the Alcázar was damaging the government's military strategy by immobilizing thousands of men who might have turned the tide at the front. They argued, Fischer urging Araquistain to use his influence with Largo Caballero to be more ruthless. On 19 September, Araquistain secured for him a pass to go to Toledo. On the way, he passed cars rushing to Madrid with wounded soldiers. Along the way, he counted five vehicles overturned in ditches and commented sourly: 'Reckless driving does not win wars.' He also witnessed a chaotic attack in which numerous militiamen died pointlessly. The lack of organization frustrated him intensely: 'There is no political work, there are no mass meetings. One hears requests for newspapers. The militias lie around all day doing nothing. That conduces to flabbiness and lack of discipline.'

Disillusioned by what he had seen in Toledo, Fischer returned to Madrid. He read in *El Socialista*, the mouthpiece of Prieto's moderate Socialists, an editorial calling for a rebirth of the initial revolutionary élan which had defeated the rebels in Madrid and so many cities on 18 July. Fischer reflected bitterly: 'Yes, where is it, I wonder. Toledo, with its nonchalant militias and hundreds of visiting automobiles, gave the impression of a carnival rather than a war. Madrid has changed its clothes but not its mood. How can the élan be revived, asks *El Socialista* and answers: by telling the people the truth.' Telling the truth, no matter how inconvenient, was to be the policy consistently adopted by Fischer in his articles. It would cause him problems with some Communist colleagues.[32]

On 20 September, Louis returned to Toledo, accompanied by Jan Yindrich, one of the Madrid correspondents of the United Press. He was surprised by the liberty afforded to correspondents: 'After showing our passes at the archway through which one enters Toledo, nobody stops us or asks any questions. We are free to wander about, visit all advanced positions, talk to the troops, make sketches, etc. It is an informal war.' He linked up with his friend, Luis Quintanilla, who had been sent by the Ministry of War to report on the progress of the siege. According to Fischer, Quintanilla 'is volatile, gesticulates, effervesces', and he got fully involved in the efforts to dislodge the besieged garrison, appearing before Fischer with singed eyelids. Like Fischer, he was frustrated by the ineffective actions of the militias, commenting with disgust: 'Too much literature and photography. The men thought this was a picnic; they wanted their picture in the paper.' On the way back to Madrid, Fischer stopped near Bargas, at the village of Olías del Rey. The biggest local landowners had been killed at the beginning of the war and their land collectivized. When Fischer asked some old peasants if they could defend themselves, they replied that their young men were away fighting with the militias and that they knew only too well that, if the rebels won, many of them would be slaughtered, as had already happened to their relatives further south. One woman told him: 'We peasants stand with the legitimate government because the alternative is death to some of us and the old degrading poverty to all of us.'[33]

Fischer's curiosity was insatiable. Everything about Madrid fascinated him – the frenetic traffic, with cars being driven around at breakneck speed by militiamen leaning on their horns, the cafés crowded with people talking revolution, the prostitutes, the street vendors. He was intrigued by a sign on a fashionable shoe store which sported a Republican flag and the statement that 'this house sympathizes with the regime. Long live the Republic.' He commented: 'What fears must have moved the owners to this avowal of faith!' On 21 September, he went out for dinner with his friend Lester Ziffren. On the way to Marichu's restaurant, they saw 'a taxi dance spot still going strong' and decided to go and explore: 'Found young girls, not at all bad looking, hoofing it around at a nickel a dance. The place was called Shanghai and it bore a sign stating that it was "seized" by the CNT and UGT. Even a civil war couldn't stop the dancing. A militiaman with a rifle sat near the door.' Typically, Fischer started asking the waitresses questions and was delighted to find one who was a Socialist who had read Marx, and another, a Basque, who said that the Catholic Basques were fighting alongside the

Socialists and Communists because their hatred for the Carlists and Fascists was greater than their disagreement with Marxism.

However, for all his curiosity about the changes in Madrid, Fischer could not keep away from Toledo despite what he had witnessed during the abortive siege of the Alcázar. Each day, he would plan to do something in the capital, and then either Jan Yindrich or Henry Buckley would ask him if he was going to Toledo and he could not resist: 'I have apparently caught a disease which I have dubbed Alcazarosis.' One day, he witnessed a visit from Largo Caballero which did little to enhance his opinion of the prime minister. After wearily watching an artillery piece fire at the Alcázar, he left and

> did not say a single word to the men who crowded around his car. He did not even raise his fist in greeting. The assault guards had certainly expected some acknowledgement of their existence on his part. They were downcast when he sped away. I am told that he always has behaved in this way, all his life. Yet he is immensely popular. In this atmosphere of around-the-Alcázar depression, he might have broken a tradition to utter a sentence which would warm and enthuse.[34]

On 21 September, Fischer did not go to Toledo because he had a meeting with Marcel Rosenberg, the recently appointed Russian Ambassador. He commented innocently: 'the appointment at this juncture has political significance. When Germany and Italy are withdrawing their embassies from Madrid, the Soviet Union registers its confidence in and friendship for the legitimate government by accrediting a special envoy to it.' He had known Rosenberg in Moscow and Paris but now as Ambassador, while friendly, he was tight-lipped:

> Rosenberg, as usual, listens but does not vouchsafe a milligram of information. I like him nevertheless as of old. His manner antagonises many people. He can be coldly cutting. But he can also be personal and cordial. In any case, I can learn much from him even when he says little. Besides, he is always wise, fathoms an idea after the first explanatory phrase, and reacts with his face or in a telling word.

After their first meeting, Fischer saw Rosenberg nearly every day until he was recalled to Moscow. Rosenberg introduced him to the dapper, English-speaking NKVD officer Colonel Alexander Orlov, and to the Military Attaché in the

Russian Embassy, General Vladimir Gorev, who was the 'Chief Rezident' in Spain of Russian Military Intelligence – the GRU.

Fischer's attitude to Soviet policy towards Spain suggested that he was far from having a particularly privileged position. His main source of information was *Pravda*, which he bought every morning. He thought it of enormous significance that, out of its total of six pages, the paper often devoted a page or more, and never less than half a page, to letters from Soviet citizens who were contributing towards food relief for Spain. With an utter lack of cynicism, he commented in his diary:

> It is obvious from the manner in which the *Pravda* features its readers'
> correspondence that Moscow is fully aware of the political importance
> to it of the Spanish situation and will therefore not stint in helping
> Madrid to suppress the rebels. Moscow has warm, natural sympathies
> with an anti-Fascist government which includes two Communists and
> is presided over by Largo Caballero who told me six months ago 'that
> there is no difference between himself and a Communist'.

Fischer realized only too well that Soviet policy was driven by national interests and he was especially acute in his analysis of the dangers that a Franco victory would mean for Russia. It was not just about the Germans coveting the Canary Islands or the Italians making themselves at home in Mallorca, but about the impact a fascist victory in Spain would have on internal politics within France. He perceived how Hitler aspired thereby to undermine the Soviet–French alliance and how the anti-Socialist prejudices of Britain's ruling classes were blinding them to the danger posed to imperial interests.[35] His relative ingenuousness in regard to Soviet policy contrasted with the sharpness revealed in his later published articles, the difference being that later he really did have the benefit of inside information.

Fischer wrote with approval of editorials in *El Socialista*, which pointed out that it was more important to win at the front than to seize automobiles and hotels in Madrid. Yet he complained about what he saw as absurd restrictions on the papers telling the truth about the Republic's parlous position. Similarly, he was indignant about the lies being produced in newspapers in Europe to the effect that the President of the Republic, Manuel Azaña, had fled to Alicante. In the same vein, he was outraged when, on 25 September, Largo Caballero refused to authorize a proclamation informing the nation of the critical military situation, writing bitterly: 'The masses ought to be stirred to enthusiasm or frightened into activity. Instead a dangerous optimism paralyzes the policy of "Business as usual". Madrid's business proceeds as usual – except that its business is often not business but pleasure.'[36]

On the previous day, 24 September, Fischer had called on his friend Juan Negrín, who three weeks earlier had become Minister of Finance. Louis had been at Toledo the day before and returned covered in blood from wounded militiamen whom he had helped tend. The talk that night in his hotel – because of artillery attacks, he had moved to the Hotel Capitol on the other side of the Gran Vía from the Florida – had been bleak. Another guest, Mikhail Koltsov, had told him that he had tried to drive beyond Toledo and got a mere fourteen kilometres before seeing signs of advancing Nationalists. Accordingly, when he met Negrín, Fischer gave him a pessimistic assessment of the situation. Negrín agreed that things had been bad, but argued that there were already improvements thanks to the new government of Largo Caballero. He went as far as to say that he was more concerned with what would happen after what he regarded as the Republic's inevitable victory. He described how he was organizing a crack force of frontier guards, the Carabineros, to protect the banks and tighten up border controls. Fischer's ability to get politicians to talk to him without inhibitions saw Negrín confide both details of the Republic's transfer of its gold reserves to the Soviet Union and his own doubts about the capacity of Largo Caballero. He argued that what was needed was 'a steel leadership. Caballero could scarcely be talked to. He would not listen to criticism. He was much too sensitive.' Fischer expressed his concerns about the press and the fact that the population was being fed lies about the real gravity of the situation.[37]

While in Madrid, Louis met and began an affair with an attractive Norwegian journalist, Gerda Grepp. She had come to Spain as correspondent for the Oslo socialist newspaper *Arbeiderbladet*, and fell passionately in love with him. She wrote to him that the twenty-nine years of her life before their meeting were meaningless in comparison with the few months since she had known him. They spent time together in Spain and elsewhere in Europe. Indeed, it was to be one of his longer-lasting affairs and one that would cause some distress to his wife. Markoosha heard about the developing relationship from one of her friends in Moscow, Elsa Wolf, who had been told about it by her husband, who was one of the Soviet advisers in Spain.[38] Throughout the years of the Spanish war, Markoosha wrote him frequent, passionate letters, in which she regularly lamented the lack of news from him. She rarely complained but occasionally her bitterness at her abandonment was evident: 'You know how loveless my life is, can't you be sometimes a bit sweeter, more personal. It is hard to blame you, after this life of constant separation, that you lose understanding, you probably have another outlet for your personal needs. But you can't desert one to one's undeserved fate.'[39]

On 25 September, Fischer and Jay Allen were given an astonishing scoop, presumably as a result of the close friendship with both Julio Álvarez del Vayo and Juan Negrín that they enjoyed. They were given permission to interview an Italian pilot who had crash-landed on 13 September and was being held at Prieto's Ministry for the Navy and Air Force. The head of the Republican air force, Ignacio Hidalgo de Cisneros, wanted to find out if the extremely frightened twenty-three-year-old with an Italian passport in the name of Vincenzo Bocalari was, in fact, as he claimed, an American national called Vincent Patriarca, born in City Island in the Bronx in New York. He spoke New York English with an Italian accent and Italian with a New York accent. Allen and Fischer assured him that they had no hostile intentions, although Fischer said: 'You're an adventurer and a damned fool and you are in a terrible mess. The government here has every right to shoot you. If you do the right thing we may be able to help you.' In response to what Allen called a 'puppy's charm', they believed his story.[40]

A barber by trade, Patriarca had gone to Italy in 1932 to fulfil his ambition to be a flyer and had served in Abyssinia before coming to Spain, tempted by the spectacular wages offered by the rebels. Crying copious tears, he begged them to save his life. He claimed to have turned against the Francoists as a result of seeing executions of labourers in the south and of the decent treatment that he had received from his Republican captors. Fischer told him that they would try to secure his release, although his diary entry suggested that he was not optimistic. Nevertheless, he and Jay Allen informed the US Embassy. Claude Bowers took up his case through the chargé d'affaires in Madrid, Eric Wendelin, in response to a press campaign in the USA mounted by a miraculously concocted 'Committee of One Thousand Mothers'. Álvarez del Vayo assured Wendelin that Patriarca would not be shot and would be well treated. He arranged for Patriarca to be placed in the custody of the embassy, where on first arrival, he cut 'a pitiful figure', according to Edward Knoblaugh of the Associated Press. However, when his confidence returned, Patriarca would watch aerial combats from the embassy gardens, shouting: 'God, if only I could be up there, I'd show them.' Wendelin secured Patriarca's repatriation to the United States, where he made a name for himself denouncing the Republicans and praising the rebels before returning to Italy and a career in Mussolini's air force.[41]

On another visit to the front, near Quismondo, south-west of Madrid, towards the advancing African columns, Fischer was appalled by the casual attitude of the militia. They were not properly dug in but merely lying behind a feeble barricade of loose earth, incapable of stopping any bullet. He noted indignantly in his diary:

> Instead of digging trenches, which they could have done with a few shovels, they loafed and ate, ate beautifully. Most of them were tearing strips of dried bacon from pigs' legs. Hills of melons, yellow and green, lent color to the scene. They drank wine. A militia man offered me a Havana cigar. Were they not earning ten pesetas a day? A good mechanic in town might be paid as much.

Returning to Madrid, near Olias del Rey, he ran into a crowd of militiamen fleeing like sheep from Toledo where there had been an air-raid. This was the incident that was described in the article whose frankness led to Fischer being berated bitterly by Cockburn and Koltsov south of Madrid. The article was written on 8 October, although it did not appear in New York until sixteen days later. That Fischer should so firmly have defended the need to tell the truth about the Republic's difficulties belies the notion that he religiously followed the Communist Party line.[42] Despite their disagreement, Fischer and Koltsov remained on good terms.

Fischer's conclusion about the loss of Toledo could not have been grimmer:

> The fact is that all the troops at Toledo ran fast when the enemy approached. The government bears a large share of the guilt. Its political work was beneath contempt. It watched with indifference as the creeping demoralisation undermined the stamina of the men. The anarchists contributed heavily by their resentment of discipline and their antagonism to the officers. But the officers were not much good either.

When he visited the front in early October, he was delighted to meet a unit made up of Spanish sportsmen, including runners, boxers, footballers and even bullfighters. However, he despaired of their lack of equipment and proper defensive fortifications as they awaited the advancing African columns, commenting:

> it might have fortified their spirit if a political leader from Madrid had come out to talk to them about the cause for which they were here, tell them what measures the government had already taken in the social and economic field to help the poor and oppressed, castigate Fascism and elaborate on the mass killings of the rebels in the south of Spain, remind

them that this awaited them and their families if the government was defeated, inspire them, enthuse them, make them think and feel. Instead, the front was neglected by propagandists and, too, by the quartermaster. Has he no more machine guns to give them? No hand grenades? Is it impossible to send out workers to build real trenches here?[43]

Fischer's analysis of the domestic problems of the Republic was especially perceptive. Rather like Koltsov, Fischer was a man of great energy, unself-conscious curiosity and utterly uninhibited about getting to see important people, then giving them his opinion or even advice. He had friends among the entire Socialist leadership, but the realities of war altered his perceptions of them. He remained enthusiastic about Julio Álvarez del Vayo but, in contrast, came to feel highly critical, not to say contemptuous, of Francisco Largo Caballero. He had not been impressed when he interviewed him during his trip to Spain in the spring of 1936 and, on 3 April, Largo Caballero told him complacently that the Right could return only through a coup d'état which he was confident would be crushed.[44] Now, Fischer was aware that comments could be heard in Madrid that a man nearing seventy was too old to be running a war.[45] On the afternoon of 11 October, Fischer attended a mass meeting in Madrid passionately addressed by Álvarez del Vayo. The audience had been delighted when the Russian Ambassador Marcel Rosenberg was brought on stage. Afterwards, Fischer visited Rosenberg at the Hotel Palace where they shared their pessimism about the conduct of the war. He decided to write a letter to the prime minister, drawing his attention to the lack of a concerted war effort: 'I banged it out feverishly in twenty minutes and took two street cars to the Foreign Office.' There he was received by Álvarez del Vayo and spoke to him with a brutal frankness born in equal measure of their personal friendship and his own commitment to the Republican cause. He told the Foreign Minister of the lack of defensive preparations that he had seen on his visits to the front. When the minister agreed that valuable time had been lost, Fischer, with typical impetuousness, blurted out: 'this is your opportunity to make history. You must assume charge of the defences of Madrid. The hell with this office. Can you not get in touch with the building unions and tell them to stop civilian work in Madrid and go out and construct trenches and gun nests? Could we not do that tomorrow?' Álvarez del Vayo said that his efforts had been impeded because only Largo Caballero had the necessary authority. Fischer read out the draft of his letter and Álvarez del Vayo urged him to send it after cutting out any reference to Largo Caballero's age, about which he was deeply sensitive.[46]

On the morning of 12 October 1936, two Spanish friends translated Fischer's letter. Although written in respectful terms, the content was devastating, particularly for a man who fancied himself as a great revolutionary. It compared the great mass mobilization that had taken place during the siege of Petrograd in 1919 with what was not happening in Madrid:

> I am profoundly disturbed by the present state of affairs here. Many measures which could easily be taken, which must be taken, are not being taken. I have been to the front often and I have inspected the environs of Madrid. Objectively, the situation is far from hopeless. There is no reason why, with your vast resources of men and enthusiasm, you should not hold the enemy at least at the present line. But what I missed most in my three weeks here is the energy and determination which should characterize a revolution. I have studied the Russian Revolution in great detail. When Petrograd was threatened in 1919 every citizen was organized. Nor did they wait for the Whites to come to them. Feverish political work accompanied tireless building of defences, mobilizing of new men, training of old soldiers, and preparation of officers' cadres. Nothing was left undone. The city worked like a powerful motor…I tell you honestly I miss this spirit here. Of course, I know your difficulties and handicaps. You lack many necessary supplies. But you must do more than you have done. History will judge as criminals the men who allow the enemy to take Madrid…I must say: if men whom I know to be sincere and faithful revolutionaries were not in this government I would be inclined to believe that traitors and saboteurs are in charge of defending this city and of holding the front intact. That is the impression an objective observer must get.

Moving from general criticisms to the specific charge made by many, Fischer pressed on:

> I want to ask you, for instance, this question: there are tens of thousands of building workers in Madrid. You have several cement and brick factories here. Why are you not building concrete trenches and dug-outs? Why do you not stop all civilian construction work in Madrid and send the working men out to erect an iron 'Hindenburg line' about thirty kilometres from Madrid which the enemy could not pass? In addition, the heights around the city should be fortified. All this could be accomplished

in a relatively short period. It would improve the morale of the soldiers if they saw that you were doing things for them, and it would give them places in which to hide from air attacks. These things are not difficult to do and they need to be done. Barbed wire entanglements charged with electricity, the mining of bridges and roads, the creation of underground artillery nests – all these and many other measures can be undertaken.

Fischer went on to point out that Largo was being criticized for not talking to the population, that they had lost confidence in him and in his military adviser, the recently promoted General José Asensio Torrado. He also asked why, with the long lines of communication of the African columns, no effort had been made to launch a guerrilla war in their rear.

Later on the same day, Fischer was summoned to the prime minister's office. A pained Largo Caballero told him that he had sent to Barcelona for shovels two months earlier and had tried to buy barbed wire in France. The excuses were feeble and were followed by the even more defeatist remark: 'As to the building operations in Madrid, you try to deal with our trade union. Their representatives were here this afternoon. They came to make demands on me.' This from the man who had been put in charge of the government precisely because of his influence over the labour movement. His principal concerns seemed to be, as it had been since 1917, that the CNT might derive some advantage to the detriment of the UGT or, even worse, that he might lose popularity and his reputation as the hero of the unions. Apparently oblivious to the different priorities imposed by the war, Largo Caballero whinged on: 'If the Socialist trade unions obey the government, the anarcho-syndicalist trade union, the CNT, will conduct propaganda against the Socialists and try to attract their members.' He ended miserably, quoting Fischer's letter back at him: 'Maybe you are right, perhaps "people in Madrid have already lost confidence" in me. Let them choose somebody else in my place.' At that point, Del Vayo kicked Fischer under the table and said: 'He is very sad. Cheer him up.' Fischer said: 'I do not think the whole country has lost confidence in you. On the contrary, there is a feeling that you are the only man for the job. But the people are not conscious of your leadership. Nobody tells them what is happening. They have a feeling that the newspapers and official communiqués lie to them. You have not made a speech to the nation since you have been in office.' Barely able to rouse himself out of his depressive torpor, Caballero's reply was equally defeatist. 'No,' he agreed. 'I haven't. I am too busy. My room is always full of people who want to see me. There are other orators and better ones. Let Del Vayo make speeches.' Fischer pleaded with him to take fifteen minutes to speak on the radio, but the prime minister simply shook his head.[47]

The tone of Fischer's diary certainly sustains his later assertions that, for all his sympathy with the Soviet experiment, he was never a Communist Party member. In 1949, responding under oath to an investigation by the US Immigration Service (in search of information about a person named Mills or Milgrom), Fischer declared:

> After I arrived in Spain I covered the front news and political news of the government – just the ordinary work the correspondent does – and I became very sympathetic to their cause because I felt that if Fascism was defeated in Spain, it would not only be a victory for Democracy and a defeat for Hitler and Mussolini who were already intervening there, but also that a victory for Democracy in Spain was the best way of preventing the Second World War which some of us already saw coming at that time.

When asked if he had ever been a member of any Communist party anywhere in the world, Fischer replied categorically 'Never'. 'In general, I am not a "joiner", even with all the political contacts that I have now and had years back. I don't think that I was a member of any so-called front organization. If I were I would have no hesitation to say so, because I even had sympathies, up to 1939, with some of these so-called front organizations.' When asked why, he replied: 'Because many of them were more or less anti-Fascist. They were doing things which I then thought would prevent the war, would bring victory over Fascism and would strengthen Democracy in various parts of the world.'[48]

Certainly, there could be no mistaking his sympathies:

> If 200 superior officers of the army had been arrested six months ago in one unexpected swoop, Spain might have been spared the 80,000 men and women, who, it is roughly estimated, have died in the last ten weeks of civil war. Azaña, however, pure-minded intellectual that he is, preferred partial action to drastic action. His land reform alarmed the landlords without seriously weakening them. His delicate transfer of some generals from Madrid to distant posts warned them of possible events to come and told them to prepare for revolt. The coincidence of the semi-feudal class's fear for its property with the militarists' fear for their positions as protectors of the classes from which they spring explains the present rising against constituted authority. Pedants may split hairs about the

legality of the situation; the reality is that the landlords, generals, fascists, and their allies are making a last effort to curb the popular revolution which started when Alfonso was driven out. It is a revolution against widespread poverty, for human rights, for progress.[49]

This was the same article which, because of its brutally realistic account of the disorganization and panic of untrained militiamen outside Toledo, earned him the virulent criticism of Mikhail Koltsov. He had argued then that his obligation to his readers was to report the facts: Koltsov, however, made it brutally clear that he believed that there were higher values than the truth. In his own diary, for instance, Koltsov played down the presence of Russian arms and advisers because he knew that this was something that was being used against the Republic. This was not a point of view shared by Fischer. In one of his articles about the International Brigades, he referred to asking the men in one unit about their machine-gun: 'The reply was "Mexican", but the characters on the gun were Russian. "Mexican" is a formula, and the word is never pronounced without a wink. I prefer my facts straight.'[50]

Fischer believed the Spanish war to be crucial to world peace and democratic freedoms: 'I had so much sympathy with the Loyalist cause that I felt it wasn't enough just to write about it. I wanted to do something more concrete so I enlisted in the International Brigades.'[51] He joined after leaving Madrid on 7 November and recalled later: 'I am as proud of that as I am of anything I have done in my life. A nation was bleeding. Machine guns were being mounted on the ivory tower. It was not enough to write.' He was briefly their quartermaster, staying for about two months, although never wore any uniform other than a corduroy jacket and trousers and never carried a weapon. His job was to organize food, clothing and equipment for the brigades. According to Martínez Amutio's fevered imagination, Fischer was Moscow's paymaster for the brigades. This was nonsense not least because Fischer's relationship with the brigades was short-lived. It came to an unhappy end when he clashed with André Marty, the paranoid and fiercely authoritarian Stalinist who really was Moscow's controller of the Internationals. Marty was fiercely jealous because Fischer spoke such good Russian and had good relations with senior Soviet advisers. He bitterly resented Fischer's open criticism of his dictatorial ways. Fischer claimed later that their conflict was inevitable 'perhaps, because I am an independent character but, chiefly, probably because I was not a Communist and couldn't be ordered around as he liked to order around all people, I felt that I wasn't wanted there. I sort of stuck out like a sore thumb and so it was just a friendly understanding that I should quit the Brigade.' Fischer himself implies that Marty manoeuvred to have him replaced. That would have been unusually subtle on Marty's part given his notoriously authoritarian tendencies and his readiness to dish out the most brutal punishments for the slightest infringements of his arbitrarily imposed discipline. On the other hand, given Fischer's connections with Rosenberg and Gorev, with Orlov and Koltsov, with Álvarez del Vayo, Negrín and Largo Caballero, Marty must have felt the need to operate more circumspectly than usual. Moreover, it is also possible that the Comintern judged, and instructed Marty, that the fellow-travelling Fischer could be of more use elsewhere.[52]

In this regard, it may well be of some significance that, in his diary, Fischer says that he brought with him from Paris 'a note of recommendation from "M"' which secured him a room at the Hotel Florida. It is probable that 'M' was Willi Münzenberg, the Comintern propaganda wizard who lived in Paris. Certainly, according to Münzenberg's wife, Babette Gross, Willi and Fischer were 'on friendly terms'.[53] He was similarly acquainted with Münzenberg's deputy, Otto Katz. Indeed, according to letters intercepted by British Intelligence, he would soon be liaising with Katz about getting the Republic's case put forward as widely as possible in England and America.[54] It is impossible to reconstruct exactly the sequence of events as to who put whom in contact with whom, but it is indisputably the case that, very shortly after his arrival in Madrid, Fischer was in touch with his old friend Julio Álvarez del Vayo, the Socialist journalist who on 4 September had become Foreign Minister in the government of Francisco Largo Caballero. One of Álvarez del Vayo's first priorities was to reverse the non-intervention policies of the democracies by getting the Republic's case before an international audience. It is hardly surprising that he should turn to Fischer for help in organizing the press and propaganda services of the Republic, nor indeed that Münzenberg and Katz should have wanted to encourage Fischer to help in this task.

Fischer wrote with indignation about what was happening to the Republic and with a burning determination to change the non-intervention policies of the democracies. In November 1936, after a week of bombing raids on Madrid, in which many children were killed, he commented: 'That Italian and German pilots should attack non-combatant Spaniards with bombs and machine-guns without provoking a protest as to force democracies to intervene to protect Spain's progressive republic is a pretty fair gauge of the world's moral calibre these days.'[55] In early December, after finding himself in the midst of the carnage produced by a bombing raid on Madrid, he wrote passionately of the wounded women, children and old people, of those left homeless and of those who piloted the waves of Junkers. He also wrote perceptively of the wider international implications:

> In Spain two vast world forces are testing each other out. So far the
> fascists have displayed more initiative and greater daring. They were
> the first to send airplanes and equipment. Now they are the first to ship
> troops. Their submarines and other naval craft spy on and interfere with
> the operations of the loyal Spanish fleet in eastern harbours. Their
> impudence is unequalled because England and France showed them in
> a score of situations – Ethiopia, the Rhineland, and so on – that he who
> dares wins. Democratic diplomacy is no match for fascist arrogance. If
> Franco conquers, Europe will be black or Europe will go to war as soon
> as Hitler and Mussolini are ready.[56]

In mid-December 1936, he went to Paris, still haunted by what he had seen in Madrid. He wrote to Freda Kirchwey: 'I wish you could do something about it. Can't you organize a committee to send relief, medicines – help in the evacuation?' He proposed going to New York to get something done to raise money for the Republic. His identification with the Republican cause was evident in his writing: '*We* need men and women – nurses – and money and materials. You mustn't allow America to get away with passivity in this great fight. Spain will suffer, but America too.'[57] That the democracies were turning a blind eye to the implications of what was happening in Spain filled Fischer with indignation. At the beginning of 1938, he would write: 'The Spanish people are paying heavily for the privilege of fighting the world's battle against fascism, paying not merely in dead, wounded, and captured, in the daily nervous strain, and in destroyed wealth, but in unrelieved undernourishment.'[58]

In his eloquent and lucid articles, Fischer returned over and over again to underline the absurdities of non-intervention. He pointed out that there was no control over Portugal whence arms flowed unimpeded to Franco. Realizing that the Germans and Italians were concerned not to antagonize Britain prematurely, indeed while Hermann Göring was in Rome discussing with Mussolini just how far they could go, Fischer wrote perceptively: 'If Great Britain called "Halt!" Hitler would mend his behaviour unwillingly and Mussolini happily.'[59] He believed that Washington's neutrality over Spain played into Hitler's hands and made American involvement in a future war inevitable. He showed how Germany and Italy could buy American arms that found their way to Franco, while the Republic was deprived of its rights under international law to buy the weaponry with which to defend itself. He wrote in vain that 'the only way to guarantee peace is to stop the fascist aggressors who alone want war. It can still be done in Spain. If Hitler and Mussolini are checked there, they will be weakened and sobered.'[60]

Fischer's friendship with Álvarez del Vayo and Negrín flourished on the basis of their shared commitment to the Republic and their belief that its survival depended on international opinion putting pressure on British, French and American politicians to abandon non-intervention. Certainly, Fischer made Herculean efforts to influence American and European public opinion in favour of a lifting of the US embargo on arms sales to the Spanish Republic. In December 1936, he went to Switzerland to cover Álvarez del Vayo's appeal to the League of Nations to scrap non-intervention. From Geneva he went to Moscow to see his family. In the course of his stay, he was treated by senior Kremlin figures as a valuable informant on Spain. He was received by Maxim Litvinov and by Georgi Dimitrov, Bela Kun's successor as head of the Comintern. He was grilled on the Spanish situation by General Semyon Petrovitch Uritsky, the chief of Soviet Military Intelligence, the GRU, who was in charge of aid to Spain. It was in Uritsky's home that Luli, the daughter of Constancia de la Mora, was staying after being evacuated to Russia. Fischer was not an agent – his relationship with these people was one of mutual benefit. He would tell them forthrightly what he thought was happening and what they should be doing. For them, his knowledge was useful, for him there was the frisson of mixing with men of power and of feeling that he was influencing them. Nevertheless, while he was in Russia, the second bout of trials of Old Bolsheviks had begun. His faith in the Soviet system was dwindling fast. For Fischer, like Koltsov, Spain seemed to be the only place where the hopes of anti-fascism could flourish: 'I was glad to leave Russia and immerse myself in a new vibrant situation where Russia showed its finest face.'[61]

From Moscow, he returned briefly to Valencia, where he reported to Prieto, Álvarez del Vayo and Largo Caballero on the meeting with Uritsky and then to Ambassador Rosenberg on their reactions. Fischer's ubiquity and influence can just be deduced from the opening of an article that he published in January 1937:

> I left Madrid on December 7 to fly to Geneva for the special Spanish
> session of the League Council. Thereafter I spent a week in Paris and
> eight days in Moscow and then flew back to Barcelona, where I arrived
> on January 6. I have now been in the Spanish capital four days, in which

time I have interviewed Prime Minister Caballero, four members of the federal cabinet, a number of party leaders and several well-informed generals.[62]

From Spain he went to the United States, where he gave several lectures. He was afflicted with an acute bout of arthritis while in New York and he used his enforced leisure to write up his material into the lengthy pamphlet *Why Spain Fights On*.[63] It was probably on this trip that Louis attended a fund-raising event for the Spanish Republic at the New York home of two Hollywood scriptwriters, the humorist and poet Dorothy Parker and Alan Campbell, her actor husband. Campbell wrote to him on the next day to comment sarcastically on his insensitivity:

> I am afraid that you misunderstand the reason for my annoyance last night. It was not the fact that you were so tactless as to mistake my wife for my mother. After all, I have been in Hollywood for the past two years and am accustomed to all kinds of stupidity and lack of perception. (Although, since the great disparity in age between my wife and myself is six years, she would have been an enterprising young girl in order to give birth to me.) The point I was trying to make is that you were at my house for presumably the same reason that I was – to get money for the Spanish Loyalists. Therefore, since I am deeply interested in the cause, I hate to see not only myself but numerous other people (names furnished on request) antagonized by your boorishness and your indiscreet comments on the people present who, after all, were here with a common interest. As to your question to Miss Parker, 'Are you as rich as Hemingway?' (and there's a way to win all hearts!), may I answer it by saying that if Hemingway's entire fortune at the moment is $825.60, the answer is 'Yes'. Because Miss Parker, like all poets, make enormous sums of money and keeps it all. In conclusion, may I suggest that you solicit funds for General Franco for the next few months. I guarantee you will thereby draw thousands of supporters to the Loyalist cause.[64]

Subsequently, Fischer sailed back to Spain with the Ambassador Fernando de los Ríos, who had not long before recruited a young Oklahoman from the Library of Congress to work for the embassy's press services. The radical librarian was Herbert Southworth, who would become a friend and collaborator of Fischer as a fellow lobbyist in the service of Negrín. At this stage, Fischer began lobbying by writing innumerable letters to politicians, including Eleanor Roosevelt.

Subsequently, he would lecture to large audiences and also address dinners of influential figures in both the United States and England.[65]

Despite Fischer's scepticism concerning Largo Caballero's capacity as war leader, under his nominal leadership – although thanks largely to Prieto and Negrín – the power of the central state was well on the way to being reasserted. In November 1936, Fischer had been permitted to attend a meeting of the inner war cabinet, perhaps in his capacity as quartermaster of the brigades but perhaps also because of his earlier letter to Largo Caballero. Prieto 'did very little talking and when he did speak he showed a marked deference to Caballero. What Prieto said was the most intelligent contribution to the entire deliberation.'[66] Largo Caballero resisted the idea of incorporating the party and trade union militias into a single regular army. His Soviet advisers had considerable difficulty in persuading him that the militia system was inefficient.[67]

It was hardly surprising that, after Largo Caballero had been replaced by Juan Negrín in May 1937, Fischer was delighted with the progress made towards the proper organization of a war effort. He wrote of Largo's 'isolation from the masses whom he refused, despite friendly pressure, to address even once during the months he was Prime Minister, his haughty behaviour towards his own colleagues and the slowness and inflexibility with which he met the problems heaped mountain-high around him, all caused many of his supporters to turn against him'. In contrast, he wrote: 'Negrín is an excellent executive, and that is what the conduct of the war needed. Things are now getting done quickly where millions can see the results – in the army. The people know that he has wiped out private violence, introduced order on the highways and streets, and created an atmosphere conducive to civil and military discipline.' He was particularly struck by Negrín's determination to maintain democratic principles despite the ongoing internal political clashes.[68]

During the summer of 1937, Fischer was in Valencia and involved in the preparation of the Anti-Fascist Writers' Congress. On one occasion, at a banquet, he was accompanied by Kate Mangan, who had been assigned to interpret for him and a visiting trade union leader.[69] He saw Kitty Bowler a couple of times. In the third week of June 1937, she wrote to her lover, the British Communist Tom Wintringham, 'Fischer had turned up again, says De los Ríos has done a grand job on Roosevelt with the result that some people in the State Department are definitely favourable'.[70] He was back in Valencia at the end of June and had dinner with the new prime minister, Juan Negrín, at Náquera near Sagunto. Negrín also arranged for him to have an interview with Azaña, although the president received him only on the strict condition that 'nothing he said was for immediate publication'. After their interview, at which Azaña had revealed to Fischer his hopes for British mediation to put an end to the war, Fischer crossed the street to have lunch with Negrín. The growing intimacy between them was reflected in the fact that some days later, Negrín invited Fischer to dinner along with Prieto, now Minister of War, Arthur Stashevsky, the Soviet trade representative, and the Communist Minister of Education, Jesús Hernández.

Afterwards, Negrín revealed to Fischer that he was about to go to Madrid. Negrín was going to be with General Rojo during the great diversionary offensive that was launched on 6 July at Brunete. Despite the blanket of secrecy that covered the operation and the exclusion of all correspondents, when Fischer appeared in Madrid, Negrín arranged for Prieto to give him a rare pass to visit the front and even put a Rolls Royce at his disposal for the journey from Valencia to Madrid. The next morning, they had breakfast and discussed Negrín's determination to move the capital to Barcelona. He also had a two-hour off-the-record interview with Azaña. He was the only foreign correspondent to visit the front during the battle of Brunete.[71] He sent two articles to *The Nation* written while in Spain, one datelined Valencia 28 June and, on 11 July, a much shorter and guarded one from Madrid.[72] A couple of days later, Louis left for Paris.

In both articles, Fischer was discreet about the level of his access to Negrín and to other politicians, such as Azaña, who spoke off the record. Nevertheless, in a long survey of the first year of the war, sent from Paris on 20 July, Fischer gave a revealing hint that his influence went far beyond that of a simple correspondent. He wrote:

> I recently walked down several central streets of Valencia with a cabinet minister at eleven o'clock in the morning and drew his attention to many hundreds of young civilian men. They were not in factories, they would be in their offices if they were government employees, and they were not in the army. All cities and villages in Loyalist Spain show a similar picture. The government needs greater power to put these vast human resources to work at winning the war. Yet the power necessary to accomplish this objective might easily become excessive and assume the quality of dictatorship. This is a delicate matter which further complicates the problem of political parties.[73]

In fact, Fischer's discretion was to cause some friction with Freda Kirchwey and *The Nation*. In response to the two tantalizing articles sent from Valencia and Madrid, she wrote on 14 July:

Your articles were interesting but they left me with a feeling of great uncertainty and a wish that I might discuss the whole inner situation with you face to face. Your second dispatch in particular was terribly provocative. I am hoping most earnestly that after you have left Spain and have no need to submit your copy for censorship, you will write a full and very frank analysis of the political situation both inside the government and between the government and its left opposition.

Concerned not just about possible official censorship, she went on to ask if there was any self-censorship on Louis' part:

Would you on account of your close personal relations with Negrín and your function as an unofficial adviser feel hesitant about writing fully? I can understand that this might be so and I would consider these reasons wholly legitimate. If such a situation exists, could you suggest a person as detached and trustworthy as, say, Brailsford who might go into the thing fully and without doing any harm.

Along similar lines, she wrote a fortnight later: 'You are really an exasperating guy. You mention a talk with Azaña and don't say anything even in private about what came out of it.'

Fischer was furious for a whole raft of reasons. He resented criticism at the best of times. He was, as always, annoyed at editorial changes to his text. Above all, he was incandescent that she should think that he would allow his relationships with politicians to affect his journalistic integrity. His letter of reply gives a vivid portrait of his way of working and of his pride in it: 'Your letter of July 14th was the most insulting I ever received from you. I hate indirection. If you don't want my contributions you can say so and I will go elsewhere.' He went on to explain how the article in which he had referred obliquely to the Brunete offensive was 'sent under special circumstances':

There was a strict censorship. No correspondent was allowed to send anything but terse official communiqués. The telephone service with abroad was suspended. No private messages could be sent. They wanted the facts of the offensive kept secret – and it was a good thing. Nobody was allowed to go to the front. I received special permission from Prieto (this is to be kept secret). When I got back in the evening I sat down to write my despatch. I knew the stiffness of the censorship. Under the circumstances I wrote more than anyone else did in that period and as much as was possible. What I said about the internal political situation was new and sensational and if you didn't appreciate it there doesn't seem to be much use going to a lot of trouble to get and forward such information to you. I was hampered by censorship and by no other circumstance, as you suggest. The proof is in the article I sent from Paris wherein I elaborated a few points touched upon in the Madrid despatch. Nobody has analysed this complicated situation, as I have.

As so often, her reply was conciliatory: 'there is no sense in getting sore or in hurling abuse at my head. I like you and your writing and we all want what you can give.'[74]

Louis' letter to Freda had been written on 5 August 1937 from Moscow, whither he had returned not having seen his family for seven months. The atmosphere of the purges there could not have been grimmer. The denunciations, arrests and shootings mounted up, and many of the victims were acquaintances of Fischer and his wife. Previously, his visits home had been the cue for lots of Russian friends to drop by in search of news. This time no one came. The only moments of political interest came when he was received by Litvinov and Dimitrov. Appalled by what he was witnessing, he was soon desperate to get away: 'I was glad there was a Spain to work in and work for. It would have been mental torture to live in Moscow's atmosphere. The alternative would have been to go away and attack the Soviet regime in my writings and lectures. I was not yet ready to do that.' Moreover, he knew that, if he attacked Russia, he would not be welcome in Spain and he could not tolerate that.[75]

His stay in Moscow was relatively short and by mid-August he was back in Paris, where it may be assumed that he conferred with Otto Katz since he was, according to letters intercepted by British Intelligence, already liaising with him about getting the Republic's case put forward as widely as possible in England and America.[76] Nevertheless, the idea that he was somehow the tool of Katz and the Comintern is unsustainable in the light of his reply to Freda Kirchwey's next letter, which contained comments on his survey of the war. She had found the article 'interesting and far more full and analytical than the one which preceded it. Even so, I find your treatment of the internal political situation a bit ambiguous. You fail to state clearly just how you think the government should deal with the various Left elements and what you think the role of the Communist Party should be.'

Louis replied with a forceful statement both of his professional ethics and of his attitude to the Communist Party:

If my article from Paris is deficient in the material you say it lacks then I am a good journalist. It is not my business to say 'how the government should deal with the various Left elements and what [I] think the role of the Communist party should be'. That would be neither news nor analysis. It would be my bias. What I advocate is not much to the point in interpreting the internal political situation. My treatment is not 'ambiguous'. It is incomplete because there can be no final summary of a phenomenon which is unfinished and which changes daily. I have said that I don't like the policy of the Communist party – which doesn't mean that I have joined the anti-Communist parade. If it weren't for the Communists in and outside of Spain, Franco would be in Barcelona.[77]

In September, he went to Nyon, near Geneva, to report on the conference called to stop Italian attacks on British shipping in the Mediterranean. Negrín came to Geneva to take the chair at the League of Nations session. Each day, Fischer would telephone him and Negrín would invite him down to his suite, where he would often find him in the bathroom shaving, clad only in his pyjama bottoms. He would then take a bath while Fischer sat on a stool or leaned against the wall chatting with him. Out of their meetings came suggestions from Fischer as to how the Republic might be able to circumvent the international embargo on its arms purchases.[78] On his way back to Spain, he stopped off in St Jean de Luz with a letter from Negrín to Claude Bowers. Throughout October 1937, Fischer remained in Spain. He had flown to Valencia for the session of the Cortes being held there and was a guest in Negrín's presidential apartments, along with Otto Katz.[79] It was during this visit that he made the intervention that saved the job of Constancia de la Mora. His observations resulted in an article in which he wrote objectively about the Communists and was firmly supportive of the tandem of Indalecio Prieto and Juan Negrín. The article on the state of Spanish politics sustains the adage that journalism is the first draft of history. He commented on the contradiction between the Republican determination to maintain a functioning democracy while trying to run the control economy necessary for an efficacious war effort, writing: 'On the whole, an astounding amount of economic laissez faire, personal freedom, and political immunity continues to testify to the vigor of democracy and its disadvantages in war time.'

Fischer's main concern, which was reflected in his tireless efforts on the international front, was to try to persuade the democracies to abandon the self-destructive policy of non-intervention. With a mixture of frustration and prescience, he wrote: 'Some day the Western democracies' deeply dormant instinct of self-preservation will be sufficiently awakened to induce them to help themselves by helping the Loyalists.' His long article ended prophetically:

> The Republic's main preoccupation is not internal politics. It is the
> foreign situation. How slow these democracies are, how difficult to shake
> them into a realization of the dangers that beset them! One merely asks
> that the British be pro-British and the French pro-French. If these
> countries lack the sense to let Loyalist Spain safeguard their interests, they
> will be forced to do the fighting themselves later on.[80]

It was during this visit to Spain that Fischer persuaded Negrín to visit the International Brigade hospital at Benicasim. Accompanied by Otto Katz, Fischer took him around the hospital where, among the wounded, they met the commander of the British battalion, the veteran Tom Wintringham.[81] It is reasonable to suppose that Katz had come to Valencia so that the three of them could discuss Fischer's report on the propaganda deficit. Fischer's work on behalf of Negrín was considerable. As he put it: 'there was never any appointment – there wasn't any designation or elevation to some rank or anything like that'. Nevertheless, his collaboration included joining Negrín on his trips to international conferences, helping with the Republic's press services and liaising with the International Brigades. In mid-March 1938, he was with Negrín when the Republican prime minister visited Paris incognito to try to talk Léon Blum into sending more aid to the Republic. To the deep frustration of both Negrín and Fischer, Blum provided nothing more than a litany of excuses.[82]

Fischer's most passionate efforts went into trying to alert public opinion in the democracies to the absurdity of their governments' policies of appeasement. Three weeks after the October 1937 visit to Negrín, Fischer went to Paris, where he attended a dinner with – among other prominent diplomats and politicians – the Spanish and Russian Ambassadors Ángel Ossorio y Gallardo and Jacob Suritz, and Joseph Paul-Boncour, the former French premier. He then moved on to London carrying a card from Negrín to the Labour leader Clement Attlee. In Negrín's name, he invited him to visit the Spanish Republic. He wrote to Otto Katz to say that he had secured the definite assurance of Attlee, the MPs Ellen Wilkinson and Philip Noel Baker and Attlee's secretary that they would go to Spain on 2 December. As he proudly told Katz, he was extremely busy seeing influential people. The long list included the Duchess of Atholl; Sir Archibald Sinclair, later Minister of Aviation during the Second World War; Sir Stafford Cripps; David Lloyd George; the strategist Basil Liddell Hart; and the Spanish and Russian

Ambassadors, Pablo de Azcárate and Ivan Maisky.[83] He returned briefly to Barcelona for the first half of December before moving on to the United States. There, he gave lectures, wrote articles and talked to senators and congressmen in an effort to get the American arms embargo lifted. At the end of January 1938, Fischer cabled Otto Katz from New York, asking him to find out if it would be possible to persuade Lloyd George and the Dean of Canterbury to go to Washington for a dinner arranged for them by about one hundred members of Congress at the end of February or the beginning of March. On 24 February, he visited Eleanor Roosevelt in the White House. He received lots of sympathetic hearings but it was all to no avail.[84]

It was not until mid-March that he returned to Paris, where he was when he heard news that Barcelona was suffering round-the-clock pounding from Italian bombers. He hastened south and reached scenes of appalling carnage. He was arrested for taking photographs, although Constancia de la Mora secured his release.[85] After the recapture of Teruel by the Francoists, the rebels had launched a massive offensive through Aragón and Castellón towards the Mediterranean. In the last week of March, they crossed the Ebro into the province of Lérida. Fischer wrote from Barcelona:

> Two hundred planes can make all the difference between a fascist and a democratic Spain, between an encircled and a protected France, between a menaced and a secure position in the Western Mediterranean for the British Empire, between a threatened and a safe Czechoslovakia, between an encouraged and a checked international fascism, between a black and a brighter Europe. But in the whole of the democratic world there are not two hundred airplanes for a cash buyer who wishes to safeguard his hearth and home and national territory against invasion. In the case of America it is a stupid law which robs the Spanish government of the wherewithal to defend itself; in the case of England it is blindness; in the case of France it is cowardice.[86]

The mixture of acute observation and passion was typical.

As the struggle went on, Fischer never lost heart. Nor did he hesitate to make his views known to cabinet ministers. One year after his first comment to a minister in Valencia on the subject of young, able-bodied non-combatants, he was still pressing his views on the same theme. In mid-April 1938, he referred to recent conversations in Barcelona with five ministers of the recently reshuffled Negrín government. A topic of conversation was that 'human reserves have scarcely been tapped (too many civilians are still on the streets), and if there is time to train them there will be no shortage of soldiers'.[87] A week later, he travelled through Catalonia and was struck by the privations of refugees. He was even more taken aback by the fact that, at El Vendrell, twenty-five kilometres north of Tarragona, he found the shops well stocked. The availability of clothes, toilet paper, soap, torches, radios, stationery and a host of goods long since disappeared from the shelves elsewhere : 'All this bespeaks reserves of material and the normal organization of life – in other words, a vast capacity for further resistance.'[88] It had led him back to his ongoing concern with resistance, regarding which he was entirely identified with Negrín's policy. The lack of restraint with which Fischer expressed his opinions to ministers may, as to some extent was the case with Koltsov, be merely a symptom of his combination of intelligence and impetuousness.

Within a month of his conversations with the members of Negrín's cabinet, he had travelled to Moscow for what would be his last trip to the Soviet Union until 1956. He arrived shortly after the trial and condemnation of Nikolai Bukharin, Alexis Rykov and a number of prominent Bolsheviks. Markoosha listed all of those they knew who had disappeared or been shot. Ostracized by virtually all of his erstwhile friends, terrified of being seen to have links with a foreigner, he received only a last visit from Koltsov, who was thirsting for news about how the Spanish Republic was holding out. Louis announced to Markoosha that he would not be returning to the Soviet Union because he could not bring himself to write favourably about what was happening and he would not be allowed to criticize it. Markoosha felt even more strongly than he did: 'Women, culture, literature, people's feelings, personal dignity were offended every day, and these, as she used to tell me when I was carried away by the success of the Five Year Plans, were more important to her than increased steel and coal production or even the construction of new cities.'

Louis had combated his doubts until now, reluctant to throw away the hopes for Russia that he had nurtured for fifteen years and because Russia was helping the Spanish Republic:

> At the front, on airfields, in hospitals, staff headquarters, and private apartments I met many of the Soviet Russians who had been sent to do their best for the Loyalists. In all the Spanish war, there were no harder workers, more valiant fighters, and more devoted partisans. They seemed to pour into the Spanish struggle the pent-up revolutionary passion which no longer found application in Russia.

He did not break openly with the Russians for fear of losing his family and of losing the ability to go on working with the Republican Government. Given the strength of the Spanish Communist Party, he feared that there would be obstacles placed in his way in Spain if he were to become *persona non grata* to the Soviets: 'I therefore limited myself to talking to Loyalist Prime Minister Negrín and a few of his close collaborators about the true horror of Russia and warning them against a dictatorship in Spain.'

The last straw was the fact that among the disappeared were men that he had known in Spain, Generals Gorev and his immediate superior General Jan Berzin, alias 'Grishin', the trade representative Artur Stashevsky, the first Ambassador Marcel Rosenberg and the Soviet representative in Catalonia, Vladimir Antonov Ovseyenko. Finally, he was ready for the break, but getting his family out would not be easy, since Markoosha was a Soviet citizen and their two sons, although American citizens, had been born in Russia. He wrote to the head of the NKVD, Yagoda, requesting the necessary documents, but was ignored. Six months passed and he asked Litvinov for help. He said he could do nothing and urged Fischer to write to Stalin. He did so in November 1938, but again received no reply. In desperation, on 3 January 1939, he asked Eleanor Roosevelt for an appointment. She saw him three days later. As a result of her intervention, passports for Markoosha, George and Victory Fischer to leave Russia appeared on 21 January.[89]

At the beginning of July 1938, Fischer was invited to England for a meeting with David Lloyd George, who sympathized with the Spanish Republic. On 12 July, he addressed a meeting at the House of Commons attended by seventy-two MPs. By the next day, Fischer was back in Paris, writing optimistically of the Spanish Republic's ability to fight on.[90] In August, he returned to Spain and visited the Ebro front. He interviewed Lieutenant Colonel Juan Modesto, the commander of the Army of the Ebro, the handsome Communist who had been challenged by Hemingway to a duel for flirting with Martha Gellhorn. En route back to Barcelona, the car in which he was travelling with Henry Buckley, Herbert Matthews and another correspondent was strafed and bombed by a rebel aircraft. On his return to Barcelona, he had lunch with Negrín. He continued to advocate the resistance policy of Negrín and del Vayo as against the inclination of Azaña and Prieto to contemplate – in vain – the prospect of a negotiated peace.[91]

On 28 November 1938, as the inexorable advance of Franco's forces spelt the end for the Republic, Fischer's optimism was replaced by a blazing indignation. He wrote a passionate account of the gruesome effects of rebel bombing raids, stressing the precision with which civilian areas in Barcelona were being targeted. It was published in Britain on 10 December and in the United States on Christmas

Eve.[92] During this visit to Barcelona, Fischer met up with Luis Araquistain and his wife Trudi, who would not talk to her sister Luisi, because of the intense hostility between their husbands. It is a tribute to Fischer's amiability that he managed to remain good friends with both sides and served as a conduit for family news between them. Not entirely seriously, Luis and Trudi used to blame Fischer for the overthrow of Largo Caballero in May 1937, as a result of which Araquistain had resigned as Spanish Ambassador in Paris. He commented:

> Because of my access to key-men in Spain and Moscow, people attributed
> to me powers and designs which I did not have. My contacts enriched my
> life. I cultivated those contacts zealously and refrained from spoiling them
> by indiscretions or boasts. My experience with men of stature helped me
> grow and I look back on them with great pleasure and gratitude. I think
> I enjoyed the confidence of Communists, non-Communists, and anti-
> Communists because I resisted party clichés and narrow loyalties. There
> is nothing heavier than a party card and I never carried one.[93]

From early 1938 onwards, along with Ernest Hemingway and the correspondents John Whitaker and Edgar Mowrer, Fischer was involved in efforts to repatriate American volunteers from the International Brigades. Fischer had secured large sums from the Republican Government to pay for American volunteers to return home. However, he declared later:

> By this time, there were wounded Americans and others who for various
> reasons wanted to go home, and Negrín, who was by this time Prime
> Minister and had a million things to do, was in no position to check on
> whether money should be paid out to this American or to that American,
> or to this American group or to that American group. He asked me if I
> would act as his intermediary with the Americans of the International
> Brigade.

When American Brigaders were to be repatriated, Fischer would draw on funds from the Negrín government's financial representative in Paris.[94] An indication of the authority wielded by Fischer can be found in a telegram among his papers to David McKelvey White, the secretary of the Friends of the Abraham Lincoln Brigade in New York. White had issued a fund-raising pamphlet calling for donations towards the $125 needed to bring home each veteran. Fischer imperiously ordered White to desist from campaigning to raise money because it was damaging the Republic's reputation. Indeed, several of those involved in the process were under the impression that Fischer was more interested in getting new volunteers in than wounded volunteers out, although he vehemently denied this when it was suggested by the American Ambassador in Paris, William Bullitt.[95]

Like Negrín, Fischer entered 1939 still believing that the Republic could hold out until the democracies came to their senses. Both believed that Franco's threats of vengeance would keep the Republican population fighting. The Caudillo had declared, on 7 November, to the vice-president of the United Press, James Miller, that he had the names of two million Republicans scheduled for execution.[96] Franco's rejection of any possibility of an amnesty for the Republicans and his loudly announced commitment to a policy of institutionalized revenge meant, according to Fischer, that for much of the population in Loyalist Spain, 'they have nothing to lose but the rope or a prison sentence. Better to fight.' He contrasted this with Negrín's announcement that the Republic would declare a complete amnesty and renounce vengeance.[97]

On 4 March 1939, Colonel Segismundo Casado, commander of the Republican Army of the Centre, staged a military coup against Negrín in the hope of ending the slaughter, a hope based on the erroneous belief that his contacts in Burgos would facilitate peace negotiations with Franco. When Casado thereby played into Franco's hands and brought Republican resistance to an end, Fischer wrote a typically perceptive and prophetic article. He pointed out that, if the Republic had been dominated by the Communists, it would have been impossible for Casado to have been successful. He explained the Casado phenomenon in terms of defeatism and war-weariness: 'The longer the war lasted, the more some Loyalists despaired of a successful conclusion; therefore they abhorred the Communists, who had faith and tenacity.' He ended his article sadly anticipating exactly what would happen among the about-to-be exiled Republicans:

> A defeat after so many lives have been lost and the country ruined must release boundless resentment. The Spaniards abroad will now proceed to cut one another's throats with denunciatory books and speeches. Services will be forgotten; the moral capital accumulated in the heroic struggle will be dissipated in an internecine war of mud-slingers. That has already begun. Each will proceed to explain how he would have saved the situation and why the others failed. What an end to a glorious struggle for freedom![98]

All that was left was to work for the Republican cause in exile. Already, Fischer had sent material on the Italian bombing raids on Barcelona to Jay Allen to help in the fight to change the US position. He had even suggested the line to take: 'While America eats Thanksgiving dinner, Barcelona is in deep mourning.' Fischer and Jay Allen, along with Herbert Southworth, had gone on lobbying for American support for the Republic even though defeat was inevitable.[99] In late August 1938, Otto Katz had written to Isabel Brown, a leading light in the British Aid Spain Movement, passing on a request from Louis for a reprint of many thousand copies of a comment in the *Evening Standard* on Juan March and anti-Semitism in Franco's Spain: 'If you agree, will you please have it made and send about 5,000 copies to Jay Allen, New York.'[100] In a similar spirit, in January 1939, Fischer had written from New York to Katz: 'Please send to me, with copies to Jay, everything, literally everything, showing pro-Loyalist sentiment on the part of European Catholics, pro-church acts and statements in Loyalist Spain, and racist, Anti-Semitic, Anti-Masonic, Anti-Protestant views in Franco territory.'[101] After the war was over, Fischer accompanied Negrín on the *Normandie* to New York, where they arrived in May 1939. He helped Negrín write speeches in English and to gain access to senior American officials, including Secretary of State Cordell Hull.

Three months later, he was back in Europe and was in Paris when Hubert Knickerbocker rang to tell him about the Nazi–Soviet pact. He was devastated, and could 'see only unrelieved blackness'.[102] Even as his horror at Soviet policy intensified, his commitment to the defeated Spanish Republic never wavered. Fischer would continue to work for Negrín and the Republic for quite some time after the Republic's defeat. Nevertheless, his main anti-fascist hopes now focused on London. In the autumn of 1939, he interviewed a wide spectrum of the British political class, including both Winston Churchill and the influential diplomat Sir Robert Vansittart. He visited the Foreign Office in London on 10 October 1939 to request that he be given confidential information to help in the production of an article. He was received by a relatively senior official, Ivo Kirkpatrick, who minuted:

> I received Mr Louis Fischer, an American journalist, today at the request of Mr Peake, who described him as a thoroughly reliable and discreet man. He writes for the American 'Nation' and other periodicals, and is in touch with the 'New Statesman' here. He worked for many years in Moscow and became infected with Bolshevik ideas; but he described himself now as disillusioned and disappointed. What he wants us to do is

supply him, either in writing or verbally, with material for an article on the course of negotiations with Russia. He is prepared to submit his article for our approval and to guarantee that he will not reveal that he obtained the information from British official sources.

Kirkpatrick responded that the British Government would come in for fierce criticism if it became known that information, withheld from Parliament, had been supplied to a foreign journalist. Fischer

retorted that his discretion was known to the authorities here and that he would not be traced to us. Moreover, he pointed out that whilst we might be well advised not to publish our side of the case for fear of treading on Soviet susceptibilities, it would, on the other hand, be good propaganda to put it out through a neutral source – particularly an organ like 'Nation', which was distinctly leftist in character and could not be accused of Conservative propaganda.

Kirkpatrick inclined to give Fischer a verbal account in return for 'the right to make any alterations we think necessary in the article which he submits for our approval'. When the issue was put to more senior figures, they decided that Fischer should be given short shrift. Orme Sargeant wrote:

I dislike this idea. We don't want at this moment to remind the public of our abortive negotiations with the Soviets, and still less do we want to 'ventilate' our grievances as to the behaviour of the Russians and their treatment of us. But unless we do bring out grievances, any account of negotiations needs present us as cutting a rather sorry figure – I should be in favour of not giving Mr Fischer any encouragement.

The Head of the Foreign Office, Sir Alexander Cadogan, brought the matter to a close when he wrote: 'I don't think we should touch this.'[103]

The fact that Fischer was seen in Paris in September 1939, in contact with French Communists and distributing funds, led a local agent of the British Secret Intelligence Services to conclude that he was a Soviet agent. This allegation appeared more than once in SIS reports, although usually on the basis of circumstantial evidence, often to do with his distribution of money.[104] It is impossible to say definitively, but it is likely that the moneys in question came, not from Moscow, but from the funds of the Spanish Government in exile, and were destined for the relief of International Brigaders. In fact, another report suggested that his main contacts had been the exiled Spanish premier Juan Negrín and the novelist André Malraux. This time, the British agent reported that the source for the idea that Fischer was a Soviet agent derived from the Trotskyist press.[105] During the visit to London when he met Churchill, he was under constant surveillance. However, his watchers reported: 'He receives a fair number of visitors when he is at the Howard Hotel, and it is understood that most of these are persons who are of a similar profession to himself. Nothing unusual in his behaviour or contacts has come under notice during the time he has been at this hotel.'[106]

Louis was now committed to the campaign to bring the USA into the war. In July 1941, he left New York with a view to spending ten weeks in London.[107] While in London, Fischer's telephone was tapped by British security services. A report on a conversation with Frederick Kuh described Fischer as 'Propaganda Manager for Dr Negrín'. In the conversation itself, Fischer reluctantly described a large luncheon party that he had attended with Brendan Bracken, Lord Cranborne and Lord Moyne. The conversation at the table had ranged over various issues, including Munich, whether the Russians could have fought to prevent the German invasion of Czechoslovakia and potential Allied help for the Soviet Union, but, to Kuh's annoyance, Fischer refused to go into detail.[108]

The 1941 publication of his memoirs in New York caused Fischer some problems with his Spanish connections. He received a letter from the one-time Spanish Republican Ambassador to London, Pablo de Azcárate, which criticized details of the book. Fischer replied at length:

I have read your letter in all friendliness as I am sure it was conceived. I would like to see you to talk about this and other matters. I suggest Wednesday right after lunch or Thursday some time. Will you 'phone me? Meanwhile, I wish to make a few comments without prejudice to our conversation. The figures about the assets of the republican treasury were printed regularly in the bulletins of the Bank of Spain. The data about debts to Russia, etc, I included to answer arguments by Araquistain and many others that Moscow had controlled all loyalist transactions…I used the interview with Azaña because he had died and death releases one from discretion. Anyway, the interpretation of the Besteiro affair reflects credit on those in the Negrín cabinet. I was perhaps wrong in using the Giral information…the 13 points story, I assumed, was correct. I got most of it from Vayo…The Vita tale did not come from a Spanish source…You are quite right about the La Baule bet and I apologise. I will try to delete it from the British edition which, however, is soon to go to press.[109]

More ferocious criticism emanated from Negrín's enemies in the Prieto wing of the Spanish Socialist Party, who accused Fischer of having received huge sums of money from Negrín to boost his image. Again this is almost certainly a reference to the sums given by Negrín for the repatriation of International Brigaders.[110]

In contrast, the book seems to have absolved Fischer from accusations of being a Soviet agent. A report from the United States received by the British Intelligence Services stated:

> Louis Fischer for many years has been considered the most prominent exponent of the Foreign Policy of the Soviet Government. He lived for many years in Russia as a correspondent of the New York 'Nation', and he married a Russian woman. His account of his disillusionment with the policy of Stalin is told at great length in his latest book 'Men and Politics', to which you refer. His political beliefs are expounded in the final chapters. He is not a party man and cannot accurately be described as a communist. He is a left intellectual. The book, which has been out three months, received most favourable reviews. Fischer has been violently attacked by the American Communists as a traitor and an agent of International Capitalism. During the past years he devoted much of his time to the Loyalist cause in Spain. Fischer has many enemies, of which Eugene Lyons is one. The latter, author of 'Assignments in Utopia' revoked Stalinism some years before Fischer, hence his dislike. Whilst it is possible that he will contact many left wing personalities during his time in England, in view of his attitude toward the war before Soviet intervention and since, there is little to suppose that his activities will be inimical to the interests of Great Britain.[111]

While in England in September 1941, Fischer interviewed Clement Attlee, now deputy prime minister. While waiting to be admitted to his presence, there took place a minor incident which revealed how irritable Fischer could be on occasions. A Mrs Phillimore, on Attlee's staff, was introduced to him and said:

> 'May I copy Miss Wilkinson's way and ask what you do?' 'Oh', he said, 'I'm attached to the *Nation* of America.' 'Oh', I said, 'of course you're Mr F.I.S.C.H.E.R., I've often read your articles. I wish I'd known.' I said, 'Have

you come from Russia?' 'No, no, I haven't been in Russia, I've been in England for five weeks.' 'Oh', I said, 'I wish I'd known. I'd so much like to have asked you to meet people.' He looked me in the eye and said: 'It would be no good. I don't like the English upper classes. I wouldn't have come.' Well, I looked at him and I said: 'You be blowed! Who do you think you're talking to? I've belonged to the Labour Party for years.' So he said: 'Oh yes, I know your sort.' So I said: 'Oh no, you don't know anything of the kind!' Then Mr Attlee sent for him. It shook me very much. I felt, 'Good gracious, I don't look like that do I?'[112]

On his return to the United States, he was appointed a contributing editor of *The Nation*, along with Norman Angell, Reinhold Niebuhr and Julio Álvarez del Vayo. This was a reflection of his commitment to persuading America to join the British in the struggle against Hitler.[113] He clinched his separation from his Russian period with a review of Walter Duranty's *The Kremlin and the People*. In the book, Duranty had portrayed the purged Bolsheviks as a kind of fifth column within the Soviet State. Fischer had dismantled this theory by pointing to the lack of any evidence to sustain it, arguing that, for Duranty, execution itself seemed to be taken as proof of guilt with the torture-induced confessions as a mere adornment. Duranty had written: 'It is unthinkable that Stalin…and the court martial could have sentenced their friends to death unless the proof of their guilt were overwhelming.' Fischer commented dryly: 'How naïve of the cynic!'[114]

After enabling his family to leave the Soviet Union, Louis did not live with them, preferring to stay in hotels when in the United States. Although his marriage did not survive, he never divorced and always remained on relatively cordial terms with Markoosha. They helped each other write their autobiographies. They maintained a voluminous correspondence from which her feelings about their marriage can be deduced. In the main, her letters were deeply loving. However, in September 1940, she wrote:

> When I saw you on Saturday, something has happened. The feeling I had for almost twenty years of inferiority and humiliation in your presence has definitely and finally revolted. I am thoroughly through and I never again am going to hear from you that what I say is unimportant or uninteresting or see the feeling of disgust on your face.

Some weeks later, as she continued to work on her book and reread letters that she had written to him, she wrote:

> Do you realize how much I have loved you and how much warmth and tenderness I have given you? You have hurt me a whole lot, Lou, these last years, much more than I deserved from you. One thing would console me. To know that this ocean of feelings I spent on you was not wasted: that you knew about it, that it has helped you, that you never had the feeling during the years we spent together that your personal life was empty.

Nothing in his short and factual letters to her suggested that he responded to what she had said.[115]

Indeed, while Markoosha concentrated on building a career as a writer and lecturer, he felt free, as he had always done, to indulge his own penchant for relationships with other women. An indication of his magnetism in this regard is revealed by the aftermath of a visit that he received in December 1942 from Mollie Oliver, a journalist who came to interview him. She was utterly entranced by his enthusiasm and charisma and wrote him a star-struck letter:

> I am sending this along to enclose the clipping of my interview on Saturday with you in Boston, after which you were kind enough to rescue my prose…My own impressions will remain clear-cut in my mind for some time. One hour's talking with you completely and seriously changed my life – the night before I was close to accepting marital obscurity, so to speak, to becoming an air corps instructor's wife, doomed to bridge afternoons and quiet ways. But now, and I don't think I'm too impulsive, I'm keen for this journalism game, realize it's the life I want. Doesn't that sound foolish? It's a sweet strangeness that shapes our lives. And thanks to your deep-tone of dynamic ideas, I have hope. And I hope to land in Russia!

They met again in the spring of 1943 and she wrote as if infatuated:

> What can I say to you? The second meeting was really something to remember. The two times I have talked to you I have felt terrifically alive, for the first times in my life, as if you were crystallizing so much for me. I can't understand the feeling, it's new but clean and good. You have an escapable vitality, such a sizzling realness about you. Life is good as you

said. Can't help but know that you did the interviewing. I did all the talking and women are supposed to be mysterious but so help me, I felt like it…Write to me.

As the correspondence progressed, it became more flirtatious and contained hints of their beginning an affair, although there is no surviving correspondence to suggest that they did.[116]

Just as Fischer had a remarkable ability to get politicians to open up to him, he apparently had a similar capacity to achieve intimacy with women, making them feel heard and understood, and, in cases like that of Mollie Oliver, encouraged or enabled to develop as writers. It had been like that with Tatiana Lestchenko and Gerda Grepp and with numerous other women in the future. However, because of his obsessive need to safeguard his independence, he ended relationships as soon as the women told him they loved or needed him. Perhaps for that reason, he had inclined to affairs with married women because he felt that they were less likely to make demands upon him. One important friendship that developed into something more was with Diana Forbes-Robinson, the wife of Jimmy Sheean. Throughout the Spanish war and after, she wrote to Louis weekly and sometimes more often. The correspondence was interrupted in 1940. After immense difficulties in her marriage, it was renewed on a more passionate basis in 1951.[117]

By the autumn of 1942, Fischer had found a new cause, that of the independence of India, and a new hero, Mahatma Gandhi. He went to India, interviewed the Mahatma, and began to write articles about the Indian situation. He wrote three books about Gandhi, one of which, a full biography, would be filmed under the direction of Sir Richard Attenborough. He tried to get President Roosevelt to back Indian independence. His articles provoked heated polemics in *The Nation* about the ethics of stirring up India while the British were still involved in the fight with Hitler. For him, the post-war peace was paramount, which led to disagreements with his friend Freda Kirchwey, who was more interested in first winning the war.[118] After an association going back to 1923, in June 1945, Fischer broke publicly with *The Nation*, resigning his position as a 'contributing editor' and accusing the editors of having a 'line' and having a 'misleading' coverage of current events, by which he meant that, in the wake of the Yalta meeting of Roosevelt, Stalin and Churchill, the magazine was becoming too pro-Soviet.[119] He began writing for small anti-Communist liberal magazines such as *The Progressive*, as a foreign correspondent and commentator on international politics, focusing on Europe and Asia, especially Communism in the Soviet Union and China, imperialism, and the problems of emerging nations. Despite this change, he always remained committed to the Spanish Republic.

The Spanish experience would always follow Fischer. In 1952, it facilitated two long interviews with Marshal Tito in Belgrade.[120] Then, in 1953, when working for the *New York Times*, Fischer was approached by Alexander Orlov, the senior NKVD agent he had met in Spain. Orlov had defected to Canada in 1938 and, after the death of Stalin, he was in New York trying to sell his memoirs to *Life* magazine for a small fortune. The editorial director of the magazine, John Shaw Billings, before parting with a substantial sum, wanted proof that Orlov really was the former NKVD general that he said he was. Having failed to make contact with Ernest Hemingway, who was in Cuba, the person Orlov chose to vouch for him was Louis Fischer. They had met in Madrid in September 1936, having been introduced by the Russian Ambassador Marcel Rosenberg. On 17 March 1953, Orlov telephoned Fischer, saying only that he was 'a friend from Spain' and requesting a meeting. Although Orlov had not identified himself, Fischer seemed to recognize him and invited him to his apartment. When he arrived, Fischer greeted him as 'my old friend Orlov' and quickly agreed to vouch for him to *Life* magazine. Orlov asked him to come to his lawyer's office, where he confirmed the former agent's real identity to Billings.[121]

The publication of the serialized book alerted the FBI to the presence of Orlov in the USA and provoked J. Edgar Hoover to initiate an investigation. In consequence, Fischer was questioned by FBI investigators on 19 May 1953 about Orlov's role in Spain. When it was Orlov's turn to be interrogated by the FBI, he attempted to divert attention from his own crimes by pointing the fingers at others. He claimed that Fischer had once been a Soviet intelligence agent. However, it has been pointed out that 'the NKVD records contain no evidence that Fischer was ever anything more than a Communist sympathizer' and that the FBI, despite its extremely thorough investigation of Orlov, chose to take no action against Fischer. Accordingly, it appears that Orlov was falsely accusing Fischer by way of revenge for, and to cast doubt on, allegations in his book *Men and Politics* about the activities of the Russian security services in Spain. Within Stalin's Russia, Fischer, far from being considered agent material, was regarded as a Trotskyist sympathizer.[122]

Fischer returned to Russia in 1956 and wrote a book about his experiences called *Russia Revisited*. He wrote biographies of Stalin, Gandhi and Lenin. The latter, *The Life and Death of Lenin*, won the National Book Award in 1964.[123] In December 1958, he was appointed a research associate at the Institute for Advanced Study in Princeton. In 1961, he became a lecturer at Princeton

University's Woodrow Wilson School of Public and International Affairs, where he taught Soviet–American relations and Soviet foreign politics. In October 1967, he wrote a letter in favour of British entry into the European Economic Community.[124]

Throughout this period, he had numerous love affairs. His correspondence contains dozens of pages of love letters from unidentified women. In 1957, 'Dede' wrote to him: 'what manner of a Man sees three women in as many hours? Who would allow such a thing? Well, I just want to be the last.'[125] The letter was from Deirdre Randall and her wish would eventually come true. The relationship with Deirdre was one of the most enduring in his life. Although forty years Louis' junior, Deirdre was deeply in love with him but tolerated his infidelities. About ten years after Louis first began to see Deirdre, another of his last relationships was especially tempestuous and involved Stalin's daughter, Svetlana Alliluyeva. At the time, Svetlana, aged forty-two, was an attractive woman with auburn hair, deep blue eyes and a seductive smile. Thirty years her senior, Louis Fischer was rather weather-beaten but still active and as alert as ever. Her years in the Kremlin, despite her problems with her father, had left her spoiled, petulant and arrogant. Having made a fortune from the sale of her book of memoirs, *Twenty Letters to a Friend*, she rented a house in Princeton in New Jersey. There in 1968 she met and fell in love with the Russian-speaking Fischer. Since she was not the only woman in his life at the time, she felt intense jealousy.[126]

Svetlana's suspicions fell inevitably on the beautiful Deirdre Randall, who had become Fischer's research assistant, certainly spent lengthy periods in his house and was effectively living with him. Svetlana was enraged after she found some of Deirdre's things in his house. On that occasion, she seems to have thrown Deirdre's clothes around. On another, Deirdre left Louis a note after Svetlana had telephoned while he was out:

> First she hung up, then curiosity got the best of her, and she asked who this was and I said, 'Deirdre. How are you?' and she said (and she talks with the elaborate sinisterness of people in Eisenstein movies, at least to me) 'and what are you doing there' and I said 'working of course' and she very sweetly, 'and are you wearing your beautiful nightgown?' and I said 'Of course not, most of the time I was in the bed naked'. Sorry I blew my top but she grabs me. I don't think she would have apologised, nor let me use her ironing board to iron the clothes she wrinkled. I think she's absolutely crackers and that one of us is going to end up with an ikon buried in her heart. My mommy told me not to fool around with married

men. If you get home at a reasonable hour, better call her. I really feel awful. I hate being bullied and I hate most of all being afraid and she's so crude I feel that I know what it was like to talk to Stalin.[127]

Svetlana's temper tantrums were the talk of Princeton's small academic community. One day, in the autumn of 1968, she arrived at Louis' house and banged furiously at the door. Inside with Deirdre Randall, Fischer ignored Svetlana as she ranted for over an hour, demanding that he return her presents to him. They amounted to a travel clock and two decorative candles. As her fury mounted, she tried to break in by smashing the windows at the side of the door. When the police arrived, they found her hysterical with blood pouring from her hands. It was the end of their relationship.[128]

The relationship with Deirdre, in contrast, was more lasting. Despite the difference in their ages, she could be critical, commenting to his son George on Louis' 'horrible hard, tough, thick-skulled frightening ego'. That perhaps made her more attractive to him, as did the fact that, while she adored him, she was something of a free-spirited child of the 1960s and did not pressure him with ambitions of monogamy. In one of her early letters to him, she wrote: 'I touch your hand. You are so vital. You've made me come alive. You are the sun. I feel you here. I am warm.'[129] With the encouragement of Deirdre, he continued to work, producing two important works on Soviet foreign policy. *Russia's Road from Peace to War: Soviet Foreign Relations, 1917–1941* was published in 1969, shortly before his death. He died on 15 January 1970, but Deirdre continued to work on the final preparation of the manuscript of the other, *The Road to Yalta: Soviet Foreign Relations, 1941–1945*, which appeared two years later.[130]

8

The Sentimental Adventurer:
George Steer and the Quest for Lost Causes

In early 1938, Martha Gellhorn wrote to her friend and mentor, Eleanor Roosevelt:

> You must read a book by a man named Steer: it is called the Tree of Gernika. It is about the fight of the Basques – he's the London Times man – and no better book has come out of the war and he says well all the things I have tried to say to you the times I saw you, after Spain. It is beautifully written and true, and few books are like that, and fewer still that deal with war. Please get it.[1]

Martha Gellhorn's judgement has more than stood the test of time. Steer was the correspondent of *The Times* whose account of the bombing of Guernica perhaps had more political impact than any single article written by any correspondent during the Spanish Civil War. The Labour Member of Parliament for Derby, Philip Noel-Baker, wrote to Steer about his reporting:

> Your telegrams from Bilbao have been of incalculable value to me, and your messages to the Times have been simply brilliant. I think no article in modern times has made so deep an impression throughout the whole country as your dispatch about the bombing of Guernica. I wish you could have heard the comments made by your Member of Parliament, Arthur Salter. I have quoted the dispatch at length in at least ten big meetings throughout the country, and it everywhere makes a tremendous impression.[2]

To a world which has witnessed the slaughter unleashed by Hitler and Stalin, to say nothing of the Korean, Vietnam and Iraq wars, the Spanish Civil War might well seem small beer. After Dresden and Hiroshima, the destruction of Guernica could appear to be no more than a second-rate piece of thuggery. Yet, for all that, the bombing of the sleepy Basque market town on 26 April 1937 has probably provoked more savage polemic than any single act of war since, and much of that polemic has revolved around Steer's article. This is partly because what happened at Guernica was perceived as the first time that aerial bombardment wiped out an undefended civilian target in Europe. In fact, the bombing of innocent civilians was a well-established practice in the colonies of the Western powers and had most recently and most thoroughly been carried out by the Italians in Abyssinia. Even in Spain, the bombing of Guernica had been preceded by the destruction of nearby Durango by German bombers at the end of March 1937. As the special envoy of *The Times* with the Republican forces in Bilbao, George Steer, who had witnessed the horrors of bombing in Abyssinia, described what was done at Durango as 'the most terrible bombardment of a civil population in the history of the world up to March 31st 1937'.[3] However, with the aid of Picasso's searing painting, it is Guernica that is now remembered as the place where the new and horrific modern warfare came of age.

It has been claimed increasingly of late that, but for Picasso, Guernica would have soon been forgotten as a regrettable but unavoidable act of war. That this is to miss much of the real drama of Guernica was one of the central points made by the most important book to be published on the atrocity, and indeed one of the most important books published on any aspect of the Spanish Civil War: *La destrucción de Guernica*, by the late Herbert Rutledge Southworth. Dr Southworth's painstaking and gripping study of the myth of Guernica and the web of lies that was constructed around it shows that the survival of the controversy owes as much to the work of George Steer as to Picasso.

Who was George Lowther Steer? As his biographer, Nick Rankin, discovered when trying to answer the question: 'Almost nothing remains of his personal letters and papers. His widow destroyed much in the 1940s before remaking her life; his parents' executors destroyed the rest in the 1950s.'[4] His life has to be reconstructed from his articles and books, from some scattered memories of people who saw him in Abyssinia, Spain or the fronts that he covered in the Second World War until his death at the end of 1944, and from his correspondence with his friend Philip Noel-Baker. What is clear from the surviving material is that Steer saw his journalism as a vehicle both to expose and thus to combat the horrors of fascism.[5] His father-in-law, Sir Sidney Barton, commented in the preface to one of Steer's books, *Sealed and Delivered*, that he had been 'at the front in the Second World War ever since this began in fact with the Italian invasion of Abyssinia on 1 October 1935'.[6]

This diminutive but brave, flame-haired reporter was born in East London, South Africa, in 1909, the son of Bernard Steer, managing editor of the important local newspaper, the *Daily Dispatch*. He was educated in England, as a scholar of Winchester College and then at Oxford University. At Christ Church, he secured a double first in Classical Greats (Mods in 1930 and Greats in 1932). He returned briefly to South Africa, working as the crime and baseball reporter for the Cape Town *Cape Argus* until 1933. He then came back to England to a job on the *Yorkshire Post*, working in the paper's London office in Fleet Street. From 1933 to 1935, he edited the 'London Letter' from the Fleet Street office, which was a mixture of stories, gossip, curiosities and theatre and other reviews sent to Yorkshire. He spent some time freelancing for the *Yorkshire Post* in the Saarland during the electoral campaign for the January 1935 referendum which saw its incorporation into Nazi Germany. Convinced that Italy was planning to invade Ethiopia, and tired of the snow in the Saarland – 'sun on yellow grass seemed better' – he returned to London and laid siege to *The Times*, which eventually hired him as a special correspondent to cover the coming Italo–Ethiopian war.[7]

After having his tonsils out and his teeth filled, he left London in June 1935, equipped with a gift from his colleagues at the *Yorkshire Post*, a topee bedecked with the colours of Winchester College. After a hazardous two-week journey, via Djibouti in French Somaliland, he arrived in Addis Ababa. He stayed at the Hotel Imperial, 'a wooden, balconied structure that looked as though it had been transplanted whole from the Yukon', where guests were expected to bring their own house-boy to clean their rooms. With typical commitment, Steer immediately began to learn the local language, Amharic. At the Imperial, he was eventually joined by a band of correspondents, among whom were several who were also to be in Spain, in particular the Australian Noel Monks, the Irishman O'Dowd Gallagher, the American Hubert R. Knickerbocker and the American-born Englishman Sir Percival Phillips. As Monks and Gallagher checked in, they were greeted by Steer, remembered by Monks as 'a short, slight man with an impish face'. The Abyssinian capital was both dusty and backward and the telegraph system particularly primitive. The censorship was crude, the cable clerks incompetent and, to save money, the correspondents invented bizarre abbreviations. Given the scarcity of news and the brevity of official communiqués, it was not surprising that others just invented their stories. Steer recalled: 'We dashed frantically about in cars between the Legations, the Foreign Ministry, the Palace and the radio, scratching together from the barren rockeries of Ethiopia a few frail seeds from which we hoped would flower exotically a story.' In early October 1935, when the Italians were about to invade, and Haile Selassie signed, but did not issue, an order for general mobilization, Hubert R. Knickerbocker produced an especially colourful account, with signals being sent by flaming beacons on the hills and beating drums in every village. In recognition of his inspiration, his fellow correspondents presented him with a small toy drum.[8] Knickerbocker would later write an equally invented account of the entry into Madrid of the military rebels some two and a half years before it actually happened.

Regarding cables from Europe and America, a messenger boy would bring a sheaf of messages to the first correspondent he met in the lobby of the Imperial. The result was that, on occasion, they were all able to read their rivals' messages and indeed to indulge in practical jokes. O'Dowd Gallagher claimed to have played a particularly effective one on Steer. He fabricated a cable purporting to be from John Jacob Astor, Lord Astor of Hever, the proprietor of *The Times*: STEER TIMES ADDIS ABABA WE NATION PROUD YOUR WORK STOP CARRY ON IN NAME YOUR KING AND COUNTRY — ASTOR. He claimed that such was the stir created by the cable that Steer was invited to interview the Emperor Haile Selassie, who gave him an unprecedentedly long interview. The story is surely apocryphal, since Steer had spoken to the Emperor for ninety minutes shortly after his own arrival and long before Gallagher appeared. By then, Haile Selassie insisted on questions being submitted in writing and seeing journalists for only a few minutes.[9]

It is certainly the case that, with or without Gallagher's mischief, Steer's sympathy with the Ethiopians led to him establishing a close personal relationship with the Emperor and being given access to his general staff throughout the war. Before the Italians invaded, he warned Monks and Gallagher: 'There's going to be a massacre unless the League of Nations get off their bottoms and stop Mussolini. These people are still living in the spear age. That's all they've got — spears.' Steer's support for such underdogs was reflected in *Caesar in Abyssinia*, which set out

> to show what was the strength and spirit of the Ethiopian armies sent against a European Great Power. My conclusions are that they had no artillery, no aviation, a pathetic proportion of automatic weapons and modern rifles, and ammunition sufficient for two days' modern battle. I have seen a child nation, ruled by a man who was both noble and intelligent, done brutally to death almost before it had begun to breathe.[10]

Moreover, as the jacket of his book proclaimed: 'The first to arrive and the last to leave, Steer was the only correspondent who saw the campaign from beginning to end.' His descriptions of Italian atrocities made his reputation as an intrepid war correspondent. They also ensured that, after the victorious forces of the Duce occupied the Addis Ababa on 5 May 1936, he would be expelled from Abyssinia merely eight days later, when Steer was accused of 'anti-Italian propaganda and espionage' on behalf of British Intelligence, and a warrant was prepared for his arrest on charges of transporting gas masks to Ethiopian troops and assisting in blowing up a road. 'It is not surprising', he told his newspaper, 'that the Italians did not succeed in finding evidence to support these charges.' The accusation derived from the fact that there had been a cargo of gas masks carried by a lorry on which he had made the perilous journey from Addis Ababa to the Emperor's northern headquarters at Dessye, just before it was occupied by the Italians.[11] On the other hand, hints of Steer's connections with the intelligence services would emerge from time to time.

Steer's nomination as special correspondent in Ethiopia had earned him the jealousy of Evelyn Waugh, who had reported for *The Times* five years earlier for the coronation of Haile Selassie, but came in August 1935 as representative of the pro-fascist *Daily Mail*. The relationship was not helped when, at their first brief encounter at a railway station, Steer failed to recognize the great novelist, taking him for just another journalist. Waugh was not exactly suited to the daily discomforts of being a war correspondent. Once, to steal a march on his colleagues, he had sent one of his despatches in Latin, a gesture which had not been well received back in London. Unlike many of his fellows, Waugh was fiercely pro-Italian, or as he described it, 'slappers with the wops', that is to say, on bottom-slapping terms with the Italians. He wrote to Diana Cooper: 'I have got to hate the ethiopians more each day goodness they are lousy & i hope the organmen gas them to buggery'. Waugh was as deficient in typing skills as in the milk of human kindness.

By his own account, Waugh was drunk much of the time in Addis Ababa and, on one occasion, he and his friend Patrick Balfour locked Steer in his room so that he would be unable to catch an important train. Bored, Waugh bought 'a very lowspirited baboon' which masturbated all day, and then, in the evenings, took it to the local nightclub, where it molested the whores. Steer would occasionally indulge in adolescent levity to make the time pass during interminable press conferences, and in the sterile meetings of the Foreign Press Association of which he was permanent secretary and Evelyn Waugh the minute-taker. However, he never reached the heights attained by Waugh. Indeed, Steer spent most of his time travelling all over Abyssinia and getting to know the country and its people. In October 1935, perhaps to escape Waugh, Steer moved out of the Hotel Imperial where he had been incarcerated in his room. It did him little good. Waugh and Balfour locked him in his new house and gave the key to the madame of a local bordello. Waugh's practical joke was not the only misfortune suffered by Steer in Ras Mulugeta Bet, as his home was named. At the beginning of May 1936, it was gutted during the looting that preceded the arrival of the Italians and he had been taken in by the family of the British Minister, Sir Sidney Barton. Waugh himself never actually made it to the front, which did not distress him overmuch since he did not take his reporting seriously. He claimed that the heaviest fighting he saw was among the journalists. Steer, he wrote, 'a very gay South African dwarf – is never without a black eye. Some say it is the altitude more than the bottle.'[12]

A mixture of grudging admiration and snobbish resentment was palpable in Waugh's review in the *Tablet* of Steer's book *Caesar in Abyssinia*:

> Mr George Steer was one of the first special correspondents to arrive in Addis Ababa in 1935, and one of the last to leave in 1936. He represented the most important newspaper in the world. He exhibited in a high degree the peculiar gifts required for that kind of journalism – keen curiosity of mind, a retentive memory, enterprise, a devotion to duty even at the expense of personal dignity and competitive zeal that was notable even in the international cut-throat rough and tumble of his colleagues.

Although the review went on to talk of liking, admiring and respecting him, the rest of Waugh's text was sharply critical. In the book, Steer had written: 'I came young, I went away older, I promised myself that I could never forgive and forget.' Not sharing Steer's anti-fascist sentiments nor his sympathy for the Ethiopians, Waugh sneered: 'Too credulous readers should remind themselves that a period of rapid adolescence is not the best time for accurate observation, nor a mood of personal resentment the best for a sober consideration of evidence.' Unable to forgive Steer either his anti-Italian stance or having pipped him to the *Times* job, Waugh complained: 'It is not enough that he thinks the war unjust. He will not allow the Italians the credit of working their destructive machinery with any skill.'[13] In his novel *Scoop*, Waugh took small revenge for Steer's hostility to the Italians and for the seriousness with which he approached his job, rendering him as 'Mr Pappenhacker of the *Twopence*'. The South African-sounding old boy of Winchester College, Pappenhacker had a profound knowledge of Greek and Latin, travelling with an Arabic grammar held close to his nose, the latter being an inaccurate reference to Steer's efforts to learn Amharic.[14]

On 4 May 1936, just nine days before the Italian expulsion order was delivered, George Steer had married Margarita Trinidad de Herrero y Hassett, who was the daughter of an English mother, a Spanish father and had been brought up in France. They had met in Abyssinia, where she had been correspondent for a Paris newspaper, *Le Journal*. She was his senior by ten years but irresistibly attractive. Small and sensuous, she was also independent and intrepid, one of the very few female correspondents in Ethiopia to cover the Italian invasion. Indeed, at one point, on visiting the victims of an Italian mustard-gas attack, she and a Spanish friend immediately volunteered to work as nurses. They had married at the British Legation in Addis Ababa while the town was being looted by marauding bandits. It was a high-spirited affair. Steer had worn a khaki shirt and trousers, a pair of old boots and a Deutsche Luft Verband cap that he purloined off an Ethiopian bystander. Margarita, in 'utilitarian woolies', carried a bouquet of lilies and daisies snatched from the legation garden. Accordingly, when the chaplain called on the couple to endow each other with all their worldly goods, there was audible merriment among the congregation. They then spent their honeymoon within the barbed-wire perimeter of the legation encampment.[15]

Barely had George and Margarita settled into a flat in Chelsea when he travelled to Spain as a 'special correspondent' for *The Times*. From 8 August to mid-September, he was at the Franco–Spanish border and witnessed the fall of the Basque town of Irún. He noted that, as Irún and Fuenterrabía were being shelled from the sea and bombed from the air, the Francoists had dropped pamphlets threatening to deal with the population as they had dealt with those in Badajoz. He produced despatches about panic-stricken refugees heading for France and on the destruction wreaked on the town by retreating anarchists enraged by their lack of ammunition.[16] Steer stayed in Spain after he ceased working for the newspaper in order to complete his book *Caesar in Abyssinia*, which was finished in Burgos. In October 1936, he drove through Old Castile and was appalled by the scale of the repression being carried out by the rebel forces in a rural area where there had been very little left-wing activity. He recalled later, when considering the relatively small scale of violence in Republican Bilbao, what he had seen in the rebel zone. He noted that 'the province of Valladolid, with a population of 300,000, a deal less therefore than Bilbao and her refugees, had lost five thousand men and women to the punitive revolvers of the Falange and the Guardia Civil and the military courts; they were still being executed at the rate of ten a day'. On the road from Palencia to Valladolid, he found graphic evidence of the terror: 'In small villages of Castile, numbering only a few thousand souls, like Venta de Baños and Dueñas, I found that the dead were one hundred and twenty-three

and one hundred and five, including "Red" schoolmistresses and wives of murdered men who had complained that their husbands were unjustly killed.'[17]

His friend and colleague, Noel Monks, would later refer to Steer having spent
six months in the Franco zone. In November 1936, Steer was seen in Toledo by
Peter Kemp, one of the very few British volunteers on the Franco side. Like so
many other correspondents, Steer was impatient of the restrictions imposed on
unescorted visits to the front. He was desperate to go north to witness the
Francoist siege of Madrid and, finally, after many complaints, permission was
granted for a trip to the capital. Kemp wrote later: 'Steer, whom I had known
before as a man of initiative and courage, could fairly be described as a natural
rebel. The incident which precipitated his expulsion is worth recording, as illus-
trating the fury of an Englishman confronted with Spanish plumbing.' As was
standard practice with the Nationalist press authorities, the journalists were
allowed to visit the Madrid front only as part of a specially conducted tour. The
large group of journalists included English, French and American correspondents, as well as the more favoured Italians and Germans. They were escorted by
a number of senior army staff officers whose job was:

> to explain the situation as it should be presented. A senior official of the
> Ministry of Press and Propaganda was in charge. A fleet of cars was
> assembled, ready to leave from the hotel at 8.30 in the morning. Soon
> after nine o'clock the party was ready to start, but there was no sign of
> Steer. After waiting a while in a fury of impatience, they were about to
> start without him when he appeared on the steps of the hotel with a set,
> exasperated expression on his face. In clear tones he addressed the
> assembled party: 'You pull-and pull-and pull-and nothing happens. You
> pull again, and the shit slowly rises. There's Spain for you,' he roared, 'in
> a nutshell.'[18]

It is, in fact, very likely that, long before his public complaint about the lava-
tories in Toledo, the Nationalist press censors were highly suspicious of Steer
because of his anti-fascist despatches from Abyssinia. Kemp remembered Steer
as 'a truly adventurous man of great initiative and charm, but a natural rebel
whose utter contempt for authority and the pomposity that too often went with
it was bound to land him in trouble'.[19] A temporary *Times* correspondent called
William F. Stirling wrote to London to complain that Luis Bolín regularly put
obstacles in the way of his work because he 'suffers from acute Anglophobia with
Times complications'. On 18 November 1936, Stirling wrote again to warn that

the Francoist authorities, by which he almost certainly meant Bolín, considered Steer to be a 'dangerous person in view of his record in Abyssinia…and his articles on Spain'.[20] Steer's book *Caesar in Abyssinia* had just been published, to the intense chagrin of the Italian military authorities, and, given the scale of their complaints, it is inconceivable that Bolín was unaware of this. Not surprisingly, Steer was expelled from the Nationalist zone in late 1936, which is why he ended up reporting on the Basque campaign from the Republican side. He told a Lieutenant Colonel Clark of the War Office that he 'was for some time at Salamanca, but was evicted owing, he thinks, to Italian influence; his book on Abyssinia has made him unpopular with them'.[21] The meeting with Clark substantiates the notion that Steer talked to British Military Intelligence even if he did not actually work for them.

Curiously, in May 1969, when Herbert Southworth tried to find out the circumstance of Steer's expulsion from the Nationalist zone, he was informed by the editor of *The Times Archives*: 'We regard with grave doubts suggestions that George Steer was once expelled from Nationalist Spain. There is nothing whatever in our papers to indicate this, and we feel sure that if he had been expelled, *The Times* would have stated so in the news columns.'[22] Yet Stirling's letters and a memoir by Steer's father discovered by Nick Rankin suggest that it was the *Times* records that were at fault. And the reason for that was simple. Having resigned from the newspaper in order to finish writing *Caesar in Abyssinia*, he was taken on again on a freelance basis. Steer's status as 'a special correspondent' actually meant that he was not on the staff, but paid by the column inch for any articles that happened to be accepted for publication.[23]

He returned to Spain, to Bilbao, at the beginning of January 1937. He met and very quickly became an admirer of the Basques in general and of their president, José Antonio de Aguirre, in particular. Indeed, he would become as partisan in favour of Aguirre as he had been about Haile Selassie. Steer was entranced by Aguirre's essential decency. Recalling the fact that, between 1924 and 1926, Aguirre had played in midfield for Athletic de Bilbao, he commented: 'he was captain of a soccer team again, and even if they lost they were going to obey the whistle and the rules. No biting; no hacking; no tripping.' The Basques came to symbolize for Steer the best elements of the fight against fascism. In his idealized and lyrical description, the Basque

> stands only for freedom between the classes, camaraderie and
> truthfulness, humanity under war conditions, unwillingness to fight for
> any extreme and violent doctrine; self-reliance, stubbornness,

straightforwardness and simplicity, dislike of propaganda on his own behalf, and an open-eyed guilelessness in face of the enemy's. He is naturally orderly, fitting into no fancy scheme of order. A big, handsome man, he is not aware of his own strength and beauty.

Steer could empathize with the Basques more than he had done with the Abyssinians and more than he could with Spain's left-wing Republicans. Indeed, Steer quickly came to share the Basques' traditional hostility to Spain, and when he spoke of 'the Spanish attack upon the Basques', he was referring both to the oppressively centralist military rebels and the forces of the Left.[24]

He reported on the bombing of Bilbao on 4 January and the consequent outburst of rage from the starving population. The Basque authorities characteristically lifted all censorship restrictions on the reporting. Having recently been expelled from the Nationalist zone himself and aware that in the Republican zone there were tight controls on what could be published, Steer was astonished and saw this as the Basques' expiation for what had happened. He was equally pleasantly surprised to find that his hotel was home to numerous right-wingers who lived without fear of molestation.[25] He visited the British Consul, who later reported:

> Mr. G. Steer, a 'Times' correspondent, who was recently expelled from insurgent territory, spent the past week in Bilbao. He was most cordially received and the President's secretary for Foreign Affairs was instructed to look after him and Madame Malaterre, a French lady of consequence in politics, and her companion, Monsieur Richard, a correspondent of 'L'Oeuvre' of Paris. A programme was arranged for visiting the prisons, the gun emplacements and fortifications constructed in a ring around the city, the tribunal in session and the historical Assembly Hall at Guernica. Mr. Steer told me that he was amazed at the frankness with which what were obviously military preparations of the most confidential nature were shown him. He expressed to me also his surprise at the orderly appearance of the city and its inhabitants which he had been led to believe, from reports circulating in insurgent territory, was showing all the symptoms of declining morale and disintegration.[26]

He had returned to London at the end of the month after receiving news that his wife Margarita was seriously ill. It was typical of the Basque Government's treatment of correspondents that a mine-sweeping trawler was placed at his disposal for the first leg of his journey, a thirteen-hour trip across a storm-tossed Bay of Biscay to Bayonne. He arrived in London to find the worst. Margarita died in premature childbirth on 29 January 1937. A funeral service was held in London, attended by Sir Sidney Barton, who had been British Minister in Addis Ababa when Steer had been there. Although devastated, Steer took advantage of his time in London to lobby government officials on behalf of the Basques. He also visited the War Office and reported in detail on the military situations in both the rebel and Republican zones. He gave detailed estimates of German and Italian positions and strengths, which may have suggested a more than casual connection with British Military Intelligence or simply reflected his determination to alert the establishment to the scale of Axis intervention. He returned to the Basque Country, burying his wife in Biarritz on 2 April.[27] His memoir, *The Tree of Gernika*, would be dedicated 'To Margarita snatched away'.

By the beginning of April, the grief-stricken Steer was back in Bilbao. On 31 March, Franco had unleashed a major assault on the Basque Country under the command of General Emilio Mola. The campaign opened with a frightening proclamation from Mola, both broadcast and printed in a leaflet dropped on the main towns: 'If submission is not immediate, I will raze Vizcaya to the ground, beginning with the industries of war. I have the means to do so.'[28] This was followed by a massive four-day artillery and aircraft bombardment in which the small picturesque country town of Durango was destroyed; 127 civilians died during the bombing and a further 131 died shortly after as a consequence of their wounds.[29]

Over the next three months, Steer was even more impressed than before by the facilities provided by the press officers of the Basque Government. The contrast with his own experience at the hands of Bolín in the rebel zone could not have been greater:

> the Basque authorities in Bilbao permitted me absolute freedom of movement and manoeuvre within their territory. I could go without hindrance or escort to any part of the front at any time. Other journalists were given the same facilities: that they did not use them as much as I did is no fault of theirs, for they had more to lose than I in the firing line.

Steer was always intrepid, not to say impetuous. Now, in the wake of the death of Margarita and his child, feeling that life had nothing to offer, he became positively foolhardy. In his visits to the front, he became so familiar with the Basque militia that, when he came to write *The Tree of Gernika*, he sometimes wrote 'we'

273

instead of 'they', something which he had also done with regard to the Ethiopian troops in *Caesar in Abyssinia*.[30]

Bilbao was starving.[31] The rebels had announced that they would permit no more supplies to enter the port. The pro-Franco British Ambassador Sir Henry Chilton had reported that the rebel fleet commanded the waters off the Basque coast and that the immediate approaches to Bilbao were mined. Since Britain had not granted belligerent rights to either side in the war, British merchant ships had the right to Royal Naval protection, at least outside Basque territorial waters. To avoid embarrassing clashes, the British Government decided on 8 April to order all British merchant vessels within one hundred miles of Bilbao to go to St Jean de Luz. Sir Henry Chilton reported that he had been informed by the Francoist authorities that they would repel by force any British merchant ships trying to enter the Nervión. Accordingly, on 10 April, the cabinet met and it was decided that the Royal Navy would not protect British shipping. There was a major uproar in the House of Commons that the world's greatest naval power should thereby admit to being unable to protect British merchantmen. The cabinet was choosing to believe unsubstantiated reports that the sea approaches to the city were mined and that Nationalist ships were operating inside the three-mile limit.

Writing from the Basque Government offices, Steer sent a telegram to his friend, Philip Noel-Baker, reporting that the blockade did not exist in any meaningful way 'for any power prepared to protect its shipping outside Spanish territorial waters'. He went on: 'Everybody here from Consul downward knows that there is not slightest danger and that blockade made out of paper and exists only in hopes Salamanca imagination Whitehall.' He reported that Basque mine-sweepers had ensured that the approaches to Bilbao were not mined. He further pointed out that Basque batteries of naval artillery with a fifteen-mile range were keeping the Nationalists at bay.[32] On the night of 19 April, the SS *Seven Seas Spray* left St Jean de Luz. Ten miles off the Basque coast, it was met by a British destroyer, which signalled the captain, William Roberts, that he entered Bilbao at his own risk and wished him good luck. On 20 April, Steer went out on a Basque trawler to meet the *Seven Seas Spray*, the first British ship successfully to run the gauntlet, and he was aboard as it made a triumphal passage down the nine miles of the river Nervión that lead to Bilbao. His moving account of the cheering crowds helped lead eventually to Royal Navy ships escorting subsequent food convoys. The British Government was forced to admit its mistake in believing that the approaches to Bilbao were mined and issued instructions to the Royal Navy to protect British merchant shipping.[33]

Steer's advice to the Basque leader, José Antonio Aguirre, to telegraph the British Government and his own numerous telegrams to Liberal and Labour members of the parliamentary opposition in London played a considerable part in reversing British policy.[34] As he wrote with a little exaggeration in *The Tree of Gernika*: 'I take to myself the credit that I, before anyone else, exposed the fake in the blockade and recovered the truth. A journalist is not a simple purveyor of news, whether sensational or controversial, or well-written, or merely funny. He is a historian of every day's events, and he has a duty to his public.' In words that echoed those of Herbert Matthews in Madrid, he continued: 'and as a historian must be filled with the most passionate and most critical attachment to the truth, so must the journalist, with the great power that he wields, see that the truth prevails'.[35]

Steer regularly went to the front, more often than not accompanying a Frenchman named Jaureghuy, who claimed jokingly to be a correspondent for the Salvation Army paper *Blood and Fire*, although he was actually a French secret service agent called Robert Monnier who was a military adviser to President Aguirre.[36] Steer continued to take far more chances than was prudent. On 26 April, along with Christopher Holme of Reuters, the Belgian Mathieu Corman of the Parisian *Ce Soir* and Noel Monks of the *Daily Express*, he spent fifteen minutes in a bomb crater at Arbacegui-Guerricaiz, west of Guernica, being strafed by the machine-guns of six Heinkel 51s. He was in Bilbao later that night in the Hotel Torrontegui having dinner with Corman, Captain Roberts and his daughter, along with Monks and Holme, when a distraught Basque official came in with news that Guernica was burning. They abandoned their table and immediately drove to Guernica, which was still ablaze when they arrived at 11 p.m. Like Monks and Holme, Steer had witnessed his share of horrors in Abyssinia and in Spain, but nothing prepared any of them for the desolation of Guernica. They watched helplessly as weeping Gudaris (Basque soldiers) frantically tried to dig the bodies out from the ruins. Steer stayed in the charred and still smoking ruins until the early hours of the morning of the 27th interviewing survivors – 'my authority for all that I have written'. He picked up three silver tubes of German incendiary devices and returned to Bilbao, where he slept on his story. The next morning, he spoke with many of the refugees who had reached the capital, before driving the fifteen miles back to Guernica to view the damage in daylight.[37]

Holme's reports appeared on 27 April in both the *Glasgow Herald* and the Manchester *Guardian*.[38] Steer's despatch was much more complete, which reflected his second visit to Guernica. His lengthy article, published on 28 April in *The Times* and the *New York Times*, subdued and unsensational in tone, was, in the opinion of Dr Southworth, probably the most important report filed by a newsman during the Civil War. More than any other commentator at the time, Steer managed to incorporate into his despatch a vivid sense not only of the scale of the atrocity, but of the extent to which it was an example of a new kind of warfare:

THE TRAGEDY OF GUERNICA

TOWN DESTROYED IN AIR ATTACK

EYE-WITNESS'S ACCOUNT

From our Special Correspondent. BILBAO, April 27

Guernica, the most ancient town of the Basques and the centre of their cultural tradition, was completely destroyed yesterday afternoon by insurgent air raiders. The bombardment of this open town far behind the lines occupied precisely three hours and a quarter, during which a powerful fleet of aeroplanes consisting of three German types, Junkers and Heinkel bombers, did not cease unloading on the town bombs weighing from 1,000 lbs. downwards and, it is calculated, more than 3,000 two-pounder aluminium incendiary projectiles. The fighters, meanwhile, plunged low from above the centre of the town to machine-gun those of the civilian population who had taken refuge in the fields.

The whole town of Guernica was soon in flames except the historic Casa de Juntas with its rich archives of the Basque race, where the ancient Basque Parliament used to sit. The famous oak of Guernica, the dried old stump of 600 years and the young new shoots of this century, was also untouched. Here the kings of Spain used to take the oath to respect the democratic rights (fueros) of Vizcaya and in return received a promise of allegiance as suzerains with the democratic title of Señor, not Rey [de] Vizcaya. The noble parish church of Santa María was also undamaged except for the beautiful chapter house, which was struck by an incendiary bomb.

At 2 a.m. to-day when I visited the town the whole of it was a horrible sight, flaming from end to end. The reflection of the flames could be seen in the clouds of smoke above the mountains from 10 miles away. Throughout the night houses were falling until the streets became long heaps of red impenetrable debris. Many of the civilian survivors took the long trek from Guernica to Bilbao in antique solid-wheeled Basque farmcarts drawn by oxen. Carts piled high with such household possessions as could be saved from the conflagration clogged the roads

Juan Negrín hosts a lunch to discuss the display of Picasso's *Guernica* at the Republican Pavilion in the forthcoming Paris Exhibition (summer 1937). From left to right, Jay Allen, Diana Sheean, Mrs Casper Whitney, Negrín, Muriel Draper and Louis Fischer.

At the League of Nations meeting in Geneva, December 1936, Louis Fischer (centre), with the Soviet and Spanish Foreign Ministers, Maxim Litvinov (left) and Julio Álvarez del Vayo (right).

(above) Tom Wintringham, Commander of the British Battalion of the International Brigades, was badly wounded at the Battle of Jarama. Here he is seen with his lover, and later wife, the American journalist Kitty Bowler, who looked after him.

(right) Safe-conduct issued to Kitty Bowler by the Catalan government, the Generalitat.

GENERALITAT DE CATALUNYA
COMISSARIAT D'INFORMACIÓ A L'ESTRANGER
BUREAU FRANÇAIS

La ciutadana Katherine Wise Bowler de nacionalitat nord-americana (E.E. U.U.) es traslladada a Catalunya per escriure informacions del nostre pais per a la premsa de Nord-Amèrica.

PREGUEM a les nostres autoritats que autoritzin la seva circulació pel territori català.

Paris 14 Novembre 1936

PER LA DELEGACIO FRANCESA DE LA COMISSARIA DE PROPAGANDA DE LA GENERALITAT de CATALUNYA

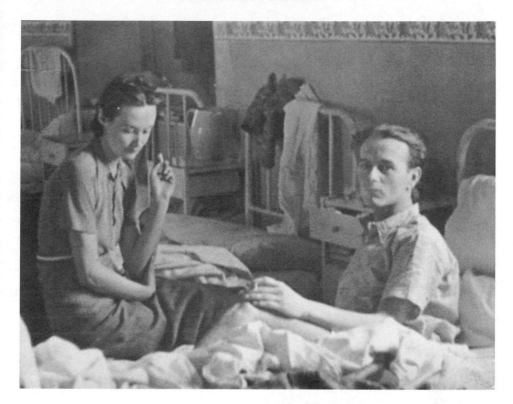

(*above*) Kate Mangan went to Spain following her lover, the German anti-Nazi Jan Kurzke who had joined the International Brigades. They are seen here in the hospital in Valencia after he was wounded.

(*right*) Kate Mangan's permission as a correspondent of the *Christian Science Monitor* to attend a meeting of the Spanish parliament in Valencia on 30 September 1937.

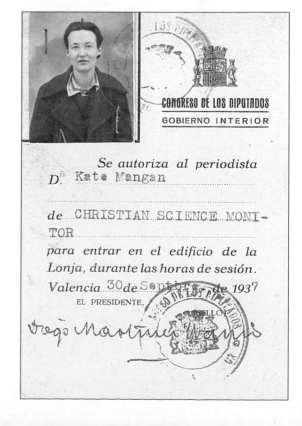

CONGRESO DE LOS DIPUTADOS

GOBIERNO INTERIOR

Se autoriza al periodista
Dª Kate Mangan

de CHRISTIAN SCIENCE MONITOR

para entrar en el edificio de la Lonja, durante las horas de sesión.
Valencia 30 de Septbre de 1937
EL PRESIDENTE,

(above left) Luis Bolín, the brutal foreign press chief in the rebel zone, showing off his uniform as honorary captain of the Foreign Legion.

(above right) Clipping of *L'Intransigeant*'s report of the murder by rebel forces in Mallorca on 17 August 1936 of its correspondent, Guy de Traversay.

(left) Left to right, the *Daily Mail* correspondent Harold Cardozo, the photographer Victor Console and the correspondent of the Havas Agency, Jean D'Hospital, accompanying Franco's columns on the Madrid front, November 1936.

CAMPAIGNING FOR THE REPUBLIC

John Dos Passos, Sydney Franklyn (back to the camera), the Dutch film-maker Joris Ivens and Ernest Hemingway in the Hotel Florida in April 1937 discussing their film *The Spanish Earth*.

Kajsa Rothman fundraising for the Republic in Stockholm.

Negrín and Louis Fischer at a meeting of the League of Nations in September 1937.

The Norwegian journalist Gerda Grepp (one of Fischer's lovers) with the Norwegian communist poet, novelist, dramatist, and journalist Nordahl Grieg (in white shirt) and Ludwig Renn, German writer and chief of staff of the XI International Brigade.

THE LAST THROW OF THE DICE

This photo, taken by Vincent Sheean with Henry Buckley's camera, shows Hemingway, Buckley, and an obscured Matthews (in beret) surveying the Ebro in November 1938.

Hemingway rows Robert Capa, Matthews and Buckley across the Ebro in November 1938.

AFTER THE WAR

(top left) Constancia de la Mora recovering after the war.
(top right) On a mission for British Intelligence in occupied France, Jay was captured by the Germans, accused of spying, sentenced to death, and imprisoned at Chalon-sur-Saône in Burgundy.
(bottom left) Arturo Barea and Ilsa Kulcsar together in their British exile.
(bottom right) Herbert Southworth in Sitges in April 1984.

all night. Other survivors were evacuated in Government lorries, but many were forced to remain round the burning town lying on mattresses or looking for lost relatives and children, while units of the fire brigades and the Basque motorized police under the personal direction of the Minister of the Interior, Senor Monzón, and his wife continued rescue work till dawn.

Church Bell Alarm

In the form of its execution and the scale of the destruction it wrought, no less than in the selection of its objective, the raid on Guernica is unparalleled in military history. Guernica was not a military objective. A factory producing war material lay outside the town and was untouched. So were two barracks some distance from the town. The town lay far behind the lines. The object of the bombardment was seemingly the demoralization of the civil population and the destruction of the cradle of the Basque race. Every fact bears out this appreciation, beginning with the day when the deed was done. Monday was the customary market day in Guernica for the country round. At 4.30 p.m., when the market was full and peasants were still coming in, the church bell rang the alarm for approaching airplanes, and the population sought refuge in cellars and in the dugouts prepared following the bombing of Durango on March 31st, which opened General Mola's offensive in the north. The people are said to have shown a good spirit.

A Catholic priest took charge and perfect order was maintained. Five minutes later a single German bomber appeared, circled over the town at a low altitude, and then dropped six heavy bombs, apparently aiming for the station. The bombs with a shower of grenades fell on a former institute and on houses and streets surrounding it. The airplane then went away. In another five minutes came a second bomber, which threw the same number of bombs into the middle of the town. About a quarter of an hour later three Junkers arrived to continue the work of demolition, and thenceforward the bombing grew in intensity and was continuous, ceasing only with the approach of dusk at 7:45. The whole town of 7000 inhabitants, plus 3000 refugees, was slowly and systematically pounded to pieces. Over a radius of five miles round a detail of the raiders' technique was to bomb separate caserios, or farmhouses. In the night these burned like little candles in the hills. All the villages around were bombed with the same intensity as the town itself, and at Múgica, a little group of houses at the head of the Guernica inlet, the population was machine-gunned for fifteen minutes.

It is impossible to state yet the number of victims. In the Bilbao Press this morning they were reported as 'fortunately small', but it is feared that this was an understatement in order not to alarm the large refugee population of Bilbao. In the hospital of Josefinas, which was one of the first places bombed, all the forty-two wounded militiamen it sheltered were killed outright. In a street leading downhill from the Casa de Juntas I saw a place where fifty people, nearly all women and children, are said to have been trapped in an air raid refuge under a mass of burning wreckage. Many were killed in the fields, and altogether the deaths may run into hundreds. An elderly priest named Arronategui was killed by a bomb while rescuing children from a burning house.

The tactics of the bombers, which may be of interest to students of the new military science, were as follows: First, small parties of airplanes threw heavy bombs and hand grenades all over the town, choosing area after area in orderly fashion. Next came fighting machines which swooped low to machine-gun those who ran in panic from dugouts, some of which had already been penetrated by 1000 lb. bombs, which make a hole 25 ft. deep. Many of these people were killed as they ran. A large herd of sheep being brought in to the market was also wiped out. The object of this move was apparently to drive the population underground again, for next as many as 12 bombers appeared at a time dropping heavy and incendiary bombs upon the ruins. The rhythm of this bombing of an open town was, therefore, a logical one: first, hand grenades and heavy bombs to stampede the population, then machine-gunning to drive them below, next heavy and incendiary bombs to wreck the houses and burn them on top of their victims.

The only counter-measures the Basques could employ, for they do not possess sufficient airplanes to face the insurgent fleet, were those provided by the heroism of the Basque clergy. These blessed and prayed for the kneeling crowds – Socialists, Anarchists, and Communists, as well as the declared faithful – in the crumbling dugouts. When I entered Guernica after midnight houses were crashing on either side, and it was utterly impossible even for firemen to enter the centre of the town. The hospitals of Josefinas and Convento de Santa Clara were glowing heaps of embers, all the churches except that of Santa Maria were destroyed, and the few houses which still stood were doomed. When I revisited Guernica this afternoon most of the town was still burning and new fires had broken out. About 30 dead were laid out in a ruined hospital.

The effect here of the bombardment of Guernica, the Basques' holy city, has been profound, and has led President Aguirre to issue the following statement in this morning's Basque Press: 'The German airmen in the service of the Spanish rebels have bombarded Guernica, burning the historic town which is held in such veneration by all Basques. They have sought to wound us in the most sensitive of our patriotic sentiments, once more making it entirely clear what Euzkadi may expect of those who do not hesitate to destroy us down to the very sanctuary which records the centuries of our liberty and our democracy. Before this outrage all we Basques must react with violence, swearing from the bottom of our hearts to defend the principles of our people with unheard of stubbornness and heroism if the case requires it. We cannot hide the gravity of the moment; but victory can never be won by the invader if, raising our spirits to heights of strength and determination, we steel ourselves to his defeat. The enemy has advanced in many parts elsewhere to be driven out of them afterwards. I do not hesitate to affirm that here the same thing will happen. May today's outrage be one spur more to do it with all speed.'

Steer's view that this was a new kind of warfare ensured that his despatch would have a more disturbing impact than those of his colleagues. The *New York Times* editorial on the following day condemned 'wholesale arson and mass murder, committed by Rebel airplanes of German type'. On 6 May, Senator William Borah of Idaho made an eloquent denunciation of the bombing in language prophetic of Picasso's painting:

> Here Fascism presents to the world its masterpiece. It has hung upon the wall of civilization a painting that will never come down – never fade out of the memories of men. So long as men and women may be interested in searching out from the pages of history outstanding acts of cruelty and instances of needless destruction of human life they will linger longest and with the greatest horror over the savage story of the fascist war in Spain.

A few days later, Bishop Francis J. McConnell, of the Methodist Episcopal Church, published an 'Appeal to the Conscience of the World' signed by several hundred prominent Americans, including senators and congressmen, professors and writers, union leaders and non-Catholic religious readers. It specifically cited

Steer as a witness. On 10 May, Congressman Jerry O'Connell of Montana quoted Steer in the House of Representatives as proof of German participation in the Spanish Civil War.[39]

More important than these echoes of Steer's report was perhaps the fact that it was reprinted in full on 29 April in the French Communist daily, *L'Humanité*, where it was read by Pablo Picasso.[40] At the time, he was working on a commission by the Spanish Republican Government to provide a mural for the great Paris Exhibition being planned for the summer of 1937. Prior to the news of the destruction of Guernica, his series of preliminary sketches had concerned the relationship between the artist and his model in the studio. On 1 May 1937, he abandoned this project, deeply affected by the reports of the bombing, and he began work on what would become his most famous painting.[41]

Despite, or rather because of, the overwhelming verisimilitude of Steer's report, the Nationalists immediately denied that Guernica had happened. The head of the Francoist foreign press bureau, Luis Bolín, spread the view that Guernica had been dynamited by Basque saboteurs. He was already beginning to experience some unpleasant press as a result of the international campaign to free Arthur Koestler, and his Guernica lie would also bring negative consequences. Nevertheless, Bolín's views were rapidly taken up by a number of English friends of the Francoist cause, Douglas Jerrold, Arnold Lunn and Robert Sencourt. The most consistent feature of their writing was the denigration of George Steer's personal and professional integrity.[42]

The Times cabled George Steer in Bilbao: VIEW OTHER SIDES DISMISSAL YOUR GUERNICA STORY FURTHER JUDICIOUS STATEMENT DESIRABLE. Steer's reply, sent on 28 April, was published the next day:

> The denial by Salamanca of all knowledge of the destruction of Gernika has created no astonishment here, since the similar but less terrible bombing of Durango was denied by them in spite of the presence of British eye-witnesses. I have spoken with hundreds of homeless and distressed people, who all give precisely the same description of the events. I have seen and measured the enormous bomb-holes at Gernika, which, since I passed through the town the day before, I can testify were not there then. Unexploded German aluminium incendiary bombs were found in Gernika marked 'Rheindorf factory, 1936'. The types of German aeroplane used were Junkers 52 (heavy bombers), Heinkel 111 (medium fast bomber), and Heinkel 51 (chasers). I was myself machine-gunned by six chasers in a large bomb-hole at Arbacegui-Gerrikaiz, when they were

returning from Gernika. According to a statement made by the German pilots captured near Ochandiano early in April at the beginning of the insurgent offensive, they are manned entirely by German pilots, while nearly all the crew are German, and the machines left Germany in February. It is maintained here that the entire insurgent air force used in this offensive against the Basques is German, except for seven Italian Fiat fighters and three Savoia 81 machines. That they bombed and destroyed Gernika is the considered judgement of your correspondent and what is more the certain knowledge if that is possible of every wretched Basque civilian who was forced to suffer it.

Fearing that *The Times* might not publish it, Steer copied his original telegram to Philip Noel-Baker, urging him to use it in the House of Commons and get the information to Lloyd George and Anthony Eden.[43] He refuted Francoist denials again in *The Times* on 6 May and, on 15 May, was able to report the shooting down near Bilbao of a German pilot whose log-book showed that he had taken part in the attack on Guernica.

Accusations that Steer had lied about Guernica continued to be made until the 1970s. In the early days, material that was found by the occupying forces in the telegraph office in Bilbao included *The Times'* cable to Steer requesting more information. It was given by Bolín to the American Catholic propagandist for Franco, Father Joseph Thorning. When he published it in 1938, Thorning claimed that it proved that *The Times* suspected the accuracy of his report. The cable was among large quantities of documents seized by the rebels in Bilbao and taken to Salamanca for sifting for information to be used in the repression. The British partisan of Franco, Major Francis Yeats-Brown, went to Salamanca, where the Francoists showed him a correspondence between 'an English MP' (Noel-Baker) and 'a journalist in Bilbao who excelled himself in describing the Guernica affair' (Steer). Without any sense of the irony of his own position as a propagandist for Franco, he wrote delightedly that the cables showed conclusively that 'both were very much mixed up in Basque affairs, too much so in fact'.[44]

Although the publication of the despatch had probably led to the Nazi expulsion of Norman Ebbutt, the *Times* man in Berlin, the paper continued to accept the veracity of Steer's report. *The Times* had published Steer's despatch in the period of the most avid appeasement demonstrated by the paper's editor, Geoffrey Dawson. In response to the virulent Anglophobia with which the controlled German press had reacted, Dawson wrote to *The Times'* acting correspondent in Berlin, H. G. Daniels:

I did my utmost, night after night, to keep out of the paper anything that might hurt their susceptibilities. I can really think of nothing that has been printed now for many months past which they could possibly take exception to as unfair comment. No doubt they were annoyed by Steer's first story of the bombing of Guernica, but its essential accuracy has never been disputed, and there has not been any attempt here to rub it in or harp upon it.

It was to no avail. As Daniels informed him, Nazi propagandists had noticed that *Times* spelt backwards is *Semit*, which was broadcast as proof that the newspaper for which Steer wrote was a Jewish-Marxist operation.[45] George Steer's name was placed on the Gestapo's Special Wanted List of 2,820 persons who were to be detained after the Germans occupied Britain in 1940.[46] Steer received threats from abroad that, if he was caught alive by the Francoists, he would be shot immediately. He continued to go to the front, carrying now a machine pistol which he did not know how to use.[47] Holme and Monks were also denounced by General Queipo de Llano in his infamous radio broadcasts.[48]

Steer stayed in what was left of Euskadi through the next six weeks of relentless bombing, going to where the fighting was thickest with Monnier and reporting almost daily on the dogged defence against the Francoist advance on Bilbao despite the lack of air cover. Indeed, aware that rebel air superiority was the key issue to the defence of the city, he bombarded Noel-Baker with requests to use his influence to get the French to permit Republican aircraft to fly over their territory. Writing from Aguirre's office, the Presidencia, he wrote:

> *We* would have cut off the Italians in Bermeo and along the western side
> of the Gernika outlet if *we* had had the aviation to deal with them.
> Considering the complete demoralisation and lack of order in the
> infantry of the last fortnight *we* resisted and counterattacked very well
> upon the new line, and with proper military elements *we* would have
> finished the offensive for ever.

Urging Noel-Baker to press Pierre Cot, the French Minister of Aviation, to breach the non-intervention agreement and send aircraft, Steer wrote revealingly: 'And tell Cot that if he has any fears of English I.S. [Intelligence Service] men reporting his naughtinesses in Bilbao, they will be idle. I am the only trusted one here, and when the time comes I can deny it all more than thrice.'[49]

That his involvement could hardly have been greater is revealed by many passages in his book along the following lines: 'I went up to Begoña to talk with the armoured car men. They were tired and angry. *Our* own artillery had fired on them and the infantry that afternoon in mistake for the enemy, causing heavy loss. *We* had been forced to withdraw to the right of the Casino in consequence, and that was the beginning of the movement that let the enemy in.' Steer accompanied the Spanish delegation that went to the League of Nations in Geneva at the end of May in search of recognition of Axis aggression. The Spanish Foreign Minister, Julio Álvarez del Vayo, produced evidence of Italian intervention, while the Basque Government produced proof of German involvement. It was to no avail and Steer wrote to Noel-Baker that 'Del Vayo was sold a pup', as well as describing a highly unsatisfactory conversation that he had had with an infuriatingly complacent Roberts, head of the Western Department of the Foreign Office. Steer also visited the American Consul in Geneva and showed him a collection of photostats of documents proving German participation in the bombing of Guernica, including an annotated map. On 13 June, he even participated at the Hotel Carlton in a meeting of the Basque Government and military high command called by Aguirre to discuss whether to defend Bilbao to the last man. When the city fell, he covered the subsequent retreat westwards into Santander. He wrote a moving account of the evacuation of 200,000 people first on trawlers and then, when the Francoists had taken the port, on lorries along the road to the west, the refugees being bombed and strafed by the Condor Legion along the way.[50]

During these last desperate days in Bilbao, he assisted the British Labour Member of Parliament, Leah Manning, who was helping the Basque Government organize the evacuation of four thousand children to Britain. She later described Steer, and another British journalist, Philip Jordan, as 'towers of strength and encouragement'.[51] The Dean of Canterbury, Hewlett Johnson, wrote to *The Times* to commend Steer, whom he described as 'your own heroic and extremely able correspondent, whom I had the privilege of meeting in Bilbao as the only British journalist at that time in that city'.[52] Philip Noel-Baker wrote to Steer that his report on Guernica had helped change British Government policy, by which he almost certainly referred to the decision to permit the evacuation of four thousand Basque children to Britain.[53]

When the Basque Government left Bilbao on 18 June, Steer went to the deserted rooms of the president and took his pen and his last notepad on which to start writing *The Tree of Gernika*. He then finished the last bottle of champagne on the premises. At dawn on the following day, he walked west until he could find a driver ready to take him along the clogged road towards Santander.[54] It was there that Steer wrote his last, long article for *The Times*, an elegiac account of

Bilbao's heroic last stand.[55] At the end of June, having lost virtually everything he owned in the retreat from Bilbao, Steer managed to find his way to Paris. He went to the gracious apartment of his friend Thomas Tucker-Edwardes Cadett, *The Times'* correspondent in France. At first, Cadett did not recognize the unshaven, malodorous tramp, in dirty clothes and *alpargatas*. When he realized it was Steer, he was alarmed to see that he was feverish and 'pretty well at the end of his tether'. After a bath and a change of clothes, he began to write in Aguirre's notebook.[56] He could not, however, just cut himself off from his beloved Basques. Having interrupted his writing to seek more material, on 18 August, he made the dangerous flight across the Bay of Biscay to Santander, where they were cornered, facing superior Italian forces. He stayed with them for a few days, flying back before their ignominious end.[57]

Steer finished his book in a remarkably short time and it was published in early 1938. The text reflected his romantic commitment to the Basque part in the battle against fascism, a battle with which he had become involved in Abyssinia. It also reflected his contempt for the farce of British commitment to non-intervention. By the time it came out, Steer was in South Africa doing research for a book on German ambitions in Africa. On the day he left London, he wrote a scribbled note to Noel-Baker: 'If you want me for any really major crisis of a war-like kind, you've only got to flash me.'[58] Noel-Baker was one of the first people to read *The Tree of Gernika*, and he wrote enthusiastically to Steer:

> What I have read I think quite brilliant. The Times gave it an extremely good review considering everything, and I am told by The Observer that it is a best seller, which I hope may be true. I lent it the other day to Morgan Jones for a speech he had to make about air bombing, and you will see he quoted it sensibly. The speech sounded better than it reads, but the best part of it was by you.[59]

The Tree of Gernika was described by James Cable, the historian of the siege of Bilbao, as

> a work of passionate engagement, a vivid, moving, exciting justification of Basque nationalism, a shrewd if slanted, analysis of the circumstances and causes of their defeat, an urgent warning to his own country-men of the wrath to come. Steer was something of an artist and his book has a quality rare in the productions of even the most brilliant journalists. The historians who have followed his version of events, however, had more

than the seduction of his style to excuse their choice. Steer had seen for himself much of what he described and, as a brave man driven to desperation by the recent loss of his first wife, he saw more than most, being particularly fascinated by the detailed conduct of military operations. Of course he also had the faults of his professional virtues. He was a journalist, not a historian, and he affected the omniscience of his trade, too often blurring the distinction between observation and deduction, evidence and hearsay. His facts are not always reliable, his judgements are occasionally hasty, his dates are slapdash. Nevertheless, anyone who takes the trouble to compare Steer's guesses with the evidence of the documents is continually astonished, not at his inevitable errors, but at the frequency with which his assumptions were correct.[60]

The Tree of Gernika is a classic of Spanish Civil War historiography. Beautifully and incisively written, it is a moving defence of Basque Nationalism and a heart-breaking account of the reasons for its defeat at the hands of Franco. It was written as a warning to the democracies of what awaited them. Romantically attached to the Basque cause, Steer wrote of his own book: 'it will, perhaps, be banned by the Basques when they get back to Bilbao'. He need not have worried. He became something of a Basque hero – and unable to see the book published in Euskadi in Franco's lifetime, exiled Basques published the book in translation in Caracas in 1963. Only after the dictator's death was it published in Spain.[61] That was hardly surprising given its deep sympathy with Basques. He wrote in the preface to the book: 'The Basques are industrious and the Spanish are idle. The Basques are all yeomen and the Spanish would all be gentlemen.'[62]

At the time, Steer's sympathy with the Basques and criticisms of the Spanish Left were the focus of a less than fulsome review of the book by George Orwell. Opening with the words, 'It goes without saying that everyone who writes of the Spanish War writes as a partisan', Orwell went on to reflect his chagrin that the object of his own partisanship, the anti-Stalinist Partido Obrero de Unificación Marxista, had had little or no success in the Basque Country. He acknowledged that Steer had been right in observing that there was no social revolution among the conservative Basques. However, he went on to comment:

Mr Steer writes entirely from the Basque standpoint, and he has, very strongly, the curious English standpoint of being unable to praise one race without damning another. Being pro-Basque, he finds it necessary to be anti-Spanish, i.e., to some extent anti-Government as well as anti-Franco. As a result his book is so full of gibes at the Asturians and other non-Basque loyalists as to make one doubtful of his reliability as a witness.

This was not entirely unfair in that Steer's sympathies lay with the Partido Nacionalista Vasco (Basque Nationalist Party), which was as hostile to the Left as it was to the Francoists, and much of what he wrote reflected that position. Despite his doubts, Orwell did recognize the immense authority with which Steer could write about Guernica.[63]

After the publication of his book, Steer remained in Africa throughout 1938, travelling and writing articles for various South African and English papers, including the *Daily Telegraph* and the Manchester *Guardian*, on the ongoing Ethiopian resistance to the Italians and on the Italian threat to poorly defended British colonies. He also collected material on German colonial ambitions, material he hoped could be used by Noel-Baker to undermine Neville Chamberlain's appeasement policies. He also indiscreetly revealed to Noel-Baker, 'for your ear alone', that he would be reporting on what he found to South African Military Intelligence. Whatever else he was doing, Steer always kept his mind on the Basque cause. On 12 October 1938, he wrote to Noel-Baker to ask for advice as to whether it would be better for him to continue to work to keep the Nazis out of Africa or else

> to come home in November and take part in any negotiations for mediation in Spain, my object being to press Basque claims. I think this is vitally important, if we are ever to have a point of concentration to resist Italo-German influence in Spain. Basque autonomy, Catalan autonomy, removal of the Italians from Majorca and the Germans from Morocco are essentials.

Not without arrogance, he added: 'I don't think anybody could press these points better on the War Office and the Air Ministry than I can.'[64]

Within a week, however, Steer had decided that Franco would never agree to international mediation and that the Spanish Republic was thus doomed. Accordingly, he wrote to Noel-Baker on 18 October: 'Henceforward, I feel, our main job is not to save Spain or Ethiopia or China or even democracy, but something far more material – to get Chamberlain out. I promise you that I will do my best to help you do this.' In another letter, he said: 'Our job is to get Chamberlain out.'[65]

Steer was still destined to see much fighting. In 1939, he travelled in North Africa and wrote a book about the threat posed by the Italians in Libya to the Egypt and to the French Empire.[66] Nevertheless, he also permitted himself finally to leave behind his grief for Margarita. On 14 July 1939, he married Esmé Barton, the younger daughter of Sir Sidney Barton, a friend since their days together in Addis Ababa. Esmé had been portrayed by Evelyn Waugh in his novel *Black Mischief* as the promiscuous 'Prudence Courteney', and her parents lampooned as the bumbling 'Sir Samson' and 'Lady Courteney'. Outraged that he should thus repay her parents' lavish hospitality to him, she had taken her revenge when she saw him in one of Addis Ababa's two ramshackle nightspots, by hurling a glass of champagne in his face. As an old friend of George Steer, she had attended the funeral of Margarita and, seeing him distraught, decided that he needed looking after and began falling in love with him. When they finally got together, their wedding was a society affair, conducted at the King's Chapel of the Savoy by the Bishop of London with three other clergymen assisting and reported in *The Times*. With George in a top hat and tails and his bride in an elaborate gown of blue crepe, it was a world away from the improvised ceremony through which he and Margarita had joked their way in the dusty legation compound in Addis Ababa. Among the guests was the head of MI5, Sir Vernon Kell, for whom Esmé worked as a secretary. On 14 May 1940, Esmé gave birth to a son. He was christened George Augustine Barton Steer in St Paul's Cathedral on 8 June 1940, with the Emperor Haile Selassie as his godfather. On 13 October 1942, they had a daughter, Caroline.[67]

As a result of his work on Africa, Steer had been hired by the *Daily Telegraph*. The outbreak of the Second World War found him honeymooning in South Africa with Esmé. He soon headed north to cover the Russian invasion of Finland, once more drawn to describe the heroic resistance of a small nation faced by a totalitarian invader. In his reporting, he drew frequent comparisons with what the Germans had done in Euskadi.[68] It was as if he was drawn always to the doomed struggle of small nations facing overwhelming odds. That commitment would lead to full-scale action when Britain became one of those small nations facing invasion. Steer remained in contact with the exiled Basque leadership in France. In the hope of getting them to England before they fell into German hands, he gave details of their whereabouts to Geoffrey Thompson, who knew Steer from his own time as Chargé d'Affaires at Hendaye during the Spanish Civil War. With the retreat from Dunkirk in full spate, Steer encouraged Philip Noel-Baker to try to persuade the British Government to bring José Antonio de Aguirre to Britain to be the focus of a Basque anti-Franco resistance.[69]

After the christening of his son, he joined his father-in-law Sir Sidney Barton, his friend Philip Noel-Baker and his son's godfather, Haile Selassie, to discuss the possibility of hitting the Italians by encouraging the resistance in Abyssinia. The Negus was keen to return to his own country to foment revolt against the Italians. This coincided with the plans of Major General Archibald Wavell, the Commander in Chief of British Forces in the Middle East. Steer, as a result of an unusually imaginative decision, was commissioned as an officer in the Intelligence Corps on the basis of his previous experience in Addis Ababa during the Italian invasion. This was organized by Geoffrey Thompson, now of the Egyptian Department of the Foreign Office. Because of the importance of his mission, Steer, 'who was of course well known to the Emperor, became a staff captain overnight' and accompanied Haile Selassie to Khartoum.[70] He did not remain long as the Emperor's *aide de camp*, but transferred to Psychological Warfare Operations, producing leaflets in Amharic which provoked plenty of desertions among the native troops recruited by the Italians. In fact, Steer turned out to be a propagandist of genius. He also organized guerrilla raids on Italian outposts. He linked up with the eccentric Colonel Orde Wingate, a buccaneering officer who shared Steer's enthusiasm for Haile Selassie. Wingate's column of Sudanese and other irregular troops kept large numbers of Italian troops occupied and eventually liberated the capital. Steer was with the Emperor when he returned to Addis Ababa on 5 May 1941.

Steer relished the opportunity to attack the Italians with his typewriter. He showed a real flair for what came to be called 'psychological warfare'. Some of his inventions aimed at rousing the Ethiopian factions were beyond what the Emperor Haile Selassie could approve, so Steer forged an imperial seal with which to issue his bulletins. This was honestly recounted in his book, *Sealed and Delivered*, and prompted Evelyn Waugh to publish a hostile review in which he went so far as to suggest that the military authorities should punish Steer for indiscretion.[71] Waugh's wish was not granted and, in fact, Steer was promoted. However, Waugh's review was used by the odious Bolín as 'proof' that Steer was a habitual liar and had therefore lied about Guernica.[72]

Steer was posted to Cairo, where his wife had managed to get herself a job with British Intelligence. He served in the North African campaign until, in 1942, he was posted to Madagascar to take part in operations to prevent the Japanese taking over the island. There was considerable competition from several sections of the Special Operations Executive for his services. Then at the beginning of 1943, now Major Steer, he was sent to India, to take part in the campaign to recover Burma from the Japanese. His inventive use of propaganda and his active participation in a number of clashes with the enemy saw him promoted to Lieutenant Colonel. He was killed, not in action but in an accident, on Christmas Day 1944, when his jeep went off the road when he was driving to watch the Christmas Day sports at his training camp.[73] It was a tragic irony that a man who had taken so many risks in such great causes should die in so banal a manner. The obituary in *The Times* recalled his exploits in Burma but not his service in Spain or Ethiopia, but commented on his books: 'Combining the research of the scholar with the experience of the fighter and the faith of the idealist, he was as frank and accurate in his writings as he was vivid and he has left a record of service to his country the cessation of which will be regretted by fellow journalists and soldiers alike.'[74]

Despite publishing five important books and a military career that saw him compared with Lawrence of Arabia, Steer is remembered, most of all, for the crucial despatch from Guernica which blew the whistle on Nazi involvement in the Spanish Civil War. From the time that he became a war correspondent in 1935, Steer had made it his business to alert the world to the imperialist ambitions and ruthless aggression of fascism. During the Italian invasion of Abyssinia and in Spain, his commitment to an apparently lost cause led him to a level of involvement that went far beyond the duties of a war correspondent. Steer's book is not just about the bombing of Guernica, but is a complete account of the entire Basque campaign. In that sense, it remains one of the ten or so most important books about the Spanish Civil War. It is also a crucial element of Steer's series of books about fascist aggression and atrocity. The book is one of the most moving and authentic tributes to the Basque people, to their suffering and their courage in the fight against Franco and his Nazi and Fascist allies. Moreover, despite his empathy with the PNV, the words of Steer summing up the Basque part in the Spanish Civil War capture the tragedy and dignity of an entire people:

> After all, the Basques were a small people, and they didn't have many guns or planes, and they did not receive any foreign aid, and they were terribly simple and guileless and unversed in warfare; but they had, throughout this painful civil war, held high the lantern of humanity and civilisation. They had not killed, or tortured, or in any way amused themselves at the expense of their prisoners. In the most cruel circumstances, they had maintained liberty of self-expression and faith. They had scrupulously and zealously observed all the laws, written and unwritten, which enjoin on man a certain respect for his neighbour. They had made no hostages; they had responded to the inhuman

methods of those who hated them by protest, nothing more. They had, as far as anyone can in war, told the truth and kept all their promises.[75]

George Steer wrote: 'In this war, the Basque fought for tolerance and free discussion, gentleness and equality.'[76] He died in a later war for those same values. Next to his body was found his most precious possession, a gold watch given to him by José Antonio de Aguirre, inscribed 'To Steer from the Basque Republic'.

9

Talking with Franco, Trouble with Hitler:
Jay Allen

In the early hours of the morning of 25 August 1936, an American journalist named Jay Allen sat typing in the tiny enclosed patio of a small pension in the white Portuguese walled town of Elvas. He couldn't sleep, partly because of the oppressive heat and partly because of the sobbing of the woman in the next room. Her husband had been one of the victims of the mass slaughter taking place just across the Spanish border at Badajoz. Jay had just come from the town and, by writing an article, was trying to come to terms with the horrors that he had seen. When published, it would do considerable damage to the cause of the military rebels in Spain. It was to be one of the most important and frequently cited chronicles of the Spanish Civil War and was to make Jay Allen the object of right-wing abuse. His commitment to the Spanish Republicans survived their defeat in 1939. In consequence, in March 1941, Jay Allen would be arrested by the German authorities in occupied France and imprisoned. He was there ostensibly as a journalist, but was trying to arrange the escape of Spanish Republican refugees and anti-fascist volunteers who had fought in the International Brigades. His fame as the man who had done so much damage to the rebel military in Spain made it difficult for American diplomats to secure his release.

Along with Henry Buckley, Jay Allen was one of the two best-informed correspondents in Spain on either side. Isabel de Palencia, who had been the Spanish minister plenipotentiary in Sweden and Finland during the Civil War, wrote: 'if I were asked who I thought was the best-informed North American on the Spanish conflict, I would unhesitatingly say, "Jay Allen". She went on to list other distinguished friends of the Spanish Republic, including Vincent Sheean, Freda Kirchwey and Elliot Paul, and concluded: 'no one has compiled the history of the Spanish war or had the patience to build up the files that Jay Allen has'.[1]

Born in Seattle on 7 July 1900, Jay Cooke Allen Junior did not have a very happy childhood. His mother, Jeanne Lynch Allen, died from tuberculosis fifteen months after he was born. A first-generation Irish Catholic, she had made her Methodist husband, Jay Cooke Allen, promise to raise their children in the Catholic Church. After Jeanne's death, her family wanted custody of Jay and, when his father refused, they kidnapped Jay. After a court battle, Jay was returned to him. The consequent bitterness in the family hurt the young Jay very deeply and may have influenced his later critical attitude towards the Catholic Church. At the same time, his relationship with his father did little to compensate him for the loss of his mother. Jay wrote years later of his father: 'When I was a kid, I never saw him sober that I remember. And in my adult years, the few occasions when we were together he was aggressive, drank too much, and though I always enjoyed his immense vitality and appreciated his honest affection, I was always ill at ease.'[2] Jay did not find emotional warmth and stability until he met the love of his life, Ruth Austin.

Chronologically and socially, Jay was part of the American 'lost generation'. He married Ruth in Woodburn, Oregon on 7 September 1924 and they left for France two weeks later for their honeymoon. During a long stay in Paris, they became good friends of Ernest Hemingway. He tipped Jay off when he was about to resign his job with the Paris office of the *Chicago Daily Tribune*. Jay applied and got the job. Between 1925 and 1934, he covered events in France, Belgium, Spain, Italy, Austria, Germany, Poland and the Balkans. Their son Michael was born on 16 October 1927. Jay was based much of the time in Geneva, although his interest in Spanish events became his all-absorbing passion because, as he constantly told his wife, 'it was the one country in Western Europe where the democratic ideal had a promise'.[3]

Jay first moved to Madrid in 1930, where he had rented an apartment from Constancia de la Mora. Jay, Ruth and son Michael had hardly moved in when Constancia turned up to inform them that, after separating from her husband, she and her infant daughter needed the apartment and to ask if they would mind leaving. To her surprise, Jay and Ruth responded with sympathy. Constancia later recalled the episode with some embarrassment:

> I had plenty of household problems to discuss with my mother. While I was still in Málaga, I had rented the apartment through Zenobia to an American newspaperman, Jay Allen, and his wife and small son. Now when I returned to Madrid, I found the paper hangers and painters busily making the apartment ready for the Americans. The Allens were impatiently waiting for the paint to dry while they stayed at a hotel. With my heart in my mouth I went to call on them to beg them to let me have

the apartment back for myself. Jay Allen was in bed when I arrived – sick, he explained cheerfully. His counterpane was covered with newspapers, books, and typing paper. His small son, dressed in long blue pants, occupied a corner of the room where he played an intricate and exceedingly noisy game with himself. Mrs. Allen, a young and charming woman, moved around the room, answering the telephone, finding books for her energetic husband, and bringing order out of the confusion that began afresh the moment she relaxed her efforts. 'I hope you will forgive me', I stammered. The Allens listened to my story and then all three, including the grave child, assured me that it was no trouble at all, of course I should have my own apartment, they would start immediately to look for another, I shouldn't waste a moment of worry for disturbing their plans – it was nothing.[4]

It was the beginning of a deep friendship that would flourish with close collaboration in putting the Republic's case during the Civil War and after, but which would end sadly in political disagreement over the strategy to be pursued in trying to help Spanish refugees.

During his visits to Spain in the late 1920s and even more so after he settled there in 1930, Jay met a wide range of Spanish politicians, including those on the extreme Right. He was a welcome guest at the Madrid home of the poet and novelist Princess Bibesco (Elizabeth Asquith, the daughter of Herbert Henry Asquith, who was British Prime Minister from 1908 to 1916). In 1919, aged twenty-two, she had married the Romanian diplomat Prince Antoine Bibesco. During her husband's posting as Ambassador to Spain from 1927 to 1931, she ran a salon where the great and the good from Madrid's literary and political elite would gather. Before the fall of the monarchy, Jay used to meet there the cousin of King Alfonso XIII, Alfonso de Orleans Borbón, and his wife, Princess Beatriz of Saxe-Coburg Gotha, a granddaughter of Queen Victoria and a cousin of Alfonso XIII's consort, Queen Victoria Eugenia. Prince Ali, as he was known in the family, was an intrepid aviator. It was at the Bibescos that Jay first met José Antonio, the son of the military dictator, General Miguel Primo de Rivera. Despite the political distance between them – José Antonio would found the Spanish fascist party, the Falange, in 1933 – they had cordial relations: 'I liked him though I hated his crowd, the señoritos and señoritas of good families who flashed their gats in the smart bars from '34 on, often pearl-handled revolvers with the Sacred Heart of Jesus on them.' Years later, Jay told Herbert Southworth: 'As I think you know, I had a sneaking sort of affection for José Antonio. I had been present when he and

Miguel [his brother] took on Queipo de Llano in a café on the Alcalá – lovely fight they had! And I used to see him all too often at Elizabeth Bibesco's. Her lover? I don't know. She was a very odd number, soggy with alcohol <u>and</u> ether.'[5] José Antonio would eventually grant Jay the last interview that he ever gave, shortly before his execution in 1936.

On several occasions, Jay met José Calvo Sotelo, the monarchist leader whose assassination on 13 July 1936 would be used as justification for the military coup launched five days later, although prepared many months before. He had a certain sympathy for Calvo Sotelo because, when Finance Minister during Primo's dictatorship, he had run into serious problems when he tried to nationalize the Spanish oil industry. Jay wrote later:

> I thought him a smoothie, rather bright so of course hailed as a great brain by his fellows (any brain at all passed as a great brain in that milieu). I confess that I did feel a little sorry for the guy who had had the rug pulled out from under him – under the peseta to be more precise – by Deterding of Shell [Henri Wilhelm August Deterding, chairman of Royal Dutch/Shell, the so-called the 'Napoleon of Oil'], among others in the international oil fraternity because he had dared set up CAMPSA, the oil monopoly under Primo.

The great international oil giants had combined to undermine the value of the peseta and Jay commented: 'I thought Calvo Sotelo a babe in the woods not to have foreseen this and I remember José Antonio once agreeing with me somewhat bitterly.'[6]

Obviously, given his deep commitment to the Republic, Jay was more at home on the Left. Through his close friend, the artist Luis Quintanilla, whom he had known in Paris, Jay developed friendships with several prominent Socialists, including the future premier Dr Juan Negrín and a number of followers of Largo Caballero, Luis Araquistain, Julio Álvarez del Vayo and Rodolfo Llopis. Indeed, in early 1931, leaders of the Spanish Socialist Party had occasionally gathered at his apartment as they plotted the overthrow of the monarchy.[7] In the early days of his time in Spain, Jay toured the country extensively and was even taken on an election campaign by Julio Álvarez del Vayo. He wrote a lengthy series of stories for the *Chicago Tribune*, which attracted a lot of attention. As he later told Herbert Southworth: 'somebody on the paper sent them in to the Pulitzer Prize Committee. The Trib's house organ ran a picture of their fair-haired boy and mentioned that he was "being considered" (whatever that means) for a Pulitzer

Prize.' The *Chicago Tribune*'s reactionary owner, Colonel R. R. McCormick, was furious. He 'erupted, informed the Pulitzer Committee that no correspondent of his wanted or needed their accolade. I have no reason to think that I would have won it although I did hear rumours.'[8]

Jay was fired in early 1934 from the *Chicago Tribune* by Colonel McCormick because he had refused to take part in a scheme to help remove a senior colleague whom he described as 'an expensive old ornament'. Having recently inherited some money, Jay began to do research for a book on Manuel de Godoy, the all-powerful minister of Carlos IV. Political events, however, would soon distract him. A right of centre coalition had come into power after the elections of November 1933 and immediately set about dismantling the reforms introduced in the previous two and a half years. Throughout 1934, a series of strikes had been deliberately provoked as what seemed to the Left to be the first step to the crushing of the labour movement and the imposition of a corporative state. The entry into the government on 6 October of the right-wing CEDA was taken by the Socialists as the next step. The response had been a revolutionary general strike.

During the repression that followed, Quintanilla brought Negrín, Araquistain, Álvarez del Vayo and Llopis, along with the Asturian miners' leader Amador Fernández, to take refuge in Jay's Madrid flat in the Calle Alcalá from 8 to 10 October. As a result of what was, at best, malicious gossip and, at worst, deliberate mischief by his neighbour, the fervently Catholic correspondent of the *New York Times*, William P. Carney, a report appeared on 9 October claiming that Jay had been arrested and charged with harbouring members of the revolutionary committee before being released with a warning that he ran the risk of expulsion from Spain. To have harboured the revolutionary committee had been fraught with risk and the report emanating from Carney put Jay in serious jeopardy. In fact, Jay had been detained, along with Leland Stowe of the *Herald Tribune* and Edmund Taylor of the *Chicago Tribune*, not because he had hidden the Socialists, but because some machine-gun-toting Guardias de Asalto claimed that they had been shot at by a sniper from the building in which he lived. After briefly holding Jay and his companions at gun-point, the Assault Guards accepted a whisky and soda and left. They obviously had some inkling that Jay was hiding the revolutionary committee because they returned shortly after and arrested him. After intervention by the American Ambassador, Claude Bowers, he was released. Leland Stowe protested to the managing editor of the *New York Times* that Carney's story was biased, false and libellous.[9]

Jay wrote later of Carney: 'I did not know then the extent to which he was tied in with the Jesuit organ *El Debate*, whose editor, now Bishop of Málaga, had worked on the *Times* on a student basis (I think I refer to Ángel Herrera – he was the eminence grise of Gil Robles).' During the Civil War, Carney would write as a fervent partisan of Franco's cause. In 1934, Jay had few friendships with right-ists other than with those he had met through Elizabeth Bibesco. Gil Robles, the leader of the Catholic authoritarian party, the Confederación Española de Derechas Autónomas, had worked hard to provoke the uprising of October 1934 in order to have an excuse to crush the organized working class. Jay recalled later: 'Gil Robles, a constipated, malevolent little man, wasn't my kettle of fish. Nor was I his.'[10] Not surprisingly, with Gil Robles' party in government, Jay was arrested again a couple of weeks later because of a story about the repression in Asturias that he had written for the *Chicago Daily News*. According to the American Ambassador, Claude Bowers, the material on the atrocities in Asturias had been provided by Indalecio Prieto. After being threatened by the police, Jay was again released. Meanwhile, Quintanilla had been arrested and Jay took part with Hemingway in efforts to drum up support for an American campaign to have him released. The episode consolidated even further Jay's close friendship with Luis Quintanilla.[11]

In 1935, Jay shelved the Godoy project, as he would do with several books that he began. This was largely because he was a meticulous perfectionist, although his friend John Whitaker claimed that his lack of productivity was because he was 'nearly as lazy as me and equally diffident when in the company of the Muse'.[12] Jay began to work on a book about the Second Republic, provisionally entitled *Revolt*. Because it was to be centred on the agrarian struggles in the south, he took Ruth to live in Torremolinos, then still an idyllic and unspoiled fishing village on the coast south-west of Málaga. They were alone because he and Ruth had decided that they wanted Michael educated in the United States and, in the late summer of 1934, she had made a brief trip to take him to be with her family in Oregon.[13] Jay was now working on at least two books – on Godoy and the Spanish Republic. His routine was writing from 7 a.m. to 12.30 p.m., when he would go with Ruth to the beach. They would have lunch at 2 p.m. followed by a walk and then more writing until dinner at 8 p.m. In mid-February, Jay wrote to Claude Bowers, invit-ing him and his wife to come and stay, but before anything came of the idea, Ruth had had to return to the United States because Michael had been taken seriously ill. Jay spent part of the spring of 1936 travelling in Extremadura collecting mate-rial for his book on the agrarian problem, accompanied for part of the time by Louis Fischer.[14] When he later revisited Badajoz after its occupation by the

Francoists in August 1936, Jay Allen recalled: 'I had been there four times in the last year to do research on a book I am working on and to try to study the operations of the agrarian reform that might have saved the Spanish Republic – a republic that, whatever it is, gave Spain schools and hope, neither of which it had known for centuries.'[15]

In the spring of 1936, Jay was deeply affected by what he saw in Badajoz and, on returning to Madrid, met with Negrín to discuss it. He recalled their meeting in a 1945 letter to the then exiled prime minister:

> I remember so vividly a conversation I had with you one night when I got back from Extremadura after a tour with Louis F. and Demetrio. I remember telling you how shocked I was at the irresponsibility of Madrid Socialists (some of them) their complete lack of any sense of the realities of the situation in the campo…And I recall your reaction. Apparently you had thought that I was committed to the Pasha's position. You seemed pleased to find out that I was not.[16]

'Demetrio' was Demetrio Delgado de Torres, a close friend of Negrín who, during the Spanish Civil War, would be his Undersecretary for the Economy at the Spanish Treasury (Ministerio de Hacienda) with responsibility for the procurement of war materials, for the management of Republican funds abroad including the transfer of gold to Russia. 'The Pasha' was Luis Araquistain, the principal spokesman and adviser of the party president Francisco Largo Caballero.

This 1945 letter revealed not only the closeness of Jay's friendship with Negrín, but also just how well informed he was about the internal politics of the Spanish Socialist party. In the spring of 1934, the PSOE was deeply split between the partisans of the Largo Caballero and those of Indalecio Prieto. Disillusioned by the limits of reform in the years of Republican–Socialist coalition from 1931 to 1933, Largo Caballero had adopted a revolutionary position, in rhetorical terms at least. From May 1934 onwards, through his theoretical journal *Leviatán*, Araquistain, who had witnessed the rise of Nazism during his time as Spanish Ambassador in Berlin, had encouraged Largo Caballero's opposition to collaboration with the liberal Republicans. Although Largo Caballero had been brought around to accepting the need for an electoral coalition in the form of the Popular Front, he was resolutely hostile to collaboration in government with the Republicans and sabotaged Prieto's opportunity to form a Republican–Socialist cabinet in mid-May 1936. Negrín believed that this fatally weakened the Popular Front Government and undermined the possibility of preventing a military uprising.[17]

What Jay saw of the explosive social situation in Extremadura in the spring of 1936 convinced him of the need for a government strong enough to implement thoroughgoing agrarian reform. Tens of thousands of land-hungry peasants living below the bread line were faced by intransigent landowners determined to cede nothing. Jay was, of course, a friend of Araquistain – hence Negrín's assumption that he supported the position of Largo Caballero – but he could see that the combination of weakening the government while spouting empty revolutionary rhetoric was dangerously irresponsible. When Largo Caballero was ousted as prime minister in May 1937, an embittered Araquistain, who had hoped to be made Foreign Minister, forgot his own revolutionary past, assumed a fervent anti-Communism stance and became a ferocious critic of Negrín. It was in reference to this that Jay commented in his letter to Negrín: 'I would never make a frontal attack on the Pasha despite all the vicious things he has said about some of us, but I still feel strongly and say so, about the irresponsibility of the Caballero crowd that spring.'[18]

When the Spanish military rebels rose on 17–18 July 1936, Jay was still living in Torremolinos, where he had established a close friendship with the expatriate English Bloomsbury Group writer, Gerald Brenan, who lived in the nearby village of Churriana. Gerald was so deeply impressed by Jay's knowledge of Spain and the energy with which he dashed around that he referred to him as 'a crack reporter'. Jay wrote to Gerald on 13 August from Gibraltar: 'I admire your guts in staying on. Don't overdo it. If you hear that the black boys are advancing – they are now reported to be at Antequera; no advance has begun from San Roque – go on a ship.' After a lengthy, and remarkably well-informed analysis of the violence, he asked Gerald to send him details of what was happening in Málaga. At the bottom of the letter, he scribbled: 'Leave please if it looks bad.' At the time of the coup, Jay was alone since, in February, Ruth had gone back to America to be with their son Michael. As soon as Jay heard the news of the coup, he set off for Gibraltar: 'I simply wanted to get to Gib to find out what was happening and file to the London News Chronicle which had asked me to cover them in the event of the rumoured rebellion taking place.' A day later, Jay Allen was reported to have been killed by the Republican army at a road block not very far from Gibraltar. He recalled years later: 'I ran into some fighting in La Línea, damned near got killed (my chauffeur's shoulder was all but shot off and next day there were 68 bullet holes in the car). Had I anticipated any such trouble, I'd have been more cautious.' His son remembered his own and his mother's distress during the hours between reading the 'news' in the Seattle paper and then learning before nightfall that he was reported to be in Gibraltar and safe:

He had borrowed a rich man's limousine and driver and was going from Torremolinos to Gibraltar. A very nervous squad of Republican soldiers opened fire. They killed the driver, who had rolled out into the street creating a pool of blood. My father rolled out also into the driver's blood. The soldiers believed he was also dead and moved away. Later my father crawled away and got to safety in Gibraltar. We all thought it deeply ironic that such a supporter of the Republic as Jay would be the first foreign casualty of the Civil War.[19]

In the course of the war, among the articles filed by Jay Allen were, along with Mario Neves' reports on the massacre of Badajoz and George Steer's report on the bombing of Guernica, three of the most important, and frequently quoted, articles written during the war. These were an exclusive interview with Franco in Tetuán on 27 July 1936, his own account of the aftermath of the Nationalist capture of Badajoz and the last ever interview given by the about-to-be executed José Antonio Primo de Rivera.

Jay Allen's interview with Franco was the first granted by the future rebel leader to a foreign correspondent. After being refused a pass to Spanish Morocco from rebel headquarters in Algeciras in the south of the province of Cádiz, he spent the night in a field near neighbouring San Roque. He was then contacted by Franco's staff and told to cross the Straits of Gibraltar and go to Tetuán. After a hazardous journey, in the High Commissioner's mansion, he was finally admitted into the presence of Franco, 'another midget who would rule'. Both Franco's optimism and his ruthless determination were revealed in this historic interview with Jay Allen. Asked how long the killing would continue now that the coup had failed, Franco replied, 'There can be no compromise, no truce. I shall go on preparing my advance to Madrid. I shall advance. I shall take the capital. I shall save Spain from marxism at whatever cost...Shortly, very shortly, my troops will have pacified the country and all of this will soon seem like a nightmare.' When Allen responded, 'That means that you will have to shoot half Spain?', a smiling Franco said: 'I said whatever the cost.'[20] In the course of the interview, Jay noticed that, on Franco's desk, there were several copies of the *Bulletin de L'Entente Internationale contre la Troisième Internationale*, a ferociously anti-Semitic and anti-Bolshevik publication which praised the achievements of fascism and military dictatorships as bulwarks against Communism. The Entente was an ultra-right-wing organization which had close contacts with Antikomintern, an organization run from Josef Goebbels' Ministry of Information. Franco pointed them out to Jay and commented on just how valuable he found them.[21]

After the interview appeared, one of Franco's staff told the American consul in Tangier that, if he were ever captured, Jay Allen would be shot. Back in Gibraltar, the British authorities informed Jay that they could not guarantee his safety and recommended that he leave. There was a price put on his head by the rebels. In late October 1936, when Dennis Weaver was arrested, along with Hank Gorrell and James Minifie, after straying behind rebel lines, news was sent to Franco's head-quarters that a *News Chronicle* correspondent had been captured. Franco ordered that he immediately be brought to Salamanca. When the Generalísimo saw him, he is reported to have said: 'No, that's not the one. The one I want is taller.'[22]

Jay Allen's report from Badajoz was secured with even greater courage than that which had taken him into the beast's lair that was Franco's headquarters. He had been in Lisbon gathering, at some risk, information on the delivery of eight hundred tons of war materiel for Franco, which was being loaded directly from the German ship *Kamerun* on to Spanish railway trucks under the supervision of Spanish officers.[23] Hearing about the massacres in Badajoz, he had set off to find out for himself. In a town in which the occupying force of legionnaires and Moorish mercenaries were killing and torturing at will, he went around incognito courageously collecting information for a lengthy article that has more than stood the test of time. What he wrote about Badajoz would cause Jay to be vilified for years after. More importantly, what he saw was to haunt him for the rest of his life. Twenty-five years later, he recalled in a letter to Louis Fischer that, when he got back across the border to the neighbouring Portuguese town of Elvas, 'I hated even thinking about what I had heard and seen at the very end of the mopping-up. As I recall I spent a couple of days on the town before I got up the courage to sit me down and write it.'[24] It was an account too that was typical of the human-ity and ethical commitment of the man, elements that were apparent from the opening paragraphs written in the sweltering heat of the patio of the Pensão Central, in the Rua dos Chilloes in Elvas. It is worth quoting in its entirety:

Elvas, Portugal, August 25, 1936
This is the most painful story it has ever been my lot to handle: I write it at four o'clock in the morning, sick at heart and in body, in the stinking patio of the Pension Central, in one of the tortuous white streets of this steep fortress town. I could never find the Pension Central again, and I shall never want to.

I have come from Badajoz, several miles away in Spain. I have been up on the roof to look back. There was a fire. They are burning bodies. Four thou-sand men and women have died at Badajoz since General Francisco Franco's

Rebel Foreign Legionnaires and Moors climbed over the bodies of their own dead through its many times blood-drenched walls.

I tried to sleep. But you can't sleep on a soiled lumpy bed in a room at the temperature of a Turkish bath, with mosquitoes and bed bugs tormenting you, and with memories of what you have seen tormenting you, with the smell of blood in your very hair, and with a woman sobbing in the room next door.

'What's wrong?' I asked the sleeping yokel who prowls around the place at night as a guard.

'She's Spanish. She came thinking her husband had escaped from Badajoz.'

'Well, didn't he?'

'Yes,' he said, and he looked at me, not sure whether to go on.

'Yes, and they sent him back. He was shot this morning.'

'But who sent him back?' I knew, but asked nevertheless.

'Our international police.'

I have seen shame and indignation in human eyes before, but not like this. And suddenly this sleepy, sweaty being, whose very presence had been an added misery, took on the dignity and nobility that a fine dog has and human beings most often have not.

I gave it up. I came down into the filthy patio, with its chickens, rabbits, and pigs, to write this and get it over with.

To begin at the beginning, I had heard dark rumors in Lisbon. Everybody there spies on everybody else. When I left my hotel at 4:00 P.M. August 23, I said I was going to Estoril to try my luck at roulette. Several people noted that down, and I hope they enjoyed their evening at Estoril.

I went to the Plaza de Rocio instead. I took the first taxi. I drove around and around and finally picked up a Portuguese friend who knows his business.

We went to the ferry that crosses the Tagus. Once on the other side we told the chauffeur, 'Elvas.' He looked mildly surprised. Elvas was 250 kilometres (about 150 miles) away. We streaked through an engaging country of sandy hills, cork oaks, peasants with side-burns, and women with little bowler hats. It was 8:30 o'clock when we pulled up the hill into Elvas, 'the lock nobody ever opened.' But Elvas knows humiliation now.

We entered a white narrow gate. That seems years ago. I have since been to Badajoz. I believe I was the first newspaperman to set foot there without a pass and the inevitable shepherding by the rebels, certainly the first newspaperman who went knowing what he was looking for.

I know Badajoz. I had been there four times in the last year to do research on a book I am working on and to try to study the operations of the agrarian reform that might have saved the Spanish Republic – a republic that, whatever it is, gave Spain schools and hope, neither of which it had known for centuries.

It had been nine days since Badajoz fell on August 14th. The Rebel armies had gone on – to a nasty defeat at Medellin, if my information was correct, as it sometimes is – and newspapermen, hand-fed and closely watched, had gone on in their wake.

Nine days is a long time in newspaper work; Badajoz is practically ancient history, but Badajoz is one of those damned spots the truth about which will not be out so soon. And so I did not mind being nine days late, if my newspaper didn't.

We began to hear the truth before we were out of the car. Two Portuguese drummers standing at the door of the hotel knew my friend. Portugal, as usual, is on the eve of a revolution. The people seemed to know who 'the others' are. That is why I took my friend along.

They whispered. This was the upshot – thousands of Republican, Socialist, and Communist militiamen and militiawomen were butchered after the fall of Badajoz for the crime of defending their Republic against the onslaught of the Generals and the landowners.

Between fifty and one hundred have been shot every day since. The Moors and Foreign Legionnaires are looting. But blackest of all: The Portuguese 'International Police,' in defiance of international usage, are turning back scores and hundreds of Republican refugees to certain death by Rebel firing squads.

This very day (August 23) a car flying the red and yellow banner of the Rebels arrived here. In it were three Phalanxists (Fascists). They were accompanied by a Portuguese lieutenant. They tore through the narrow streets to the hospital where Senor Granado, Republican Civil Governor of Badajoz, was lying. Senor Granado, with his military commander, Col. Puigdengola, ran out on the Loyalist militia two days before the fall of Badajoz.

The Fascists ran up the stairs, strode down a corridor with guns drawn, and into the governor's room. The governor was out of his mind with the horror of the thing. The director of the hospital, Dr. Pabgeno, threw himself over his helpless patient and howled for help. So he saved a life.

The day before, the mayor of Badajoz, Madroñero, and the Socialist deputy Nicolás de Pablo, were handed over to the rebels. On Tuesday, 40 republican refugees were escorted to the Spanish frontier. Thirty-two were shot the next morning. Four hundred men, women and children were taken by cavalry escorts through the frontier post of Caia to the Spanish lines. Of these, close to 300 were executed.

Getting back in the car, we drove to Campo Maior, which is only seven kilometres (about four miles) from Badajoz on the Portuguese side. A talkative frontier policeman said: 'Of course, we are handing them back. They are dangerous for us. We can't have Reds in Portugal at such a moment.'

'What about the right of asylum?'

'Oh,' he said, 'Badajoz asks extradition.'

'There is no such thing as extradition for a political offense.'

'It's being done all up and down the frontier on orders of Lisbon,' he said belligerently.

We cleared out. We drove back to Elvas. I met friends who are as much Portuguese and vice versa.

'Do you want to go to Badajoz?' they asked.

'No,' I said, 'because the Portuguese say their frontier is closed and I would be hung up.'

I had another reason. The rebels do not like newspapermen who see both sides. But they offered to take me through and back again without complications. So we started. Suddenly we drove out of the lane on to a bridge that leads across the Guadiana River into the town where Wellington's troops ran amok in the Peninsular wars, where now is just another tragedy.

Now we were in Spain. My friends were known. The extra person in the car (myself) passed unnoticed. We were not stopped.

We drove straight to the Plaza. Here are my notes: Cathedral is intact. No it isn't. Driving around the side I see half a great square tower shot away.

'The Reds had machine-guns there and our artillery was obliged to fire,' my friends said.

Here yesterday there was a ceremonial, symbolical shooting. Seven leading Republicans of the Popular Front (Loyalists), shot with a band and everything before three thousand people. To prove that Rebel generals didn't shoot only workers and peasants. There is no favouritism to be shown between the Popular Fronters.

We stopped at the corner of the narrow Calle de San Juan, too narrow for traffic. Through here fled the loyalist militiamen to take refuge in a Moorish fortress on a hill when the descendants of those who built it broke through the Trinidad gate. They were caught by Legionnaires coming up from the gate by the river and shot in batches on the street corners. Every other shop seemed to have been wrecked. The conquerors looted as they went. All this week in Badajoz, Portuguese have been buying watches and jewelry for practically nothing. Most shops belong to the Rightists. It is the war tax they pay for salvation, a Rebel officer told me grimly. The massive outlines of the Alcázar fortress showed at the end of the Calle de San Juan. There the town's defenders, who sought refuge in the tower of 'Espantaperros' were smoked out and shot down.

We passed a big dry goods shop that seems to have been through an earthquake. 'La Campana,' my friends said. 'It belonged to Don Mariano, a leading Azañista (follower of Manuel Azaña, President of Spain). It was sacked yesterday after Mariano was shot.'

We drove by the office of the Agrarian Reform, where in June I saw the Chief Agronomist, Jorge Montojo, distributing land, incurring naturally the hatred of the landowners and, because he was a technician following strictly bourgeois canons of law, the enmity of the Socialists, too. He had taken arms in defense of the Republic, and so –

Suddenly we saw two Phalanxists halt a strapping fellow in a workman's blouse and hold him while a third pulled back his shirt, baring his right shoulder. The black and blue marks of a rifle butt could be seen. Even after a week they showed. The report was unfavourable. To the bull ring with him.

We drove out along the walls to the ring in question. Its sandstone walls looked over the fertile valley of Guadiana. It is a fine ring of white plaster and red brick. I saw Juan Belmonte (bullfight idol) here once on the eve of the fight, on a night like this, when he came down to watch the bulls brought in. This night the fodder for tomorrow's show was being brought in, too. Files of men, arms in the air.

They were young, mostly peasants in blue blouses, mechanics in jumpers. 'The Reds.' They are still being rounded up. At four o'clock in the morning they are turned out into the ring through the gate by which the initial parade of the bullfight enters. There machine guns awaited them.

After the first night the blood was supposed to be palm deep on the far side of the lane. I don't doubt it. Eighteen hundred men – there were women, too – were mowed down there in some twelve hours. There is more blood than you would think in eighteen hundred bodies.

In a bullfight when the beast or some unlucky horse bleeds copiously, 'wise monkeys' come along and scatter fresh sand. Yet on hot afternoons you smell blood. It is all very invigorating. We were stopped at the main gate of the plaza, my friends talking to Phalanxists. It was a hot night. There was a smell. I can't describe and won't describe it. The 'wise monkeys' will have a lot of work to do to make this ring presentable for a ceremonial slaughter bullfight. As for me, no more bullfights – ever.

We came to the Trinidad gate through these once invulnerable fortifications. The moon shone through. A week ago a battalion of 280 legionnaires stormed in. Twenty-two live to tell the tale of how they strode over their dead, and, with hand grenades and knives, silenced those two murderous machine guns. Where were the government planes? That is one of the mysteries. It makes one quake for Madrid.

We drove back to town past the republic's fine new school and sanitary institute. The men who built these are dead, shot as 'Reds' because they sought to defend them.

We passed a corner.

'Until yesterday there was a pool blackened with blood here,' said my friends. 'All the loyal military were shot here and their bodies left for days as an example.'

They were told to come out, so they rushed out of the house to greet the conquerors and were shot down and their houses looted. The Moors played no favorites.

Back at the Plaza. During the executions here Mario Pires went off his head. He had tried to save a pretty fifteen year old girl caught with a rifle in her hands. The Moor was adamant. Mario saw her shot. Now he is under medical care at Lisbon.

I know there are horrors on the other side aplenty. Almendra Lejo, Rightist, was crucified, drenched with gasoline, and burned alive. I know people who saw charred bodies. I know that. I know hundreds and even thousands of innocent persons died at the hands of revengeful masses. But I know who it was who rose to 'save Spain' and so aroused the masses to a defense that is as savage as it is valiant.

Anyway, I am reporting Badajoz. Here a dozen or more rightists were executed every day during the siege. But – back in Elvas in the casino I asked diplomatically: 'When the Reds burned the jail, how many died?'

'But they didn't burn the jail.' I had read in the Lisbon and Seville papers that they had.

'No, the brothers Plá prevented it.'

I knew Luis and Carlos Plá, rich young men of good family, who had the

305

best garage in southwestern Spain. They were Socialists because they said the Socialist Party was the only instrument which could break the power of Spain's feudal masters.

'They harangued the crowd that wanted to burn the three hundred Rightists in the jail just before the Moors entered, saying they were going to die in defence of our Republic, but they were not assassins. They themselves opened the doors to let these people escape.'

'What happened to the Plás?'

'Shot.'

'Why?'

No answer.

There is no answer. All these people could have been allowed to escape to Portugal three miles away, but they weren't.

I heard Gen. Queipo de Llano announcing on the radio that Barcarrota had been taken and that 'rigorous justice' was dispensed with the Reds there. I know Barcarrota. I asked the peasants there in June if, now that they were given land, they would not be capitalist.

'No,' indignantly.

'Why?'

'Because we only get enough for our own use, not enough to be able to exploit others.'

'But it's yours.'

'Of course.'

'What do you want from the republic now?'

'Money for seed. And schools.'

I thought then, 'God help anybody who tries to prevent this.'

I was wrong. Or was I? At the casino here, which is frequented mostly by landowners and rich merchants, I ventured to inquire what the situation was before the rebellion.

'Terrible. The peasants were getting 12 pesetas for a 7 hour day, and nobody could pay it.'

That is true. It was more than the land could stand. But they had been getting from 2 to 3 pesetas from sunup to sundown before. Twenty Spaniards with red and yellow ribbons in their buttonholes sat around the casino and from the fact that they were here I assumed that they did not feel Franco had yet made Spain quite safe.

On the moon-drenched streets there was a smell of jasmine, but I had another smell in my nostrils. Sweet, too horribly sweet.

On the foothill in the white Plaza by a fountain, a youth leaning against the wall with his feet crossed was playing his guitar and a soft tenor sang a melting Portuguese love song.

At Badajoz in June boys still sang beneath balconies. It will be a long time before they do again.

Suddenly through the square shot a car with a red and yellow flag. We halted. Our drummers came to meet us.

'They are searching the hotel.'

'For whom?'

'Don't know.'

We shall go away, as soon as it is light. People who ask questions are not popular near this frontier, if it can be called a frontier.[25]

Jay might have hoped to gain a Pulitzer for such an important article but his boss Colonel McCormick, the owner of the *Chicago Daily Tribune*, refused to submit it. In fact, this and other articles convinced the Colonel that Jay was too left-wing and in October 1936, he would dismiss him along with other liberal members of the paper's foreign staff.[26] The article had outraged the American Catholic hierarchy, which was trying to present Franco and the rebels as saintly crusaders. Accordingly, Jay was attacked on the grounds that he was not actually present during the massacre. What is clear from a close reading of the article is that Jay was driven into and around Badajoz, at very considerable risk, by his Portuguese friends. He appears to have remained more or less hidden in the car for most of the time, listening to the conversations of his friends with their local acquaintances. The chronicle was assembled from what he read in the Portuguese press, from what he saw and heard while in Badajoz and from what both his Portuguese friends and Spanish refugees told him in Elvas, between his arrival on 23 August and beginning to write the article in the early hours of the morning of the 25th.

A man who was to make a business out of impugning Jay's credibility, Father Joseph F. Thorning, of Mount St Mary's College, claimed that the massacre was no more than a 'stupid story'. In a pamphlet, he wrote: 'The story of Mr Jay Allen may be disregarded inasmuch as he himself acknowledges that he arrived eight days later.' Thorning, on the other hand, had no difficulty in believing the statement, 'I went thoroughly into that question and satisfied myself that no Red who surrendered at Badajos [sic] was shot', from Francis McCullagh, who was in the town ten weeks after the bodies had been removed.[27] Jay's account gives plenty of details that he did know about, what he saw in Portugal with the terrified refugees, the bodies in the cemetery, interviews with Francoists. What he had to say is, in any case, sustained by the other great eye-witnesses, Mario Neves, who wrote on 15 August of the scenes of desolation and dread that he had witnessed, and Mario Pires, who was so traumatized by what he saw that he had to be admitted to the San José mental clinic in Lisbon. Jay's account is also substantiated by subsequent scholarship.[28]

Herbert Southworth commented on errors in the printed despatch on the Badajoz massacre:

> It was originally sent from a cable office in Tangier. At one place it reads, as published: 'I know there are horrors on the other side aplenty. Almendra Lejo, rightist, was crucified, drenched with gasoline and burned alive.' Jay Allen obviously cabled something like the following: 'ALMENDRALEJO RIGHTIST CRUCIFIED...' which should have been decoded from the cablese as follows: 'A rightist of Almendralejo [Andalusian town] was crucified.' [...] Any news report, technically transmitted by telegraph, telephone, radio, and so on, has a built-in possibility for errors, and this fact should be taken into consideration when judging news dispatches as historical sources.[29]

On 10 September, Gerald Brenan accompanied Jay to Lisbon to investigate rumours of a mutiny and to gather material on the way in which the Spanish rebels were being supplied through Portugal. By 13 September, they were back in Tangier and Jay was immediately flying to Gibraltar and then Madrid. On 16 September 1936, he reached the capital and spent the evening with Lester Ziffren, recounting tales of the plight of foreign correspondents in the rebel-held south. He later met up with Louis Fischer and told him about what he had seen in Badajoz. Fischer recalled: 'We visited Badajoz together last April on an automobile trip through Spain to study Azaña's agrarian reform.' Jay told him that when he had entered the bullring, he saw 'the arena covered with a layer, seven inches thick, of black hardened human blood. Every home in this small town mourned a member or relative. The population, he states, looked grim and sullen. It looked no one in the eye.' Jay brought news that, after the columns of Yagüe had moved on to Madrid, the cleaning-up operations to the south of Badajoz had started in earnest and taken their toll of the small town of Barcarrota, 'where we attended a Socialist meeting in April'.[30]

His friend and colleague, John Whitaker, after commenting that Jay had 'generally proved himself the best informed journalist in Spain', noted with respect to this historic report: 'His story was denied and he was vilified by paid speakers from one end of the United States to the other.'[31] An interesting and perhaps representative example of this vilification would be found in a wildly inaccurate letter from Father Thomas V. Shannon to the editor of the New York Catholic magazine, *The Tablet*:

> Naturally, like all American writers abroad, Duranty, Gunther, Farson, he was pretty far to the left. Incongruous as it may seem, Allen represented the most conservative, not to say reactionary paper in the country. In a way, he was a free-lance. Colonel McCormick of the *Tribune* picked him up in Europe: he had not been sent abroad. He was dropped once, due to violent protests by Notre Dame, and a second time on protest from another source. He did not quit.

Shannon claimed that Jay Allen was born and brought up as a Catholic until he was nine-years-old and thus saw his later political position as a betrayal:

> In Madrid, he fell in with Azaña and his crew. He was frankly committed to that regime, and so wrote. He approved with glee of confiscation and took particular delight in the plight of the Jesuits. He had been filled with all sorts of information about Jesuit wealth, all based on hearsay. He wasn't in the least shocked with the pillage and arson in Madrid or Malaga. All of this he wrote to whatever American paper would accept his stuff. After the revolt of 1936, he became increasingly violent, and long before Badajoz had been letting his imagination run riot. He finally became a bitter partisan. The transition was not difficult. He was in the mood for this five years ago when I met him in Madrid.[32]

Shannon's character assassination of Jay was widely circulated. It was part of a concerted effort by the Catholic hierarchy to smear those who supported the Spanish Republic.[33] A copy of it eventually reached Jay. The public assault on Jay was carried out by Dr Joseph F. Thorning, one of Franco's most tireless propagandists in the United States. Thorning was an odd choice of champion to put up against Jay, since he was a man who had no prior knowledge of Spain. Jay recalled later:

> Dr Joseph Thorning popped up from where I wouldn't know, originally with an S.J. after his name. These initials were later dropped for reasons never made clear to me although I did hear something about an

inheritance. Poverty, chastity and obedience seemed not to apply to him, not the first two anyway and I know whereof I speak.[34]

In 1938, Thorning, hearing that Jay was preparing to write more fully on what had happened at Badajoz, wrote sarcastically: 'The mere fact that he finds this necessary 18 months after his first efforts indicates that his original story didn't impress the more thoughtful readers. The unfortunate truth (for Mr Allen) is that, arriving 8 days late, he missed the boat. Hearsay evidence is a poor substitute.' Thorning's own account was based on the book of Major McNeil-Moss, who was never there.[35] The success of the Catholic campaign may be measured in the fact that there were references in the American provincial press to 'the Bolshevik Jay Allen' and claims that he was earning huge sums in Moscow gold.[36] More specifically, Jay's beloved aunt, his mother's sister, turned against him because of the poisonous criticisms of Joseph Thorning. Among other things, Thorning had acquired and published a letter from Jay's godmother, Mrs J. Ham Lewis, to the effect that, after the death of his mother, he had been raised in godless and alcoholic surroundings.[37]

Although the Badajoz article will probably be Jay Allen's most important legacy, also quite remarkable was his achievement in securing, on 3 October 1936, the last ever interview given by the imprisoned Falangist leader José Antonio Primo de Rivera. When rumours abounded that José Antonio was dead, Jay was able to interview him in Alicante jail as a result of an invitation from Rodolfo Llopis, who was now the undersecretary to prime minister Francisco Largo Caballero. In order to gain access to the prisoner, Jay had first to convince the local anarchist-dominated Public Order Committee. Over two fraught meetings, he managed to persuade them by saying that, if they did not permit the interview, he would have to write that the Republican Government had no authority. On entering the exercise patio of the prison, Jay Allen found José Antonio and his brother Miguel in good physical condition. The Falangist leader reacted furiously when told that the rebels' defence of privileged interests had swamped his party's rhetorical ambitions for sweeping social change, saying: 'If it turns out to be nothing but reaction, then I'll withdraw my Falangists and I'll, I'll probably be back here in this or another prison in a very few months. If that is so, they're wrong. They'll provoke still worse reaction. They'll precipitate Spain into an abyss. They'll have to cope with me. You know that I've always fought them. They called me a heretic and bolshevik.'[38] José Antonio may have been exaggerating his revolutionary aims to curry favour with his jailers, but his barefaced denials of the activities of Falangist gunmen before the war and of

Falangist complicity in atrocities since was clearly infuriating the anarchists who had witnessed the interview.

In view of José Antonio's anything but conciliatory attitude, Jay felt obliged to terminate the interview 'because of the astounding indiscretions of Primo'.[39] He later told Claude Bowers' biographer, Holman Hamilton:

> I believe that in the Fall of '36 when I went to see him in prison in Alicante just before his execution, I was the last foreigner he spoke to and perhaps the last human being apart from his jailers, a wild and woolly lot calling themselves a Committee of Public Safety – which was before Negrín put a stop to that sort of thing.[40]

In fact, there was more to the visit to Alicante than there seemed at the time or than Jay was prepared to tell Hamilton. In fact, as he recalled to Herbert Southworth:

> As I believe you know, Negrín had urged me to see JA and then go on to France or England and try to promote an exchange. For Caballero's son, although Caballero had refused to consider that. I did my damnedest bit but, as you know, I accomplished nothing. Negrín's idea was that José Antonio was a patriot by his lights and bull-headed besides and that he would cause Franco a lot of trouble. Maybe. But, thinking back on the mood of the Committee of Public Safety in Alicante, I doubt whether they would have let José Antonio out of their grasp regardless of what Madrid asked or ordered.[41]

In April 1937, Jay made a speech to the Chicago Council on Foreign Relations. He started off saying: 'When I came out of Spain I could not talk about it at all to anybody. It was like a nightmare, a four months long nightmare, the only difference being that from a nightmare you awake.' He talked about the horror unleashed when the military coup provoked the collapse of the Republican state and opened the way to violence in Republican territory. He tried to explain why the Republic had such a bad press in the United States, arguing powerfully that the truth does not come out of rebel Spain:

> No correspondent can write it and stay there…What the rebels do the world does not know, perhaps does not care to know. But every last atrocity on the loyalist side has been told amply and more often than

not without any explanation at all. There is another reason why the truth has not been told. Most of the correspondents who went to Spain were ignorant of the Spanish scene. They knew all about fascism and communism, the issue about which everyone nowadays is so glib, and they knew nothing about Spain. They took stock in Franco's crusade to save Spain from the 'reds'. Franco's rebellion is in reality the French revolution in reverse. But how can you expect a correspondent whose stock in trade is communism and fascism to deal in anything so démodé as the French revolution? They do not know. Then there is another reason. There are elements in this country, press services and organizations, that have sought to draw some profit from the red issue.

Stressing that 'It has been a great tragedy, a great tragedy!', he ended: 'I ask as someone about to return to this "horror" that people in this democracy of ours try to read about Spain with open minds. And I ask too that in this country of ours interested groups not be allowed to muzzle truth, to stifle press, to pin "red" labels on correspondents who are writing the truth as they see it. They, we, can do no more.'[42]

Catholic efforts to discredit Jay Allen and Herbert Matthews were partly based on material supplied by William Carney and Edward Knoblaugh. Thorning distributed to a wide network of correspondents a statement from Edward Knoblaugh about Jay:

It is not exactly a secret among the foreign correspondents in Spain that Mr Allen, ardent Socialist, did a considerable amount of stumping (some uncharitable souls might call it 'agitating') in Spain for the Leftist revolt cause long before the war. Close friend of Socialist leader Del Vayo, and of Leftist revolt leader Luis Quintanilla, the painter, Allen was arrested during the 1936 [sic] revolt for allegedly harbouring the revolutionary executive committee in his apartment. Files of the New York Times during that month will reveal that he was warned by Ambassador Bowers to keep out of Spanish politics. The article in question (I do not recall the exact date) was written by Mr Carney, and resulted in a bitter feud between the two during the remainder of their assignment in Madrid.[43]

Knoblaugh himself published extremely dubious atrocity propaganda for the Francoists and contributed to the cover-up on Guernica. According to Jay Allen, the entire book written by Knoblaugh was a fabrication: 'As you know, some

Jesuit or other helped him with his book. He was hardly literate. If you remember the book, it was a very special production, wildly untrue. Of course, Eddie did have some odd ideas and his powers of observation were not exceptional but it was odd that his "memoires" came out in that special pattern.'[44] In 1942, Jay met him in Peoria, where he was working on the local paper, the *Peoria Star*. When Jay raised the issue of the letter, Knoblaugh, who was not very bright, replied that it had been 'taken care of', by which he meant that he had written to Thorning to protest that personal letters should not be circulated freely. Jay retorted that 'the matter may have been "taken care of" with the man of God but not yet with me, seeing as how the letter had been written and was about me and, among other things, was quite wrong'.[45] In a similar effort to convince Milly Bennett that his slanders were of no importance, Knoblaugh wrote: 'I am happy to say that not a single statement of fact that I made in the book about the forces that were at work was challenged by those who would most have liked to have torn me to pieces. I knew what I was talking about and the Loyalist supporters knew that I knew.' This was far from the truth, but it was hardly surprising that it was the view of someone who could write: 'I think I have read almost every book out on the war, and believe me, I have never seen such a mess of junk as some of them are. Others have a modicum of fact, but it seems that no one tried to be objective and impartial except myself.' Since Knoblaugh believed that the Russians were behind the Asturian miners' uprising of 1934, his views could hardly be described as objective.[46]

After Jay lost his job with the *Chicago Daily Tribune* in October 1936, he did some work for the *New York Times* but was principally occupied in various tasks on behalf of the Republic, including trying to buy arms. Gerald Brenan wrote to his friend Ralph Partridge that, on 4 November in London, he had watched Jay make a deal for the purchase for the Spanish Republic of twenty Austrian Army tanks, thousand-pound notes fluttering about 'like postage stamps'.[47] However, his principal task consisted of lobbying in Washington. In April 1937, he sailed for France first class on the *Normandie* with his wife Ruth and son Michael. David A. Smart, the publisher of the hugely successful men's magazine, *Esquire*, and the editor Arnold Gingrich, were on board. Smart wanted to launch a new fortnightly magazine, to be called *Ken – The Insider's World* ('ken' from the Scottish 'to know'), and aimed at giving the public the 'lowdown' on world events as seen by 'insiders'. At first, Smart was attracted to the idea of the new venture being radical and militantly anti-fascist and told Jay: 'this magazine will be the first big break the under-dog in America has had'. Jay's reputation for scoops and his Washington connections made him the ideal editor, hence the trip to Europe to collect material for the first issue. From Paris, Jay wrote to Smart explaining the Popular Front in France and suggesting that *Ken* would be the magazine for the future Popular Front in America, as 'a united front of all decent and intelligent liberal and progressive elements'. Smart was 'thrilled' and authorized Jay to engage various journalists. During the summer of 1937, Jay and Ruth stayed in St Jean de Luz, close to the Spanish border, from where Jay made a succession of forays into Spain. On his return to New York, taking Smart at his word, Jay engaged editors, researchers and commissioned investigations. The dummy for the first issue contained a 20,000-word feature on the fascist assault on democracy. Smart did not like it and it was scrapped in favour of more short items. Smart did not like that either. Jay's concept was too serious and too radical, which did not please potential advertisers. In October 1937, Jay was replaced by George Seldes, who was only slightly more populist and hardly less radical. Seldes wrote later:

> I have seen the dummies, layouts, stories, illustrations, and photographs which Allen prepared, all accurate and interesting pieces, superior to anything which has yet appeared in *Ken*, and yet I have heard Smart sneer about spending forty or fifty thousand dollars on the Allen regime 'and not having a damn story to show for it'.

Seldes told Hemingway that advertisers had threatened to withdraw from *Esquire* if *Ken* published pro-union material. Seldes was reduced to the rank of contributor and wrote to Hemingway that 'Smart has the coldest feet in America. In addition to cold feet he is a dirty hypocrite.' Learning that Smart had commissioned 'red-baiting' cartoons to please the advertising agencies, Seldes wrote that Smart was 'a doublecrossing son of a bitch'. The first issue did not appear until 31 March 1938, with Hemingway and Paul de Kruif roped in as token editors.[48]

In the autumn, while still working on *Ken* at the New York offices of *Esquire*, Jay was also acting on behalf of Negrín. It is clear from a rather oblique letter to Claude Bowers about an abortive meeting with the Secretary of State, Cordell Hull, that Jay would appear in Washington from time to time as a lobbyist for the Spanish Republican government. In the same letter, he referred to a meeting in Poughkeepsie with the President's son, James Roosevelt, to discuss 'a quite remarkable set of proposals' from Negrín. He explained what had happened in a later letter to Hemingway's biographer, Carlos Baker: 'I myself happened to be the messenger designated to hand to FDR in the early Fall of 1937 a letter stating in black and white how he felt, stating (if memory serves) that the Russians would all too happily crawl back off the limb they were on, IF we would do something to enable the Republic to buy the arms it was entitled to buy under international law.' Having learned that there was apparently no copy of the letter in the Roosevelt archive at Hyde Park, Jay wrote: 'All I know is that I handed it to Jimmie Roosevelt in Poughkeepsie when he was seated beside his father in the automobile in which they were about to take off on a vacation.'[49]

On 7 May 1938, Roosevelt's Secretary of the Interior, Harold L. Ickes, wrote in his diary:

> Jay Allen came to see me yesterday. Allen used to be a foreign correspondent for *The Chicago Tribune*, but he was fired while he was covering the Spanish war for that paper. He is outraged over our embargo on munitions of war to Loyalist Spain. He thinks, and I agree with him, that this is a black page in our history. He believes that President Roosevelt has been imposed upon by the career men who sit at the feet of Great Britain and think that all wisdom in international affairs begins and ends with the British Foreign Office. He regards the Loyalists' brave fight as a real stand for democratic principles. As he put it, neutrality has been made an instrumentality of wanton destruction...More and more letters of protest are coming to my desk against this embargo. *The New York Times* had a front-page story a few days ago to the effect that the President was getting ready to lift the embargo. Allen thinks that this story was a deliberate plant in order to stir up the Catholics to protest against its lifting and thus make it impossible for the President to act.

When Ickes called on Roosevelt to lift the arms embargo, the president replied that to do so 'would mean the loss of every Catholic vote next fall and that the Democratic members of Congress were jittery about it and didn't want it done. This was the cat that was actually in the bag, and it is the mangiest, scabbiest cat ever.'[50] Jay discovered years later that the story had been written by Arthur Krock of the *New York Times'* Washington bureau. Given Krock's close relationship with Joseph Kennedy, the pro-Franco Ambassador in London, Jay believed that the article had been written precisely to stir up Catholic opinion and kill any chance of the embargo being lifted.[51]

Jay often managed to see Eleanor Roosevelt and on one occasion, he was able for half an hour to put the case for the lifting of the arms embargo to FDR himself. He had carefully prepared for the moment, polishing and rehearsing his remarks. When the day came, he went to Hyde Park and delivered his speech.

When he finished, believing that he had said it all, and said it well, he was thrown into confusion by Roosevelt's laconic response: 'Mr Allen, I could not hear you!' Jay was nonplussed. Had the president really not heard him? Had he not spoken loudly enough? Had he indeed failed at this critical juncture in his life and the life of the Spanish Republic? Seeing his dismay, the president explained: 'Mr Allen, I can hear the Roman Catholic Church and all their allies very well. They speak very loudly. Could you and your friends speak a little louder, please?'[52]

Years later, when trying to fill out his own recollections, Jay made an oblique reference in a letter to Herbert Southworth which reflected the frustrations of their joint lobbying activities:

> Do your files contain any precision about the run-around we got from FDR in June or July '38 – remember when Corcoran got hold of Drew Pearson and a deal was suggested by which WE should lay off a propaganda line that was getting Protestant bishops excited – with cause – and the State Department would go easy on a shipment of plane parts from Canada. Eleanor invited Ruth and me to Hyde Park, if you remember, to tell me in almost those very words that FDR had welshed.[53]

'Corcoran' was the lobbyist Thomas G. Corcoran (known to his friends as 'Tommy the Cork'). Along with Felix Frankfurter, a law professor at Harvard and an informal adviser to Roosevelt, Corcoran was one of Jay's most important contacts in Washington. Drew Pearson was a well-known columnist. Both were members of what was called 'the Roosevelt brains trust'. Pearson was aware that the reactionary wing of the Catholic Church in the United States was conducting one of the most efficient lobbies ever to operate on Capitol Hill.

Before then, Jay had briefly been back in Spain during the winter of 1937–38 and was at the battle for Teruel. He reached Barcelona from Paris on Christmas Day 1937, the battle having begun just over a week before. He spent a hair-raising time in Teruel with Hemingway and Matthews. He wrote to Carlos Baker: 'At Teruel, where it was bitterly cold, EH saved my eardrums when we were on a granite hilltop with no place to hide and being bombed to hell by tri-motor Savoias by showing me how to hold my mouth open by means of a pencil between my teeth.' Hemingway got annoyed when Jay refused to help move an artillery piece mired in the mud, saying: 'I was hired to write, not fight this war!' Jay went on to irritate Hemingway further by reminding him that, under the Geneva

Convention, he had no right to wear sidearms. Jay commented: 'I know, I ran quite a risk of being labelled chicken. But I did not care much; I could think of maybe eight occasions when, if I had been armed, I'd have been a dead duck with no chance to argue.'[54]

On board ship en route home, he wrote an optimistic cable to Bowers:

> I feel that even if Franco takes back Teruel he will have suffered a fearful loss, prisoners, material, prestige and most important of all, his fire has been drawn. They made him strike where they wanted him to strike. Elsewhere would have been more dangerous. Short of busting through our lines east of Teruel he can't recoup. I wouldn't be surprised to see a hot government offensive a long ways from Teruel and then the way of Teruel will be clear. Matthews, Hemingway and I can testify that no prisoners were shot.

He commented with approval: 'I was interested in the cold shouldering of the Communists. They are being pushed out all along the line. They will stand for that and more, I think, because they want to win the war unlike Caballero.' Nevertheless, he ended: 'I still won't buy any stock in your Mr Azaña. The republicans are in the saddle but I don't think that when it is over the war will have been fought entirely to make Spain safe for the Marcelino Domingos et al.'[55]

Given that Thorning and other Catholic propagandists continued to claim that his article on Badajoz was a fake, in the course of 1938, Jay had begun to write a lengthy justification proving from other sources, especially the contemporary Portuguese and Spanish rebel press, that the massacre had happened as he described it. In early 1939, he wrote to George S. Messersmith, Assistant Secretary of State:

> I find myself in the strange position of being obliged to prove that I saw what I saw (and I am proving it for publication with documents from rebel sources exclusively…I have finished a job on the 'bullring massacre' at Badajoz in August 1936, which it was my misfortune to cover. This has been dismissed as a simple lie by Franquist friends. I have gone back to Rebel and to Portuguese papers to prove it. And I find I have thrown myself open to a charge of much greater gravity, for a *Chicago Tribune* correspondent, than lying; I am guilty, it would seem from my own findings, of the most serious offence on the Tribune calendar, namely UNDERSTATEMENT.

The manuscript on Badajoz was an exhaustive piece of work, utterly vindicated by later scholarship, yet Jay never published it. He distributed copies to his contacts in the American press and politics, among whom it created little echo. In the 1960s, when he began to toy with doing something about it, he had to ask Louis Fischer for a copy. In the end, it was Herbert Southworth who had kept a copy and proposed that they expand and publish it.[56]

The work on the Badajoz massacre was intended not just to counter the smears of Thorning and other Catholic propagandists, but was part of a much more ambitious project. This was eventually intended to be the definitive history of the Spanish Civil War. As a preliminary step, Jay wanted to establish a detailed, hour-by-hour, day-by-day, chronology of what had happened all over Spain. When he could spare time from his other activities, he worked, at his office in the front of his home in New York City, with Herbert Southworth (whom he always called 'Fritz'), and a young radical journalist Barbara Wertheim (who would later find fame as historian Barbara Tuchman). What has survived of their work, the Badajoz manuscript, the preliminary notes for the chronology and the chronology itself suggest that, had the project been finished, it would have been a work of supreme importance.[57] During this time, through the house at 21 Washington Square North came a constant parade of Spanish refugees and representatives of Negrín's government. Some, such as Luis Quintanilla or Constancia de La Mora, stayed for lengthy periods. Others were guests at Ruth Allen's endlessly hospitable table, where more often than not the languages spoken were Spanish and French.[58]

When the Western Powers acquiesced in the betrayal of Czechoslovakia at Munich, Jay was shattered. He knew it spelt the end for the Spanish Republic. Years later, he wrote to Herbert Southworth: 'Munich took the guts out of me.'[59] As the Civil War reached its end, Jay Allen worked feverishly to get help for the hundreds of thousands of refugees who had trekked into France and to raise awareness of the threat hanging over the defeated from the victorious Francoists. When Constancia de la Mora arrived in New York in February 1939, he roped her into his campaigns. They lobbied influential and powerful people, and Jay Allen made contact with politicians in Washington to discuss the refugee crisis and Franco's Law of Political Responsibilities. The assistant to Henry A. Wallace, the Secretary of Agriculture, wrote to say that he and Secretary Wallace (who would later be vice-president in Roosevelt's second term) agreed entirely with the points put to them by Allen and Constancia de la Mora.[60] They each wrote letters to the National Labor Relations Board in Washington describing the situation of the defeated Republicans, facing hunger and terror in equal measure.[61] In mid-March, Jay organized a fund-raising dinner of the North American Committee to Aid Spanish Democracy. According to Mrs Vincent Sheean [Diana Forbes-Robertson], Jay chaired 'beautifully' a forum which was addressed by himself, Jimmy Sheean, Leland Stowe, George Seldes, John Whitaker and other correspondents who had been in Spain. Dorothy Parker, W. H. Auden and Ralph Bates also spoke. The event was such a success that it was repeated several times.[62]

Jay was devastated by the final defeat of the Republic at the end of March 1939. His son Michael, twelve years old at the time, recalled: 'The night the Spanish Republic fell was the darkest night I remember in my life. My mother and father were unreachable, gone, lost in grief or depression – and now I think this was probably the beginning of my father's depression.'[63] Nevertheless, Jay knuckled down and went on fighting for the Republic.

The British journalist Henry Buckley, who had started his career in Spain as a stringer for Jay, was not surprised by this. He later wrote of him with affection for the man and admiration for his political commitment:

> I wish there were more people in the world like Jay and I wish I were a good enough writer to describe him adequately. But for me his company is always a wonderful tonic. Conversation with him is like drinking at a cool, refreshing wayside fountain. Jay, like myself, has as far as I know never belonged to any political party. His father is a prosperous lawyer in Portland, Oregon, and Jay has been sailor, Harvard graduate and, finally, foreign correspondent. He has an X-ray mind which goes to the heart of the most intricate questions. And he can, and does, explain them clearly. I am morally lazy. I know that it is all wrong that a Spanish peasant should toil endlessly and remain half-starved and that factory workers should sicken and die of consumption because hygienic conditions are not looked after, and I know all the sordid beastliness of poverty, but I am very apt to just forget about it and to feel that after all I am not to blame and that instead of pointing out the dark spots of our civilisation in my writing as a reporter it is so much simpler to gloss over this and pat the man in power on the back and thus sit pretty with the people who count. But Jay does not have my faculty for putting my conscience into a twilight sleep. His alert and vigorous mind sweeps the cobwebs from the problems of the day.[64]

One of Jay's ideas was that Constancia de la Mora should write an autobiographical account of her part in the Spanish Civil War and thereby bring the cause of the Spanish Republicans to a much wider audience. It was a brilliant idea. Connie was not only an eye-witness, but was a woman who had lived through the war and could tell a dramatic story of her own flight from an aristocratic background to commitment to the Republicans. She was taken in by Jay and Ruth Allen in their house at 21 Washington Square. Constancia de la Mora's biographer, Soledad Fox, has revealed that Jay arranged for a ghost-writer in the form of Ruth McKenney to put Constancia's story into its eventual form. In fact, doubts about the authorship were expressed at the time by the exiled poet Pedro Salinas.

In a letter to his friend, Katherine Whitmore, a professor of Spanish with whom he was in love, Salinas wrote:

> Did you like Connie de la Mora's book? I haven't read it totally but I have flicked through it slowly. Hers? I doubt it. I suspect that it is a collective product of the group that hangs around Jay Allen, a great friend of hers and her husband...The whole thing has the whiff of a political-literary clique. The last time I was in New York, in the home of Jay Allen (a man, incidentally, of the highest intelligence and quite a character) I promised myself not to go back because of the mixture of guests, pseudo-communists and pseudo-writers, who mix everything up. It goes without saying that Connie is not capable of writing the book on her own.

The book was an immense success both commercially and in terms of putting the Republican case to the American public. Thereafter, when a hostile reviewer accused her of pro-Communist partisanship – which was evidently damaging to the Spanish Republican position in the United States – she turned to Jay Allen to orchestrate her defence. He did so again when the Robles case was resuscitated with damaging implications for the Republic as a whole and for Constancia's press office in particular.[65]

Not long after the arrival of Constancia, in May 1939, Jay Allen accompanied Negrín as interpreter when he made the rounds of American politicians.[66] To his intense disappointment, two appointments set up with President Roosevelt were cancelled at short notice. Eleanor Roosevelt invited them to tea by way of feeble consolation. Jay made frantic, but ultimately unsuccessful, efforts to arrange a meeting with the president. His efforts were hampered by continued allegations from both American Catholics and some Spanish Republicans that Negrín was in the pocket of the Communists. Jay wrote to Bowers: 'Anyone who tries to raise the "Red" bugaboo in connection with this migration must be called a liar.' He was understandably distressed that the ever more frenetic anti-Communist stance of both Indalecio Prieto and the ex-Spanish Ambassador to Washington, Fernando de los Ríos, was unjustly damaging the prestige of Negrín.[67] Jay also took part, along with Constancia and with Mrs Luisi Álvarez del Vayo, in an unending stream of meetings on behalf of the Spanish Refugee Relief Campaign to raise awareness of the refugee crisis. He also made regular representations to the State Department in an effort to get the American Government to provide shipping to get the refugees out of France to Mexico. This was something that he would go on doing throughout the Second World War whenever he was in the United States. In 1943, he conducted a public conversation on the subject with Isabel de Palencia before a large audience in the New York Town Hall.[68]

Through his work on behalf of Spanish refugees, Jay had a serious falling-out with Constancia. The occasion of their estrangement was the revelation in the United States of the appalling conditions in which the Spanish exiles were still being kept in French concentration camps. Short of food, water, clothing and proper shelter, and deprived of medical care, thousands were dying each week. To make matters worse, the French authorities had raided and closed down the headquarters of the Servicio de Evacuación de los Refugiados Españoles. The Reverend Herman F. Reissig, the executive secretary of the North American Committee to Aid Spanish Democracy, which had become the Spanish Refugee Relief Committee with which Jay and Constancia were working, cabled the Department of State requesting that the American Government make an official protest. Constancia interceded with Eleanor Roosevelt in the hope of getting her intervention. It was made clear that the American policy of non-intervention remained in place, not least, in this case, because of suspicions about the SERE's Communist connections.[69]

However, things would get worse when the French Government made a decision – known as the 'Ménard decree' after General Jean Ménard, the superintendent of the camps – to send the Spanish refugees back across the Pyrenees. Communist veterans of the Abraham Lincoln Battalion of the International Brigades demonstrated against the decision in front of the French Consulate in New York. Several were arrested, including Milt Wolff, the last commander of the battalion, and Lou Ornitz, who, it will be recalled, had been in the Francoist prison at San Pedro de Cardeña, where he had clashed with William Carney. In the context of the Hitler–Stalin pact, Herman Reissig and Jay Allen did not believe that it was prudent to be associated with Communist-inspired actions nor indeed to provoke the French Government against the refugees. Accordingly, they and the majority of the Spanish Refugee Relief Committee voted against participation in the protests. In consequence, an outraged

Constancia wrote from Mexico City an open letter to Jay on 9 April 1940 that destroyed their friendship: 'Dear Jay Allen, Because I know the excellent work you did in America during the two and a half years of the war in Spain and even afterwards, because I witnessed your clear understanding of the treason that handed over Madrid and its heroic population to Franco, I cannot now comprehend what has come over you.' She went on to accuse Jay of accepting the French denial that the Ménard order had actually been issued and thereby abandoning the Spanish refugees 'in this their hour of greatest need'. She ended with an accusation that he was lying in order to safeguard a comfortable living.[70]

A week after seeing the letter, a deeply mortified Jay wrote to Claude Bowers:

> The Spanish Refugee Relief Campaign, a development of the old North American Committee and the Friends of Spanish Democracy, was supposed to be non-political in character. Our enemies called us 'communists'. We were not, or at least not since I went on the Board last May. It was I who insisted that our funds be expended in France through the Quakers last October when our regular agencies over there broke down. In the past six weeks there has been an effort on the part of our communist friends to run the organization to suit themselves and in ways that would have discredited us and, what is more, prove retroactively the truth of charges against us. I stood my ground and was aided by my valiant colleague, Mrs Vincent Sheean. A bust-up resulted and the communists withdrew to a rival organization of their own creation in which I wish them much success. There was a hell of a row over the Menard expulsion order which Daladier stupidly saw fit to deny as a 'fake'. It was not a fake. But I saw no reason to allow the communists to come out in front and compromise all of our friends in behalf of the refugees. To have done so would have been to discredit Don Juan [Negrín] and Vayo and the other Spanish Republicans.

Constancia de la Mora was absent from the meeting at which the decision was taken to channel funds through the Quakers and incandescent with rage. Her consequent attack on Jay was especially painful:

> I am now considered Public Enemy No.1 by our communist friends and the recipient of an open letter from a lady whom I have always known as Connie but who signs herself 'Constancia de la Mora'. I enclose it for your perusal. Let me say that I have answered it with a personal letter to

Connie and signed Jay in which I point out that I find it difficult to answer an open letter from a friend, particularly an open letter ending as hers ends.[71]

Over twenty years later, Jay was still smarting from the injustice of her accusations and wrote to Louis Fischer:

I did indeed express myself...about what I considered to be the harshness of the French towards the Spanish refugees but also about the ghastly unwisdom of the Lincoln Brigade boys picketing the French consulate in New York. On this subject I had several times spoken my piece in public. (Incidentally, I find a letter from Ernest Hemingway at that time saying that while the French were bastards any other nation would have simply called out the cavalry and driven our people back to Franco.)

Jay felt so bitter that when Constancia asked for help to return to the United States, he refused: 'I sent her a message by a mutual friend to the effect that I worshipped her memory and hated her guts. And this was fairly accurate.'[72]

Jay was also accused by the veterans' association of being 'more friendly to the French Government than to the Spanish refugees'. He was linked with Ralph Bates, now denounced as a red-baiting liar, and with the Dies Committee, as the House of Un-American Activities Committee was known. Around this time, he met Earl Browder, the Secretary-General of the Communist Party of the USA, and told him that 'there was little difference between his attitude towards his "liberal" allies and that of Congressman Martin Dies: they both considered us to be stooges'.[73] After all he had done for the Republican cause, it must have been unutterably saddening to read in the veterans' newsletter that 'the Spanish refugees can expect only betrayal, imprisonment and death from these defenders of British and French Imperialism'.[74] In fact, Juan Negrín had insisted that the plight of the refugees never be used against the French. Accordingly, he wrote to Negrín: 'I am very glad that we took the position we did, in spite of having lost many friends like Connie. Had we not taken that position we would never again have had this country's ear.' He went on to say:

if today this country does not view with alarm the activities in behalf of the Spanish Refugees it is not because of any intelligent action taken by Connie and her friends. And may I also say that I view as nothing short of criminal any action that would tend to label Spanish Republican refugees with a label that, in many parts of the world, is the equivalent of a death sentence. With us, it was not a question of 'defending Daladier' as Connie seemed to think but of defending the refugees. That is still our position and we are doing all we can.[75]

At the time, Jay and Ruth were looking out for Negrín's estranged wife and their three sons, Juan, Rómulo and Miguel.[76]

In the spring of 1940, Jay was immensely moved when the German novelist, and International Brigade commissar, Gustav Regler, dedicated his novel *The Great Crusade* to him. He was trying, along with Hemingway and Eleanor Roosevelt, to help Regler get from France, where he had been held in a concentration camp, to Mexico.[77] In October 1940, Jay wrote to his friend, the Supreme Court judge Justice Felix Frankfurter, who had been a supporter of the Spanish Republic and was now taking part in Roosevelt's campaign to be re-elected for a third term. His letter both reflected his life-long doubts about whether to write a book about the Spanish war and also revealed just how much hope he had tied up in the struggle for democracy in general and in Spain in particular. He wrote:

I am very glad that you found time to read Regler's book. He did not let us down. Also it is a true book. There are so few true books. Hemingway's too is a true book. It is also a miraculous book. That is the way Spain was. Reading it, I am not unhappy that I have written so little but that little was true. I think that I could not have written the kind of book that I was always being urged to write and that I was sometimes tempted to write, and kept it as rigorously, as imaginatively true as Gustav and Ernest, great artists and great spirits both, have known how to do. It may seem silly to say this but to have a good conscience in 1940 is something.

In the letter, he made a passionate statement of his own political position. He recounted his indignation when Adolf B. Berle Jr, the Assistant Secretary of State, an admirer of Franco, had suggested to him that the supporters of the Republic were Communists. He was particularly outraged in the context of the Nazi–Soviet Pact:

If we were all Communists how come that Negrín and Álvarez del Vayo are so passionately pro-British? How come that Regler and Gustavo Durán, two of the great heroes of that incredible holding action, men who accepted Communist discipline for the duration because it was the only

<u>discipline</u> and because <u>we</u> of the western democracies threw Spain into the arms of Stalin, how come that today they are as passionately anti-Nazi as ever? The Communists aren't anti-Nazi. How come that all of the correspondents, Ernest, Jimmie Sheean, Lee Stowe, Matthews, Edgar Mowrer, Fernsworth, Whitaker, Buckley and your servant feel as we do about this war?

He asked Frankfurter to suggest to Berle that he read Regler and Hemingway:

If for no other reason, to find out why one people in Europe, a rabble, poorly armed, facing hideous odds, betrayed by the world, could fight for two years and a half and hold, never giving in until the British and the French and Mr Kennedy's little boy and God knows who else conspired to kick the last prop out from under them.[78]

One week later, Jay Allen went to occupied France, with a commission from the North American Newspaper Alliance, although he had also been asked to work with a committee devoted to helping anti-fascist intellectuals and artists escape from occupied France. What neither NANA nor the American Emergency Rescue Committee knew was that Jay had also been commissioned by British Intelligence to make contact with the nascent French underground to determine the whereabouts of British troops left behind at Dunkirk.[79] The American Emergency Rescue Committee was run from New York with its local office, the Centre Américain, in Marseilles, administered since the summer of 1940 by Varian Fry, a rather prickly American journalist and classical scholar. The New York headquarters had been unhappy with Fry for some time both because of the scale of expenditure that he was incurring and also because of a touchy irritability reflected in numerous petulant and insulting messages. In one letter to his wife on 17 October 1940, Fry referred to Mildred Adams Kenyon, the secretary of the AERC, and her colleagues as 'those boobs in New York', 'those blithering idiots in New York' and 'those imbeciles in New York'.[80] He refused to rein in his expenditure and, in consequence, they had been looking for a replacement. Mildred Adams had been a journalist during the Spanish Civil War, had met and admired Jay Allen and now worked with him in helping Spanish refugees. She therefore thought that he would be an ideal replacement for Fry. Jay was prepared to take on the job because he hoped to be able to extend his work on behalf of Spanish Republican refugees and International Brigaders in captivity. Hemingway had given him a list of names of men whom he particularly wanted to be helped.

In late November 1940, the New York headquarters of the AERC had informed Varian Fry that a replacement was en route. At the end of the year, he received a message at the office, asking him to go to the Hotel Splendide at a certain time, 'to meet a "friend" at the bar'. The emissary was Jay Allen, whom he found sitting with a large Scotch and soda before him. That Jay should have whisky was the first brick in the wall of Fry's hostility ('he must have brought the Scotch from Lisbon, for Marseille's supply had long since run out'). If he took an instant dislike to Jay, Fry was hardly less taken by his companion: 'an American woman of more than middle years whom he introduced as Margaret Palmer'. Fry's hostility had little to do with anything that Margaret Palmer did or said. Henry Buckley recalled meeting her in Jay's apartment in 1934 and described her then as 'a charming American who has lived in Madrid for more years than she cares to recall'.[81]

Jay had travelled to France via Casablanca, to avoid passing through Spain. On 5 December 1940, in Marrakech, he had managed to get an interview with General Weygand, the seventy-four-year-old commander of Vichy French North Africa. Although the published article was anodyne, it clearly made the point about Weygand's commitment to Pétain and Vichy. In a deeply perceptive unpublished account, written shortly after, Jay wrote critically of Weygand's defeatism in June 1940. Comparing him unfavourably with De Gaulle, he made it quite clear that Weygand was utterly unreliable as a potential ally. On the following day, Jay interviewed General Charles Auguste Paul Noguès, the Commander of French forces in Morocco. The interview as published has not survived but Jay's own private account presented Noguès as a cunning and deceitful opportunist, if anything less trustworthy than Weygand.[82]

Jay was also planning to go into Vichy in order to interview Marshal Pétain. He aimed to combine his work for NANA with that of the committee and hoped that his journalist's credentials would be a good cover for his more clandestine activities. To establish distance between himself and the committee, Jay had put Miss Palmer in charge as the filter through which he could keep in touch and also issue instructions to the staff, whom he specifically avoided meeting. After their first meeting, Jay wrote to Fry:

> Following up our conversation today, let me say: First: That I assumed that you are making preparations to leave, with the clear understanding that your work here will be carried on to the best of my ability, without however doing it necessarily in your way and, if possible, expanding in other directions. Second: That, because I have a certain responsibility in

all of this, you will consider me in charge as of January 1. Naturally, you will do what you think best in matters already begun, but you will inform me. I suggest a brief memo <u>daily</u> no matter how cryptic. In this way, we will be able to put Allen au courant. This memo to be left with MP.

He went on to call for a record of all expenditure to be kept and that copies of all correspondence be passed to him via Margaret Palmer.[83]

Fry resented the proposed arrangement, reluctant to hand over his operation, in part because of a fear that Jay, as a journalist, would be under close surveillance by the police. Accordingly, he ignored Jay's instructions, failed to pass on correspondence in and out of the ERC office and exceeded the budget. Jay wrote sternly: 'I must ask you to reread your letter from the Committee which I brought you from New York. You will also reread my note of January 2, please. In the meantime, I must request you <u>formally</u> to do nothing without discussing this further with me; otherwise I shall take <u>effective</u> steps to make you realize what your present position with the ERC actually is.'[84] The nervous and hypersensitive Fry could hardly have been more different from the worldly and battle-hardened Jay Allen. Fry's resentment of Jay grew by the day. He complained to the AERC headquarters in New York about the tone of Jay's note. He justified his opposition to Jay on the grounds that he was 'altogether too impatient, too bossy, too unwilling to listen to others or to benefit by the experience – often painful and costly – of others'. By others, he meant himself. Fry wrote to his wife in embittered terms that make it difficult to recognize Jay Allen: 'The Friend is dictatorial and stupid. He is incapable of listening to anyone (proverbially) and he is utterly uninformed about what we are doing and apparently quite uninterested in learning. He just keeps bullying me into going, without ever stopping to consider the consequences.' During the transition period, Fry informed Margaret Palmer about the cases he had worked on, legally and illegally. Every night she would return to the Hotel Splendide to inform Jay about what she had learned during the day.[85]

Obviously Fry was too volatile to be trusted with information about Jay's work on behalf of the British. In his ignorance and obsessed with his own status, Fry was seething about Jay's arrival and wrote to his wife on 5 January that the New York committee 'seem like a bunch of blithering, slobbering idiots'. Moreover, to Jay's annoyance, he continued to act as if he were in charge of the office. It may be that Jay was not giving the organization the detailed supervision that it needed, but his behaviour was hardly that of the dictatorial 'bullying, pig-headed' bungler portrayed by Fry.[86] Part of the problem was that Fry, apart from being egotistically protective of what he saw as his little empire, was interested only in artists and intellectuals. Jay, inevitably, was concerned with the wider anti-fascist struggle, and was keen to organize the passage into Spain of British military personnel and International Brigaders on the run from the Germans.[87] When Jay Allen went into Vichy, he was surprised, having been told that Marshal Pétain was 'ga-ga', to find him, on 13 January 1941, in a period of considerable lucidity. The result was the first interview given to a foreign journalist since he became head of the French state. After the formal interview, Pétain, whom Jay found to be anything but senile, took him to one side. The Marshal then poured out a heartfelt, indeed venomous, critique of his Foreign Minister, Pierre Laval. He went on to recount how he had summarily dismissed Laval and subsequently suffered intense German pressure to reinstate him. The bulk of the published interview, however, consisted of Pétain justifying the French capitulation in June 1940 and praising the 'progress' made since. In February, Jay toured French North Africa. In Algeria, he interviewed the Governor General, Admiral Jean Marie Abrial, and produced an anodyne article merely reporting the Admiral's words.[88]

In fact, such articles were a cover for his efforts to make contact with people who were helping the Rescue Committee, particularly his old friend Randolfo Pacciardi, who had commanded the Italian Garibaldi Battalion in the International Brigades. The British Special Operations Executive were keen to get him to London to take part in the creation of an Italian Legion to fight alongside the Allies and thereby help undermine the Fascist regime. Pacciardi was in a Vichy prison, and the British had hatched a scheme to get him out and across the desert to the harbour of Oran in Tunisia. Jay's job was to buy a boat that would take Pacciardi at an appointed time out to a waiting British submarine. When Jay went to interview Marshal Pétain, whom he had met many years earlier, he asked him for help in seeing the 'good works' the Vichy Government had achieved in Oran. Delighted, the Marshal said he would provide him with a military police captain as his guide, a four-door open touring car, and six MPs on motorcycles to escort him. With sirens blaring, they went around the town, with the captain showing Jay all the 'good works' achieved by the Vichy regime. When they reached the harbour, Jay saw a cluster of fishing boats at the water's edge and asked the captain if he might interview these simple fishermen about their good lives under Vichy. The captain, delighted that Jay was so interested, urged him on. In full view of the smiling captain and his men, Jay proceeded to buy a boat in which Pacciardi that very night would rendezvous with the British submarine. He pulled out a roll of bills and counted out the substantial sum required for so risky a mission. He shook the fisherman's hand, waved to the captain and returned to the touring car. And off they went, sirens blaring once more, to finish the tour of Pétain's 'good works'.[89]

Things came to a head between Jay and Fry in mid-February 1941 when Jay visited Fry's office at the Centre Américain. Jay's version of the confrontation is not known. According to the anything but reliable Fry, there was a shouting match in which

> He [Jay] said he would like to break my neck. He promised to do the utmost against me as soon as he got back to New York...All during our conversation he boasted how important he was and how successful ('...I'm a bit of a success...') and promised to have me fired out on my ear the minute he got back. He said he had never hated anyone so much in his life, that I was slippery and dishonest, that I was a 'careerist' (what is a 'careerist'?), that I was 'washed up,' that he would 'show me'...It was a regular tornado he let loose in my office...Miss Palmer says he is a genius, but I am inclined to think he is slightly nuts.

In mid-March, to the unconcealed delight of Fry, Jay was caught by the Germans. He had crossed the demarcation line without permission and went to Paris, where he met several people under Gestapo surveillance. He was then followed as he travelled back south and arrested as he tried to cross back into Vichy France. He believed that he had been denounced by an American official with fascist sympathies who had bumped into him on the Champs-Elysées. When arrested, Jay was carrying incriminating notes with the names, ranks and serial numbers of the British troops he had located. To avoid them falling into the hands of the Gestapo, he told the border police that he was sick and needed to go to the bathroom, where he tore up the notes and flushed them down the toilet. When the Gestapo arrived, he handed over notebooks full of relatively innocuous journalistic scribblings. Nevertheless, Jay was accused of spying, sentenced to death, and imprisoned at Chalon-sur-Saône.[90]

When he received the news, Fry wrote to his wife with gloating *schadenfreude*: 'Suppose they torture him? Will he be able to keep his mouth shut about us and our work? Or will he break down and talk when the matches are pushed up under his fingernails and the fire bites into his flesh?' Ten days after Jay's arrest, an operation that he had discussed earlier with Randolfo Pacciardi had ended in catastrophe. The idea was to set up a shuttle to take Spanish and Italian anti-fascist refugees from Oran to Gibraltar, but the Vichy police had got wind of it and set a trap. Bursting with self-satisfaction, Fry wrote to his wife: 'Naturally I was kinda pleased. It was too perfect an end for a boasting, blustering fool not to give observers the moral satisfaction of seeing someone reap his just rewards.' With breathtaking insensitivity, he went on:

> I feel sorry for him not so much because of the discomforts he must be suffering as for the ludicrousness of his career here: it was loudmouthed, spectacular, reckless and brief, and it ended suddenly and foolishly. He must be bursting with hatred for me right now and so, I suppose, are his backers at home. But the fact remains that I was right and he was terribly, incredibly and stupendously wrong.[91]

Admiral William D. Leahy, the American Ambassador to Vichy, and a strongly conservative admirer of Pétain, was irritated by Jay's activities. His initial response was to leave him to rot in Gestapo custody. However, he was shaken out of his lethargy by a telegram from the State Department informing him that 'A very great amount of anxiety has been created in various circles here because of the arrest of Jay Allen. Mrs Roosevelt is personally interested in the matter as well as many other prominent persons', and urging him to report what the Embassy could do to expedite his release. Leahy consulted the French authorities and replied nonchalantly to Washington: 'You will appreciate since Allen went to the occupied zone without any authorisation whatsoever and since he is in the custody of the German authorities, the French are in no position to help in obtaining his release.' He reported that he had asked his first secretary, Maynard B. Barnes, 'to take every appropriate step which in his judgement will facilitate obtaining Allen's release and he is also endeavouring to obtain permission for a member of the Embassy staff to visit Allen. Under the circumstances I can see nothing further that can be done.' Barnes requested the American Press Association in Paris to write to the German occupation authorities requesting that 'all consideration possible be given to the fact that Allen was merely doing what any enterprising newspaper correspondent would like to do'.[92]

In fact, Jay had been doing rather more than that, as was acknowledged by Lord Halifax, the British Ambassador in Washington. It was hardly surprising then that, despite the Press Association doing what Barnes suggested, Jay remained in captivity. A week later, Leahy reported complacently to the State Department that Barnes had written to the German Embassy that

> it was my understanding that the general practice of the military authorities at the line of demarcation is to impose only mild penalties on

those persons who clandestinely cross the demarcation line and that I also understood that of the 60 or more persons arrested in the same vicinity as Allen on the day that he was arrested nearly all have been released either upon the payment of a fine or the completion of a short prison sentence.

Leahy's perception of Jay was that he was an irritant and he was unaware that, for the Germans, he was a prisoner of some significance – a man whose journalistic activities during the Spanish Civil War had significantly helped the Republic. Leahy was happy to accept assurances from the Germans that Allen 'would not be subjected either to worse or better treatment because of being a newspaperman or an American'. In fact, Jay was being repeatedly interrogated by both the Gestapo and Vichy police, who wanted him to admit to being a British agent.[93]

Barnes kept pressing the German Embassy in Paris without success. The response, a clear delaying tactic, was that 'if the American Government intends to express to the Government of the Reich a special desire concerning the case of Mr. Allen' it should do so through the American Embassy in Berlin. It was clear to Cordell Hull that Jay was 'being subjected to more severe treatment than that accorded other persons similarly situated'. Washington formally requested the German Government both to permit a US diplomat to visit Jay and to expedite his early release. Berlin's delays were further related to the arrest in the United States of various German seamen and two propagandists, Dr Manfred Zapp and Günther Tonn. Since Zapp was a close friend of the Nazi Foreign Minister Joaquim von Ribbentrop and Hitler himself had taken an interest in his case, the idea of a prisoner exchange began to take shape. However, things were further complicated by the existence of a French arrest order for Jay on charges of espionage. The French alleged that, while in Vichy, Jay had paid a journalist to steal a compromising ministerial document. On 23 June, for the illegal crossing of the demarcation line, the Germans sentenced Jay to four months' imprisonment, for which only one of the three months already served would be counted. In consequence, Jay was moved from Chalon-sur-Saône to the altogether harsher prison at Dijon. Finally, in mid-July an agreement was reached on a prisoner exchange. That the State Department pursued the case at all and that Attorney General Robert H. Jackson permitted the prisoner exchange was thanks in large part to the Herculean efforts of Ruth Allen. Because of the complications regarding the French accusations, Jay was kept in captivity until August 1941.[94]

On 24 August, shortly after his return, Jay was interviewed by Rex Stout for 'Speaking Liberty Series' on the NBC Red Network for the USA and South America. He related how he had been arrested:

Five months ago, last month, I had crossed over from Free France into the Occupied Zone. The Nazis caught me as I was getting out. A peasant, who had got me in, was to smuggle me out, and when I was looking for him (I learned later he had been arrested) I was picked up by a German customs guard on the demarcation line. These guards are very efficient, they use police dogs and they have a nasty habit of planting land-mines in places where they suspect people are slipping through. I crossed over because I wanted to see what the Nazis were doing in Occupied France. I found out all right in four and a half months in their prison. There, in a military prison in Chalons I found out more than I could have possibly uncovered had I been free.

Perhaps most significantly in terms of his own state of mind, he said that, while in prison, he was constantly asked whether Americans knew what the Germans were doing in France, and commented: 'I used to tell my fellow jail-birds that we were waking up, but now that I'm home I wonder if it is true.' When he was asked if Weygand would be able to resist pressure to throw France actively into the Axis camp, he replied: 'I'm a reporter, not a crystal gazer but my considered opinion is this: resistance to the Nazis, to Franco–German collaboration in North Africa as well as in France itself comes from people who steadfastly refuse to believe that Germany can win, and their resistance is precisely as strong as hope for a democratic victory is strong.'[95]

He soon began to work on a book about his experiences with the title *My Trouble with Hitler*. It was going to be published by Harper, but his inveterate perfectionism consistently delayed the project. He also went on a speaking circuit with the Colsten Leigh agency and the book was often mentioned in the publicity for the lectures. After the Japanese attack on Pearl Harbor, on 7 December 1941, brought the USA into the war, Jay wanted to work again as a war correspondent. However, his friend Robert Sherwood, now in government service, asked him to 'do a job for the Army during the invasion of North Africa, specifically the invasion of Morocco'. Although he would have preferred to be working as a newspaperman, he accepted. Indeed, as Luisi del Vayo wrote to Louis Fischer,

Jay left very mysteriously in an unknown direction. The whole thing was decided apparently in hours and without leaving him more time than to call the friends on the phone to tell them good-bye. Friends' commentary was: at least that settles the book! He sounds very happy and excited, suffering only a little bit of not being able to give more details.[96]

When, on Sunday 8 November 1942, Operation Torch saw Allied forces land in North Africa, Jay found himself the head of the Psychological Warfare Branch of the US Army in Morocco. Admiral Leahy, who in July 1942 had become Chief of Staff to Roosevelt, was not pleased. He had enormous sympathy for Pétain and disapproved of Jay's activities. In his diary notes for 20 October 1942, Admiral Leahy wrote:

> Robert Sherwood of the Office of War Information called to discuss a report which I received from the State Department that Mr Jay Allen was scheduled to go to North Africa, Mr Allen was imprisoned in the occupied zone for travelling without the proper visas. He was then working with General George C. Patton. Mr Allen had initiative and energy, but he lacked discretion.[97]

Officially, Jay was attached to General Eisenhower's headquarters in Algiers with the rank of 'assimilated' colonel. He was actually working under General George C. Patton in Morocco. He coincided there with his friend, Herbert Southworth, who was already in the services working for the Office of War Information. That coincidence aside, war service in North Africa would not be a happy experience for Jay. As he put it himself:

> His distaste for the State Department's policy of appeasing the Vichy crowd, in the persons of Darlan and Giraud, he could not hide, but insists he took orders and followed them 'like any soldier'. He was particularly outraged by what he calls the 'virulent anti-Semitism' of our commanders, coupled with an attitude which he says approached adulation of the Arabs.

He was appalled by a senior officer who told him that he did not understand what was wrong with the 'Nazzees'. More shocking was his discovery that Vichy prison camps held members of the French resistance and ex-International Brigaders. The American high command were not interested in doing anything about this because they accepted the Vichy French explanation that they were dangerous communists. Jay was most shocked by the experience of his close friend, Colonel Arthur 'Michel' Roseborough, of the OSS, stationed in Algiers and in charge of liaison with the French underground. Colonel Roseborough was under orders not to communicate with the Gaullist underground because they were reds. He worked in his office all day doing meaningless things. As Jay related later to his son, the Colonel went to the officers' club and got stinking drunk every night, and then staggered to his office and secretly communicated with the Gaullists. Drunkenness, so called, was his cover.[98]

On 17 December 1942, Eisenhower's friend and aide, Captain Harry C. Butcher, recalled an alarming report from Jay to General Patton regarding the pro-German attitudes of the Vichy French commander in North Africa, General Charles Auguste Paul Noguès and his staff. He claimed in the report that the American policy of appeasement towards Darlan went 'beyond the limits required supposedly by "military expediency" and that our continued support of discredited Vichy-minded generals and bureaucrats would cost us the confidence of the French people on whom we would have to depend during the invasion'.[99] In January 1943, just before Franklyn D. Roosevelt was due to meet Churchill at the Casablanca conference, Jay expressed his concerns about American relations with the pro-Fascist Vichy elements to General Eisenhower, who dismissed him with the brusque statement that there was a war to be won. Jay resigned from the OWI and returned to the USA in February 1943, 'not because he failed to carry out orders he thought morally wrong and politically inexpedient but because his personal sentiments made him a marked man with men, many of them old associates of his, at headquarters.'[100]

After the US embargo on the Spanish Republic and appeasement of the dictators, it was another step on the road to Jay's total disillusionment. His son was shocked by his demeanour: 'When I saw him, I knew something was very wrong. And it got worse.' He was no longer interested in finishing the book, since the war was no longer his war, the war that had started on 18 July 1936 in Spain. As his son put it: 'He had suffered too many defeats. He fought for justice and peace. He fought well. And he was shot down. He said to me more than once, "Michael, don't get on the barricades too soon!" By which I know he meant, "Do not get shot down too soon."' Nevertheless, when he returned to the United States, despite the beginnings of a deep depression from which he would never entirely recover, he undertook another lecture tour and argued his point vigorously, 'hundreds of times, over the radio and in magazine articles'. He commented later: 'it wasn't very glorious but perhaps there was some small contribution in all this to the awakening that eventually came about'.[101]

Hemingway wrote to him about the time that he returned from North Africa. Apparently, Martha Gellhorn had offered to edit the manuscript *My Trouble with Hitler*, and had put off starting a novel until it arrived. Despairing of the endless wait, she began her novel. Hemingway wrote: 'I would have been glad to do it and read several chapters of the manuscript with great interest and admiration.'

However, his other commitments prevented him taking it on: 'I thought there was wonderful stuff in it and I would have been very proud to have been any use to you in preparing it for publication. But it was impossible for me to undertake it at this time.' The next sentence was a priceless example of Hemingway's insensitivity: 'I write you now about something of importance' – this being his need for Jay to provide some information about the pro-Franco activities of Edward Knoblaugh, who had appeared in Havana claiming to be a friend of Jay. Having just told Jay that he could not help with his book because he was busy, he wrote: 'Also, Jay, will you please let me have this at once, no matter how many other things you have to do.' Jay immediately complied.[102]

Jay dabbled with his books on nineteenth-century Spain, on his experiences in the German prison and on the Spanish Civil War. On 20 March 1943, it was announced in the *New York Times* that Jay Allen, recently returned from N. Africa, had delivered a book to Harpers which would be published by summer 1943 under the title *The Day Will End: a personal adventure behind Nazi lines*. This was clearly 'My Trouble with Hitler'. Nothing more was heard of it. Apparently, dissatisfied with the editorial changes that Harpers had suggested, Jay had withdrawn the manuscript and continued to work on it. He and Ruth moved to Seattle during 1944 to take care of his father and his father's estate. His spirits were sustained by the hope that, when Hitler and Mussolini were defeated, something would be done about the Franco dictatorship. He hoped to return to a free Spain, not least to collect the several thousand books that he had had to leave in Torremolinos when he had set off for Gibraltar in July 1936. His great hope was to see the Republic re-established and 'to resume where we left off'. This he thought possible 'if we keep our heads on our shoulders and realize that far more potent than the atom bomb for our defense would be a forthright, courageous policy of support, economic and political, in countries like Spain, where people have come to doubt our intentions'.[103] When that did not happen, and the United States colluded in the survival of Franco, Jay essentially retired. What happened exactly remains a mystery but it appears that there were few commissions coming his way, because he seems to have been blacklisted. After his father died, he began to live off his inheritance. In 1946 he moved to Carmel, and remained there with frequent visits to New York.[104]

In many respects, Jay Allen, the courageous journalist, disappeared. The defeat of the Spanish Republic, the attrition of trying to alert America to the danger of fascism, his experience in a Gestapo prison, and the anti-leftist backlash that poisoned American life in the late 1940s, all conspired to drain away his optimism and determination to go on fighting for what he believed in. His son wrote an article in which it is impossible not to see a reference to a downcast and disillusioned Jay:

> I knew men who fought to preserve the freedom of the Spanish Republic.
> Here were men who lived an ideal of democracy, freedom, opportunity.
> They saw a vision of a new Spain. And then Spain fell and with it their
> dreams. With the dreams were destroyed their lives. I was a small boy
> when that war was fought. Perhaps then the memory is stronger. My
> mind was less cluttered. I saw tragedy more clearly, so death was more
> vivid. Then there were those who sought to awaken America to the threat
> of Hitler's fascism. They loved this country too much to see it betrayed to
> sordid fears and petty ambitions. They saw that our borders lay on the
> Rhine and that our hopes were centred in Paris as well as Milwaukee. But
> they too went down. Premature anti-fascists they were called.

Similarly, he was surely thinking of his father when he wrote of the pain of those 'who nursed the sorrow of blunted goals. These were men who watched their most cherished desires disintegrate piece by piece.'[105]

It was a feeling that seemed to grow as Jay worked on a book about the Spanish Civil War in an attempt to explain what he and others had been fighting for. He wrote to Negrín, along with a lengthy series of detailed queries which revealed just how closely they had worked during the war: 'My trouble has been due in part to something Ruth calls defeatism. I don't care for her choice of words but – need I explain?' He went on bitterly: 'I made a serious mistake going to North Africa and passing up a fat lecture season in 42–43. I have never recovered financially from this. I had the quaint idea that I was serving my country. Imagine!'[106] Explicitly, Michael Allen wrote of Jay: 'My father was a journalist who breathed the air of Spain until it became his country too. Loyal to his nation and all her hopes, he fought for the Spanish Republic. At a very early age I saw the fullness of life reflected in my own home – the fullness that comes alone from dedication to some ideal beyond our limited beings.'[107]

Throughout this time, Jay dabbled in his ongoing interest in nineteenth-century Spain. He told Bowers in 1948 that he was writing a life of Isabel II and again in 1957. However, as with the book on the Spanish Civil War, his perfectionism stood in the way of completion. His research was meticulous but he dithered about sending Bowers a couple of chapters: 'I never seemed to get them into good enough shape. I value your opinion highly and I'd rather pass for a sluggard than for a no account historian.' He and Ruth put a great effort into helping their friend Margaret Palmer, who had lost everything in Spain and was destitute.[108]

In the 1960s Jay watched the revival of interest in the Spanish Civil War stimulated by the publication of Hugh Thomas' book. Interested only in seeing the truth, he urged Herbert Southworth to send Thomas a copy of his manuscript on the activities of the African columns as they occupied Badajoz. Thomas had consulted Southworth in the preparation of his book but, surprisingly, not Jay Allen: 'You are the person to get in touch with him. Despite the suggestions of Ham Armstrong and others he never did look me up.' He was somewhat hurt, but concerned only that Thomas be given the means of getting his facts right: 'I would find it difficult to write Thomas out of the blue. "Pride" maybe.' In fact, thinking about Thomas' book resuscitated regrets that he had never properly finished his own book, of which the splendid section on Badajoz might have formed part. He dabbled with some of his notes in the light of Thomas' text and even wrote to Herbert about whether it was worth trying to do something substantial with the 'Chronology'.

In fact, his heart was not in finishing the book. His depression at what he perceived as the endless betrayals, the American arms embargo, Munich, defeat of the Spanish Republic, stood in the way. Just as his experiences in Vichy had undermined his enthusiasm for publishing *My Trouble with Hitler*, now he could not summon the energy to finish the Spanish Civil War project. One difficulty was that he had agreed to a request from the Hoover Institution at Stanford to deposit his considerable library on Spain there. Apparently, Princeton University wanted to buy it for a considerable sum but, living in Carmel, California, 'I preferred to have it where I could conveniently consult it and so gave it to Hoover. When I diffidently raised the question of remuneration, they seemed shocked. "But we never pay for such collections!" My collection is hidden away in a cellar.'[109] In a letter to Herbert, he made a sad and revealing comment that applied not just to the book but to his political activities on behalf of the Republic:

> Looking back (which I do frequently but not too often lest I cut my throat) I realize that I was hideously at fault in not finishing it. But what good would it have done, except to my morale and that of my friends? As I said at the time, it was like repapering the inside of a barrel going over Niagara. As you know Munich spelt doom to me and I wasn't far wrong.[110]

Nevertheless, Jay could never entirely put aside the idea of doing something on the Spanish Civil War. He was greatly inspired by Herbert's two books, *El mito de la cruzada de Franco* and *Antifalange*, the latter of which was dedicated to him. In letter after letter to Herbert, he talked of what he had seen in Badajoz and his distress that he had been doubted. He was also inspired by Herbert to think in terms of doing something with the 'Chronology'. In late 1967, he started to work on a resumé of it with a view to sending it to Herbert for him to correct.[111] Jay never did finish the great book on the Spanish Civil War. He faced money problems. Somewhat envious of the huge sums made by friends like John Gunther and William Shirer, he wrote to Herbert: 'Money, money, money. Why don't we ever get our hands on it in any sizeable sums? John Gunther says that I have the Midas touch in reverse. Everything I touch turns to pennies.'[112] Jay's health deteriorated and he wrote to Herbert on 28 May 1967 that he had lost thirty pounds in weight. He had the first of a number of increasingly debilitating strokes in the early summer of 1968. He wrote to Herbert that it had affected his left side and his voice box. He continued to keep abreast of publications on the war and went on tinkering with the manuscript of the Chronology, which he was surprised to find more incomplete than he had remembered.[113] It was eventually donated to Brandeis University. He had another stroke in the autumn of 1972 and yet another in December. He died five days before Christmas. Ruth wrote to Herbert: 'It broke my heart to have Jay go without ever having put his vast knowledge of Spain into printable form.' In response, Herbert made considerable efforts to find a publisher for *My Trouble with Hitler*, and Ruth worked hard to piece together into a coherent whole the many versions and amendments left by Jay. Unfortunately, it was not possible to find a publisher prepared to undertake what she called 'the enormous editing job necessary'.[114] Consequently, the most substantial literary monument to Jay Allen remained his newspaper articles during the Spanish Civil War.

PART THREE

AFTER THE WAR

10

The Humane Observer: Henry Buckley

It is said that when Hemingway returned to Madrid after the civil war, he would always turn to Henry Buckley in order to find out what was really going on in Franco's Spain.[1] When Hugh Thomas published his pioneering and monumental history of the Spanish Civil War, he thanked Buckley for allowing him 'to pick his brains remorselessly'.[2] William Forrest, who was in Spain during the war, representing first the *Daily Express* and later the *News Chronicle*, wrote that 'Buckley saw more of the Civil War than any foreign correspondent of any country and reported it with a scrupulous adherence to the truth that won the respect even of those who sometimes might have preferred the truth to remain uncovered'.[3] Henry Buckley may not have written any of the most famous chronicles of the war, like Jay Allen's account of the massacre of Badajoz or George Steer's account of Guernica. Nevertheless, in addition to his sober news items throughout the war and to the help freely dispensed to less experienced colleagues, he did produce one of the most enduring records of the Spanish Republic and the civil war, a monumental testimony to his work as a correspondent.

Henry Buckley's *Life and Death of the Spanish Republic* constitutes a unique account of Spanish politics throughout the entire life of the Second Republic, from its foundation on 14 April 1931 to its defeat at the end of March 1939. Here was a book that covered the entire period, combining personal recollections of meetings with the great politicians of the day with eye-witness accounts of dramatic events, and recounted the complex experience in vivid prose laced with humour, pity for human suffering and outrage at those whom he considered to be responsible for the tragedy of Spain. It summed up his work as a correspondent during the Spanish Civil War representing the *Daily Telegraph*. It was an ironic commentary on the experiences recounted in the book that, not long after it had been published in 1940, the warehouse in London containing stocks of the book was hit by German incendiary bombs and all the unsold copies were destroyed.

Henry Buckley was born in Urmstow near Manchester in November 1904 and, after stints in Berlin and Paris, he had come to Spain to represent the now defunct *Daily Chronicle*. He returned to Spain after the Second World War with his Catalan wife and lived in Spain until his death. Despite his record as a fervent supporter of the Second Republic, he managed to go back as a correspondent after the Second World War. Ironically, he was regularly received by General Franco in the formal audience granted annually to the Foreign Press Association.

Henry Buckley was a devout Roman Catholic, with radical social instincts. It was human empathy, rather than ideology, that accounted for his support for the struggles of the industrial workers and the landless peasants in the 1930s. This is something that is clear throughout his book. As befitted a conservative, he was an enormous admirer of General Miguel Primo de Rivera, whom he once passed on one of his nocturnal strolls: 'This very great Andalusian gentleman' – 'Rather than a dictator, Primo was a national Father Christmas'. He disliked Alfonso XIII – 'his face showing cleverness, cunning perhaps, but not intelligence' – and that was partly because he felt that the King had betrayed Don Miguel Primo de Rivera. Buckley was a determinedly honest man. He liked the dictator's son, José Antonio, although he was disturbed by the paid thugs who belonged to the Falange, he sympathized with Franco's brother-in-law, Ramón Serrano Suñer, and didn't really like the Republican leader, Manuel Azaña.

He was disappointed by his first sight of Spain, and by the shabbiness and poverty of the peasants, yet was also fiercely self-critical of the complacency implicit in reporting on a country of which he knew nothing in 1929. He writes throughout with a humorous awareness of his own deficiencies, describing himself, on leaving Paris for Madrid, as 'a rather crotchety and thin-blooded virgin'. His eye for female beauty is always open but tempered with a sense of his own male ridiculousness. He tells us of a German girlfriend who fainted in his arms every time he kissed her: 'a result due I am afraid to her weakness of heart and not to my prowess in this direction'.[4]

Buckley may have been ignorant on his arrival, but he set out to learn and learn he did. Initially, he was working as stringer for Jay Allen, who was the principal European correspondent for the *Chicago Daily Tribune* and was based at the time in Paris.[5] Henry Buckley disliked Madrid as 'bleak and draughty and monotonous', and was outraged by a situation in which 'one million Spaniards live at the expense of the rest of the nation'. Yet, as is shown by his account of the siege of the capital during the war, he came to love the city and admire its inhabitants. It seemed like a conservative Englishman speaking when he said: 'I feel that the democratic system adopted by the Republic when King Alfonso left the country was in no small part responsible for Spain's tragedy'. But it was soon apparent that his view was based on the rather radical belief that the Republicans were insufficiently dictatorial to engage in a thorough reform of the country's ancient economy.[6]

The overwhelming value of his wonderful book is that it provides an objective picture of a crucial decade of contemporary Spanish history, based on an abundance of the eye-witness material that only a really assiduous resident correspondent could garner. Perceptive and revealing anecdotes abound. With Republican crowds surging through the streets of Madrid, Buckley, waiting in the bitter cold on the night of 13 April outside Palacio de Oriente, asks a porter what the Royal Family was doing: 'I imagined its members in anxious conclave, calling up friends, consulting desperately. The answer was calm and measured: "Their Majesties are attending a cinematographic performance in the salon recently fitted up with a sound apparatus."' On the next day, he witnesses the then unknown Dr Negrín calming an impatient crowd by arranging for a Republican flag to be draped on a balcony of the Palacio de Oriente. In Chicote's bar in the Gran Vía, 'a polished British-public-school-educated son of a Spanish banker tells him "the only future the Republicans and Socialists will have will be on the gallows or in gaol"'. In the autumn of 1931, he sees the wife of Niceto Alcalá Zamora refused entry to the Palacio de Oriente on the day of her husband's investiture as President of the Republic, something which he sees as emblematic of the status of women.[7]

One of the greatest joys of Buckley's prose is to be found in his immensely perceptive portraits of the major political and military figures of the day. Buckley's knowledge led to perceptions which have profoundly coloured the later judgements of historians. On Julián Besteiro as President of the Cortes, whose misguided judgements stood in the way of agrarian reform, he wrote with mordant irony: 'he showed fine tolerance, quick to hurry to the support of the weak – in this case the representatives of feudalism who had ridden rough-shod over their opponents for many a century'. In the aftermath of the massacre by security forces of anarchist peasants at Casas Viejas in the province of Cádiz on 8 January 1933, Buckley describes Carlos Esplá, then subsecretario de Gobernación, as a 'superlatively inefficient and muddle-headed Republican', and goes a long way to explaining the weakness of the Republic because of its politicians' inability to deal with the high-handed brutality of the Civil Guard. Despite lack of sympathy for his politics, Buckley admired the political efficacy of the CEDA leader, José María Gil Robles – 'truculent, forceful, an excellent executive and with considerable judgement in men and politics'. In contrast, he saw Largo Caballero's alleged revolutionism in 1934 as utterly false. He referred to General

Gonzalo Queipo de Llano as 'an excitable and irascible officer' and described Alcalá Zamora's vacuous oratory in satirical terms.[8]

Henry Buckley knew every politician of note in 1930s Spain. Cedric Salter, who also wrote for the *Daily Telegraph*, visited Madrid in the spring of 1937 and wrote later of a meeting with Buckley, whom he described as 'small, observant, with a one-sided smile and a passionate admiration for Negrín'.[9] Buckley certainly admired Negrín, but he was utterly bowled over by Dolores Ibárruri. After meeting her in Valencia in May 1937 and being subjected to a passionate harangue, he wrote: 'But what a woman! She was, I think, the only Spanish politician I ever met; and I think I know most of those who have any call on fame during this generation, and she is the only one who really did impress me as being a great person.' He liked Indalecio Prieto and admired his untiring work as minister during the civil war, but was aware that not all of his feverish work was as productive as it might have been since he insisted on dealing with every minor detail, even to the extent of personally examining journalists' applications for visits to the front. Buckley notes with exasperation how Prieto's secretary, Cruz Salido, simply referred everything back to Prieto.[10]

Of Valentín González, el Campesino, his view confirms that of other observers: 'He had the strangely magnetic eyes of a madman.' In contrast, few observers would expect it to be said of the brutal Stalinist Enrique Líster that he appreciated the importance of good food – 'He had a cook who had been with Wagon-Lits restaurant cars before the war and in the various times in various retreats in which I managed to pick up a meal at Líster's headquarters I do not think I ever had a bad one.' Buckley could also admire Líster 'handling the remains of an Army corps with coolness and considerable skill'. The greatest admiration is reserved for Negrín, not only for his dynamism but also for his essential kindness:

> My chief impression of him was of his strong pity for human suffering. He would look at the newsboy from whom he was buying an evening paper and say 'Having those eyes treated, sonny? No? Well go to Dr So-and-So at such-and-such a clinic and give him this card and he'll see that you get treated right away.' Or out in the country, he would stop in small villages and talk to the peasants, look in at their miserable homes, peer behind the easy mask of picturesqueness which veils so much disease and suffering in Spain. Before leaving he would slip some money or a card which would ensure free medical treatment into the hand of the woman of the house. That was Negrín as I knew him.[11]

Buckley's eye for the telling detail brings the politics of the Second Republic to life. During the run-up to the November 1933 elections, Buckley visited CEDA headquarters and noted the lavish quality of the posters used in Gil Robles' campaign. On 21 April 1934, he attended the rain-soaked rally of the Juventud de Acción Popular at El Escorial. The parading, saluting and chanting led Buckley to see it as the trial for the creation of fascist shock troops. A turn-out of 50,000 had been expected but, despite the transport facilities, the giant publicity campaign and the large sums spent, fewer than half that number arrived. Besides, as Buckley observed, 'there were too many peasants at El Escorial who told reporters quite cheerfully that they had been sent by the local political boss with fare and expenses paid'. On the eve of the miners' insurrection in Asturias, on the night of 5 October, Buckley was with the Socialists Luis Araquistain, Juan Negrín and Julio Álvarez del Vayo in a bar in Alcalá discussing the wisdom of Largo Caballero's strategy. During the siege of Madrid, he described how the Hotel Palace was turned into a hospital. During the battle of Guadalajara, he interviewed Italian regular troops who had gone to Spain in response to formal military orders. At the end of May 1937, he hastened to Almería to examine the damage done by the German warship *Admiral Scheer* on 31 May 1937 in reprisal for the Republican bombing of the cruiser *Deutschland* on 29 May 1937, and produced a grim description of damage wreaked on the working-class districts of this undefended port.

As a witness to such scenes, Buckley was overcome with moral indignation, although his sympathies for the poor of Spain were engaged as early as 1931. Reflecting on the situation of Alfonso XIII on the night before his departure from Madrid, he asks rhetorically: 'Where are your friends? Can anyone believe that this fine people of Spain have hearts of stone? No. If you had ever shown generosity or comprehension of their aches and struggles they would not leave you friendless tonight. You never did.' Although a practising Catholic throughout his life, Buckley wavered in his Catholic faith because of right-wing Catholic hostility to the Republic, commenting: 'Much as I disliked the mob violence and the burning of churches I felt that the people in Spain who professed most loudly their Catholic faith were the most to blame for the existence of illiterate masses and a threadbare national economy.' His humanity was brought into conflict with his religious faith, as can be seen in his vivid accounts of the daily lives of near-starving *braceros* in the south.

To some degree, the greatest object of Buckley's indignation was the role of the British Government and the diplomatic corps. He commented:

When I did talk to any of our diplomatic officers I found them very complaisantly disposed towards the Spanish Right. They looked upon them as a guarantee against Bolshevism, much preferable to have them in power than either Socialists or Republicans for this reason, and they would gently pooh-pooh any suggestion that the Spanish Right might one day side with Germany and Italy and we might suddenly find our Empire routes in danger.

He was hardly surprised to be told by his friend, Jay Allen, that he had seen Italian pilots landing in Gibraltar and allowed by British officials with courtesy and facility to pass through on to Seville. After the bombing of the German battle-cruiser *Deutschland*, the German crew members killed were buried with full military honours in Gibraltar. After the German revenge attack on an undefended Almería, Buckley witnessed the funeral of one of the victims. Looking at the worn faces and gnarled hands of those who followed the coffin, he wondered 'how it is that so few people care how much the working masses suffer'. He was appalled that, while the port of Gandía was bombed by German aircraft and British ships were destroyed, the Royal Navy destroyer standing nearby in Valencia was ordered to do nothing. Effectively, the picture painted by Buckley is one of the British establishment putting its class prejudices before its strategic interests. In this regard, he quotes a British diplomat who says: 'The essential thing to remember in the case of Spain is that it is a civil conflict and that it is very necessary that we stand by our class.'[12]

Buckley certainly did not share the anti-Communist hysteria of the British middle classes. He was sceptical of claims that the Soviet Union wanted to create a Spanish satellite:

Even supposing the case that the Communist Party succeeded in obtaining complete control of Government and nation, it would still, presumably, be composed of Spaniards; it seemed to me that it would be very difficult for Russia to impose any particular line of conduct not approved by Spaniards as a whole…Russia had, of course, every interest in saving the Republic but I do not think that apart from a natural desire to see the Spanish Communist Party as powerful as possible and to spread its ideas as much as possible, the Russians had any idea of making Spain into a subject state of their own and I fail entirely to see how they could have done so at such a long distance…A good deal has been written about Russian activities in Spain during the civil war but I certainly did not see any numbers of Russians about either in the police force or as private persons, except for the diplomatic staff, a few journalists, and a few military advisers. There were also a number of aviators and tank experts from October 1936 for some time until most of them were gradually replaced, but all of these latter kept very much to themselves.

For that reason, he was less than convinced by Colonel Segismundo Casado, commander of the Republican Army of the Centre, when he argued that his coup on 4 March 1939 was intended 'to save Spain from Communism'.[13]

While working for the *Daily Telegraph*, Henry Buckley established friendships with many of the most prominent war correspondents who worked in Spain, including Jay Allen, Vincent Sheehan, Lawrence Fernsworth, Herbert Matthews and Ernest Hemingway. Quietly spoken – one Spanish journalist commented that his speaking voice was '*casi un susurro*' (almost a sigh) – Buckley was extremely popular among his colleagues, who called him 'Enrique'. Kitty Bowler made a trip to Madrid in October 1936, which she described as 'a nightmare', but it was made bearable by Henry Buckley. He rescued her from the unwelcome attentions of men in her hotel and she later wrote of him as 'the sweetest reporter in Spain. His everyday banter acted like a welcome cocktail.'[14] Josephine Herbst met him in April 1937 and remembered him as 'a wonderful fellow, and with more background about Spain's past than any other correspondent in Spain'.[15] The young Geoffrey Cox remembered 'a small, quietly spoken, highly able man who showed himself remarkably resistant to propaganda pressures from all sides'.[16] Constancia de la Mora described Henry Buckley as 'a little sandy-haired man, with a shy face and a little tic at the corner of the mouth which gave his dry humour a sardonic twist'.[17]

Yet his quiet manner belied the courage which saw him visiting every front at considerable risk to himself. In the latter stages of the battle of the Ebro, on 5 November 1938, he crossed the river in a boat with Ernest Hemingway, Vincent Sheean, Robert Capa and Herbert Matthews. He commented later:

> We were sent out to cover the news on Líster's front – Hemingway was then reporting to the North American Newspaper Alliance. At that time, virtually all the bridges across the Ebro had been smashed by the fighting and a series of treacherous spikes had been sunk in the river to discourage all navigation on it. However, since there was no other way of getting to the front, the five of us set out in a boat with the idea of rowing along the shore until we got to the deepest part of the river, then crossing, and

rowing back to the opposite shore. The trouble was that we got caught in the current and started drifting into the centre. With every moment that passed, the situation became more menacing, for, once on the spikes, the bottom of the boat was certain to be ripped out; almost as certain was that we would drown once the boat had capsized. It was Hemingway who saved the situation, for he pulled on the oars like a hero, and with such fury that he got us safely across.

Buckley would later joke that Hemingway 'was a terrific person, kindly, almost infantile at times. I think he almost loved the war, exactly like some of the characters in his own books.'[18]

Buckley was, of course, playing down his own bravery. Hemingway described him during the war as 'a lion of courage, though a very slight, even frail creature with (or so he says in his book) jittery nerves'.[19] The eternally cynical Cedric Salter, who occasionally accompanied him in the last stages of the war, commented that Buckley 'was always quietly gay when things looked bad, but perhaps because he is made in a more sensitive mold than the others I always felt that in order to do the things he did required more real moral courage for him than from the others'.[20] Salter's insight is substantiated by Buckley's own account. He recalled a conversation with several colleagues after a visit to the front. With considerable understatement, he wrote:

> Our dangers came from long-distance shelling and from the constant bombing and machine-gunning of the roads behind the lines. The risk was actually not very great. I had no hesitation in saying that I always felt highly nervous when getting near the front. Nor had I any shame in confessing that when I lay in some field and watched bombers coming towards the point where I was lying and heard the 'whur-whur-whur' as the bombs came speeding down, was I ever anything but thoroughly frightened. Even more terrifying, I think, is being machine-gunned. You know that a bomb must practically fall on top of you in an open field in order to hurt you. But it is only rarely that any shelter against machine-gunning can be found when one dives haphazard from a car with the planes coming over and minutes or even seconds in which to throw oneself into the best shelter available.[21]

After the capture of Catalonia by the rebel forces at the end of January 1939, Buckley, along with Herbert Matthews and Vincent Sheean and other correspondents, had joined the exodus of refugees. He and Matthews established themselves in a hotel in Perpignan and devoted themselves to reporting on the appalling conditions in the concentration camps improvised by the French authorities into which the refugees had been herded. They managed to intervene to rescue people they knew from the groups being taken to the camps.[22]

Although he says little of his own role, Buckley's pages are alive with fury when he reaches his horrendous account of refugees arriving at the French frontier. He was outraged that Britain and France did not do more:

> The whole world was excited about the rescuing of some 600 chefs d'oeuvres of Spanish and Italian art which were being guarded near Figueras after their long odyssey. But we cared nothing about the soul of a people which was being trampled on. We did not come to cheer them; to encourage them. To have taken these half million and cherished them and given them work and comfort in Britain and France and their colonies, that indeed would have been culture in its real sense of the word. I love El Greco, I have spent countless hours just sitting looking at the Prado Titians and some of Velázquez's works fascinate me, but frankly I think that it would have been better for mankind if they had all been burnt in a pyre if the loving and warm attention that was lavished on them could have been devoted to this half-million sufferers. Better still if we had hearts big enough to cherish both, but since apparently we have not, it would at least have been a happier omen if such drops of the milk of human kindness which we still possess could have gone to the human sufferers. Yet while men well known in Catalan and Spanish cultural life in addition to tens of thousands of unknown persons were lying exposed to the elements and an average of sixty persons a week were dying of sickness and disease among the refugees in and around Perpignan, the art treasures left for Geneva in 1,842 cases on February 13; they were well protected from wind and rain. Women and children and sick and wounded men could sleep in the open air, almost uncared for. But the twenty trucks of Prado pictures had great tarpaulin covers and the care of a score of experts.[23]

In the summer of 1938, Henry Buckley had gone to Sitges with Luis Quintanilla and Herbert Matthews. Quintanilla introduced him to the Catalan painter Joaquim Sunyer. He in turn presented Buckley to a Catalan girl, María Planas. They fell in love and quickly decided to marry. Despite the fact that the Catholic

Church was still proscribed in Republican Spain, Constancia de la Mora used her influence to permit them to be married in a chapel used by the Basques exiled in Catalonia. After the Spanish Civil War, Buckley was posted to Berlin, where he worked until two days before the outbreak of the Second World War, when he was invited to leave by Hitler's government. After a brief time in Amsterdam covering the German invasion, he then spent a year and a half in Lisbon before becoming a war correspondent for the *Daily Express* with the British forces. Thereafter, he and María were able to see each other just once a year in Gibraltar. As a correspondent for Reuters, he landed with British forces at the Anzio beachhead and was very badly wounded when a German shell exploded near a jeep in which he was riding on the drive on Rome. As a consequence, he was left with shrapnel in his right side and was in acute pain for the rest of his life. Immediately after the war, he was attached to the Allied forces in Berlin, and was later Reuters correspondent in Madrid and during 1947 and 1948 in Rome.

In 1949, he returned to Madrid as director of the Reuters office there, where he remained until September 1966 apart from brief assignments to Morocco, Portugal and Algeria. On 11 January 1961, along with other members of the *junta directiva* of the Agrupación de Corresponsales de Prensa Extranjeros de España, he was received by General Franco. In 1962, he covered the last stand of the OAS in Oran. He maintained his friendship with Hemingway and they would meet whenever the American novelist visited Madrid. After thirty years in Spain, the Spanish Government marked his retirement in 1966 with the award of the Cruz de Caballero de la Orden de Isabel la Católica, which was given him by the then Foreign Minister Fernando María Castiella. In January 1968, Queen Elizabeth II of England appointed him Member of the Order of the British Empire, which was conferred upon him by the then British Ambassador, Sir Alan Williams.

After 1966, Henry Buckley retired to live in Sitges, but continued to work for the BBC as an occasional correspondent. He died on 9 November 1972. He was much loved and admired by his professional colleagues for his honesty and gentleness of manner. No less a figure than the great Francoist journalist Manuel Aznar wrote in *La Vanguardia*: 'Being an Englishman of a distinguished kind, he was for us an example of courtesy. If only all the English were like that when they are with us.' The Spanish journalists who knew him heard little of his experiences during the Civil War or of his friendship with Negrín. For Hemingway, Hugh Thomas and others, he was a living archive of the war. Fortunately for those who could not consult him personally, he left *Life and Death of the Spanish Republic*, a worthy monument to a great correspondent.

11

A Lifetime's Struggle: Herbert Rutledge Southworth and the Undermining of the Franco Regime

In 1963, the Franco dictatorship set up a special department to counter the subversive effect of the work of a man called Herbert Rutledge Southworth. Yet, until that date, hardly anyone had heard of Herbert Southworth outside of the small circle of Jay Allen, Louis Fischer and Constancia de la Mora. Yet his published work struck so hard at the dictatorship's complex justification of its own existence that the regime's efforts merely to prevent his work entering Spain were deemed to be insufficient. The partisan accounts of recent Spanish history that were used to vindicate a brutal regime were, as a result of his writing, no longer sustainable. The principal task of the new department was to come up with more plausible and modernized versions. This inevitably involved the implicit recognition that its earlier accounts were untrue. Once the dam had been breached, of course, there was no going back. The subsequent attempts were even more easily ridiculed. In this sense, Herbert Southworth, who had once been a part of the pro-Republican group that lobbied for the Spanish Republic in the United States, would do more for the anti-Franco cause than any of his more famous friends. Long after they had been forgotten, he made his presence felt to the extent of being denominated the Franco regime's public enemy number one.

Southworth struck this blow, and thus became a major figure in the historiography of the Spanish Civil War, as a result of the publication in Paris in 1963 of his book, *El mito de la cruzada de Franco*. It was issued by Ediciones Ruedo Ibérico, the great publishing house of the Spanish anti-Franco exile run by an eccentric and massively well-read anarchist, José Martínez Guerricabeitia. Smuggled into Spain and sold clandestinely, Ruedo Ibérico's books had enormous impact, particularly after the publication of a Spanish translation of Hugh

Thomas' classic work on the Spanish Civil War. From the first moments of the conspiracy that became the military coup of 18 July 1936, the rebels were falsifying their own history and that of their enemies. Hugh Thomas' book recounted the history of the war in a readable and objective style – in itself a devastating blow for the partisans of what they called Franco's crusade – and was therefore devoured hungrily by anyone who could get hold of a copy. Southworth's book was infinitely less immediately popular, but much more devastating. It did not narrate the war but rather dismantled, line by line, the structures of lies that the Franco regime had erected to justify its existence. The consequence of the arrival in Spain of both books was an attempt by the then Minister of Information, the dynamic Manuel Fraga Iribarne, to seal the frontier against the arrival of more copies and to counteract the intellectual and moral impact of both – but especially of the Southworth book, for its corrosive effect on the regime's self-image.

In fact, the book by Thomas had arrived first and had been smuggled into Spain in large quantities. Its success saw a tightening of frontier restrictions. Herbert's book was sent to the Canary Islands, where the customs were much slacker and from there entry into the mainland was relatively easy. This meant that the price when it was finally sold, under the counter, in Spanish bookshops, was more than double that in France. The profit went to the smuggler and the bookseller. Herbert wrote to Jay Allen: 'I have been writing for more than three years and I have not earned a single centime, a new or an old franc. I have not even recovered the money I advanced to publish the first book in Spanish. It has sold more than 3000 copies, which in view of the difficulties in getting it into Spain is not too bad.'[1] Nevertheless, those three thousand copies that filtered in were enough to provoke the creation, within the Ministry of Information, of the special department under the name Sección de Estudios sobre la Guerra de España.

To direct it, Fraga chose a clever young functionary of the ministry, a chemist who had trained to be a Jesuit before leaving to marry, Ricardo de la Cierva y de Hoces. He came from a famous conservative family; his grandfather had been Minister of the Interior in the governments of the monarchy, his uncle had invented the autogiro and his father had been killed by the Republicans during the Spanish Civil War. His job was, broadly speaking, to bring up to date the official historiography of the regime in order to repel the attacks coming from Paris. The principal weapon in the armoury of this new unit of intellectual warfare was provided by the purchase of the magnificent library on the Spanish Civil War, built up over many years by the Italian journalist, Cesare Gullino, who had originally been sent to Spain by Mussolini. Southworth quickly became the department's main enemy. In comparison with Hugh Thomas, who was already well known after the world-wide success of his book on the Spanish war, Herbert Southworth was virtually unknown. However, there was another crucial difference between the two men. Thomas had written his great book on the conflict, but the Spanish Civil War was not going to be the central objective of his life. He was already working on his monumental history of Cuba. Southworth, in contrast, dedicated his life to the study of the Spanish Civil War. Moreover, against de la Cierva, who had the staff and resources of a ministry at his disposal, Southworth had his own arsenal: one of the world's greatest collections of books on the war.

As well as being an anti-Francoist author, Southworth was one of the investors who made possible the survival of the important Spanish publishing house in Paris, Editions Ruedo Ibérico.[2] That Ricardo de la Cierva y de Hoces saw Southworth as an opponent to be feared was soon revealed. In 1965, de la Cierva had written to him, saying: 'I have great respect for you as an expert on the bibliography of our war and many people have been made aware of your book thanks to me. But I sincerely believe, Mr Southworth, that if you were to eliminate all the passion and prejudice that is found in your pages, your work would achieve the status that it deserves' (*Tengo una gran estima por Vd. Como especialista en la bibliografía de nuestra Guerra y muchas personas han conocido su libro por mi medio. Pero creo sinceramente, Mr Southworth, que si Vd suprimiera toda la pasión y todo el partidisimo que rebosa en sus páginas, su obra alcanzaría todo el valor que se merece*).[3] They met in Madrid in 1965 and de la Cierva invited him to dinner. Southworth told me later that de la Cierva had proudly recounted to him how the police had orders to seize copies of *El mito de la cruzada,* found when searching bookshops and the homes of political suspects. De la Cierva confided that he recommended and even gave to his friends confiscated copies of the book, proceeding to distribute copies to the other dinner guests. However, in Franco's Spain, what was said in private was often far removed from what was said in public. Ricardo de la Cierva wrote:

> H. R. Southworth is, without argument, the great expert on the bibliography of our war, as seen from the Republican side…His library on our war is the world's most important private collection: more than seven thousand titles. I am almost certain that he has read all seven thousand. And he keeps, in a tremendous photographic memory, all the important facts and all the relevant cross-references between these books.[4]

De la Cierva had underestimated the numerical size of the library, but not Southworth's detailed knowledge of its contents. This praise was immediately followed by some ferocious, but superficial, attacks on the alleged deficiencies of Southworth's methodology.

Who was this Herbert Southworth, the legendary book-collector who for many years to come would be the legendary intellectual scourge of General Franco's dictatorship? His books would be quarried by the most serious specialists on the Spanish Civil War and his study of the bombing of Guernica would be one of the three or four most important of the many thousands of volumes written on the conflict. Even so, few people knew who he was because, not having a position in a university, he lacked an easy label. Nevertheless, he had had an extraordinary existence. His passage from poverty in the American West to crusading left-wing journalist during the Spanish Civil War had elements of a John Steinbeck novel. His later transformation into successful radio station magnate and then into a scholar of world-wide reputation was reminiscent of one of Theodore Dreiser's self-made heroes.

He was born in Canton, a tiny Oklahama town, on 6 February 1908. When the town bank owned by his father failed in 1917, the family moved briefly to Tulsa in eastern Oklahoma. They stayed longer in Abilene, Texas, where his father prospected for oil. Herbert's principal memory of that time was reading his father's collection of the Harvard Classics. The theft of one of the volumes when he was twelve affected him so deeply that it was perhaps the beginning of his own obsessive book-collecting. He educated himself among the stacks of the Carnegie Public Library in Abilene. There, after months of reading *The Nation* and *The New Republic*, he decided to abandon Protestantism and the conservative Republicanism of the Bible belt. He became a socialist and an avid lifetime reader of what he joyfully called 'the muckraker's school of journalism'. It was to be the basis of his astonishing transformation into a formidable scholar in Europe.[5]

He went to secondary school in Abilene until the age of fifteen. He worked at various jobs in the construction industry in Texas and then in a copper mine in Morenci, Arizona. There, he learned Spanish working with Mexican miners. The collapse of the price of copper after the Wall Street crash left him unemployed. He then decided to work his way through Arizona University and when his savings ran out, he went to the Texas Technological College in Lubbock – better known as the birthplace of Buddy Holly. There, he lived in acute poverty, paying for his studies by working in the college library. He majored in history with a minor in Spanish. The work in the library had deepened his love for books. With the encouragement of the college librarian, he left, in 1934, with only one thought in mind: to seek work in the world's most important book collection, the Library of

Congress in Washington, DC. When he finally got a post in the Document Department, it was at a salary of less than half of what he had received in the copper mines. Yet, although it barely allowed him to eat, he was happy just to be able to pass his days among the bookshelves.[6]

When the Spanish Civil War broke out, he began to review books on the conflict and write the occasional article for the *Washington Post*. The articles were immensely well informed and based on thorough study of the international press.[7] The reviews foreshadowed both the sardonic humour and the hawk-eyed critical acuity that were to be the hallmarks of his later writing. Reviewing Theo Rogers' *Spain: A Tragic Journey*, he wrote:

> There is a frightening confusion about this book. I mean the careless, perhaps deliberate, confusing of the words Anarchist and Communist. There is a wide difference between the two and intelligent people recognize it. As Mr Rogers uses the words, they betray the worried indignation of his mind; they do not convey information. It is not fair to speak vaguely of people bought with 'Moscow gold' and offer no specific proofs. It is disingenuous to deny that Franco is a fascist and then add that he merely believes in the 'totalitarian state'.

He ended his article with the suggestion that readers would 'doubtless open Mr Rogers' book (if they open it at all) with hearty approval of the strange words of Sir Wilmott Lewis, who contributes the foreword: "I know nothing save the title of the book for which this is written as a foreword, and with its conclusions, if it draws any, I imagine I should strongly disagree".'[8]

His review of Harold Cardozo's *The March of a Nation* noted the contradictions between a series of statements: that on 18 July Queipo de Llano had 'barely 180 trained soldiers on whom he could depend' and had to use 'this handful of men' cunningly in order 'to overawe the teeming population'; that 'the ready supply of volunteers, 300,000 in all, within the first few months of the war, was the best proof that the Army movement was really a national one', and that in October, 'General Varela was very short of men. His march to Toledo had been a daring feat of bluff and his march to Madrid was to be even more daring. The African expeditionary force itself did not number much more than fourteen to fifteen thousand men, and it was by shuffling the unit from one side to another that General Varela was able to appear in strength.'[9]

Already emotionally affected by the struggle between fascism and anti-fascism, he always said thereafter that the events in Spain gave direction to his life. His articles brought him to the notice of the Republic's Ambassador, Fernando de los Ríos, who asked him to work for the Spanish Information Bureau. He eagerly left his ill-paid but secure government post in the library and moved to New York. There he worked with passion and wrote regular press articles and pamphlets, including *Franco's Mein Kampf*, his anonymous demolition of José Pemartín's attempt to provide a formal doctrine for Francoism, *Qué es 'lo nuevo'… Consideraciones sobre el momento español presente.*[10] During this time, he took a Masters degree at Columbia University and formed an enduring friendship with his colleague Jay Allen, the distinguished war correspondent. Jay, Barbara Wertheim (later famous as Barbara Tuchman) and Louis Fischer all knew him as 'Fritz' because his rotund figure and blond hair reminded them of the keeper of a German *bierkeller*. Jay wrote later of the man from Oklahoma whose slow drawl made him sound like a Texan: '

> He worked with me as a research assistant in New York in '38 and '39. He felt much as I did, was willing to go along with the CP as long as they were going our way but not after the Pact. A Texan and, I believe, a Baptist, he had and still has some very prickly ideas about the Roman Church, ideas shared by anti-clerical Catholics generally.[11]

Southworth's views were summed up in a brilliant article on the political power of the Catholic press published in late 1939.[12]

While in New York, Southworth also met and married a beautiful young Puerto Rican woman, Camelia Colón, although it was not to be a happy marriage. Herbert was devastated by the defeat of the Republic although, after the war ended, he and Jay continued to work for the exiled premier Juan Negrín. With Barbara Wertheim, he worked on a massive, minutely detailed chronology of the Spanish Civil War, which was intended to be the basis for a book on the war by Jay, never to be finished. With Jay, Herbert helped many prominent Spanish exiles who passed through New York, including Ramón J. Sender and Constancia de la Mora. Herbert also worked sporadically throughout the 1940s on a book about the Spanish fascist party, the Falange, which was eventually rejected by publishers on the grounds that it was too scholarly. In May 1946, he wrote to Jay about the difficulty of doing research while trying to earn a living and, in December 1948, he reported: 'I keep playing with the idea of a book on the Spanish Phalanx. I have mountains of material and maybe in a year or so, I shall have the time to sit down and put it together.'[13] It would be 1967 before he eventually produced his remarkable work *Antifalange*, dedicated to Jay Allen.

A Lifetime's Struggle

In the summer of 1941, the office in New York run by Jay Allen on behalf of the Spanish Republic was forced to close down, and Herbert was recruited by the State Department because his anti-fascist credentials were assumed to be of utility in the anticipated war against the dictatorships. Shortly after Pearl Harbor, the section where he worked was converted into the US Office of War Information. In April 1943, he was sent to Algeria to work for the Office of Psychological Warfare. Because of his knowledge of the Spanish situation, he was posted to Rabat in Morocco, where he spent most of the war directing Spanish-language broadcasts to Franco's Spain.[14] At the end of the war, he stayed on for a while working for the State Department until, in May 1946, he was fired. He wrote to Jay: 'I am told by a friend inside that I have been placed on a State Department blacklist and will never be employed by the Department. This is a bit bothersome for a man of 38 whose greatest claim to employment is the five years he has spent in American information work.' The anti-fascist qualifications that had secured him his original employment were a serious disadvantage in the context of the Cold War. Nevertheless, Herbert believed that 'the basis of the charges against me lies not in my pro-Spanish Republicanism, nor in my lack of anti-Soviet feeling, but in my activity against the political manoeuvres of the Roman Church'.[15]

He decided not to use his demobilization air passage home but stay in Rabat, partly to await the fall of Franco but largely because he had fallen in love with a strikingly handsome and powerfully intelligent French lawyer, Suzanne Maury. He had already separated from his wife Camelia, although they did not divorce until 1948. Suzanne too had problems separating from her husband. When both were free to do so, they married in 1948. Knowing that there were no controls on broadcasting from Tangier, Suzanne advised him to buy a quantity of US Army surplus radio equipment with which he founded Radio Tangier. He remained in frequent contact with Jay Allen and, like his friend, continued to hope for the fall of the Franco regime.

At the end of December 1948, he wrote to Jay:

> We spent a month in Paris in October and November. I saw Vayo and half promised to do something on Spain, but I don't do it. What do you think of something starting like this: a political objective is not unlike a military objective. No general would use the same strategy to take a trench that he would use to take a castle, and the forces thrown against a barn would differ from those deployed against an atomic city. In the efforts to overthrow Franco, all the ammunition is being used against a fascist regime, which no longer exists. To admit this will compel many an

emotional wrench etc. ...As you can see, I am incapable of writing anything without getting profound and ideological.[16]

During these years, he travelled regularly to Spain in search of material for what would become the largest ever collection of books and pamphlets on the Spanish Civil War (which now resides at the University of California at La Jolla, San Diego). In his December 1948 letter to Jay, he commented: 'I crossed Spain twice, once by Malaga–Barcelona and the other time by San Sebastian, Burgos, Valladolid, Madrid, Cordoba. I really think that a little blockade would topple Franco in three weeks if not sooner.'[17]

The radio station was nationalized by the Moroccan Government at midnight on 31 December 1960. Herbert and Suzanne had already gone to live in Paris. He continued to buy books through an enormous world-wide network of booksellers. Occasionally, he bought the libraries of some Spanish exiles, among them that of the President de la Generalitat de Catalunya, Josep Tarradellas. He also established a close relationship with Father Marc Taxonera, the tall, gaunt librarian of the Monastir de Montserrat, with whom he would exchange spare copies of books.[18] Herbert lost money in a vain effort to launch the potato crisp in France. That, the problems of finding an apartment big enough to house his library, which was deposited in a garage, together with an incident in which he was beaten up by policemen during a left-wing demonstration, inclined him to leave the capital. The problem of his by now enormous library saw him move south, where property was cheaper. In 1960, he and Suzanne bought the rundown Château de Puy in Villedieu sur Indre. He never really liked the area, writing jokily to Jay Allen: 'You have missed nothing in not knowing this part of France. I would gladly participate in the next war against the peasants.'[19] Some years later, in September 1970, they would move to the faded magnificence of the secluded Château de Roche, in Concrémiers near Le Blanc. He wrote to Jay Allen: 'we have passed six months heroically trying to get this house in order. We are now in fair condition. Confusion reigns. Worrying about roofs, heating and WCs has impeded my work.'[20] Finally, in the centre of the huge run-down château was a relatively modernized core, the equivalent of a four-bedroom house, where they lived. On the third floor and the other wings lived the books and the bats.

Once established at Puy, he began to publish the series of books that obliged the Franco regime to change its falsified version of its own past. The most celebrated was the first, *The Myth of Franco's Crusade*, the devastating exposé of right-wing propaganda about the Spanish Civil War.[21] By putting up the money for Ruedo Ibérico, to publish it, he inadvertently saved the house from financial collapse. In fact, because the French printer had little experience of typesetting in Spanish, the first edition contained so many errors that it had to be pulped.[22] Nevertheless, it appeared in 1963 and a year later in a much expanded French edition, it was decisive in persuading Manuel Fraga to set up the department solely dedicated to the modernization of regime historiography. Its director, Ricardo de la Cierva, in a losing battle with Southworth, went on to write over one hundred books in defence of the Franco regime. This feat was achieved by dint of having the resources of the Ministry of Information at his disposal until the death of Franco, and by a lack of inhibition about self-repetition. Jay Allen sent a copy of *El mito* to Louis Fischer, describing the book as 'an extremely detailed and able job'. Aware that Herbert was facing significant financial problems, Jay asked Louis in his capacity as a distinguished professor in Princeton if he could use his influence to persuade the university to acquire the Southworth collection 'and Fritz along with it'.

In 1967, Southworth wrote a second book, *Antifalange*, also published by Ruedo Ibérico, a massively erudite commentary on the process whereby Franco converted the Falange into the single party of his regime. It had significantly less commercial impact than *El mito*, because it was a minutely detailed line-by-line commentary on a book by a Falangist writer, Maximiano García Venero, *Falange en la guerra de España: la Unificación y Hedilla*. García Venero was the ghost-writer for the wartime Falangist leader, Manuel Hedilla, who had opposed Franco's take-over of the single party in April 1937.[23] Having been condemned to years of imprisonment, internal exile and penury, Hedilla saw the book as an attempt to revindicate his role in the war. José Martínez, the director of Ruedo Ibérico, asked Herbert to provide detailed notes expanding on the things that García Venero had chosen not to say about Falangist violence. Given his exhaustive knowledge of the Falange, those notes eventually grew to a scale that required their publication in an accompanying volume. Meanwhile, Manuel Fraga had become aware of the imminent publication, and had ensured that the Spanish Embassy in Paris put pressure on García Venero to prevent publication and indeed cause fatal damage to Ruedo Ibérico. Since the enormous book had already been typeset at great expense, José Martínez refused and, after labyrinthine legal complications, the two books were released.[24] Southworth's devastating demolition of García Venero's text revealed such knowledge of the interstices of the Falange that it provoked considerable surprise and admiration among many senior Falangists. As a result of his prior research for his projected book on the Falange, Southworth had long since been engaged in a flourishing correspondence with major Falangists, among them Ernesto Giménez Caballero, Jesús Suevos and

Ángel Alcázar de Velasco. This continued until his death and was notable for the tone of respect with which many of them treated him.

In the mid-1960s, Herbert had entered into contact with the great French hispanist, Pierre Vilar, who had persuaded him of the utility of presenting a doctoral thesis at the Sorbonne. Initially, he had planned to do so with a complete annotated bibliography of the Spanish Civil War along the lines of a vastly expanded version of *Le mythe de la croisade de Franco*. As he worked on this, however, he got more and more involved in one element, the propaganda battle over the bombing of Guernica.[25] In 1975, Herbert Southworth's masterpiece appeared in Paris as *La destruction de Guernica. Journalisme, diplomatie, propagande et histoire*, to be followed shortly afterwards by a Spanish translation. The English original appeared as *Guernica! Guernica! A Study of Journalism, Diplomacy, Propaganda and History*. Based on a staggering array of sources, it is an astonishing reconstruction of the effort by Franco's propagandists and admirers to wipe out the atrocity at Guernica – and it thus had a very considerable impact in the Basque Country. The book did not reconstruct the bombing itself, but actually begins with the arrival in Guernica from Bilbao of the *Times* correspondent, George L. Steer, together with three other foreign journalists.

It is a work of the most fascinating and meticulous research, which reconstructs the web of lies and half-truths that falsified what really happened at Guernica. The most exaggerated Francoist version, which blamed the destruction of the town on sabotaging miners from Asturias, was the invention of Luis Bolín, the head of Franco's foreign press office. To evaluate the work of Bolín and the subsequent manipulation of international opinion about the event, Southworth carefully reconstructed the conditions under which foreign correspondents were obliged to work in the Nationalist zone. He showed how Bolín frequently threatened to have shot any correspondent whose despatches did not follow the Francoist propaganda line. After a detailed demolition of the line peddled by Bolín, Southworth went on to dismantle the inconsistencies in the writings of Bolín's English allies, Douglas Jerrold, Arnold Lunn and Robert Sencourt.

It might normally be expected that a detailed account of the historiography of a subject would be the arid labour of the narrow specialist. However, Southworth managed, with unique mastery, to turn his study of the complex construction of a huge lie into a highly readable book. Among the most interesting and important pages of the book there is an analysis of the relationship between Francoist writing on Guernica and the growth of the Basque problem in the 1970s. Southworth demonstrated that there was an effort being carried out to lower the tension between Madrid and Euzkadi by means of the elaboration of a new version of what happened in Guernica. For this, it was crucial for neo-Francoist historiography to accept that Guernica had been bombed and not destroyed by Red saboteurs. Having conceded that the atrocity was largely the work of the Luftwaffe, in total contradiction of the regime's previous orthodoxy, it became important for the official historians to free the Nationalist high command from all blame. This task required a high degree of sophistry, since the Germans were in Spain in the first place at the request of Francisco Franco. Nevertheless, the neo-Francoists set out to distinguish between what they portrayed as independent German initiative and the innocence of Franco and the commander in the north, General Emilio Mola. Therefore, Southworth analysed the massive literature on the subject to advance a clear hypothesis: Guernica was bombed by the Condor Legion at the request of the Francoist high command in order to destroy Basque morale and undermine the defence of Bilbao.

This conclusion was not apparently remarkable, scarcely went beyond the first chronicle sent to *The Times* by George Steer and was no more than had been regarded as axiomatic by the majority of Basques since 1937. However, the great French historian, Pierre Vilar, in his prologue to the book, pointed out the importance of what Southworth had achieved in returning to the event itself and removing layer after layer of untruth laid on by censorship, by diplomats serving vested interests and determined propagandists of Franco. In Vilar's view, what gave Southworth's work an importance far beyond the confines of the historiography of the Spanish Civil War was his determined quest for the truth, and his exposure of the way in which journalists, censors, propagandists and diplomats distorted history. In a terrain in which truth has always been the first casualty, the 'passionate objectivity' of Southworth rose up like a beacon and made it an object lesson in methodology. Southworth's research was based on an astonishing array of sources in seven languages, amassed in many countries. On the advice of Pierre Vilar, the manuscript was presented in 1975 – successfully – as a doctoral thesis at the Sorbonne. He had already lectured in universities in Britain and France, but this was the beginning of a belated academic recognition of Southworth's work in his own country. In the mid-1970s, he became Regents Professor at the University of California.

Herbert was never fully welcome in the US academic community, because of his inveterate subversiveness and his mischievous humour. He made no secret of his contempt for Washington's policies in Latin America, which evoked for him the betrayal of the Spanish Republic. Every day, as an avid observer of what he considered to be the hypocrisy of political theatre, he devoured a stack of French and American newspapers. Along with his political passion, he had a wonderful sense of the absurd and an irresistibly infectious laugh. He was particularly keen on multilingual puns, never ceasing to be tickled by the delivery to any restaurant table in Spain of a bottle of mineral water with its label '*sin gas*'. I remember on one occasion at a conference in Germany, the assembled participants were led by the director of the host foundation to see a sumptuous carpet which, we were proudly told, had once belonged to Adolf Hitler. Herbert dropped to his knees and began shuffling around, peering closely at the pile. Herr Direktor asked with concern what the matter was and was completely nonplussed when Herbert replied in his slow Texan drawl: 'I'm looking for the teeth marks!' His demolition of the fake scholarship of others was often extremely amusing, most notably in his chapter entitled 'Spanica Zwischen Todnu Gabriet', in which he traced minutely how Francoist author after Francoist author cited a book they had never read (Peter Merin's *Spanien zwischen Tod und Geburt* (*Spain between Life and Death*)), but merely mis-copied its title. He once asked me to ensure that his gravestone carried the epitaph 'HIS WRITINGS WERE NOT HOLY WRIT / BUT NEITHER WERE THEY WHOLLY SHIT'. Despite his austere inquisitorial style, he was a rotund and jolly trencherman.

After the death of Franco, Herbert was regularly invited to give lectures at Spanish universities, where he was a major cult figure. His influence was seen in the work of a new generation of British and Spanish scholars. Southworth's remorselessly forensic writings imposed new standards of seriousness on writing about the war. A pugnacious polemicist, he regularly took part in literary arguments, most notably with Burnett Bolloten and Hugh Thomas. Regarding his great Francoist opponent, Ricardo de la Cierva, he had already published a devastating demolition of his sloppy scholarship, 'Los bibliófobos: Ricardo de la Cierva y sus colaboradores'.[26] Herbert wrote to Jay: 'People say I am destructive and ill-tempered and never say a good word about anybody, but somebody has to say who are the sons of bitches and the good guys. In the academic world, all is politeness and you scratch my back and turn around. I like to think of myself as a fresh current of air.'[27] However, he ceased publishing for a time because he was working on his massive study of Guernica. As his letters revealed, he also faced severe financial problems. In 1970, he saw that his outgoings on books dramatically exceeded income and he decided that he must sell the collection. It was sold to the University of California at San Diego as 'The Southworth Collection' and remains the world's single most important library on the Spanish Civil War. With income from savings dwindling, he and Suzanne also had to sell the Château de Roche in 1978.

I had assumed that, as they had both entered their seventies, they would move to a modern house. Instead, they bought a medieval priory in the village of St Benoît du Sault, an intriguing but inconvenient house in which every room was on a different level and whose long and narrow stone spiral staircase led eventually to another bat-infested study. Inevitably, Herbert began to rebuild his collection and had started to write again. He enjoyed the friendship of the Pierre Vilar, of numerous Spanish scholars and of the venerable Dutch anarchist thinker, Arthur Lehning. They lived happily in St Benoît until Suzanne's health broke down in 1994. Herbert nursed her devotedly until her death on 24 August 1996. He never recovered fully from that blow and, after a subsequent stroke, his health deteriorated dramatically. Nevertheless, although bed-ridden, with the devoted help of an English neighbour, Susan Mason-Walstra, he continued to work.

Initially, he had intended to revise *El mito de la Cruzada de Franco*. However, just as an earlier attempt had seen the research expand until it became his monumental book on Guernica, now something similar happened. The consequence was a two-fold final historiographical legacy. In 1996, he published a long analysis of the way that the ex-Trotskyist Julián Gorkín had, through his work for the Congress for Cultural Freedom and his falsification of the memoirs of Communist dissidents, distorted the historiography of the Spanish Civil War. The Welsh historian Burnett Bolloten was also the target of devastating criticisms. Bolloten had been a United Press correspondent during the war and was close to Constancia de la Mora. He had set out to write a history of the war which was initially pro-Negrinista, but he had become fiercely anti-Communist as a result of the assassination of Trotsky. His subsequent writings had been somewhat influenced by Gorkín, something mercilessly pilloried by Southworth.[28] Then, only three days before his death on 30 October 1999 in the hospital at Le Blanc, Indre, Herbert Southworth delivered the manuscript of his last book, a detailed analysis of two related elements of the military coup of 1936: the fabrication of a Communist plot to take over Spain in order to justify the coup and the influence on Franco himself of his relationship with the extreme rightist Entente Internationale contre la Troisième Internationale.[29] The book was a more fitting epitaph than that quoted above.

12

Epilogue: Buried Treasure

'**Y**ou are eternally right in saying that for the Spanish crimes the three great democracies must take full responsibility in history.' Thus, on 7 August 1939, Josephus Daniels, under whom FDR had served as Assistant Secretary of the Navy during the First World War, wrote to Claude Bowers.[1] For the duration of the Spanish Civil War, despite the reports of their own diplomats and of countless correspondents in Spain, the governments of Britain, France and the United States chose to ignore the fact that Hitler and Mussolini were sending unstinting help to the rebels and tilting the balance of international power against the democracies. Despite the fact that it was normal practice under international law to permit an established friendly government to purchase arms and supplies, all three governments denied this right to the Spanish Republic. Neither Anglo-French non-intervention nor the American 'moral' embargo and the subsequent extension of the 1935 Neutrality Act to encompass Spain were neutral in their consequences.[2] They damaged the cause of Spain's legally elected government, limited the Republic's capacity to defend itself and threw it into the arms of the Soviet Union.

The fact that Leon Blum frequently burst into tears when reminded that, if the Spanish Republic was crushed, France and the rest of Europe would be next, suggests that he was tortured by regrets about his policy, without needing the reminders of journalists such as Louis Delaprée.[3] There is no record of Neville Chamberlain ever expressing regret for his betrayal of the Spanish Republic, although it was a significant stepping stone on the way to his loss of power in June 1940. In contrast, when Claude Bowers went to report to Franklin D. Roosevelt on Franco's victory, a crestfallen president told him: 'We have made a mistake. You have been right all along.'[4] In 1944, the Assistant Secretary of State, Sumner Welles, recognized that 'Of all our blind isolationist policies, the most disastrous was our attitude on the Spanish Civil War', and 'in the long history of the foreign policy of the Roosevelt Administration, there has been, I think, no more cardinal error than the policy adopted during the civil war in Spain'.[5] At least Roosevelt felt regret, but it can have been as nothing in comparison with the bitterness felt by the many liberals and leftists in America and Europe who had watched the policy of the democratic powers strangle the Spanish Republic and hasten the triumph of fascism.

Through their despatches, the correspondents, and in the case of Jay Allen, Louis Fischer and George Steer, through their campaigning activities, had tried to bring this home. Thanks in large part to the correspondents, millions of people who knew little about Spain came to feel in their hearts that the Spanish Republic's struggle for survival was somehow their struggle. The work of the correspondents and their letters to his wife Eleanor had an impact on President Roosevelt's thinking about the threat of fascism. In turn, the fact that he placed electoral interests before wider moral issues had an impact on them. It contributed to Jay Allen's plunge into depression and Louis Fischer's turn to Gandhian pacifism. Herbert Matthews wrote bitterly that Roosevelt was 'too intelligent and experienced to fool himself about the moral issues involved' and that his 'overriding consideration was not what was right or wrong, but what was best for the United States and, incidentally, for himself and the Democratic party'.[6]

The Spanish Republic was a defensive bulwark against the threat of fascist aggression. But its appeal was not just negative. In the grey and cynical world of the depression years, the cultural and educational achievements of the Spanish Republic seemed to be an exciting experiment. However, for most of the correspondents, the most important element of their support for the Republic was the fight to defend democracy against the advance of fascism. To their disappointments in Spain were added vilification at home from those who believed that Franco was conducting a crusade in defence of true religion against Bolshevik bestiality. The consequence was what F. Jay Taylor called 'one of this generation's most impassioned political and religious controversies'. Indeed, so intensely conflictive was the polemic provoked within the United States that the British Consul in New York reported in February 1938 that the city was 'almost assuming the likeness of a miniature Spain'.[7] Nearly thirty-five years after the defeat of the Republic, Herbert Matthews declared: 'No event in the outside world, before or since, aroused Americans in time to such religious controversy and such burning emotions'.[8]

Yet despite vilification, defeat and the bitter frustration of witnessing the culpable negligence of the democracies, almost all those who supported the cause of the Spanish Republic carried for the rest of their lives the conviction that they had participated in a struggle that mattered. It was a feeling shared even by George Orwell, whose memoir of his brief time in Spain has given much succour to those who wish to claim, whether from the far Left or the far Right, that the defeat of the Spanish Republic was somehow more the responsibility of Stalin than of Franco, Hitler, Mussolini or Neville Chamberlain. On leaving Spain, Orwell stayed for three days in the French fishing port of Banyuls. He and his wife 'thought, talked, dreamed incessantly of Spain'. Although bitter about what he had seen as a foot soldier with the semi-Trotskyist POUM, Orwell claimed to feel neither disillusionment nor cynicism: 'Curiously enough the whole experience has left me with not less but more belief in the decency of human beings.'[9]

As late as the mid-1980s, Alfred Kazin could still view the war in Spain as 'the wound that will not heal'. In words that could have been uttered by Jay Allen or Louis Fischer or Mikhail Koltsov or George Steer or Henry Buckley or Herbert Southworth, Kazin wrote:

> Spain is not my country, the Spanish Civil War, like what followed, was *my* war. In the course of it I lost friends. I lost hope that Hitler could be stopped before the Second World War. I lost whatever tolerance for communists was left in me after the Moscow purge trials. Nevertheless, the destroyers of the Spanish Republic would always be my enemies.[10]

However, no one has summed up better the meaning of the Spanish war for so many of the writers and journalists who witnessed the heroic struggle of the Republic than Josephine Herbst. In February 1966, Josie went to see the Spanish Civil War documentary *Mourir à Madrid*, by the French director Frédéric Rossif. She wrote that night to some friends:

> I wouldn't have wanted anyone I knew to be seated near me, not unless they too had gone through the same experience. I not only felt as if I were dying but that I had died. And afterward, I sat in the lobby for a good while, trying to pull myself together, smoking, and the whole scene outside, and on the street when I got there, seemed completely unreal. I couldn't connect with anything or feel that it meant anything, somewhat in the same way that I had felt when I got down from the plane in Toulouse after I flew out of Barcelona and had expected to enjoy ordering a real lunch for a change and instead sat sobbing over an omelet – all I could bear to try to eat – and wine – and looking at people calmly passing by as if I had entered into a nightmare where the 'real' world had

suddenly been wiped off with a sponge and vanished forever. And actually, sitting in the lobby, smoking, it came to me that in the most real sense my most vital life did indeed end with Spain. Nothing so vital, either in my personal life or in the life of the world, has ever come again. And in a deep sense, it has all been a shadow picture for years and years. In Toulouse, though the war had not yet ended, I knew it would end and with defeat. And that nothing was going to stop World War II. Nothing. And most of the time since then has been lived on buried treasure of earlier years, on a kind of bounty I could still take nourishment from.[11]

Notes

Chapter 1: The Wound that Will Not Heal

1   Sefton Delmer, *Trail Sinister. An Autobiography* (London: Secker & Warburg, 1961), pp. 264–8. Delmer had married Isabel Nichols in 1935. After they divorced, she later married the British composer Constant Lambert and after his death married another composer, Alan Rawsthorne, in 1955.
2   *Daily Express*, 21 July 1936.
3   *Daily Express*, 22 July 1936.
4   *Daily Express*, 27 July 1936.
5   James M. Minifie, *Expatriate* (Toronto: Macmillan of Canada, 1976), p. 57.
6   King to Eden, 1 August 1936, FO 371/20525. On King, see the splendid account by Maria Thomas, 'The Front Line Albion's Perfidy. Inputs into the Making of British Policy Towards Spain: The Racism and Snobbery of Norman King', *International Journal of Iberian Studies*, vol. 20, no. 2.
7   King to FO, 4, 6 August 1936, FO 371/20527, FO 371/20526; King to Eden, 26 August 1936, FO 371/20536.
8   King to Seymour, 2 September, Seymour to King, 5 September, PRO FO371/20537, W10719/62/41; King to Western Department, 10 September, PRO FO371/20538, W11209/62/41; King to Roberts, 11 September 1936, PRO FO371/20539, W11527/62/41; King to Western Department, 3 October 1936, and enclosure, Companys to King, 30 September, PRO FO371/20542, W13083/62/41.
9   *The Times*, 23, 24 July 1936.
10 Lawrence A. Fernsworth, 'Terrorism in Barcelona Today', *Washington Post*, 10 June 1937; Lawrence Fernsworth, 'Revolution on the Ramblas', in Frank C. Hanighen (ed.), *Nothing but Danger* (New York: National Travel Club, 1939), pp. 28–9, 34–5; Lawrence Fernsworth, *Spain's Struggle for Freedom* (Boston, MA: Beacon Press, 1957), pp. 192–200.
11 Lawrence Fernsworth, 'Revolution on the Ramblas', in Hanighen, *Nothing but Danger*, pp. 46–7.
12 *Daily Mail*, 13, 18 July 1936.
13 *Daily Mail*, 20 July 1936.
14 *Daily Mail*, 21 July 1936.
15 *Daily Mail*, 25 July 1936.

16 *Daily Mail*, 27, 28 July 1936.

17 John Langdon-Davies, *Behind the Spanish Barricades* (London: Secker & Warburg, 1936), p. 97.

18 L. Fernsworth, *Spain's Struggle*, p. 188.

19 Langdon-Davies, *Barricades*, p. 97.

20 Cedric Salter, *Try-out in Spain* (New York: Harper Brothers, 1943), pp. 33–4, 68–9.

21 Langdon-Davies, *Barricades*, p. 121.

22 Langdon-Davies, *Barricades*, pp. vii–viii.

23 C. Salter, *Try-out in Spain*, pp. xix–xxi.

24 F. C. Hanighen (ed.), *Nothing but Danger* (New York: National Travel Club, 1939), p. 7.

25 Louis Fischer, *Men and Politics. An Autobiography* (London: Jonathan Cape, 1941), p. 438.

26 A list of 948 men and women was compiled by José Mario Armero, *España fue noticia. Corresponsales extranjeros en la guerra civil española* (Madrid: Sedmay Ediciones, 1976), pp. 409–36. The list is defective in many ways, not least in the omission of many correspondents known to have been in Spain, but it is indicative of the numbers.

27 Vernon Bartlett, *This is My Life* (London: Chatto & Windus, 1938), p. 301.

28 Louis Delaprée, *Le martyre de Madrid. Témoinages inédits de Louis Delaprée* (Madrid: No publisher, 1937), p. 21.

29 Martha Gellhorn, *The Face of War*, 5th edn (London: Granta Books, 1993), p. 17.

30 Peter Wyden, *The Passionate War. The Narrative History of The Spanish Civil War* (New York: Simon + Schuster, 1983), p. 29; Philip Knightley, *The First Casualty. The War Correspondent as Hero, Propagandist, and Myth Maker from the Crimea to Vietnam* (London: André Deutsch, 1975), pp. 192–5.

31 Louis Fischer, in Richard Crossman (ed.), *The God That Failed. Six Studies in Communism* (London: Hamish Hamilton, 1950), p. 220.

32 Hanighen, *Nothing but Danger*, p. 7.

33 Edmond Taylor, 'Assignment in Hell', in Hanighen, *Nothing but Danger*, pp. 58–60; Webb Miller, *I Found No Peace* (London: Book Club, 1937), pp. 325–7.

34 Minifie, *Expatriate*, pp. 53–4.

35 'To Aid Spanish Fascists', *New York Times*, 1 December 1936; Laurel Leff, *Buried by The Times. The Holocaust and America's Most Important Newspaper* (New York: Cambridge University Press, 2005), p. 179.

36 William Braasch Watson, 'Hemingway's Civil War Dispatches', *The Hemingway Review*, vol. VII, no. 2, Spring 1988, pp. 4–12, 26–9, 39, 60.

37 George Seldes, '"Treason" on the Times', *The New Republic*, 7 September 1938.

38 Herbert L. Matthews, *A World in Revolution. A Newspaperman's Memoir* (New York: Charles Scribner's Sons, 1971), pp. 19–20, 62; Leff, *Buried by the Times*, pp. 165–9, 180–1, 399; Guy Talese, *The Kingdom and the Power* (New York: The World Publishing Co., 1969), pp. 57–61.

39 Matthews, *A World in Revolution*, pp. 19–21, 25–30; George Seldes, *The Catholic Crisis* (New York: Julian Messner, 1939), pp. 195–9.

40 Matthews, *A World in Revolution*, pp. 11–12, 17–18. For descriptions of Matthews, see Delmer, *Trail Sinister*, p. 328, and Carlos Baker, *Ernest Hemingway. A Life Story* (London: Collins, 1969), p. 369.

41 Matthews, *A World in Revolution*, pp. 30–2. Herbert L. Matthews, *The Education of a Correspondent* (New York: Harcourt Brace, 1946), pp. 130–1, 142–3.
42 Gellhorn, *The Face of War*, p. 17.
43 Matthews, *A World in Revolution*, p. 19.

Chapter 2: The Capital of the World

1 Paul Preston, *Franco: A Biography* (London: HarperCollins, 1993), pp. 171–84; H. R. Knickerbocker, *The Siege of the Alcazar: A War-Log of the Spanish Revolution* (London: Hutchinson, n.d. [1937]), pp. 172–3; Webb Miller, *I Found No Peace* (London: The Book Club, 1937), pp. 329–30, 336–8; Herbert L. Matthews, *The Yoke and the Arrows* (London: Heinemann, 1958), p. 176; Claude Bowers, *My Mission to Spain* (London: Victor Gollancz, 1954), p. 313.
2 *Washington Post*, 14 September 1936; *Syracuse Herald*, 14 September 1936.
3 Gorrell to Wendelin, US Embassy, 5 October; Ziffren log, 5 October 1936; diary entry 22 September 1936, Ziffren, 'Diary of a Civil War Correspondent' (all Lester Ziffren papers). I am indebted to David Wurtzel, who provided me with copies of these documents. On Ziffren, see David Wurtzel, 'Lester Ziffren and the Road to War in Spain', *International Journal of Iberian Studies*, vol. 19, no. 1, pp. 73–83.
4 *News Chronicle*, 27 October; *Washington Post*, 25, 28 October 1936. The story about rebel courtesy was published in the American provincial press, see for example *Sheboygan Press*, 28 October 1936. Denis Weaver, 'Through the Enemy's Lines', in Frank C. Hanighen (ed.), *Nothing but Danger* (New York: National Travel Club, 1939), pp. 101–15; A Journalist, *Foreign Journalists under Franco's Terror* (London: United Editorial, 1937), p. 16; James M. Minifie, *Expatriate* (Toronto: Macmillan of Canada, 1976), pp. 70–5; Hull to Bowers, 28 October 1936, *Foreign Relations of the United States 1936*, vol. II (Washington, DC: Government Printing Office, 1954), p. 748; Bowers, *My Mission*, pp. 325–6.
5 Lester Ziffren, 'The Correspondent in Spain', *Public Opinion Quarterly*, vol. 1, no. 3, July 1937, p. 113.
6 Jan H. Yindrich, 'Seen from a Skyscraper', in Hanighen, *Nothing but Danger*, pp. 145–50, 156–9; Josephine Herbst, *The Starched Blue Sky of Spain and Other Memoirs* (New York: HarperCollins, 1991), pp. 134–5; Arturo Barea, *The Forging of a Rebel* (London: Davis-Poynter, 1972), pp. 603, 655; Keith Scott Watson, *Single to Spain* (London: Arthur Barker, 1937), pp. 158–60.
7 Ziffren, diary entry, 18 September 1936; Lester Ziffren, 'The Correspondent in Spain', *Public Opinion Quarterly*, vol. 1, no. 3, July 1937, p. 114.
8 Julio Álvarez del Vayo, *The Last Optimist* (London: Putnam, 1950), pp. 41–4, 53–66, 111–23.
9 Ziffren, diary entry, 18 September 1936; Sefton Delmer, *Trail Sinister. An Autobiography* (London: Secker & Warburg, 1961), p. 290.
10 Spanish diary, manuscript, pp. 53–4, Louis Fischer Papers, Seeley G. Mudd Manuscript Library, Princeton University (henceforth Fischer Papers).
11 Ziffren, 'The Correspondent', pp. 113–14.
12 Spanish diary, manuscript, p. 95, Fischer Papers.

13 Mijail Koltsov, *Diario de la guerra de España* (Paris: Ruedo Ibérico, 1963), p. 93.

14 Ziffren, 'The Correspondent', p. 112.

15 Jan Kurzke and Kate Mangan, 'The Good Comrade', pp. 104–6 (unpublished ms, Jan Kurzke Papers, Archives of the International Institute for Social History, Amsterdam).

16 Lester Ziffren, 'I Lived in Madrid', *Current History*, April 1937, pp. 35–6.

17 Louis Fischer, Spanish diary, manuscript, p. 90, Fischer Papers.

18 Henry Buckley, *Life and Death of the Spanish Republic* (London: Hamish Hamilton, 1940), p. 269; Delmer, *Trail Sinister*, pp. 287–8.

19 Geoffrey Cox, taped interview, Imperial War Museum, Sound Archive, Spanish Civil War Collection, 10059/4; Geoffrey Cox, *Eyewitness. A Memoir of Europe in the 1930s* (Dunedin: University of Otago Press, 1999), pp. 203–5; Sir Geoffrey Cox interview with author, 2006.

20 Cox, *Eyewitness*, pp. 205, 213; Cox interview.

21 Cox, *Eyewitness*, pp. 211–12; Delmer, *Trail Sinister*, p. 289.

22 Barea, *The Forging*, pp. 569–70, 573–4.

23 H. Edward Knoblaugh, *Correspondent in Spain* (London and New York: Sheed & Ward, 1937), p. 135; Virginia Cowles, *Looking for Trouble* (London: Hamish Hamilton, 1941), p. 24; Barea, *The Forging*, p. 577.

24 Herbert L. Matthews, *The Education of a Correspondent* (New York: Harcourt Brace, 1946), p. 119; Vincent Sheean, *Not Peace but a Sword* (New York: Doubleday, Doran, 1939), p. 79.

25 Barea, *The Forging*, pp. 581–7.

26 Knoblaugh, *Correspondent*, pp. 145–6.

27 Delmer, *Trail Sinister*, pp. 290–3; Cox, *Eyewitness*, p. 215.

28 Barea, *The Forging*, p. 628.

29 Cox, *Eyewitness*, pp. 215–16. The book was *Defence of Madrid* (London: Victor Gollancz, 1937).

30 Claude Bowers, *My Mission to Spain* (London: Victor Gollancz, 1954), p. 320.

31 Frances Davis, *My Shadow in the Sun* (New York: Carrick & Evans, 1940), p. 163.

32 Harold G. Cardozo, *The March of a Nation* (London: The Right Book Club, 1937), p. 179.

33 Buckley, *Life and Death*, pp. 261–3; Cox, *Eyewitness*, p. 219; 'Street Fighting', *News Chronicle*, 9 November 1936.

34 Barea, *The Forging*, pp. 588–96. On Koltsov's relationship with Álvarez del Vayo and the Office of War Commissars, see the chapter 'Stalin's Eyes and Ears in Madrid? The Rise and Fall of Mikhail Koltsov'.

35 Barea, *The Forging*, pp. 596–8.

36 Barea, *The Forging*, pp. 597–99.

37 Barea, *The Forging*, pp. 598–9; Yindrich, 'Seen from a Skyscraper', p. 151.

38 Delmer, *Trail Sinister*, p. 296; Barea, *The Forging*, pp. 601–5, 615–17, 640.

39 Michael Eaude, *Arturo Barea. Triunfo en la medianoche del siglo* (Mérida: Editora Regional de Extremadura, 2001), pp. 243–9; Barea, *The Forging*, pp. 603–12.

40 Louis Delaprée, 'Une visite au "front de Babel" avec la brigade internationale', *Paris-Soir*, 24 November 1936; Barbro Alving, 'Utlandsbrigaden har vänt bladet', *Dagens*

Nyheter, 9 December 1936; Herbert Matthews, 'Free Lances of Madrid', *New York Times Magazine*, 3 January 1937; Louis Fischer, 'Spain's "Red" Foreign Legion', 'Madrid's Foreign Defenders', *The Nation*, 9 January, 4 September 1937.

41 Koltsov, *Diario*, pp. 265, 269, 273; David Wingeate Pike, *Les français et la guerre d'Espagne 1936–1939* (Paris: Presses Universitaires de France, 1975), p. 39; Barea, *The Forging*, p. 632; Cox, *Defence of Madrid*, pp. 203–6; Delmer, *Trail Sinister*, pp. 269, 275, 322–6; Louis Delaprée, *Le martyre de Madrid. Témoinages inédits de Louis Delaprée* (Madrid: No publisher, 1937), pp. 46–7.

42 *Paris-Soir*, 19 November 1936; Delaprée, *Le martyre*, pp. 11–15.

43 On Rubio Hidalgo's tortuous relations with both Arturo and Ilsa, see *The Forging*, pp. 626, 631–9, 682–6, 693–5.

44 Burnett Bolloten to Arturo Barea, 10 June; Arturo Barea to Bolloten, 21 June; Ilsa Barea to Bolloten, 22 June 1950 (Bolloten Collection, Box 10, Folder 7, Hoover Institution, Stanford University); Barea, *The Forging*, pp. 640–2.

45 On the meeting with Dos Passos, p. 665; John Dos Passos, 'Room and Bath at the Hotel Florida', *Esquire*, January 1938, also reprinted in *Journeys Between Wars* (New York: Harcourt, Brace, 1938), pp. 364–74; Barea, *The Forging*, p. 665.

46 Barea, *The Forging*, p. 684. On Rosario del Olmo, see Geoffrey Brereton, *Inside Spain* (London: Quality Press, 1938), pp. 36–8. See also Jay Allen to Carlos Baker, 6 March 1963, Jay Allen Papers.

47 Francis McCullagh, *In Franco's Spain* (London: Burns, Oates & Washbourne, 1937), pp. 108–9.

48 Fischer, *Men and Politics*, pp. 242–5.

49 Babette Gross, *Willi Münzenburg. A Political Biography* (East Lansing, MI: Michigan State University Press, 1974), p. 272.

50 For sympathetic portraits of Katz, see Arthur Koestler, *The Invisible Writing*, 2nd edn (London: Hutchinson, 1969), pp. 255–8, 400; Claud Cockburn, *A Discord of Trumpets* (New York: Simon + Schuster, 1956), pp. 305–9. For a splenetically hostile one, see Stephen Koch, *Double Lives. Spies and Writers in the Secret Soviet War of Ideas against the West* (New York: The Free Press, 1994), pp. 74ff. On the creation of the Agence Espagne, see Gross, *Münzenberg*, pp. 311–12.

51 Cockburn, *A Discord*, p. 306. The book, *Prince Hubertus Friedrich of Loewenstein, a Catholic in Republican Spain* (London: Victor Gollancz, 1937), was an objective examination of the Republic's policy towards the Church once Manuel Irujo became Minister of Justice.

52 Barea, *The Forging*, p. 661; Gustav Regler, entry for 17 April 1937, 'Civil War Diary' (Southworth Papers), p. 24.

53 Fischer, *Men and Politics*, p. 430; Gross, *Münzenburg*, p. 312.

54 Koestler, *The Invisible Writing*, p. 409.

55 Constancia de la Mora, *In Place of Splendor. The Autobiography of a Spanish Woman* (New York: Harcourt, Brace, 1939), pp. 289, 291–2; Kurzke and Mangan, 'The Good Comrade', pp. 298, 300, 303, 309; Lawrence Fernsworth, *Spain's Struggle for Freedom* (Boston, MA: Beacon Press, 1957), pp. 200–39.

56 Gustav Regler, *The Owl of Minerva* (London: Rupert Hart-Davis, 1959), p. 274.

57 Martha Gellhorn, 'Memory', *London Review of Books*, 12 December 1996, p. 3.

58 Regler, *The Owl*, p. 284.

59 Herbert L. Matthews, *The Education of a Correspondent* (New York: Harcourt, Brace and Co., 1946), pp. 3–22; Herbert L. Matthews, *A World in Revolution: A Newspaperman's Memoir* (New York: Charles Scribner, 1972), pp. 54–69.

60 Herbert Matthews, 'Italians Foresee Stand by Seyoum', *New York Times*, 26 October 1935; Matthews, *Education of a Correspondent*, pp. 28–9; Herbert L. Matthews, *Two Wars and More to Come* (New York: Carrick & Evans, 1938), p. 18.

61 Matthews, *Education of a Correspondent*, pp. 62–3.

62 Matthews, *Two Wars*, pp. 18, 185.

63 Matthews, *The Education of a Correspondent*, pp. 67–8.

64 Sheean, *Not Peace but a Sword*, p. 199.

65 Cox, *Defence of Madrid*, p. 208; Geoffrey Cox taped interview, Imperial War Museum, Sound Archive, Spanish Civil War Collection, 13161/3/2.

66 Vernon Bartlett, *This is My Life* (London: Chatto & Windus, 1938), pp. 300–1.

67 Delmer, *Trail Sinister*, p. 299.

68 Arthur Koestler, *Spanish Testament* (London: Victor Gollancz, 1937), p. 177.

69 Matthews, *Two Wars*, pp. 281–2; Matthews, *The Education of a Correspondent*, p. 95; Dos Passos, *Journeys*, p. 369; Carlos Baker, *Ernest Hemingway. A Life Story* (London: Collins, 1969), pp. 370–1.

70 John Dos Passos, *Century's Ebb: The Thirteenth Chronicle* (Boston, MA: Gambit, 1975), pp. 89–90; Jason Gurney, *Crusade in Spain* (London: Faber & Faber, 1974), p. 145.

71 Delmer, *Trail Sinister*, pp. 315–16.

72 Gellhorn interview with Peter Wyden, *The Passionate War. The Narrative History of the Spanish Civil War* (New York: Simon + Schuster, 1983), p. 321; Herbst, *The Starched Blue Sky*, p. 138; Dos Passos, *Century's Ebb*, p. 83.

73 Anne Sebba, *Battling for News. The Rise of the Woman Reporter* (London: Hodder & Stoughton, 1994), pp. 93–7; Herbst, *The Starched Blue Sky*, pp. 169–70.

74 Cowles, *Looking for Trouble*, pp. 16–22.

75 Herbst, *The Starched Blue Sky*, pp. 136–7, 152–3; Roman Karmen, *¡No pasarán!* (Moscow: Editorial Progreso, 1976), pp. 303–4, 326. Franklin appears as 'Cookie' in the autobiographical novel, Dos Passos, *Century's Ebb*, p. 37.

76 Ilya Ehrenburg, *Eve of War 1933–1941* (London: MacGibbon & Kee, 1963), pp. 153–4. It is possible to put a date on this incident thanks to Gustav Regler, 'Civil War Diary', p. 59.

77 Gellhorn, 'Memory', p. 3.

78 Cowles, *Looking for Trouble*, pp. 23, 35–7; Matthews, *The Education of a Correspondent*, p. 122; Regler, entry for 3–6 April 1937, 'Civil War Diary', p. 64; Cedric Salter, *Try-out in Spain* (New York: Harper Brothers, 1943), pp. 108–11; Delmer, *Trail Sinister*, p. 316.

79 Kitty Bowler, 'Memoirs', Chapter 9, p. 8, LHCMA, Wintringham papers, 1, Folder 3; Viscount Churchill, *All My Sins Remembered* (London: William Heinemann, 1964), p. 171.

80 Patricia Cockburn, *The Years of the Week* (London: MacDonald, 1968), pp. 202–5; Frank Pitcairn, *Reporter in Spain* (London: Lawrence & Wishart, 1936), pp. 26–9, 55–6, 103–38. For a highly critical account of Cockburn's sectarianism, see Kurzke and Mangan, 'The Good Comrade', pp. 274–8.

81 Cockburn, *A Discord*, pp. 307–9; Phillip Knightley, *The First Casualty* (London: André Deutsch, 1975), p. 196.

82 Imperial War Museum, *The Spanish Civil War Collection. Sound Archive Oral History Recordings* (London: Imperial War Museum, 1996), p. 258; Kurzke and Mangan, 'The Good Comrade', pp. 63, 91, 112–13.

83 Slater's International Brigade files, 4A, 4160, Russian Centre for the Preservation and Study of Recent Historical Documents, Moscow, Fond. 545, Opus 6, 201 (copy held by International Brigades Memorial Trust, London) (henceforth RCPSRHD/IBMT). See also Richard Baxell, *British Volunteers in the Spanish Civil War. The British Battalion in the International Brigades, 1936–1939* (London: Routledge/Cañada Blanch, 2004), p. 89; James K. Hopkins, *Into the Heart of the Fire: The British in the Spanish Civil War* (Stanford, CA: Stanford University Press, 1998), pp. 226–7, 246, 406; Fred Thomas, *To Tilt at Windmills. A Memoir of the Spanish Civil War* (East Lansing, MI: Michigan State University Press, 1996), pp. 18, 23, 53, 105. Tony McLean's remark can be found in his testimony to the Imperial War Museum Oral History Project, 838/5.

84 Louis Fischer, 'On Madrid's Front Line', *The Nation*, 24 October 1936.

85 Cockburn, *The Years of the Week*, pp. 208–11.

86 Ehrenburg, *Eve of War*, p. 148.

87 *Chicago Daily Tribune*, 28, 29 July 1936. Slightly different versions of these articles were printed in the *News Chronicle*, 29 July, 1 August 1936.

88 *Chicago Daily Tribune*, 30 August 1936; John T. Whitaker, *We Cannot Escape History* (New York: Macmillan, 1943), p. 113.

89 M. L. Stein, *Under Fire: The Story of American War Correspondents* (New York: Julian Messner, 1968), p. 87.

90 Minifie, *Expatriate*, p. 76.

91 *New York Times*, 7 December 1936.

92 William P. Carney, 'No democratic government in Spain', 'Russia's part in Spain's civil war' and 'Murder and anti-religion in Spain' (New York: The America Press, 1937); Herbert Rutledge Southworth, *Guernica! Guernica!: A Study of Journalism, Propaganda and History* (Berkeley: CA: University of California Press, 1977), p. 431.

93 William P. Carney, 'Life in Madrid: A City of Stalking Death', *New York Times*, 24 January 1937.

94 De la Mora, *In Place of Splendor*, pp. 258, 286.

95 Josephine Herbst, unpublished diary, entry for 29 April 1937, 'Journal Spain', Za Herbst Collection, Beinecke Library, Yale University, pp. 51–2; Regler, diary entry for 29 April 1937, 'Civil War Diary', pp. 84–5.

96 Ernest Hemingway, *By-Line. Ernest Hemingway: Selected Articles and Dispatches of Four Decades* (London: William Collins, 1968), pp. 308–11; Carl Rollyson, *Nothing Ever Happens to the Brave. The Story of Martha Gellhorn* (New York: St Martin's Press, 1990), p. 103. On the Republic's efforts to restore order, see Paul Preston, *The Spanish Civil War. Reaction, Revolution, Revenge* (London: HarperCollins, 2006), pp. 231–4, 259–63.

97 Noel Monks, 'I Hate War', in Hanighen, *Nothing but Danger*, pp. 90–3.

98 On Steer see Southworth, *Guernica! Guernica!, passim*; Paul Preston, 'prólogo', George L. Steer, *El árbol de Gernika. Un ensayo sobre la guerra moderna* (Tafalla:

Txalaparta, 2002), pp. 7–18; Nick Rankin, *Telegram from Guernica. The Extraordinary Life of George Steer, War Correspondent* (London: Faber & Faber, 2003).

99 Sheean, *Not Peace*, pp. 162–6; Brereton, *Inside Spain*, p. 37.

100 Allen to Southworth, 17 January 1964, 7 August 1967, Southworth Papers, Museo de Guernica.

101 Lester Ziffren, 'I Lived in Madrid', *Current History*, April 1937, p. 41.

102 Author's interview with Geoffrey Cox, 2006.

103 O. D. Gallagher, 'Five Waited for a City to Die', in Hanighen, *Nothing but Danger*, pp. 228–40.

104 *Daily Express*, 27, 29 March 1939.

105 Knightly, *The First Casualty*, p. 214. Gallagher died many years later on the banks of Loch Ness, where he had been posted as correspondent.

Chapter 3: The Lost Generation Divided

1 Josephine Herbst, unpublished diary, 'Journal Spain', Za Herbst Collection, Beinecke Library, Yale University, pp. 4–8; Josephine Herbst, *The Starched Blue Sky of Spain and Other Memoirs* (New York: HarperCollins, 1991), pp. 152–4; Caroline Moorehead, *Martha Gellhorn, A Life* (London: Chatto & Windus, 2003), p. 141; John Dos Passos, *Journeys Between Wars* (New York: Harcourt, Brace, 1938), pp. 364–5. Delmer's remarks come, not from his memoirs, but from a letter to Carlos Baker, *Ernest Hemingway. A Life Story* (London: Collins, 1969), p. 371.

2 Herbst, 'Journal Spain', pp. 11–12.

3 The most extreme example is Stephen Koch, *The Breaking Point. Hemingway, Dos Passos and the Murder of José Robles* (New York: Counterpoint, 2005). See also the more measured version by Ignacio Martínez de Pisón, *Enterrar a los muertos* (Barcelona: Seix Barral, 2005).

4 John Dos Passos, *The Theme is Freedom* (New York: Dodd & Mead, 1956), pp. 127–8; Townsend Ludington, *John Dos Passos. A Twentieth-Century Odyssey* (New York: E. P. Dutton, 1980), p. 102.

5 John Dos Passos, letter to the editors of the *New Republic*, July 1939, *The Fourteenth Chronicle. Letters and Diaries* (Boston, MA: Gambit Incorporated, 1973), p. 527; Ludington, *John Dos Passos*, p. 366; Martínez de Pisón, *Enterrar a los muertos*, pp. 25–9.

6 Louis Fischer, *Men and Politics* (London: Jonathan Cape, 1941), pp. 374, 406.

7 Daniel Kowalsky, *La Unión Soviética y la guerra civil española. Una revisión crítica* (Barcelona: Editorial Crítica, 2003), pp. 28–9, 256–8, 284–9; Paulina y Adelina Abramson, *Mosaico roto* (Madrid: Compañía Literaria, 1994), pp. 63, 251.

8 Francisco Ayala, *Recuerdos y olvidos (1906–2006)* (Madrid: Alianza Editorial, 2006), p. 230.

9 Fischer, *Men and Politics*, p. 406.

10 I am indebted to Ángel Viñas for this observation. Fuqua's views, Bowers to Dos Passos, 27 August 1937, Papers of Claude Bowers, Lilly Library, Indiana University (henceforth Bowers Papers).

11 Ministerio de la Guerra, Estado Mayor Central, *Anuario Militar de España 1936* (Madrid: Imprenta y Talleres del Ministerio de la Guerra, 1936), p. 181.

12 Cf. Martínez de Pisón, *Enterrar a los muertos*, pp. 84–5, 101, 107–10, who speculates that the decision to kill Robles was taken by Alexander Orlov (Leiba Lazarevich Feldbin), the NKVD resident in Spain.

13 On Grigulevich, see Germán Sánchez, 'El misterio Grigulévich', *Historia 16*, no. 233, September 1995; Boris Volardsky, *KGB: The West Side Story* (forthcoming), Chapter 16; Christopher Andrew and Vasili Mitrokhin, *The Sword and the Shield: The Mitrokhin Archive and the Secret History of the KGB* (New York: Basic Books, 1999), p. 300; Marjorie Ross, *El secreto encanto de la KGB. Las cinco vidas de Iósif Griguliévich* (Heredia, Costa Rica: Farben Grupo Editorial Norma, 2004); Ángel Viñas, *El escudo de la República* (Barcelona: Editorial Crítica, 2007), pp. 60–6, 74–8, 544–6, 609–19.

14 *Hoja de Servicios del general Ramón Robles Pazos*, Archivo Militar General, Segovia. Ramon's treatment at the hands of the Republicans contrasted dramatically with the immediate execution that awaited any officer who refused to serve the rebels.

15 José Robles to Lancaster, 20 October 1936 and undated, Robles Papers, Sheridan Libraries, Johns Hopkins University, Ms 47.

16 Bowers to Dos Passos, 27 August 1937, Bowers Papers; Francisco Ayala, *Recuerdos y olvidos (1906–2006)* (Madrid: Alianza Editorial, 2006), pp. 229–30; Martínez de Pisón, *Enterrar a los muertos*, p. 32.

17 Francisco Robles to Lancaster, 6 January 1937, Robles Papers, Sheridan Libraries, Johns Hopkins University, Ms 47.

18 Fischer, *Men and Politics*, p. 406.

19 Dos Passos, *The Theme*, pp. 115–16, 128; Ludington, *John Dos Passos*, p. 366; Kurzke and Mangan, 'The Good Comrade', p. 419 (Jan Kurzke Papers, Archives of the International Institute for Social History, Amsterdam). On Barry, see Harriet Ward, *A Man of Small Importance. My Father Griffin Barry* (Debenham, Suffolk: Dormouse Books, 2003).

20 Dos Passos, letter to *New Republic*, *The Fourteenth Chronicle*, pp. 527–9; Dos Passos, *The Theme*, p. 128.

21 Dos Passos to Lancaster, undated 1938, Robles Papers, Ms 47.

22 According to the Spanish novelist Ignacio Martínez de Pisón, this devastating revelation was made to Coco by Luis Rubio Hidalgo in late February or early March. According to Dos Passos himself, it was made by Liston Oak on the same day that Márgara Villegas asked him to investigate her husband's disappearance, that is to say, on or about 9 April. Martínez de Pisón, *Enterrar a los muertos*, p. 35; Dos Passos to Lancaster, undated 1938, Robles Papers Ms 47; Dos Passos, *The Fourteenth Chronicle*, p. 528; Ludington, *Dos Passos*, pp. 367, 371.

23 Kurzke and Mangan, 'The Good Comrade', pp. 419–20.

24 Coco Robles to Lancaster, 20 April, 17 July; Coindreau to Lancaster, 14 May 1937, Robles Papers, Ms 47.

25 He describes their meeting in his autobiographical novel, John Dos Passos, *Century's Ebb: The Thirteenth Chronicle* (Boston, MA: Gambit, 1975), pp. 77–9; Kurzke and Mangan, 'The Good Comrade', p. 246.

Notes

26 John Dos Passos, *Journeys Between Wars* (New York: Harcourt, Brace, 1938), pp. 359–60.

27 Dos Passos, *New Republic, The Fourteenth Chronicle*, p. 528; Dos Passos, *Century's Ebb*, pp. 73–7. See also Koch, *The Breaking Point*, pp. 106–10, 114–15. Koch takes Dos Passos' later novel literally on this point and assumes that a fictional character, Alfredo Posada (in fact, based very loosely on Dos Passos' friend Luis Quintanilla), was a real functionary of the Ministry of Foreign Affairs in Valencia, something that Luis Quintanilla never was.

28 Ludington, *Dos Passos*, pp. 365–9.

29 Dos Passos, *Century's Ebb*, p. 81.

30 Herbst, 'Notes on Spain'/'Journal Spain', p. 1.

31 Herbst, *The Starched Blue Sky*, pp. 150–1.

32 Dos Passos, *Century's Ebb*, p. 82.

33 Ilse Katz to Herbst, 20 March 1937; the text of the broadcast, both in Za Herbst Collection, Beinecke Library, Yale University; Stephen Koch, *Double Lives. Spies and Writers in the Secret Soviet War of Ideas against the West* (New York: The Free Press, 1994), pp. 231–4, 291–2. For a brilliant refutation of Koch's speculation, see Elinor Langer, 'The Secret Drawer', *The Nation*, 30 May 1994, pp. 752–60.

34 Herbst, *The Starched Blue Sky*, p. 139.

35 Koch, *The Breaking Point*, pp. 102–5, 292–3; Herbst, *The Starched Blue Sky*, pp. 139, 154; Herbst to Bliven, 30 June 1939, Za Herbst Collection, Beinecke Library, Yale University; Soledad Fox, *Constancia de la Mora in War and Exile. International Voice for the Spanish Republic* (Brighton: Sussex Academic Press, 2007), pp. 96–9.

36 Elinor Langor, *Josephine Herbst* (Boston: Little, Brown, 1984), pp. 211–12. The safe-conduct is reproduced in Langor's book among the photographs between pp. 182 and 183.

37 Herbst, *The Starched Blue Sky*, pp. 154–5; Langor, *Josephine Herbst*, pp. 221–2. Koch's novelized account of the conversation, Koch, *The Breaking Point*, pp. 141–6, 153–5.

38 Coindreau to Lancaster, 1 June 1937, Robles Papers, Ms 47; Dos Passos to Bowers, 21 July 1937, Bowers Papers.

39 Herbst to Bliven, 30 June 1939, Za Herbst Collection, Beinecke Library, Yale University.

40 Dos Passos, *Century's Ebb*, pp. 90–4; Ludington, *Dos Passos*, pp. 370–1; 'The Fiesta at the Fifteenth Brigade', Dos Passos, *Journeys*, pp. 375–81; Herbst, *The Starched Blue Sky*, p. 157.

41 Dos Passos, *Century's Ebb*, pp. 90–4; Dos Passos to *New Republic*, p. 528. Luis Quintanilla's view reported by José Nieto.

42 Ludington, *Dos Passos*, p. 371; Herbst, *The Starched Blue Sky*, pp. 156–7. The most florid, and largely invented account, Koch, *The Breaking Point*, pp. 147–59.

43 Koch, *The Breaking Point*, p. 146.

44 Herbst, 'Journal Spain', pp. 13–14.

45 Cowles, *Looking for Trouble*, pp. 34–5; Herbst, 'Journal Spain', pp. 126–8; Herbst, *The Starched Blue Sky*, pp. 167–71.

46 Dos Passos to Lancaster, 26 June, Coindreau to Lancaster, 28 May 1937, Robles Papers, Ms 47.

47 Dos Passos to Bowers, 21 July 1937, Bowers Papers.

48 Kurzke and Mangan, 'The Good Comrade', p. 364. On the photograph, see Koch, *The Breaking Point*, p. 301.

49 Dos Passos, *Journeys*, pp. 391–2.

50 Dos Passos, *Century's Ebb*, pp. 94–6, 98.

51 Dos Passos, *The Theme*, p. 145.

52 Koch, *The Breaking Point*, p. 175.

53 Liston Oak, 'Behind Barcelona Barricades', *The New Statesman and Nation*, 15 May 1937. Orwell to Cyril Connolly, 8 June 1937, George Orwell, *Orwell in Spain* (London: Penguin Books, 2001), p. 23.

54 *Investigation of Un-American Propaganda Activities*, Special Committee on Un-American Propaganda Activities, House of Representatives, 76th Congress, 1st Session, 1939, vol. 11, pp. 6544–52; Pierre Broué, *Staline et la révolution. Le cas espagnol (1936–1939)* (Paris: Librairie Arthème Fayard, 1993), p. 178; Harvey Klehr, *The Heyday of American Communism. The Depression Decade* (New York: Basic Books, 1984), p. 440; Paulina y Adelina Abramson, *Mosaico roto* (Madrid: Compañía Literaria, 1994), p. 259. On the Comintern's work in seamen's unions, see Jan Valtin, *Out of the Night*, 2nd edn (London: Fortress Books, 1988).

55 Koch, *The Breaking Point*, pp. 175–7, 191–8.

56 Dos Passos, *Century's Ebb*, p. 96. For an entirely invented account of their meeting, see Koch, *The Breaking Point*, pp. 200–4.

57 Kurzke and Mangan, 'The Good Comrade', p. 365; Bowler to Wintringham, 22 June 1937, Russian Centre for the Preservation and Study of Recent Historical Documents, Moscow, Fond. 545, Opus 6, 216 (copy held by International Brigades Memorial Trust, London).

58 Koch, *The Breaking Point*, p. 176. On his return to Spain, he published 'What Happened in Barcelona'; 'A Spanish Incident'; 'Stalinist "Cheka" Method in Spain Destroys Unity of Anti-Fascist Struggle' (with Sam Baron); 'The Tragic Death of Nin is a Result of the Policy of Spanish Communists' (with Sam Baron), *Socialist Call*, 5 June, 3 July, 14 August, 11 September 1937, and 'Balance Sheet of the Spanish Revolution', *Socialist Review*, September 1937; Trotsky, 'Stalinism and Bolshevism', reprinted in *Living Marxism* (no. 18, April 1990); 'Their Morals and Ours', *The New International*, vol. IV, no. 6, June 1938.

59 Oak, 'I am Exposed as a Spy', *Socialist Call*, 18 December 1937.

60 Ludington, *Dos Passos*, p. 374; Dos Passos, *Century's Ebb*, pp. 98–9.

61 Coindreau to Lancaster, 28 May 1937, Robles Papers, Ms 47.

62 Coindreau to Lancaster, 28 May 1937; Márgara to Esther Crooks, 5, 23 August 1937, Robles Papers, Ms 47.

63 Márgara to Esther Crooks, 6 June, Márgara to Lancaster, 24 July 1937, Robles Papers, Ms 47.

64 De la Mora, *In Place of Splendor*, pp. 295–6.

65 Martínez de Pisón, *Enterrar a los muertos*, pp. 166–79; Fischer, *Men and Politics*, pp. 406–7; De la Mora, *In Place of Splendor*, p. 296; Kurzke and Mangan, 'The Good Comrade', p. 420; Herbst to Bliven, 30 June 1939, Za Herbst Collection, Beinecke Library, Yale University.

66 For an analysis of the dismissal and a facsimile of Porter's FBI testimony, see Langor, *Josephine Herbst*, pp. 248–59.

67 Ludington, *Dos Passos*, pp. 378–84.

68 Dos Passos, *Journeys Between Wars*, pp. 359–60, 378.

69 Hemingway to Dos Passos, both undated, Ernest Hemingway Papers, Outgoing Correspondence, John F. Kennedy Presidential Library and Museum.

70 Ludington, *Dos Passos*, p. 374.

71 Malcolm Cowley, 'Disillusionment', *New Republic*, 14 June 1939; Dos Passos to Macdonald and letter to *New Republic*, both July 1939, *The Fourteenth Chronicle*, pp. 526–9; Cowley to Elinor Langer, 13 April 1976, Za Herbst Collection, Beinecke Library, Yale University.

72 Dos Passos, *The Theme*, pp. 128, 130.

73 Dos Passos, *Century's Ebb*, pp. 74–7.

74 The Dos Passos remark was made to José Nieto. It is difficult to corroborate this. The Gustav Regler remark in Herbst to Watson, 25 July 1967, Za Herbst Collection, Beinecke Library, Yale University.

Chapter 4: Love and Politics

1 Constancia de la Mora, *In Place of Splendor. The Autobiography of a Spanish Woman* (New York: Harcourt, Brace, 1939), pp. 241–53, 279–80; Louis Fischer, *Men and Politics. An Autobiography* (London: Jonathan Cape, 1941), pp. 306, 432; Ignacio Hidalgo de Cisneros, *Cambio de Rumbo*, 2 vols (Bucharest: Colección Ebro, 1964, 1970), II, p. 212; Soledad Fox, *Constancia de la Mora in War and Exile. International Voice for the Spanish Republic* (Brighton: Sussex Academic Press, 2007), pp. 11–13.

2 De la Mora, *In Place of Splendor*, pp. 281–3.

3 De la Mora, *In Place of Splendor*, pp. 279–81; Jan Kurzke and Kate Mangan, 'The Good Comrade' (Jan Kurzke Papers, Archives of the International Institute for Social History, Amsterdam), p. 261; John Dos Passos, *Journeys Between Wars* (New York: Harcourt, Brace, 1938), p. 357.

4 Arturo Barea, *The Forging of a Rebel* (London: Davis-Paynter, 1972), pp. 673–4, 684.

5 Vincent Sheean, *Not Peace but a Sword* (New York: Doubleday, Doran, 1939), pp. 147–8.

6 Joseph North, *No Men are Strangers* (New York: International Publishers, 1958), pp. 129–32.

7 Fischer, *Men and Politics*, pp. 432–6; Burnett Bolloten, *The Spanish Civil War: Revolution and Counterrevolution* (Hemel Hempstead: Harvester Wheatsheaf, 1991), pp. 539–40.

8 De la Mora, *In Place of Splendour*, pp. 339–40.

9 Fischer to Negrín, 9 November 1937, Fischer Papers, Series 1 General Correspondence, Box 10, Folder 29.

10 Kurzke and Mangan, 'The Good Comrade', p. 414.

11 Mangan to Bennett, 7 November 1937, Milly Bennett Papers, Box 3, Folder 18, Hoover Institution Archives.

12 Fischer notes on 'October 1937 Benicasim visit with Negrín'; Fischer to Negrín, 7 October 1937, Fischer Papers, Series 1 General Correspondence, Box 10, Folder 29.

13 Fischer to Negrín, 9 November 1937, Fischer Papers, Series 1 General Correspondence, Box 10, Folder 29.

14 Virginia Cowles, *Looking for Trouble* (London: Hamish Hamilton, 1941), p. 17.

15 De la Mora, *In Place of Splendour*, pp. 290–1; Sefton Delmer, *Trail Sinister. An Autobiography* (London: Secker & Warburg, 1961), p. 328.

16 Delmer, *Trail Sinister*, p. 259.

17 Author's conversation with Sir Geoffrey Cox, 9 September 2006.

18 Author's conversation with Sam Russell, 9 September 2006.

19 De la Mora, *In Place of Splendor*, pp. 287–8.

20 De la Mora, *In Place of Splendor*, p. 289.

21 Louis Fischer, *Men and Politics*, p. 432; Philip Jordan, *There is No Return* (London: Cresset Press, 1938), pp. 287–8.

22 Viscount Churchill, *All My Sins Remembered* (London: William Heinemann, 1964), pp. 170–1.

23 Kurzke and Mangan, 'The Good Comrade', pp. 414, 419.

24 Jordan, *There is No Return*, p. 18.

25 Stephen Spender, *World within World* (London: Readers Union, 1953), p. 197.

26 E. O. Deeble, 'In Valencia. December Scene', *Washington Post*, 4 January 1937.

27 Jordan, *There is No Return*, pp. 18–19.

28 Sheean, *Not Peace*, pp. 140–1.

29 I am indebted to Charlotte Kurzke for information about her mother.

30 Jan Kurzke and Kate Mangan, 'The Good Comrade' (unpublished ms, Jan Kurzke Papers, Archives of the International Institute for Social History, Amsterdam), pp. 81, 88, 228–9, 275 and notes by Charlotte Kurzke, p. x. On Kate's relations with Slater, Mangan to Bennett, 13 February 1938, Milly Bennett Papers, Box 3, Folder 18, Hoover Institution Archives.

31 Kurzke and Mangan, 'The Good Comrade', pp. 92, 228–9. That 'Louise Mallory' was Kitty is evident from the manuscript by Louis Fischer, 'Oct. 1937 Benicasim Visit with Negrín', Fischer Papers, Series 1 General Correspondence, Box 10, Folder 29. See also Hugh Purcell, *The Last English Revolutionary. A Biography of Tom Wintringham 1898–1949* (Stroud: Sutton Publishing, 2004), p. 97.

32 Clipping from *Old Colony Memorial*, 25 August 1937, Liddell Hart Centre for Military Archives, King's College, London, Wintringham Collection, Spanish Civil War (henceforth LHCMA, Wintringham papers), folder 10.

33 Duranty to Bowler, 18 February, 10 April 1937, LHCMA, Wintringham papers, folder 10; Bowler to Wintringham, 1 July 1937, Russian Centre for the Preservation and Study of Recent Historical Documents, Moscow, Fond. 545, Opus 6, 216 (copy held by International Brigades Memorial Trust, London) (henceforth RCPSRHD/IBMT).

34 Bowler to Charlotte Everett Miller Bowler (her mother), 8 September 1936, LHCMA, Wintringham papers, Folder 3; Kitty Bowler, 'Memoirs', Chapter 1, pp. 1–4, Chapter 2, pp. 1–3, Chapter 4, pp. 1–7, LHCMA, Wintringham papers, 1, folder 3.

35 Kitty Bowler, 'Memoirs', Chapter 5, pp. 6–8, LHCMA, Wintringham papers, 1, folder 3.

36 Wintringham, manuscript 'An improbable chapter', LHCMA, Wintringham papers, folder 11.

37 Bowler to Joe Pass (editor of *Fight*), 26 November Bowler to North, 26 November 1936, LHCMA, Wintringham papers, folder 1. On the Comissariat de Propaganda, see Francesc Poblet, 'El Comissariat de Propaganda. Un organisme pioneer de la propaganda governamental a l'Estat espanyol', in Josep Maria Solé i Sabaté, Joan Villarroya and Eduard Voltes (eds), *La Guerra civil a Catalunya*, 4 vols (Barcelona: Edicions 62, 2004), I, pp. 243–7.

38 Bowler to North, 26 November 1936, LHCMA, Wintringham papers, folder 1; Kitty Bowler, 'Memoirs', Chapter 9, p. 5, LHCMA, Wintringham papers, 1, Folder 3.

39 The great majority of her articles were published without a by-line. An exception was Katherine Bowler, 'The Bombing of the Prado', *Guardian*, 30 January 1937.

40 Purcell, *Wintringham*, p. 110.

41 Sinclair Loutit to David Fernbach, 7 July 1978 (courtesy of David Fernbach); Wintringham to Victor Gollancz, 10 August 1941, LHCMA, Wintringham papers, 1, folder 18. For a slightly different version, see Purcell, *Wintringham*, p. 114. Wintringham eventually divorced his wife and married Kitty. The British Communist Party demanded that he leave her and he chose instead to leave the party.

42 Margaret Wintringham to Bowler, 15 October 1937, LHCMA, Wintringham papers, folder 10.

43 Purcell, *Wintringham*, pp. 113–14.

44 Wintringham to Victor Gollancz, 10 August 1941, LHCMA, Wintringham papers, 1, folder 18.

45 Bowler to Charlotte Bowler, 4 December 1936, LHCMA, Wintringham papers, folder 3.

46 Bowler to 'P', 12 December 1936; Bowler to Charlotte Bowler, 7 February 1937, LHCMA, Wintringham papers, folders 3 and 1; Bowler to Wintringham, 18, 20 December 1936, and a further undated letter which, from internal evidence, seems to have been written on 21 December, RCPSRHD/IBMT, F.545, O.6/216.

47 Saklatvala Battalion order, 'Comrade Bowler will be carried on the Battalion strength', LHCMA, Wintringham papers, folder 12; Wintringham to Victor Gollancz, 10 August 1941, LHCMA, Wintringham papers, 1, folder 18; Kurzke and Mangan, 'The Good Comrade', pp. 254–5, 261–3.

48 Bowler, Memoirs, LHCMA, Wintringham papers, 1, folder 3.

49 Wintringham to Victor Gollancz, 10 August 1941, LHCMA, Wintringham papers, 1, folder 18.

50 Wintringham to Fein, 24 February; Kerrigan to Wintringham, 15 March, Wintringham to 'Shaya', 7 April 1937, RCPSRHD/IBMT, F.545, O.6/216; Purcell, *Wintringham*, pp. 122–4. The fact that the letters were confiscated accounts for their presence in the Wintringham files of the International Brigades archive in Moscow.

51 Author's interview with Sam Russell, 21 October 2006.

52 Wintringham to Bowler, undated, LHCMA, Wintringham papers, folder 11.

53 Bowler to Wintringham, 27 January 1937, RCPSRHD/IBMT, F.545, O.6/216.

54 In an effort to have the order rescinded, Wintringham wrote a report taking responsibility for her presence in Madrigueras, 'Report – Kitty Bowler', 4 July 1937,

RCPSRHD/IBMT, F.545, O.6/216. See also Kurzke and Mangan, 'The Good Comrade', pp. 262–3; Russell interview.

55 Wintringham to Kerrigan, 4 March; Bowler to Kerrigan, 12 March 1937, RCPSRHD/IBMT, F.545, O.6/216; Patience Edney taped interview, Imperial War Museum, Sound Archive, Spanish Civil War Collection, 8398/13; Purcell, *Wintringham*, pp. 139–44; Deeble to Bowler, 4 June 1937, LHCMA, Wintringham papers, folder 10; Kurzke and Mangan, 'The Good Comrade', pp. 341–3.

56 Harriet Ward, *A Man of Small Importance. My Father Griffin Barry* (Debenham, Suffolk: Dormouse Books, 2003), p. 180; Purcell, *Wintringham*, p. 112; Kurzke and Mangan, 'The Good Comrade', pp. 413–14.

57 Bowler to Wintringham, 25 June 1937, and attached report sent to Kerrigan, RCPSRHD/IBMT, F.545, O.6/ 216.

58 Bowler to Wintringham, 9 July 1937, RCPSRHD/IBMT, F.545, O.6/ 216.

59 Wintringham to Victor Gollancz, 10 August 1941, LHCMA, Wintringham papers, 1, folder 18.

60 Bowler to Wintringham, 8 February, 'Had a nice long letter from Kate', 28 June 1937, RCPSRHD/IBMT, F.545, O.6/ 216; Kurzke & Mangan, 'The Good Comrade', pp. 397–8, 408.

61 Kurzke and Mangan, 'The Good Comrade', pp. 230–1, 244. On Kitty, Mangan to Bennett, undated, but mid-1938, Milly Bennet Papers, Box 3, Folder 18, Hoover Institution Archives.

62 Wintringham to Bowler, 2 November 1936, LHCMA, Wintringham papers, folder 11; Bowler to Wintringham, 27 January 1937, RCPSRHD/IBMT, F.545, O.6/216.

63 Kurzke and Mangan, 'The Good Comrade', pp. 244–5, 292.

64 Kurzke and Mangan, 'The Good Comrade', p. 364. Ironically, Kate's estranged husband, Sherry Mangan, was himself a prominent Trotskyist and he wrote about the POUM in 1939: see *The Spanish Civil War: The View from the Left*, Special Issue of *Revolutionary History*, vol. 4, nos 1/2, 1991, pp. 303–13.

65 Stephen Koch, *The Breaking Point. Hemingway, Dos Passos and the Murder of José Robles* (New York: Counterpoint, 2005), pp. 115–18; Kurzke and Mangan, 'The Good Comrade', p. 245.

66 Kurzke and Mangan, 'The Good Comrade', p. 247; De la Mora, *In Place of Splendor*, pp. 295–6.

67 Kurzke and Mangan, 'The Good Comrade', p. 248.

68 Kate Mangan to Sherry Mangan, 16 April 1937, papers of Charlotte Kurzke.

69 Cowles, *Looking for Trouble*, p.36; Lucy Viedma, 'Everything you have done for us Spanish children', *The World in the Basement* (Stockholm: Arbetarrörelsens Arkiv och Bibliotek, 2003) p. 37; 'Kajsa kämpade för Spaniens barn' in *Varmlands Folkblad*, 27 November 2004.

70 On Fernanda Jacobsen's activities, see C. E. Lucas Phillips, *The Spanish Pimpernel* (London: Heinemann, 1960), pp. 85–8, 104–17; Delmer, *Trail Sinister*, pp. 344–6; Salter, *Try-Out in Spain*, pp. 117–33. The security report is 'Informe sobre la actuación de la Delegación Canadiense en España: Antecedentes de Kajsa', in Mackenzie-Papineau Collection, Nacional Archives, Canada. I am deeply grateful to Larry Hannant who sent me a copy of this document.

Notes

71 Hazen Size to Bethune, 25 February 1937, Osler Medical History Library, McGill University; Moller to Hedda Hopper, 28 January 1943, UCLA Library, Special Collections, Collection 877, Box 30, Folder 1. Kenneth Macgowan Papers. I am grateful to David Lethbridge who sent me copies of both documents. See also Larry Hannant (ed.), *The Politics of Passion. Norman Bethune's Writing and Art* (Toronto: University of Toronto Press, 1998), pp. 125–7, 361–4 (where there is an English translation of the 'Informe'); T. C. Worsley, *Behind the Battle* (London: Robert Hale, 1939), pp. 247–8.

72 Kurzke & Mangan, 'The Good Comrade', p. 339. Josephine Herbst, unpublished diary, Za Herbst Collection, Beinecke Library, Yale University, pp. 11, 13, 27, 39, 42, 46–7; Cowles, *Looking for Trouble*, p. 36.

73 Moller to Hopper, quoted above; Félix Schlayer, *Diplomático en el Madrid rojo* (Sevilla: Espuela de Plata, 2008), pp. 248–53. On Kajsa after leaving the press office, see Viedma, 'Everything', p. 37; 'Kajsa åter i Spanien', *Solidaritet*, no. 1, 1938; 'Kajsa kämpade för Spaniens barn' in *Varmlands Folkblad*, 27 November 2004.

74 On Anna Louise Strong, see Marion Merriman and Warren Lerude, *American Commander in Spain: Robert Hale Merriman and the Abraham Lincoln Brigade* (Reno, NV: University of Nevada Press, 1986), pp. 40–1. Milly's movements can be traced from the various letters of recommendation and safe-conducts preserved among her papers in the Hoover Institution Archives.

75 Kurzke and Mangan, 'The Good Comrade', pp. 246–8; Peter N. Carroll, *The Odyssey of the Abraham Lincoln Brigade: Americans in the Spanish Civil War* (Stanford, CA: Stanford University Press, 1994), pp. 74, 92, 157; Merriman and Lerude, *American Commander*, pp. 40–2, 53–7, 75, 79, 145, 151, 167; A. Tom Grunfeld, letter to *The Volunteer*, December 2004; James M. Minifie, *Expatriate* (Toronto: Macmillan of Canada, 1976), p. 69; Delmer, *Trail Sinister*, pp. 332–3.

76 Kurzke and Mangan, 'The Good Comrade', pp. 250, 344–9.

77 H. Edward Knoblaugh, *Correspondent in Spain* (London and New York: Sheed & Ward, 1937), pp. 176–8.

78 Knoblaugh to Bennett, 7 November 1939, Milly Bennett Papers, Box 3, Folder 7, Hoover Institution Archives.

79 Kurzke and Mangan, 'The Good Comrade', pp. 309–10.

80 *The Times*, 17, 24 February, 3 March 1937; T. C. Worsley, *Behind the Battle* (London: Robert Hale, 1939), pp. 275–7.

81 Deeble to Bowler, 4 June 1937, LHCMA, Wintringham papers, folder 11.

82 Kurzke and Mangan, 'The Good Comrade', pp. 259–61.

83 Kurzke and Mangan, 'The Good Comrade', p. 364.

84 There exist three versions of the demise of Basil Murray, of which only that by Kate Mangan is entirely reliable. Kurzke and Mangan, 'The Good Comrade', pp. 349–54; Delmer, *Trail Sinister*, pp. 337–43; Claud Cockburn, 'Spies and Two Deaths in Spain', *Grand Street*, no. 2, 1981.

85 Articles by Matthews, *New York Times*, 20, 26 December 1937, 5, 9, 11, 16, 28, 31 January, 4, 6 February 1938; by William P. Carney, *New York Times*, 31 December 1937, 18, 22, 23 January, 8, 23 February 1938; Herbert L. Matthews, *A World in Revolution. A Newspaperman's Memoir* (New York: Charles Scribner's Sons, 1971), pp. 28–30.

86 Ernest Hemingway to 'Madug', undated January 1938, Louis Henry and Marguerite Cohn Hemingway Collection, Special Collections, University of Delaware Library. Herbert L. Matthews, *Two Wars and More to Come* (New York: Carrick & Evans, 1938), jacket copy.

87 Salter, *Try-out in Spain*, pp. 227–30.

88 The story of Jim Lardner is movingly recounted by Sheean, *Not Peace*, pp. 235–66.

89 Sheean, *Not Peace*, pp. 141–2, 240–2.

90 Salter, *Try-out in Spain*, pp. 182–3.

91 Josephine Herbst, unpublished memoir, 'Journal Spain', Za Herbst Collection, Beinecke Library, Yale University, pp. 8, 11; De la Mora, *In Place of Splendor*, p. 293. On Kajsa, Cowles, *Looking for Trouble*, p. 36.

92 Bernard Knox, *Essays Ancient and Modern* (Baltimore, MD: Johns Hopkins University Press, 1989), p. 248.

93 Salter, *Try-out in Spain*, p. 210.

94 North, *No Men are Strangers*, p. 142.

95 Peter Besas, 'Henry Buckley, Reporter and 40-year Veteran of Madrid', *Guidepost*, 1970, pp. 17–18; Herbert L. Matthews, *The Education of a Correspondent* (New York: Harcourt Brace, 1946), p. 138; Sheean, *Not Peace*, pp. 336–7.

96 Herbert Matthews, 'Rebels Intensify Bombing of Roads', *New York Times*, 16 January 1939.

97 Matthews, *A World in Revolution*, p. 97.

98 Salter, *Try-out in Spain*, pp. 240–9.

99 Herbert Matthews, 'Figueras Capital of Loyalist Spain', 'Conflict to Go On', 'Toll of 500 Feared in Figueras Raids', *New York Times*, 28 January, 4, 6 February 1939.

100 Sheean, *Not Peace*, pp. 350–63.

101 Herbert Matthews, '130,000 Refugees Enter France', *New York Times*, 7 February 1939.

102 Matthews, *The Education*, p. 192.

Chapter 5: The Rebel Zone

1 Kate Mangan to Sherry Mangan, 16 April 1937, papers of Charlotte Kurzke.

2 Radio Nacional de España, *Guerra civil y Radio Nacional. Salamanca 1936–1938* (Madrid: Instituto Oficial de Radio y Televisión, 2006), pp. 8–11, 65–7.

3 Eugenio Vegas Latapie, *Los caminos del desengaño. Memorias políticas 2: 1936–1938* (Madrid: Ediciones Giner, 1987), pp. 172–3; Ángel Viñas, *La Alemania nazi y el 18 de julio* (Madrid: Alianza Editorial, 1974), pp. 167–8; Gonzalo Álvarez Chillida, *El antisemitismo en España. La imagen del judío (1812–2002)* (Madrid: Marcial Pons, 2002), pp. 312–13, 361–2; María Cruz Seoane and María Dolores Sáiz, *Historia del periodismo en España 3. El siglo XX: 1898–1936* (Madrid: Alianza Editorial, 1998), pp. 348–9, 426–7; Herbert Rutledge Southworth, *Guernica! Guernica!: A Study of Journalism, Propaganda and History* (Berkeley, CA: University of California Press, 1977), pp. 411, 498.

4 *ABC* (Sevilla), 14, 18 August 1936; Francisco Franco Salgado-Araujo, *Mi vida junto a Franco* (Barcelona: Editorial Planeta, 1976), p. 190; Vegas Latapie, *Los caminos*, p. 173.

5 Rafael Abella, *La vida cotidiana durante la guerra civil 1) La España nacional* (Barcelona: Editorial Planeta, 1978), p. 109.

6 Vegas Latapie, *Los caminos*, p. 175; Francis McCullagh, *In Franco's Spain* (London: Burns, Oates & Washbourne, 1937), pp. 104–7.

7 Noel Monks, *Eyewitness* (London: Frederick Muller, 1955), p. 73.

8 McCullagh, *In Franco's Spain*, p. 107. The pseudonym given Bolín in McCullagh's book was Bustamente.

9 Arthur Koestler, *Spanish Testament* (London: Victor Gollancz, 1937), pp. 26–8, 220; Southworth, *Guernica! Guernica!*, pp. 415–16.

10 'A Journalist', *Foreign Journalists under Franco's Terror* (London: United Editorial, 1937), pp. 8–12; Major Geoffrey McNeill-Moss, *The Epic of the Alcazar* (London: Rich & Cowan, 1937), pp. 309–15.

11 Josep Massot i Muntaner, *El desembarcament de Bayo a Mallorca, Agost–Setembre de 1936* (Barcelona: Publicacions de l'Abadia de Montserrat, 1987), pp. 337–40; Georges Bernanos, *Els grans cementeris sota la lluna* (Barcelona: Curiel Edicions Catalanes, 1981), pp. 186–8; Jaume Miravitlles, *Episodis de la guerra civil espanyola* (Barcelona: Editorial Pòrtic, 1972), pp. 241–2; Southworth, *Guernica! Guernica!*, p. 416.

12 Webb Miller, *I Found No Peace* (London: The Book Club, 1937), pp. 325–7.

13 H. R. Knickerbocker, *The Siege of the Alcazar: A War-Log of the Spanish Revolution* (London: Hutchinson, n.d. [1937]), pp. 172–3; Webb Miller, *I Found No Peace* (London: The Book Club, 1937), pp. 329–30; Herbert L. Matthews, *The Yoke and the Arrows: A Report on Spain* (London: Heinemann, 1958), p. 176.

14 Luis Bolín, *Spain: The Vital Years* (Philadelphia, PA: Lippincott, 1967), pp. 196–7; Harold Cardozo, 'Alcazar Chief "You Must Die" to Son', *Daily Mail*, 30 September 1936. The story is deconstructed in Herbert Rutledge Southworth, *El mito de la cruzada de Franco* (Paris: Ediciones Ruedo Ibérico, 1963), pp. 49–56.

15 Miller, *I Found No Peace*, pp. 336–7; Allen to Southworth, 17 January 1964, 7 August 1967, Southworth Papers, Museo de Guernica.

16 'Denis Weaver Captured by Franco. "News Chronicle" War Correspondent taken with 4 Companions. Chauffeur Shot Dead', *News Chronicle*, 27 October; 'Britons Captured by Rebels', *Guardian*, 27 October 1936; Denis Weaver, 'Through the Enemy's Lines', in Hanighen, *Nothing but Danger*, pp. 98–115; 'A Journalist', *Foreign Journalists*, pp. 15–16; James M. Minifie, *Expatriate* (Toronto: Macmillan of Canada, 1976), pp. 70–5; Claude Bowers, *My Mission to Spain* (London: Victor Gollancz, 1954), pp. 325–6. Some discrepancies between the published versions of Weaver and Minifie may be explained by the fact that the latter's memoirs were completed after his death by his wife on the basis of taped reminiscences.

17 *News Chronicle*, 29 October 1936.

18 Geoffrey Cox, *Eyewitness. A Memoir of Europe in the 1930s* (Dunedin: University of Otago Press, 1999), pp. 200–1.

19 Cox, *Eyewitness*, p. 204.

20 C. E. Lucas Phillips, *The Spanish Pimpernel* (London: Heinemann, 1960), pp. 70–80.

21 'A Journalist', *Foreign Journalists*, pp. 14, 17; Koestler, *Spanish Testament*, p. 220.

22 *Guardian*, 22 February 1937; Southworth, *Guernica! Guernica!*, pp. 54–5, 421–2.

23 Koestler, *The Invisible Writing*, 2nd edn (London: Hutchinson, 1969), pp. 382–9.

24 Koestler, *Spanish Testament*, p. 34.

25 Koestler, *The Invisible Writing*, pp. 389–93.

26 Koestler, *The Invisible Writing*, pp. 400–9; David Cesarani, *Arthur Koestler. The Homeless Mind* (New York: The Free Press, 1998), pp. 120–3, 135–41; K. W. Watkins, *Britain Divided* (London: Nelson, 1963), pp. 46–7, 55–6. The book, written by Otto Katz, but published under the name of Emile Burns, was *The Nazi Conspiracy in Spain* (London: Victor Gollancz, 1937).

27 Koestler, *Spanish Testament*, pp. 223–31; Koestler, *The Invisible Writing*, pp. 413–27, 443–6; Sir Peter Chalmers-Mitchell, *My House in Malaga* (London: Faber & Faber, 1938), pp. 269–89; Bolín, *Spain: the Vital Years*, pp. 247–9; Shiela Grant Duff, 'A Very Brief Visit', in Philip Toynbee (ed.), *The Distant Drum. Reflections on the Spanish Civil War* (London: Sidgwick & Jackson, 1976), pp. 76–86; Cesarani, *Arthur Koestler*, pp. 123–35. In his account, Regler, *Owl of Minerva*, pp. 276–7, conflates the arrest of Denis Weaver in late October 1936 with that of Koestler. There was no Comintern campaign in favour of Weaver.

28 Marcel Junod, *Warrior without Weapons* (London: Jonathan Cape, 1951), pp. 123–5.

29 McCullagh, *In Franco's Spain*, pp. 104–29; Monks, *Eyewitness*, pp. 79–84, 105–6.

30 On Merry del Val, see RNE, *Guerra civil y Radio Nacional*, p. 50, and Judith Keene, *Fighting for Franco. International Volunteers in Nationalist Spain during the Spanish Civil War, 1936–1939* (London: Leicester University Press, 2001), p. 56; Peter Kemp, *Mine were of Trouble* (London: Cassell, 1957), p. 67; Alan Dick, *Inside Story* (London: George Allen & Unwin, 1943), p. 109.

31 Luis Moure Mariño, *La generación del 36: memorias de Salamanca y Burgos* (La Coruña: Ediciós do Castro, 1989), pp. 73–9; Luis Portillo, 'Unamuno's Last Lecture', Cyril Connolly, *The Golden Horizon* (London: Weidenfeld & Nicolson, 1953), pp. 397–403; Carlos Rojas, *¡Muera la inteligencia! ¡Viva la muerte! Salamanca, 1936. Unamuno y Millán Astray frente a frente* (Barcelona: Planeta, 1995), pp. 134–9.

32 Ernesto Giménez Caballero, *Memorias de un dictador* (Barcelona: Planeta, 1979), pp. 88–90; Francisco Franco Salgado-Araujo, *Mis conversaciones privadas con Franco* (Barcelona: Editorial Planeta, 1976), p. 431.

33 Vegas Latapie, *Los caminos*, pp. 182–5; Ángel Viñas, *Franco, Hitler y el estallido de la guerra civil. Antecedentes y consecuencias* (Madrid: Alianza Editorial, 2001), pp. 178–89; Álvarez Chillida, *El antisemitismo*, p. 311. On Gay Forner and Arias Paz, see RNE, *Guerra civil y Radio Nacional*, pp. 25–33, 75–81.

34 On Aguilera, see Paul Preston, 'The Answer lies in the Sewers: Captain Aguilera and the Mentality of the Francoist Officer Corps', *Science & Society*, vol. 68, no. 3, Fall 2004, pp. 277–312.

35 Ministerio de la Guerra, Sección Personal, 21 November 1932, Legajo 416, Gonzalo Aguilera Munro, Archivo General Militar de Segovia. Michael Alpert, *La reforma militar de Azaña (1931–1933)* (Madrid: Siglo XXI, 1982), pp. 133–49.

36 Informe sobre el Capitán de Caballería retirado, D. Gonzalo de Aguilera Munro, Ministerio de la Guerra, Sección Personal, Legajo 416, Gonzalo Aguilera Munro, Archivo General Militar de Segovia (henceforth Informe GAM, leg. 416, AGMS).

37 Informe GAM, leg. 416, AGMS.

38 H. R. Knickerbocker, *The Siege of the Alcazar* (London: Hutchinson, n.d. [1937]), p. 136; Harold G. Cardozo, *The March of a Nation: My Year of Spain's Civil War* (London: The Right Book Club, 1937), pp. 284–6.

39 Frances Davis, *My Shadow in the Sun* (New York: Carrick & Evans), pp. 130–1, 165, 171; McCullagh, *In Franco's Spain* (London: Burns, Oates & Washbourne, 1937), pp. 111–12; Cardozo, *The March of a Nation*, pp. 220–1.

40 See safe-conduct issued Salamanca, 23 November 1936, Legajo 416, Gonzalo Aguilera Munro, Archivo General Militar de Segovia; Cardozo, *The March of a Nation*, p. 286.

41 Sefton Delmer, *Trail Sinister. An Autobiography* (London: Secker & Warburg, 1961), pp. 143–91; Cox, *Eyewitness*, pp. 224–5.

42 Delmer, *Trail Sinister*, pp. 268–76.

43 Delmer, *Trail Sinister*, pp. 277–8; Virginia Cowles, *Looking for Trouble* (London: Hamish Hamilton, 1941), p. 17.

44 Delmer, *Trail Sinister*, pp. 274–8.

45 Davis, *My Shadow*, p. 61 and *passim*.

46 Edmond Taylor, 'Assignment in Hell', in Frank C. Hanighen, *Nothing but Danger* (London: Harrap, 1940), p. 56.

47 Nigel Tangye, *Red, White and Spain* (London: Rich & Cowan, 1937), pp. 75–80; Nicholas Rankin, *Telegram from Guernica. The Extraordinary Life of George Steer, War Correspondent* (London: Faber & Faber, 2003), pp. 84–5.

48 Cardozo, *The March of a Nation*, pp. 221–3; McCullagh, *In Franco's Spain*, pp. 106–8.

49 McCullagh, *In Franco's Spain*, pp. 98, 110–11, 116; 'A Journalist', *Foreign Journalists under Franco's Terror* (London: United Editorial, 1937), p. 30.

50 Arnold Lunn, *Spanish Rehearsal* (London: Hutchinson, 1937), p. 43.

51 Luis Moure Mariño, *La generación del 36: memorias de Salamanca y Burgos* (La Coruña: Ediciós do Castro, 1989), p. 69; Vegas Latapie, *Los caminos*, p. 175.

52 McCullagh, *In Franco's Spain*, pp. 112–13.

53 Monks, *Eyewitness*, p. 68.

54 Frances Davis, *A Fearful Innocence* (Kent, OH: Kent State University Press, 1981), pp. 140–6; Davis, *My Shadow*, pp. 84–7.

55 Taylor, 'Assignment in Hell', pp. 63–6.

56 Davis, *My Shadow*, pp. 129–33; Cowles, *Looking for Trouble*, p. 70. Oddly, and presumably as a result of a lapse of memory, in her much later memoirs, Davis attributes the threat to Aguilera, Davis, *A Fearful Innocence*, p. 150.

57 Arturo Barea, *The Forging of a Rebel* (London: Davis-Paynter, 1972), pp. 653–4; Keene, *Fighting for Franco*, p. 67.

58 'A Journalist', *Foreign Journalists*, pp. 26–30. Cf. Southworth, *Guernica! Guernica!*, pp. 52, 420, n. 62.

59 Curio Mortari, *Con gli insorti in Marocco e Spagna* (Milano: Fratelli Treves Editori, 1937), pp. 19, 99–112, 223–60.

60 Castejón column, *Diario de la Manhã*, 11 August; Correia broadcast, *ABC* (Sevilla), 9 August; interview with Franco, *Diario de Lisboa*, 10 August 1936.

61 Leopoldo Nunes, *La guerra en España (Dos meses de reportaje en los frentes de Andalucia y Extremadura)* (Granada: Librería Prieto, 1937), pp. 127–33; *O Seculo*,

27 August 1936, reproduced in *ibid.*, pp. 133–6; broadcast *La Unión* (Seville), 28 August 1936.

62 RNE, *Guerra civil y Radio Nacional*, p. 46.

63 McCullagh, *In Franco's Spain*, p. 98.

64 *Il Messagero*, 19 August 1937; Indro Montanelli, *Memorias de un periodista* (Barcelona: RBA Libros, 2002), pp. 32–3. The official line can be seen in *Il Popolo*, 27 August 1937, which proclaimed '*il contributo di sangue italiano*' in a '*splendida vittoria italiana*' (the tribute of Italian blood in a splendid Italian victory).

65 Lunn, *Spanish Rehearsal*, pp. 40–1.

66 Southworth, *Guernica! Guernica!*, pp. 53–4; Tangye, *Red, White and Spain*, pp. 10–15, 67–8, 75–81, 154.

67 Reynolds and Emily Packard, *Balcony Empire. Fascist Italy at War* (New York: Oxford University Press, 1942), pp. 53–4.

68 Packard, *Balcony Empire*, p. 54; Cowles, *Looking for Trouble*, pp. 90–4; Cardozo, *The March of a Nation*, pp. 296, 301; Dick, *Inside Story*, pp. 127–31; Southworth, *Guernica! Guernica!*, pp. 50, 418.

69 John Whitaker, 'Prelude to World War: A Witness from Spain', *Foreign Affairs*, vol. 21, no. 1, October 1942, p. 109.

70 Cecil Gerahty, *The Road to Madrid* (London: Hutchinson, 1937), pp. 60–3.

71 F. Theo Rogers, *Spain: A Tragic Journey* (New York: The Macaulay Company, 1937), pp. vii, xiii–xiv, 15–16, 20, 62, 67–8, 104–7.

72 George Seldes, 'Treason on *The Times*', *The New Republic*, 7 September 1938.

73 De la Mora, *In Place of Splendor*, pp. 258, 286.

74 Constancia de la Mora to Jay Allen, 31 December 1939 (Papers of Jay Allen). This episode is recounted in more detail in Soledad Fox, *Constancia de la Mora in War and Exile. International Spokesperson for the Spanish Republic* (Brighton: Sussex Academic Press, 2006), Chapter 3.

75 Carl Geiser, *Prisoners of the Good Fight: The Spanish Civil War 1936–1939* (Westport, CT: Lawrence Hill & Co., 1986), p. 22.

76 Southworth, *Conspiracy*, p. 202, n. 84.

77 George Seldes, *The Catholic Crisis* (New York: Julian Messner, 1939), p. 196; *New York Times*, 27 April 1937.

78 *New York Times*, 30 April 1937.

79 *New York Times*, 23 July 1937; Geiser, *Prisoners*, pp. 28–9.

80 *New York Times*, 31 December 1937, 2, 5 January 1938; Matthews, *The Education of a Correspondent*, pp. 108–11; Seldes, *The Catholic Crisis*, pp. 196–7. The version by Knightley, *The First Casualty*, p. 199, is slightly inaccurate.

81 Allen to Hemingway, 8 January 1938 (Hemingway Collection, JFK Library, Boston); Herbert L. Matthews, *A World in Revolution. A Newspaperman's Memoir* (New York: Charles Scribner's Sons, 1971), pp. 28–30.

82 Geiser, *Prisoners*, pp. 96–7, 125–6, *New York Times*, 4 April, 29 May 1938.

83 Bob Doyle, *Memorias de un rebelde sin pausa* (Madrid: Asociación de Amigos de las Brigadas Internacionales, 2002), p. 78; Cecil Eby, *Between the Bullet and the Lie* (New York: Holt, Rinehart, Winston, 1969), pp. 252–6; Geiser, *Prisoners*, pp. 136–40; *New York Times*, 11 July 1938.

84 Bill Alexander, *British Volunteers for Liberty: Spain 1936–1939* (London: Lawrence & Wishart, 1982), pp. 188–91; Richard Baxell, *British Volunteers in the Spanish Civil War. The British Battalion in the International Brigades, 1936–1939* (London: Routledge/Cañada Blanch, 2004), pp. 125–6; Geiser, *Prisoners*, pp. 139–40.

85 Geiser, *Prisoners*, pp. 172–3; *New York Times*, 9 October 1938.

86 'A Journalist', *Foreign Journalists*, p. 7.

87 Pujol (Burgos), to Franco, 22 August 1936, Archivo de Palacio, Sección Burgos, Legajo 115.

88 Bowers to Hull, 12 April 1937, *Foreign Relations of the United States 1937*, vol. I (Washington, DC: United States Government Printing Office, 1954), pp. 279–80.

89 *Appendix to the Congressional Record*, 11 May 1937; Southworth, *Guernica! Guernica!*, pp. 52, 419–20, nn. 59, 60.

90 Barry Faris, editor International News Service, telegram to Franco, April 1938, Archivo de Palacio, Sección Burgos, Legajo 115.

91 Christopher Andrew and Vasili Mitrokhin, *The Sword and the Shield: The Mitrokhin Archive and the Secret History of the KGB* (New York: Basic Books, 1999), pp. 58–62; John Costello and Oleg Tsarev, *Deadly Illusions* (New York: Crown Publishers, 1993), pp. 131–8, 147–51.

92 Winston S. Churchill, *Step by Step* (London: Odhams Press, 1947), pp. 220–1; Costello and Tsarev, *Deadly Illusions*, pp. 159–64; Andrew and Mitrokhin, *The Mitrokhin Archive*, pp. 66–7.

93 Kim Philby, *My Silent War* (London: MacGibbon & Kee, 1968), p. xxiii; Costello and Tsarev, *Deadly Illusions*, pp. 165–6.

94 Philby, *My Silent War*, pp. xxiii–xxv; Costello and Tsarev, *Deadly Illusions*, pp. 166–7.

95 *New York Times*, 1, 2, 3, 12 January 1938; Packard, *Balcony Empire*, p. 56. The best account is by Judith Keene, *Fighting for Franco. International Volunteers in Nationalist Spain during the Spanish Civil War, 1936–1939* (London: Leicester University Press, 2001), pp. 74–6.

96 Southworth, *Guernica! Guernica!*, pp. 430, 494; Costello and Tsarev, *Deadly Illusions*, pp. 168–76; Bruce Page, David Leitch and Philip Knightley, *Philby. The Spy Who Betrayed a Generation* (London: Sphere Books, 1977), pp. 71–5, 116–17; Andrew and Mitrokhin, *The Mitrokhin Archive*, p. 67.

97 Southworth, *Guernica! Guernica!*, p. 499.

98 *Dez anos de política externa (1936–1947). A nação portuguesa e a segunda guerra mundial*, IV (Lisbon: Imprensa Nacional, 1965), pp. 333–4; Del Moral to Duque de Alba, mayo de 1937, AGA, Exteriores, 54/6.803. I am grateful to Dr Hugo García for information regarding the role of Arias Paz in the removal of Bolín. The meeting with Franco in RNE, *Guerra civil y Radio Nacional*, pp. 48–9.

99 Southworth, *Guernica! Guernica!*, pp. 62–8, 334–7, 427.

100 Southworth, *Guernica! Guernica!*, pp. 64–7, 334–5, 337.

101 Informe GAM, leg. 416, AGMS.

102 Informe GAM, leg. 416, AGMS; Kemp, *Mine were of Trouble*, pp. 99–101; General Sagardía, *Del Alto Ebro a las Fuentes del Llobregat. Treinta y dos meses de guerra de la 62 División* (Barcelona: Editora Nacional, 1940), p. 106.

103 Cowles, *Looking for Trouble*, pp. 86–7.
104 Cowles, *Looking for Trouble*, p. 90.
105 Cowles, *Looking for Trouble*, p. 77.
106 Cowles, *Looking for Trouble*, pp. 96–9.
107 Cedric Salter, *Try-out in Spain* (New York: Harper Brothers, 1943), pp. 250–65.

Chapter 6: Stalin's Eyes and Ears in Madrid?

1 Arkadi Vaksberg, *Hotel Lux. Les partis frères au service de l'Internationale Communiste* (Paris: Éditions Fayard, 1993), p. 151; Carlos García-Alix, *Madrid–Moscú* (Madrid: T Ediciones, 2003), p. 176. Mikhail Koltsov, *Khochu letat'* (Moscow: Voengiz, 1931).

2 On Soslovsky, see Isaac Deutscher, *The Prophet Unarmed. Trotsky: 1921–1929* (London: Oxford University Press, 1959), pp. 113, 203, 421, 428–30. On the incident in the Bolshoi, see Pierre Broué, *Staline et la révolution. Le cas espagnol (1936–1939)* (Paris: Librairie Arthème Fayard, 1993), p. 105.

3 Robert C. Tucker, *Stalin as Revolutionary, 1879–1929* (New York: W. W. Norton, 1973), pp. 469–70.

4 Reinhold Görling, *'Dinamita Celebral' Politischer Prozeß und ästhetische Praxis im Spanischen Bürgerkrieg (1936–1939)* (Frankfurt: Verlag Klaus Dieter Vervuert, 1986), p. 311.

5 Viktor Shklovsky, *Mayakovsky and His Circle* (London: Pluto Press, 1972), pp. 202, 220.

6 Paulina and Adelina Abramson, *Mosaico roto* (Madrid: Compañía Literaria, 1994), p. 36.

7 Arthur Koestler, *The Invisible Writing* 2nd edn (London: Hutchinson, 1969), pp. 368, 372.

8 Gustav Regler, *The Owl of Minerva* (London: Rupert Hart-Davis, 1959), pp. 236–9.

9 Yuri Rybalkin, *Stalin y España. La ayuda militar soviética a la República* (Madrid: Marcial Pons Historia, 2007) p. 50.

10 Mijail Koltsov, *Diario de la guerra de España* (Paris: Ruedo Ibérico, 1963), p. 14. All subsequent references to *Diario* are to this edition. See also Jonathan Haslam, *The Soviet Union and the Struggle for Collective Security in Europe 1933–39* (London: Macmillan Press, 1984), p. 108.

11 Koltsov, *Diario*, pp. 412–24; Mikhail Koltsov, *Ispanskaya vesna* (Leningrad: Izdatel'stvo pisatelei v Leningrade, 1933).

12 Koltsov, *Diario*, pp. 12, 15–18, 23, 29, 33–4.

13 Koltsov, *Diario*, pp. 39–42, 50–1, 55–8.

14 Koltsov, *Diario*, pp. 77–9.

15 Ursula El-Akramy, *Transit Moskau: Margarete Steffin und Maria Osten* (Hamburg: Europäische Verlagsanstalt, 1998), pp. 195–6.

16 Cockburn recounted the episode with the telephone extension to Peter Wyden, *The Passionate War. The Narrative History of the Spanish Civil War* (New York: Simon + Schuster, 1983), pp. 328, 537. The untitled article by Claud Cockburn, in Philip Toynbee (ed.), *The Distant Drum. Reflections on The Spanish Civil War* (London:

Notes

Sidgwick & Jackson, 1976), p. 53; Patricia Cockburn, *The Years of the Week* (London: MacDonald, 1968), p. 208. A meeting with Cockburn is described by Koltsov, *Diario*, pp. 264–5.

17 Koltsov to Stalin, 4 December 1937. I am immensely grateful to Ángel Viñas for providing me with a copy of this document.

18 Santiago Carrillo, interview with the author, 20 September 2006. On transmissions, see Koltsov, *Diario*, pp. 202, 205, 217. I am equally grateful to Dr Ángel Viñas for his help on this point.

19 Louis Fischer, *Russia's Road from Peace to War. Soviet Foreign Relations 1917–1941* (New York: Harper & Row, 1969), p. 273.

20 Ernest Hemingway, *For Whom the Bell Tolls* (London: Jonathan Cape, 1941), p. 397.

21 Ilya Ehrenburg, *Eve of War 1933–1941* (London: MacGibbon & Kee, 1963), p. 148; José Fernández Sánchez, 'El ultimo destino de Mijail Koltsov', *Historia 16*, no. 170, junio 1990, p. 21.

22 Alexander Orlov, *The March of Time. Reminiscences* (London: St Ermin's Press, 2004), p. 215.

23 Hugh Thomas, *The Spanish Civil War*, 3rd edn (London: Hamish Hamilton, 1977), p. 393; Olga Novikova, 'Las visiones de España en la Unión Soviética durante la guerra civil española', unpublished manuscript.

24 Koltsov, *Diario*, pp. 9, 66 (glasses); pp. 66, 68, 147, 366 (WWI and Russian Civil War).

25 Koltsov, *Diario*, pp. 9–12, 404 (threatening Guides), p. 59 (*Mundo Obrero*), pp. 71, 87, 197 (María Teresa's pistol). José Fernández Sánchez, 'Introducción', Mijail Koltsov, *Diario de la guerra de España* (Madrid: Akal Editor, 1978), pp. 5–6.

26 Boris Efimov, in *Mikhail' Kol'tsov, kakim on byl. Vospominaniya* (Moscow: Sovetskii Pisatel', 1965), p. 65; A. Rubashkin, *Mikhail' Kol'tsov. Kritiko-biograficheskii ocherk* (Moscow: Khudozhestvennaya literatura, 1971), p. 174; Gleb Skorokhodov, *Mikhail' Kol'tsov. Kritiko-biograficheskii ocherk* (Moscow: Sovetskii Pisatel', 1959), pp. 160–3. The most convincing identification of Koltsov with 'Miguel Martínez' can be found in Ian Gibson, *Paracuellos: cómo fue* (Barcelona: Argos Vergara, 1983), pp. 55–9. See also Broué, *Staline et la révolution*, p. 105; Günther Schmigalle, *André Malraux und der spanische Bürgerkrieg: Zur Genese, Funktion und Bedeutung von 'L'Espoir'* (Bonn: Bouvier Verlag Herbert Grundmann, 1980), p. 160; Carlos Serrano, *L'enjeu espagnol: PCF et guerre d'Espagne* (Paris: Messidor/Éditions Sociales, 1987), p. 52. I am immensely grateful to my friend Dr Frank Schauff for his inestimable help with the Russian references cited in this chapter.

27 General Vicente Rojo, *Así fue la defensa de Madrid* (México D.F.: Ediciones Era, 1967), p. 214; Koltsov, *Diario*, pp. 275–8; José Andrés Rojo, *Vicente Rojo. Retrato de un general republicano* (Barcelona: Tusquets Editores, 2006), pp. 87–8.

28 Boris Volodarsky, *KGB: The West Side Story* (unpublished manuscript); Ángel Viñas, *El escudo de la República, El oro de España, la apuesta soviética y los hechos de mayo de 1937* (Barcelona: Crítica, 2007) pp. 57–68. On Grigulevich, see Marjorie Ross, *El secreto encanto de la KGB. Las cinco vidas de Iósif Griguliévich* (Heredia, Costa Rica: Farben Grupo Editorial Norma, 2004) pp. 40–67; Christopher Andrew & Vasili Mitrokhin, *The Sword and the Shield: The Mitrokhin Archive and the Secret History of the KGB* (New York: Basic Books, 1999) pp. 99, 162. The claim that Koltsov had links with the GRU derives from Novikova, 'Las visiones'.

29 Koltsov, *Diario*, pp. 99–100 (Maqueda), p. 142 (Álvarez del Vayo), pp. 145–6 (radio intercepts), pp. 158–9 (5º Regimiento).

30 Koltsov, *Diario*, pp. 114, 167, 176–8, 185–6, 192.

31 Boris Volodarsky, *KGB: The West Side Story*, Chapter 16.

32 Andrew and Mitrokhin, *The Sword and the Shield*, p. 300; Germán Sánchez, 'El misterio Grigulévich', *Historia 16*, no. 233, septiembre de 1995, p. 118. On Koltsov and Paracuellos, see Viñas, *El escudo*, pp. 57–74.

33 Koltsov, *Diario*, pp. 196, 281–3.

34 Gleb Skorokhodov, *Mikhail' Kol'tsov. Kritiko-biograficheskii ocherk* (Moscow: Sovetskii Pisatel', 1959), pp. 154–5.

35 Santiago Álvarez, *Los Comisarios Políticos en el Ejército Popular de la República* (Sada-A Coruña: Ediciós do Castro, 1989), pp. 93–7, 115–27; Juan Andrés Blanco Rodríguez, *El Quinto Regimiento en la política militar del P. C.E. en la guerra civil* (Madrid: UNED, 1993), pp. 171–93.

36 *Milicia Popular*, 2, 3, 8, 11, 13, 14, 15, 20, 21 October 1936.

37 Koltsov, *Diario*, p. 151.

38 Stéphane Courtois and Jean-Louis Panné, 'The Shadow of the NKVD in Spain', in Stéphane Courtois et al., *The Black Book of Communism. Crimes, Terror, Repression* (Cambridge, MA: Harvard University Press, 1999), p. 337.

39 Arturo Barea, *The Forging of a Rebel* (London: Davis-Poynter, 1972), pp. 596–7.

40 Regler, *The Owl*, p. 276.

41 Skorokhodov, *Mikhail' Kol'tsov*, pp. 158–60.

42 Orlov, *The March*, p. 231.

43 Communication from Boris Volodarsky; Emma Wolf in *Mikhail' Kol'tsov, kakim on byl'*, pp. 305–7. On the collaboration between Gorev and Koltsov, see Frank Schauff, *Der verspielte Sieg. Sowjetunion, Kommunistische Internationale und Spanischer Bürgerkrieg 1936–1939* (Frankfurt: Campus, 2005), p. 238.

44 Abramson, *Mosaico roto*, pp. 63–5.

45 Sefton Delmer, *Trail Sinister. An Autobiography* (London: Secker & Warburg, 1961), p. 387.

46 Orlov, *The March*, p. 229. I am grateful to Dr Ángel Viñas, who pointed out that, by June 1937, only seventeen such decorations had been awarded in total and that it was highly unlikely that eleven of them were for a minor tank skirmish.

47 Schmigalle, *André Malraux*, p. 159; Hugh Thomas, *The Spanish Civil War*, 3rd edn (London: Hamish Hamilton, 1977), p. 495. See Koltsov, *Diario*, pp. 257–9, 303, 339.

48 Abramson, *Mosaico roto*, p. 62.

49 Haslam, *The Soviet Union*, p. 262.

50 Boris Efimov, in *Mikhail' Kol'tsov, kakim on byl'*, p. 65; Abramson, *Mosaico roto*, p. 62.

51 Roman Karmen, *¡No pasarán!* (Moscow: Editorial Progreso, 1976), pp. 249–53.

52 Abramson, *Mosaico roto*, pp. 61, 91–100; Koltsov, *Diario*, pp. 123–41; Karmen, *¡No pasarán!*, pp. 265, 277.

53 Karmen, *¡No pasarán!*, pp. 272–3.

54 Karmen, *¡No pasarán!*, pp. 276–8.

55 Karmen, *¡No pasarán!*, pp. 277–81, 301.

56 Karmen, *¡No pasarán!*, pp. 303, 307; Koltsov, *Diario*, pp. 93, 118.

57 Hemingway, *For Whom the Bell Tolls*, p. 221.

58 Abramson, *Mosaico roto*, pp. 175–82.

59 Edward P. Gazur, *Secret Assignment. The FBI's KGB General* (London: St Ermin's Press, 2001), pp. 139–40.

60 Martha Gellhorn, 'Memory', *London Review of Books*, 12 December 1996, p. 3.

61 Claud Cockburn, *A Discord of Trumpets* (New York: Simon + Schuster, 1956), p. 304.

62 Abramson, *Mosaico roto*, p. 62.

63 Broué, *Staline et la révolution*, p. 105.

64 Koltsov, *Diario*, p. 202.

65 El-Akramy, *Transit Moskau*, pp. 93–7, 125–9, 135, 173, 329–30; Vaksberg, *Hotel Lux*, p. 161. Koltsov's involvement in the writing of *Hubert im Wonderland* in David Pike, *German Writers in Soviet Exile, 1933–1945* (Chapel Hill, NC: University of North Carolina Press, 1982), p. 340.

66 Delmer, *Trail Sinister*, p. 387.

67 Gustav Regler, 'Civil War Diary', unpublished manuscript (Southworth Papers), entry for 14 March 1937, p. 44.

68 Ehrenburg, *Eve of War*, pp. 148–9.

69 Regler, *The Owl*, p. 294.

70 Regler, *The Owl*, pp. 294–6.

71 Stephen Koch, *The Breaking Point. Hemingway, Dos Passos and the Murder of José Robles* (New York: Counterpoint, 2005), p. 99.

72 Vaksberg, *Hotel Lux*, pp. 52, 64.

73 Ronald Radosh, Mary R. Habeck and Grigory Sevostianov (eds), *Spain Betrayed. The Soviet Union in the Spanish Civil War* (New Haven, CT: Yale University Press, 2001), pp. 267, 521 n. 60. See also Simon Sebag Montefiore, *Stalin. The Court of the Red Czar* (London: Weidenfeld & Nicolson, 2003), p. 208.

74 'A book that has not yet been written', Mikhail Koltsov, *The Man in Uniform* (Moscow: Cooperative Publishing Society of Foreign Workers in the USSR, 1933), pp. 43–5, 48, 53.

75 David Cotterill (ed.), *The Serge-Trotsky Papers* (London: Pluto Press, 1994), p. 139; Miquel Koltzov, *Proves de la traició trotskista* (Barcelona: Secretariat de Propaganda del C.E., 1937), Broué, *Staline et la revolution*, pp. 171–3.

76 Walter Held, 'Le Stalinisme et le POUM dans la Révolution espagnole', reprinted in Trotsky, *La Revolution espagnole*, p. 688.

77 Broué, *Staline et la revolution*, p. 183.

78 Koltsov, *Diario*, pp. 311–16, 414, 425–7.

79 Koltsov, *Diario*, pp. 366–7; V. P. Verevkin, *Mikhail' Efimovich Kol'tsov* (Moscow: Mysl', 1977), p. 77.

80 *Posetiteli kremlovskogo kabineta I. V. Stalina [1936–1937], Istoričeskij archiv*, 4/1995, p. 50.

81 Orlov, *The March*, p. 338.

82 Boris Efimov, in *Mikhail' Kol'tsov, kakim on byl'*, p. 66; Abramson, *Mosaico roto*, p. 62; Fernández Sánchez, 'El ultimo destino', p. 21.

83 Alexander Orlov, *The Secret History of Stalin's Crimes* (London: Jarrolds, 1954), p. 196.

84 El-Akramy, *Transit Moskau*, pp. 197–202; Orlov, *The March*, p. 250; Gazur, *Secret Assignment*, pp. 96–7. It is likely that Orlov is confusing the adoption by Koltsov and Osten with the fact the child adopted by the Yezhovs was a girl, which probably had nothing to do with Koltsov.

85 Dmitri Volkogonov, *Stalin. Triumph and Tragedy* (London: Weidenfeld & Nicolson, 1991), p. 330.

86 On Yezhov's degeneracy, see Sebag Montefiore, *Stalin*, pp. 150–3, 211.

87 *Posetiteli kremlovskogo kabineta I. V. Stalina [1936–1937]*, in *Istoričeskij archiv*, 4/1995, p. 52.

88 Koltsov, *Diario*, pp. 376–406.

89 Stephen Spender, *World within World* (London: Readers Union, 1953), pp. 205–10; Jef Last, *The Spanish Tragedy* (London: Routledge, 1939), pp. 196–8.

90 Koltsov, *Diario*, pp. 435–40; *El Sol*, 8 July 1937. For a long commentary on this, see Görling, '*Dinamita Cerebral*', pp. 337–46.

91 Hemingway, *For Whom the Bell Tolls*, pp. 234–5.

92 Ehrenburg, *Eve of War*, p. 180.

93 Schauff, *Der verspielte Sieg*, p. 104.

94 Cockburn, *A Discord*, pp. 304–5.

95 Lord Chilston (Moscow) to FO, 16 September 1937, FO 371/21300, W17349/1/41. The article is not reproduced in the diary.

96 Trotsky's attack from an article written in November 1937, Leon Trotsky, *La Revolution espagnole 1930–40*, Pierre Broué (ed.) (Paris: Les Éditions de Minuit, 1975) p .466. The recall and Koltsov's reaction, Koltsov, *Diario*, p. 485; Vaksberg, *Hotel Lux*, pp. 161–2.

97 *Posetiteli kremlovskogo kabineta I. V. Stalina [1936–1937]*, in *Istoričeskij archiv*, 4/1995, p. 69.

98 Görling, *Dinamita Cerebral*, p. 312.

99 Robert C. Tucker, *Stalin in Power. The Revolution from Above, 1928–1941* (New York: W. W. Norton, 1990), pp. 463–4; Roy Medvedev, *Let History Judge. The Origins and Consequences of Stalinism* (London: Macmillan, 1971), p. 354.

100 Emma Vol'f, *Mikhail' Kol'tsov, kakim on byl*, p. 310.

101 Pike, *German Writers*, p. 194.

102 Louis Fischer, *Men and Politics. An Autobiography* (London: Jonathan Cape, 1941), p. 467.

103 Fernández Sánchez, 'El ultimo destino', p. 22.

104 Boris Efimov, *Mikhail' Kol'tsov, kakim on byl*, p. 70.

105 Efimov, *Mikhail' Kol'tsov, kakim on byl*, pp. 71–2; Medvedev, *Let History Judge*, p. 402.

106 Gleb Skorokhodov, *Mikhail' Kol'tsov. Kritiko-biograficheskii ocherk* (Moscow: Sovetskii Pisatel', 1959), pp. 229–30.

107 Cockburn, *A Discord*, pp. 310–11.

108 Cockburn, *A Discord*, pp. 311–12.

109 Cockburn, *A Discord*, p. 314; Cockburn, *The Years*, pp. 258–9. On Russian policy towards Czechoslovakia, see Fischer, *Russia's Road*, pp. 311–15; *Men and Politics*, pp. 524, 537. On Russian aircraft deliveries, see Hugh Ragsdale, *The Soviets, the Munich Crisis, and the Coming of World War II* (Cambridge: Cambridge University Press,

2004), pp. 82–6, 120, 140–8. For Western accounts of the Soviet response to the Munich crisis, see Jiri Hochman, *The Soviet Union and the Failure of Collective Security, 1934–1938* (Ithaca, NY: Cornell University Press, 1984), pp. 144–75; Igor Lukes, 'Stalin and Czechoslovakia in 1938–39: An autopsy of a myth', *Diplomacy & Statecraft*, vol, 10, nos 2 & 3, July 1999.

110 Stephen F. Cohen, *Bukharin and the Bolshevik Revolution. A Political Biography 1888–1938* (London: Wildwood House, 1974), pp. 360, 368.

111 Fischer, *Russia's Road*, p. 306.

112 Martha Gellhorn, 'Memory', *London Review of Books*, 12 December 1996, p. 3.

113 Cockburn, *The Years*, pp. 257–61; Cockburn, *A Discord*, pp. 311–14.

114 Vaksberg, *Hotel Lux*, p. 162.

115 Boris Efimov, in *Mikhail' Kol'tsov, kakim on byl*, p. 73.

116 Efimov, in *Mikhail' Kol'tsov, kakim on byl*, pp. 73–6. Fernández Sánchez, 'El ultimo destino', p. 22, gives the date as 12 October but all other sources agree on 12 December: Rayfield, *Stalin and His Hangmen*, p. 352; Tucker, *Stalin in Power*, p. 524; Medvedev, *Let History Judge*, p. 231; Robert Conquest, *The Great Terror. Stalin's Purge of the Thirties*, 2nd edn (Harmondsworth: Pelican Books, 1971), p. 441; Abramson, *Mosaico roto*, pp. 63, 101; Skorokhodov, *Mikhail' Kol'tsov*, p. 2.

117 Fischer, *Russia's Road*, p. 300; Conquest, *The Great Terror*, p. 118.

118 Regler, *The Owl*, pp. 277–9.

119 Hemingway, *For Whom the Bell Tolls*, pp. 397–9; Herbst to Watson, 2 August 1967, Za Herbst Collection, Beinecke Library, Yale University.

120 Author's interview with Adelina Kondratieva in Madrid in 1998; Vaksberg, *Hotel Lux*, p. 152.

121 Volkogonov, *Stalin*, p. 317.

122 Broué, *Staline et la révolution*, pp. 142–3.

123 Fischer, *Russia's Road*, p. 273.

124 Tucker, *Stalin in Power*, p. 463.

125 Geoffrey Roberts, *The Unholy Alliance. Stalin's Pact with Hitler* (London: I.B. Tauris, 1989), pp. 109–19.

126 *Lubyanka. Stalin i glavnoe upravlenie Gosbesopasnosti NKVD 1937–1939* (Moscow: Mezhdunarodnyi fond 'Demokratiya', 2004), pp. 556–61; Vaksberg, *Hotel Lux*, pp. 154–8. Koltsov's life of Gorki was published in 1938 as *Burevestnik: zhizn'I smert'Maksima Gorkoga*.

127 Vaksberg, *Hotel Lux*, pp. 159–60.

128 Sebag Montefiore, *Stalin*, pp. 236, 287.

129 Donald Rayfield, *Stalin and His Hangmen. An Authoritative Portrait of a Tyrant and Those Who Served Him* (London: Viking, 2004), pp. 249–50.

130 Rayfield, *Stalin and His Hangmen*, pp. 351–2; Regler, *The Owl*, pp. 230–3; Victor Serge, *Memoirs of a Revolutionary 1901–1941* (London: Oxford University Press, 1963), pp. 317–18; Conquest, *The Great Terror*, pp. 666–7; Vaksberg, *Hotel Lux*, pp. 73–5.

131 Leonid Maximenkov and Christopher Barnes, 'Boris Pasternak in August 1936', *Toronto Slavic Quarterly*, no.17, 2003.

132 Moscow Chancery to Northern Department, 30 December 1938. FO 371/22287, N6398/26/38.

133 Evgenii Gnedin, *Sebya ne poteryat'* in *Novyi Mir*, no. 7/1988 (pp. 173–209), pp. 193–4.

134 Rayfield, *Stalin and His Hangmen*, pp. 353–4.

135 Fernández Sánchez, 'Introducción', p. 6.

136 Konstantin Simonov, *Glazami Cheloveka Moego Pokoleniya (Razmyshleniya o I. V. Staline), Znamya*, no. 3, March 1988, pp. 3–66; Robert Conquest, *Stalin. Breaker of Nations* (London: Weidenfeld & Nicolson, 1991), p. 323.

137 Document of 4 November 1954, *Reabilitatsiya. Kak eto bylo. Fevral' 1956 – nachalo 80-ch godov*, vol. I (Moscow: Mezhdunarodnyi fond 'Demokratiya', 2000), p. 173.

138 Simonov, *Glazami Cheloveka Moego Pokoleniya*, pp. 31–2.

139 Boris Efimov, in *Mikhail' Kol'tsov, kakim on byl*, pp. 75–6; Rayfield, *Stalin and His Hangmen*, pp. 352–3; Tucker, *Stalin in Power*, pp. 524, 575.

140 Abramson, *Mosaico roto*, p. 101.

141 Ehrenburg, *Eve of War*, p. 239.

142 Vaksberg, *Hotel Lux*, pp. 163–4; El-Akramy, *Transit Moskau*, pp. 267–9, 301–3; Pike, *German Writers*, pp. 340–1. Vaksberg gives the date of her execution as 8 August, El-Akramy as 16 September. On Ignacio Hidalgo de Cisneros' friendship with Maria Osten, there is a letter in the Moscow archives from Mikhail Suslov to Soledad Sancha of the Spanish Republican Embassy, dated 9 July 1939. I am grateful to Dr Soledad Fox for her kindness in drawing my attention to this document.

Chapter 7: A Man of Influence

1 Phillip Knightley, *The First Casualty. The War Correspondent as Hero, Propagandist, and Myth Maker from the Crimea to Vietnam* (London: André Deutsch, 1975), p. 194.

2 Stephen Koch, *Double Lives. Spies and Writers in the Secret Soviet War of Ideas against the West* (New York: The Free Press, 1994), pp. 27, 286, 306.

3 Justo Martínez Amutio, *Chantaje a un pueblo* (Madrid: G. del Toro, 1974), pp. 367–71. On the long-term origins and consequences of the May Days, see Helen Graham, '"Against the State": A Genealogy of the Barcelona May Days (1937)', in *European History Quarterly*, vol. 29, no. 4, 1999, and Helen Graham, *The Spanish Republic at War 1936–1939* (Cambridge: Cambridge University Press, 2002), pp. 254–315.

4 Stanley G. Payne, *The Spanish Civil War, The Soviet Union, and Communism* (New Haven, CT: Yale University Press, 2004), p. 349.

5 SIS Report on Fischer, 22 December 1939, Security and intelligence records releases, National Archives, Kew, Personal [PF Series] files. KV2/1910, 125A; Louis Fischer, *Men and Politics. An Autobiography* (London: Jonathan Cape, 1941), pp. 230–3.

6 Lestchenko to Fischer, 12 May 1931, 18 April 1932 (Box 7, Folder 14, Louis Fischer Papers), Seeley G. Mudd Manuscript Library, Princeton University (henceforth Fischer Papers). The story of Tatiana Lestchenko was recounted in *Washington Post*, 12 June 1949, and in George Fischer to Nancy Bressler, 12 March 1976 (also Box 7, Folder 14).

7 Fischer, *Men and Politics*, pp. 60–3.

8 Kirchwey to Fischer, 7 December 1920, Fischer Papers, Box 6, Folder 12.

9 Fischer, *Men and Politics*, pp. 70–1, 89–91, 99–100, 115, 306.

10 Fischer, *Men and Politics*, pp. 184–93.

11 Fischer to Kirchwey, 21 September 1934, Fischer Papers, Box 6, Folder 12.

12 Malcolm Muggeridge, *Chronicles of Wasted Time. An Autobiography* (Vancouver: Regent College Publishing, 2006), pp. 242–50.

13 Fischer to Kirchwey, 1 January 1934, Fischer Papers, Box 6, Folder 12; Sara Alpern, *Freda Kirchwey: A Woman of The Nation* (Cambridge, MA: Harvard University Press, 1987), p. 118.

14 S. J. Taylor, *Stalin's Apologist. Walter Duranty: The New York Times's Man in Moscow* (New York: Oxford University Press, 1990), pp. 227, 235–7; Fischer, *Men and Politics*, pp. 208–29.

15 Fischer, *Men and Politics*, pp. 119–21.

16 Fischer, *Men and Politics*, pp. 124–43, 146–8, 204–6.

17 Fischer, *Men and Politics*, pp. 149–51, 155–6, 200–1.

18 Liddell to IPI, 27 September 1934, Security and intelligence records releases, Personal [PF Series] files, KV2/984, 173A.

19 Fischer, *Men and Politics*, p. 155; Fischer to Kuh, 21 April 1934, Security and intelligence records releases, Personal [PF Series] files, KV2/984, 165A.

20 Fischer to Kirchwey, 1, 7 March, 4 April 1934, Fischer Papers, Box 6, Folder 12.

21 On Largo Caballero and Araquistáin, see Paul Preston, *The Coming of the Spanish Civil War: Reform Reaction and Revolution in the Second Spanish Republic 1931– 1936*, 2nd edn (London: Routledge, 1994), *passim*; 'Prólogo', *Leviatán: antología* (Madrid: Ediciones Turner, 1976); 'The Struggle against Fascism in Spain: The Contradictions of the PSOE Left', in *European Studies Review*, vol. 9, no. 1, 1979; Marta Bizcarrondo, *Araquistain y la crisis socialista en la II República. Leviatán (1934–1936)* (Madrid: Siglo XXI, 1975); *Leviatán y el socialismo de Luis Araquistain* (Glashütten im Taunus: Auvermann, 1974).

22 Fischer, *Men and Politics*, pp. 242–5.

23 Louis Fischer, 'Class War in Spain', *The Nation*, 18 April 1934; Fischer, *Men and Politics*, pp. 245–7; Spanish diary, manuscript, pp. 58–9, Fischer Papers, Box 25, Folder 2.

24 Fischer (Moscow) to Kirchwey, 30 September, 7 November; Kirchwey to Fischer, 22 October 1935, Box 10, Folder 169, Freda Kirchwey Papers, Schlesinger Library, Radcliffe Institute for Advanced Study, Harvard University (henceforth Kirchwey Papers); Fischer (Geneva) to Kirchwey, 24 October, from Paris, 26 November 1934, Fischer Papers, Box 6, Folder 12.

25 Fischer, *Men and Politics*, pp. 249–83, 294–5.

26 Fischer to Kirchwey, 31 August 1935, Fischer Papers, Box 6, Folder 12; Kirchwey to Fischer, 9, 24 December 1935, 23 January, 26 February, 7 May 1936; Fischer to Kirchwey, from Vienna, 16 December 1935, from Moscow, 29 January, from Madrid, 10 April 1936 (all Kirchwey Papers, Box 10, Folder 169).

27 Fischer to Kirchwey, 4 April 1936, Fischer Papers, Box 6, Folder 12; Kirchwey to Fischer, 7 May 1936 (Kirchwey Papers, Box 10, Folder 169).

28 Fischer (Madrid) to Kirchwey, 10 April 1936, Kirchwey Papers, Box 10, Folder 169; Jay Allen, 'Fragment of Memoirs', papers of Dean Michael Allen; Louis Fischer in

Richard Crossman (ed.), *The God That Failed. Six Studies in Communism* (London: Hamish Hamilton, 1950), p. 219; Fischer, *Men and Politics*, p. 309.

29 Fischer to Kirchwey, 4 April 1936, Fischer Papers, Box 6, Folder 12 (from Genoa), 17 April 1936; Kirchwey to Fischer, 7 May 1936, Kirchwey Papers, Box 10, Folder 169.

30 Fischer, *The God*, p. 219.

31 Fischer, Spanish Diary, p. 12.

32 Fischer, Spanish Diary, pp. 20–30.

33 Fischer, Spanish Diary, pp. 32, 36–7.

34 Lester Ziffren, diary entry for 21 September 1936, 'Diary of a Civil War Correspondent', Ziffren Papers; Fischer, Spanish Diary, pp. 42–5, 50; *Men and Politics*, p. 341.

35 Fischer, Spanish Diary, pp. 45–6; *Men and Politics*, pp. 342–3.

36 Fischer, Spanish Diary, pp. 53–8.

37 Fischer, Spanish Diary, pp. 69–74.

38 Gerda Grepp correspondence with Fischer, Fischer papers, Box 4, Folder 29; Fischer, *Men and Politics*, pp. 363, 365.

39 Markoosha to Fischer, 18 October 1938, Fischer Papers, Box 41, Folder 2.

40 Fischer, Spanish Diary, pp. 79–83; Jay Allen, 'U.S. Boy Bomber, Wet-eyed, Tells a Story of War', *Chicago Daily Tribune*, 30 September 1936.

41 *Chicago Daily Tribune*, 1, 11 October 1936; Hull to Wendelin, 12 October, Wendelin to Hull, 13 October, 6 November 1936, *Foreign Relations of the United States 1936*, vol. II (Washington, DC: Government Printing Office, 1954), pp. 735–7, 752–3; H. Edward Knoblaugh, *Correspondent in Spain* (London and New York: Sheed & Ward, 1937), pp. 114–15; Judith Keene, *Fighting for Franco. International Volunteers in Nationalist Spain during the Spanish Civil War, 1936–1939* (London: Leicester University Press, 2001), pp. 95–9.

42 Fischer, Spanish Diary, pp. 84–7; Louis Fischer, 'On Madrid's Front Line', *The Nation*, 24 October 1936. See Chapter 1.

43 Fischer, Spanish Diary, pp. 90, 94.

44 Fischer, *Men and Politics*, p. 309.

45 Fischer, *Men and Politics*, p. 352.

46 Fischer, Spanish Diary, pp. 95–101.

47 Fischer, Spanish Diary, pp. 102–4; Fischer, *Men and Politics*, pp. 352–7. On Asensio, see Antonio Cordón, *Trayectoria (Recuerdos de un artillero)* (Paris: Colección Ebro, 1971), pp. 261–2.

48 'Examination of Louis Fischer by Laurence G. Parr, Investigator', pp. 3, 11, in Fischer Papers, Series 2, Subject Correspondence, Box 16, Folder 1, 'International Journeys and Correspondence: Spain (1936–1939, 1949)'.

49 Louis Fischer, 'On Madrid's Front Line', *The Nation*, 24 October 1936.

50 Louis Fischer, 'Madrid's Foreign Defenders', *The Nation*, 4 September 1937.

51 'Examination of Louis Fischer', p. 3.

52 Martínez Amutio, *Chantaje*, pp. 368–9; 'Examination of Louis Fischer', pp. 3–4; Fischer, *Men and Politics*, pp. 366–80.

53 Babette Gross, *Willi Münzenberg. A Political Biography* (East Lansing, MI: Michigan State University Press, 1974), p. 306.

Notes

54 Katz's secretary to Isabel Brown, 1 March 1937, Security and intelligence records releases, Personal [PF Series] files. KV2/1910, 88A.

55 Louis Fischer, 'Madrid Keeps Its Nerve', *The Nation*, 7 November 1936.

56 Louis Fischer, 'Under Fire in Madrid', *The Nation*, 12 December 1936.

57 Fischer to Kirchwey, 16 December 1936, Fischer Papers, Box 6, Folder 12.

58 Louis Fischer, 'The Loyalists Push Ahead', *The Nation*, 1 January 1938.

59 Louis Fischer, 'Can Madrid Hold On?', *The Nation*, 16 January 1937.

60 Louis Fischer, 'Keeping America Out of War', *The Nation*, 27 March 1937.

61 Uritsky Report to Voroshilov on visit by Fischer, reprinted in Ronald Radosh, Mary R. Habeck and Grigory Sevostianov (eds), *Spain Betrayed. The Soviet Union in the Spanish Civil War* (New Haven, CT: Yale University Press, 2001), pp. 108–20; Fischer, *Men and Politics*, pp. 381–6, 391.

62 Louis Fischer, 'Can Madrid Hold On?', 'The Road to Peace', *The Nation*, 16 January 1937, 26 February 1938; *Men and Politics*, pp. 390–1.

63 Louis Fischer, *Why Spain Fights On* (London: Union of Democratic Control, 1938).

64 Campbell to Fischer, undated, Fischer Papers.

65 There is a voluminous correspondence with Eleanor Roosevelt in the Fischer Papers, Series 1 General Correspondence, Box 10, Folder 19; Fischer to Director of United Press, 16 April 1937; Fischer to Director of *Le Temps*, 23 August 1938; Fischer to Editor of *New Republic*, 2 September 1938; Bowers to Fischer, 18 February 1939, Fischer Papers, Series 2, Subject Correspondence, Box 16, Folder 1; Fischer, *Men and Politics*, pp. 392, 453–65.

66 Fischer, *Men and Politics*, p. 371.

67 Fischer, *Men and Politics*, p. 336.

68 Louis Fischer, 'Loyalist Spain Gathers Its Strength', *The Nation*, 3 July 1937.

69 Jan Kurzke and Kate Mangan, 'The Good Comrade', pp. 104–6 (unpublished ms, Jan Kurzke Papers, Archives of the International Institute for Social History, Amsterdam), p. 416.

70 Bowler to Wintringham, 22, 28 June 1937, Russian Centre for the Preservation and Study of Recent Historical Documents, Moscow, Fond. 545, Opus 6, 216 (copy held by International Brigades Memorial Trust, London) (henceforth RCPSRHD/IBMT).

71 Fischer to Kirchwey, 6, 20 July 1937, Fischer Papers, Box 6, Folder 12. He refrained from referring to their conversation until he published 'Internal Politics in Spain', *The Nation*, 30 October 1937, and mentioned both it and the interview with Azaña in Fischer, *Men and Politics*, pp. 393–403.

72 The two articles were published as 'Loyalist Spain Gathers Its Strength' and 'Loyalist Spain Takes the Offensive', *The Nation*, 3, 17 July 1937.

73 Louis Fischer, 'Franco Cannot Win', *The Nation*, 7 August 1937.

74 Freda's comments in Kirchwey to Fischer, 14, 28 July, 17 August; Fischer's reply, Fischer (Moscow) to Kirchwey, 5 August 1937, Kirchwey Papers, Box 10, Folder 171.

75 Fischer, *Men and Politics*, pp. 409–19.

76 Katz's secretary to Isabel Brown, 1 March 1937, Security and intelligence records releases, Personal [PF Series] files. KV2/1910, 88A.

77 Kirchwey to Fischer, 28 July; Fischer (Paris) to Kirchwey, 17 August 1937, Kirchwey Papers, Box 10, Folder 171.

78 Fischer, *Men and Politics*, pp. 425–8; Fischer (Geneva) to Kirchwey, 15 September 1937, Kirchwey Papers, Box 10, Folder 171.

79 Negrín to Bowers, 20 September 1937, Papers of Claude Bowers, Lilly Library, Indiana University (henceforth Bowers Papers); Fischer, *Men and Politics*, p. 430.

80 Louis Fischer, 'Internal Politics in Spain', *The Nation*, 30 October 1937.

81 Fischer notes on 'October 1937 Benicasim visit with Negrín'; Fischer to Negrín, 7 October 1937, Fischer Papers, Series 1 General Correspondence, Box 8, Folder 29.

82 Louis Fischer, 'Paris in the Crisis', *The New Statesman and Nation*, 26 March 1938.

83 Fischer to Katz, 24 November 1937, intercepted by the Secret Intelligence Service, DGW to Major Vivian, 27 November 1937, Security and intelligence records releases, Personal [PF Series] files. KV2/1910, 95A, KV2/1383, 228A; Fischer, *Men and Politics*, pp. 439–42.

84 Katz to Isabel Brown, 27 January 1938, Security and intelligence records releases, Personal [PF Series] files. KV2/1910, 99A; Fischer, *Men and Politics*, pp. 446–9.

85 Herbert L. Matthews, *The Education of a Correspondent* (New York: Harcourt Brace, 1946), pp. 123–8; Fischer, *Men and Politics*, pp. 449–51.

86 Louis Fischer, 'Barcelona Holds Out', *The Nation*, 2 April 1938.

87 Louis Fischer, 'A Cable from the Front', *The Nation*, 23 April; 'Catalonia Fights On', *The New Statesman and Nation*, 30 April 1938.

88 Louis Fischer, 'Spain Won't Surrender', *The Nation*, 30 April 1938.

89 Fischer, *The God*, pp. 221–2; Fischer, *Men and Politics*, pp. 466–73, 500, 551–4.

90 Louis Fischer, 'Spain's Tragic Anniversary', 30 July 1938; *Men and Politics*, pp. 502–9.

91 Fischer to Kirchwey, 16 August 1938, Fischer Papers, Box 6, Folder 12; Louis Fischer, 'The War in Spain', *The New Statesman and Nation*, 20 August; 'The Drive Along the Ebro', *The Nation*, 3 September 1938; *Men and Politics*, p. 511.

92 Louis Fischer, 'Peace on Earth, Good Will to Men', *The New Statesman and Nation*, 10 December; 'Peace on Earth', *The Nation*, 24 December 1938.

93 Fischer, *Men and Politics*, pp. 548–9.

94 'Examination of Louis Fischer', pp. 4–9; Bowers to Hull, 1 April, Bullitt to Hull, 26 May, 10 June, 27 June, Murphy to Hull, 8 August 1938, *Foreign Relations of the United States 1938*, vol. 1 (Washington, DC: United States Government Printing Office, 1955), pp. 279, 287, 294, 304–7, 317.

95 Selligman to Fischer, 15 February, 17 March 1937, Fischer Papers. There are several receipts for sums ranging from $15,000 to one million French francs in his papers, dated from 30 July 1938 to 25 April 1939, signed by David Amariglio and Peter C. Rhodes (representatives of the Friends of the Abraham Lincoln Brigade, see New York Times, 9 October 1938); Fischer to White, 25 October 1938; *Friends of the Abraham Lincoln Brigade pamphlet $125 will bring one wounded boy home!* (Fischer Papers, Series 2, Subject Correspondence, Box 16, Folder 1). Peter N. Carroll, *The Odyssey of the Abraham Lincoln Brigade: Americans in the Spanish Civil War* (Stanford, CA: Stanford University Press, 1994), p. 219.

96 Francisco Franco Bahamonde, *Palabras del Caudillo 19 abril 1937–7 diciembre 1942* (Madrid: Ediciones de la Vicesecretaría de Educación Popular, 1943), p. 476.

97 Louis Fischer, 'Thirty Months of War in Spain', *The Nation*, 7 January 1939.

98 Louis Fischer, 'Spain's Final Tragedy', 18 March 1939.

99 Eleanor Roosevelt to Jay Allen, 7 March, 10, 22 July, 17 August 1940 (Rayner Special Collections Library, Dartmouth College, Hanover, New Hampshire).

100 Katz to Brown, 28 August 1938, letter intercepted by SIS, Security and intelligence records releases, Personal [PF Series] files, KV2/1384, 264A.

101 Fischer to Allen, 24 November 1938; Fischer to Otto Simon (pseudonym of Katz), 19 January 1939, Fischer Papers, Series 2, Subject Correspondence, Box 16, Folder 1.

102 Fischer, *Men and Politics*, pp. 565, 568–9; Alpern, *Freda Kirchwey*, p. 134.

103 Foreign Office Minutes (Mr Kirkpatrick), 10 October 1939, FO 371/23074/ C16202/3356/18; Fischer, *Men and Politics*, pp. 582–90.

104 SIS Reports on Fischer, 25 September, 9 December, 22 December 1939, Security and intelligence records releases, Personal [PF Series] files. KV2/1910, 115A, 124A, 125A.

105 SIS Report on Fischer, 20 November 1939, Security and intelligence records releases, Personal [PF Series] files. KV2/1910, 123A.

106 Report on Fischer, 2 October 1939, Security and intelligence records releases, Personal [PF Series] files. KV2/1910, 118A.

107 *The Times*, 23 July 1941.

108 Extracts from telephone check, Kuh to Fischer, 18 September 1941. Security and intelligence records releases, Personal [PF Series] files. KV2/985, 333A.

109 Fischer to Azcárate, 9 August 1941, Security and intelligence records releases, Personal [PF Series] files. KV2/1910, 132C.

110 Memorandum 'Building up a Prime Minister', 5 August 1941, Security and intelligence records releases, Personal [PF Series] files. KV2/1910, 132X.

111 SIS Report on Fischer, 21 September 1941, Security and intelligence records releases, Personal [PF Series] files. KV2/1910, 138A.

112 SIS Report on Fischer, 30 September 1941, Security and intelligence records releases, Personal [PF Series] files. KV2/1910, 142A.

113 Alpern, *Freda Kirchwey*, p. 137.

114 Louis Fischer, 'Still the Enigma', *Saturday Review of Literature*, 6 December 1941; Taylor, *Stalin's Apologist*, p. 298.

115 Markoosha to Fischer, 23 September 1940, undated letter, Fischer Papers, Box 41, Folder 4.

116 Mollie Oliver to Fischer, 13 December 1942, undated Spring, 6, 12 May 1943, Box 9, Folder 2, Fischer Papers.

117 Diana Sheean to Fischer, 11 May 1951, Fischer Papers, Box 11, Folder 19.

118 Alpern, *Freda Kirchwey*, pp. 145–7; Louis Fischer, *A Week with Gandhi* (London: Allen & Unwin, 1943); *Gandhi and Stalin: Two Signs at the World's Crossroads* (New York: Harper, 1947); *The Life of Mahatma Gandhi* (New York: Harper, 1950).

119 Alpern, *Freda Kirchwey*, pp. 162–4.

120 Fischer to Luisi del Vayo, 5 June 1952, Fischer Papers, Box 12, Folder 43.

121 Edward P. Gazur, *Secret Assignment. The FBI's KGB General* (London: St Ermin's Press, 2001), pp. 315–16.

122 John Costello and Oleg Tsarev, *Deadly Illusions* (New York: Crown Publishers, 1993), pp. 340–53, 478–80.

123 Obituary in *The Times*, 23 January 1970.

124 *The Times*, 1 February 1985.

125 'Dede' (Deirdre Randall) to Fischer, undated (1957), Box 10, Folder 1, Fischer Papers.

126 Svetlana Alliluyeva to Fischer, 5 April, 14 June 1968, Box 1, Folder 7, Fischer Papers.

127 Alliluyeva to Fischer, 17 September 1968, Box 1, Folder 7; Randall to Fischer, 22 October (1968), Box 10, Folder 4, Fischer Papers.

128 Patricia Blake, 'The Saga of Stalin's "Little Sparrow". Svetlana's Tormented Journey from East to West and Back Again', *Time Magazine*, 28 January 1985. A slightly different version of the same article, 'Svetlana – Embraced by Stalin's Ghost', was published in *The Times*, 1 February 1985.

129 Deirdre Randall to Fischer, undated, Box 10, Folder 1, Fischer Papers.

130 Louis Fischer, *Russia's Road from Peace to War: Soviet Foreign Relations, 1917–1941* (New York: Harper, 1969), and *The Road to Yalta: Soviet Foreign Relations, 1941–1945* (New York: Harper, 1972).

Chapter 8: The Sentimental Adventurer

1 Gellhorn to Roosevelt, undated, 1938, Franklin D. Roosevelt Presidential Library.

2 Noel Baker to Steer, 6 March 1937, Noel-Baker Papers, Churchill Archives Centre, Churchill College, Cambridge (henceforth CAC), NBKR, 4/2. The letter is clearly misdated March when the content points clearly to it being written in May.

3 G. L. Steer, *The Tree of Gernika: A Field Study of Modern War* (London: Hodder & Stoughton, 1938), pp. 161–8.

4 Nicholas Rankin, *Telegram from Guernica. The Extraordinary Life of George Steer, War Correspondent* (London: Faber & Faber, 2003), p. 5.

5 For a critical examination of Steer's work, see Tom Buchanan, *The Impact of the Spanish Civil War on Britain. War, Loss and Memory* (Brighton: Sussex Academic Press, 2007), p. 25.

6 Sidney Barton, Preface, G. L. Steer, *Sealed and Delivered* (London: Hodder & Stoughton, 1942), p. 1.

7 *Who was Who 1941–1950* (London: Adam & Charles Black, 1951), p. 1097; George Steer, *Caesar in Abyssinia* (Boston, MA: Little, Brown & Co., 1937), p. 19.

8 Steer, *Caesar in Abyssinia*, pp. 20–2, 130, 153–4; Noel Monks, *Eye-Witness* (London: Frederick Muller, 1955), p. 35.

9 Phillip Knightley, *The First Casualty. The War Correspondent as Hero, Propagandist, and Myth Maker from the Crimea to Vietnam* (London: André Deutsch, 1975), pp. 174–5; Steer, *Caesar in Abyssinia*, pp. 37–41.

10 Steer, *Caesar in Abyssinia*, pp. 7–8.

11 *The Times*, 18 May 1936; Steer, *Caesar in Abyssinia*, pp. 286–93, 404.

12 Waugh's letters from September to November 1935 in Artemis Cooper (ed.), *Mr Wu & Mrs Stitch. The Letters of Evelyn Waugh and Diana Cooper* (London: Hodder & Stoughton, 1991), pp. 52–7. The meetings with Steer, *Caesar in Abyssinia*, pp. 73, 154, the fate of the house, pp. 370–87.

Notes

13 *Tablet*, 23 January 1937, reprinted in Donald Gallagher (ed.), *The Essays, Articles and Reviews of Evelyn Waugh* (London: Methuen, 1983), pp. 188–9.

14 Evelyn Waugh, *Scoop* (Boston, MA: Littlebrown, 1977) [1st edn, 1937], pp. 61–3, 115–16.

15 Steer, *Caesar in Abyssinia*, pp. 393–7; Rankin, *Telegram*, pp. 38–40, 70–1, 97.

16 *The Times*, 29, 31 August, 1, 2, 4, 5 September 1936.

17 Steer, *Gernika*, pp. 13, 139.

18 Monks, *Eye-Witness*, p. 94; Peter Kemp, *Mine were of Trouble* (London: Cassell, 1957), pp. 41, 52–3.

19 Peter Kemp, *The Thorns of Memory* (London: Sinclair Stevenson, 1990), p. 21.

20 Rankin, *Telegram*, pp. 84–5.

21 Clark, War Office, to Roberts, FO, 8 February 1937, TNA FO 371/21284, W 2902/1/41.

22 Herbert Rutledge Southworth, *Guernica! Guernica!: A Study of Journalism, Propaganda and History* (Berkeley, CA: University of California Press, 1977), p. 402.

23 Rankin, *Telegram*, pp. 85–6, 104.

24 Steer, *Gernika*, pp. 12–13, 134–8.

25 Steer, *Gernika*, pp. 113–19, 126.

26 Stevenson to Chilton, 31 January 1937, TNA FO 371/21284, FO 371/21284, W 2827/1/41.

27 *The Times*, 30 January 1937; James Cable, *The Royal Navy and the Siege of Bilbao* (Cambridge: Cambridge University Press, 1979), p. 75; Steer, *Gernika*, p. 132; Rankin, *Telegram*, pp. 96–7, 103; Clark, War Office, to Roberts, FO, 8 February 1937, TNA FO 371/21284, W 2902/1/41.

28 Steer, *Gernika*, p. 159; Bowers to Hull, 30 April 1937, *Foreign Relations of the United States 1937* (Washington: United States Government Printing Office, 1954), I, p. 291.

29 Steer, *Gernika*, pp. 160–70; Southworth, *Guernica!*, pp. 368–9; Jesús Salas Larrazabal, *La guerra de España desde el aire*, 2nd edn (Barcelona: Ariel, 1972), pp. 187–8.

30 Steer, *Gernika*, p. 14.

31 *The Times*, 14 April 1937.

32 Steer to Noel-Baker, 19 April 1937, Noel-Baker Papers, CAC, NBKR, 4x/118.

33 *The Times*, 15, 21, 24 April 1937; P. M. Heaton, *Welsh Blockade Runners in the Spanish Civil War* (Newport, Gwent: The Starling Press, 1985), pp. 35–50; Cable, *Siege of Bilbao*, pp. 55–76; Steer, *Gernika*, pp. 190–4; Rankin, *Telegram*, pp. 105–8.

34 Cable, *Siege of Bilbao*, pp. 67–8.

35 Steer, *Gernika*, pp. 208–9.

36 Steer, *Gernika*, pp. 228–33.

37 Steer, *Gernika*, pp. 234–45.

38 Christopher Holme, 'The Reporter at Guernica', *British Journalism Review*, vol. 6, no. 2, pp. 46–51.

39 Southworth, *Guernica!*, pp. 181–7.

40 Gijs van Hensbergen, *Guernica. The Biography of a Twentieth-Century Icon* (London: Bloomsbury, 2004), p. 45.

41 Herschel B. Chipp, *Picasso's Guernica. History, Transformations, Meanings* (Berkeley, CA: University of California Press, 1988), pp. 58–70.

42 Luis Bolín, *Spain: The Vital Years* (Philadelphia, PA: Lippincott, 1967), pp. 279–80; Robert Sencourt, *Spain's Ordeal. A Documented Survey of Recent Events* (London: Longmans, Green and Co., 1938), pp. 237–45.

43 *The Times*, 29 April 1937; Steer to Noel-Baker, 29 April 1937, CAC, NBKR, 4x/118; Rankin, *Telegram*, pp. 127, 137.

44 Joseph F. Thorning, *Why the Press Failed on Spain* (New York: International Catholic Truth Society, 1938), pp. 10–11; Southworth, *Guernica!*, p. 442; Rankin, *Telegram*, p. 137.

45 Franklin Reid Gannon, *The British Press and Nazi Germany 1936–1939* (Oxford: Clarendon Press, 1971), pp. 113–16.

46 Rankin, *Telegram*, p. 4.

47 Steer, *Gernika*, p. 250.

48 *ABC* (Sevilla), 4, 5 May 1937.

49 Steer to Noel-Baker, 8 May; Noel-Baker to unknown Minister, 13 May 1937, CAC, NBKR, 4x/118, 4/660.

50 *The Times*, 1, 3, 4, 7, 10, 12, 15, 17, 18, 19, 20, 21, 22, 26, 27 May, 1, 4, 7, 12, 14, 15, 16 June 1937; Steer, *Gernika*, pp. 265–316, 322–4, 328–31, 354; Steer to Noel-Baker, 31 May 1937, CAC, NBKR, 4x/118; Gilbert to Hull, 29 May 1937, *Foreign Relations of the United States 1937*, vol. I, pp. 305–6.

51 Leah Manning, *A Life for Education. An Autobiography* (London: Gollancz, 1970), p. 125.

52 *The Times*, 5 May 1937.

53 Noel-Baker to Steer, 29 April 1937, CCA, NBKR, 4/660.

54 Steer, *Gernika*, p. 359.

55 *The Times*, 21 June 1937.

56 Rankin, *Telegram*, p. 137.

57 Steer, *Gernika*, pp. 372–83; Steer to Noel-Baker, no day, August 1937, CCA, NBKR, 4/2. For a highly critical account of the Basques' military failure, see Xuan Cándano, *El pacto de Santoña (1937). La rendición del nacionalismo vasco al fascismo* (Madrid: La Esfera de los Libros, 2006), Chapter II.

58 Steer to Noel-Baker, 12 November 1937, CCA, NBKR, 9/64.

59 Noel-Baker to Steer, 7 February 1938, CCA, NBKR, 9/64.

60 Cable, *Siege of Bilbao*, pp. 5–6.

61 G. L. Steer, *El árbol de Guernica* (n.p. [Caracas]: Ediciones Gudari, 1963); George L. Steer, *El árbol de Gernika. Un ensayo sobre la guerra moderna* (Tafalla: Txalaparta, 2002).

62 Steer, *Gernika*, pp. 12–13.

63 George Orwell, *Time and Tide*, 5 February 1938, reprinted in *Orwell in Spain* (London: Penguin Books, 2001), pp. 263–4.

64 Steer to Noel-Baker, 12 October 1938, CCA, NBKR, 4/8.

65 Steer to Noel-Baker, 18 October, 26 November 1938, CCA, NBKR, 4/8.

66 G. L. Steer, *Judgment on German Africa* (London: Hodder & Stoughton, 1939); G. L. Steer, *A Date in the Desert* (London: Hodder & Stoughton, 1939).

67 *The Times*, 15 July 1939, 15 May, 10 June 1940, 22 October 1942; Rankin, *Telegram*, pp. 31, 39, 103.

68 Rankin, *Telegram*, pp. 166–70.

69 Noel-Baker to R. A. Butler, 4, 18 June 1940, CCA, NBKR, 4/663.
70 Sir Geoffrey Thompson, *Front Line Diplomat* (London: Hutchinson, 1959), pp. 154–5.
71 *Tablet*, 26 September 1942, reprinted in Gallagher, *Reviews of Evelyn Waugh*, pp. 271–2.
72 Luis Bolín, *Spain: The Vital Years* (Philadelphia, PA: Lippincott, 1967), pp. 279–80.
73 Steer SOE file, TNA HS9/1410/9, 22666/A.
74 *The Times*, 5 January 1945.
75 Steer, *Gernika*, p. 365.
76 Steer, *Gernika*, p. 13.

Chapter 9: Talking with Franco, Trouble with Hitler

1 Isabel de Palencia, *Smouldering Freedom. The Story of the Spanish Republicans in Exile* (London: Victor Gollancz, 1946), p. 153.
2 Allen to Juan Negrín, 14 December no year (1945), Archivo Juan Negrín, Las Palmas de Gran Canaria, Carpeta AJN 29, 33-33J.
3 Allen, 'Autobiographical summary'. Although written anonymously and in the third person, this document was almost certainly compiled by Jay Allen himself.
4 Constancia de la Mora, *In Place of Splendor. The Autobiography of a Spanish Woman* (New York: Harcourt, Brace, 1939), pp. 135–6.
5 Allen to Holman Hamilton, 28 February 1963, Jay Allen Papers; Allen to Southworth, 2 June 1967, Southworth Papers.
6 Allen to Southworth, 18 June 1964, Jay Allen Papers.
7 Michael Allen to Preston, 1 November 2006; Santiago Álvarez, *Negrín, personalidad histórica. Documentos* (Madrid: Ediciones de la Torre, 1994), p. 277.
8 Allen to Southworth, 7 August 1967, Southworth Papers.
9 Jay Allen, 'Fragment of Memoirs', papers of Dean Michael Allen; Alden Whitman, 'Jay Allen, News Correspondent in Trenchcoat Tradition, Dead', *New York Times*, 22 December 1972; Claude Bowers, *My Mission to Spain* (London: Victor Gollancz, 1954), p. 101; Bruno Vargas, *Rodolfo Llopis (1895–1983). Una biografía política* (Barcelona: Planeta, 1999), p. 88; George Seldes, 'Treason on *The Times*', *The New Republic*, 7 September 1938.
10 Allen to Hamilton, 7 October 1963, Jay Allen Papers.
11 Quintanilla to Allen, undated, 25 May, 13 June, 20, 23 July 1935, Luis Quintanilla Papers.
12 Whitaker to Allen, 30 March 1935, Jay Allen Papers.
13 Ruth Allen to Honoria Murphy, 7 January 1982, Jay Allen Papers. Among these papers there is a correspondence with Walter B. Boyce, an Englishman from whom he was renting a house.
14 Allen to Bowers, 14 February 1936, Papers of Claude Bowers, Lilly Library, Indiana University (henceforth Bowers Papers); Bowers, *My Mission*, p. 103; Fischer, *Men and Politics*, pp. 309–10.
15 Michael Allen to Preston, 29 December 2006; Jay Allen, 'Slaughter of 4,000 at Badajoz, City of Horrors', *Chicago Daily Tribune*, 30 August 1936.

16 Allen to Negrín, 14 December 1945, Archivo Negrín, Carpeta AJN 29, 33-33J.

17 On Araquistain and Leviatán, see Paul Preston, 'The Struggle Against Fascism in Spain: The Contradictions of the PSOE Left', in *European Studies Review*, vol. 9, no. 1, 1979, and 'Prólogo', *Leviatán: antología* (Madrid: Ediciones Turner, 1976). On Largo Caballero's prevention of a Prieto cabinet, see Paul Preston, *The Coming of the Spanish Civil War: Reform Reaction and Revolution in the Second Spanish Republic 1931–1936*, 2nd edn (London: Routledge, 1994), pp. 262–5.

18 Allen to Negrín, 14 December 1945, Archivo Negrín, Carpeta AJN 29, 33-33J.

19 Jay Allen, notes on reading John Spencer Churchill's book, *A Churchill Canvas* (Boston, MA: Little, Brown, 1961); Michael Allen to author, 1 April 2006. On the relationship with Brenan, see Jonathan Gathorne-Hardy, *The Interior Castle. A Life of Gerald Brenan* (London: Sinclair-Stevenson, 1992), pp. 301–5; Jay to Brenan, 13 August 1936, Brenan archive, Harry Ransome Research Centre, University of Texas at Austin.

20 *Chicago Daily Tribune*, 28, 29 July 1936. Very slightly different versions of these articles were printed in *The News Chronicle*, 29 July, 1 August 1936.

21 Allen to Negrín, 14 December 1945, Archivo Juan Negrín, AJN 29, 33-33J.

22 Allen undated memo to Carlos Baker, Jay Allen Papers.

23 'Portugal lets Nazi ship unload arms for Spain', *Chicago Daily Tribune*, 23 August 1936.

24 Allen to Fischer, 9 July 1962, Jay Allen Papers.

25 *Chicago Daily Tribune*, 30 August 1936.

26 Michael Allen to author, 1 April 2006.

27 Father Joseph Thorning, *Why the Press Failed on Spain!* (Brooklyn: International Catholic Truth Society, 1937), p. 5; Francis McCullagh, *In Franco's Spain* (London: Burns, Oates & Washbourne, 1937), pp. 48–56.

28 On Pires, see the report of the Spanish Ambassador to Portugal, Claudio Sánchez Albornoz, 18 August 1936, in José Luis Martín (ed.), *Claudio Sánchez Albornoz. Embajador de España en Portugal, mayo–octubre 1936* (Ávila: Fundación Sánchez Albornoz, 1995), pp. 157–60; Alberto Pena Rodríguez, *El gran aliado de Franco. Portugal y la guerra civil española: prensa, radio, cine y propaganda* (Sada-A Coruña: Ediciós do Castro, 1998), pp. 283–6; Francisco Espinosa Maestre, *La columna de la muerte. El avance del ejército franquista de Sevilla a Badajoz* (Barcelona: Editorial Crítica, 2003), p. 209.

29 Herbert Rutledge Southworth, *Guernica! Guernica!: A Study of Journalism, Propaganda and History* (Berkeley, CA: University of California Press, 1977), p. 133. Omitted from the quotation above is the following sentence: 'In another part of this article, Jay Allen referred to the Portuguese correspondent Mario Neves. This name was garbled in transmission, printed in the *Chicago Daily Tribune* as "Mario Pires", and has continued to be spelled that way at least five times subsequently in anthologies.' In fact, on this point, it was Southworth who was mistaken. See previous footnote.

30 Lester Ziffren, 'Diary', entry for 16 September 1936; Fischer, Spanish Diary, pp. 48–9; Gathorne-Hardy, *The Interior Castle*, p. 311.

31 John T. Whitaker, *We Cannot Escape History* (New York: Macmillan, 1943), p. 113.

32 Shannon to Scanlan, 18 December 1937, Bowers Papers.

Notes

33 Representative of the campaign were the pamphlets of Father Joseph B. Code, *The Spanish Civil War and Lying Propaganda* (New York: Paulist Press, 1938); Father Joseph Thorning, *Why the Press Failed on Spain!* (Brooklyn, NY: International Catholic Truth Society); Father Joseph Thorning, *Mercy and Justice!* (New York: Peninsular News Service, 1939); Father Joseph Thorning, *Fernando de los Ríos Refutes Himself* (New York: Paulist Press, 1939).

34 Allen to Hamilton, 16 January 1964, Jay Allen Papers.

35 Thorning to Weir, 5, 15 March 1938, Bowers Papers.

36 *The Fresno Bee*, 1 April, *Modesto Bee*, 4 April 1938.

37 Allen to Baker, 6 March 1963, 9 January 1969, Jay Allen Papers.

38 *Chicago Daily Tribune*, 9 October 1936 (also reproduced in *The News Chronicle*, 24 October 1936); Ian Gibson, *En busca de José Antonio* (Barcelona: Planeta, 1980), pp. 161–70; Herbert Rutledge Southworth, *Antifalange; estudio crítico de 'Falange en la guerra de España' de Maximiano García Venero* (Paris: Ediciones Ruedo Ibérico, 1967), pp. 144–8.

39 Claude G. Bowers to Acting Secretary of State, 20 November 1936, *Foreign Relations of the United States 1936*, vol. II (Washington, DC: US Government Printing Office, 1954), p. 568.

40 Allen to Hamilton, 28 February 1963, Jay Allen Papers.

41 Allen to Southworth, 2 June 1967, Southworth Papers.

42 Jay Allen, 'The Spanish Nightmare', Speech to Chicago Council on Foreign Relations. Text sent from British Library of Information, New York, 22 April 1937, FO 371/21291 W 8895/1/41.

43 'Confidential Information from E. H. Knoblaugh', distributed by Joseph Thorning, copy sent by Jay Allen to Claude Bowers, Bowers Papers.

44 Knightley, *The First Casualty*, pp. 200–1; Allen, 'Fragments of Memoirs'; Herbert Rutledge Southworth, *Guernica! Guernica!: A Study of Journalism, Propaganda and History* (Berkeley, CA: University of California Press, 1977), pp. 109–18, 441; Marta Rey García, *Stars for Spain. La guerra civil española en los Estados Unidos* (Sada-A Coruña: Ediciós do Castro, 1997), pp. 65, 118–19; H. Edward Knoblaugh, *Correspondent in Spain* (London and New York: Sheed & Ward, 1937), pp. 82–99.

45 Allen to Hemingway, 17 March 1943, Hemingway Collection, John F. Kennedy Presidential Library and Museum, Boston (henceforth Hemingway Papers); Allen to Carlos Baker, 9 January 1969, Jay Allen Papers.

46 Knoblaugh to Bennett, 16 November 1939, Milly Bennett Papers, Box 3, Folder 7, Hoover Institution Archives.

47 Gathorne-Hardy, *The Interior Castle*, p. 314.

48 Seldes to Hemingway, 24 February 1938, Hemingway Collection, John F. Kennedy Presidential Library and Museum, Boston; George Seldes, '"Ken", the Inside Story', *The Nation*, 30 April 1938; 'Insiders', *Time*, 21 March 1938; Michael Allen to author, 1 April 2006.

49 Allen to Bowers, 28 September 1937, Bowers Papers; Peter J. Sehlinger and Holman Hamilton, *Spokesman for Democracy. Claude G. Bowers 1878–1958* (Indianapolis, IN: Indiana Historical Society, 2000), p. 198; Allen to Baker, 6 March 1963, Jay Allen Papers.

50 Diary entry for 7 May 1938, Harold L. Ickes, *The Secret Diary of Harold L. Ickes, Volume II, The Inside Struggle* (New York: Simon + Schuster, 1954), pp. 388–90.

51 Allen to Southworth, 7 August 1967, Southworth Papers.

52 Michael Allen to author, 1 November 2006.

53 Allen to Southworth, 6 January 1964, Allen Papers.

54 Allen to Baker, 9 January 1969, Jay Allen Papers.

55 Allen to Bowers, 13 January 1938, Bowers Papers.

56 Allen to Messersmith, 8 January 1939, Allen to Fischer, 9 July 1962, Allen to Southworth, 6 January, Southworth to Allen, 20 January 1964, Jay Allen Papers.

57 The process is referred to in many subsequent letters between Jay and Herbert. I am indebted to Michael Allen for his recollections. I also draw on my own conversations with Herbert Southworth. There are substantial fragments of the chronology in the ALBA Collection of the Tamiment Library, at New York University. I am grateful to Gail Malmgreen and Dr Isabelle Rohr for help in locating this material.

58 Michael Allen to author, 1 April 2006.

59 Allen to Southworth, 28 May 1967, Southworth Papers.

60 Letter from J. D. LeCron to Jay Allen, 16 March 1939. Papers of Jay Allen; Soledad Fox, *Constancia de la Mora in War and Exile. International Voice for the Spanish Republic* (Brighton: Sussex Academic Press, 2007), pp. 84–7.

61 Letter signed 'Blank' from the National Labor Relations Board to Jay Allen, 25 March 1939. Papers of Jay Allen.

62 Diana Sheean to Fischer, 21 March, 10 April 1939, Fischer Papers, Box 11, Folder 19.

63 Michael Allen to author, 30 November 2006.

64 Buckley, *Life and Death*, pp. 171–2.

65 Fox, *Constancia de la Mora*, pp. 89–95, 98–9, 103–5. For Salinas' comments, see Pedro Salinas, *Cartas a Katherine Whitmore (1932–1947)* (Barcelona: Tusquets Editores, 2002), p. 358. Jay himself commented on the issue in a letter to Carlos Baker, 6 March 1963, Jay Allen Papers.

66 Diary entry for 13 May 1939, Ickes, *The Secret Diary*, p. 633.

67 Allen to Bowers, 3, 13 July 1939, Bowers Papers.

68 Memorandum by Chief of Division of European Affairs, 27 March 1939, *Foreign Relations of the United States 1939*, vol. II (Washington, DC: Government Printing Office, 1956), pp. 767–8; Palencia, *Smouldering Freedom*, pp. 152–3.

69 Fox, *Constancia de la Mora*, pp. 110–11, 120.

70 Constancia de la Mora to Jay Allen, 9 April 1940; Fondo Amaro del Rosal, Archivo Histórico de la Fundación Pablo Iglesias. I am indebted to Soledad Fox for drawing my attention to this document.

71 Allen to Bowers, 19 April 1940, Bowers Papers; Allen to Baker, 9 January 1963, Allen Papers.

72 Allen to Fischer, 9 July 1962, Papers of Jay Allen; Fox, *Constancia de la Mora*, pp. 124–31.

73 Allen to Baker, 6 March 1963, 9 January 1963, Allen Papers.

74 *The Volunteer for Liberty*, vol. II, no. 3, May 1940, pp. 1–2.

75 Allen to Baker, 6 March 1963, Allen Papers; Allen to Negrín, 12 July 1940, Archivo Negrín, AJN 55, 75A–75D.

76 Allen to Negrín, 12 July 1940, Archivo Negrín, AJN 55, 75C.

77 Allen to Bowers, 19 April 1940, Bowers Papers.

78 Allen to Frankfurter, 24 October 1940, Jay Allen Papers.

79 Jay Allen, undated memo to Carlos Baker, Jay Allen Papers; Michael Allen to author, 21 July 2006.

80 Andy Marino, *A Quiet American: The Secret War of Varian Fry* (New York: St Martin's Press, 1999), pp. 210–13; Varian Fry, *Surrender on Demand* (New York: Random House, 1945), pp. 154–5.

81 Buckley, *Life and Death*, p. 164; Fry, *Surrender*, p. 155. Jay's first meeting with Fry seems to have been on 2 January 1941.

82 Jay Allen, 'Weygand Denies Rifts with Pétain', *New York Times*, 12 December 1940; Hull to Murphy, 13 December 1940, *Foreign Relations of the United States 1940*, vol. II (Washington, DC: United States Government Printing Office, 1957), p. 420; Jay Allen, untitled manuscript on Weygand and Noguès, Allen Papers, pp. 3–16.

83 Allen to Fry, 2 January 1941, Varian Fry Papers, Columbia University.

84 Allen to Fry, 20 January 1941, Varian Fry Papers.

85 Fry to AERC HQ, New York, 21 January 1941, Varian Fry Papers; Fry, *Surrender*, p. 155; Marino, *A Quiet American*, p. 253.

86 Marino, *A Quiet American*, pp. 255–8.

87 Lt Colonel Richard Broad to Allen, undated (but probably 1947); Ruth Allen to Priscilla Allen, 11 May 1980, Jay Allen Papers.

88 The account of the interview by Jay Allen, 'Pétain Sees France Part of New Order'; 'Algeria's Loyalty Pledged to Pétain', *New York Times*, 18 January, 18 February 1941.

89 SOE War Diary, 6, 16, 17, 29, 30 March 1941, TNA: PRO, HS 7/214; Michael Allen to author, 27 September 2006.

90 Acting Secretary of State to Admiral Leahy, 17 March, Chargé in Germany to Secretary of State, 21 March 1941, *FRUS 1940*, vol. II, pp. 597–8, 601; Michael Allen to Preston, 21 July 2006; Marino, *A Quiet American*, p. 265.

91 Fry, *Surrender*, p. 208; Marino, *A Quiet American*, pp. 265–7.

92 Acting Secretary of State to Leahy, 20 March, Leahy to Secretary of State (Hull), 22, 24 March 1941, *FRUS 1940*, vol. II, pp. 601–3.

93 Halifax to FO, 30 May 1941, TNA: PRO, FO 371/29022, W6858; Leahy to Hull, 28 March 1941, *FRUS 1940*, vol. II, pp. 603–4; Jay Allen, 'The Prisoners of Chalon', *Harper's Magazine*, September 1940.

94 Leahy to Hull, 16 April, 19 May, 23 June; Hull to Chargé in Berlin (Morris), 25, 26 April, 6 May; Morris to Hull, 2, 10 May, 10 June Berle to Morris, 23 June 1941, *FRUS 1940*, vol. II, pp. 606–19; Jay Allen, 'The Prisoners of Chalon'; Jay Allen, 'Autobiographical summary'; Ruth Allen to her parents, 3 April 1941 Ruth Allen, 'Family Chronology', Jay Allen Papers.

95 Transcript, TNA: PRO, FO 371, 2874, Z 7458/45/17.

96 Luisi del Vayo to Fischer, 21 October 1942, Fischer Papers, Box 12, Folder 43.

97 Fleet Admiral William D. Leahy, *I was There* (London: Victor Gollancz, 1950), p. 124.

98 Michael Allen to author, 6 November 2006; Jay Allen, 'Autobiographical summary', Jay Allen Papers.
99 Captain Harry C. Butcher, *My Three Years with Eisenhower* (London: William Heinemann, 1946), p. 192.
100 Michael Allen to author, 6 November 2006; Jay Allen, 'Autobiographical summary', Jay Allen Papers.
101 Michael Allen to author, 6 November 2006; Jay Allen, 'Autobiographical summary', Jay Allen Papers.
102 Hemingway to Allen, 17 February 1943, Hemingway Papers.
103 Jay Allen, 'Autobiographical summary', Jay Allen Papers.
104 Michael Allen to author, 27 September 2006.
105 Michael Allen, 'An Answer', *Episcopal Church News*, 22 January 1956.
106 Allen to Negrín, 14 December 1945, Archivo Negrín, AJN 29, 33-33J.
107 Michael Allen, 'An Answer', *Episcopal Church News*, 22 January 1956.
108 Allen to Bowers, 30 November 1948, 19 January, 12 September 1957, Bowers Papers.
109 Allen to Morris, University of Missouri Press, 23 December 1965, Southworth Papers.
110 Allen to Southworth, 6 January 1964, Allen Papers.
111 Allen to Southworth, 7 November, 15 December 1967, Southworth Papers.
112 Allen To Southworth, 14 December 1964, Southworth Papers.
113 Allen to Southworth, 28 May 1967, Southworth Papers; 21 June 1968, 23 June 1971, Allen Papers; Southworth to Allen, 13 July 1968, Southworth Papers.
114 Ruth Allen to Southworth, 1 November 1971, 22 December 1972, 16 August 1973, 28 October 1979; Southworth to Ruth Allen, 29 August 1973, 14 November, 7 December 1979, 27 January, 7 July, 2 September 1980; Alain Hénon (University of California Press) to Ruth Allen, 24 September 1979, Southworth Papers.

Chapter 10: The Humane Observer

1 William Forrest, 'Mr Henry Buckley', *The Times*, 15 November 1972.
2 Hugh Thomas, *The Spanish Civil War* (London: Eyre & Spottiswoode, 1961), p. xxi.
3 Forrest, 'Mr Henry Buckley', *The Times*, 15 November 1972.
4 Henry Buckley, *Life and Death of the Spanish Republic* (London: Hamish Hamilton, 1940), pp. 15, 33.
5 Constancia de la Mora, *In Place of Splendor. The Autobiography of a Spanish Woman* (New York: Harcourt, Brace, 1939), p. 291.
6 Buckley, *Life and Death*, pp. 13–17.
7 Buckley, *Life and Death*, pp. 34–6, 46–7, 75, 80.
8 Buckley, *Life and Death*, pp. 30 (Queipo de Llano), 73 (Besteiro), 83–4 (Alcalá Zamora), 97–8 (Esplá), 109 (Gil Robles), 133 (Largo Caballero).
9 Cedric Salter, *Try-out in Spain* (New York: Harper Brothers, 1943), p. 113.
10 Buckley, *Life and Death*, pp. 312–14 (Ibárruri), 336–7 (Prieto).
11 Buckley, *Life and Death*, pp. 364 (Campesino), 370 (Líster), 397–8 (Negrín).

12 Buckley, *Life and Death*, pp. 321–4, 330–3, 382–4.
13 Buckley, *Life and Death*, pp. 420–3.
14 Kitty Bowler, 'Memoirs', Chapter 7, p. 8; LHCMA, Wintringham papers, 1, Folder 3.
15 Herbst to Watson, 2 August 1967, Za Herbst Collection, Beinecke Library, Yale University.
16 Geoffrey Cox, *Eyewitness. A Memoir of Europe in the 1930s* (Dunedin: University of Otago Press, 1999), p. 214.
17 De la Mora, *In Place of Splendor*, p. 291.
18 Peter Besas, 'Henry Buckley, Reporter and 40-year Veteran of Madrid', *Guidepost*, 1970, pp. 17–18; Herbert L. Matthews, *The Education of a Correspondent* (New York: Harcourt Brace, 1946), p. 138; Sheean, *Not Peace*, pp. 336–7.
19 Allen to Baker, 2 February 1964, Jay Allen Papers.
20 Cedric Salter, *Try-out in Spain* (New York: Harper Brothers, 1943), p. 211.
21 Buckley, *Life and Death*, pp. 376–7.
22 De la Mora, *In Place of Splendor*, p. 408.
23 Buckley, *Life and Death*, p. 419.

Chapter 11: A Lifetime's Struggle

1 Southworth to Allen, 21 December 1965, Jay Allen Papers.
2 Albert Forment, *José Martínez: La epopeya de Ruedo Ibérico* (Barcelona: Editorial Anagrama, 2000), pp. 238, 241.
3 Quoted in Southworth to Allen, 21 December 1965, Jay Allen Papers.
4 Ricardo de la Cierva y de Hoces, *Cien libros básicos sobre la guerra de España* (Madrid: Publicaciones Españolas, 1966), p. 40.
5 Herbert R. Southworth, 'A modo de prólogo', *El mito de la cruzada de Franco* (Barcelona: Plaza y Janés, 1986), pp. 10–12.
6 Southworth, 'A modo de prólogo', pp. 13–14; conversations with Paul Preston over many years.
7 Herbert R. Southworth, 'Franco Draws Italians, Nazis and Portuguese', *Washington Post*, 14 November 1937.
8 Herbert R. Southworth, 'Apology for Revolt', *Washington Post*, 7 July 1937; F. Theo Rogers, *Spain: A Tragic Journey* (New York: The Macaulay Company, 1937), p. ix.
9 Herbert R. Southworth, 'Franco's Friend', *Washington Post*, 24 November 1937; Harold G. Cardozo, *The March of a Nation: My Year of Spain's Civil War* (London: The Right Book Club, 1937), pp. 11, 59, 74, 157.
10 *Franco's Mein Kampf. A Fascist State in Rebel Spain* (New York: no publisher given, 1939), José Pemartín, *Qué es 'lo nuevo'…Consideraciones sobre el momento español presente*, 2nd edn (Madrid: Espasa-Calpe, 1940).
11 Jay Allen to Holman Hamilton, 16 January 1964, Jay Allen Papers.
12 H. Rutledge Southworth, 'The Catholic Press', *The Nation*, 16 December 1939.
13 Southworth to Allen, 25 May 1946, 28–29 December 1948, Jay Allen Papers.
14 Southworth, 'A modo de prólogo', p. 19.
15 Southworth to Allen, 25 May 1946, Jay Allen Papers.

16 Southworth to Allen, 28–29 December 1948, Jay Allen Papers.

17 Southworth to Allen, 28–29 December 1948, Jay Allen Papers.

18 Southworth to Allen, 29 January 1964, Jay Allen Papers.

19 Southworth to Allen, 20 January 1964, Jay Allen Papers.

20 Southworth to Allen, 7 May 1971, Jay Allen Papers.

21 Herbert Rutledge Southworth, *El mito de la cruzada de Franco* (Paris: Ediciones Ruedo Ibérico, 1963); Herbert Rutledge Southworth, *Le mythe de la croisade de Franco* (Paris: Ediciones Ruedo Ibérico, 1964). This expanded edition was published in Spanish as *El mito de la cruzada de Franco* (Barcelona: Plaza y Janés, 1986).

22 Forment, *Ruedo Ibérico*, pp. 241–2.

23 Herbert Rutledge Southworth, *Antifalange; estudio crítico de 'Falange en la guerra de España' de Maximiano García Venero* (Paris: Ediciones Ruedo Ibérico, 1967).

24 Forment, *Ruedo Ibérico*, pp. 257–8, 263–4, 272–3, 305–6, 311–12.

25 Southworth to Allen, 21 December 1965, 12 December 1968, Jay Allen Papers.

26 Herbert R. Southworth, 'Los bibliófobos: Ricardo de la Cierva y sus colaboradores', *Cuadernos de Ruedo Ibérico*, pp. 28–9 (diciembre 1970 y marzo 1971).

27 Southworth to Allen, 7 May 1971, Jay Allen Papers.

28 Herbert Rutledge Southworth, '"The Grand Camouflage": Julián Gorkín, Burnett Bolloten and the Spanish Civil War', in Paul Preston and Ann Mackenzie (eds), *The Republic Besieged: Civil War in Spain 1936–1939* (Edinburgh: Edinburgh University Press, 1996), pp. 260–310; author's interviews with Burnett Bolloten.

29 Herbert R. Southworth, *Conspiracy and the Spanish Civil War: The Brainwashing of Francisco Franco* (London: Routledge-Cañada Blanch Studies, 2002), translated into Spanish as *El lavado de cerebro de Francisco Franco. Conspiración y guerra civil* (Barcelona: Editorial Crítica, 2000).

Epilogue: Buried Treasure

1 Peter J. Sehlinger and Holman Hamilton, *Spokesman for Democracy. Claude G. Bowers 1878–1958* (Indianapolis, IN: Indiana Historical Society, 2000), p. 200.

2 Sumner Welles, *The Times for Decision* (New York: Harper & Brothers, 1944), p. 59; Dante A. Puzzo, *Spain and the Great Powers, 1936–1941* (New York: Columbia University Press, 1962), pp. 149–60.

3 Dolores Ibárruri, *El único camino* (Madrid: Editorial Castalia, 1992), pp. 423–5; Herbert L. Matthews, *A World in Revolution: A Newspaperman's Memoir* (New York: Charles Scribner, 1972), p. 75.

4 Dominic Tierney, *FDR and the Spanish Civil War. Neutrality and Commitment in the Struggle that Divided America* (Durham, NC and London: Duke University Press, 2007), pp. 1, 139–40; Richard P. Traina, *American Diplomacy and the Spanish Civil War* (Bloomington, IN: Indiana University Press, 1968), pp. 230–2.

5 Welles, *The Times for Decision*, pp. 57, 61.

6 Herbert L. Matthews, *Half of Spain Died. A Reappraisal of the Spanish Civil War* (New York: Charles Scribner's Sons, 1973), p. 176.

7 Tierney, *FDR & SCW*, p. 89.

Notes

8 F. Jay Taylor, *The United States and the Spanish Civil War 1936–1939* (New York: Bookman Associates, 1956), p. 7; Matthews, *Half of Spain Died*, p. 173.

9 George Orwell, *Homage to Catalonia* (London: Secker & Warburg, 1971), pp. 246–7.

10 Alfred Kazin, 'The Wound That Will Not Heal', *The New Republic*, 25 August 1986.

11 Herbst to Mary and Neal Daniels, 17 February 1966, Za Herbst Collection, Beinecke Library, Yale University. It is reprinted in its entirety in Elinor Langor, *Josephine Herbst* (Boston, MA: Little, Brown, 1984), pp. ix–x.

Bibliography

Archival Sources

ALBA Collection of the Tamiment Library, at New York University

Allen, Jay, Papers (courtesy of Very Rev. Michael Allen)

— correspondence with Juan Negrín, Archivo Juan Negrín, Las Palmas de Gran Canaria

Bennett, Millie, Papers, Hoover Institution Archives, Stanford

Bolloten, Burnett, Papers, Hoover Institution Archives, Stanford

Bowers, Claude, Papers, Lilly Library, Indiana University

British Battalion, International Brigade files, Russian Centre for the Preservation and Study of Recent Historical Documents, Moscow, Fond. 545, Opus 6, 201 (copy held by International Brigades Memorial Trust, London)

Fischer, Louis, Papers, Seeley G. Mudd Manuscript Library, Princeton University

Fondo Amaro del Rosal, Archivo Histórico de la Fundación Pablo Iglesias

Fry, Varian, Papers, Rare Book and Manuscript Library, Columbia University

Gellhorn, Martha, correspondence with Eleanor Roosevelt, Franklin D. Roosevelt Presidential Library, Hyde Park

Hemingway, Ernest, Papers, Hemingway Collection, John F. Kennedy Presidential Library and Museum, Boston

Herbst, Josephine, Papers, Za Herbst Collection, Beinecke Library, Yale University

Kirchwey, Freda, Papers, Schlesinger Library, Radcliffe Institute for Advanced Study, Harvard University

Mangan, Kate, Papers (courtesy of Charlotte Kurzke)

Ministerio de la Guerra, Archivo Militar General, Segovia, Sección Personal

National Archives, Public Record Office: Foreign Office Correspondence FO371; Security and intelligence records releases, Personal files; SOE War Diary

Negrín, Juan, Papers, Archivo Juan Negrín, Las Palmas de Gran Canaria

Noel-Baker, Philip, Papers, Churchill Archives Centre, Churchill College, Cambridge

Quintanilla, Luis, Papers (courtesy of Paul Quintanilla)

Robles Pazos, José, Papers, Sheridan Libraries, Johns Hopkins University

Wintringham, Tom, Papers, Liddell Hart Centre For Military Archives, King's College, London

Ziffren, Lester, Papers (courtesy of David Wurtzel)

Unpublished Manuscripts

Bowler, Kitty, 'Spanish Civil War Memoirs', Wintringham Collection, Liddell Hart Centre
 for Military Archives, King's College, London
Fischer, Louis, 'Spanish diary', Louis Fischer Papers, Seeley G. Mudd Manuscript Library,
 Princeton University
Herbst, Josephine, Spanish diary, 'Journal Spain', Za Herbst Collection, Beinecke Library,
 Yale University
Kurzke, Jan and Kate Mangan, 'The Good Comrade' (Jan Kurzke Papers, Archives of the
 International Institute for Social History, Amsterdam)
Regler, Gustav, 'Civil War Diary', Southworth Papers
Volodarsky, Boris, *KGB: The West Side Story* (forthcoming)

Interviews

1) Author's Interviews: Sir Geoffrey Cox, Charlotte Kurzke, Sam Lessor, Ben Wintringham
2) Imperial War Museum, Sound Archive, Spanish Civil War Collection, 8398/13: Geoffrey
 Cox, Tony McLean, Patience Edney

Published Documents

Congressional Record
Dez anos de política externa (1936–1947). A nação portuguesa e a segunda guerra mundial,
 IV (Lisbon: Imprensa Nacional, 1965)
Foreign Relations of the United States 1936, vol. II (Washington, DC: Government Printing
 Office, 1954)
Foreign Relations of the United States 1937, vol. I (Washington, DC: United States
 Government Printing Office, 1954)
Foreign Relations of the United States 1938, vol. 1 (Washington, DC: United States
 Government Printing Office, 1955)
Foreign Relations of the United States 1939, vol. II (Washington, DC: United States
 Government Printing Office, 1956)
Foreign Relations of the United States 1940, vol. II (Washington, DC: United States
 Government Printing Office, 1957)
Foreign Relations of the United States 1941, vol. II (Washington, DC: United States
 Government Printing Office, 1959)
Investigation of Un-American Propaganda Activities, Special Committee on Un-American
 Propaganda Activities, House of Representatives, 76th Congress, 1939
Ministerio de la Guerra, Estado Mayor Central, *Anuario Militar de España 1936* (Madrid:
 Imprenta y Talleres del Ministerio de la Guerra, 1936)
The Serge–Trotsky Papers, ed. by David Cotterill (London: Pluto Press, 1994)

Newspapers and Magazines

ABC (Sevilla)
Chicago Daily Tribune
Daily Express
Daily Mail
Diario de la Manhã
Diario de Lisboa
Esquire
Manchester Guardian
Il Messagero
The Nation
The New International
The New Republic
The New Statesman and Nation
News Chronicle

New York Times
Paris-Soir
Sheboygan Press
O Seculo
Socialist Call
Socialist Review
Syracuse Herald
Time Magazine
The Times
La Unión (Sevilla)
The Volunteer
The Volunteer for Liberty
Washington Post

Books and Articles

Abella, Rafael, *La vida cotidiana durante la guerra civil 1) La España nacional* (Barcelona: Editorial Planeta, 1978)

Abramson, Paulina and Adelina, *Mosaico roto* (Madrid: Compañía Literaria, 1994)

Alexander, Bill, *British Volunteers for Liberty: Spain 1936–1939* (London: Lawrence & Wishart, 1982)

Alpern, Sara, *Freda Kirchwey: A Woman of The Nation* (Cambridge, MA: Harvard University Press, 1987)

Alpert, Michael, *La reforma militar de Azaña (1931–1933)* (Madrid: Siglo XXI, 1982)

Álvarez, Santiago, *Los Comisarios Políticos en el Ejército Popular de la República* (Sada-A Coruña: Ediciós do Castro, 1989)

— *Negrín, personalidad histórica. Documentos* (Madrid: Ediciones de la Torre, 1994)

Álvarez Chillida, Gonzalo, *El antisemitismo en España. La imagen del judío (1812–2002)* (Madrid: Marcial Pons, 2002)

Alvarez del Vayo, Julio, *The Last Optimist* (London: Putnam, 1950)

Andrew, Christopher and Vasili Mitrokhin, *The Sword and the Shield: The Mitrokhin Archive and the Secret History of the KGB* (New York: Basic Books, 1999)

Armero, José Mario, *España fue noticia. Corresponsales extranjeros en la guerra civil española* (Madrid: Sedmay Ediciones, 1976)

Ayala, Francisco, *Recuerdos y olvidos (1906–2006)* (Madrid: Alianza Editorial, 2006)

Baker, Carlos, *Ernest Hemingway. A Life Story* (London: Collins, 1969)

Barea, Arturo, *The Forging of a Rebel* (London: Davis-Poynter, 1972)

Bartlett, Vernon, *This is My Life* (London: Chatto & Windus, 1938)

Baxell, Richard, *British Volunteers in the Spanish Civil War. The British Battalion in the International Brigades, 1936–1939* (London: Routledge/Cañada Blanch, 2004)

Berga, Miquel, *John Langdon-Davies (1897–1971). Una biografia anglo-catalana* (Barcelona: Editorial Pòrtic, 1991)

Bibliography

Bernanos, Georges, *Els grans cementeris sota la lluna* (Barcelona: Curiel Edicions Catalanes, 1981)

Bizcarrondo, Marta, *Araquistain y la crisis socialista en la II República. Leviatán (1934–1936)* (Madrid: Siglo XXI, 1975)

Blanco Rodríguez, Juan Andrés, *El Quinto Regimiento en la política militar del P.C.E. en la guerra civil* (Madrid: UNED, 1993)

Bolín, Luis, *Spain: The Vital Years* (Philadelphia, PA: Lippincott, 1967)

Bolloten, Burnett, *The Spanish Civil War: Revolution and Counterrevolution* (Hemel Hempstead: Harvester Wheatsheaf, 1991)

Bowers, Claude, *My Mission to Spain* (London: Victor Gollancz, 1954)

Brereton, Geoffrey, *Inside Spain* (London: Quality Press, 1938)

Broué, Pierre, *Staline et la révolution. Le cas espagnol (1936–1939)* (Paris: Librairie Arthème Fayard, 1993)

Buchanan, Tom, *Britain and the Spanish Civil War* (Cambridge: Cambridge University Press, 1997)

— *The Impact of the Spanish Civil War on Britain. War, Loss and Memory* (Brighton: Sussex Academic Press, 2007)

Buckley, Henry, *Life and Death of the Spanish Republic* (London: Hamish Hamilton, 1940)

Burns, Emile, *The Nazi Conspiracy in Spain* (London: Victor Gollancz, 1937)

Cable, James, *The Royal Navy and the Siege of Bilbao* (Cambridge: Cambridge University Press, 1979)

Cándano, Xuan, *El pacto de Santoña (1937). La rendición del nacionalismo vasco al fascismo* (Madrid: La Esfera de los Libros, 2006)

Cardozo, Harold G., *The March of a Nation* (London: The Right Book Club, 1937)

Carney, William P., *No democratic government in Spain* (New York: The America Press, 1937)

Carroll, Peter N., *The Odyssey of the Abraham Lincoln Brigade: Americans in the Spanish Civil War* (Stanford, CA: Stanford University Press, 1994)

Cesarani, David, *Arthur Koestler. The Homeless Mind* (New York: The Free Press, 1998)

Chipp, Herschel B., *Picasso's Guernica. History, Transformations, Meanings* (Berkeley, CA: University of California Press, 1988)

Churchill, Viscount Peter, *All My Sins Remembered* (London: William Heinemann, 1964)

Churchill, Winston S., *Step by Step* (London: Odhams Press, 1947)

Cockburn, Claud, *A Discord of Trumpets* (New York: Simon & Schuster, 1956)

Cockburn, Patricia, *The Years of the Week* (London: MacDonald, 1968)

Code, Father Joseph B., *The Spanish Civil War and Lying Propaganda* (New York: Paulist Press, 1938)

Cohen, Stephen F., *Bukharin and the Bolshevik Revolution. A Political Biography 1888–1938* (London: Wildwood House, 1974)

Connolly, Cyril, *The Golden Horizon* (London: Weidenfeld & Nicolson, 1953)

Conquest, Robert. *Stalin. Breaker of Nations* (London: Weidenfeld & Nicolson, 1991)

— *The Great Terror. Stalin's Purge of the Thirties*, 2nd edn (Harmondsworth: Pelican Books, 1971)

Cordón, Antonio, *Trayectoria (Recuerdos de un artillero)* (Paris: Colección Ebro, 1971)

Costello, John and Oleg Tsarev, *Deadly Illusions* (New York: Crown Publishers, 1993)

Courtois, Stéphane et al., *The Black Book of Communism. Crimes, Terror, Repression* (Cambridge, MA: Harvard University Press, 1999)

Cowles, Virginia, *Looking for Trouble* (London: Hamish Hamilton, 1941)

Cox, Geoffrey, *Defence of Madrid* (London: Victor Gollancz, 1937)

— *Eyewitness. A Memoir of Europe in the 1930s* (Dunedin: University of Otago Press, 1999)

Crossman, Richard (ed.), *The God that Failed. Six Studies in Communism* (London: Hamish Hamilton, 1950)

Cruz Seoane, María and María Dolores Sáiz, *Historia del periodismo en España 3. El siglo XX: 1898–1936* (Madrid: Alianza Editorial, 1998)

Davis, Frances, *A Fearful Innocence* (Kent, OH: Kent State University Press, 1981)

— *My Shadow in the Sun* (New York: Carrick & Evans, 1940)

Delaprée, Louis, *Le martyre de Madrid. Témoinages inédits de Louis Delaprée* (Madrid: No publisher, 1937)

Delmer, Sefton, *Trail Sinister. An Autobiography* (London: Secker & Warburg, 1961)

Deutscher, Isaac, *The Prophet Unarmed. Trotsky: 1921–1929* (London: Oxford University Press, 1959)

Dick, Alan, *Inside Story* (London: George Allen & Unwin, 1943)

Dos Passos, John, *Century's Ebb: The Thirteenth Chronicle* (Boston, MA: Gambit, 1975)

— *Journeys Between Wars* (New York: Harcourt, Brace, 1938)

— *The Fourteenth Chronicle. Letters and Diaries* (ed. Townsend Ludington) (Boston, MA: Gambit Incorporated, 1973)

— *The Theme is Freedom* (New York: Dodd & Mead, 1956)

Doyle, Bob, *Memorias de un rebelde sin pausa* (Madrid: Asociación de Amigos de las Brigadas Internacionales, 2002)

Eby, Cecil, *Between the Bullet and the Lie* (New York: Holt, Rinehart, Winston, 1969)

Ehrenburg, Ilya, *Eve of War 1933–1941* (London: MacGibbon & Kee, 1963)

El-Akramy, Ursula, *Transit Moskau: Margarete Steffin und Maria Osten* (Hamburg: Europäische Verlagsanstalt, 1998)

Espinosa Maestre, Francisco, *La columna de la muerte. El avance del ejército franquista de Sevilla a Badajoz* (Barcelona: Editorial Crítica, 2003)

Fernández Sánchez, José, 'El ultimo destino de Mijail Koltsov', *Historia 16*, no. 170, junio 1990

Fernsworth, Lawrence, *Spain's Struggle for Freedom* (Boston, MA: Beacon Press, 1957)

Fischer, Louis, *Gandhi and Stalin: Two Signs at the World's Crossroads* (New York: Harper, 1947)

— *The Life of Mahatma Gandhi* (New York: Harper, 1950)

— *Men and Politics. An Autobiography* (London: Jonathan Cape, 1941)

— *Russia's Road from Peace to War. Soviet Foreign Relations 1917–1941* (New York: Harper & Row, 1969)

— *A Week with Gandhi* (London: Allen & Unwin, 1943)

— *Why Spain Fights On* (London: Union of Democratic Control, 1938)

Fox, Soledad, *Constancia de la Mora in War and Exile. International Voice for the Spanish Republic* (Brighton: Sussex Academic Press, 2007)

Franco Bahamonde, Francisco, *Palabras del Caudillo 19 abril 1937–7 diciembre 1942* (Madrid: Ediciones de la Vicesecretaría de Educación Popular, 1943)

Bibliography

Franco Salgado-Araujo, Francisco, *Mi vida junto a Franco* (Barcelona: Editorial Planeta, 1976)

Friedland, Boris Efimovich et al., *Mikhail' Kol'tsov, kakim on byl. Vospominaniya* (Moscow: Sovetskii Pisatel', 1965)

Fry, Varian, *Surrender on Demand* (New York: Random House, 1945)

Gannon, Franklin Reid, *The British Press and Nazi Germany 1936–1939* (Oxford: Clarendon Press, 1971)

García, Hugo, *Mentiras necesarias. La batalla por la opinión británica durante la Guerra Civil* (Madrid: Biblioteca Nueva, 2008)

García-Alix, Carlos, *Madrid-Moscú* (Madrid: T Ediciones, 2003)

Gazur, Edward P., *Secret Assignment. The FBI's KGB General* (London: St Ermin's Press, 2001)

Geiser, Carl, *Prisoners of the Good Fight: The Spanish Civil War 1936–1939* (Westport, CT: Lawrence Hill & Co., 1986)

Gellhorn, Martha, *The Face of War*, 5th edn (London: Granta Books, 1993)

— 'Memory', *London Review of Books*, 12 December 1996

Gerahty, Cecil, *The Road to Madrid* (London: Hutchinson, 1937)

Gibson, Ian, *En busca de José Antonio* (Barcelona: Planeta, 1980)

— *Paracuellos: cómo fue* (Barcelona: Argos Vergara, 1983)

Giméncz Caballero, Ernesto, *Memorias de un dictador* (Barcelona: Planeta, 1979)

Gnedin, Evgenii, *Sebya ne poteryat'* in *Novyi Mir*, no. 7/1988

Görling, Reinhold, *'Dinamita Celebral' Politischer Prozeß und ästhetische Praxis im Spanischen Bürgerkrieg (1936–1939)* (Frankfurt: Verlag Klaus Dieter Vervuert, 1986)

Graham, Helen, 'Against the State': A Genealogy of the Barcelona May Days (1937) in *European History Quarterly*, vol. 29, no. 4, 1999

— *The Spanish Republic at War 1936–1939* (Cambridge: Cambridge University Press, 2002)

Gross, Babette, *Willi Münzenburg. A Political Biography* (East Lansing, MI: Michigan State University Press, 1974)

Gurney, Jason, *Crusade in Spain* (London: Faber & Faber, 1974)

Guttmann, Allen, *The Wound in the Heart. America and the Spanish Civil War* (New York: The Free Press of Glencoe, 1962)

Hanighen, Frank C. (ed.), *Nothing but Danger* (New York: National Travel Club, 1939)

Haslam, Jonathan, *The Soviet Union and the Struggle for Collective Security in Europe 1933–39* (London: Macmillan Press, 1984)

Heaton, P. M., *Welsh Blockade Runners in the Spanish Civil War* (Newport, Gwent: The Starling Press, 1985)

Hemingway, Ernest, *By-Line. Ernest Hemingway: Selected Articles and Dispatches of Four Decades* (London: William Collins, 1968)

— *The Fifth Column* (New York: Scribner, 2003)

— *For Whom the Bell Tolls* (London: Jonathan Cape, 1941)

Hensbergen, Gijs van, *Guernica. The Biography of a Twentieth-Century Icon* (London: Bloomsbury, 2004)

Herbst, Josephine, *The Starched Blue Sky of Spain and Other Memoirs* (New York: HarperCollins, 1991)

Hidalgo de Cisneros, Ignacio, *Cambio de Rumbo*, 2 vols (Bucharest: Colección Ebro, 1964, 1970)

Hochman, Jiri, *The Soviet Union and the Failure of Collective Security, 1934–1938* (Ithaca, NY: Cornell University Press, 1984)

Hopkins, James K., *Into the Heart of the Fire: The British in the Spanish Civil War* (Stanford, CA: Stanford University Press, 1998)

Ickes, Harold L., *The Secret Diary of Harold L. Ickes, Volume II, The Inside Struggle* (New York: Simon & Schuster, 1954)

Imperial War Museum, *The Spanish Civil War Collection. Sound Archive Oral History Recordings* (London: Imperial War Museum, 1996)

Jordan, Philip, *There is No Return* (London: Cresset Press, 1938)

Journalist, A, *Foreign Journalists under Franco's Terror* (London: United Editorial, 1937)

Junod, Marcel, *Warrior without Weapons* (London: Jonathan Cape, 1951)

Karmen, Roman, *¡No pasarán!* (Moscow: Editorial Progreso, 1976)

Keene, Judith, *Fighting for Franco. International Volunteers in Nationalist Spain during the Spanish Civil War, 1936–1939* (London: Leicester University Press, 2001)

Kemp, Peter, *Mine were of Trouble* (London: Cassell, 1957)

— *The Thorns of Memory* (London: Sinclair Stevenson, 1990)

Klehr, Harvey, *The Heyday of American Communism. The Depression Decade* (New York: Basic Books, 1984)

Knickerbocker, H. R., *The Siege of the Alcazar: A War-Log of the Spanish Revolution* (London: Hutchinson, n.d. [1937])

Knightley, Phillip, *The First Casualty. The War Correspondent as Hero, Propagandist, and Myth Maker from the Crimea to Vietnam* (London: André Deutsch, 1975)

Knoblaugh, H. Edward, *Correspondent in Spain* (London and New York: Sheed & Ward, 1937)

Knox, Bernard, *Essays Ancient and Modern* (Baltimore, MD: Johns Hopkins University Press, 1989)

Koch, Stephen, *The Breaking Point. Hemingway, Dos Passos and the Murder of José Robles* (New York: Counterpoint, 2005)

— *Double Lives. Spies and Writers in the Secret Soviet War of Ideas against the West* (New York: The Free Press, 1994)

Koestler, Arthur, *The Invisible Writing*, 2nd edn (London: Hutchinson, 1969)

— *Spanish Testament* (London: Victor Gollancz, 1937)

Koltsov, Mijail, *Diario de la guerra de España* (Paris: Ruedo Ibérico, 1963)

— *The Man in Uniform* (Moscow: Cooperative Publishing Society of Foreign Workers in the USSR, 1933)

— *Proves de la traició trotskista* (Barcelona: Secretariat de Propaganda del C.E., 1937)

Kowalsky, Daniel, *La Unión Soviética y la guerra civil española. Una revisión crítica* (Barcelona: Editorial Crítica, 2003)

Langdon-Davies, John, *Behind the Spanish Barricades* (London: Secker & Warburg, 1936)

Langor, Elinor, *Josephine Herbst* (Boston, MA: Little, Brown, 1984)

Last, Jef, *The Spanish Tragedy* (London: Routledge, 1939)

Leahy, Fleet Admiral William D., *I Was There* (London: Victor Gollancz, 1950)

Lefebvre, Michel, *Kessel/Moral. Deux reporters dans la guerre d'Espagne* (Paris: Éditions Tallandier, 2006)

Bibliography

Leff, Laurel, *Buried by The Times. The Holocaust and America's Most Important Newspaper* (New York: Cambridge University Press, 2005)

Loewenstein, Prince Hubertus Friedrich von, *A Catholic in Republican Spain* (London: Victor Gollancz, 1937)

Lucas Phillips, C. E., *The Spanish Pimpernel* (London: Heinemann, 1960)

Ludington, Townsend, *John Dos Passos. A Twentieth-Century Odyssey* (New York: E. P. Dutton, 1980)

Lunn, Arnold, *Spanish Rehearsal* (London: Hutchinson, 1937)

McCullagh, Francis, *In Franco's Spain* (London: Burns, Oates & Washbourne, 1937)

McNeill-Moss, Major Geoffrey, *The Epic of the Alcazar* (London: Rich & Cowan, 1937)

Manning, Leah, *A Life for Education. An Autobiography* (London: Gollancz, 1970)

Marino, Andy, *A Quiet American: The Secret War of Varian Fry* (New York: St Martin's Press, 1999)

Martín, José-Luis (ed.), *Claudio Sánchez Albornoz. Embajador de España en Portugal, mayo–octubre 1936* (Ávila: Fundación Sánchez Albornoz, 1995)

Martínez Amutio, Justo, *Chantaje a un pueblo* (Madrid: G. del Toro, 1974)

Martínez de Pisón, Ignacio, *Enterrar a los muertos* (Barcelona: Seix Barral, 2005)

Massot i Muntaner, Josep, *El desembarcament de Bayo a Mallorca, Agost–Setembre de 1936* (Barcelona: Publicacions de l'Abadia de Montserrat, 1987)

Matthews, Herbert L., *The Education of a Correspondent* (New York: Harcourt Brace, 1946)

— *Half of Spain Died. A Reappraisal of the Spanish Civil War* (New York: Charles Scribner's Sons, 1973)

— *Two Wars and More to Come* (New York: Carrick & Evans, 1938)

— *The Yoke and the Arrows* (London: Heinemann, 1958)

— *A World in Revolution. A Newspaperman's Memoir* (New York: Charles Scribner's Sons, 1971)

Maximenkov, Leonid and Christopher Barnes, 'Boris Pasternak in August 1936', *Toronto Slavic Quarterly*, no. 17, 2003

Medvedev, Roy, *Let History Judge. The Origins and Consequences of Stalinism* (London: Macmillan, 1971)

Merriman, Marion and Warren Lerude, *American Commander in Spain: Robert Hale Merriman and the Abraham Lincoln Brigade* (Reno, NV: University of Nevada Press, 1986)

Miller, Webb, *I Found No Peace* (London: The Book Club, 1937)

Minifie, James M., *Expatriate* (Toronto: Macmillan of Canada, 1976)

Miravitlles, Jaume, *Episodis de la guerra civil espanyola* (Barcelona: Editorial Pòrtic, 1972)

Moa Rodríguez, Pío, *Los mitos de la guerra civil* (Madrid: La Esfera de los Libros, 2003)

Monks, Noel, *Eyewitness* (London: Frederick Muller, 1955)

Montanelli, Indro, *Memorias de un periodista* (Barcelona: RBA Libros, 2002)

Moorehead, Caroline, *Martha Gellhorn, A Life* (London: Chatto & Windus, 2003)

Mora, Constancia de la, *In Place of Splendor. The Autobiography of a Spanish Woman* (New York: Harcourt, Brace, 1939)

Mortari, Curio, *Con gli insorti in Marocco e Spagna* (Milano: Fratelli Treves Editori, 1937)

Moure Mariño, Luis, *La generación del 36: memorias de Salamanca y Burgos* (La Coruña: Ediciós do Castro, 1989)

Muggeridge, Malcolm, *Chronicles of Wasted Time. An Autobiography* (Vancouver: Regent College Publishing, 2006)

North, Joseph, *No Men are Strangers* (New York: International Publishers, 1958)

Nunes, Leopoldo, *La guerra en España (Dos meses de reportaje en los frentes de Andalucia y Extremadura)* (Granada: Librería Prieto, 1937)

Orlov, Alexander, *The March of Time. Reminiscences* (London: St Ermin's Press, 2004)

— *The Secret History of Stalin's Crimes* (London: Jarrolds, 1954)

Orwell, George, *Homage to Catalonia* (London: Secker & Warburg, 1971)

— *Orwell in Spain* (London: Penguin Books, 2001)

Packard, Reynolds and Eleanor, *Balcony Empire. Fascist Italy at War* (New York: Oxford University Press, 1942)

Page, Bruce, David Leitch and Phillip Knightley, *Philby. The Spy Who Betrayed a Generation* (London: Sphere Books, 1977)

Palencia, Isabel de, *Smouldering Freedom. The Story of the Spanish Republicans in Exile* (London: Victor Gollancz, 1946)

Payne, Stanley G., *The Spanish Civil War, the Soviet Union, and Communism* (New Haven, CT: Yale University Press, 2004)

Pena Rodríguez, Alberto, *El gran aliado de Franco. Portugal y la guerra civil española: prensa, radio, cine y propaganda* (Sada-A Coruña: Ediciós do Castro, 1998)

Petrou, Michael, *Renegades. Canadians in the Spanish Civil War* (Vancouver: University of British Columbia Press, 2008)

Philby, Kim, *My Silent War* (London: MacGibbon & Kee, 1968)

Pike, David, *German Writers in Soviet Exile, 1933–1945* (Chapel Hill, NC: University of North Carolina Press, 1982)

— *Les français et la guerre d'Espagne 1936–1939* (Paris: Presses Universitaires de France, 1975)

Pitcairn, Frank, *Reporter in Spain* (London: Lawrence & Wishart, 1936)

Preston, Paul, *The Coming of the Spanish Civil War: Reform Reaction and Revolution in the Second Spanish Republic 1931–1936*, 2nd edn (London: Routledge, 1994)

— *Franco: A Biography* (London: HarperCollins, 1993)

— *The Spanish Civil War. Reaction, Revolution, Revenge* (London: HarperCollins, 2006)

— 'The Answer lies in the Sewers: Captain Aguilera and the Mentality of the Francoist Officer Corps', *Science & Society*, vol. 68, no. 3, Fall 2004, pp. 277–312

— (ed.), *Leviatán: antología* (Madrid: Ediciones Turner, 1976)

— 'The Struggle Against Fascism in Spain: The Contradictions of the PSOE Left', in *European Studies Review*, vol. 9, no. 1, 1979

Pruszyński, Ksawery, *En la España roja* (Barcelona: Alba Editorial, 2007)

Purcell, Hugh, *The Last English Revolutionary. A Biography of Tom Wintringham 1898–1949* (Stroud: Sutton Publishing, 2004)

Puzzo, Dante A., *Spain and the Great Powers, 1936–1941* (New York: Columbia University Press, 1962)

Radio Nacional de España, *Guerra civil y Radio Nacional. Salamanca 1936–1938* (Madrid: Instituto Oficial de Radio y Televisión, 2006)

Radosh, Ronald, Mary R. Habeck and Grigory Sevostianov (eds), *Spain Betrayed. The Soviet Union in the Spanish Civil War* (New Haven, CT: Yale University Press, 2001)

Bibliography

Ragsdale, Hugh, *The Soviets, the Munich Crisis, and the Coming of World War II* (Cambridge University Press, 2004)

Rankin, Nick, *Telegram from Guernica. The Extraordinary Life of George Steer, War Correspondent* (London: Faber & Faber, 2003)

Rayfield, Donald, *Stalin and His Hangmen. An Authoritative Portrait of a Tyrant and Those Who Served Him* (London: Viking, 2004)

Regler, Gustav, *The Great Crusade* (New York: Longmans, Green & Co., 1940)

— *The Owl of Minerva* (London: Rupert Hart-Davis, 1959)

Rey García, Marta, *Stars for Spain. La guerra civil española en los Estados Unidos* (Sada-A Coruña: Ediciós do Castro, 1997)

Roberts, Geoffrey, *The Unholy Alliance. Stalin's Pact with Hitler* (London: I.B. Tauris, 1989)

Rogers, F. Theo, *Spain: A Tragic Journey* (New York: The Macaulay Company, 1937)

Rojas, Carlos, *¡Muera la inteligencia! ¡Viva la muerte! Salamanca, 1936. Unamuno y Millán Astray frente a frente* (Barcelona: Planeta, 1995)

Rojo, General Vicente, *Así fue la defensa de Madrid* (México D.F.: Ediciones Era, 1967)

Rojo, José Andrés, *Vicente Rojo. Retrato de un general republicano* (Barcelona: Tusquets Editores, 2006)

Rollyson, Carl, *Nothing Ever Happens to the Brave. The Story of Martha Gellhorn* (New York: St Martin's Press, 1990)

Ross, Marjorie, *El secreto encanto de la KGB. Las cinco vidas de Iósif Griguliévich* (Heredia, Costa Rica: Farben Grupo Editorial Norma, 2004)

Rubashkin, A., *Mikhail' Kol'tsov. Kritiko-biograficheskii ocherk* (Moscow: Khudozhestvennaya literatura 1971)

Rybalkin, Yuri, *Stalin y España. La ayuda militar soviética a la República* (Madrid: Marcial Pons Historia, 2007)

Sagardía, General, *Del Alto Ebro a las Fuentes del Llobregat. Treinta y dos meses de guerra de la 62 División* (Barcelona: Editora Nacional, 1940)

Salas Larrazabal, Jesús, *La guerra de España desde el aire*, 2a edición (Barcelona: Ariel, 1972)

Salter, Cedric, *Try-out in Spain* (New York: Harper Brothers, 1943)

Sánchez, Germán, 'El misterio Grigulévich', *Historia 16*, no. 233, septiembre de 1995

Schauff, Frank, *Der verspielte Sieg. Sowjetunion, Kommunistische Internationale und Spanischer Bürgerkrieg 1936–1939* (Frankfurt: Campus, 2005)

Schmigalle, Günther, *André Malraux und der spanische Bürgerkrieg: Zur Genese, Funktion und Bedeutung von 'L'Espoir'* (Bonn: Bouvier Verlag Herbert Grundmann, 1980)

Scott Watson, Keith, *Single to Spain* (London: Arthur Barker, 1937)

Sebag Montefiore, Simon, *Stalin. The Court of the Red Czar* (London: Weidenfeld & Nicolson, 2003)

Sebba, Anne, *Battling for News. The Rise of the Woman Reporter* (London: Hodder & Stoughton, 1994)

Sehlinger, Peter J. and Holman Hamilton, *Spokesman for Democracy. Claude G. Bowers 1878–1958* (Indianapolis, IN: Indiana Historical Society, 2000)

Seldes, George, *The Catholic Crisis* (New York: Julian Messner, 1939)

Sencourt, Robert, *Spain's Ordeal. A Documented Survey of Recent Events* (London: Longmans, Green and Co., 1938)

Serge, Victor, *Memoirs of a Revolutionary 1901–1941* (London: Oxford University Press, 1963)

Serrano, Carlos, *L'enjeu espagnol: PCF et guerre d'Espagne* (Paris: Messidor/Éditions Sociales, 1987)

Sheean, Vincent, *Not Peace but a Sword* (New York: Doubleday, Doran, 1939)

Shklovsky, Viktor, *Mayakovsky and His Circle* (London: Pluto Press, 1972)

Skorokhodov, Gleb, *Mikhail' Kol'tsov. Kritiko-biograficheskii ocherk* (Moscow: Sovetskii Pisatel', 1959)

Solé i Sabaté, Josep Maria, Joan Villarroya and Eduard Voltes, (eds), *La Guerra civil a Catalunya*, 4 vols (Barcelona: Edicions 62, 2004)

Southworth, Herbert Rutledge, *Antifalange; estudio crítico de 'Falange en la guerra de España' de Maximiano García Venero* (Paris: Ediciones Ruedo Ibérico, 1967)

— *Conspiracy and the Spanish Civil War: The Brainwashing of Francisco Franco* (London: Routledge, 2002)

— *Guernica! Guernica!: A Study of Journalism, Propaganda and History* (Berkeley, CA: University of California Press, 1977)

— *El mito de la cruzada de Franco* (Paris: Ediciones Ruedo Ibérico, 1963)

Spender, Stephen, *World within World* (London: Readers Union, 1953)

Steer, G. L., *Caesar in Abyssinia* (Boston, MA: Little, Brown & Co., 1937)

— *A Date in the Desert* (London: Hodder and Stoughton, 1939)

— *Judgment on German Africa* (London: Hodder and Stoughton, 1939)

— *Sealed and Delivered* (London: Hodder & Stoughton, 1942)

— *The Tree of Gernika: A Field Study of Modern War* (London: Hodder & Stoughton, 1938)

Tangye, Nigel, *Red, White and Spain* (London: Rich & Cowan, 1937)

Taylor, F. Jay, *The United States and the Spanish Civil War 1936–1939* (New York: Bookman Associates, 1956)

Taylor, S. J., *Stalin's Apologist. Walter Duranty: The New York Times's Man in Moscow* (New York: Oxford University Press, 1990)

Thomas, Fred, *To Tilt at Windmills. A Memoir of the Spanish Civil War* (East Lansing, MI: Michigan State University Press, 1996)

Thomas, Hugh, *The Spanish Civil War*, 3rd edn (London: Hamish Hamilton, 1977)

Thompson, Sir Geoffrey, *Front Line Diplomat* (London: Hutchinson, 1959)

Thorning, Joseph F., *Mercy and Justice!* (New York: Peninsular News Service, 1939)

— *Fernando de los Ríos Refutes Himself* (New York: Paulist Press, 1939)

— *Why the Press Failed on Spain* (New York: International Catholic Truth Society, 1938)

Tierney, Dominic, *FDR and the Spanish Civil War. Neutrality and Commitment in the Struggle that Divided America* (Durham, NC and London: Duke University Press, 2007)

Toynbee, Philip (ed.), *The Distant Drum. Reflections on the Spanish Civil War* (London: Sidgwick & Jackson, 1976)

Traina, Richard P., *American Diplomacy and the Spanish Civil War* (Bloomington, IN: Indiana University Press, 1968)

Trotsky, Leon, *La Revolution espagnole 1930–40* (ed. Pierre Broué) (Paris: Les Éditions de Minuit, 1975)

Bibliography

Tucker, Robert C., *Stalin in Power. The Revolution from Above, 1928–1941* (New York: W. W. Norton, 1990)

— *Stalin as Revolutionary, 1879–1929* (New York: W. W. Norton, 1973)

Vaksberg, Arkadi, *Hotel Lux. Les partis frères au service de l'Internationale Communiste* (Paris: Éditions Fayard, 1993)

Valtin, Jan, *Out of the Night*, 2nd edn (London: Fortress Books, 1988)

Vargas, Bruno, *Rodolfo Llopis (1895–1983). Una biografía política* (Barcelona: Planeta, 1999)

Vegas Latapie, Eugenio, *Los caminos del desengaño. Memorias políticas 2: 1936–1938* (Madrid: Ediciones Giner, 1987)

Verevkin, V. P., *Mikhail' Efimovich Kol'tsov* (Moscow: Mysl', 1977)

Vidal, César, *Paracuellos-Katyn. Un ensayo sobre el genocidio de la izquierda* (Madrid: LibrosLibres, 2005)

Viñas, Ángel, *La Alemania nazi y el 18 de julio* (Madrid: Alianza Editorial, 1974)

— *El escudo de la República. El oro de España, la apuesta soviética y los hechos de mayo de 1937* (Barcelona: Crítica, 2007)

— *La soledad de la República. El abandono de las democracias y el viraje hacia la Unión Soviética* (Barcelona: Crítica, 2006)

— *Franco, Hitler y el estallido de la guerra civil. Antecedentes y consecuencias* (Madrid: Alianza Editorial, 2001)

Volkogonov, Dmitri, *Stalin. Triumph and Tragedy* (London: Weidenfeld & Nicolson, 1991)

Ward, Harriet, *A Man of Small Importance. My Father Griffin Barry* (Debenham, Suffolk: Dormouse Books, 2003)

Watkins, K. W., *Britain Divided* (London: Nelson, 1963)

Watson, William Braasch, 'Hemingway's Civil War Dispatches', *The Hemingway Review*, vol. VII, no. 2, Spring 1988

Waugh, Evelyn, *The Essays, Articles and Reviews of Evelyn Waugh* (ed. Donald Gallagher) (London: Methuen, 1983)

— *Mr Wu & Mrs Stitch. The Letters of Evelyn Waugh and Diana Cooper* (ed. Artemis Cooper) (London: Hodder & Stoughton, 1991)

— *Scoop* (Boston, MA: Little Brown, 1977)

Whitaker, John T., *We Cannot Escape History* (New York: Macmillan, 1943)

Worsley, T. C., *Behind the Battle* (London: Robert Hale, 1939)

Wurtzel, David, 'Lester Ziffren and the Road to War in Spain', *International Journal of Iberian Studies*, vol. 19, no. 1

Wyden, Peter, *The Passionate War. The Narrative History of the Spanish Civil War* (New York: Simon + Schuster, 1983)

Ziffren, Lester, 'The Correspondent in Spain', *Public Opinion Quarterly*, vol. 1, no. 3, July 1937

—, 'I Lived in Madrid', *Current History*, April 1937

Index

Abramson, Paulina 65, 155, 185
Acción Española 134, 140
Action Française 140
Adams Kenyon, Mildred 325–6
Adventures of a Young Man, The (Dos
   Passos) 91
Agence Espagne 42, 76, 96–7, 143
Aguilera y Yeltes, Gonzalo 137, 147–9,
   162–3, 167, 193
Akers-Douglas, Aretas (Viscount
   Chilston) 196
Albacete 37, 110–11, 214
Alfonso XIII, King 293, 342
Allen, Jay 54–6, 291–338
   arrests/release 295–6, 300, 331–2
   on Badajoz massacre 300–8, 318
   books/research of 295–6, 332, 334–8
   contacts/friends 293–4, 297–8, 308–9,
      314–16, 321–3
   criticism of 309–12, 330–1
   early life/career 291–2
   entertaining revolutionaries 294–5, 318
   and Fry 325–7, 329–30
   interviews of 310–11, 326, 328
   lectures/speeches 311–12, 332
   lobbying for Republic 17, 21, 314–16,
      318–19, 321–4
   on Nazis in Czechoslovakia 318–19
   in North Africa 326, 328, 332–3
   political sympathies of 18, 294–5, 318
   private life 292–3, 296, 298, 313, 335,
      337–8
   and Pulitzer Prize Committee 294–5,
      307

Allen, Ruth 292, 296–8, 313–14, 318, 324,
   331, 335–8
Alliluyeva, Svetlana 261–2
Alving, Barbro 'Bang' 30, 37
Amariglio, David 160–1
American Emergency Rescue Committee
   325, 328
Amutio, Justo Martínez 214–15, 237
Anglo-Russian Trade Gazette 163
Antifalange (Southworth) 338, 356, 359
Anti-Fascist Writers' Congress 193, 242
anti-semitism 134, 146, 151, 163, 206–7,
   253, 282, 299, 333
Antonov-Ovseenko, Vladimir 190, 206
'Appeal to the Conscience of the World'
   279–80
Araquisatain, Luis 214, 221, 225–6, 251,
   297
Arbeiderbladet 230
Arias Paz, Manuel 147, 166
Associated Press 120, 165, 231
Astray, José Millán 135, 146, 150–1, 166
Asturias 4, 360
Attlee, Clement 247, 256–7
Ayala, Francisco 65, 69
Azaña, Manuel 147, 243, 342

Babel, Isaak 207–8
Badajoz 6, 22–3, 54–5, 136, 291, 299,
   300–8, 318
Barcelona 4, 7–14, 84–5, 105, 131, 165,
   169, 253
   press office 88, 96, 126–7
Barea, Arturo 30–7, 39–40, 60, 182

Index

Barry, Gerald 138–9
Barry, Griffin 71, 112
Bartlett, Vernon 16, 46–7
Barton, Sidney 264, 287–8
Basque 166–7, 195
  blockade of Nervión river 274–5
  Steer on 271–9, 283–4
Bates, Ralph 108, 319, 323
Behind the Spanish Barricades (Langdon-
  Davies) 13
Belchite 126
Beneš, Eduoard 201–2
Benicasim 97, 247
Bennett, Milly 114, 118–21, 313
Beria, Lavrenti 204–5, 209
Bernanos, Georges 136
Berniard, Georges 166–7
Bertodano y Wilson, Frederick Ramón 166
Bethune, Norman 112–14, 116, 122–3
Bibesco, Antoine 293
Bibesco, Elizabeth 293–4, 296
Bliven, Bruce 77, 79–80
Blum, Léon 6, 247, 364
Bocalari, Vincenzo 231
Bolín, Luis 24, 59, 93, 155, 166, 360
  and foreign correspondents 134–8,
    141–3, 149–50, 270–1
Bolloten, Burnett 94, 362–3
Bolshevism and the Jews 206–7
Botto, Georges 167
Bowers, Claude 43, 82, 157–8, 364
Bowler, Kitty 85, 97, 104–14, 347
Brenan, Gerald 298, 308, 313
Brigada Especial 67, 71, 79
Britain, non-intervention policy 74, 97,
  238–40, 246–8
Brunete 126, 243
Brut, René 136
Buckley, Henry 27, 33
  assignments 341–5, 348–50
  awards 350
  early life/career 342–3
  friends/contacts 343–4, 347, 349–50
  political sympathies 43, 343–4, 345–7
Bujaraloz 176
Bukharin, Nikolai 198, 202, 249
*Bulletin de L'Entente Internationale contre
  La Troisième Internationale* 299

Bullitt, William 252
Burgos 137, 139, 148–9

Caballero, Ernesto Giménez 146, 359
Caballero, Fransico Largo 4–5, 11, 177,
  229, 233, 242, 343
Cable, James 284–5
Caesar in Abyssinia (Steer) 266–9, 271,
  274
Café Rambla, Barcelona 105
Camus, Albert 3
Capa, Robert 126, 130–1, 158, 347
Cardozo, Harold 11, 33, 137, 149, 151,
  355
Carney, William P. 19–20, 55–7, 98, 321
  false reporting by 157–61, 295–6
  and Herbert Matthews 55–6, 126–7,
    131–2, 159, 312
  political sympathies 157–9
Carrillo, Santiago 178, 181
Casa de los Sabios, Valencia 73
Casa Viejas 343
Casado, Segismundo 61, 252, 347
Catalonia 3–4, 6, 9–10, 12, 74, 130–1, 158
Catholic Church, censorship of 18–20,
  126–7, 154, 309–12, 317
Catholic Mind (Carney) 57
Ce Soir 59
censorship
  in Madrid press office 31, 33–7
  methods of avoiding 31, 57–8, 99–100,
    144–5
  in rebel zone 95, 144–5, 149–54,
    309–12, 317
  of US Catholic lobby 18–20, 126–7
  in Valencia press office 95
Century's Ebb (Dos Passos) 48, 76, 85, 92
Chalmers-Mitchell, Peter 143–4
Chamberlain, Neville 132, 286–7, 364
Chicago Council of Foreign Relations
  311–12
Chicago Daily Tribune 18, 29, 292, 295,
  307, 313
Chicherin, Georgi 219–20
Chilton, Henry 139, 274
Chudak 174
Churchill, Randolph 150, 161
Churchill, Winston 144, 253

Index

Civil War 7
  background to 3–7
  foreign perceptions of 6–7, 13–14
Claridad 225
Cockburn, Claud 42, 51–2, 177, 200–3
Coindreau, Maurice 72–3, 86, 89, 91–2
Commission of Inquiry into Alleged
  Breaches of the Non-Intervention
  Agreement in Spain 142
'Committee of One Thousand Mothers'
  231
Common Sense 90, 92
'Communist Party and the War Spirit: a
  Letter to a Friend who is Probably a
  Party Member' 90
communists 226–9, 320–1, 324–5, 346–7
  and censorship 95, 245–6
  and foreign correspondents 43, 51–2,
    141–3, 177, 214–15, 363
  influence in Republic 74–5, 89–90, 156,
    160, 179–81, 205–6
  rumours of control by 11–12, 14, 156,
    363
Companys, Lluís 9, 13
concentration camps 132, 159–60, 321,
  324, 349
Confederación Española de Derechas
  Autónomas (CEDA) 4–5, 134, 296
Corcoran, Thomas G. 316
Correspondent in Spain 120
Cowles, Virginia 49, 81–2, 155, 167–9
Cox, Geoffrey 29–30, 32–4, 46, 138–9
Crooks, Esther 87, 89
Curran, Edward Lodge 19
Czechoslovakia 200–4, 255, 318

Dagens Nyheter 37
Dahl, Harold 158
Daily Chronicle 342
Daily Despatch 265
Daily Express 7, 12, 30, 60, 132, 135, 148,
  275
Daily Herald 221
Daily Mail 11–12, 128–9, 137, 149–50,
  156, 169
Daily Telegraph 13, 41, 128, 135–6, 145,
  341, 347
Daily Worker 50, 95, 104, 106–7, 130

Dancing Catalans (Langdon-Davies) 12
Davis, Frances 33, 151
Dawson, Geoffrey 281–2
'Day in the Life of Trotsky' 174
*Day Will End: a personal adventure behind
  Nazi lines, The* (Allen) 335
de Aguirre, José Antonio 185, 275, 287,
  293–4
de Azcárate, Pablo 255–6
de Cisneros, Ignacio Hidalgo 93–4, 204,
  211
de Herrero y Hassett, Margarita Trinidad
  269, 272–3
de la Cierva y de Hoces, Ricardo 352–4,
  359, 362
de la Mora, Constancia 248
  autobiography 319–20
  on correspondents reporting truth
    98–101
  correspondents' views on 99–102, 128
  and Jay Allen 321–3
  private life 93–4
  and Rubio Hidalgo 40, 93–5
  in Valencia press office 93–6
de Llano, Quiepo 141–2, 152–3, 156,
  343–4
de los Ríos, Fernando 321, 356
de Palencia, Isabel 291, 321
de Rivera, Miguel Primo 12, 293, 310, 342
de Traversay, Guy 18, 38, 136
de Valencia, Luis *see* Gay Forner, Vincente
de Villegas, Mágara Fernández 69, 71–3,
  82, 87–9
Deeble, Elizabeth 107, 123
del Olmo, Rosario 40, 60
del Vayo, Julio Álvarez 25, 34, 41–2, 74,
  218, 222, 233, 238
  and Koltsov/Martinez 182
  and Robles family 88–9
del Vayo, Luisi 88, 131–2, 222, 321
Delaprée, Louis 14, 37–8, 148
Delegación para Prensa y Propaganda
  146–7, 166–7
Delmer, Sefton 'Tom' 7–8, 29, 37, 47,
  98–9, 99–100, 119–20, 148–9
Deutsche Zentral Zeitung 188, 197
d'Hospital, Jean 136, 140
Diario de la Manhã 152–3

Diario de Lisboa 152–3
Dick, Alan 145–6, 155
Dimitrov, Georgi 240, 245
Djhordis, Mink 84–6
Dos Passos, John 40, 71, 74, 102
  feud with Hemingway 64–5, 74–6, 80–
    3, 86–7, 90–2
Dos Passos, Katy 75
Doyle, Bob 159–60
Durango 115, 273, 280
Duranty, Walter 104–5, 257

Ebbutt, Norman 281
Ebro, battle of 127, 347–8
Ediciones Ruedo Ibérico 351–3, 358–9
Ehrenberg, Ilya 49–50, 102
El Debate 145, 296
El mito de la cruzado de Franco
    (Southworth) 338, 351, 353, 359, 363
El Socialista 226, 229
El Vendrell 131, 249
elections (1933–1936) 4, 156, 294–5, 345
English Review 154
Esquire 313–14
Ethiopia 265–8
'Evidence of the Trotskyist
    Treachery'(Koltsov) 191

*Falange en la guerra de España: La
    unificatión y Hedilla* (Venero) 359
Falange Española 5, 54, 293, 356, 359–60
'Farewell to Europe' (Dos Passos) 89
fascism *see* Falange; Franco; Nazis
Feigenberg, Yevgenia 193, 207
Fernsworth, Lawrence 9–12, 43, 122–3
Fiesta, for XV Brigade 78–9, 81, 90, 92
Fifth Column, The (Hemingway) 81–2
Figaro 140
Fight 106–7
Figueras 131, 349
Fischer, Bertha 'Markoosha' 215–16, 220,
    224–5, 230–1, 249–50, 257–8
Fischer, Louis 15, 17, 21, 26–7, 37, 41,
    224–5
  books by 219–20, 240–1, 260, 262
  contacts and influence of 213–15,
    217–20, 223, 225, 238
  criticisms of Caballero 233–6

on disappearance of Robles 70–1
early life and career 215–16
ethics of 53–4, 232, 237, 243–6
on Franco's victory 250–1
in Germany and Russia 216, 218–19,
    240
lectures/lobbying in United States
    241–2, 248, 251–3, 255, 260–1
and Negrín 97–8, 213, 215, 222, 230,
    240, 242–3, 253
on non-intervention policies of Britain
    and France 238–40, 246–8
political sympathies of 214, 217, 220–1,
    225–6, 236–7, 245–6, 259
private life 215–16, 220, 230, 250,
    257–9, 260–2
on Russian policy in Spain 229–30,
    249–50
whether Soviet agent 254–6
writing for *The Nation* 222–4, 257, 259
For Whom the Bell Tolls (Hemingway) 21,
    90, 120, 186–7, 195, 205
Forbes-Robinson, Diana 259, 319
foreign correspondents 10–11, 21
  dangers faced by 17–18, 27, 58, 130, 165
  ethics of 10–11, 19–20, 42–3, 53–7, 154,
    237
  exclusion of 15, 18, 30, 150, 243
  expulsion of 24–5, 37, 98, 107, 138,
    145, 148–9, 152, 162, 271–2
  and foreign perceptions of War 6–7,
    13–14
  and non-intervention policies 16–17,
    74, 97, 238–40, 246–8, 282, 321,
    364–5
  portrayed as fictional characters 21, 48,
    75–6, 80, 92, 186–7, 195, 205
  sympathies of 16–18, 21, 43–6, 83, 180
  treatment in rebel zone 134, 148–55,
    166–9
Forrest, William 30, 32, 129, 131–2
Fragga Iribarne, Manuel 352, 359
France, non-intervention policy of 74, 97,
    238–40, 246–8, 282, 364
Franco, Francisco 5–6, 22, 54–5
  African columns of 5–6, 22–4, 67,
    135–6, 147
  changing military objectives of 93

interviews with 54, 299
pamphleting campaign of 269
treatment of foreign correspondents
under 134–7, 144–6, 148–55, 166–9,
270–1
and Troskyists 196
Franco, Nicolás 141
Franco's Mein Kampf (Southworth) 356
Frankfurter, Felix 316, 324–5
Friends of the Abraham Lincoln Brigade
160–1, 251
Fry, Varian 325–7, 329–30
Fuqua, Stephen O. 64–5, 68, 79

Gabinete de Prensa 134, 161
Gallagher, O'Dowd 60–1, 131, 265–6
Gandhi, Mahatma 259–60
Gay Forner, Vincente 146–7, 166
Gelhorn, Martha 16–17, 20, 44, 62, 75, 81,
112, 263, 334–5
Geopolitics 164
Germany 152–3
activities in Spain 18, 141–3, 217,
280–1, 289, 297, 364
Gernika *see* Guernica
Gide, André 193–4, 208
Gil Robles, José María 141, 296, 343
Giral, José 5–6, 95–6, 177
Glasgow Herald 275
Gnedin, Evgeni 209–11
Gorev, Vladimir Efimovich 39, 64–5, 69,
176, 181, 183, 229, 250
Gorrell, Henry T. 'Hank' 23–5, 138, 300
Grepp, Gerda 230, 259
Greßhöner, Maria *see* Osten, Maria
Grigulevich, Iosif Romualdovich 67,
181–2
Gross, Babette 42–3, 238
Guadalajara, battle of 93, 144
Guernica, bombing of 54, 59
rebel denial of 158, 166–8, 280–2,
312–13
Southworth on 354, 360–1
Steer on 263–79, 299
Guerricabeitia, José Martinez 351, 359

Hanighen, Frank 15, 17–18
Havas Agency 136, 140

Hemingway, Ernest 314, 316–17, 348
in Barcelona 127, 130
at battle-front 48, 126
on Catholic lobby's censorship 19
feud with Dos Passos 64, 71, 74–6,
80–3, 86–7, 90–2
lobbying 21, 251, 296, 324–5
in Madrid 47–50, 62–4, 118
political sympathies of 17, 21
private life 75
and *Spanish Earth* 74–5, 102
For Whom the Bell Tolls 21, 90, 120,
186–7, 195, 205
Hemingway, Pauline 75
Hendaye 138, 160–1
Herbst, Josie 62–4, 75–82, 89, 347, 366–7
Hidalgo, Luis Rubio 24, 26, 31, 35, 39, 93–5
Hitler, Adolf 132, 217, 331
Holme, Christopher 59, 275, 282
Homage to Catalonia (Orwell) 190
Honolulu Star-Bulletin 118

Ibárruri, Dolores 176, 191–2, 344
Ideal Room 69
Il Messagero 153
Imprecor (International Press
Correspondence) 52–3
Informacciones 134, 146
International Brigade 21, 41–2, 52–3,
79–81, 90, 92, 159, 237, 251, 255–6,
333
Irún 140, 152
'Ispanskii dnevnik' 197
Italy 6, 15, 23, 134, 152–3, 228, 231,
239–40, 265, 346
Ivens, Joris 71, 102
Izvestiya 188, 198–9

James, Edwin L. 'Jimmy/Dressy' 19, 126,
159
Jarama, battle of 93, 189
Jews 173, 186–7, 206–7, 215–16, 282
John Hopkins University 64, 68–70, 86
Johnson, Hewlett (Dean of Canterbury)
115, 248, 283
Jordan, Philip 101, 103–4, 283
Journey Between Wars 90, 92
Juventudes Unificadas Socialistas 88, 181

Karmen, Roman 183, 185
Katz, Otto 42–3, 97, 142
Kemp, Peter 145, 270
Ken – The Insider's World 200, 313
Khochu letat (I want to fly)(Koltsov)
   173–4
King, Norman 9, 12–13
Kirchwey, Freda 217, 222–4, 243–5, 259
Kirkpatrick, Ivo 253–4
Knickerbocker, Hubert Renfro 'Red' 33,
   148, 161–2, 253, 265–6
Knoblaugh, Edward H. 'Doaks' 31, 120–2,
   312–13, 335
Koch, Stephen 76–8, 186
Koestler, Arthur 47, 51, 141–4, 280
Koestler, Dorothy 144
Koltsov, Boris Efimovic Friedand 179,
   184–5, 193, 209
Koltsov, Elisabeta 187, 207
Koltsov, José 'Jusik' 193, 211–12
Koltsov, Mikhail Efimovich Frieldand 21,
   34, 50, 53–4, 173–212
  advisory role, in Spain 176–8, 184–5,
   190
  arrest 173, 200–1, 204, 208–11
  awards received 173, 204
  and censorship 177
  character of 186–7
  on Czechoslovakia 199–203
  early life and career 173–4
  ethics of 237
  History of the Bolshevik Party
   (lecture) 173, 194–5, 204
  as Jew 206–7
  as Karkov in *For Whom the Bell Tolls*
   21, 186–7, 195, 205
  and Miguel Martínez 179–83
  political activities of 173–5, 190–1,
   200–3, 210–11
  private life 187–9, 193, 197, 203, 207,
   209, 211–12
  and the purges 182–3, 198–9, 204
  relationship with Stalin 173–4, 177–8,
   180, 182, 191–5, 198, 204–5, 208
  on role of Soviet security services
   190–1
  Spanish Spring 176
Kork, Avgust 198–9

Kremlin and the People, The (Duranty)
   256
Krokodil 174
Kuh, Frederick 221, 255
Kulcsar, Ilsa 36–41, 40–1, 44
Kurzke, Jan 104, 113–14

*La destruction de Guernica! A Study of
   Journalism, Diplomacy, Propaganda
   and History* (Southworth) 264,
   360–1
La Petite Gironde 166
La revolución nacional–socialista (de
   Valencia) 147
La Stampa 152
Lambarri y Yanguas, Manuel 155, 169
Lancaster, Henry Carrington 68–70, 72,
   86–9
Lance, Christopher 'Spanish Pimpernel'
   139–40
Langdon-Davies, John 12–14
Langer, Elinor 76–7
Lardner, Jim 127
Le Journal 140, 269
Le mythe de las croisade de Franco
   (Southworth) 360
League Against War and Fascism 106
League of Nations 242, 283
Leahy, William D. 330–1
Lenin, Vladimir 260
L'Espagne ensanglantée (Koestler) 142–3
Lestchenko, Tatiana 216, 259
Leviatán 226, 297
L'Hoste, Hubert 188, 211–12
L'Humanité 37, 280
Life and Death of Lenin, The (Fischer)
   260
Life and Death of the Spanish Republic
   (Buckley) 341, 343, 350
L'Intransigeant 18, 38, 62, 136
Lister, Enrique 179, 181, 344
Literatunaya Gazeta 197
Litinov, Maxim 175, 207, 213, 220, 240,
   245, 250
Lloyd George, David 248, 250, 281
London *Evening News* 149, 154
London *Evening Standard* 164, 253
Lunn, Arnold 150, 154, 360

Index

MacCaw, Raymond 19–20
McConnell, Francis J. 279–80
McCormick, R.R. 295, 307
McNeill-Moss, Geoffrey 136, 310
Madrid
  censorship 31, 33–7, 57–8, 61
  evacuation of government 28, 31–2, 96
  fall of, rumours 33
  last correspondents in 60–1
  living conditions in 28–32, 42, 48–50,
    59–61, 186
  press office 24, 30
  siege of 25–63
Malet-Dauban, Henri 140, 167
Malraux, André 208, 210
Manchester *Guardian* 57–8, 110, 218, 275
Mangan, Kate 52, 71, 73, 85, 94, 104,
  112–14, 117–18
March of a Nation, The (Cardozo) 355
Martínez, Miguel 179–83
Marty, André 110, 205–6, 208, 237–8
Mason-Walstra, Suzanne 363
Matthews, Herbert Lionel 19–21, 31, 37,
  44–6, 100–1, 130, 365
  and William Carney 55–6, 126–7,
    131–2, 159
Men and Politics (Fischer) 260
Menschenopfer Unerhört (Koestler) 142–3
Merriman, Robert 119–20
Merry del Val, Pablo 145–6, 164–7, 169
Miaja Menant, José 61, 65, 183
Milicia Popular 182
Miller, Webb 22, 60, 136–7
Minifie, James M. 9, 18–19, 24, 119,
  137–8, 300
Mink, George 84–6
Miravitlles, Jaume 106, 123, 236
Modesto, Juan 248
Mola, Emilio 5, 6, 136–7, 273
Mollet 7–8
Molotov, Vyacheslav 192, 193
Monks, Noel 58–9, 135, 144–5, 265, 282
Monnier, Robert 275, 282
Morocco 5–6, 11, 52, 134, 152, 326,
  332–3, 350, 357
Moscardó Ituarte, Luis 137
Moscow Daily News 115, 118–19
Mourir à Madrid (film) 366–7

Mulliner, Mary 125
Mundo Obrero 179
Münzenberg, Willi 42, 142, 238
Murray, Basil 110, 121, 125–6
My Trouble with Hitler (Allen) 332,
  334–5, 337–8
Myth of Franco's Crusade, The
  (Southworth) 358

Nation, The 37, 41, 213, 216–17, 222, 243,
  257
Nazi Conspiracy in Spain, The (Katz) 142–3
Nazis
  activities in Spain 18, 142–3, 217,
    280–1, 289, 297, 364
  in Czechoslovakia 200–3, 318–19
  in North Africa 332–3
  and Russia, pact 324–5
Negrín, Juan 41, 213, 242, 324, 343–4
  coup against 61, 252
  and Fischer 97–8, 213, 215, 222, 230,
    240, 242–3, 253
Nervión river 274–5
Neves, Mario 299, 308
New Masses 106–7
New Republic 77, 79, 91
New Statesman and Nation 213
New York Evening Post 216
New York Herald Tribune 18–19, 24,
  136–8, 295
New York Times 19, 37, 44, 119, 260, 275
News Chronicle 12, 16, 24, 29, 46, 128,
  137–8, 141, 300
Newsweek 165
Nin, Andreu 83–4, 190–1, 196
NKVD (People's Commissariat for
  Internal Security) 163, 173–4, 177–8,
  192–3, 198–9, 207–8, 210, 260
Noel-Baker, Philip 247, 263, 274, 281–2,
  287–8
North, Joseph 95, 106, 130
North Africa 287–8, 326, 328, 332–3
North American Committee to Aid
  Spanish Democracy 159, 321
Novyi Mir 197

O Secule 153
Oak, Liston 72, 77, 82–6, 114–15, 124

Index

O'Connell, Jerry J. 162, 280
Oficine de Prensa y Propaganda 134–5, 146, 166
Ogonyok 174
Oil Imperialism: The International Struggle for Petroleum (Fischer) 219
Olías del Rey/Teninete 22–4, 227, 232
Oliver, Mollie 258–9
Orlov, Alexander 163–4, 178, 183, 210, 228, 260
Ornitz, Lou 160, 321
Orwell, George 83–4, 190, 285–6, 366
Osten, Maria 188, 197, 203, 207, 209, 211–12

Pacciardi, Randolfo 328–9
Packard, Reynolds 136, 155
Paris-Soir 16, 37–8, 148
Parker, Dorothy 241, 319
Partido Obrero de Unificación Marxista (POUM) 72, 83–4, 154, 191, 196–7, 209–10, 366
Partisan Review 91
Pathé newsreels 136
Patriarca, Vincent 231
Paul, Elliott 88–9
Pemartin, José 356
People's Press 105
Pester Lloyd 140
Pétain, Philippe 326, 328, 330
Philby, Kim (Harold A.R.) 159, 163–5, 167
Philippines Free Press 156
Phillips, Percival 40–1, 135–6, 150–1, 265
Picasso, Pablo 264, 279–80
Pitcairn, Frank *See* Cockburn, Claud
Planas, María 349–50
Pollitt, Harry 107–9, 113
Popular Front 4–6, 113, 156, 185, 226, 297, 303, 314
Portugal 15, 134, 141, 152–3, 239, 302, 306, 308, 350
POUM *see* Partido Obrero de Unificación Marxista
Pravda 34, 173, 176–8, 197, 199–200, 203
Prieto, Indalecio 5, 95–6, 177, 321, 344
Progressive, The 259

propaganda 3, 19–20, 89, 106, 125, 195, 238, 247, 255 *see also* censorship
  denial of Guernica 158, 166–8, 280–2, 312–13, 360
  of rebels 85, 134–5, 137, 146–7, 158, 166–7, 269, 358
  Spain as basis for Russian 195–7
  truth as counter to 98–9
Propaganda Department, Ministry of Foreign Affairs 96
Pujol, Juan Martinez 134–5, 161
Pulitzer Prize Committee 294–5, 307

Quintanilla, Luis 74, 80, 222, 296
Quintanilla, Pepe 74, 78–82, 91

Radek, Karl 174, 207, 210
Radio Tangier 357–8
Rakovsky, Kristian 220
Randall, Deirdre 261–2
rebels *see* Franco
refugees
  campaigns for 318–19, 321–4
  reporting on 121–3, 131–2, 249, 277–8
Regler, Gustav 42–3, 175–6, 189–90, 324
Republic
  and background to Civil War 5–7
  establishment of 3–4
Republican–Socialist coalition 4, 295, 297
Retour de l'URSS (Gide) 193–4, 208
Reuters 8, 59, 128, 165, 275, 350
Review of Reviews 163
Revolt (Allen) 296
Rice, F.A. 150, 152
Ripoll 12–13
Road to Yalta: Soviet Foreign Relations, 1941–1945, The (Fischer) 262
Robles Pazos, Francisco 'Coco' 69–70, 72–3, 88–9, 115, 124
Robles Pazos, José 66–7, 124
  and brother Ramón 66–8
  disappearance, mystery of 67, 70–3, 77–9, 82, 86–7, 89
  Dos Passos/Hemingway feud 64, 71, 74–6, 80–3, 86–7, 90–2
  service in Russia 67–8
  in Soviet Military Intelligence 64–5

Robles Pazos, Margarita 'Miggie' 73, 88–9
Robles Pazos, Ramón 66–7
Robson, Karl 152
Rogers, F. Theo 156–7, 355
Rojo, Vicente 179–80, 183
Roosevelt, Eleanor 248, 250, 315, 320–1, 324, 365
Roosevelt, Franklin D. 163, 259, 315–16, 320, 364–5
Roosevelt, James 314–15
Roosevelt, Theodore 156
Rosenberg, Marcel 56, 178, 206, 223, 228, 233, 250, 333–4
Rossif, Frédéric 366–7
Russell, Sam 99
Russia 39, 177 *see also* NKVD
  and Czechoslovakia 201–4
  influence on Republic 11–12, 17, 26, 64–6, 154–6, 206–7, 217–18
  and Nazis, pact with 324–5
  purges in 182–3, 198–9, 204, 209, 240, 249
  restrictions on press in/by 41, 54, 57, 190, 194–7, 218
  Spanish policy of 155–6, 178, 180–4, 229–30, 237, 249–50, 346, 364
Russia Revisited (Fischer) 260
Russia's Road from Peace to War: Soviet Foreign Relations, 1917–1941 (Fischer) 262

safe conducts 9, 77, 141, 152–3
Sagunto 95
Salter, Cedric 13–14, 50–1, 128–9, 131, 169, 344, 348
San Pedro Daily News 160
Schauff, Frank 195
Scoop (Waugh) 268
Sealed and Delivered (Steer) 264, 288
Selassie, Haile 265–7, 287–8
Seldes, George 314, 319
Sencourt, Robert 360
Serge, Victor 208
Serrano, Suñer, Ramón 147, 342
Seseña 24, 138
Shannon, Thomas V. 309
Sheean, Vincent 'Jimmy' 31, 46, 60, 95, 127–8, 130–2, 319

Shorokhodov, Gleb 183
Siege of the Alcazar: A War Log of the Spanish Revolution, The (Knickerbocker) 161
Simone, André *see* Katz, Otto
Sitges 349–50
Slater, Humphrey 'Hugh' 52–3, 104
Small, Alex 139–40
Smart, David A. 313–14
Sorbonne 360
Sosnovsky, Lev 174
Sotelo, José Calvo 5, 294
Southworth, Herbert Routledge 241, 271, 308
  early life/career 354–6
  Falangist contacts of 359–60
  as Franco's public enemy number one 351–2
  on Guernica 264, 354, 360–1
  lobbying 253
  in Morocco 333, 357
  private libraries of 353, 358, 362
  private life 356–7
  scholarship of 360–2
  writings of 351, 353, 355–6, 358–60, 363
Soviet Construction 208
Soviets in World Affairs, The (Fischer) 219–20
Spain: A Tragic Journey (Rogers) 156–7, 355
Spanish Civil War, The (Thomas) 351–3
Spanish Earth, The (film) 71, 74–5, 82, 102
'Spanish Lenin' *see* Caballero, Francisco Largo
Spanish Refugee Relief Campaign 321–3
Spanish Spring (Koltsov) 176
Spencer, Peter (Viscount Churchill) 50, 101
Stalin, Joseph 85–6, 207, 217, 260
  and Koltsov 173–4, 177–8, 180, 182, 191–5, 198, 204–5, 208
Starched Blue Sky of Spain, The (Herbst) 76, 79
Steer, George Lowther 21, 59, 263–90, 360–1
  and the Basques 271–4, 283–5, 289–90

Steer, George Lowther (*cont.*)
  in Ethiopia 265–8, 288
  on Guernica 263–79, 283–6, 299
  military service of 288–9
  in North Africa 287–8
  private life 264–5, 269, 272–3, 287
  in rebel Spain 269–71
Stirling, William F. 149–50, 270
Stowe, Leland 295, 319
strikes 4, 295

Tablet, The 309
Talavera 24, 145, 164, 179–80
Tangye, Nigel 149, 154
Taylor, Edmund 151, 295
Taylor, F. Jay 365
Telefónica *see* Madrid, press office
Teruel 52, 126–7, 159, 165, 248, 316–17
Tetuàn, revolt at 52, 54
Thomas, Hugh 337, 341, 351–3, 362
Thompson, Geoffrey 'Tommy' 169, 287
Thorning, Joesph 281, 307–10, 312, 317
Times, The 149–50, 165, 275, 281–2, 361
Tito, Josip Broz 259
Toledo, massacre in 22, 136–7, 185,
  226–8, 355
Tolstoi, Aleksi 210
Tree of Gernika, The (Steer) 263–4, 273–5,
  283–5
Trotsky, Leon 67, 85, 174, 180
Tuchman, Barbara *see* Wertheim,
  Barbara
Two Wars and More to Come (Matthews)
  127

Ulbrechy, Walter 211–12
Ulrikh, Vasily 211
Umanskii, Konstantin A. 210–11
United Press 22–4, 24, 30, 94, 120, 136–8,
  155, 220–2, 227, 363
United States
  arms embargo 95, 315, 334
  Catholic lobby 18–19, 309–12, 317
    Fischer's lecture in 240

House Committee of Un-American
  Activities 84, 89, 323
  non-intervention policy 321, 364–5
  repatriating US volunteers 251–2
Uritsky, Semyon Petrovitch 240

Vaksberg, Arkadi 190, 205
Valencia 32, 73, 93–103, 130–1
Varela, José 24, 133, 355
Vegas Latapié, Eugenio 147
Venero, Manuel 359
Vilar, Pierre 360–1, 363
Voigt, Frederick 57–8
Volkogonov, Dimitri 206
Volodarsky, Boris 179–81, 183
von Ribbentrop, Joaquim 165, 331
von Rothman , Kajsa 115–18, 129

Washington Post 162
Waugh, Evelyn 267–8, 288
Weaver, Dennis 24, 137–9, 300
Week, The 50, 200
Welles, Sumner 364–5
Wells, H.G. 144
Wendelin, Eric 231
Wertheim, Barbara 318, 356
Whitaker, John 155, 308–9, 319
Why Spain Fights on (Fischer) 241
Wilkinson, Ellen 247
Wintringham, Tom 97, 104–9, 112–13,
  247
Wolf, Emma 65, 183, 198
Worsley, T.C. 116–17, 123

Yagoda, Genrikh 174, 192, 208–9, 250
Yeats-Brown, Francis 281
Yezhov, Nikolai 193, 199, 204, 207, 209
Yindrich, Jan 30, 227
Yorkshire Post 265

Za rubezhom 174
Zamora, Niceto Alcalá 343–4
Zapp, Manfred 331
Ziffren, Lester 24, 25–6, 308